the
inclusive
hebrew
scriptures

volume III: the writings

the inclusive hebrew scriptures

volume III: the writings

Co-sponsors' edition

PRIESTS FOR EQUALITY
Brentwood, Maryland

PRIESTS FOR EQUALITY
P.O. Box 5243
W. Hyattsville, MD 20782-0243

Printed in the United States of America
2000 01   5 4 3 2nd printing

Cover illustration by Melissa Cooper
Book designed by Craig R. Smith
Typeset in Book Antiqua and FC American Uncial

Library of Congress Catalog Card Number: 99-74682
ISBN 0-9644279-5-8

table of contents

septuagint canon order

literary genre order

this book is dedicated

to
Virginia Williams, SL,
A woman with a pulsing, welcoming heart,
A feminist who gently challenged
Everyone
With her words and life
To respect the rights of women,
To live the gospel's message of equality,
To move mountains
Nation—world—church—
Toward justice, peace and human rights.

Virginia Williams, SL was a reader for this volume before her death on February 16, 1999. She was a member of the Loretto Community and served on its Executive Committee.

CR   CR   CR

acknowledgments

the spirit of wisdom fills this book. she has made her presence known not only in the words that fill these pages, but also in our journey towards the publication of these texts. She has guided us throughout this project—even at times when we were unaware of her presence or ignored her promptings. She has appeared to us with different faces and provided us with companions and guides along the way. She has given us many gifts. And so, as we begin this book, I would like to acknowledge the many gifts that we have received.

The first is the gift of community. This is especially present among our colleagues at the Quixote Center: Tony Banout, Joseph Byrne, Bill Callahan, John Clark, Marie Clarke, Maureen Fiedler, Jane Henderson, Trisha Kendall, Ellen Lynch, Melinda Miles, Dolly Pomerleau, Tim Scanlon and Tammy Williams. Every one of them has encouraged us on the way to keep the Quixote vision alive—all the while making sure that our feet were firmly planted on the ground. We are especially grateful to Maureen Fiedler and Tony Banout, who serve as members of the Priests for Equality Steering Committee. Both have been very generous to us in both time and resources. Maureen's tireless efforts at fundraising have kept us on a steady path to completion of this book.

Besides the members of the Quixote Center staff, we were also blessed with the skills of three talented part-time fundraisers: John Judge, Jayme Mathias and Robert Christian Holaday. They spent many hours on the phone raising the funding to make this book possible.

We continue to find Wisdom in the sage advice and critical eyes of our readers who reviewed the texts. Each of these women possesses a profound commitment to equality and love of language. They made sure that we were true to our purpose of producing a truly inclusive text that read smoothly:

Barbara Marian (Feminist Theology, Liturgy) again brought her expertise as a liturgist and her keen sensibilities with the cadence of the spoken word to help craft the text.

Anne Patrick Ware, SL (Feminist Theology) provided a sharp theological and grammatical reading of key texts. Her insights about "power language" helped us to think through issues with which we had struggled in our previous works.

Virginia Williams, SL (Feminist Theology) served as a reader for the books of *Ruth* and *Lamentations* before her untimely death in February, 1999. This volume is dedicated to her memory.

Mary Ann Cunningham, SL (Feminist Theology) served as a reader for *Chronicles* and *Proverbs*. She brought a sense of humor and careful editor's eye to the task.

Mary Dougherty (Feminist Theology, Ecumenism) gave us many insights into how inclusive language is being used in a number of faith traditions.

Kate Barfield (Feminism) once again brought her careful attention to detail and sensitivity to the nuances of language to the task.

And finally, we celebrate the gifts of talent and commitment that came together in the team that produce this book. From the very beginning, we have been blessed with a very special group of people who have been directly involved in the creation of this text. These people came together from many walks of life and represent a variety of disciplines:

Nicholas Vittum (Editor) brought a fresh and vibrant voice to the shaping of the texts. A published poet, Nick's skills are evident throughout *The Writings*; in particular, his poetic sensibilites come through most clearly in *Song of Songs* which is, we think, one of the jewels of this volume. He will be publishing his original vision of the translation separately under the title *Solomon's Song*.

The Rev. Elizabeth Anderson (Feminist Theology, Editor) joined us once again, bringing to the text the meticulous attention of an expert editor and insights of a feminist scholar. She made sure that the text read smoothly and cross-checked each verse of the text to make sure that nothing was left out.

Mark Buckley (Systematic Theology, Scripture) worked on the rough draft for most of these texts, providing invaluable and insightful up-to-the-minute scripture research along the way.

Craig R. Smith (Scripture, Layout and Design, and Executive Editor) continued to serve as our independent scripture scholar and designer for this book, as well as the project editor. Words cannot begin to describe what an invaluable resource Craig is. Craig's encyclopedic knowledge and love of scripture translation, his passion for words expressed clearly, vividly and powerfully, as well as his creative design of this book, is reflected on each and every page.

Rev. Joseph A. Dearborn,
National Secretary

co-sponsors

Everyone dreams, but not equally:
Those who dream at night with their eyes closed
awake to find it was all fantasy.
But the dreamers of the day are the dangerous ones
that they live their dreams with open eyes
and make them possible.

—T.E. Lawrence (of Arabia)

It is our great honor to list the names the following people whose contributions made this book possible. For these individuals, and countless others who have supported us over the years, you are the true dreamers of the day.

❖ Robert L. Anstey ❖ Robert J. Anthony/Dignity, NY ❖ Dorothy Armbruster ❖ Patti Armstrong ❖ Jane Audrey-Neuhauser ❖ Kathy Ault ❖ Marsha Bade ❖ Susan Barnes ❖ Catherine A. Barry ❖ Frank Basler ❖ Annette, Andy, Tara, & Rachel Batzer ❖ Theresa & Daniel Bauer ❖ Gary B. Beebe ❖ Benedictine Sisters, Duluth, MN ❖ Raymond Bernabo ❖ Elsie Bernauer, OP ❖ Christopher Bingham ❖ Selena Blackwell and Dorothy Many ❖ Tony Blaufuss ❖ Rev. Kathleen A. Bleyaert ❖ Lois Blosser ❖ Mary L. Boland ❖ Theresa Bowden ❖ Good Shepherd Parish MCC ❖ Rev. Joseph P. Breen ❖ Mary Brennan ❖ Joyce Bettencourt ❖ Dr. Keith I. Brown ❖ Joseph F. Buckley ❖ Rev. Gene Buhr ❖ H. Roslyn Taylor ❖ Ligeia C Cannon ❖ Ann Carberry & James E. Brown ❖ Ann Carberry & James E. Brown ❖ Mary Lou Carlson, O.S.F. Clinton Iowa Franciscan❖ Valerie J. Carlton ❖ Rev. Jean Carmichael ❖ Madeline Casey ❖ Sr. Mary Chamberlain ❖ Ann

M. Chambers ❖ Genevieve D. Chavez ❖ Cynthia Cheski ❖ Joan Chittister, O.S.B. ❖ Rosalie E. Cieply ❖ Patricia & Donald Clausen ❖ Rev. Victor Clore ❖ Ann Coleman ❖ Sr. Jane Ann Comerford ❖ Dorothy M. Concesion ❖ Anne & Tony Conway ❖ Marie L. Corr, BVM ❖ Ruth A. Cox ❖ Mary Ann Cunningham, SL ❖ Rosemary & Tom Daily ❖ Rev. Norbert P. Dall ❖ William V. D'Antonio ❖ Dorothy "Dody" Davies ❖ Charles N. Davis ❖ Gail Davis ❖ Kathleen & John DeFeo ❖ Peter K. Dennis, SS.CC ❖ Nancy J. Derycke ❖ Robert D. Di Censo ❖ Dignity/Maine ❖ Frances Doak ❖ Sr Laverne Dolphin, BVM ❖ Dominican Sisters, Great Bend, KS ❖ Jeanette K. Duquette ❖ Margaret Dostal ❖ Susan F. Dougherty ❖ Mary Dougherty ❖ Maureen Dougherty ❖ Anonymous ❖ Diane Drufenbrock, OSF ❖ Gwen Dubois ❖ Deborah Ann Durand ❖ Anthony M. Durante ❖ The Rev. Hope H. Eakins, Rector St. John's Episcopal Church, Essex, CT ❖ Robert Edgerly ❖ Christine Eheman ❖ Anonymous ❖ Maureen Fiedler, SL ❖ Rita M Flynn ❖ Anne McDonald Flynn ❖ Leadership of the Franciscan Sisters of Little Falls, MN ❖ Jimilee Franzee ❖ James Markunas Society ❖ Mary C. Freeman ❖ Samuel W. Gage II ❖ Alida M. Gall ❖ Eileen Garavente ❖ Mary Geraghty, CSJ ❖ Mary Glover ❖ Jeanette Rosenberg Goetz ❖ Mary Goudreau ❖ Col. Roseanne Greco ❖ Dorothy Gremillion ❖ Lucille J. Grow ❖ Alexandra Guliano ❖ Betty Rogers Kunz ❖ Dave & Christie Bernklau Halvor ❖ Pixie Koestline Hammond ❖ Pauline Harding ❖ Kathleen A. & Richard L. Hauke ❖ Nancy Healy, S.F.C.C. ❖ Eloise Heimann ❖ Mary F. Hempel ❖ Julie A. Henkener ❖ Alex Herrera ❖ Cheryl Huber Lee ❖ Joan M. Huntenburg ❖ Posy Jackson ❖ Rev. William James ❖ Rev. Balty Janacek ❖ Elizabeth Jarnagin ❖ S. Maureen Jessnik ❖ Celeste N. Jirles ❖ Mary Beth Jones ❖ Elizabeth Joyce, SP ❖ Rev. Julie Yarborough & Rev. Jeff Markay ❖ Anonymous ❖ Janet Houlihan Kain ❖ Mary Beth Kelly, S.C.L. ❖ Kathleen Rose Kennedy ❖ Rev. Eugene M. Kilbride ❖ Barbara Killian ❖ Margaret M. W. Kinsey ❖ Reinhold Kissner, Serra Club ❖ Alice L. Knopf ❖ Lorraine & Frank Koehler ❖ Peter Kohler ❖ Jennifer Konecny-Costa ❖ Arthur R. Koth ❖ Kenneth J. LaBudde ❖ Richard J. Lang ❖ Cynthia Lapp ❖ Joanna Laven ❖ Louise H. Lawler ❖ David Lee ❖ Katherine McNeil Leighton ❖ The Rev. Karyl J. Leslie ❖ Jean Levtzow ❖ Anonymous ❖ Light of Christ Community Church ❖ Mary D. Lindstrom ❖ David & Ann Lodge ❖ Bernadette Lohse ❖ Sr. Pauline Lorch, OSU ❖ Loretto Community ❖ Pat Love ❖ Theresa Lucier, SP ❖ Robert & Dorothy MacDonald ❖ Sebastian MacDonald ❖ Anonymous ❖ Sr. Marie V. Marnell, CSJP ❖ Helen J Maronda ❖ Angela C. Martin ❖ Patsy & Woods Martin ❖ Mary & Newell Witherspoon ❖ Nancy Mason ❖ Barbara A. Maurer ❖ Carol Mayes ❖ Mary Jo & Joseph McLaughlin ❖ Mary McMahon ❖ Katherine McNeil Leighton ❖ Bridget Mary Meehan—

SOFIA: Spirituality of the Feminine in Action❖ Joseph M. Messina ❖ Carol J. Meyer ❖ Rev. James L. Meyer ❖ Mary Igoe Meyers ❖ Lois A. Michelin ❖ Rose M. Miller ❖ Eleanore Mitchell ❖ Rita & Jim Mize ❖ Robert A. Mockus ❖ Dr. Virginia R. Mollenkott ❖ Joe Moniz ❖ Patricia A. Moore ❖ The Rev. Grace Jones Moore ❖ Neil M Mulock ❖ Mary Jo Neal ❖ Patricia Nemec ❖ Rev. Barbara B. Nish ❖ Margaret Novinski ❖ Ann Novo ❖ Kathleen O'Connell ❖ Rae C. O'Connor ❖ Diane K. O'Donnell ❖ Stephanie & Bill O'Grady ❖ Kathy & Joel Olah ❖ Kay O'Neil, PBVM & Michelle Meyers, PBVM ❖ Walter R. O'Neil ❖ Carol Palmer ❖ Sr. Virginia Patrick, CDP ❖ Therese Pavilonis, HM ❖ Patricia Peach, BVM ❖ Ann Penick ❖ Lillian Pereyra ❖ Virginia B. Peters ❖ Anonymous ❖ Elizabeth Phillips ❖ Anonymous ❖ J. William Potter, Jr ❖ Kathleen Powers ❖ Mary Anne Psumas-Jackloski ❖ Elizabeth W. Ravenscroft ❖ Kathy & Robert Redig ❖ Religious of the Sacred Heart of Mary, Western American Province ❖ Katherine Rhoda ❖ Jeanne & Stuart Riddle ❖ Sr. Frances Roberts, SSJ ❖ Rochester Franciscan Community ❖ Jeannette Rosenberg Goetz ❖ Anne Russell, OP ❖ Audrey & Bernard Rutkowski ❖ Rev. William Ryan ❖ Joan Coffey Ryder ❖ Marie C. Sandberg ❖ Louise & Donald Sandercock ❖ Kenneth J. Schaefer ❖ Joel L. Schmiegel ❖ Susie Schnelle ❖ Jean Mackel Schoonmaker ❖ Paul A. Schumacher ❖ Lisa Senuta ❖ Rebecca Shaw ❖ The Rev. Martha A. Siegel ❖ Sisters of St. Joseph, Concordia, KS ❖ Barbara M. Sitko, HM ❖ Katherine Smith, SP ❖ Penny Smith ❖ Al Smith, OSFS ❖ Margaret M. Snell ❖ Margery Sonntag ❖ Jerome G Sowul ❖ Benedictine Sisters McCabe Renewal Center, Duluth, MN❖ Genira & Bruce Stephens-Hotopp ❖ Margaret Sterchi ❖ Virginia Sullivan Finn ❖ Sisters of Divine Providence, Pittsburgh ❖ Rhoda Swanner ❖ Anonymous ❖ Beth Taneyhill ❖ Louise S. Tanner ❖ Lisa Ten ❖ Nancy J Tennessen ❖ Anonymous ❖ In Memoriam Sean P. Thompson ❖ Anonymous ❖ In Memory of My Sister, Margaret ❖ Rev. Maren C. Tirabassi ❖ Rev. Irvin Udulutsch, OFM Cap ❖ J. Thomas Uranker, Pittsburgh, PA ❖ In Memory of Rev. Giles J. Krysmalski, Pittsburgh, PA ❖ Joseph Sequeira Vera ❖ Margaret & Dan Villanueva ❖ Fr. Will Votraw ❖ Roger A. Waha ❖ Karen Walther, SSND ❖ Anne Marie & Henry Weiler ❖ Beata Weiss, ASC ❖ Linda Werner ❖ Martha J. Wicklund ❖ Joyce Wilkerson ❖ Eleanor Willhard ❖ Anonymous ❖ Rawson L. Wood ❖ Ann E. Wright ❖ Mary & Jerome Wuller ❖ Sue Yarger and Daughters ❖ David Yenko ❖ Julie & Sandy Zito

ℛ   ℛ   ℛ

introduction

the inclusive hebrew scriptures is part
of a series of inclusive language scripture translations by Priests for Equality.
Our goal is to translate the entire Bible into gender-inclusive language by
July of 2001, the twenty-fifth anniversary of our founding.

Background

Our work on inclusive language scriptures began in 1988 when we
received permission to distribute a collection of lectionary readings produced
by Dignity–San Francisco. We initially offered the readings at cost to our
supporters, asking only that they use the texts and let us know what they
thought of them. Feedback about the texts—from both spontaneous and
formal surveys conducted by PFE—flooded in, and prompted us to revise
the texts. These surveys told us that one of the major concerns with inclusive
language was the revision of the "God language."

As we continued to work on the texts, the work took on a life of its own.
We formed a four-person editorial committee, with each member having
an area of expertise in either scripture, feminist theory, theology or pastoral
ministry. We then moved from revising already-existing texts to doing our
own translation work from the original languages. As our work progressed,
we began to replace existing revised texts with fresh, original inclusive
translations. Since then, PFE has produced inclusive language lectionaries,
which are used in parishes, religious houses, intentional communities, and
campus ministries in the United States and throughout the world.

From the very beginning of our translation work, we dreamed of producing a complete inclusive language Bible. This dream remained on the back burner for a few years as we produced the lectionary texts. At some point in early 1994, however, we realized that we had significant portions of the New Testament translated, and we began to see our dream as an achievable task. At this point, the editorial committee set about the task of translating the remaining passages of the New Testament. By December 1994, PFE had produced the first all-inclusive New Testament text.

The initial response to *The Inclusive New Testament* was enthusiastic, and to date, the book has gone through three printings. Along with these positive responses, more and more people began to ask us when we were going to finish "the rest of the Bible." Our dream—and the dream of many others—had merged into a mission, and we set about the task of translating the Hebrew Scriptures.

Our first installment of *The Inclusive Hebrew Scriptures*, published in 1997, was a stand-alone edition of the Psalms which could be used for personal and public prayer. In the lectionaries, we used *Psalms Anew*, by Nancy Schreck and Maureen Leech. These texts served us well as responsorial psalms, which were then used in liturgies throughout the world. Yet our intention was to create our own translation. So we set about working on our own translation of the psalms in late 1996. *The Inclusive Psalms* were published in May of 1997.

We plan to publish the Hebrew Scriptures in three volumes, using the categories in which the books are arranged in Jewish tradition: the Law (*Torah*), the Prophets (*Nevi'im*) and the Writings (*Ketuvim*).

The first of the three volumes, *The Inclusive Writings*, includes the version of the Psalms we published previously, as well as other books of the Hebrew canon. However, our version also includes the Deuterocanonical books (also called the Apocrypha) which are included in standard Catholic editions.

The Writings

The term "The Writings" may be unfamiliar to many people, particularly those who did not grow up in the Jewish tradition. The term refers to the third section of the Hebrew Scriptures, a miscellaneous collection which includes the Psalms, which had become the songbook of the restored Temple; the wisdom books of *Job, Ecclesiastes*, and *Proverbs*—texts that struggle with questions of human existence in the light of God's covenant; the *Song of Songs, Ruth, Lamentations,* and *Esther,* four of the five books which were read on certain festivals (*Lamentations* is the fifth); *Daniel,* which represents a new form of literature, known as apocalyptic, that emerged after the Babylonian Exile; and the historical works of *Chronicles, Ezra* and *Nehemiah.*

How these books came to be placed together is a highly disputed question. In ancient Israel, only the *Torah* was considered to be divinely revealed—a tradition maintained to this day by the Samaritan community. The Prophets (which, in the Jewish arrangement, includes the historical books of *Joshua, Judges, Samuel* and *Kings*) were later accepted into the Hebrew canon as divinely revealed, with The Writings being added during the period just prior to, and following, the coming of Christianity. The evolution of the three-part division of Scripture indicates historical developments within Judaism from its ancient origins up to the Christian era.

As might be expected of such latecomers, the Writings often did not enjoy the same level of respect accorded to the Law and Prophets. In the 2nd century BCE, when the Deuterocanonical book of Sirach was written, the Jewish community spoke not only of the Law and Prophets, but also of "the rest of the books of our ancestors," though no one is certain what comprises the "rest of the books." And while their use inside the Jewish community became commonplace, their contents were hotly debated among various Jewish parties—debates which reflected a series of splits in the Palestinian Jewish community which was exacerbated between the Maccabean revolt in 67 BCE and the destruction of the Temple in 70 CE.

It isn't until much later that we begin to find references to a distinct collection of books called The Writings. Vague references to these "other" books until the 1st century CE is a sign that Judaism did not yet have a sharply-defined collection.

By the 1st century CE, there is a little more clarity about what these books might have been. The name "the Writings" first appears in the Babylonian Talmud—a collection of rabbinical commentaries compiled about the same time as the New Testament—where a complete list of the books of the Bible is included. Luke 24:44 refers to a tripartite division of "The Law of Moses, the Prophets and the Psalms." This agrees with the philosopher Philo of Alexandria's* reference to the "Law, the prophetic works and hymns, and other works by which knowledge and piety may be increased and perfected." The historian Josephus (ca. 37 BCE—100 CE) refers to five books of Moses, thirteen prophetic books, and four books containing "hymns to God and precepts for the conduct of life." These are thought to have been the Psalms, the *Song of Songs, Proverbs*, and *Ecclesiastes*. No specific name is given to this collection, though.

---

* Jewish philosopher who lived between 25 BCE and 50 CE. Philo worked out a synthesis of Judaism and Middle Platonic philosophy that had a great influence on many early Christian thinkers.

Why the Different Ordering of the Books?

In *The Inclusive Writings*, we have used the order of the books found in the Hebrew Bible. Since this is very different from the ordering of books that are found in Christian Bibles, a brief explanation of how the different orderings came to be may be in order. There were, however, many historical and political factors involved, and covering them all would take volumes.

Ancient civilizations customarily preserved their cultural and religious writings, and the Hebrews were no exception. Efforts began very early in the Jewish community to collect and preserve authoritative sacred literature. The 1st century Jewish historian, Josephus, records, "Our ancestors took no less care about writing records....They committed that matter to their high priests and to their prophets....These records have been written all along down to our own times with the utmost accuracy. That we have here an authoritative body of literature can be seen in the fact that the written Law was to 'serve as a witness' against the Israelites (*Deuteronomy* 31:19-27)."

The development of a set canon* for the Hebrew Scriptures took many centuries and was not settled until well into the Christian era. Josephus speaks of a rabbinical tradition which holds that the canon was closed with the book of *Ezra*, but this claim cannot be substantiated. Another tradition holds that the canon was set at the Synod of Jamnia in Palestine about 100 BCE, but there is little reliable evidence to support this claim, either.

What became known as the Palestinian canon is contained in the Masoretic text (the term refers to the body of Jewish tradition relating to the correct textual reading of the scriptures; the text itself contains critical textual notes and variations). It consists of twenty-four books, as shown in the following table:

The Law (*Torah*, or "instruction")
> *Genesis*
> *Exodus*
> *Leviticus*
> *Numbers*
> *Deuteronomy*

---

* "Canon" comes from the Greek *kanon* and the Hebrew word *kaneh*, both of which mean "reed." The word came to refer to a rod of a specific length that was used in measurement—the ancient equivalent to our yardstick. Canon refers to the measure used in a given locale to indicate the authoritative unit of distance for that region. It was first applied to Scripture by St. Athanasius in the *Decree of the Synod of Nicea* (350 CE) to refer to the set of books considered authoritative and inspired, and recognized by the believing community as being the source of revealed doctrine and containing ideals by which the community live, especially with regard to its religious life.

The Prophets ("Beards")

The Earlier Prophets

Joshua

Judges

1 and 2 *Samuel* (counted as one book)

1 and 2 *Kings* (counted as one book)

The Later Prophets

Isaiah

Jeremiah

Ezekiel

The Twelve (counted as one book)

Hosea

Joel

Amos

Obadiah

Jonah

Micah

Nahum

Habakkuk

Zephaniah

Haggai

Zechariah

Malachi

The Writings

The Books of Truth

Psalms

Job

Proverbs

The Scrolls

The Song of Songs (read on the eighth day of Passover)

Ruth (read on the second day of the Feast of Weeks, or Pentecost)

Lamentations (read on the ninth day of the Hebrew month of Ab, in mourning for the destruction of Solomon's Temple)

Ecclesiastes (read on the third day of the Feast of Tabernacles)

Esther (read on the Feast of Purim)

The Rest

Daniel

Ezra and *Nehemiah* (counted as one book)
1 and 2 *Chronicles* (counted as one book)

Sometimes Ruth was attached to Judges, since the book was set during the time of the Judges, and Lamentations was attached to Jeremiah, since the book was attributed to Jeremiah's authorship. Thus, sometimes the Hebrew canon consisted of twenty-two books rather than the more usual twenty-four. Many who favored this arrangement found a meaningful coincidence in the twenty-two letters in the Hebrew alphabet.

In 586 BCE, the Jewish community was taken into exile by the Babylonians; many of them remained assimilated in Gentile nations throughout successive ruling empires. By the time of the Greeks (4th century BCE), they had difficulty reading Hebrew and needed a version more easily understood by the masses. So in the late 3rd and early 2nd centuries BCE, the rabbis of Alexandria, Egypt, translated the Hebrew Scriptures into *koiné* (or common) Greek. This text became known as the Septuagint, or "Seventy" (abbreviated LXX), because of a legend that seventy elders completed the translation in seventy days.

The Septuagint divided the texts in a different manner from that found in the Hebrew version, and contained books and sections of books not found in the Hebrew canon. There were four main divisions, as seen in the following table (the Deuterocanonical books, which were written at a later date and generally reflect the influence of Greek philosophical ideas, are marked with an obelisk †):

The Pentateuch (The "five vessels" or scroll casings)
Genesis
Exodus
Leviticus
Numbers
Deuteronomy

The Historical Books
Joshua
Judges
Ruth
I Samuel
II Samuel
I Kings
II Kings
I Chronicles
II Chronicles

Ezra
Nehemiah
† *Tobit*
† *Judith*
Esther, with † additions
† *1 Maccabees*
† *2 Maccabees*

The Books of Poetry and Wisdom

Job
Psalms
Proverbs
Ecclesiastes
The Song of Songs
† *The Wisdom of Solomon*
† *Sirach* (or *Ecclesiasticus*)

The Prophets

The Major (i.e., longer) Prophets
　　Isaiah
　　Jeremiah
　　Lamentations
　　Ezekiel
　　Daniel, with † additions
The Minor (i.e., shorter) Prophets
　　Hosea
　　Joel
　　Amos
　　Obadiah
　　Jonah
　　Micah
　　Nahum
　　Habakkuk
　　Zephaniah
　　Haggai
　　Zechariah
　　Malachi

The rearrangement of the texts into four distinct literary genres—legal, historical, poetic/didactic, and prophetic writings—further demonstrates that there was no set ordering of the books up through the second century BCE.

The Septuagint was a highly respected volume among the Greek-speaking Jewish communities through the 1st century CE, when it became the standard text of the Christian community, though there were continuing arguments over the inclusion of the Deuterocanonical books and passages. It was at this time that the the Septuagint's ordering of the books became the standard for the Christian community from the time of Paul, and the Palestinian canon's ordering became the arrangement for the Jewish community.

This would seem to indicate that there was no set collection of books at that time, and given the close ties that the rabbis in Alexandria had with Jerusalem, it is difficult to imagine that they would have developed an entirely different canon. It is accepted by most scholars that there was no set Hebrew canon prior to the Christian era, when disputes with Christians over the status of their scriptures made it necessary to determine a canon.

What books should be included in the canon of Scripture sparked much debate, especially in the early Christian community. Two schools of thought developed. That favored by Augustine-accepted the Septuagint collection ("the Alexandrian canon"), which it was claimed had been in use among the Christian community from the time of St. Paul. The other group followed the lead of St. Jerome, whose studies with Jewish scholars led him to prefer the shorter Hebrew canon and express serious doubts about whether the additional books were of the same inspired status as the other parts of scripture. These two schools of thought coexisted for centuries, until the Council of Florence (1441) adopted the Alexandrian canon as the standard for Christians.

The two schools of thought became an additional source of division during the Reformation. The Reformation scholars, wishing to return to a more primitive faith, followed St. Jerome, limiting the number of books of the Old Testament to those found in the Hebrew canon. The other books were called "Apocryphal"—meaning "secret" or "hidden," because their authorship or authenticity was questioned. The Catholic scholars, following the Council of Florence, accepted the additional books as inspired, though they recognized that they were later additions to the Bible. That is why, in Catholic circles, the texts are known as "Deuterocanonical," meaning a "second canon," recognizing that the acceptance of these books was hotly debated.

These books, because of their more philosophical themes (such as immortality of the soul, and the doctrine of Purgatory) and formalistic styles, came to be used in Catholic theology and liturgies, adding additional support for their inclusion in the Bible. The final version of the Catholic canon of Scripture was codified by the Council of Trent (1545-1563).

In our version, we have adopted the ordering of the books found in the Hebrew canon, and, with two notable exceptions, placed the Apocryphal/ Deuterocanonical books in a separate section. The two exceptions are the books of Daniel and Esther. We have combined into the texts the sections of Esther and Daniel found in the Greek text but not in the Hebrew rather than treat them separately. We have done this simply to make them more understandable by placing them in the context of the appropriate book. These sections have been set off by brackets.

Inclusive Language

When the rabbis of Alexandria translated the Hebrew Scriptures into *koiné* Greek, they did much more than merely transpose one language to another. The Greek translation of the Hebrew Scriptures marked an interpretive innovation from the Hebrew text. The translators were Greek-speaking Jews living in a Hellenistic culture and influenced by the ideas of that culture, and thus brought a whole new framework to the translation of Scripture.

This marked a shift from a more concrete orientation to a more conceptual and speculative one. For instance, much of the concrete anthropomorphisms found in early Hebrew literature were changed— "hand of God" became "power of God"; "God our Rock" became "God our Help." Also, the proper name for God, YHWH, was replaced by the Greek political term, *Kyrios* (Lord or Sovereign). This circumlocution actually followed Jewish practice. Devout Jews no longer pronounced the Name, in an effort to keep from breaking the third commandment, but substituted the word *Adonai*. While *Adonai* is usually translated "Lord," it is the everyday term of respect for someone who is due deference ("sir").

The significance of this shift should not be lost to us today. Every translation is an interpretation. While faithfulness to the text was important for the Greek-speaking translators of the Hebrew Scriptures, they easily made cultural adaptations for their readers.

This kind of adaptation was not unique to the Greek-speaking Jewish community. Other translations and paraphrase versions of the scriptures flourished in the ancient world. The Targums, for instance, are Aramaic paraphrasings of the Hebrew text written at a later date for the Jewish community in Palestine, Syria and Babylonia, for whom knowledge of Hebrew had been lost. Similarly, there were versions of the scriptures in Old Syriac, known as the Peshitta, for other Jewish communities. Years before Jerome translated the Bible into Latin, Western Christianity relied on versions of the Bible in Old Latin, often poorly translated, but written for a community that was quite different from the Greek-speaking community from which the original texts came.

In developing scripture translations today, translators still bring in the biases of their own culture. For two millennia, standard biblical translations have reflected Western, male-centered attitudes and prejudices. Words and phrases, such as "brotherhood of man," which are claimed to include all people, carry with them the implication that maleness is the standard for being human. The language used in such translations does not merely describe sexual biases and prejudices; it also prescribes a course of behavior that fits into such an understanding. Biblical translations have been used to justify patriarchal and exclusionary practices and oppressive measures against women.

This is changing rapidly in our own culture as a growing consciousness of equality develops. As women of faith became more conscious of their exclusion, they have sought to recover their place in the religious traditions. For them, inclusive language—using words and phrases that are not sexist or classist—is a vital and attitude-changing tool in the church. And as inclusive language becomes more accepted in general use—particularly in the media and in public speeches—the need for inclusive language in religious texts becomes more apparent than ever.

With this shift in consciousness came a shift in language. Inclusive language is more than a corrective to the language of patriarchy—it is a form of language that expresses a vision of inclusion. Inclusive language is itself an issue of social justice as well as a means of achieving it. To use inclusive language is to challenge deeply ingrained biases and educate people in the habit of equality. In short, inclusive language is an essential consciousness-raising tool that can foster change in the Church and in society at large.

Developing Inclusive Language Translations

Imagine yourself learning a new language, like French. At first, you find yourself just struggling with the vocabulary and grammar, learning to construct simple sentences and stammering out awkward phrases. As time goes on, and you continue to practice the language, you find it easier to construct sentences which express complex ideas. Finally, after a good deal of time and practice, you find yourself communicating confidently in the language.

In many ways, using inclusive language is a lot like learning another language. It requires one to think outside of the patriarchal worldview into which we have been born. When we first started working on inclusive language texts back in 1987, we struggled with learning to speak the language of inclusion. We faltered and fell many times in our initial efforts—as we still sometimes falter. Thanks primarily to the encouragement and suggestions of women and men who share our vision of equality, we began to develop a degree of confidence—and, we feel, more at ease with the language of equality.

Along the way, we developed a set of guiding principles to make sure that we were consistent in our use of inclusive language. These principles are:

◆ **To create a "critical feminist biblical interpretation" of sacred Scripture that is inclusive in both content and style.**

From the beginning of the project, our efforts have involved grassroots feedback, the guidance of feminist theology and scripture scholarship, and an editorial process that involves both women and men who are skilled in both the theological and the social aspects of feminist, pastoral and scriptural critique.

◆ **To present the text in a layout that enhances the flow of the text, emphasizing the particular literary form that the test uses, while retaining the traditional chapters and verses.**

The modern divisions of the Bible into chapters most likely happened in the 13th century; separating the text into numbered verses occurred in the 16th century. While we have retained the traditional chapter and verse numbering throughout *The Inclusive Writings,* we have sought to present the text in its appropriate literary style: poetry looks like poetry, stories look like stories, genealogies are recognizable as genealogies, etc. In *Song of Songs,* for instance, the text is divided into three parts, traditionally designated as "The Groom," "The Bride" and "The Friends." These designations do not appear in Hebrew and were added to the text by later translators. Instead of adding to the text what is not there, we have chosen to lay out the text in such a way that one can see at a glance when there is a different speaker or speakers. In doing so, we have attempted to maintain the lyrical integrity of the text without sacrificing readability.

◆ **To make a clear distinction between linguistic convention and overt bias in passages that appear sexist, and to distinguish between those passages which simply exclude women and those which actively vilify women.**

This is probably the most difficult problem we have had to face in our translation work. Nonetheless, we have sought to determine whether the text is using a mere linguistic convention that seems sexist to our modern sensibilities, or whether the underlying meaning of the text is inherently sexist.

A case in point is the book of *Lamentations*, which is a dirge over the destruction of Jerusalem. The city has traditionally been personified as a woman, and in many contexts that personification is inoffensive. But in *Lamentations*, the incessant characterization of Jerusalem as a woman shamed, abandoned, defiled, raped, and enslaved is offensive in the extreme. In this case, because we could not alter the content of the original text, we chose to cast the poem in the second person: "How desolate you lie" instead of "how desolate she lies."

In all circumstances, we seek to recover the original meaning of the text without perpetuating the sexist or classist idiom. To do this, we have employed some of the most current biblical scholarship and feminist critique available today.

❖ *To use terminology that acknowledges the many forms in which God appears in our lives, and to restore the role of women and of feminine images of God in Scripture.*

Through our many surveys and countless written responses, people who use our inclusive language texts have told us that the biggest concern in inclusive scripture is "God language"—words and images that describe the Divine Mystery. God is spirit, and the words and images we use to describe God are approximations, drawn from our experience, to describe a Mystery. Drawing upon imagery that is exclusively male violates both our experience and the Divine Mystery. We simply do not rely on exclusively male role models as the standard for human experience—why then would we limit God to exclusively male images?

The Writings and the Apocryphal/Deuterocanonical texts offer a special opportunity to recover feminine images of God and the role of women in Scripture. The books of *Ruth, Esther*, and *Judith* feature strong and independent women, central characters who are leaders or whose actions are pivotal to the survival of a nation.

Moreover, because the character of Sophia (Wisdom) plays such a primary role in the books of *Proverbs* and *Wisdom*, appearing not only as God's companion but as the very manifestation of the divine to human beings, it is a clear and powerful evocation of the feminine aspects of God. Accordingly, we have capitalized the pronouns relating to Wisdom wherever they occur, to emphasize the image of the Divine Feminine.

❖ *To maintain a preferential option for those relegated to society's margins.*

It is becoming fairly standard practice to avoid characterizing people by a particular accident of birth or fortune. Our goal is to humanize individuals and declare God's preferential option for those on the margins of society. To that end, we strive to acknowledge the dignity of each individual by the simple expedient of how we address that person.

One way we do this in our translation is to prefer terms which emphasize social justice over moral rectitude. For example, the same Hebrew word can be translated "justice" and "righteousness"; "wickedness" can just as easily be translated "corruption." While traditional translations have preferred terms underscoring morality and virtue (or lack there of), we believe the original Hebrew concepts are more correctly translated by terms which talk about personal ethics, the quality of interpersonal relationships, and just (or unjust) social structures.

◆ *To stress an underlying mutuality and equality in human relationships.*

Another area of the translation work that proved somewhat problematic was how to handle what is often referred to as "power language." This is language which reflects power relations among human beings and between human beings and the divine. Such language has been used to perpetuate such injustices as sexism, classism and ethnocentrism. Use of power language reflects the inequalities in society where individuals and groups dominate other individuals and groups.

The ancient world was filled with inequalities that are reflected in the text: there were kings and servants, masters and slaves. God is portrayed as a ruler very much like the despots of the ancient world. Over the past few years, there has been a growing concern about the role of power language in the perpetuation of sexist and classist structures. People of conscience have begun to work with substitutes, many of which we have incorporated in our translation.

In our translation, we have attempted to eradicate power language that might be used to perpetuate forms of injustice such as sexism and racism, and to find ways of mitigating it in other circumstances. In our text, we have attempted to find "functional" substitutes for social roles—terms which describe what a person does, but don't define who the person is. For example, we have in most cases translated "kings" as "rulers" or "leaders." "Masters" and "servants" frequently become "employers" and "laborers."

This is not always easy to do. We have found no way to eliminate power language from the text entirely, since it is often integral to the way God is portrayed—and sometimes that portrayal is very much at odds with our sensibilities. As one of our readers commented on one of the drafts of *Chronicles*, "This God could be named Mary Ann and still not be feminist." Images of power and domination sometimes fill the texts, and we often found ourselves frustrated in finding some way to express what was being said in less offensive language. The *Psalms*, for example, are so rife with blatant militarism and the stereotypical vengeful God that we had three choices: change what the text clearly says and means, and produce an unfaithful translation; delete the references altogether, and become censors; or change what we can and leave the rest to speak as its own commentary—not only on humankind's penchant for brutality and warmongering, but on its need to cast God in a role that affirms such destructiveness. We have taken that third path, but we have walked it in the realization that the translation which results will occasionally reflect the harshness of the original text.

Where we were describing historical conditions and events, we wanted to reflect these circumstances as they were—even with the inequalities built into the society. We attempted to use language that describes the social roles and conditions then present, rather than prescribe the way things ought to be, but even here we may not have done this to the extent that would make everyone happy. Our intention is always to provide a text that is both faithful to the original *and* reflective of the values of justice and equality that we hold so dear. We humbly leave it to the reader to determine whether we have fulfilled in our intent.

Conclusion

Translating scripture into inclusive language is not an easy task. It requires faithful attention to the past, the present, and the future, all at the same time. It requires that one pay attention to the past, to remain faithful to the text of the scriptures and the traditions and histories through with they developed. It requires that one be faithful to the present, reading the signs of the times and responding prophetically to people's hopes and dreams and concerns. And finally, it requires that one be faithful to the future—to a vision of equality and inclusion.

To be inclusive, inclusive language translations of scripture must keep all three elements in a dynamic balance. A translation that sticks doggedly to the past will bring with it all the baggage from the past—sexism and patriarchy as well as other forms of inequality. Such translations continue to be stumbling blocks for women and men today. A translation in which vision dominates will be rootless—lacking identity because it will have lost any sense of whence it came. And a translation which is not attentive to the signs of the times will not speak to people and touch their lives.

In *The Inclusive Writings*, we have attempted to maintain a balance among all three. Our commitment to the full and equal participation of women and men in the church and society is our guiding vision, one that inspires us to find new ways of expressing old truths. Our dedication to produce quality texts is what impels us to study the texts carefully, and uncover the intention behind each passage so that we might faithfully render it. And our bond of solidarity with women and men struggling to build just churches and social structures has been our constant touchstone for this translation. If this book can help deepen faith, open eyes, or strengthen commitment to effect change, our labors will not have been in vain.

CR   CR   CR

the psalms

book I

1   Happiness comes to those
    who reject the path of violence,
who refuse to associate with criminals
    or even to sit with people who belittle others.
2   Happiness comes to those
    who delight in the Law of Our God
    and meditate on it day and night.
3   They're like trees planted by flowing water—
    they bear fruit in every season,
and their leaves never wither:
    everything they do will prosper.

4   But not wrongdoers!
    They're like chaff that the wind blows away.
5   They won't have a taproot to anchor them
    when judgment comes,
nor will corrupt individuals be given a place
    at the gathering of the Just.

6   Our God watches over the steps
    of those who do justice;
but those on a path of violence and injustice
    will find themselves irretrievably lost.

1 Why are the nations creating such an uproar?
   Why all this commotion among the peoples?
2 Those who hold power
      are taking their stand,
   gathering their forces against Our God,
      against God's Anointed One.
3 "Let's break their chains!" they say.
   "Let's throw off their shackles!"

4 But the One who sits enthroned in the heavens laughs;
      the Sovereign One derides them,
5 then rebukes them in anger
      and, enraged, terrifies them:
6 "It is *I* who installed my ruler on Zion,
      on the mountain of my holiness!"

7 I will proclaim God's decree—
      Our God said to me:
   "You are my own;
      I've given birth to you today.
8 Just ask—I'll give you the nations as your inheritance!
      I'll give you the ends of the earth as your possession!
9 You'll break them with an iron scepter;
      you'll shatter them as easily as a clay pot."

10 So, you rulers, be wise!
      And you who hold power, stand warned!
11 Serve Our God and rejoice—
      but do so with fear and trembling.
12 Pay homage to God's Own
      lest you be destroyed on your way in a blaze of anger—
      for God's passion can flare up without warning.

   Happiness comes to those
      who make God their refuge!

3

A psalm of David
Written when he fled from his son Absalom

1 O God, so many people have turned against me!
  So many are in open rebellion!
2 More and more are telling me,
  "No deliverance is coming to you from your God!"
  —— *Selah* ——

3 But you, Adonai, are my protection, my glory,
  the One who helps me hold up my head.
4 I cry aloud to you, Adonai,
  and you answer me from the mountain of your holiness.
  —— *Selah* ——
5 Now I can lie down and sleep, and then awake again,
  for you have hold of me—
6 no fear now of those tens of thousands
  who stand against me wherever I turn.

7 Arise, Adonai!
  Save me, my God!
  You struck all my enemies with a blow to the jaw,
  and broke the teeth of the violent.

8 From you, Adonai—deliverance;
  to your people—blessing.

4

To the conductor: for strings
A psalm of David

1 Answer me when I call, God of my justice!
  Give me relief from my distress!
2 Have mercy!
  Hear my prayer!

How long will you people dishonor me before God?
  How long will you love delusion and pursue lies?
—— *Selah* ——
3 Know that those who love Our God
  have been set apart by divine will—
  Our God will hear me when I call!
4 Tremble, and stop your sinning;
  search your heart,
  alone and silent in your room.
5 Offer sacrifices of justice,
  and put your trust in Our God.

6 So many are asking,
  "Does good even exist anymore?"
Let the light of your face, Adonai,
  shine on us!
7 You put joy in my heart—
  a joy greater than being full
  of bread and new wine.
8 In peace I'll lie down,
  in peace I will sleep:
for you alone, Adonai,
  keep me perfectly safe.

To the conductor: for wind instruments
A psalm of David

1 Take note of my words, Adonai!
   Understand my sighs!
2 Listen to my cry for help, my Ruler, my God—
   for it is to you that I pray.
3 Adonai, every morning you hear my voice,
   every morning I put my requests before you, and I wait.

4 You're not a God who delights in treachery—
   evil cannot live with you.
5 Arrogant people cannot stand in your presence;
   you hate all who twist the truth;
6 you destroy those who lie,
   and abhor the bloodthirsty and deceitful.

7 But I, because of your great love,
   will enter your House;
I will worship in your holy Temple
   in awe and reverence.
8 Because of my enemies, guide me in your justice;
   make straight your way before me.

9 For nothing they say can be trusted:
   their hearts teem with treacheries,
their throats are open graves,
   and their tongues speak nothing but deceit.
10 Pronounce sentence on them, O God!
   Let them fall by their own devices!
Because they fall away from your word, banish them,
   for they've been in open rebellion against you.

11 But let all who take refuge in you
   be glad and rejoice forever.
Protect them,
   so that those who love your Name
   will rejoice in you.
12 As for the just, Adonai,
   you surround them with the shield of your will.

To the conductor: for strings, tuned an octave higher
A psalm of David

1   Adonai, don't rebuke me in your anger,
        don't chastise me in your wrath.
2   Have mercy on me, Adonai,
        for my strength is gone.
     Heal me,
        for I am afraid to my very bones,
3   and my soul is full of anguish.

     And you, Adonai—how long?
4   Turn, Adonai! Save my life!
     Deliver me because of your love.
5   For in death no one remembers you.
        Who can give you praise from the tomb?
6   I am exhausted from crying;
        every night I flood my bed with tears,
        I drench my couch with my weeping.
7   I'm nearly blind with grief;
        my eyes are weak because of all my foes.

8   Get away from me, all you who incite to violence,
        for Adonai has heard the sound of my weeping.
9   Adonai has heard my supplication
        and accepts my prayer.
10   May all my enemies be ashamed and panic-stricken!
        May they turn back in sudden disgrace!

A frenzied musical rant, which David sang to Our God
about Cush, of the tribe of Benjamin

1 Adonai, my God, I take refuge in you.
   Save me from those who hound me!
2 Rescue me, or my enemies will tear me to pieces like a lion
   and rip me to shreds, with no one to save me.

3 O God, if my hands have done wrong,
4   if I have done evil to someone who was at peace with me,
   or was dishonest even with my enemy,
5 then let my foe pursue and overtake me
   and trample my life to the ground!
   Let my honor sleep in the dust!
                —— Selah ——

6 Wake up, Adonai!
   Rise up in your anger
   against the fury of my enemies!
   Awake, my God,
   and give me justice!
7 Let the company of nations gather around you,
   and rule over them from on high.
8 Let Our God judge the peoples fairly—
   and judge me fairly as well, Most High!
   Prove my innocence and integrity!

9 Put an end to the violence all around me!
   Make the just feel secure, O God of justice,
   you who test mind and heart!
10 You are my shield, God Most High,
   who saves the upright of heart.

11 God, you are a just judge,
   a God whose anger would blaze forth every day
12   if you were not so forgiving!
   Even so, you sharpen your sword
   and bend and string your bow.
13 You have prepared your deadly weapons
   and readied your flaming arrows.

¹⁴ Those who are full of malice and conceive evil
      bring forth nothing but disillusionment.
¹⁵ Those who dig deep pitfalls for others
      will fall into their own traps.
¹⁶ Their malice recoils right back on them,
      and their violence will fall on their own head.

¹⁷ I thank Our God for being so just!
      I sing praise to the Name of Adonai Most High!

8

To the conductor: to be played on the Gittite harp
A psalm of David

¹ Adonai, Our God, how majestic is your Name in all the earth!
      You have placed your glory above the heavens!
² From the lips of infants and children
      you bring forth words of power and praise,
   to answer your adversaries
      and to silence the hostile and vengeful.

³ When I behold your heavens, the work of your fingers,
      the moon and the stars which you have set in place—
⁴ what is humanity that you should be mindful of us?
      Who are we that you should care for us?
⁵ You have made us barely less than God,
      and crowned us with glory and honor.
⁶ You have made us responsible
      for the works of your hands,
      putting all things at our feet—
⁷ all sheep and oxen,
      yes, even the beasts of the field,
⁸ the birds of the air, the fish of the sea
      and whatever swims the paths of the seas.

⁹ Adonai, Our God,
      how majestic is your Name in all the earth!

1 I will praise you, Adonai, with my whole heart;
 I will tell of all your marvelous works!
2 I will be glad and rejoice in you,
 I will sing praise to your Name, Most High!

3 When my enemies are turned back,
 they stumble and are lost in your presence.
4 For you have maintained my right and my cause;
 you occupy the judgment seat, a righteous judge.
5 You have rebuked the nations, and destroyed the violent.
 You blotted out their name forever and ever.
6 The enemy has been cut down;
 their ruins are endless.
You have overthrown their cities,
 and even the memory of them has vanished.

7 But you, Adonai, reign forever
 and have established your throne of judgment.
8 You will judge the world in justice
 and govern the peoples with equity.
9 For you, Adonai, are a refuge for the oppressed,
 a stronghold in times of trouble.
10 Those who know your Name trust in you,
 for you have never forsaken those who seek you, Adonai.

11 Sing praise to Our God enthroned in Zion,
 declare God's work among the nations!
12 For the One who avenges blood remembers them,
 and doesn't ignore the cry of the afflicted.

13 Have mercy on me, Adonai!
 See what I suffer from those who hate me!
Lift me up from the gates of death,
14 that I may recount all your praises—

---

* Psalms 9 and 10 were originally a single poem. Together they form an acrostic poem: the first letter of each stanza begins with a subsequent letter of the Hebrew alphabet.

that in the gates of the Daughter of Zion
    I may rejoice in your deliverance!
15 The nations have fallen into the pit they dug,
    the net they set caught their own feet.
16 In passing sentence, you are manifest;
    you are known, Adonai, for your just judgments:
the violent are trapped
    by the work of their own hands.
           —— *Selah; meditation* ——

17 Sheol will become the home of the godless—
    all those who forget Our God.
18 But the needy will not always be forgotten,
    the hope of the poor will not be lost forever.

19 Arise, Adonai! Don't let them be victorious!
    Let the nations be judged in your presence!
20 Strike them with terror, Adonai,
    and let the nations know that they are only human.
           —— *Selah* ——

10:1 Why do you stand aloof, Adonai?
    Why do you seem to hide yourself in times of trouble?
2 The violent arrogantly pursue the weak
    and catch them in craftily designed schemes.
3 The impious boast of the desires of their hearts;
    they bless Greed, yet renounce you, Adonai.
4 With their noses in the air they never seek you;
    they think and say, "There is no God!"
5 Though their ways always prosper,
    your judgments are on high, out of their sight;
haughtily they keep your laws far away from themselves,
    and they sneer at all their enemies.
6 They think in their hearts, "We will not be moved;
    throughout all generations, we'll be happy and untroubled."
7 Their mouths are filled with cursing and deceit and oppression;
    under their tongues are mischief and iniquity.
8 They sit in ambush in the villages;
    they ambush the innocent and murder them;
    they stalk their victims in secret.

9   They lie in wait like a lion in the bushes;
        they lie in wait to catch the helpless:
        they catch the poor by drawing them into their net.
10 Their victims are crushed,
        they collapse and fall under their oppressors' strength.
11 But the violent only say, "God has forgotten,"
        or, "God is looking the other way and will never see this."

12 Wake up, Adonai! O God, lift up your hand!
        Don't forget those who are helpless!
13 Why do the violent renounce you, God?
        Why do they say in their hearts,
        "You won't call me to account"?
14 But you *do* see;
        you see every trouble, every cause for grief;
        you ponder it and take it into your hand.
    The helpless commit themselves to you;
        you are the helper of the orphan.
15 Break the arm of the violent and the evildoer!
        Seek out corruption till you find no more!

16 You will rule forever and ever, Adonai,
        and those who don't acknowledge you
        will perish from the land.
17 Adonai, you hear the desire of the meek;
        you strengthen their hearts
        and bend your ear to them,
18 to do justice to the orphan and the oppressed
        so that those born of earth may strike terror no more.

11

For the conductor
By David

1 I take refuge in Our God,
   yet this is what I hear from everyone:
"Bird, fly back to your mountain refuge and hide!"
2 Or: "See how the violent are bending their bows
   and fitting their arrows to the string,
   ready to ambush the innocent from the shadows!"
3 Or: "When the foundations are being destroyed,
   what can an honest person do?"

4 But I say:
Our God is in the holy Temple,
   Our God rules from heaven!
The eyes of God see all,
   and examine the human condition.
5 Our God watches over the just,
   but stands against the oppressor and those who love violence,
6 raining down fire and brimstone on the ruthless;
   a scorching wind is all they'll get to eat or drink.
7 For Our God is just, and loves justice—
   the upright will see God's face.

12

To the conductor: tune one octave higher
A psalm of David

1 Help, Adonai! No one is loving any more;
   faithfulness has vanished from the peoples.
2 Neighbor lies to neighbor;
   their words are smooth and duplicitous.
3 May Our God destroy all smooth talkers,
   every boastful tongue, and those who say,

4 "We can talk our way out of anything!
    We know *just* how to twist our words,
    so that no one can challenge us."

5 "Because they oppress the helpless,
    because poor people sigh and moan,
    now I will rise up!" says Our God.
6 The promises of Our God are flawless,
    like refined silver, freed from dross, purified seven times over.
7 You, Adonai, will keep us safe and protect us always
    from this generation—
8 where corrupt people strut proudly around,
    and the scum of the earth hold high office.

13

For the conductor
A psalm of David

1 How long, Adonai? Will you forget me forever?
    How long will you hide your face from me?
2 How long must I wrestle with my anguish,
    and wallow in despair all day long?
    How long will my enemy win over me?

3 Look at me! Answer me, Adonai, my God!
    Give light to my eyes, lest I sleep the sleep of death,
4 lest my enemy say, "I have prevailed,"
    lest my foes rejoice when I fall.

5 I trust in your love;
    my heart rejoices in the deliverance you bring.
6 I'll sing to you, Adonai,
    for being so good to me.

14

For the conductor
By David

1 Only fools say to themselves.
    "There is no God!"
They're all corrupt,
    they've done terrible things,
    and no one does what is right.
2 Our God looks down from heaven upon the peoples
    to see if anyone understands,
    if anyone seeks God.
3 But they are all lost,
    they are all equally corrupt;
not one of them does what is right,
    not a single one.
4 Will they never learn?
They eat up my people like bread
    and never give God a thought.
5 I see them now, consumed with fear,
    because God is on the side of those who do justice.
6 They frustrate the progress of poor people at every turn,
    but Our God is the refuge of those in need.

7 Who will God bring us from Zion?
    Who will be the Deliverance of Israel?
When Our God makes the faithful prosperous again,
    what joy and celebration will be ours
    as children of Leah and Rachel and Jacob!

By David

1 Who has the right to enter your tent, Adonai,
      or to live on your holy mountain?
2 Those who conduct themselves with integrity,
      and work for justice;
   who speak the truth from their heart,
3   and do not use their tongues for slander;
   who do not wrong their neighbors,
      and cast no discredit on their friends;
4 who look with contempt on the corrupt,
      but honor those who revere Our God;
   who always keep their promises
      even when it hurts;
5 who don't demand interest on loans,
      and cannot be bribed to exploit the innocent.

If people do these things,
   nothing can ever shake them.

A poem of David

1   O God, keep me safe—
      you are my refuge!
2   I said to Our God, "You are my God;
      there is nothing good for me apart from you."

3   The holy people of my land are wonderful!
      My greatest pleasure is to be with them.
4   But those who rush after other gods
      will bring many troubles upon themselves.
    I will not take part in their sacrifices;
      I won't even speak the names of their gods.

5   You, Adonai, are all that I have,
      you are my food and drink.
    My life is safe in your hands.
6   Within the boundaries you set for me
      there are nothing but pleasant places!
    What a delightful inheritance I have!

7   I praise Our God, who guides me;
      even at night my heart teaches me.
8   I'm always aware of your presence;
      you are right by my side, and nothing can shake me.
9   My heart is happy and my tongue sings for joy;
      I feel completely safe with you,
10 because you won't abandon me to the Grave;
      you won't let your loved one see decay.
11 You show me the path to Life;
      your presence fills me with joy,
      and by your side I find enduring pleasure.

1 Adonai, I plead for a just cause!
   Listen to my cry!
Turn your ear to my prayer,
   for my lips are free from untruth.
2 Prove my integrity—
   let your eyes see what is true!
3 You search my heart,
   you visit me by night.
You test me and find nothing wrong:
   I determined that my mouth wouldn't sin!
4 And as for my actions,
   because of the word you spoke to me,
I was able to avoid a path
   that leads to violence.
5 I kept my feet firmly on your road,
   and my steps never faltered.

6 Now I am the one calling to you—
   and you, O God, will answer me.
Turn your ear to me
   and hear my prayer.
7 Show me your steadfast love—
   and your great strength.
Save those who take refuge in you
   from those who hate them.
8 Guard me as the apple of your eye;
   hide me in the shadow of your wings,
9 and from violent and ruthless attacks—
   from my enemies who surround me with deadly intent.
10 They close their hearts to compassion,
   but open their mouths in arrogance.
11 They've tracked me down;
   now they surround me.
 Their eyes are alert,
   ready to strike me to the ground
12 as though they were hungry lions about to pounce
   or a young lion crouched in the bushes.

¹³ Adonai, arise! Confront them, strike them down!
     Rescue me from the violent with your sword!
¹⁴ Let your hand rescue me from such people,
     from such a world,
     from people whose only reward is in this present life.

You fill the bellies of those you cherish;
     their children will have plenty,
     and will store up wealth for *their* children.
¹⁵ And me? When I look at justice I see your face;
     and when I awake, I'll be content just to see your likeness.

18

For the conductor
By David, God's faithful one, who sang Adonai this song
the day God saved him from the hand of all his enemies—
from the hand of Saul. This is what he sang:

¹ I love you, Adonai,
     my strength.
² Adonai—
     my mountain crag,
     my fortress,
     my rescuer,
     my God,
     my rock behind whom I take refuge,
     my shield,
     my horn of deliverance,
     my stronghold!
³ The One whom I praise,
     and to whom I call,
is Adonai—
     and from the enemy I am saved!

⁴ The waves of Death enclosed me,
     the torrents of Destruction devoured me;
⁵ the snares of Sheol entangled me,
     the traps of Death drew me down.

6   In my distress I called you, Adonai;
      to you, my God, I cried for help.

    From your Temple you heard my voice,
      and my cry to you reached your ears.
7   Then the netherworld reeled and rocked;
      the mountains trembled to their foundations
    in the presence of your anger.
8   Smoke billowed from your nostrils
      and a consuming fire spewed forth from your mouth;
    glowing coals erupted into flames.
9   You tore through the heavens and came down;
      thick darkness was under your feet.
10   You rode upon the backs of cherubim,
      and soared on the wings of the wind.
11   You made the night your cloak;
      you covered yourself in a canopy of storm clouds.
12   From the brightness before you
      your clouds surged forth
    with hailstones and lightning bolts.
13   You thundered in the heavens,
      and your voice, Most High, resounded
    with hailstones and bolts of lightning.
14   You shot your arrows and scattered my enemies;
      you scattered your lightning bolts and routed them.
15   Then the channels of the sea were exposed,
      and the foundations of the world were laid bare
  at your rebuke, Adonai,
    at a snort from your nostrils.
16   You reached from on high and took hold of me,
      and pulled me out of deep water.
17   You rescued me from my strong enemy,
      and from my foes who were too powerful for me.
18   They fell upon me in the day of my calamity,
      but you, Adonai, were my support.
19   You brought me out of the vast netherworld;
      you rescued me, because you delighted in me.

20   Adonai, you set everything right again because I was just;
      you rewarded me because my hands were clean.
21   For I kept your ways, Adonai:
      I didn't do evil—I didn't leave you, my God.

22   For all your laws were in front of me,
  and I didn't turn away from a single decree.
23   I was blameless before you,
  and I kept myself from evil—
24   you rewarded me because I was just,
  because I kept my hands clean.

25   To those who love,
  you show yourself loving;
  to those who are blameless,
  you show yourself blameless;
26   to those who are single-hearted,
  you show yourself single-hearted;
  to those who are crooked,
  you show yourself...shrewd!
27   You save humble people,
  but force the arrogant to lower their eyes.
28   You are my ever-burning lamp, Adonai!
  My God, you lighten my darkness!
29   Yes, with you I can crush a brigade,
  and with my God I can scale ramparts.

30   O God, your way is perfect;
  your promise, Adonai, proves true:
  you are a shield for all who take refuge in you.
31   For who is God, but you?
  And who is a rock except our God?—
32   the God who arms me with strength
  and makes my path perfectly safe,
33   who gives me the sure footing of a mountain goat,
  and sets me on heights of my own,
34   who trains my hands for battle
  so that my arms can bend a bow of bronze.
35   You have given me your shield of victory
  and your strong hand supported me;
  you stoop to make me great.
36   You make my road wide and smooth,
  so that I never twist an ankle.

37   I pursued my enemies and overtook them,
  and did not relent until they were destroyed.
38   I crushed them, so they couldn't get up;
  they fell beneath my feet.

39 For you armed me with strength for the battle;
        you made my assailants sink beneath me.
40 You made my enemies turn back and run,
        and I destroyed my opponents.
41 They cried for help, but there was none to save them;
        they cried to God, but God didn't answer them.
42 I beat them as fine as dust in the square;
        I stomped on them like mud in the streets.
43 You delivered me from the attacks of an unbelieving people;
        you made me a leader of the nations.
    A people whom I had not known
        are now subject to me.
44 As soon as they hear of me, they obey me—
        nations come cringing!
45 The nations come cowering,
        and come trembling from their strongholds.

46 Our God lives! Blessed be my rock!
        And let the God of my salvation be exalted—
47 the God who gave me vengeance
        and subdued my attackers under me,
48   who delivered me from defamers!
49 For this I will extol you among the nations, Adonai,
        and sing praises to your Name.
50 You give great victories to your leader,
        and show unfailing love to your Anointed,
        to David and his descendants forever.

19

1 The heavens herald your glory, O God,
   and the skies display your handiwork.
2 Day after day they tell their story,
   and night after night they reveal
   the depth of their understanding.
3 Without speech, without words,
   without even an audible voice,
4 their cry echoes through all the world,
   and their message reaches the ends of the earth.
   For in the heavens
   the sun has pitched a tent.
5 It comes forth with the grandeur of a wedding procession,
   with the eagerness of an athlete ready to race.
6 It rises at one end of the sky
   and travels to the other end,
   and nothing escapes its warmth.

7 Your law, Adonai, is perfect;
   it refreshes the soul.
   Your rule is to be trusted;
   it gives wisdom to the naive.
8 Your purposes, O God, are right;
   they gladden the heart.
   Your command is clear;
   it gives light to the eyes.
9 Holding you in awe, Adonai, is purifying;
   it endures.
   Your decrees are steadfast,
   and all of them just.
10 They are more precious than gold,
   than the purest of gold,
   and sweeter than honey,
   than honey fresh from the comb.
11 In them your faithful people find instruction;
   there is great reward in keeping them.

12   But who can detect one's own failings?
        Forgive the misdeeds I don't even know about!
13   Keep your faithful one from presumption as well,
        so that my faults never control me.
     Then I will be blameless
        and innocent of a grave error.

14   May the words of my mouth
        and the thoughts of my heart
     be pleasing in your sight, Adonai,
        my rock and my redeemer!

20

1   May Our God answer you in the day of distress!
       May the Name of the God
       of Leah, Rachel and Jacob protect you!
2   May God send you help from the sanctuary
       and sustain you from Zion!
3   May God remember all your sacrifices,
       and accept your burnt offerings!
                  —— *Selah* ——
4   May God give you your heart's desires
       and fulfill all your dreams!
5   We will shout for joy over your triumph
       and in the Name of our God wave our banners—
       may Our God grant all your petitions!

6   Now I know that Our God saves the anointed,
       answering from holy heaven with saving power.
7   Some trust in political power, some in military might,
       but we trust in the Name of Adonai, our God!
8   With only human resources, they fall;
       but we have risen, and we stand firm.

9   Save us, Adonai, our Ruler!
       Answer when we call.

For the conductor
A psalm of David

¹ This ruler, Adonai, rejoices in your strength!
      How great is my joy in your victory!
² You've given me my heart's desire
      and did not deny me the wish of my lips.
—— *Selah* ——
³ You greeted me with lavish blessings,
      and placed on my head a crown of pure gold.
⁴ I asked you for life;
      you gave me length of days forever and ever.
⁵ Great is my glory in your victory;
      you bestowed majesty and splendor upon me.
⁶ You gave me a boon forever:
      you gladdened me with the joy of your presence.
⁷ For this ruler trusts in you, Adonai;
      because of your love, I stand unshaken.

⁸ May your hand reach all my enemies,
      your right hand reach my foes!
⁹ They'll look like a fiery furnace when you appear—
      you, O God, will consume them in anger,
      and fire will devour them.
¹⁰ You'll wipe their progeny from the earth,
      their posterity from among the peoples.
¹¹ Though they concoct heinous plots against you,
      the schemes they devise cannot succeed—
¹² for you will put them to flight
      and all they will see
      are your arrows flying at them.

¹³ Be exalted, Adonai, in your strength!
      We will sing the praise of your might!

To the conductor: to the tune of "Doe of the Morning"
A psalm of David

1   My God, my God,
    why have you forsaken me?
Why are you so far away,
    so far from saving me,
    so far from the words of my groaning?
2   I cry all day, my God, but you never answer;
    I call all night long, and sleep deserts me.

3   But you, Holy One—
    you sit enthroned on the praises of Israel.
4   Our ancestors put their trust in you,
    they trusted and you rescued them;
5   they cried to you and were saved,
    they trusted you and were never disappointed.

6   Yet here I am, more worm than human,
    the scorn of humanity, an object of ridicule:
7   all who see me mock me,
    they shake their heads and sneer,
8   "You trust in God? Ha! Let God save you now!
    If God is your friend, let God rescue you!"
9   Yet you drew me out of the womb,
    you nestled me in my mother's bosom;
10 you cradled me in your lap from my birth,
    from my mother's womb you have been my God.
11 Don't stand aside now that trouble is near—
    I have no one to help me!

12 My enemies are like a herd of bulls surrounding me,
    like the strong bulls of Bashan closing in on me;
13 with jaws open wide to swallow me,
    they're like lions tearing their prey, and roaring.
14 I am like water draining away,
    my bones are all disjointed,
    my heart is like wax melting inside me.
15 My strength is dried up like a piece of clay pottery
    and my tongue is stuck to the roof of my mouth:
    you lay me down in dusty death.

16 A pack of dogs surrounds me,
   a gang of brigands close me in;
   they pierce my hands and feet.
17 I can count every one of my bones,
   and there they stare at me, gloating.
18 They divide my garments among them
   and cast lots for my clothes.

19 But you, Adonai, don't be far off!
   My strength, hurry to help me!
20 Rescue my life from the sword,
   my dear life from the power of these dogs!
21 Save me from the lion's mouth,
   my poor soul from the wild bull's horns!

22 Then I will proclaim your Name to my sisters and brothers,
   and praise you in the full assembly:
23 "You who worship Our God, give praise!
   Daughters of Leah, daughters of Rachel, glorify Our God!
   Sons of Jacob, fall down and worship!
24 For God has not despised—not disdained—
   the suffering of those in pain!
   God didn't hide
   but answered them when they cried for help!"
25 You are the theme of my praise in the Great Assembly,
   and I will fulfill my vows in the presence of your worshipers.
26 Those who are poor will eat and be satisfied,
   those who seek you will give you praise—
   long life to their hearts!
27 The whole earth, from one end to the other,
   will remember and come back to you;
   all the families of the nations
   will bow down to you.
28 For yours is the kindom,
   you Ruler of nations!
29 Those who had feasted and devoured the poor—
   now they'll bow down;
   the most affluent in the land
   will kneel before you.
   They all go down to the dust
   and none can keep themselves alive.

30 But my children will be faithful to you,
  and they will be told about Our God for generations to come.
31 They will come and proclaim your justice
  to a people yet unborn:
  "All this Our God has done!"

23

A psalm of David

1 Adonai, you are my shepherd—
  I want nothing more.
2 You let me lie down in green meadows,
  you lead me beside restful waters:
3   you refresh my soul.
  You guide me to lush pastures
  for the sake of your Name.
4 Even if I'm surrounded by shadows of Death,
    I fear no danger,
    for you are with me.
  Your rod and your staff—
    they give me courage.
5 You spread a table for me
    in the presence of my enemies,
  and you anoint my head with oil—
    my cup overflows!
6 Only goodness and love will follow me
    all the days of my life,
  and I will dwell in your house, Adonai,
    for days without end.

1 The earth and everything on it—
   the world and all who live in it—
   belong to Our God.
2 Our God built it on the deep waters,
   laying its foundations in the ocean depths.

3 Who has the right to ascend Our God's mountain?
   Who is allowed to enter Our God's holy place?
4 Those whose hands are clean and whose hearts are pure,
   who do not worship idols, or make false promises.
5 Our God will bless them;
   God their savior will declare them innocent.
6 Such are the people who seek Our God,
   who seek your face, God of our ancestors.
         —— *Selah* ——

7 Fling wide the gates,
   open the ancient doors,
   and the Glorious Liberator will come in!
8 Who is this "Glorious Liberator"?
   Adonai, strong and mighty,
   Our God, victorious in battle!
9 Fling wide the gates,
   open the ancient doors,
   and the Glorious Liberator will come in!
10 Who is this "Glorious Liberator"?
   Adonai Sabaoth is our Glorious Liberator!
         —— *Selah* ——

1 To you, Adonai,
    I lift up my soul.
2 My God, I trust in you;
    don't let me be ashamed,
    don't let my enemies triumph over me.
3 No—none who hope in you will be ashamed,
    but shame will come to the wantonly treacherous.

4 Show me your ways, Adonai!
    Teach me your paths!
5 Lead me in your truth and teach me,
    for you are the God of my salvation.
    I wait all the day long for you.
6 Remember your mercies, Adonai, your love—
    your ancient and unwavering love!
7 Pardon the sins of my youth
    and my rebellious ways;
remember me because of your love,
    because of your goodness, Adonai!

8 And how good and upright you are, Adonai!
    You instruct sinners in the path,
9 you guide the humble in what is right,
    and teach them your way.
10 All of your paths, Adonai,
    are full of love and faithfulness
    for those who keep your Covenant and Testimonies.

11 For the sake of your Name, Adonai,
    pardon my guilt, for it is great.
12 Who are those who revere you?
    They are the ones you teach
    which way you want them to go.
13 Their lives will be spent in prosperity,
    and their children will possess the land.
14 Our God becomes friends with those who show reverence,
    and reveals the Covenant to them.

¹⁵ My eyes are always on you, Adonai,
   for you will pluck my feet out of the snare.
¹⁶ Turn to me, be gracious to me,
   for I am lonely and anguished.
¹⁷ How heavy are the troubles of my heart!
   Free me from my distress!
¹⁸ Look at my affliction and my trouble,
   and mend all my brokenness.
¹⁹ See how my enemies keep multiplying,
   how they hate me so violently!
²⁰ O guard of my life, rescue me!
   Don't let me be put to shame,
   for I take refuge in you.
²¹ May integrity and uprightness protect me,
   for you are my only hope.

²² Ransom Israel, O God,
   from all trouble!

By David

1 Do me justice, Adonai!
     For I have walked in integrity
     and I have trusted in you without wavering.
2 Search me, Adonai, and test me;
     examine my heart and my mind.
3 For your love is before my eyes,
     and I walk in your truth.
4 I don't sit with deceitful people,
     nor do I consort with hypocrites.
5 I avoid places where troublemakers gather,
     and have nothing to do with violent people.
6 I wash my hands in innocence
     and minister at your altar, Adonai,
7 giving voice to my praise
     and recounting all your wondrous deeds.
8 Adonai, I love the house in which you dwell,
     the dwelling place of your glory.
9 Don't sweep me away with sinners,
     or take my life along with the bloodthirsty!
10 They hatch terrible schemes with their left hand,
     and take bribes with their right.
11 But I walk in integrity;
     ransom me, and have pity on me.
12 My foot stands on level ground;
     in the assemblies I will bless Adonai.

By David

1   Adonai, you are my light, my salvation—
         whom will I fear?
     You are the fortress of my life—
         of whom will I be afraid?
2   When my enemies attack me,
         spreading vicious lies about me wherever they go,
     they, my adversaries and foes,
         will stumble and fall.
3   Though an army mounts a siege against me,
         my heart will not fear;
     though war break out against me,
         I'll still be confident.

4   One thing I ask of you, Adonai,
         one thing I seek:
     that I may dwell in your house
         all the days of my life,
     to gaze on your beauty
         and to meditate in your Temple.
5   You will keep me safe in your shelter
         when trouble arises,
     you will hide me under the cover of your Tabernacle—
         you'll set me on a rock, high and out of reach.
6   Then I'll be able to hold my head up,
         even with my enemies surrounding me.
     I will offer in your Tabernacle
         sacrifices of great joy—
         I'll sing and make music to you, Adonai!

7   Hear me when I call, Adonai!
         Have mercy on me and answer me!
8   You say to my heart, "Seek my face,"
         and so it is your face I seek!
9   Don't hide your face from me,
         don't turn your faithful one away in anger.
     Don't reject me, don't desert me,
         O God of my salvation,
         for you are my only help.

10   Even if my own parents reject me,
      you, Adonai, will accept me.
11   Teach me your way, Adonai,
      and lead me on a straight path because of my enemies.
12   Don't surrender me to the will of my enemies;
      for defamers rise up against me breathing violence.

13   Even so I have confidence
      that I'll see the goodness of Our God
      in the land of the living!
14   Wait for God—stand tall
      and let your heart take courage!
      Yes, wait for Our God!

28

By David

1   To you, Adonai, I call—
      my rock, don't turn a deaf ear to me!
    If you don't heed my cry,
      I'll become like those who go to the Pit.
2   Hear the voice of my pleading
      as I call to you for help,
    as I lift up my hands in prayer
      toward your Most Holy Place!
3   Don't drag me away with the violent,
      with the evildoers,
    who speak words of peace to their neighbors
      but have evil in their hearts.
4   Repay them as their actions deserve,
      for the malice of their deeds
    and for the work of their hands—
      give them their deserts!
5   For they ignore your deeds, Adonai
      and the work of your hands.

6   I will bless you, Adonai, for you have heard
      my cries for mercy.

7   You are my strength and my shield;
        in you my heart trusts.
    You revived me—my heart rejoices,
        and I praise you with my song.
8   You are the strength of your people,
        the stronghold where your anointed find salvation.
9   Save your people, and bless Israel your inheritance!
        Be their shepherd and carry them forever!

29

A psalm of David

1   Give glory to Our God, you heavenly court,
        give Our God glory and strength!
2   Give forth the glory that God's Name deserves,
        and worship Our God in the splendor of holiness!

3   The voice of Our God resounds over the waters;
        the God of glory thunders over the raging seas.
4   God's voice is powerful,
        God's voice is full of majesty.
5   The voice of Our God snaps the cedars,
        shatters the cedars of Lebanon.
6   It makes Lebanon skip like a calf,
        and Sirion like a young wild ox.
7   The voice of Our God strikes with bolts of lightning;
8   the voice of Our God shakes the wilderness,
        the wilderness of Kadesh.
9   The voice of God twists the oaks,
        and strips the forests bare;
        and in God's Temple all cry, "Glory!"
10 Our God sits in judgment over the flood;
        Adonai is its Ruler forever.
11 Give strength to your people, Adonai!
        Bless your people with peace!

A psalm
A song for the dedication of the Temple
By David

1   I praise you, O God, because you raised me up
     and kept my enemies from gloating over me.
2   I cried to you for help, Adonai my God,
     and you healed me.
3   You brought me back from the realm of the dead, Adonai;
     you spared me from going down into the Pit.

4   Sing to Adonai, you who love God!
     Praise God's holy Name!
5   Our God's anger is fleeting,
     but God's favor endures forever.
  There may be tears during the night,
     but joy comes in the morning.

6   When I presumed I was secure, I boasted,
     "I will never be defeated!"
7   When I stood in your favor, Adonai,
     I stood as firm as a mountain.
  But then you hid yourself from me,
     and I was filled with terror.
8   So I called to you, Adonai,
     I pleaded for your help:
9   "What good will come from my destruction,
     from my going to the grave?
  Does dust praise you, Adonai?
     Can the dead proclaim your unfailing goodness?
10   Hear me, Adonai, and be merciful!
     Help me, Adonai!"

11   Then you changed my despair into a dance—
     you stripped me of my death shroud
     and clothed me with joy.
12   That's why my heart sings to you,
     that's why I can't keep silent—
  Adonai, you are my God,
     and I will thank you forever!

1 In you, Adonai, I took refuge;
    never let me be disgraced!
    In your justice, deliver me!
2 Turn your ear to me!
    Hurry! Rescue me!
Be the rock I hide behind,
    be the walled fortress that saves me!
3 Because you are my rock, my fortress,
    and for the sake of your Name,
    lead me, guide me!
4 Pull me out of the trap they set for me,
    for you are my refuge!

5 Into your hands I commit my spirit;
    deliver me, Adonai, God of truth!
6 I hate those who cling to useless idols;
    but I trust in you.
7 I'll be happy,
    I'll rejoice in your love—
for you saw my despair,
    you knew the dark night of my soul.
8 You didn't hand me over to the enemy,
    but gave my feet boundless freedom.

9 Now take pity on me, Adonai,
    for I'm in trouble again.
I cried so much that I'm exhausted—
    and not only my eyes, but my mind and body as well.
10 My life is consumed by sorrow,
    my years are worn out with my sighs;
my strength fails me because of my despair,
    my bones are getting weaker.
11 Because of all my oppressors
    I'm held in utter contempt, even by my neighbors;
 my friends are afraid of me,
    and people who see me on the street hurry past me.
12 I am forgotten, as good as dead in their hearts,
    like something that has outlived its usefulness.

13   I hear their endless slanders,
     and threats from every quarter
  as they conspire against me,
     plotting to take my life.

14   But I put my trust in you, Adonai;
     I say, "You are my God!"
15   My times are in your hand,
     save me from the hands of my enemies and persecutors.
16   Smile on your faithful one,
     save me in your love!
17   Don't let me be disgraced, Adonai,
     for I cried to you;
  let disgrace fall instead on the corrupt—
     in their silence, let them go to Sheol,
18   their lying lips sealed shut
     because of their sneering contempt for those who do right,
     because of their overwhelming pride and arrogance.

19   How great is the goodness
     reserved for those who revere you!
  You bestow it—in front of everyone—
     on those who take refuge in you.
20   Safe in your presence,
     you hide them from the world's insidious schemes;
  inside your tent, you shelter them,
     far from the war of tongues!
21   Blessed are you, Adonai,
     for you showed your wonderful love to me
     in a city under siege!
22   In my alarm I exclaimed,
     "I've been snatched from your sight!"
  Yet you heard the sound of my cries
     when I called to you for help.

23   Revel in your love for God,
     you whom God has touched!
  For Our God protects the faithful
     but will repay the arrogant in full.
24   Be strong, let your heart be bold,
     you who hope in Our God.

32

By David
A teaching poem

1 Happiness comes from having your rebellion taken away,
   from having your failure completely covered.
2 Happiness comes from Our God not counting your mistakes,
   from having nothing to hide.
3 As long as I kept my stubborn silence,
   my bones grew weak because of my constant complaints.
4 Day and night your hand was heavy upon me;
   my strength was sapped by a summer's heat.
                —— *Selah* ——
5 Finally I admitted my sin to you,
   and stopped hiding my guilt.
   I said, "I confess my rebellion, Adonai,"
   and you took away the guilt of my sin.
                —— *Selah* ——
6 That's why people of faith everywhere
   should pray to you—they'll find you.
   Even when the flood begins rising,
   it will never touch them.
7 You are my hiding place;
   you'll protect me from trouble
   and surround me with songs of freedom.
                —— *Selah* ——

8 "I'll teach you
   and show you the way you should walk;
   I will counsel you,
   and keep watch over you.
9 Be wise!
   Don't be like horses and mules,
   who need to be harnessed with bit and bridle
   before they'll come to you."

10 Wrongdoers are prone to many sorrows,
   but those who trust in Our God
   are surrounded with unfailing love.
11 Be glad in Our God and rejoice, you who love justice!
   Exult, you upright of heart!

1 Sing out your joy to Our God, you who love justice—
   praise is fitting for loyal hearts.
2 Praise Our God with the harp,
   and play music with a ten-stringed lyre!
3 Sing God a new song,
   play with all your skill, and with shouts of joy!
4 For the word of Our God is true
   and everything God does can be trusted.
5 Our God loves justice and right
   and fills the earth with love.

6 By your word, Adonai, the heavens were made,
   by the breath of your mouth all the stars.
7 You gather the seas together and control them,
   putting the Deep into its vault.
8 Let all the earth revere Our God,
   let all who live in the world tremble before you!
9 You spoke, and everything came to be;
   commanded, and it all sprang into being.
10 You frustrate the designs of the nations,
   defeat the plans of the peoples.
11 But your own plan will stand firm forever,
   the designs of your heart from age to age.
12 Happy is the nation whose God is Adonai!
   Happy the people you choose as your own inheritance!
13 From the heavens you look forth, Adonai,
   and see all of humankind.
14 From your dwelling place you watch over
   all the peoples of the earth.
15 You shape the hearts of them all
   and consider all their deeds.

16 A ruler isn't saved by the size of an army;
   a warrior doesn't escape because of strength.
17 Trust in the horse for your deliverance
   and you'll be disappointed—
   despite its might,
      it cannot save.
18 The eyes of Our God look on those who stand in reverence,
   on those who hope in God's love

¹⁹ to rescue them from death,
    or to keep them alive during famine.
²⁰ And so we wait for Our God,
    our help and our shield.
²¹ For in you our hearts find joy;
    we trust in your holy Name.
²² May your love be upon us, Adonai,
    as we place all our hope in you.

34*

By David
Written when he pretended to be insane in front of Abimelech,
who drove him away and he escaped

1 I will bless Our God always,
    praise will continually be on my lips!
2 My soul will boast about Our God—
    let the oppressed hear it and be glad!
3 Glorify Our God with me,
    and let us exalt God's Name together!
4 I sought Our God, who answered me
    and freed me from all my fears.
5 Those who look to Our God are radiant,
    and their faces are never covered with shame.
6 The poor called out; Our God heard
    and saved them from all their troubles.
7 The angel of Our God encamps around those
    who revere God, and rescues them.
8 Taste and see how good Our God is!
    Happiness comes to those who take refuge in Our God.
9 Holy people of God, revere Adonai—
    for those who stand in awe of God lack nothing.
10 The young lion may grow weak and hungry,
    but those who seek Our God will lack no good thing.

---

* This psalm is an acrostic poem: the first letter of each verse begins with a subsequent letter of the Hebrew alphabet.

11 Come, children, listen to me!
   I will teach you reverence for Our God.
12 Which of you loves life,
   and wants to enjoy a long life of prosperity?
13 Then keep your tongue from gossip
   and your lips from telling lies;
14 turn away from bad and practice good;
   seek peace and pursue it.

15 The eyes of Our God are on those who do justice,
   and God's ears are open to their cry.
16 The face of Our God is turned against evildoers
   to cut off their memory from the earth.
17 But the just cry out, and Our God hears,
   and saves them from all their troubles.
18 Our God is close to the brokenhearted
   and rescues those whose spirits are crushed.
19 Many are the afflictions of the just;
   but Our God delivers them from all their troubles.
20 Our God protects their very bones,
   and not one of them will be broken.
21 Calamity will strike down these vicious curs,
   and the haters of justice will be condemned.
22 Our God ransoms the lives of the faithful,
   and none who take refuge in God will see punishment.

1   Accuse my accusers, Adonai,
    attack my attackers!
2   Grip your shield and sword,
    arise and help me!
3   Brandish your spear and javelin
    in the faces of my pursuers!
Say to me,
    "I am your victory!"

4   Shame and infamy on those
    who are out to kill me!
Turn them back,
    and confuse those who plot my downfall!
5   Let them be like chaff in the wind,
    with the angel of Our God driving them!
6   Let them walk a dark and slippery road
    with the angel of Our God hounding their heels!
7   Without provocation, they spread their net for me;
    unprovoked, they dug a pit for me.
8   But let ruin overtake them unawares—
    let the net they spread for me catch them instead,
    let them fall into their own pit.

9   Then I'll rejoice in Our God,
    exult that God has saved me.
10 All my bones will exclaim,
    "Adonai, who can compare to you?
You rescue the oppressed from their oppressors,
    the vulnerable from their exploiters!"

11 Perjurers take the stand against me;
    people I don't even know accuse me falsely.
12 They repay my kindness with violence,
    and I am left desolate.
13 Yet when they were sick, I wore sackcloth;
    I even humbled my soul with fasting
    when my prayers for them went unanswered.
14 I went around weeping for them like a grieving parent,
    I mourned as though for a friend or relative.

15 But when I stumbled, they were full of glee,
      and flocked to jeer at me;
   strangers I never even knew flocked to the stand,
      to deride and slander me without ceasing;
16 my treacherous foes circled around me,
      mocking me and grinding their teeth at me.

17 How much longer, Adonai, will you look on?
      Rescue me from their onslaughts,
      my dear life from these lions!
18 I will give thanks in the Great Assembly,
      praise you where the people throng.
19 Don't let these liars gloat over me,
      don't let those who hate me for no reason
      exchange sly glances!
20 They do not speak of peace,
      but attack the most vulnerable of the land.
21 They hatch vicious plans to slander me,
      and spread lies about me through the land—
   "Aha! Aha!" they say.
      "With our own eyes we witnessed your crime!"

22 But you're the one, Adonai, who witnessed everything.
      Don't remain silent, don't be far from me!
23 Wake up! Arise to my defense!
      Adonai, my God, side with me!
24 Vindicate me in your justice, Adonai my God,
      and don't let them gloat over me.
25 Don't let them think,
      "We've got you just where we wanted!"
   Don't let them say,
      "We've swallowed you whole!"
26 Let all who gloat over my misfortune
      be put to shame and confusion;
   let all who profit at my expense
      be clothed with shame and infamy!

27 But let those who delight in my vindication
      shout for joy and be glad;
   let those who delight in the well-being of your faithful one
      continually say, "Our God be praised!"
28 Then my tongue will tell of your justice,
      and sing your praises all day long.

36

For the conductor
By David, loyal subject of Our God

1   Deep in the heart of the violent,
      perversity is the only oracle they hear.
    They never view God
      with awe or reverence.
2   They flatter themselves in their own eyes so much
      that they can't see—can't hate—their own guilt.
3   In their mouths are mischief and deceit;
      all wisdom, all goodness is gone.
4   They hatch devious plots
      as they lie on their beds.
    They set their feet on ways that aren't good;
      they cling to what is evil.

5   Your love, Adonai, reaches to the heavens,
      your faithfulness to the skies.
6   Your justice is like the mountains in their splendor,
      Your judgments like the great deep.
    Whether human or animal, Adonai,
      you keep us all in your care.
7   How precious is your love!
    Whether creatures of heaven or children of earth,
      we all find refuge in the shadow of your wings.
8   We feast on the bounty of your estate,
      and drink from the stream of your delights.
9   In you is the wellspring of Life,
      and in your light we become enlightened.
10 Prolong your love for those who know you,
      and your justice for upright hearts.

11 Don't let the foot of the proud crush me
      nor the hand of the evildoer drive me away.
12 See how the violent have fallen—
      Flung down, unable to rise again!

1　Don't be vexed by evildoers,
　　　and don't be envious of the corrupt!
2　They'll soon fade like the grass,
　　　and wither away like unwatered plants.

3　Trust in Our God, and do good,
　　　and you'll dwell in the land and enjoy security.
4　Delight in Adonai,
　　　and you'll be given the desires of your heart.

5　Commit your way to Adonai, and trust in Our God;
　　　God *will* take action,
6　making your vindication as sure as the dawn
　　　and your integrity as bright as noonday.

7　Be still before Our God and wait patiently;
　　　don't fret about those who amass great fortunes
　　　and carry out their schemes unchallenged.

8　Let go of your anger,
　　　and leave resentment behind.
　　And stop worrying!
　　　It produces nothing but evil,
9　　and evildoers will be cut off.
　　But those who put their hope in Our God—
　　　they will inherit the land.

10　A little while longer,
　　　and the violent will be no more;
　　no matter how hard you look for them,
　　　they will not be found.
11　But the gentle will inherit the land,
　　　and will enjoy abundant peace.

12　Unscrupulous people plot against the just,
　　　and gnash their teeth at them;

---

* This psalm is an acrostic poem: the first letter of each stanza begins with a subsequent letter of the Hebrew alphabet.

¹³ but the Sovereign One laughs at them,
    knowing that their day is coming.

¹⁴ They draw their sword and bend their bow
    to slaughter the poor and needy,
    to murder those who walk uprightly;
¹⁵ but they will be pierced through the heart with their own sword,
    and their bows will be broken.

¹⁶ Better the little that honest people have saved
    than the ill-gotten gains amassed by the corrupt.
¹⁷ The power of the corrupt will be broken;
    but Our God champions the just.

¹⁸ Our God safeguards the possessions of the honest,
    and their inheritance will last forever;
¹⁹ they will not wither in the days of drought,
    and when famine comes, they will have abundance.

²⁰ But the corrupt will shrivel up;
    the enemies of Our God are like blazing fields—they vanish,
    they vanish more quickly than smoke.

²¹ The corrupt borrow and never pay back,
    but the righteous are generous and giving;
²² for those blessed by God will inherit the land,
    but the accursed will be slashed down.

²³ Our steps are steadied by Adonai,
    who secures our path.
²⁴ Though we stumble, we won't fall,
    for God is holding our hand.

²⁵ I was once young, and now I am old;
    but I have never seen the just forsaken
    nor their children begging bread.
²⁶ All day long they're generous and lend willingly,
    and their children become a blessing.

²⁷ Turn from evil and do good,
    and you'll always live securely.
²⁸ For Our God loves justice
    and will never forsake the faithful,
    but the progeny of the corrupt will be cut down.

29 The just will inherit the land,
   and dwell in it forever.

30 The mouth of the just utters wisdom,
   and their tongue speaks justice.
31 The Law of God is in their heart;
   their feet don't slip.

32 Violent criminals lie in ambush for the just,
   and seek to massacre them.
33 But Our God will not surrender them
   to the power of evil,
   or let them be condemned
   when they're brought to trial.

34 Wait for Adonai, and keep Our God's way,
   and God will raise you up
   so that you can possess the land,
   where you will witness the destruction of the corrupt.

35 I have witnessed the corrupt become powerful,
   and flourish like trees born for this soil.
36 Then suddenly they vanished and were gone—
   I looked for them, but they couldn't be found.

37 But take note of the blameless—behold the upright,
   for there is a future for peacemakers.
38 But those who insist on rebellion will be utterly destroyed;
   the future of the corrupt will be cut short.

39 The safety of the just is from Our God,
   their refuge when trouble comes.
40 Adonai helps them and rescues them—
   rescues them from the violent and saves them,
   because they take refuge in Our God.

1   Adonai, don't rebuke me in your anger
        or chastise me in your wrath!
2   For your arrows hit their mark,
        and I've felt the blows from your hand.
3   There is no health in my body
        because of your indignation;
    there is no wholeness to my bones
        because of my sin.
4   For my guilt has overwhelmed me;
        it's a heavy burden, too onerous for me to carry.
5   My wounds stink and fester;
        and all because I was such a fool.
6   I am completely broken;
        bent low, I walk around in anguish all day.
7   For my loins are filled with inflammation,
        and there is no health to my body.
8   I am utterly exhausted and crushed;
        I scream because my heart and mind are filled with discord.
9   Adonai, you know everything I long for,
        and my groans aren't hidden from you.
10 My heart is fever-racked, my strength fails me;
        even my eyes look dull and dead.
11 My friends and companions avoid me like the plague,
        and my neighbors stay far away.
12 Those who seek my life lay their snares,
        the ones who want to hurt me threaten ruin
        and plot their treachery all day long.
13 But I act like I'm deaf and can't hear,
        like I'm mute and can't speak:
14 I don't listen to what they're saying,
        and there are no retorts in my mouth.
15 It's because I wait for you, Adonai,
        and you'll answer me, my God, my Sovereign.
16 I said, "Don't let them gloat over me,
        don't let them get the advantage when my foot slips!"

17 But now I'm ready to fall,
   and my pain never leaves me.
18 I confess my transgression,
   I am sorry that I rebelled against you.
19 I have many mortal enemies,
   and those who hate me without reason are numerous.
20 Those who repay good with evil
   slander me for pursuing good.
21 Don't desert me too!
   My God, don't be far away from me!
22 Hurry and help me,
   my Sovereign, my Liberator!

For the conductor
Dedicated to Jeduthun
A psalm of David

1 I said, "I'll watch my words
    so that I don't stumble over my tongue.
I'll muzzle my mouth
    whenever corrupt people are nearby."
2 So I stood silent and still
    not even saying anything good—
and my anguish began to grow.
3 My heart grew hot inside me,
    my thoughts burned like a fire—
until I finally spoke:

4 Show me my end, Adonai!
    How many more days do I have?
    How fleeting is my life?
5 My life is as short as a hand's breadth,
    its span is nothing in your sight.
Each person is a mere mist;
    everyone's life but a fading mirage.
—— *Selah* ——
6 People roam through the streets like ghosts,
    in restless pursuit of vainglory;
they build storehouses of great wealth,
    without thought of who will get
    their fortune after they vanish.

7 But now, my God, what is there to wait for?
    You are everything I hope for.
8 Set me free from all my sins;
    don't make me the taunt of fools!
9 I was silent, not opening my mouth,
    because this was all your doing.
10 Put away the whips you've used on me;
    I'm crushed by the blows of your hand.
11 You discipline people
    and correct them because of their error—

like the moth, you devour everything they treasure;
 each person is a mere mist.
12 Hear my prayer, Adonai, and my cry for help!
 Listen to my weeping, and don't ignore me.
 I'm an alien with you, a stranger, as were all my ancestors.
13 Look away from me and let me rejoice once again,
 or I'll leave this life and be no more!

40

For the conductor
A psalm of David

1 Unyielding, I called to you, Adonai,
 now at last you have stooped to me
 and answered my cry for help.
2 You have pulled me out of the Pit of Destruction,
 out of its mud and quicksand;
you set my feet on a rock
 and made my steps firm.
3 You put a new song in my mouth,
 a song of praise to you.
Many will look on in wonder
 and so will put their trust in you.
4 Happiness comes to those
 who put their trust in Our God,
instead of in human egos
 or people blind to the truth!

5 How many wonders you've worked for us,
 Adonai, my God!
 How many plans you've made for us;
 you have no equal!
I want to recount them again and again,
 but their number is too great.
6 You don't desire sacrifice or oblation,
 instead you made my ears receptive to you;
you asked no burnt offering
 or sacrifice for sins from me.

7 And so I declared,
   "Here I am! I have come!
8 In the scroll of the book
   it is written about me."
   I desire to do your will, my God,
   and your law is written in my heart.
9 I'll proclaim your justice
   in the Great Assembly,
   and I won't keep my mouth shut,
   as you well know.
10 I have never kept your generosity to myself,
   but announce your faithfulness and saving action;
   I have made no secret of your love and faithfulness
   in the Great Assembly.

11 For your part, Adonai, don't withhold your love from me!
   Let your kindness and faithfulness constantly protect me!
12 Misfortunes surround me, far more than I can count;
   my sins entrap me and I am unable to escape.
   They outnumber the hairs on my head,
   and my courage is drained.
13 Hurry! Come to my rescue, Adonai!
   Be swift to help me!

14 Shame and confusion on all
   who are out to destroy me!
   Turn them back and heap disgrace
   on those who enjoy my misfortune!
15 May they be horrified at their shame,
   those who say to me, "Aha! Aha!"
16 May there be joy and gladness
   for all who seek you!
   May all who love your saving power
   have constant cause to say, "God is great!"

17 Now I am poor and needy.
   May Adonai think of me!
   You are my helper and deliverer—
   come swiftly!

1 Happiness comes to those who tell the truth;
    Our God will defend them when they are in trouble.

2 Our God will protect and preserve them,
    giving them long life and happiness in the land,
    and will not abandon them to the desires of their enemies.

3 Our God will nourish them on their sickbed,
    and restore them to health.

4 I said, "Have mercy on me, Adonai, and heal me,
    for I have rebelled against you!"

5 My enemies spew curses at me,
    like, "Why don't you just die
    and disappear along with your name!"

6 Those who visit me are duplicitous;
    they come only to gather bad news about me,
    and when they leave, they gossip everywhere.

7 My enemies whisper to each other behind my back;
    they fabricate horrible lies about me.

8 They say, "You have a vile disease
    and you'll never leave your bed again!"

9 Even my best friend, the one I trusted most,
    the one who broke bread at my table,
    spins slanderous tales about me.

10 Be merciful to me, Adonai!
    Raise me up so that I can pay them back!

11 I will know you're pleased with me
    if my enemy doesn't triumph over me.

12 You uphold me through my integrity,
    and set me in your presence forever.

13 Blessed be Our God, the God of Israel,
    forever and ever!
    Amen, amen!

book II

1 Like a stag, a doe, longing for streams of cool water,
    my whole being longs for you, my God.
2 My soul aches with thirst for God, for a god that lives!
    When can I go and see God face to face?
3 My only food, day or night, is my tears;
    they recriminate me:
    "Where is your God?" they say.

4 These things I remember
    as I pour out my soul like water—
how I'd go with the crowds
    and lead them into God's house,
amid cries of gladness and thanksgiving,
    drunk with the dance of celebration.

5 *"Why so dispirited?" I ask myself.*
    "Why so churned up inside? Hope in God!"
I know I'll praise God once again,
    for you are my Deliverance;
    you are my God.

6 This is why my heart despairs:
    I remember other days with you,
in the land of Jordan, on Mount Hermon
    and the Hill of Mizar.
7 The primeval Deep is echoing
    in the sound of your waterfalls;

---

[*] Psalms 42 and 43 were originally a single poem.

your torrents rage and break over me,
    overwhelming me.
8 Every day, Adonai, you ordain your love toward me,
    and during the night you bring me your song.
In my prayers to the God of my life,
9   I say to God, my rock:
"Why have you forgotten me?
    Why do you keep me in mourning,
    oppressed by an unseen enemy?"
10 My bones are shattered by their words,
    foes taunt me constantly:
    "Where is your God?" they say.

11 *"Why so dispirited?" I ask myself.*
    "Why so churned up inside? Hope in God!"
I know I'll praise God once again,
    for you are my Deliverance;
    you are my God.

43:1 Vindicate me, God!
    Plead my cause before unjust judges!
Rescue me from a lying, deceitful accuser.
2   For you, O God, are my stronghold, my defense.
Why have you forgotten me?
    Why do you keep me in mourning,
    oppressed by an unseen enemy?

3 Send forth your light and your truth—
    let them guide me,
let them bring me to your holy mountain,
    to your dwelling place.
4 Then at last I'll go up again
    to the altar of God,
    the God of my joy and delight.
My harp and lyre will sing your praise once again,
    O God, my God.

5 *"Why so dispirited?" I ask myself.*
    "Why so churned up inside? Hope in God!"
I know I'll praise God once again,
    for you are my Deliverance;
    you are my God.

For the conductor
By the disciples of Qorach
A teaching psalm

1 O God, we heard with our own ears—
        our ancestors told us
    all the things you did in their days,
        in days of old.
2 Your hand drove the nations out
        and planted them instead.
    You crushed the peoples,
        yet made our forebears take root.
3 It was not our ancestors' swords that won them the land,
            nor their arm that gave them the victory,
    but your mighty hand
        and your arm,
    the light of your presence—
        and your love for them.

4 You are my ruler, my God!
        At your bidding the children of Israel are victorious.
5 Through you we push back our enemies,
        in your Name we march over our adversaries.
6 I won't trust in my bow,
        nor will my sword win me the victory;
7 but it is you who makes us victorious over our enemies
        and puts our foes to shame.
8 We boast about you all day long, O God,
        and will praise your Name forever.
                —— *Selah* ——

9 But now you've rejected and chastened us
        and no longer lead our armies into battle.
10 You made us retreat before our enemy,
        and our foes pillage freely.
11 You've abandoned us to be butchered like sheep,
        and scattered us among the nations.

12 You have sold your people off for a pittance
    and did not consider them of much value.
13 You have made us the mockery of our neighbors,
    the scorn and contempt of those around us.
14 You've made us an example, a warning for the nations,
    and an object of ridicule among the peoples.

15 I brood on my disgrace all day long,
    and the shame on my face is exposed to all,
16 as my enemies assail me with taunts and abuse
    and take their revenge on me.
17 Every possible indignation has befallen us
    even though we didn't forget you
    or betray your Covenant;
18 we have not gone back on our word,
    nor did our feet stray from your path.
19 Yet you've broken us and thrust us into a pit of jackals,
    and covered us with a death pall.
20 If we had forgotten the Name of our God,
    or spread our hands in prayer to a god we've never known,
21 wouldn't you have discovered it, Adonai,
    since you know the hidden recesses of our heart?
22 Because of you we face a bloodbath all day long,
    and are treated as sheep for slaughter.

23 Wake up! Why do you sleep, Adonai?
    Rouse yourself! Don't reject us forever!
24 Why do you turn your face from us
    and ignore our misery and oppression?
25 We're falling down to the dust,
    we're lying in the dirt.
26 Arise and come to our help!
    Ransom us in your great love!

45

For the conductor
To the tune of "Lilies"
A teaching psalm by the disciples of Qorach
A wedding song

1   My heart is stirred with this sweet melody;
      I serenade you with my verse, my leader:
      my tongue is like the pen of a skillful writer.

2   Over all the earth, you are the most stately in manner,
      and the most charming of speakers,
      because God has blessed you forever.
3   Gird your sword upon your thigh, my champion,
      triumph by your splendor
      and subdue by your grandeur!
4   In your majesty ride forth
      for the cause of truth and the defense of the just.
      Let your right hand proclaim
      your awesome deeds!
5   Your arrows are sharp;
      they pierce the hearts of your enemies
      and make the nations cower before you.
6   For God has enthroned you forever and ever,
      and your royal scepter is a rod of justice.
7   And because you love justice and hate corruption,
      God, your God, has set you above your companions
      and anointed you with the oil of gladness.
8   Your robes are all fragrant with myrrh, aloes and cassia.
      Stringed instruments entertain you in ivory palaces.
9   Daughters of dignitaries are in your retinue,
      and at your right hand stands the queen in gold from Ophir.

10   Listen, my daughter! Give this your full attention:
      forget your country and your ancestral home,
11   for the ruler is enthralled by your beauty;
      give honor as you would to your sovereign.
12   A Tyrian robe is among your gifts,
      and great dignitaries will court your favor with jewels.
13   You, my daughter, will be gloriously dressed
      in a gown woven with gold.

14 Adorned in splendid robes you make your way to the ruler,
    and arrive with your friends as your attendants.
15 With joy and gladness you go in procession
    as you enter the palace of the ruler.

16 Your children will take the place of your ancestors,
    and you'll make them rulers throughout all the earth.
17 And I will make your name remembered
    from one generation to another,
so that the nations will praise you
    forever and ever.

46

For the conductor
By the disciples of Qorach
A song for soprano voices

1 God is our refuge and our strength,
    who from of old has helped us in our distress.
2 Therefore we fear nothing—
    even if the earth should open up in front of us
    and mountains plunge into the depths of the sea,
3 even if the earth's waters rage and foam
    and the mountains tumble with its heaving.

4 There's a river whose streams gladden the city of God,
    the holy dwelling of the Most High.
5 God is in its midst;
    it will never fall—
    God will help it at daybreak.
6 Though nations are in turmoil and empires crumble,
    God's voice resounds, and it melts the earth.

7 *Adonai Sabaoth is with us—*
    our stronghold is the God of Israel!

8 Come, see what Our God has done—
    God makes the earth bounteous!

9   God has put an end to war,
      from one end of the earth to the other,
   breaking bows, splintering spears,
      and setting chariots on fire.

10 "Be still, and know that I am God!
      I will be exalted among the nations;
      I will be exalted upon the earth."

11 *Adonai Sabaoth is with us;*
      our stronghold is the God of Israel!

47

For the conductor
By the disciples of Qorach
A psalm

1   People everywhere—clap your hands!
      Shout to God with a joyful voice!

2   For Our God Most High is awe-inspiring,
      the great Ruler over the whole earth.

3   God subdues peoples for us,
      and puts the nations under our feet.

4   God chooses our inheritance for us,
      the pride of Leah, Rachel and Jacob,
      the object of God's love.

5   God ascended the throne with a shout,
      with trumpet blasts!

6   Sing praise to God, sing praise!
      sing praise to our Ruler, sing praise!

7   For God rules over all the earth—
      sing praise and understand!

8   God rules over the nations;
      God sits on the throne of holiness.

9   World leaders are gathered,
      and so are the people of Sarah and Abraham's God,
   for Our God reigns over all the earth,
      and is exalted above all.

A song of praise
By the disciples of Qorach

1 How great is Adonai, how worthy of praise
    in the city of Our God, on God's holy mountain—
2 beautiful and lofty, the joy of all the earth!
  Mount Zion, "the heart of the earth,"
    is the city of the great Ruler.
3 And for all its citadels,
    God is Zion's true fortress.

4 Look—the rulers joined forces
    and made their attack.
5 But when they saw Zion,
    they were terrified and fled,
6 quaking in their boots,
    screaming in pain like a woman in labor.
7 Just as we had heard reports
    that you smashed the ships of Tarshish
    with a strong east wind,
8 so we now see with our own eyes
    in the city of Adonai Sabaoth,
  in the city of our God:
    it is God who makes Zion secure forever.
                —— *Selah* ——

9 O God, we meditate on your love
    within your Temple.
10 As your Name reaches the ends of the earth, O God,
    so does your praise;
    justice fills your right hand.
11 Mount Zion rejoices,
    and the villages of Judah celebrate
    because of your judgments.
12 Walk throughout Zion—make the rounds
    and count the towers!
13 Ponder its ramparts, examine its citadels,
    so that you can tell a future generation
14 that God is our God, forever and ever—
    and God will guide us even to our last day.

49

For the conductor
By the disciples of Qorach
A psalm of praise

1 Hear this, everyone!
　　Listen, all who live on the earth—
2 both women and men,
　　rich and poor alike!
3 My mouth will speak wisdom,
　　and my heart will utter knowledge.
4 I'll sing you a riddle,
　　and with my harp I'll explain its meaning:

5 Why should I be afraid in times of danger,
　　or when I'm surrounded by those who lie and deceive?
6 They trust only in their money,
　　and boast of nothing but their great wealth.
7 Yet even they cannot redeem another person—
　　no one can pay God the ransom for someone else,
8 　　because the payment for a life is too great.
What they can pay will never be enough
9 　　to keep them from the grave,
　　to let them live forever.
10 They see that even the wise die,
　　as do the foolish and stupid.
They all perish
　　and leave their riches to others.
11 Their graves will be their homes forever;
　　there they'll live from one generation to the next,
　　even though they once had lands of their own.
12 Their prosperity cannot keep them from death;
　　they'll die just like any animal.
13 This is the fate of those who trust in themselves,
　　and of their like-minded followers:
14 they are doomed to die like sheep,
　　and death will be their shepherd.
The righteous will rule over them in the morning,
　　as their bodies decay in the land of the dead,
　　far away from their mansions.

15 But God will redeem me,
    and will pluck me out of Death's control.

16 So don't be envious when people become rich,
    when they make their homes even grander—
17 because they can't take it with them when they die;
    their splendor will not join them in the grave.
18 Even though they're successful in this life,
    and are praised because they prosper,
19 they'll join all their ancestors in death,
    where the darkness lasts forever.
20 Those who are prosperous but without understanding
    will die just like any animal.

50

1 Adonai, Our God,
    speaks and summons the earth
  from the rising of the sun
    to its setting.
2 Out of Zion, the perfection of beauty,
    God shines forth.
3 Our God comes, and won't be silent:
    a devouring fire goes before God,
    while storms rage all around.
4 God summons heaven and earth
    to the trial of God's people:
5 "Gather to me my faithful ones,
    who make their covenant with me by sacrifice!"
6 The heavens affirm God's justice
    because it is God who is the judge!
                —— *Selah* ——

7 "Hear, O my people, and I will speak!
    Hear, O Israel, and I will testify against you!
    I am God—your God.
8 I don't fault you for your sacrifices—
    on the contrary, your burnt offerings are always before me.
9 It's just that I don't need oxen from your stall,

or goats from your folds,
10 since every beast of the forest is mine already;
   I have cattle on a thousand hills!
11 I know every bird in the mountains,
   and all that moves in the field is mine.
12 If I were hungry, I wouldn't tell you,
   for the world and all that is in it is mine.
13 Do I eat the flesh of oxen,
   or drink the blood of goats?
14 Offer me a sacrifice of thanksgiving instead,
   and fulfill the vow you make to me!
15 Then call upon me in the day of trouble—
   I will deliver you, and you will honor me."

16 But to the corrupt God says:
   "What right have you to recite my statutes
      or take my covenant on your lips?
17 For you hate discipline,
   and you throw away my words as if they were trash.
18 If you see a thief, you join in the thieving;
   and you cheat alongside other adulterers.
19 You give your mouth free rein for evil,
   and your tongue frames deceit.
20 You sit and speak against your sisters and brothers,
   and you slander your own siblings.
21 I didn't say a word while you did those things—
   you thought that I was just like you.
   But now I rebuke you
      and accuse you to your face.
22 So consider this, you who forget me—
   or I'll tear you to pieces with no hope of rescue!
23 Those who bring thanksgiving as their sacrifice
   honor me and prepare my road.
   To these I will reveal my salvation."

51

For the conductor
A psalm of David
Written when the prophet Nathan came to him
after David had relations with Bathsheba

1 O God, have mercy on me!
    Because of your love and your great compassion,
      wipe away my faults;
2 wash me clean of my guilt,
      purify me of my sin.
3 For I am aware of my faults,
      and have my sin constantly in mind.
4 I sinned against you alone,
      and did what is evil in your sight.
    You are just when you pass sentence on me,
      blameless when you give judgment.

5 I was born in sin,
      conceived in sin—
6 yet you want truth to live in my innermost being.
      Teach me your wisdom!
7 Purify me with hyssop until I am clean;
      wash me until I am purer than new-fallen snow.
8 Instill some joy and gladness into me,
      let the bones you have crushed rejoice again.
9 Turn your face from my sins,
      and wipe out all my guilt.

10 O God, create a clean heart in me,
      put into me a new and steadfast spirit;
11 do not banish me from your presence,
      do not deprive me of your holy Spirit!
12 Be my savior again, renew my joy,
      keep my spirit steady and willing;
13 and I will teach transgressors your ways,
      and sinners will return to you.

14 Save me from bloodshed, O God, God of my salvation—
      and my tongue will acclaim your justice.
15 Open my lips, Adonai,
      and my mouth will declare your praise.

16 Sacrifice gives you no pleasure;
  were I to present a burnt offering,
  you would not have it.
17 My sacrifice, O God, is a broken spirit;
  you will not scorn this crushed and broken heart.

18 Make Zion prosper through your favor,
  and rebuild the walls of Jerusalem.
19 Then there will be proper sacrifice to please you—
  burnt offerings and whole oblations,
  and young bulls to be offered on your altar.

52

For the conductor
A teaching psalm by David
Written when Doeg the Edomite went to Saul and said,
"David has gone to Ahimelech's house"

1 How can you boast
  about how corrupt you are, you tyrant?
Even against God's beloved
2   you forge wild lies all day long—
your slanderous tongue
  is sharp as a razor!
3 You love evil, not good;
  falsehood, not truth-telling.
    —— *Selah* ——
4 You enjoy cruel gossip
  and slanderous talk.
5 So God will pull you down to the ground forever,
  sweep you away, leave you ruined and homeless
  and uprooted from the land of the living!
6 The righteous will look on, awestruck,
  and they will laugh at your plight.
7 "This is the one," they'll say,
  "who didn't seek refuge in God,
but trusted in great wealth
  and grew strong by destroying others."

8   I am an olive tree flourishing in God's house,
      for I trust in God's love forever and ever.
9   I will praise you forever for what you have done;
      among your faithful I will put my trust in your Name,
      for it is good.

53

For the conductor
About sickness
A teaching psalm by David

1   Fools say in their hearts,
      "There is no God."
   They are corrupt, and do despicable wrongs—
      there is none who does good.
2   God looks down from heaven
      on all of humankind,
   to see whether any
      are wise or seek God.
3   But they've all turned away;
      they all became corrupt together.
   None of them does good—
      not a single one.
4   Will they never learn, these evildoers
      who devour my people like bread,
      and never call upon God?
5   There they are, consumed with fear—
      when there was never anything to fear!
   For God scattered the bones of those who attacked you, Israel—
      you put them to shame,
      for God had rejected them.

6   Who will come from Zion
      to bring the deliverance of Israel?
   When God's people are brought back from captivity,
      the descendants of Leah, Rachel and Jacob will rejoice;
      the children of Israel will be glad.

54

To the conductor: for strings
A teaching psalm by David
Written when the Ziphites went to Saul and said,
"David is hidden among us!"

1 O God, save me by the power of your Name,
  defend me by your might!
2 God, hear my prayer,
  listen to the words of my mouth.
3 Strangers attack me,
  ruthless scoundrels seek my life;
  they don't give God a single thought.
            —— *Selah* ——
4 For you are my helper,
  the One who sustains my life.
5 May their own malice recoil on my slanderers;
  silence them with your truth.
6 I will offer you a willing sacrifice
  and praise your Name, Adonai, for it is good.
7 You have rescued me from every trouble;
  I have seen my enemies' downfall with my own eyes.

1 O God, hear my prayer—
   don't ignore my pleas!
2 Hear me! Answer me!
   My mind is tortured and I am distraught
3 at the sound of my enemies,
   at their vicious oppression.
   They engulf me with their treachery
   and assault me in anger.
4 My heart is tortured inside me;
   terrors of death assail me.
5 Fear and trembling invade me;
   horror overwhelms me.

6 So I said, "If only I had the wings of a dove!
   Then I'd fly away and find rest.
7 Yes, I'd fly far away,
   and find rest in the desert.
                —— *Selah* ——
8 I'd hurry to my place of refuge,
   far from this raging wind and storm."

9 Confound them, Adonai, confuse their speech,
   for I see nothing but violence and strife in the city.
10 Day and night they prowl its borders;
   malice and trouble roam its streets.
11 Violence fills the city,
   fraud and deceit never leave its marketplace.

12 For it is not an enemy who reviles me—
   I could bear that!
   It is not a foe who taunts me—
   or I could hide and be safe.
13 No, it is you, my other self,
   my companion, my bosom friend!—
14 we who together held sweet communion;
   we walked to God's house amid the festive throng!

¹⁵ Let Destruction seize them without warning!
   Let Sheol swallow them alive!
   For Corruption will make its home with them
      wherever they are.
¹⁶ As for me, I will call on God
      and God will save me.
¹⁷ Evening, morning and noon
      I lament and groan
      and my Liberator hears my voice.
¹⁸ God ransoms me whole
      from those who wage war against me,
      though many oppose me.
¹⁹ God will hear me and overthrow them—
      the One who has reigned from the beginning—
            —— *Selah* ——
   because they will never change:
      they have no reverence for God.

²⁰ And you, my former friend—
      you even attack your soulmates
      and violate your covenant with them.
²¹ Your talk is as smooth as butter,
      but in your heart there is war;
   your words are more soothing than oil,
      yet they conceal the drawn sword.

²² Cast your burden on God,
      who will sustain you,
      and will never allow the righteous to be overthrown.
²³ But God will bring your enemies down
      to the pit of destruction;
   those murderous deceivers will not live out half their days.
      Adonai, I will trust in you!

To the conductor: to the tune of "A Dove on the Far Oaks"
By David
A poem written when the Philistines seized him in Gath

1 O God, have mercy on me, for the enemy persecutes me,
 my assailants harass me all day long.
2 All day long my slanderers persecute me;
 countless are those who assail me, Exalted One.

3 *When I am afraid,*
 I will trust in you.
4 *In you I will shout defiance!*
 In you I will trust and let go of my fear—
 what can mortals do to me?

5 All day long they twist my words,
 all their thoughts are hostile.
6 They plot, they wait in ambush,
 they watch my every move,
 eager to take my life.
7 Don't let them escape!
 O God, in your anger bring ruin to the nations.
8 You write down all my laments,
 and store every tear in your wineskin—
 have you counted each one?
9 Then my enemies will turn back
 on the day I call upon you;
10 this I know—
 that God is on my side.

 In you I will shout defiance!
11 *In you I will trust and let go of my fear—*
 what can mortals do to me?

12 I have bound myself with vows to you, O God,
 and will redeem them with thank-offerings;
13 for you have rescued me from death
 and kept my feet from stumbling,
 to walk in your presence,
 in the light of life.

To the conductor: to the tune of "Do Not Destroy"
By David
A poem, written when he ran from Saul and hid in a cave

1 Have mercy on me, O God, have mercy on me!
In you my soul takes shelter;
I take shelter in the shadow of your wings
until the destroying storm is over.

2 I call on God the Most High,
on God who has done everything for me,

3 to send help from heaven to save me,
to stop them from persecuting me.
—— *Selah* ——
O God, send me your love
and your faithfulness.

4 I'm surrounded by lions
greedy for human prey,
their teeth are spears and arrows,
their tongue a sharp sword.

5 Rise high above the heavens, O God,
and let your glory cover the earth!

6 They laid a net where I was walking
when I was bowed with care;
they dug a pit for me
but fell into it themselves.
—— *Selah* ——

7 My heart is ready, O God,
my heart is ready;
I will sing and play for you.

8 Awake, my muse!
Awake, lyre and harp!
I will awaken the dawn!

9 I will thank you among the peoples, Adonai,
and sing of you among the nations;

10 your love is high as heaven,
your faithfulness reaches to the skies.

11 Rise high above the heavens, O God,
let your glory cover the earth!

To the conductor: to the tune of "Do Not Destroy"
By David
A poem

1 Do you really make just decisions, you leaders?
  Do you judge everyone fairly?
2 No! You think only of the injustice you will do;
  you commit crimes of violence in the land.
3 You've done wrong all your lives,
  and lied from the day you were born.
4 You are full of poison, like snakes;
  you stop up your ears, like a deaf cobra
5 that doesn't hear the voice of the snake charmer
  or the incantation of the fakir.

6 Break their teeth, Adonai!
  Tear out the fangs of these fierce lions!
7 Let them disappear like water draining away;
  Let them be crushed like weeds on the path.
8 Let them be like snails that dissolve into slime;
  let them be like a baby born dead
  that never sees the light.
9 Before these thorns can grow into brambles
  they'll be swept away
  whether they are green or dry.
10 The just will be glad when they see the corrupt punished;
  they will wade through the blood of the wicked.
11 People will say, "The just really are rewarded;
  there is indeed a God who judges the world!"

To the conductor: to the tune of "Do Not Destroy"
By David
A poem written when Saul sent guards to
watch David's house and try to kill him

1 Rescue me from my enemies, my God!
   Protect me from those who attack me!
2 Rescue me from those who love violence,
   and save me from this bloodthirsty gang!
3 Look! They lie in wait for my life;
   the powerful conspire against me
for no reason at all—
   I didn't do anything wrong, Adonai!
4 Though I committed no sin, they rush to take their stand.
   Awake, come to my aid and see!
5 You, Our God, God of Hosts, Israel's God—
   rise up and punish the nations;
   show no mercy to these evil traitors!
      —— Selah ——

6 Each evening they come back like dogs;
   they howl and roam the city.
[They prowl in search of food,
   they snarl till they've had their fill.] *

7 See what they spew from their mouths—
   their lips are filled with words that cut like a sword.
   "For who," they say, "will hear us?"
8 But you, Adonai, will laugh at them—
   you scoff at all the nations.

9 O my strength, I watch for you,
   for you, O God, are my stronghold.
10 The God who loves me
   will go before me;
God will let me gloat
   over the ones who slander me now.

---

* This part of the verse is found in the Greek version of the text, but is missing from the standard Hebrew version.

11 O God, kill them, lest my people be seduced!
   By your power, scatter them and lay them low—
   you who are our shield, Adonai!
12 For the sins of their mouths and their lips,
   for the curses and lies that they speak,
   let them be caught in their pride.
13 Destroy them in your anger!
   Destroy them until they are no more!
   Then all will know that God rules in Israel
   and to the ends of the earth.
                  —— *Selah* ——

14 Each evening they come back like dogs.
   They howl and roam the city,
15 they prowl in search of food,
   they snarl till they have had their fill.

16 As for me, I will sing of your strength
   and each morning acclaim your love;
   for you have been my stronghold,
   a refuge in the day of my distress.
17 O God my strength,
   it is you that I praise,
   for you, O God, are my stronghold—
   the God who loves.

60

To the conductor: To the tune of "The Lily of the Covenant"
A poem of David, for teaching
Written when he fought the Arameans of Mesopotamia and Syria, when
Joab returned and killed twelve thousand Edomites in the Valley of Salt

1 O God, you have rejected us
   and broken our defenses.
   You have been angry;
      restore us!
2 You have rocked the land and split it open;
      now repair the cracks that your earthquakes are causing!
3 You have made your people feel hardship,
      and given us stupefying wine.
4 Now raise a banner for those who revere you
      to which they may flee, out of bowshot,
5 that your loved ones may escape;
      help us by your mighty hand and answer us!

6 God promised in the sanctuary:
   "In triumph I will divide up Shechem,
      and measure off the Succoth Valley.
7 Gilead is mine,
      and so is Manasseh;
   Ephraim is the helmet for my head,
      and Judah is my scepter;
8 Moab will serve as my washbowl,
      upon Edom I will set my shoes,
   and over Philistia
      I will shout my triumph!"

9 Who will bring me into the fortified city?
      Who will lead me to Edom?
10 Isn't it you who have rejected us, O God,
      and no longer go forth with our armies?
11 Give us aid against the enemy,
      for all other help is worthless.
12 With God we will triumph;
      God will trample our enemies.

61

To the conductor: for strings
By David

1 O God, hear my cry;
   listen to my prayer!
2 From the end of the earth I call to you,
   and now my heart grows weak.
   Set me on a rock
   that is higher than I.
3 For you have been my shelter,
   a tower of strength when I am in danger.
4 In your tent I will make my home forever,
   and take shelter under the cover of your wings.
—— *Selah* ——

5 For you've heard my vows, O God,
   and given me the inheritance
   reserved for those who revere your Name.
6 To my life as a ruler, add one day, then another,
   then year upon year and generation upon generation.
7 Let me rule in God's presence forever,
   and let love and faithfulness be my protectors.
8 Then I will sing praises forever to your Name
   as I fulfill my vows day after day.

62

To the conductor: for Jeduthun
A psalm of David

1 In God alone my soul finds rest,
      for my deliverance comes from God,
2 who alone is my rock, my salvation, my fortress:
      I will never be shaken.

3 How long will you besiege me
      as though I were a crumbling wall
      or a tottering fence?
4 They connive to push me off a cliff,
      they delight in telling lies.
   With their mouths they utter blessing,
      but in their hearts they curse.
                —— *Selah* ——

5 In God alone my soul finds rest,
      for my deliverance comes from God,
6 who alone is my rock, my salvation, my fortress:
      I will never be shaken.

7 Only in God—my deliverance, my glory—
      my refuge is God.
8 Trust in God always, my people;
      pour out your hearts before God our refuge.
9 Humankind is but a breath,
      mortals are just an illusion.
   Put them on the scales and the balance is thrown off:
      they weigh less than a breath.
10 Do not trust in extortion,
      or put false hopes in stolen goods;
   do not set your heart on riches
      even when they increase.

11 For God has said only one thing,
      only two do I know:
   that to God alone belongs power,
12   and that you, Adonai, are loving—
   you repay all people
      according to their deeds.

1 Adonai, my God,
    you are the One I seek.
My soul thirsts for you,
    my body longs for you
in this dry and weary land
    where there is no water.
2 So I look to you in the sanctuary
    to see your power and glory;
3 because your love is better than life,
    my lips will glorify you.

4 And so I bless you while I live;
    in your Name I lift up my hands.
5 My soul will be sated as with a sumptuous feast,
    and with euphoric cries I will praise you.
6 I remember you when I'm in bed;
    through sleepless nights I meditate on you,
7 because you are my help,
    and in the shadow of your wings I sing for joy.
8 My soul clings to you;
    your mighty hand upholds me.

9 But those who seek my life will be destroyed,
    they'll be cast into the bowels of the earth;
10 they will be delivered over to the sword,
    and will become food for jackals.
11 But I will rejoice in God,
    everyone who swears by God will rejoice,
but the mouths of those who tell lies
    will be silenced.

For the conductor
A psalm of David

1 O God, hear the voice of my lament!
   Keep me safe from the threats of the enemy.
2 Hide me from that vicious gang,
   from that mob of evildoers
3 who sharpen their tongues like swords
   and wing their cruel words like arrows
4 to ambush the innocent like a sniper,
   shooting without warning, themselves unseen.
5 They encourage each other in their evil plans
   and brag about how they hide their snares,
   secure that no one will see them;
6 they plot their secret injustices with skill and cunning,
   with evil purpose and deep design.

7 But God's arrows hit their mark,
   and their downfall will be sudden.
8 Their own mischievous tongues will be their undoing,
   and all who see them will recoil in horror.
9 All humankind will be afraid:
   "This is God's doing," they'll say,
   and they'll learn their lesson from what God has done.

10 But the just will rejoice and seek refuge in Our God;
   let the upright in heart give praise!

For the conductor
A psalm of David
A song

¹ O God, to you we owe hymns of praise in Zion;
   to you our vows must be fulfilled,
² you who hear our prayers
   and before whom all flesh must stand.
³ When we are overcome by our sins,
   you provide the atonement for them.
⁴ Happy are those you choose, those you draw near
   to dwell in your courts!
We are filled with the blessings of your house,
   the holy things of your Temple!

⁵ With powerful deeds of justice
   you answer us, God our Deliverer,
in whom all the ends of the earth
   and the farthest seas put their trust.
⁶ You set the mountains in place by your power,
   having armed yourself with might.
⁷ You still the roaring of the seas,
   the roaring of the waves, and the tumult of the peoples.
⁸ And those who dwell at the ends of the earth
   stand in awe of your marvels;
   you make the sunrise and sunset shout for joy!
⁹ You nourish and water the land—
   greatly you have enriched it.
The streams of God are full of water;
   you provide us with grain as you ordained.
¹⁰ Thus have you prepared the land:
   drenching its furrows,
breaking up its clods, softening it with showers,
   blessing its yield.
¹¹ You have crowned the year with your bounty
   and your paths overflow with a rich harvest;
¹² the untilled meadows overflow with abundance,
   and rejoicing clothes the hills.
¹³ The fields are covered with flocks
   and the valleys are blanketed with grain.
   They shout and sing for joy!

1 Shout to God,
    all the earth!
2 Sing the glory of God's Name—
    give glorious praise!
3 Say to God,
    "How awesome are your deeds!
    Your enemies cower before your great strength!
4 The whole earth worships you
    and sings praises to you—
    all creation praises your Name!"
           —— *Selah* ——

5 Come and see the works of God—
    God's deeds on our behalf are wondrous.
6 God turned the sea into dry land;
    and people passed through the river on foot.
There we rejoiced in God,
7   whose reign of power lasts forever,
whose eyes keep watch on the nations
    so that the rebellious don't exalt themselves before God.

8 Bless our God, all you peoples,
    let the sound of God's praise be heard!
9 God has kept us among the living,
    and has not let our feet slip.
10 For you have tested us, O God—
    you have refined us as silver is refined.
11 You put us in prisons
    and laid burdens on our backs;
12 you let people ride over our heads;
    we went through fire and through water—
    and you brought us to a place of abundance and space.

13 I will come to your house with burnt offerings;
    I will pay my vows to you,
14 the ones my lips uttered
    and my mouth promised when I was in trouble.

15 I will present you burnt offerings of fatlings,
     with the smoke of burning rams;
     I will make an offering of bulls and goats.
            —— *Selah* ——
16 Come and hear, all who revere God,
     and I will tell what the Holy One has done for me.
17 I cried aloud to God,
     and praise was on my tongue.
18 If I had nursed evil in my heart,
     God would not have listened.
19 But God did listen,
     and heeded the voice of my prayer.
20 Blessed be God,
     who has not rejected my prayer
     or stopped loving me!

67

To the conductor: for strings
A song of praise

1 O God, show us kindness and bless us,
     and make your face smile on us!
            —— *Selah* ——
2 For then the earth will acknowledge your ways,
     and all the nations will know of your power to save.
3 Let the peoples praise you, O God,
     let all the peoples praise you!
4 Let the nations shout and sing for joy,
     for you dispense true justice to the world—
     you guide the nations of the earth!
5 Let the peoples shout and sing for joy,
     let all the peoples praise you!
6 The land has given its harvest:
     God, our God, has blessed us.
7 May God bless us, and may God be revered
     even to the ends of the earth!

To the conductor
By David
A song of praise

1   Arise, O God, and scatter your enemies!
    Make your enemies flee before you!

2   As smoke disappears in the air, so make them disappear!
    As wax melts in fire, let the violent vanish before you!

3   But let the righteous be joyful!
    Let them exult before God,
    let them be jubilant with joy!

4   Sing praise to the Rider of the Clouds
    whose Name is Adonai!
    Exult before God!

5   A parent to the orphan
    and protector of the defenseless
    is our God, who dwells in holiness!

6   God creates families for those who are alone,
    and leads captives to freedom;
    but the rebellious dwell in a parched land.

7   O God, when you went forth before your people,
    when you marched through the wilderness,
        —— *Selah* ——

8   the earth quaked, the heavens poured down rain
    before you, the One of Sinai—
    before you, the God of Israel.

9   You gave rain in abundance, O God,
    you restored the land—our inheritance—when it languished;

10   your tribe found a dwelling in it,
    in your goodness, O God, you provided for the needy.

11   Adonai gave the command,
    and the women who carried the good news
    were a great throng:

12   "The rulers and their armies,
    they flee, they flee!

13   And women who have no standing
    are dividing the spoil;

and even for those of you who sleep in the sheepfolds,
    there are wings of a dove—with pinions of fine gold—
    in a silver sheath!
14 When Shaddai scattered the rulers in Zalmon,
    it looked like a snowstorm had swept through!"

15 Mountain of majesty, mountain of Bashan!
    Mountain of tall peaks, mountain of Bashan!
16 Why look with envy, you many-peaked mountain,
    toward the mount where God chose to reign,
    where Adonai will dwell forever?
17 With God's Chariot—
    and with twenty thousand, and thousands more—
    Adonai came from Sinai into the sanctuary.
18 When you ascended the high mount,
    you led captives in your train
and received tribute
    from those you conquered—
even from those who rebel
    against the Most High God who lives there.

19 Blessed be Our God, who supports us day by day—
    God alone is our Savior!
           —— *Selah* ——
20 Our God is a God of salvation,
    since to Adonai we owe our escape from death.
21 God will strike down the rulers of your enemies,
    their leaders who continue in their guilty ways.
22 God said,
    "I who stifled the Serpent
    and muzzled the Deep Sea
23 will let you walk away unscathed
    and leave your enemies to the dogs."

24 Your solemn processions are coming into view now, O God—
    the processions of my God, my Ruler,
    have come into the sanctuary—
25 the singers in front, then the musicians,
    and all around them the young people playing tambourines.
26 "Bless God in your great congregation," they sing,
    "you who are Israel's fountain!"

27 Then comes little Benjamin, leading the rest:
    the royalty of Judah in their throng,
    then the royalty of Zebulun and of Naphtali.

28 Summon your power, O God;
    show the strength that you have shown to us before, O God!
29 Because of your Temple at Jerusalem,
    rulers bring you gifts.
30 Rebuke the Beast of the Reeds!
    It is a herd of bulls inciting its calves—the nations—
    to stampede over people for lust of silver.
God will scatter the nations whose lust creates war,
31   and Egypt's wealthy will come bearing tribute,
    Cush will hurry to God with gifts in hand.

32 Sing to God, all the earth's realms!
    Sing praises to Adonai!
      —— *Selah* ——
33 Sing to the Rider of the ancient skies,
    who thunders forth with a powerful voice!
34 Proclaim the power of God,
    whose majesty is over Israel,
    in the skies!
35 O God, how awesome you are in your sanctuary!
    The God of Israel gives power and strength to the people.
Blessed be God!

To the conductor: to the tune of "Lilies"
By David

1 O God, save me,
    for the waters are up to my neck!
2 I'm sinking into a deep swamp
    and can't find a foothold!
  I'm in very deep water,
    and its torrents are overwhelming me.
3 I'm exhausted from crying,
    my throat is raw;
  and my sight is blurring
    from looking for my God.
4 Those who hate me for no reason
    outnumber the hairs of my head.
  So many would destroy me,
    so many accuse me without cause,
  and force me to restore
    what I didn't steal!

5 O God, you know how foolish I've been,
    and my faults are not hidden from you.
6 Don't let those who look to you be disappointed because of me,
    Sovereign God of Hosts!
  Don't let those who seek you be ashamed because of me,
    O God of Israel,
7 since it is for your sake that I bear insult,
    that shame covers my face.
8 I've become an outcast in my own family,
    a stranger to my mother's children—
9 and because I am consumed with zeal for your House,
    the insults of those who ridicule you
    fall upon me.
10 When I weep and fast,
    I receive nothing but abuse.
11 When I dress in sackcloth,
    I am called a buffoon.
12 They sit at the gate gossiping about me,
    and drunks make me the butt of their songs.

¹³ But I pray to you, Adonai,
   for the time of your favor, O God!
   In your great love, answer me!
      With you is sure deliverance!
¹⁴ Rescue me from the quicksand—
      don't let me sink!
   Let me be rescued from my enemies,
      and from the watery depths.
¹⁵ Don't let the raging flood engulf me,
      don't let the abyss swallow me up,
      or the pit close its mouth over me.
¹⁶ Answer me, Adonai, for your love is wonderful!
      In your great mercy, turn toward me.
¹⁷ Don't hide your face from your faithful one;
      I am in trouble—hurry and answer me!
¹⁸ Come and ransom my life;
      as an answer to my enemies, redeem me.

¹⁹ You know my torment, my shame and my dishonor;
      You see how my enemies treat me.
²⁰ My heart aches from their insults and I am helpless;
      I look for sympathy, but to no avail;
      for comforters, but find none.
²¹ Instead, they poisoned my food,
      and for my thirst they gave me vinegar to drink.
²² May they be trapped by the table they set;
      may their own friends be caught in its snare!
²³ May their eyes grow dim so that they cannot see,
      and their backs become increasingly feeble!
²⁴ Pour out your wrath upon them;
      let the fury of your anger sweep them away!
²⁵ Let their encampment become deserted;
      let their tents stand empty!
²⁶ For they persecute the one you struck,
      and add insult to the pain of the one you wounded.
²⁷ Charge them with crime upon crime,
      and don't let them share in your promise!
²⁸ Erase their names from the Book of the Living,
      and don't record them among the just!

²⁹ I am suffering and in pain—
      let your saving help protect me, God!

30 Then I will praise your Name in song,
    and glorify you with thanksgiving.
31 This will please you more than oxen
    or bulls with their horns and hooves.
32 See and be glad, you who have nothing!
    You who seek God, take heart!
33 For Our God hears the poor;
    God has not neglected those who are captives.
34 Let heaven and earth praise God,
    the seas and all that moves in them!
35 For God will free Zion
    and rebuild the cities of Judah,
and those who were expelled from the land
    will return at last.
36 The descendants of God's faithful ones will inherit it,
    and those who love God's Name will inhabit it.

70

To the conductor
By David
A petition

1 O God, save me!
    Adonai, help me, and hurry!
2 Let those who seek my life
    be humiliated and dazed!
Let those who wish me harm
    flee in disgrace!
3 Those who jeer, "Aha! Aha!"—
    make them retreat, covered with shame!
4 Let all who seek you
    rejoice and be glad in you!
Let those who love your salvation
    forever say, "God is great!"
5 As for me, I am wretched and poor, my God—
    hurry to my side!
You are my rescuer, my help;
    Adonai, do not delay.

1 In you, Adonai, I take shelter—
   let me never be disappointed.
2 In your justice, rescue me, deliver me,
   turn your ear to me and save me!
3 Be mine, O mountain of strength!
   Send your decree—deliver me,
   for you are my rock, my fortress!
4 O God, rescue me from the hands of the violent,
   from the clutches of the thief and outlaw!

5 For you alone are my hope, Adonai my sovereign—
   I have trusted you since my youth.
6 I have relied on you from the womb;
   you sustained me from my mother's breast;
   to you I give constant praise.
7 I have become a target for many,
   but you are my firm refuge.
8 My mouth is filled with your praise,
   full of your splendor all day long.
9 Don't throw me away now that I am old,
   nor desert me now that my strength is failing.

10 For my enemies are spying on me,
   and those who are waiting for me to die
   are hatching conspiracies.
11 They say, "God has forsaken you!
   We will pursue you, then catch you—
   for there is no one to rescue you."
12 O God, don't be far from me!
   My God, come quickly and help me!
13 May those who slander me be utterly humiliated;
   let those who want to hurt me
   be covered with insult and disgrace.

14 As for me, I'll always have hope,
   and I will add to all your praises.
15 My lips will proclaim your deeds of justice and salvation
   all day long, even though they are innumerable.

16 O God, I will enter your mighty Temple
       and there proclaim your justice.

17 You taught me when I was young,
       and I am still proclaiming your marvels.
18 Now that I am old and gray,
       O God, do not desert me;
    let me live to tell the coming generation
       about your strength and power.

19 Your justice, O God, is higher than the heavens.
       You have done great things;
       who is comparable to you?
20 Though you have sent me much misery and hardship,
       you will give me life again,
    you will raise me up again
       from the depths of the earth;
21 you'll increase my honor
       and once again comfort me.

22 And so on the lyre I'll praise you,
       my ever-faithful God;
    I will play the harp in your honor,
       Holy One of Israel.
23 My lips will sing for joy while I play for you—
       my whole being, which you have redeemed, will sing.
24 And all day long, my tongue will speak of your beneficence—
       how those who wanted to hurt me
       were put to shame and humiliated!

1 O God, give your anointed one your judgment—
    and your justice.
2 Teach your chosen one to govern your people rightly
    and bring justice to the oppressed.
3 The mountains will bring the people peace
    and the hills justice!
4 Your anointed will defend the oppressed among the people,
    save the children of the poor,
    and crush the oppressor.
5 The reign of your anointed will endure
    as long as the sun and moon—
    throughout all generations.
6 The rule of the chosen one will be
    like rain coming down on the meadow,
    like showers watering the earth.
7 Justice will flower through the days, and profound peace,
    until the moon be no more.

8 Your anointed will rule from sea to sea,
    and from the Euphrates to the ends of the earth.
9 The desert tribes will bow before the throne
    and the enemies of your chosen one will lick the dust.
10 Tarshish and the Isles will offer gifts;
    Arabia and Sheba will bring tribute.
11 All rulers will pay homage,
    and all the nations will serve your anointed.
12 Your anointed will rescue the poor when they cry out,
    and the oppressed when there is no one to help them.
13 Your chosen one
    will take pity on the lowly and the poor,
    and will save their lives.
14 Your chosen one
    will rescue them all from violence and oppression,
    and will treat their blood as precious.

¹⁵ Long live the anointed one!
    Bring a tribute of gold from Sheba!
Let the ruler be prayed for continually,
    and blessed day after day!
¹⁶ Let there be an abundance of grain upon the earth—
    let it rustle on the mountaintops!
Let the crops flourish like the forests of Lebanon;
    let them thrive like the grass of the fields.
¹⁷ May the name of your anointed one endure forever,
    and continue as long as the sun.
In your chosen the nations of earth will be blessed,
    and they will bless the anointed in return.

¹⁸ Blessed be Our God, the God of Israel,
    who alone does wondrous deeds!
¹⁹ And blessed forever be God's glorious Name;
    may the whole earth be filled with God's glory.
    Amen, amen!

²⁰ Here end the prayers of David begot of Jesse.

book III

1   Israel, how good your God is
      to those who are single-hearted!

2   My feet had almost strayed—
      a little farther and I would have slipped,
3   for I had envied those who boast of their success
      and begrudged the prosperity of the corrupt.
4   They have no struggles,
      their bodies are healthy and strong;
5   they don't suffer as others do,
      they're not afflicted like the rest of humanity!
6   So pride is their badge of honor,
      violence is the robe that covers them;
7   their eyes gorge themselves on new luxuries,
      their taste for extravagance knows no limits.
8   They cynically attribute evil to God,
      and blame all oppression on the Most High;
9   they think their mouth speaks for heaven,
      that their tongue can dictate on earth.

10 This is why my people turn to them
      and lap up all they say,
11 asking, "How will God ever find out?
      Does the Most High know everything?
12 Look at them: these are the corrupt,
      yet they are well off and still getting richer!

13 What's the use of keeping my own heart pure,
        and washing my hands in innocence,
14 if God still plagues me all day long
        and brings new punishments every morning?"

15 Had I dared to say things like that,
        I would have been false to the circle of your disciples.
16 Instead, I sought to probe the problem of injustice,
        but found it nearly impossible—
17 until the day I entered God's sanctuary
        and saw the end in store for them.
18 They will certainly fall into Perdition;
        you urge them on to their own destruction
19 until they suddenly fall,
        done for, terrified to death.
20 Like waking up from a dream, Adonai,
        their fantasies will be dashed in an instant.

21 But since my heart was aggrieved,
        and I had a gut full of anger,
22 I became a stupid fool before you;
        I acted like a jackass, and I am sorry.
23 Even so, you were always at my side
        holding me by the hand.
24 Now lead me with your counsel
        and in the end, bring me into your glory.
25 I look to no one else in heaven,
        I delight in nothing else on earth.
26 My body and mind may fail
        and my heart may pine for love,
    but God is my heart's rock,
        and my portion forever.

27 So then: those who are far from you will be lost,
        and you will destroy those who break faith with you.
28 But as for me, my joy lies in being close to God.
        I have taken refuge in you, Adonai my Sovereign,
        proclaiming without end what you have done.

1 O God, why have you cast us off forever?
      Why does your anger smolder
      against the sheep of your pasture?
2 Remember the flock you made yours so long ago—
      the tribe you ransomed as your inheritance—
      and Mount Zion, where you dwelled.

3 Pick your way through these utter ruins,
      all this damage the enemy has done in the sanctuary.
4 Your foes roar triumphantly in your Temple;
      they have set up their tokens of victory.
5 They are like people coming up with axes
      to a thicket of trees—
6 and now with chisel and hammer
      they hack away at its carved paneling.
7 They set your sanctuary on fire,
      burned it to the ground,
      and profaned the place where your Name abides.
8 They said in their hearts,
      "Let's destroy them,
      and burn all the shrines of God in their land!"

9 We have been given no signs;
      there is no prophet now,
      and no one understands the evidence before us.
10 O God, how long will the enemy mock you?
      Will the enemy revile your Name forever?
11 Why hold back your hand, your right hand?
      Take it from the folds of your cloak and destroy them!

12 O God, my Sovereign of old,
      you bring deliverance throughout all the earth—
13 you stirred up the sea by your might;
      you smashed the heads of dragons in the waters,
14 you crushed the heads of Leviathan,
      and offered it to the desert tribes for food.

15 You released the springs and torrents;
   you brought dry land out of the primeval waters.
16 Yours is the day, and yours the night;
   you established the moon and the sun.
17 You fixed all the limits of the land;
   summer and winter you made.

18 Now remember how the enemy has blasphemed you, Adonai,
   and how a stupid people has reviled your Name!
19 Don't give the vulture the life of your dove;
   don't ignore forever the lives of your little ones!
20 Look to your Covenant,
   because the dark places in the land
   are filled with haunts of violence!
21 Don't let the downtrodden turn away in disappointment—
   let the oppressed and poor praise your Name!
22 Arise, O God, and champion your cause;
   remember how the fool mocks you day after day!
23 Don't ignore the shouts of your enemies—
   the uproar of those who rebel against you
   is getting louder and louder.

To the conductor: to the tune of "Do Not Destroy"
A psalm of Asaph
A song

1 Thank you, O God, thank you!
     For your presence—your Name—is near
     when we hear of your wonderful deeds.

2 "I choose the right time—
     I who judge with absolute justice.
3 When the earth quakes and shakes all who live on it,
     I'm the one who makes its pillars firm."

4 To the arrogant I say,
     "Forsake your pride!"
   and to the corrupt,
     "Do not raise your proud horns!
5 Don't raise your horns against the Exalted One
     or speak arrogantly against the Rock of Ages."

6 No power from the east or west
     or even from the wilderness
     can raise a person up—
7 God alone is judge;
     God brings one down and raises up another.
8 In the hand of Our God there is a cup,
     and the wine foams in it, hot with spice;
   Our God pours it out,
     and all the wicked of the earth drink it
     and drain it to its very dregs.

9 As for me, I will declare all this forever;
     I will sing praises to the God of our ancestors.
10 "I will break off the horns of the wicked,
     but the horns of the righteous will be lifted high."

To the conductor: for strings
By Asaph
A song

1 O God, you made yourself known in Judah;
      your Name is great in Israel—
2 you set up your tent in Salem,
      and Zion is your home.
3 There you broke the fiery arrows,
      the shield, the sword, the weapons of war.
                —— *Selah* ——
4 You are resplendent with light,
      majestic on the mountains of the Lion:
5 their bravest warriors, despoiled, slept in death;
      not a single warrior was able to lift a hand.
6 At your blast, O God of our ancestors,
      both horse and chariots lie still.
7 You and you alone are to be worshiped.
      Who can stand when your anger is roused?
8 You pronounced your sentence from the heavens;
      the earth in terror was silent
9 when you arose to execute judgment,
      to save the lowly of the earth.
10 Indeed, they will praise you
      for the wrath you pour out on others,
   and those who escape your wrath
      will gather around you.

11 So make vows to Adonai, your God—
      and fulfill them.
   Let neighboring lands bring their tribute
      to the One who strikes terror,
12 who cuts short the breath of their leaders,
      and strikes terror in the rulers of the earth.

To the conductor: for Jeduthun
By Asaph
A psalm

1 I cried to God for help,
     I cried out to God to hear me.
2 In the day of my distress I sought you, Adonai,
     and by night I lifted my outstretched hand in prayer.
  I lay sweating and nothing would cool me,
     nothing could comfort me.
3 When I called you to mind, I groaned;
     as I lay thinking, gloom overcame my spirit.
       —— *Selah* ——
4 You kept my eyes open all night;
     I was so troubled I couldn't speak.
5 My thoughts went back to times now distant,
     to years long past;
6   I remembered my songs in the night.
  As I lay thinking,
     my spirit pondered:
7 "Adonai, will you reject us forever and ever?
     Will you never again show your favor?
8 Has your unfailing love now vanished forever?
     Will your promise remain unfulfilled
     generation after generation?
9 Have you forgotten how to show mercy, O God?
     Has your anger blotted out your compassion?"
       —— *Selah* ——

10 Then I thought: "This is the cause of my infirmity—
     it is another visitation of the right hand of the Most High!"
11 And then I remember your deeds, Adonai—
     yes, I will call to mind your wonderful acts of long ago.
12 I will meditate on all your works,
     and think about all you have done.
13 O God, your way is holy;
     what god is as great as Our God?
14 You are the God who worked miracles;
     you have shown the nations your power.

15 With your strong arm you redeemed your people,
   the descendants of Israel and their children's children.
16 The waters saw you, O God,
   they saw you and trembled,
   and the ocean depths quaked.
17 The clouds coursed their waters,
   the skies echoed with your voice,
   your arrows flashed all around.
18 The sound of your thunder was in the whirlwind,
   your lightning lit up the world,
   and the earth shook and quaked.
19 You made your path through the sea,
   and walked through the mighty waters,
   yet no one could find your footsteps.
20 You guided your people like a flock of sheep,
   by the hand of Moses and Miriam and Aaron.

An instructional psalm
By Asaph

1 My people, hear my teaching;
　　listen to the words of my mouth!
2 I will open my mouth in parables,
　　I will utter things hidden from of old—
3 the things we have heard and known,
　　things our ancestors have told us.
4 We won't hide them from our children,
　　we will tell the next generation.

We'll tell them of your praiseworthy deeds, Adonai,
　　your power, and the wonders you have performed.
5 You set up statutes for our forebears,
　　and established the Law in Israel,
　　which you commanded our ancestors to teach their children
6 so the next generation would know them—
　　children yet to be born—
and as they come up,
　　they would tell their own children.
7 Then they would put their trust in you
　　and not forget your deeds, but keep your commandments—
8 unlike their ancestors,
　　a stubborn and defiant generation,
whose hearts were fickle,
　　whose spirits were unfaithful to God.

9 Like the Ephraimite archers
　　who turned tail in the day of battle,
10 they didn't keep your Covenant,
　　and refused to live by your Law.
11 They forgot your deeds,
　　the wonders you showed them.
12 In the sight of their ancestors, you performed miracles
　　in the land of Egypt, on the plain of Zoan.

13 You split the sea and led them through it;
     you made the water stand like a wall.
14 You guided them with a cloud by day,
     and by night with the light of a fire.
15 You split the rock in the wilderness
     and gave them water that gushed like the great seas—
16 you brought streams out of the rocky crag,
     and made water flow down like rivers.

17 But still they sinned against you,
     defying the Most High in the wilderness.
18 They willfully challenged God
     by demanding food for themselves.
19 They spoke against you:
     they said, "Can God prepare a feast in the wilderness?
20 True, Moses struck the rock and water gushed out,
     and streams flowed abundantly.
   But can God also give us bread
     and provide meat for the people?"
21 When you heard them, Adonai, you were enraged;
     your fire blazed up against the people,
     and your wrath erupted against Israel
22 because they didn't believe in you
     or trust that you would deliver them.

23 Yet you gave a command to the skies above
     and opened the doors of the heavens;
24 you rained down manna for them to eat,
     and gave them grain from heaven.
25 Mere mortals ate the bread of angels;
     you sent them food in abundance.
26 You loosed the east wind in the heavens
     and drove the south wind by your power.
27 You rained meat down on them like dust,
     winged fowl like sand on the seashore.
28 You made birds come down into their camp
     and around their tents.
29 They ate until they were fully satisfied;
     you gave them what they craved.

30 And still they did not desist from complaining—
   even while it was still in their mouths.
31 So you rose in anger against them,
   killing the strongest among them,
   and striking down the youth of Israel.
32 Even so, they kept on sinning;
   in spite of your wonders, they didn't believe,
33 so you made their days vanish like a vapor,
   and their years pass by like a phantom in the night.

34 Whenever you struck them down, they would turn to you;
   they became eager for you again.
35 They remembered that God was their rock,
   that God Most High was their redeemer.
36 But then they would deceive you with their speech,
   and lie to you with their lips;
37 their hearts were fickle,
   they were unfaithful to your Covenant.

38 But you were merciful;
   you forgave their wrongs
   and didn't destroy them.
   Time and again, you held back your anger
   and didn't give vent to your full wrath.
39 You remembered that they were but flesh,
   a passing breath that never returns.

40 How often they rebelled against you in the wilderness,
   and grieved you in the wasteland!
41 Again and again they challenged you;
   they pushed the Holy One of Israel to the limit.
42 They didn't remember your power
   or the day you ransomed them from the oppressor,
43 the day you displayed your miraculous signs in Egypt,
   or your wonders in the plain of Zoan.

44 You turned their rivers to blood,
   and made their streams undrinkable.
45 You sent swarms of flies to devour them
   and frogs to devastate them.
46 You gave their crops to grasshoppers,
   and their produce to locusts.

⁴⁷ You killed their vines with hail
    and their sycamores with sleet.
⁴⁸ You abandoned their cattle to the hail,
    and their livestock to lightning bolts.
⁴⁹ You unleashed your blazing anger against them—
    your fury, rage and havoc—
  with an escort of avenging angels
⁵⁰   who cleared a path for your anger.
  You didn't spare them from death,
    but gave them over to pestilence.
⁵¹ You struck down all Egypt's firstborn,
    the firstfruits of their vigor in the tents of Ham.
⁵² But you led your people like a flock,
    and guided them like sheep through the wilderness.
⁵³ You led them to safety, so they were not afraid,
    while the seas covered their enemies.
⁵⁴ You brought them to the foot of your holy hill,
    to the mountain your right hand had won.
⁵⁵ You drove out nations before them;
    you allotted their lands to them as an inheritance.
  You settled the tribes of Israel in their tents.

⁵⁶ But again they challenged and defied you;
    they did not keep your statutes.
⁵⁷ Like their ancestors they were fickle and cynical,
    they recoiled like a faulty bow.
⁵⁸ They angered you with their hillside altars,
    and aroused your jealousy with their idols.
⁵⁹ When you heard them, you were enraged,
    and utterly rejected Israel.
⁶⁰ You abandoned the tabernacle at Shiloh,
    the tent you had pitched in their midst.
⁶¹ You let the ark of your might go into captivity,
    your glory into the hands of the enemy.
⁶² You gave over your people to the sword,
    you were furious with the people of your inheritance.
⁶³ Fire consumed their young men,
    and their young women sang no wedding songs;
⁶⁴ their priests fell by the sword,
    and their widows had no tears left to cry.

⁶⁵ Then you awoke as from sleep,
    as a warrior wakes from the stupor of wine.
⁶⁶ You beat back their enemies
    and put them to everlasting shame.
⁶⁷ Then you rejected the clan of Joseph,
    you did not choose the tribe of Ephraim;
⁶⁸ instead, you chose the tribe of Judah,
    Mount Zion, which you loved.
⁶⁹ You built your sanctuary like the high heavens,
    like the earth that you established forever;
⁷⁰ you chose David, your faithful one
    and took him from the sheepfolds;
⁷¹ you took him from tending nursing ewes
    to be the shepherd of your chosen people, Israel.
⁷² And David tended them with blameless heart;
    leading them with skillful hands.

1 O God, the nations have invaded your domain,
  they have defiled your holy Temple!
  They have reduced Jerusalem to a pile of ruins!
2 They have left the corpses of your faithful ones
  to the birds of the air,
  and the flesh of your devout to the beasts of the earth.
3 They have shed blood like water throughout Jerusalem,
  with no one left to bury the dead!
4 And now we're insulted by our neighbors,
  the laughingstock of those around us, the butt of their jokes.

5 How much longer will you be angry with us, Adonai?
  Forever?
  Will your jealousy go on smoldering like a fire?
6 Redirect your anger to the nations,
  who do not acknowledge you,
  and to those dominions
  that do not call on your Name,
7 for they have devoured your people
  and reduced their home to desolation.
8 Don't hold our former sins against us.
  In your tenderness, quickly intervene,
  for we can hardly be crushed lower.
9 Help us, O God of our salvation,
  for the sake of your glorious Name!
  Deliver us! Atone for our sins
  and rescue us for your Name's sake!
10 Why should the nations ask, "Where is their God?"
  Soon, let us see the nations learn what vengeance you exact
  for the blood of your faithful shed there.
11 May the groans of the captives reach you;
  with your long arm, rescue those condemned to death.
12 Pay back our neighbors sevenfold, and strike them to the heart
  for the monstrous insults they hurled at you, Adonai.
13 Then we, your people, the flock of your pasture
  will give you everlasting thanks;
  we will recount your praises
  forever and ever.

To the conductor: to the tune of "Lilies of the Covenant"
By Asaph
A psalm

1 Shepherd of Israel, hear us,
    you who lead Joseph like a flock!
You who are enthroned on the cherubim, shine out!
2   Shine out before Ephraim, Benjamin and Manasseh!
Awaken your power
    and come to save us!

3 *O God, return to us—*
    let your face smile on us, and we will be saved!

4 Adonai, God of Hosts,
    how much longer will you fume
    while your people pray?
5 You fed us on the bread of tears,
    and made us drink our tears in such measure;
6 you now let our neighbors ridicule us
    and our enemies treat us with scorn.

7 *O God of Hosts, return to us—*
    let your face smile on us and we will be saved!

8 There was a vine:
    you uprooted it from Egypt;
    to plant it, you drove out other nations.
9 You cleared a space where it could grow;
    it took root and filled the land—
10 it covered the mountains with its shade,
    and its branches were like the cedars of God;
11 its tendrils stretched out to the Sea,
    its offshoots all the way to the Euphrates.
12 Why, then, have you destroyed its wall
    so that all who pass can steal its grapes?
13 The forest boar can trample it
    and creatures of the field can eat it.

¹⁴ Please, O God of Hosts, come back!
  Look down from heaven,
  and watch over this vine,
¹⁵ the root planted by your own hand,
  the shoot you have raised up as your own.
¹⁶ It is now cut down and thrown into the fire,
  consumed by the flames of your rebuke.
¹⁷ Let your hand rest upon the One at your right side,
  the Chosen One you raised up for yourself.
¹⁸ Then we'll never turn from you again;
  our life renewed, we will invoke your Name.

¹⁹ *Adonai, God of Hosts, return to us—*
  let your face smile on us and we will be saved!

81

To the conductor: for the Gittite harp
By Asaph

¹ Sing out in praise of God our strength,
  acclaim the God of our ancestors!
² Begin the music, take up the tambourine,
  the tuneful harp and the lyre!
³ Blow the trumpet on the New Moon,
  and on the Full Moon, the day of our Feast.
⁴ For this is a law for Israel,
  a decree of the God of our forebears,
⁵ laid as a solemn charge on Joseph
  when he went from the land of Egypt.

Then I heard language
  too great to comprehend:
⁶ "When I lifted the burden from your shoulders,
  your hands were freed from the builder's basket.
⁷ When you cried to me in distress,
  I rescued you.

I answered you cloaked in thunder;
    and even though you challenged me
    by the waters of Meribah.
—— *Selah* ——

8 Listen, my people, while I accuse you—
    if only you would listen to me, Israel!

9 You will have no alien god among you
    nor bow down to any foreign god.

10 I am Adonai, your God,
    who brought you out of the land of Egypt!

11 But my people did not listen to my voice
    and Israel would not obey me;

12 so I gave them over to their willful hearts,
    to follow their own devices.

13 If only my people would listen to me,
    if Israel would follow my paths,

14 I would subdue their enemies at once
    and turn my hand against their persecutors.

15 Those who hate me will come cringing before me,
    and meet with everlasting punishment.

16 And I will feed Israel with the finest wheat
    and satisfy you with honey from the rock."

1   God presides in the divine assembly
     and pronounces judgment among the "gods":

2   "How long will you defend the unjust
     and show partiality to the corrupt?
3   Defend the lowly and the orphaned,
     render justice to the oppressed and the destitute!
4   Rescue the weak and the poor,
     and save them from the hand of violence!
5   But you know nothing and you understand nothing—
     you walk in darkness,
and the foundations of the earth
     are shaking because of your ignorance!
6   I said, 'You are "gods," all of you—
     children of the Most High!'
7   But you will die as any mortal,
     and fall like any ruler!"

8   Rise up, O God, and bring justice to the earth,
     for all the nations are your possession!

1 O God, don't be silent;
    don't be aloof, don't be quiet, O God!
2 Look what an uproar your enemies are making!
    Your foes have reared their ugly heads.
3 They cunningly plot against your people
    and conspire against those you cherish.
4 They say, "Come, let's destroy them as a nation;
    let the name of Israel be remembered no more!"
5 Indeed, they lay their plans with a single purpose
    and form an alliance against you—
6 the tents of Edom and the Ishmaelites,
    Moab and the descendants of Hagar,
7 Byblos, Ammon and Amalek,
    Philistia with the inhabitants of Tyre—
8 even Assyria has joined them,
    lending support to the children of Lot.
9 Treat them as you did Midian,
    as you treated Sisera and Jabin at the river Kishon,
10 who were destroyed at Endor
    and became dung for the field.
11 Treat their nobles like Oreb and Zeeb,
    and their people like Zebah and Zalmunna,
12 who said, "Let's take possession
    of the pastures of God."
13 My God, make them like whirling dust,
    like chaff blown by the wind!
14 As fire consumes a forest
    and flame sets the hills ablaze,
15 pursue them with your storm
    and terrify them with your whirlwind!
16 Fill their faces with shame,
    and make them seek your Name, Adonai!
17 Let them always be frustrated and terrified,
    and let them perish in disgrace.
18 Make them know that your Name alone—Adonai—
    is supreme over all the earth.

84

To the conductor: for the Gittite harp
By the disciples of Qorach

1 How I love your dwelling place,
    Adonai Sabaoth!
2 How my soul yearns and pines
    for your courts, Adonai!
My heart and my flesh sing for joy
    to you, the living God.
3 The sparrow has found its home at last,
    the swallow a nest for its young—
on your altars, Adonai Sabaoth,
    my Sovereign, my God!
4 Happiness belongs to those who live in your house
    and can praise you all day long;
      —— *Selah* ——
5 and happy the pilgrims who find refuge in you
    as they set their hearts on the Ascents!
6 As they go through the Valley of the Weeper,
    they make it a place of springs,
    clothed in blessings by the early rains.
7 From there they make their way from village to village,
    until each one appears before God in Zion.

8 Adonai, God of Hosts, hear my prayer;
    Listen, O God of our ancestors!
      —— *Selah* ——
9 O God, our shield, show us your favor
    and look upon the face of your Anointed—
10 for a single day in your courts
    is worth more than a thousand anywhere else;
better to be a humble doorkeeper in God's house
    than to live richly in the tents of the corrupt.
11 For you, Adonai our God, are a battlement and shield,
    bestowing grace and glory;
Our God withholds nothing good
    from those whose walk is blameless.
12 Adonai Sabaoth,
    happy are those who put their trust in you!

For the conductor
By the disciples of Qorach
A psalm

1 Adonai, favor your land once again
       and restore the fortunes of Israel;
2 forgive the guilt of your people
       and cover all their sins.
3 Set aside all your anger,
       and calm the heat of your rage.
4 Return to us, O God of our deliverance!
       Put an end to your displeasure with us.
5 Will you be angry with us forever,
       will your wrath continue from one generation to the next?
6 Won't you revive us again
       so that your people can rejoice in you?
7 Let us see your mercy, Adonai,
       and grant us your deliverance.

8 I will listen to what you have to say, Adonai—
       a voice that speaks of peace,
   peace for your people and your friends
       so long as they don't return to their folly.
9 Your salvation is near for those who revere you
       and your glory will dwell in our land.
10 Love and faithfulness have met;
       justice and peace have embraced.
11 Fidelity will sprout from the earth
       and justice will lean down from heaven.
12 Our God will give us what is good,
       and our land will yield its harvest.
13 Justice will march before you, Adonai,
       and peace will prepare the way for your steps.

A prayer of David

1 Open your ears, Adonai, and answer me,
     for I am weak and helpless.
2 Save me from death,
     for I am loyal to you;
  protect your faithful one,
     for you are my God and I trust in you.
3 Have mercy on me, Adonai,
     for I pray to you all day long.
4 Make your faithful one glad,
     for I lift my soul to you, Adonai.

5 You are good and forgiving, Adonai,
     full of constant love for all who call on you.
6 Listen to my prayer, Adonai,
     hear my cries for help.
7 I call to you in times of trouble
     because you answer my prayer.
8 There is no other god like you, Adonai,
     not one who can do what you do.
9 When you act, all the nations will come
     and bow down before you, Adonai,
     and will pay honor to your Name.
10 How great you are, Worker of Marvels;
     you alone are God!
11 Teach me your way, Adonai,
     so that I may walk with you alone;
     make me single-hearted in reverence for your Name.
12 I will praise you with all my heart, Adonai;
     I will glorify your Name forever.
13 How great is your constant love for me!
     You have rescued me from the depths of Sheol.

14 O God, the arrogant are coming against me;
     a ruthless gang is trying to kill me—
     they don't care that you are my Leader.
15 But you, Adonai, are a compassionate and merciful God,
     slow to anger, overflowing with love and fidelity.

¹⁶ Turn to me and have mercy on me;
    grant me strength, for I am faithful to you
    just as my parents were.
¹⁷ Give me a sign of your favor,
    then those who hate me will be frustrated
when they see that you, Adonai,
    have given me comfort and help.

87

By the disciples of Qorach
A psalm
A song

¹ Our God loves this city
    founded on the holy mountain;
² God loves the gates of Zion
    more than all the dwellings of Israel,
³ and glorious predictions are made about you,
    the city of God:
        —— *Selah* ——
⁴ "I will add monstrous Egypt, and Babylon
    to the nations that acknowledge me.
Philistia, Tyre, Ethiopia—
    each of them was born there."
⁵ Indeed, it will be said that everyone
    was born in Zion,
and the Most High will be the one
    who brings it all to pass.
⁶ Our God will write in the register of the peoples,
    "This one too was born there."
⁷ People in Zion will dance as they sing,
    "Everything I am has its source in you."

88

A song
A psalm by the disciples of Qorach
To the conductor: to the tune of "Sickness and Depression"
A teaching psalm by Heman the Ezraite

1 Adonai, God of my deliverance,
    by day I cry out to you,
    in the night I am before you.
2 Let my prayer reach you;
    turn your ear to my cry!
3 Troubles fill me to the brim,
    and my life is on the brink of Sheol;
4 I am numbered among those who go down into the Pit,
    all my strength is drained from me.
5 I am alone, down among the dead,
    like a body lying in its grave—
I'm like someone you no longer remember,
    someone cut off from your care.
6 You have plunged me into the lowest part of the Pit,
    into its deepest and darkest regions,
7 with the weight of your anger pulling me down,
    drowning me beneath the waves of your fury.
        —— *Selah* ——
8 You have turned my friends against me
    and made me repulsive to them;
I am in prison and there is no escape,
9   and my eyes ache from crying.

Adonai, I call you all day long,
    I stretch out my hands to you.
10 Are your wonders meant for the dead?
    Can ghosts rise up to praise you?
11 Who declares your love in the grave,
    or your fidelity from the place of destruction?
12 Do they hear about your marvels in the netherworld,
    about your justice in the Land of the Forgotten?
13 But I am here, calling for your help,
    praying to Adonai every morning.

14 Why do you reject me, Adonai?
 Why do you hide your face from me?
15 I am close to death and in despair—
 I've suffered your terrors since I was a child.
16 You consumed me with your anger
 and destroyed me with your terrors;
17 they surrounded me like a flood all day long,
 and engulfed me altogether.
18 You've turned my friends and loved ones against me;
 now night is my closest companion.

89

A teaching psalm by Ethan the Ezraite

1 Forever I will sing the wonders of your love, Adonai,
 proclaiming your faithfulness to all generations!
2 I'll tell them that your love stands firm forever,
 your fidelity is fixed in the heavens.
3 "I have made a covenant with my chosen;
 sworn an oath to David, my faithful one:
4 'I will establish your line forever,
 and make your throne firm throughout all generations.' "

5 The heavens praise your wonders, Adonai,
 and the council of the holy ones declares your fidelity.
6 Who in the skies can be compared to Our God?
 Who is like Adonai among the gods—
7 a God who is revered in the council of the holy ones
 great and awesome above all others?
8 Adonai Sabaoth, who is like you?
 Power and faithfulness surround you!
9 You rule the surging sea,
 calming the turmoil of its waves.
10 You crush the monster Rahab with a mortal blow,
 and scatter your enemies with your strong arm.
11 The heavens are yours, and so is the earth—
 you established the world and all it contains.

12 You created North and South;
  Mounts Tabor and Hermon echo your Name.
13 Your arm is powerful, your hand is strong,
  your right hand is lifted high.
14 Your judgment seat is built on righteousness and justice,
  love and fidelity stand in your presence.

15 Happy are those who have learned to praise you, Adonai,
  who walk in the light of your presence!
16 They will rejoice in your Name all day long,
  uplifted by your justice.
17 You are the strength in which they glory;
  through your favor we hold our heads high.
18 Our God is our shield;
  the holy One of Israel is our ruler.

19 One day a vision came
  and you announced this to your faithful ones:
  "I have bestowed power on a warrior
  and raised up a youth from among the people.
20 I have discovered David,
  who is faithful to me.
  David, I anoint you with my holy oil.
21   My hand will be ready to help you,
  and my arm to give you strength.
22 No enemy will oppress you
  and no rebel will bring you low;
23 I will shatter your foes before you,
  and strike down those who hate you.
24 My fidelity and love will be with you,
  and through my Name your strength will increase.
25 I will extend your rule to the Sea
  and your dominion as far as the Euphrates.
26 You will say to me,
  'You are my Abba, my God,
  my rock and my deliverance.'
27 And I will appoint you my firstborn,
  higher than all the earth's rulers.
28 I will maintain my love for you forever
  and my covenant with you will never fail.
29 I will establish your line forever
  and your throne as long as the heavens endure.

30 If your descendants forsake my Law
   and do not live by my rules,
31 if they renounce my teachings
   and do not observe my commands,
32 I will punish their disobedience with the rod
   and their iniquity with lashes.
33 But I will never deprive them of my steadfast love—
   I'll never betray my faithfulness.
34 I will not violate my Covenant
   or change what my lips have promised.
35 I have sworn by my holiness once and for all,
   I will not break my word.
36 Your line will continue forever,
   your throne will stand before me like the sun.
37 It will be established forever,
   as faithful as the moon's witness in the skies."
                  —— *Selah* ——

38 Yet you have rejected and spurned
   and raged against your Anointed!
39 You have repudiated the Covenant with your faithful ones,
   defiled the crown and flung it to the ground.
40 You have breached my walls
   and left my fortresses in ruin;
41 all who pass by plunder me
   and I have become the laughingstock of my neighbors.
42 You have increased the power of my enemies
   and made my adversaries rejoice;
43 you have blunted my sword
   and refused to help me in battle.
44 You have put an end to a glorious reign
   and hurled my throne to the ground.
45 You have cut short the days of my youth
   and covered me with shame.
                  —— *Selah* ——

46 How long, Adonai, will you hide yourself from sight?
   Will your wrath blaze like fire forever?
47 Remember how fleeting life is—
   have you created humankind in vain?

48   Who can live and not see death
        or save themselves from the power of Sheol?
49   Where is your steadfast love of old, Adonai,
        those faithful promises you swore to David?
50   Remember the abuse hurled at your faithful one, Adonai,
        how I have borne in my heart the taunts of entire nations;
51   how your enemies have vilified us, Adonai,
        vilified your Anointed at every step!

52   Blessed be Our God forever!
        Amen, amen!

book IV

90

A prayer of Moses, chosen one of God

1 Adonai, you have been our refuge
   from one generation to the next.
2 Before the mountains were born,
   you brought forth the earth and the world,
   you are God without beginning or end.
3 You turn humankind back into dust
   and say: "Go back, creatures of the earth!"
4 For in your sight a thousand years
   are like yesterday, come and gone,
   no more than a watch in the night.
5 You sweep us away like a dream,
   fleeting as the grass that springs up in the morning—
6 in the morning it sprouts,
   but by evening it has withered and died.

7 In the same way, we are consumed—
   terrified by your anger and indignation.
8 Our guilt lies open before you;
   our secrets are revealed in the light of your presence.
9 All our days pass away under your anger,
   and our life is over like a sigh.
10 The span of our life is but seventy years—
   perhaps eighty if we're strong—
   but the best of them are nothing but sorrow and pain;
   they pass swiftly and we are gone.
11 Who understands the power of your anger?
   We fear the strength of your wrath.

12 Make us realize how short life is
   that we may gain wisdom of heart.

13 Adonai, relent!
   How long before you have mercy on your faithful ones?
14 When morning comes, fill us with your love,
   and we will celebrate all our days.
15 Give us joy for as many days as you afflicted us,
   for as many years as we knew misfortune!
16 Let your work be seen by your faithful,
   your glory be witnessed by their children.
17 Let our God's favor be upon us!
   Grant success to the work of our hands,
   success to the work of our hands!

91

1 You who dwell in the shelter of the Most High
   and pass the night in the shadow of Shaddai,
2 say: "Adonai, my refuge and my mountain fortress,
   my God in whom I trust!"
3 For Our God says:
   "I will rescue you from the snare,
   and shield you from poisoned arrows.
4 I will cover you with my pinions;
   under my wings you will take refuge;
   my faithfulness will shield you.
5 You have no need to fear the prowlers of the night
   or the arrow that flies by day,
6 the plague that lurks in the shadows
   or the scourge that stalks at noon.
7 Though a thousand fall at your left side
   and ten thousand at your right,
   it will never come near you.
8 You will see it pass you by,
   and witness the punishment of the corrupt
   with your own eyes.
9 Because you have made me your refuge

and have me as your stronghold,
10   no evil will befall you,
     and no disaster will come near your tent.
11   For I will command my angels
     to guard you wherever you go.
12   They'll carry you in their hands
     so you don't hurt your foot on a stone.
13   You'll tread on the young lion as easily as one does a cobra;
     you'll trample down both lion and serpent.
14   Because you love me, I will deliver you;
     I will rescue you because you acknowledge my Name.
15   You will call upon me, and I will answer you;
     I will be with you in trouble;
     I will deliver you and honor you.
16   I will satisfy you with a long life
     and show you my salvation."

92

A psalm
A song for the Sabbath

1 It is good to praise you, Adonai,
     and celebrate your Name in song, Most High—
2 to proclaim your love in the morning
     and your fidelity through the watches of the night,
3 to the music of a ten-stringed lyre
     and the melody of the harp.
4 Your deeds, Adonai, fill me with joy;
     I shout in triumph over the work of your hands.
5 How great are your works, Adonai!
     How profound your thoughts!

6 Those who don't realize this are senseless;
     they are fools because they can't understand
7 that though the corrupt keep springing up like grass
     and all evildoers blossom and flourish,
   it is only so that they will be destroyed forever—
8   while you, Adonai, reign on high forever!
9 Come and watch your foes, Adonai,
     come and watch your foes perish
     and all evildoers will be scattered.
10 I have raised my horn high,
     strong as the wild ox;
     I am anointed with fine oil.
11 With my own eyes I've seen the defeat of my enemies,
     and I've heard the downfall of my cruel foes.

12 The just flourish like a palm tree,
     and grow as tall as the cedars of Lebanon;
13 transplanted in the house of Our God,
     they flourish in the courts of the Most High—
14 still full of sap in old age,
     they still produce abundant fruit,
15 eager to declare that Our God is just—
     my rock, in whom there is no wrong.

1   Our God reigns, robed in splendor!
      You are robed, Adonai, and armed with strength.
  The world stands firm and cannot be moved;
2   your throne stands firm from ages past,
     from eternity you exist.
3   The seas are shouting, Adonai—
     the seas raise their voices,
     the seas shout with pounding waves.
4   Stronger than the thunder of the great waters,
     mightier than the breakers of the sea,
     mightiest of all is Our God!
5   Your reign was made known from of old;
     the holy ones praise you in your Temple,
     Adonai, for days without end.

1   Adonai, God our avenger—
     reveal yourself, God our avenger!
2   Rise up, judge of the earth,
     and give the arrogant what they deserve!
3   How long will these violent gangs, Adonai,
     how long will these violent gangs be jubilant?
4   Arrogance pours forth from their speech
     as they boast about all their crimes.
5   They crush your people, Adonai!
     They oppress those most dear to you!
6   They prey on the elderly and attack foreigners,
     and murder children who beg in the streets.
7   They say, "God doesn't see us;
     the God of Israel doesn't notice!"

8   Wise up, you fools!

You idiots! When will you ever learn?
9   Can't the One who fashioned the ear, hear?
    Can't the Maker of the eye, see?
10 Do you think that the One who disciplines entire nations
    won't punish a guilty individual?
    Do you think the Teacher of humankind
    doesn't already know?
11 Our God knows what people think—
    and knows just how vapid their reasoning is!

12 Those you instruct are the fortunate ones, Adonai,
    because you teach them from your Law—
13 to give them tranquility in times of trouble,
    until a pitfall is dug for the treacherous.
14 Our God will not abandon the faithful
    and will not desert those who belong to the Covenant.
15 The Tribunal of Justice will restore equity,
    and all who are upright in heart will follow it.

16 I said, "Who will take my side against the corrupt?
    Who will stand by me against the violent?"
17 If Our God had not helped me,
    I would have gone quickly to the land of silence.
18 I said, "I am falling,"
    but your constant love, Adonai, upheld me.
19 When I am anxious and worried,
    you comfort me and bring me joy.
20 You have nothing to do with those
    who sit on the thrones of iniquity,
    nor do those who cause strife
    receive your protection.
21 They plotted against the life of the just,
    and sentenced the innocent to death from their hiding places.
22 But Adonai is my fortress;
    my God is my rock of refuge.
23 God will make their evil recoil upon them,
    and destroy them through their corruption;
    Adonai, Our God, will utterly destroy them.

1 Come, let us sing joyfully to God!
   Raise a shout to our rock, our deliverance!
2 Let us come into God's presence with thanksgiving,
   and sing our praises with joy.
3 For Our God is a great God,
   the great Ruler, above all gods.
4 O God, in your hands are the depths of the earth,
   and the mountain peaks are yours.
5 Yours is the sea, for you made it,
   the dry land as well, for your hands formed it.
6 Come, let us bow down in worship;
   let us kneel before Adonai, our Maker.
7 For you are our God,
   and we are the people you shepherd,
   the flock under your care.

If only you would hear God's voice today!
8 "Harden not your hearts as at Meribah,
   as in the days of Massah in the desert,
9 where your ancestors tested me;
   they tested me even though they had seen my works.
10 For forty years that generation provoked me,
   until I said, 'The hearts of these people go astray,
   and they do not know my ways.'
11 Then I took an oath in anger,
   'They will never come to my place of rest.' "

1 Sing to Our God a new song!
   Sing to Our God, all the earth!
2 Sing to Our God, bless God's Name!
   Proclaim God's salvation day after day;
3 declare God's glory among the nations,
   God's marvels to every people.
4 Our God is great, most worthy of praise,
   Our God is to be revered above all gods.
5 The gods of the nations are nothing, they don't exist—
   but Our God created the universe.
6 In God's presence are splendor and majesty,
   in God's sanctuary power and beauty.
7 Pay tribute to Our God, you tribes of the people,
   pay tribute to the God of glory and power.
8 Pay tribute to the glorious Name of Our God;
   bring out the offering, and carry it into God's courts.
9 Worship Our God, majestic in holiness,
   tremble in God's presence, all the earth!
10 Say among the nations,
   "Our God reigns supreme!"
   The world stands firm and unshakable:
   Our God will judge each nation with strict justice.
11 Let the heavens be glad, let the earth rejoice,
   let the sea roar and all that it holds!
12 Let the fields exult and all that is in them!
   Let all the trees of the forest sing for joy
13 at the presence of Our God, for God is coming,
   God is coming to rule the earth—
   to rule the world with justice
   and its peoples with truth!

1 Our God reigns!
   Let the earth rejoice;
   let the many coastlands be glad!

2 Clouds and thick darkness surround you, Adonai;
   righteousness and justice
   are the foundation of your judgment seat.
3 Fire goes before you
   and destroys your enemies on every side.
4 Your lightning bolts light up the world;
   the earth sees, and trembles.
5 The mountains melt like wax at your sight,
   at the sight of the God of all the earth.

6 The heavens proclaim your justice,
   and all the peoples see your glory.
7 All who worship images are put to shame,
   who make their boast in worthless idols,
   all gods bow down before you.
8 Zion hears and is glad,
   and the women of Judah rejoice
   because of your judgments, Adonai.
9 For you, Adonai, are Most High over all the earth;
   you are exalted far above all gods.

10 Adonai, you love those who hate evil;
   preserve the lives of your faithful ones
   and deliver them from the hands of the wicked.
11 Light dawns for the just,
   and joy for the upright in heart.
12 Rejoice in Our God, you just,
   and give praise to God's holy Name!

1   Sing a new song to Our God,
        who has worked wonders,
    whose right hand and holy arm
        have brought deliverance!
2   Our God has made salvation known
        and shown divine justice to the nations,
3   and has remembered in truth and love
        the house of Israel.
    All the ends of the earth have seen
        the salvation of our God.
4   Shout to the Most High, all the earth,
        break into joyous songs of praise!
5   Sing praise to Our God with the harp,
        with the harp and melodious singing!
6   With trumpets and the blast of the shofar,
        raise a shout to Our God, Ruler of All.
7   Let the sea and all within it thunder;
        the world and all its peoples.
8   Let the rivers clap their hands
        and the hills ring out their joy
9   before Our God, who comes to judge the earth,
        who will rule the world with justice
        and its peoples with equity.

1   Our God reigns,
     and the nations tremble!
  You who are enthroned on the cherubim,
     let the earth quake!
2   Our God is even higher than Zion,
     and exalted above all the nations;
3   let them praise your Name,
     Great and Awesome One:

  "You are holy 4 and mighty,
     a Leader who loves justice,
  who established honesty, justice and righteousness in Israel!
     You have done this!
5   We exalt you, Adonai, Our God,
     and we worship at your footstool.
     You are holy!"

6   Miriam, Moses and Aaron were among them,
     and Samuel too was among those who invoked the Name;
  they called on Our God
     and God answered them.
7   Adonai spoke to them in the pillar of cloud;
     they obeyed the decrees and statutes God gave them.
8   Adonai, Our God, you answered them.
     For them, you became God the Forgiver
     even though you punished their evil deeds.

9   "We exalt you, Adonai our God,
     and we worship at your holy mountain;
     for you, Adonai our God, are holy!"

100

1 Acclaim Our God with joy,
    all the earth!
2 Serve Our God with gladness!
    Enter into God's presence with a joyful song!
3 Know that Adonai is God!
    Our God made us, and we belong to the Creator;
we are God's people
    and the sheep of God's pasture.
4 Enter God's gates with thanksgiving
    and the courts with praise!
Give thanks to God!
    Bless God's Name!
5 For Our God is good;
    God's steadfast love endures forever,
and God's faithfulness
    to all generations.

1 I sing of your love and justice—
     Adonai, I sing to you!
2 I will be faithful in my pursuit of you;
     when will you come to me?
   I will strive to live in purity of heart among my peers;
3 I will not look upon any injustice without acting.
     I hate crooked dealing, and will have none of it.
4 Twisted thoughts are far from me—
     I will have nothing to do with evil.
5 Those backbiters who slander their neighbor—
     I will silence them;
   those with haughty looks and proud hearts—
     I will not tolerate them.
6 I look to those who keep faith with the land
     to make up my household;
   only those who follow a blameless path
     will I allow in my company.
7 There is no room in my house for any deceiver;
     no liars will stand in my presence.
8 Morning after morning I will silence
     all who are corrupt in the land,
   and cut off all evildoers
     from the City of God.

A prayer of someone depressed and fainting
A lament poured out before God

1   Adonai, hear my prayer,
      let my cry for help reach you;
2   do not hide your face from me
      when I am in trouble;
    turn your ear to me,
      when I call, be quick to answer me!
3   For my days are vanishing like smoke,
      my bones smoulder like logs,
4   my heart is withering like grass in the scorching sun
      and Death is consuming me;
5   whenever I heave a sigh,
      my bones stick through my skin.
6   I have become a vulture roaming the wilderness;
      a screech owl living in the ruins—
7   I lie awake lamenting,
      like a lone bird that chatters to itself on the roof.
8   My enemies taunt me all day long;
      those who used to praise me
      now use my name as a curse.
9   Ashes are the bread I eat,
      and everything I drink is laced with tears.
10 In your fury and your wrath,
      you picked me up only to toss me aside;
11 my days fade away like a shadow,
      and I am as dry as hay.

12 But you, Adonai, sit enthroned,
      and your renown lasts from one generation to the next!
13 Arise, and take pity on Zion!
      The time has come to have mercy on it,
      indeed, the hour has come;
14 for your faithful ones prize its stones
      and are moved to pity by its dust.
15 The nations revere your Name, Adonai,
      and all rulers of the earth stand in awe of your glory.
16 When you build Zion anew,
      your glory will be revealed;

[17] Adonai, you will answer the prayer of the abandoned,
and will not scorn their petitions.
[18] Put this on record for the next generation,
so that a people not yet born can praise Our God:
[19] "Adonai has leaned down
from the sanctuary on high,
has looked down at earth from heaven,
[20] to hear the groans of the captive,
and to set free those condemned to death."
[21] So the Name of Our God will be proclaimed in Zion
and God's praise in Jerusalem;
[22] nations and realms will be united
and offer worship to Our God together.

[23] You've broken my strength in mid-course,
you have shortened my days.
[24] Don't take me before my time,
when your own life lasts forever!
[25] Aeons ago you laid the earth's foundations,
and the heavens are the work of your hands;
[26] yet they will vanish, while you remain—
they'll all wear out like a garment,
you'll change them like clothing,
and then toss them away.
[27] But you never change,
and your years are unending.
[28] The children of your faithful ones
will have a permanent home,
and their descendants will be
in your presence always.

1 Bless Adonai, my soul!
  All that is in me, bless God's holy Name!
2 Bless Adonai, my soul,
  and remember all God's kindnesses!
3 The One who forgives all your sins
  is the One who heals all your diseases;
4 the One who ransoms your life from the Pit
  is the One who crowns you with love and tenderness.
5 The One who fills your years with prosperity
  also gives you an eagle's youthful energy.

6 How you love justice, Adonai!
  You are always on the side of the oppressed.
7 You revealed your intentions to Moses,
  your deeds to Israel.
8 You are tender and compassionate, Adonai—
  slow to anger, and always loving;
9 your indignation doesn't endure forever,
  and your anger lasts only for a short time.
10 You never treat us as our sins deserve;
  you don't repay us in kind for the injustices we do.
11 For as high as heaven is above the earth,
  so great is the love for those who revere you.
12 As far away as the east is from the west,
  that's how far you remove our sins from us!
13 As tenderly as parents treat their children,
  that's how tenderly you treat your worshipers, Adonai!
14 For you know what we are made of—
  you remember that we're nothing but dust.
15 We last no longer than grass,
  live no longer than a wildflower;
16 one gust of wind and we're gone,
  never to be seen again.
17 Yet your love lasts from age to age
  for those who revere you, Adonai,
  as does your goodness to our children's children,
18 and to those who keep your Covenant
  and remember to obey your precepts.

¹⁹ You have established your judgment seat in the heavens,
   and your reign extends over everything.

²⁰ Bless Our God, you angels,
      you powers who do God's bidding,
      attentive to every word of command!
²¹ Bless Our God, you heavenly host,
      you faithful ones who enforce God's will!
²² Bless Our God, all creation,
       to the far reaches of God's reign!
     Bless Adonai, my soul!

1 Bless Our God, my soul!
   Adonai, my God, how great you are!
Clothed in majesty and glory,
2   wrapped in a robe of light,
   you stretch the heavens out like a tent.
3 You lay the beams for your palace on the waters above;
   you use the clouds as your chariot
   and ride on the wings of the wind;
4 you use the winds as messengers
   and fiery flames as attendants.
5 You fixed the earth on its foundations
   so it can never totter,
6 and wrapped it with the Deep as with a robe,
   the waters overtopping the mountains.
7 At your rebuke the waters bolted,
   fleeing at the sound of your thunder,
8 cascading over the mountains, into the valleys,
   down to the reservoir you made for them;
9 you imposed boundaries they must never cross
   so they would never again flood the land.
10 You set springs gushing in ravines,
   running down between the mountains,
11 supplying water for wild animals
   and attracting the thirsty wild donkeys;
12 the birds of the air make their nests by these waters
   and sing among the branches.
13 From your palace you water the highlands
   until the ground is sated by the fruit of your work;
14 you make fresh grass grow for cattle
   and plants for us to cultivate
   to get food from the soil—
15 wine to cheer our hearts,
   oil to make our faces shine,
   and bread to sustain our life.
16 The trees of Our God drink their fill—
   those cedars of Lebanon,
17 where birds build their nests
   and, on the highest branches, the stork makes its home.

18 For the wild goats there are the high mountains,
   and in the crags the rock badgers hide.
19 You made the moon to tell the seasons,
   and the sun knows when to set:
20 you bring darkness on, night falls,
   and all the forest animals come out—
21 savage lions roaring for their prey,
   claiming their food from God.
22 The sun rises, they retire,
   going back to lie down in their lairs,
23 and people go out to work,
   to labor again until evening.
24 Adonai, what variety you have created,
   arranging everything so wisely!
   The earth is filled with your creativity!
25 There's the vast expanse of the Sea,
   teeming with countless creatures,
   living things large and small,
26 with the ships going to and fro
   and Leviathan whom you made to frolic there.
27 All creatures depend on you
   to feed them at the proper time.
28 Give it to them—they gather it up.
   Open your hand—they are well satisfied.
29 Hide your face—they are terrified.
   Take away their breath—they die and return to dust.
30 Send back your breath—fresh life begins
   and you renew the face of the earth.
31 Glory forever to Our God!
   May you find joy in your creation!
32 You glance at the earth and it trembles,
   you touch the mountains and they smoke!

33 I will sing to you all my life,
   I will make music for my God as long as I live.
34 May these reflections of mine give God
   as much pleasure as God gives me!
35 May the corrupt vanish from the earth
   and the violent exist no longer!
   Bless Our God, my soul!
   Alleluia!

1 Alleluia!
Give thanks to Our God,
and call on God's Name;
proclaim God's deeds among the peoples!
2 Sing to God, sing praise,
and tell of all God's marvels!
3 Glory in God's holy Name;
let the hearts that seek Our God rejoice!
4 Turn to Our God—to God's strength—
and seek God's presence constantly.
5 Remember the marvels God has done—
the wonders performed and the judgments pronounced—
6 you descendants of Sarah and Abraham,
God's faithful ones,
7 you offspring of Leah, Rachel and Jacob,
who are God's chosen.
Adonai is our God,
whose authority covers all the earth.

8 God remembers the Covenant forever,
the promise God made for a thousand generations,
9 the pact made with Sarah and Abraham,
the oath to Rebecca and Isaac,
10 the decree confirmed to Leah, Rachel and Jacob,
an everlasting covenant for Israel.
11 "I give you the land of Canaan," said God,
"as the portion you will inherit."
12 There they were fewer in number,
no more than a handful, strangers to the country.
13 They roamed from nation to nation,
from one land to another;
14 God let no one oppress them,
and punished rulers on their behalf.
15 "Do not touch my anointed ones!" God said,
"Do not harm my prophets!"
16 God called down a famine on the country
and destroyed their supply of food.

17 Then God sent Joseph ahead of them,
    to be sold as a slave.
18 They put shackles on his feet,
    and placed an iron collar around his neck,
19 until Joseph's prophecy came to pass,
    and the word of Our God proved him true.
20 Pharaoh gave orders to release him;
    the ruler of Egypt set him free
21 and made him head of the royal household,
    and placed him in charge of the imperial treasury:
22 Joseph was to discipline the officials as he saw fit
    and to teach the elders wisdom.

23 Then Israel migrated to Egypt,
    and settled in the land of Ham.
24 Our God made the people fertile
    and more numerous than their oppressors,
25 whose hearts were turned to detest God's people
    and to conspire against God's faithful.
26 God sent Moses, Miriam and Aaron,
    God's faithful chosen ones,
27 and they performed God's miraculous signs among them—
    God's wonders in the land of Ham.
28 God sent darkness and darkness fell—
    for hadn't they defied God's word?
29 God turned their rivers into blood,
    which killed all their fish.
30 Their country was overrun with frogs,
    even in the Pharaoh's bedroom;
31 God spoke, and swarms of flies appeared,
    and clouds of mosquitoes infested the whole country.
32 God sent them hail instead of rain,
    and lightning across their land;
33 God leveled their vines and fig trees,
    and splintered the trees of their country.
34 God spoke and there came locusts and grasshoppers,
    more than you could count,
35 eating every green thing in the land,
    every blade their soil produced.
36 Then God struck down all the firstborn in the land,
    the entire firstfruits of their posterity;

37 and led Israel out with silver and gold,
  and not one among their tribes was left behind.
38 Egypt was glad to see them go,
  for Israel had filled them with dread.
39 God spread a cloud to cover them,
  and a fire to give light at night.
40 They demanded food, and God sent them quail
  and satisfied them with the bread of heaven;
41 God opened the rock, and waters gushed out,
  flowing through the desert like a river.
42 Yes, faithful to the sacred promise
  given to Sarah and Abraham,
43 God led the people out joyfully,
  singing their glad songs,
44 and gave them the lands of the nations.
  Where others had toiled, they took possession,
45 on condition that they kept God's statutes
  and obeyed the Laws.
  Alleluia!

1 Alleluia!
Give thanks for Adonai's goodness;
   God's love endures forever!
2 Who can proclaim the mighty deeds of Our God,
   or show forth enough praise?
3 Happy are those who act justly,
   who do what is right always!
4 Remember me, Adonai,
   when you show favor to your people.
Help me when you deliver them,
5   that I may enjoy the prosperity of your chosen ones,
share the joy of your nation,
   and join with your own people in giving praise.

6 We have sinned the way our forebears did;
   gone astray and given in to corruption.
7 Our ancestors, when they were in Egypt,
   didn't perceive your wondrous works,
didn't remember your abundant love,
   but there by the sea, by the Sea of Reeds, they rebelled.
8 Yet you saved them, O God, for the sake of your Name,
   to make your mighty power known.
9 You rebuked the Sea of Reeds, and it became dry;
   you led them through the deep as if it were a desert.
10 So God saved them from the hand of the adversary,
   delivered them from the power of the enemy.
11 The waters covered their foes,
   and not one of them was left.
12 Then they believed your promises
   and sang your praise.
13 But they soon forgot your works,
   would not wait to learn your plan,
14 and gave in to their craving in the wilderness,
   putting you to the test in the wasteland;
15 so you gave them what they asked for,
   then sent a wasting disease among them.
16 In the camp they grew jealous of
   Moses, Miriam and Aaron, your holy ones,

17 so the earth opened up and swallowed Dathan,
    and buried the followers of Abiram.
18 Fire broke out among their throng,
    a flame that consumed these corrupt people.
19 At Horeb they made a calf
    and worshiped a molten image.
20 They exchanged your glory
    for the image of an ox that eats grass.
21 They forgot you, their Liberator,
    who had done such great things in Egypt,
22 wondrous works in the land of Ham,
    and awe-inspiring deeds at the Sea of Reeds.
23 You would have destroyed them,
    but Moses, your chosen one,
stood in the breach before you
    and averted your destructive wrath.
24 Then they despised the pleasant land,
    and did not believe your promise.
25 They grumbled in their tents,
    and did not obey your voice.
26 So you swore with upraised hand
    that they would fall in the wilderness,
27 and their descendants would be dispersed among the nations,
    scattered throughout the lands.
28 Then they attached themselves to the Baal of Peor,
    and ate sacrifices offered to lifeless gods;
29 they provoked you to anger with their doings,
    and a plague broke out among them.
30 Then Phinehas stood up and intervened,
    and the plague was stopped—
31 and it has been remembered as a just act
    from generation to generation forever.
32 They angered you at the waters of Meribah,
    and Moses suffered on their account;
33 for they rebelled against your Spirit
    and Moses spoke rashly.
34 They did not destroy the peoples
    as you had commanded them,
35 but they mingled with the nations
    and learned to do as they did.
36 They worshiped their idols,
    which became a snare to them.

37 They sacrificed their own children,
   sacrificed them to demons;
38 they shed innocent blood,
   the blood of their children,
   whom they sacrificed to the idols of Canaan;
   and the land was polluted with blood.
39 Thus they became unclean by their acts,
   and debauched by their deeds.
40 Therefore, you became angry with your people
   and you abhorred your inheritance,
41 and handed them over to the nations,
   so that their enemies ruled over them.
42 Their foes oppressed them,
   and subjected them to their power.
43 You delivered them again and again,
   but they were willfully rebellious,
   and were brought low through their sin.
44 But when you heard their cry
   you saw that they were in distress;
45 you remembered your Covenant for their sake
   and out of your great love, relented.
46 You made all their captors
   take pity on them.

47 Save us, Adonai, our God,
   and gather us from among the nations,
   that we may give thanks to your holy Name
   and glory in your praise!

48 Blessed be Our God, the God of Israel,
   from everlasting to everlasting!
   And let all the people say,
   "Amen, alleluia!"

book ʊ

1 "Give thanks for Adonai's goodness;
      God's love endures forever!"
2 Let these be the words of Adonai's redeemed,
      those redeemed from the oppressor's clutches,
3 those brought home from foreign lands,
      from east and west, from northern lands and southern seas.

4 Some lost their way in the wilderness, in the wasteland,
      not knowing how to reach an inhabited town;
5 they were hungry and thirsty,
      and their courage was running low.
6 They called to Our God in their trouble,
      and God rescued them from their sufferings,
7 guiding them by a direct route
      to an inhabited town.
8 Let them thank Adonai for this great love,
      for the marvels done for all people—
9 for God has satisfied the thirsty
      and filled the hungry with good things.

10 Some were living in gloom and darkness,
      prisoners suffering in iron chains
11 because they defied God's word,
      and scorned the advice of the Most High.
12 God humbled their hearts with suffering;
      they stumbled and there was no one to help them.
13 Then they called to Our God in their trouble
      and God rescued them from their sufferings,
14 releasing them from gloom and darkness

and shattering their chains.
15 Let them thank Adonai for this great love,
for the marvels done for all people—
16 for breaking bronze gates open
and smashing iron bars.

17 Some were fools who suffered because of their rebellion,
because of their own sins,
18 until they were so sick, nearly at death's door,
that food became repugnant.
19 Then they called to Our God in their trouble
and God rescued them from their sufferings,
20 sending a word to heal them,
and snatching them from the Pit.
21 Let them thank Adonai for this great love,
for the marvels done for all people.
22 Let them offer sacrifices of thanksgiving
and recount what God has done in joyful song.

23 Some went down to the sea in ships,
plying their trade across the ocean;
24 they too saw the works of Our God,
the wonders that God worked on the Deep!
25 God spoke and raised a storm wind,
lashing up towering waves.
26 Flung to the sky, then plunged to the depths,
in the ordeal their courage melted away.
27 They staggered and reeled like drunkards
with all their skill adrift.
28 Then they called to Our God in their trouble,
and God rescued them from their sufferings,
29 reducing the storm to a whisper
until the waves of the sea were hushed;
30 overjoyed with the calm,
they were brought safe to the port they were bound for.
31 Let them thank God for this great love,
for the marvels done for all people.
32 Let them praise God in the Great Assembly
and give praise in the Council of Elders.

33 Sometimes God turned rivers into desert,
   springs of water into arid ground,
34 or a fertile country into salt flats,
   because the people living there were corrupt.
35 So God would turn desert into pools of water,
   or an arid country into flowing springs
36 to give the hungry a home,
   a place to build and call their own.
37 There they sow fields and plant vineyards
   that yield a plentiful harvest.
38 God blesses them, their numbers grow,
   · and their livestock never decrease.
39 Or their numbers dwindle,
   with oppression, disaster and hardship taking their toll.
40 God pours contempt upon the nobly born
   and leaves them to wander in trackless wastes,
41 but lifts the needy out of their misery,
   and increases their families like flocks.

42 The upright see it and rejoice,
   but all wrongdoers shut their mouths.
43 If you are wise, study these things
   and realize the great love of Our God.

108

A song
A psalm of David

1   My heart is ready, Adonai,
      and I will sing, sing your praise,
      with all my heart.
2   Awake, lyre and harp—
      I will wake the dawn!
3   I will thank you, Adonai, among the peoples,
      among the nations I will praise you,
4   for your love reaches to the heavens
      and your truth to the skies.
5   Adonai, go even higher than the heavens,
      and let your glory be over the earth
6   so that those you love will be delivered!
   Let your right hand become our deliverance
      and answer me!

7   From the holy place God has made this promise:
   "In my joy I will apportion Shechem
      and measure out the valley of Succoth.
8   Gilead is mine,
      and Manasseh is mine as well.
    Ephraim I take for my helmet,
      Judah for my scepter.
9   Moab I will use for my washbowl,
      on Edom I will plant my shoe;
      and over Philistia I will shout in triumph."

10 But who will lead me to conquer the fortress?
      Who will bring me face to face with Edom?
11 Will you completely reject us, Adonai,
      and no longer march with us?
12 Give us help against the enemy,
      for our own power is useless.
13 With you we will fight valiantly,
      and it is you who will trample our foes.

1 O God of my praise,
    break your silence,
2 now that the corrupt and the deceitful
    are accusing and defaming me,
3 saying malicious things about me,
    attacking me for no reason.
4 In return for my friendship, they denounce me,
    though all I had done was pray for them;
5 they have repaid my kindness with evil,
    my love with hatred.

6 Let *them* stand before a corrupt judge,
    and let *them* be framed with false accusations;
7 when they are judged, make sure they are found guilty,
    and let their prayer be construed as a crime!
8 Let their life be cut short
    and let someone else take their office;
9 let their children be orphaned
    and their spouses bereft!
10 Let their children be homeless beggars,
    searching for food far from their ruined homes;
11 let their creditors seize their possessions
    and foreigners swallow their profits!
12 Let no one be left to show them kindness,
    let no one look after their orphans!
13 Let their family die out,
    their name disappear in one generation!
14 Let the crimes of their ancestors
    be held against them before God,
    and their parents' sins never be erased;
15 let Our God bear them constantly in mind,
    and wipe their memory from the earth!
16 They never thought of being kind,
    but persecuted the poor, the needy and the brokenhearted
    and hounded them to death.
17 They loved pronouncing curses, so curses came to them gladly;
    they had no taste for blessing, so it will shun them.

¹⁸ They wrapped themselves up in their curses,
which soaked right into them like water,
deep into their bones like oil—
¹⁹ and now those same curses envelop them like a cloak,
belted around their waists forever.
²⁰ This is the way God will repay all my accusers,
all who speak evil against me!

²¹ Adonai, defend me for the sake of your Name,
rescue me in the generosity of your love!
²² Reduced to affliction and poverty,
my heart is wounded within me.
²³ I am dwindling away like a shadow,
I have been shaken off like a locust.
²⁴ My knees are weak for lack of food,
my body is thin and gaunt;
²⁵ I have become an object of derision;
people shake their heads when they see me.
²⁶ Help me, Adonai, my God,
save me because of your love!
²⁷ Let them know that this is your hand,
that it was you, Adonai, who has done all this.
²⁸ Counter their curses with your blessing,
shame my aggressors when they arise,
and make your faithful one glad!
²⁹ Clothe my accusers in disgrace,
cover them with a cloak of their own shame.

³⁰ I will give thanks aloud to Our God,
and proclaim God's praise in the Assembly—
³¹ for taking the side of poor people,
defending them against those
who would sentence them to death.

1 Our God said to my Sovereign One:
"Sit at my right hand,
    until I make your enemies your footstool."

2 Adonai, stretch forth your mighty scepter from Zion,
    and rule in the midst of your enemies!

3 Your people will offer themselves freely
    on the day you lead your host
    upon the holy mountains.
From the womb of the morning
    your young people will come to you, plentiful as the dew.

4 Our God has sworn and will not retract:
    "You are a priest forever
    in the line of Melchizedek."

5 With God at your side
    you will shatter rulers on the day of wrath.

6 You will execute judgment among the nations,
    filling them with corpses;
    you will shatter chiefs over the wide earth.

7 And because you will drink from the brook along the way,
    you will be strengthened and victorious!

1   Alleluia!
      I will thank you, Adonai, with all my heart
      in the meeting of the just and their assembly.

2   Great are your works,
      to be pondered by all who love them.

3   Majestic and glorious are your works,
      and your justice stands firm forever.

4   You make us remember your wonders—
      you are compassion and love.

5   You give food to those who revere you,
      keeping your Covenant ever in mind.

6   You reveal to your people the power of your actions
      by giving them the lands of the nations as their inheritance.

7   The works of your hands are truth and justice,
      and all your precepts are sure,

8   standing firm forever and ever,
      and carried out uprightly and faithfully.

9   You have sent deliverance to your people
      and established your Covenant forever.
      Your Name is holy and awe-inspiring!

10   Reverence for Our God is the beginning of wisdom—
      and those who have it prove themselves wise.
      Your praise will last forever!

---

* This psalm is an acrostic poem: the first letter of each line begins with a subsequent letter of the Hebrew alphabet.

1   Alleluia!
    Happiness comes to those who revere Our God,
        who revel in God's commands!

2   Their children hold power on earth;
        the descendants of the just will always be blessed.

3   There will be riches and wealth for their families,
        and God's justice can never be changed.

4   For the just, Our God shines like a lamp in the dark,
        God is merciful, compassionate and righteous.

5   Good people are generous, and lend money without interest;
        they are honest in all their dealings.

6   They are never shaken, because they love justice
        and will leave an imperishable memory behind them.

7   They never fear bad news,
        because their unwavering hearts trust in Our God.

8   With peaceful hearts, they fear nothing;
        and in the end they will triumph over their enemies.

9   Quick to be generous, they give to the poor,
        doing justice always and forever;
        their horn will always be lifted in honor.

10 The corrupt become infuriated when they see this;
        they grind their teeth and waste away,
        finally vanishing like their empty dreams.

---

* This psalm is an acrostic poem: the first letter of each line begins with a subsequent letter of the Hebrew alphabet.

"the great hallel"
psalms 113-118

1 Alleluia!
   You faithful of Our God, give praise,
      praise the Name of Our God!
2 Blessed be the Name of Our God,
      from now and for all times!
3 From the rising of the sun to its setting,
      praised be the Name of Our God!
4 You are high over all nations, Adonai!
      Your glory transcends the heavens!
5 Who is like you, Adonai, our God?
      Enthroned so high,
6 you need to stoop
      to see the sky and the earth!
7 You raise the poor from the dust,
      and lift the needy from the dung heap
8 to give them a place at the table with rulers,
      with the leaders of your people.
9 You give the childless couple a home
      filled with the joy of many children.
   Alleluia!

1 Alleluia!
When Israel came out of Egypt,
from a people who spoke an alien tongue,
2 Judah became God's Temple,
Israel became God's domain.
3 The sea fled at the sight:
the Jordan turned back on its course,
4 the mountains leapt like rams,
and the hills like yearling sheep.
5 Why was it, sea, that you fled—
that you turned back, Jordan, on your course?
6 Mountains, why did you leap like rams—
you hills, like yearling sheep?
7 Earth, tremble before your Maker,
before the God of Israel,
8 who turned the rock into a pool of water
and flint into a bubbling fountain!

1 Not to us, Adonai, not to us,
but to your Name give the glory
for the sake of your love and faithfulness.
2 Why do the nations say,
"Where is their God?"
3 But you, Adonai, are in the heavens,
doing whatever you will.
4 Their idols are silver and gold,
the work of human hands.
5 These "gods" have mouths but they cannot speak;
they have eyes but they cannot see;
6 they have ears but they cannot hear;
they have noses but they cannot smell.
7 They have hands but they cannot feel;

they have feet but they cannot walk—
and no sound comes from their throats.

8   Their makers will become just like them,
and so will all who trust in them!

9   Descendants of Israel, trust in Our God,
who is your help and your shield.
10 Daughters of Miriam, Sons of Aaron, trust in Our God,
who is your help and your shield.
11 You who revere Adonai, trust in Our God,
who is your help and your shield.

12 Our God remembers us and blesses us;
Our God will bless the children of Israel,
the children of the Covenant.
13 Those who revere Our God will be blessed,
the humble no less than the great;
14 may Our God increase you,
you and all your children.
15 May you be blessed by Our God,
who made heaven and earth!
16 The heavens, the heavens belong to Our God,
but the earth God has given to humankind.
17 The dead will not praise Our God,
nor those who go down into silence.
18 But we who live bless Our God,
now and forever.
Alleluia!

116

1   I love you, Adonai, for you have heard
my cry for mercy.
2   You have listened to me;
I will call on you all my days.
3   The bands of Death encircled me;
the messengers of Sheol ambushed me,

I was overcome with trouble and sorrow.
4 Then I called your Name, Adonai—
"Help, Adonai, save me!"

5 You are gracious, Adonai, and just;
Our God is compassionate.
6 You protect those without guile;
when I was brought low, you saved me.
7 Be at rest once again, my soul,
for Our God has been good to you.
8 You have rescued my soul from Death,
my eyes from Tears,
and my feet from Banishment.
9 I walk before you, Adonai,
in the land of the living.
10 I believed even when I said,
"I am completely crushed,"
11 and in despair said,
"No one can be trusted."

12 How can I repay you, Adonai,
for all your goodness to me?
13 I raise the cup of deliverance,
and call on the Name of Our God.
14 I will fulfill my vows to you
in the presence of all your people.
15 The death of your faithful
is precious in your sight.
16 Adonai, I am your faithful one—
I am faithful to you alone,
the child of your fidelity.
You have freed me from my chains.
17 I will offer you the sacrifice of praise,
and call on the Name of Our God.
18 I will fulfill my vows to you
in the presence of all your people,
19 in the courts of the house of Our God,
in the midst of Jerusalem.
Alleluia!

1   Praise Our God, all you nations,
      extol God, all you mighty ones.
2   For God's love toward us is great,
      God's faithfulness, eternal.
    Alleluia!

1   I thank you, Adonai, for your goodness!
      Your love is everlasting!
2   Let Israel say it:
      "Your love is everlasting!"
3   Let the House of Aaron say it:
      "Your love is everlasting!"
4   Let those who revere Our God say it:
      "Your love is everlasting!"

5   In anguish, I cried to you, Adonai,
      and you answered me with freedom.
6   Because Our God is with me, I'm not afraid—
      what can anyone do to me?
7   Because Our God is with me as my Helper,
      I can triumph over my enemies.
8   Better to take refuge in Our God
      than to trust in human beings;
9   better to take refuge in Our God
      than to follow leaders.
10 The nations were swarming round me,
      but I stood my ground in the Name of Our God.
11 They swarmed round me closer and closer,
      but I stood my ground in the Name of Our God;
12 They swarmed round me like bees,
      but they died like thorns in a bonfire;
      I stood my ground in the Name of Our God.
13 I was pressed, pressed, about to fall,
      but Our God came to my help.

14 God is my strength and my song;
   God has become my salvation!
15 Raise shouts of joy and victory
   in the tents of the upright:
   Our God's right hand is doing mighty acts!
16 Our God's right hand is winning,
   Our God's right hand is doing mighty acts!
17 No, I will not die—
   I will live to proclaim the deeds of Our God;
18 though Our God has disciplined me often,
   I am not abandoned to Death.
19 Open the gates of justice for me,
   let me come in and thank you, Adonai!
20 This is the gate of Our God,
   and only the upright can enter!
21 Thank you for hearing me,
   for saving me.
22 It was the stone which the builders rejected
   that became the keystone;
23 this is Our God's doing,
   and it is wonderful to see.
24 This is the day Our God has made—
   let us celebrate with joy!

25 Please, Adonai, please save us!
   Please, Adonai, give us prosperity now!
26 Blessings on the one who comes in the Name of Our God!
   We bless you from Adonai's Temple!
27 Adonai is God
   and God has enlightened us.
   Join the festal procession!
   With palm fronds in hand, go up to the horns of the altar!
28 You are my God, and I thank you;
   you are my God, and I exalt you.
   Thank you for hearing me,
   for saving me.
29 Thank you, Adonai, for your goodness!
   Your love is everlasting!

aleph

1 Happiness comes to those whose way is blameless,
   who walk in your Law, Adonai.
2 Happiness comes to those who keep your decrees,
   and seek you with all their heart,
3 and do no wrong,
   but walk in your ways.
4 You have commanded that your precepts
   be kept diligently—
5 if only I were more faithful
   in keeping your statutes!
6 Then I wouldn't feel so ashamed
   when I look at all your commands.
7 I will thank you with an upright heart,
   when I truly learn to be as just as you want me to be.
8 I will obey your statutes;
   do not utterly forsake me.

beth

9 How can young people keep themselves
   on the straight and narrow?
   By keeping to your words!
10 With all my heart I seek you;
   let me not stray from your commands.
11 In my heart I treasure your promise
   so that I keep from sinning against you.
12 Blessed are you, Adonai—
   teach me your statutes!
13 With my lips I declare
   every ordinance you've spoken.
14 I rejoice in the path you decree
   as much as I'd rejoice in great wealth.
15 I meditate on your precepts
   and ponder your ways.

---

* This psalm is an acrostic poem: the first word of each stanza begins with a subsequent letter of the Hebrew alphabet.

¹⁶ I delight in your statutes;
   I will not forget your words.

ghimel

¹⁷ Be good to your faithful one,
   that I may live and keep your words.
¹⁸ Open my eyes, and let me ponder
   the wonders of your Law.
¹⁹ No matter where I am on earth, I am a foreigner;
   don't hide your commands from me.
²⁰ I am eaten up with longing
   for your ordinances all the time.
²¹ You rebuke the arrogant with a curse,
   for turning away from your commands.
²² Take scorn and contempt away from me,
   for I keep your decrees.
²³ Though tyrants conspire and testify against me,
   your faithful one meditates on your statutes.
²⁴ Yes, your decrees are my delight—
   they are my counselors.

daleth

²⁵ Down in the dust I lie;
   give me life according to your word.
²⁶ I was honest about my past ways, and you answered me;
   teach me your statutes.
²⁷ Make me understand the way of your precepts,
   and I will meditate on your wondrous deeds.
²⁸ My soul is weary with sorrow;
   strengthen me according to your word.
²⁹ Keep me from the habit of telling lies,
   and give me grace through your Law.
³⁰ I choose the path of truth;
   I have set my heart on your ordinances.
³¹ I cling to your decrees;
   Adonai, don't let me be ashamed.
³² I will run headlong down the road of your commands,
   for you have set my heart free.

he

33 Educate me, Adonai, in the way of your statutes,
   and I'll keep them to the end.
34 Give me discernment, that I may observe your Law
   and obey it with all my heart.
35 Lead me in the path of your commands—
   that is where I'll find joy.
36 Draw my heart to your decrees
   and not toward selfish gain.
37 Turn my eyes away from looking at worthless things;
   make me alive in your way.
38 Fulfill for your faithful
   your promise to those who fear you.
39 Take away the reproach which I dread,
   for your ordinances are good.
40 See how I long for your precepts!
   In your justice give me life.

waw

41 Fulfill your promise, Adonai,
   and let your love, your salvation come to me.
42 Then I'll have a word for those who taunt me,
   for it is *your* word that I trust.
43 Don't steal the word of truth from my mouth completely;
   for I put my hope in your ordinances.
44 And I will obey your Law continually,
   forever and ever.
45 I will walk in freedom,
   because I seek your precepts.
46 I will speak of your decrees before heads of state,
   and I will not be ashamed.
47 I delight in your commands,
   because I love them.
48 I will lift up my hands to your commands because I love them,
   and I'll meditate on your statutes.

zayin

49 Grant to your faithful one the fulfillment of your word,
   for you have given me hope.
50 Your life-giving promise
   has been great comfort during my torment.

51 Though the proud scoff bitterly at me,
   I do not turn away from your Law.
52 I remember your ancient ordinances, Adonai,
   and I am comforted.
53 Indignation seizes me
   because of the corrupt who reject your Law.
54 Your statutes are all I sing about
   in my wayfarer's shelter.
55 I remember you in the night, Adonai,
   and I will keep your Law.
56 For it has been my fortune
   to obey your precepts.

heth

57 Did I not say, Adonai, that my role
   is to keep your words?
58 I sought your face with all my heart;
   give me grace, as you promised.
59 I examined my own ways,
   and turned my feet to your decrees.
60 I'll be prompt and will not hesitate
   in keeping your commands.
61 Though the ropes of violent people bind me hand and foot,
   I won't forget your Law.
62 When I wake up in the middle of the night
   I thank you for your just ordinances.
63 I am a friend to all who revere you
   and keep your precepts.
64 Your love, Adonai, fills the earth;
   teach me your statutes!

teth

65 In keeping with your promise,
   do good to your faithful one.
66 Give me insight and understanding,
   for I trust in your commands.
67 Before I was disciplined I went astray,
   but now I obey your word.
68 You are good and what you do is good;
   teach me your statutes.
69 Though arrogant people smear me with lies,
   I observe your precepts with all my heart.

⁷⁰ Their heart has become calloused and bloated,
  but I delight in your Law.
⁷¹ It was good for me to have been afflicted,
  because through it I learned your statutes.
⁷² The law of your mouth is more precious to me
  than gold and silver coins by the thousands.

yod

⁷³ Just as your hands made me and shaped me,
  give me discernment, that I may learn your commands.
⁷⁴ Those who revere you will rejoice when they see me,
  because I hope in your word.
⁷⁵ I know, Adonai, that your ordinances are just,
  and that you afflicted me only because of your faithfulness.
⁷⁶ Let your love comfort me now,
  as you promised your faithful one.
⁷⁷ Let your compassion come to me and breathe life back into me,
  for your Law is my delight.
⁷⁸ Let the arrogant be put to shame for oppressing me unjustly;
  as for me, I'll meditate on your precepts.
⁷⁹ Let those who revere you turn to me,
  those who acknowledge your decrees.
⁸⁰ Let my heart be perfect in your statutes,
  so that I will never be put to shame.

kaph

⁸¹ Keenly I long for your salvation;
  I hope in your word.
⁸² My eyes strain, looking for your promise—
  when will you comfort me?
⁸³ Though I'm as shriveled as an old withered wineskin,
  I have not forgotten your statutes.
⁸⁴ How long must your faithful one wait?
  When will you pass sentence on my persecutors?
⁸⁵ They have set their traps in my path,
  arrogantly ignoring your Law.
⁸⁶ But all your commands are trustworthy,
  and they persecute me without cause! Help me!
⁸⁷ They almost wiped me off the face of the earth,
  but I haven't forsaken your precepts.
⁸⁸ In your love, keep me alive,
  and I will obey everything you say.

lamed

89 Like the heavens in their constancy,
   your word, Adonai, endures forever.
90 Through one generation to the next, your faithfulness continues,
   as firmly established as the earth itself.
91 Your ordinances endure to this day
   for all who are faithful to you.
92 If your Law hadn't been my delight,
   I'd have been lost in my affliction.
93 I will never forget your precepts,
   for through them you gave me life.
94 I am yours—save me,
   for I have sought your precepts!
95 Violent people wait to destroy me,
   but I pay heed to your decrees.
96 Even perfection has its limits, I see—
   but your command is absolutely limitless.

mem

97 My meditation all day long is your Law—
   how I love it!
98 Your commands make me wiser than my enemies,
   for they are always with me.
99 I have more insight than all my teachers,
   for your decrees are my meditation.
100 I understand more than the elders,
   because I obey your precepts.
101 I've kept my feet from straying onto any evil path,
   so that I could obey your words.
102 I have never turned away from your ordinances,
   for you yourself have taught me.
103 How sweet is the taste of your promises—
   sweeter than honey in my mouth!
104 Through your precepts, I gain discernment,
   and because of them I hate every wrong path.

nun

105 Now I know your word is a lamp for my steps,
   for the path just ahead of me.
106 I resolve and swear
   to keep your ordinances of justice.

107 I have suffered much, Adonai—
  give me life as you have promised.
108 Please accept my heartfelt praises, Adonai,
  and teach me your decrees.
109 Though constantly I take my life in my hands,
  I never forgot your Law.
110 The corrupt laid their traps for me,
  but I haven't strayed from your precepts.
111 Your decrees are all the inheritance I'll ever want—
  they're the joy of my heart.
112 I set my heart to keep your statutes,
  forever and to the letter.

samekh

113 Oh, how I hate duplicitous people!
  But I love your Law.
114 You are my refuge and my shield;
  in your word I hope.
115 Get away from me, you reprobates,
  so that I can keep the commands of my God!
116 Sustain me as you have promised, that I may live;
  don't let me be ashamed for hoping in you.
117 Help me and I will be safe,
  and forever delight in your statutes.
118 You reject all who stray from your statutes,
  they know nothing but emptiness and deceit.
119 You sweep the corrupt away like a pile of ashes—
  that is why I love your decrees.
120 My body trembles in awe of you,
  and I revere your ordinances.

ayin

121 Please don't abandon me to my oppressors,
  for I have done what is upright and just.
122 Ensure the well-being of your faithful one,
  don't let the arrogant oppress me.
123 My eyes strain looking for your salvation
  and your just promise.
124 Deal with your faithful one out of your love,
  and teach me your statutes.
125 I am faithful to you;
  give me discernment so that I can understand your decrees.

¹²⁶ It's time to act, Adonai!
    They're breaking your Law!
¹²⁷ That is why I love your commands more than gold,
    more than the purest gold.
¹²⁸ This is why I trust all your precepts
    and hate every destructive path.

pe

¹²⁹ Quite wonderful are your decrees—
    that is why I obey them.
¹³⁰ The revelation of your words sheds light,
    giving understanding to the guileless.
¹³¹ I pant with open mouth
    in my longing for your commands.
¹³² Turn to me, have mercy on me,
    as you turn to those who love your Name.
¹³³ Direct my footsteps as you promise,
    and don't let sin govern my life.
¹³⁴ Ransom me from all oppression,
    that I can keep your precepts.
¹³⁵ Let your face shine upon your faithful one,
    and teach me your statutes.
¹³⁶ Streams of tears flow from my eyes
    because others do not obey your Law.

tsadhe

¹³⁷ Righteous are you, Adonai,
    and your ordinance is just.
¹³⁸ You have pronounced your decrees in justice
    and in perfect faithfulness.
¹³⁹ My zeal consumes me
    because my foes forget your words.
¹⁴⁰ Your promise is absolutely trustworthy,
    and your faithful one loves it.
¹⁴¹ I am lowly and contemptible,
    but I have never forgotten you.
¹⁴² Your justice is everlasting justice,
    and your Law is truth itself.
¹⁴³ Though distress and anguish come upon me,
    your commands are my delight.
¹⁴⁴ Your decrees are forever just;
    make me understand them, that I might live.

qoph

145 So I call out with all my heart—answer me, Adonai,
    and I will obey your statutes.
146 I call upon you—save me,
    and I will keep your decrees!
147 I wake before the dawn and cry out for help;
    I hope in your words.
148 My eyes greet the night watches
    in meditation on your promise.
149 Hear my voice because of your love, Adonai,
    and give me life through your ordinances.
150 Malicious schemers are near me,
    but they are far from your Law.
151 You, Adonai, are near,
    and all your commands endure forever.
152 Long ago I learned your decrees,
    and you planted them for all time.

resh

153 Behold my affliction, and rescue me,
    for I have not forgotten your Law.
154 Plead my cause and ransom me!
    Give me life, as you promised!
155 Deliverance is far from the corrupt
    because they don't seek your statutes.
156 Your compassion is great, Adonai,
    give me life, as your ordinances promise.
157 Though my persecutors and enemies are many,
    I haven't turned from your decrees.
158 I look upon the faithless with loathing,
    because they do not obey your word.
159 See how I love your precepts, Adonai!
    In your great love, give me life.
160 Your word is true above all else;
    all of your just ordinances are everlasting.

shin

161 Unjustly, I am persecuted by our leaders,
    but my heart stands in awe of your word.
162 I rejoice at your promise,
    like one who has found rich plunder.

¹⁶³ I hate lies—I abhor them!
　　But I love your Law.
¹⁶⁴ Seven times a day I praise you
　　for your just ordinances.
¹⁶⁵ Those who love your Law have great peace,
　　and for them there is no stumbling block.
¹⁶⁶ I wait for your salvation, Adonai,
　　and I follow your commands.
¹⁶⁷ I keep your decrees
　　and love them deeply.
¹⁶⁸ I obey your precepts and decrees,
　　for all my ways are before you.

taw

¹⁶⁹ View my petition when it comes before you, Adonai;
　　in keeping with your word give me discernment.
¹⁷⁰ Let my supplication reach you;
　　rescue me as you promised.
¹⁷¹ Let my lips pour forth your praise
　　because you teach me your statutes.
¹⁷² Let my tongue sing of your promise,
　　for all your commands are just.
¹⁷³ Let your hand be ready to help me,
　　for I have chosen your precepts.
¹⁷⁴ I long for your salvation, Adonai,
　　and your Law is my delight.
¹⁷⁵ Let me live to praise you,
　　and let your ordinances sustain me.
¹⁷⁶ I've gone astray like a lost sheep—search for your faithful one,
　　because I have never forgotten your commands.

the songs of ascents
psalms 120-134

120

A Song of Ascents

1 When I was in trouble, I called to you, Adonai,
      and you answered me.
2 Save me from these liars
      and from all these double-crossers!
3 What will God do to you, you foul liar?
      How will God punish you?
4 You'll be shot through with arrows,
      or burned with blazing coals!
5 Living among you is as bad as living in Mesech
      or among the people of Kedar!

6 I have lived too long
      with belligerent people!
7 I stand for peace,
      but when I talk of peace, they want war!

121

A Song of Ascents

1 I lift my eyes to the mountains—
      from where will my help come?
2 My help comes from Our God,
      who made heaven and earth!
3 Our God won't let our footsteps slip:
      our Guardian never sleeps.
4 The Guardian of Israel
      will never slumber, never sleep!

5   Our God is our Guardian,
        Our God is our shade:
    with God by our side,
6   the sun cannot overpower us by day,
        nor the moon at night.
7   Our God guards us from harm,
        guards our lives.
8   Our God guards our leaving and our coming back,
        now and forever.

122

A Song of Ascents
By David

1   How I rejoiced when they said to me,
        "Let us go to the house of Our God!"
2   And now our feet are standing
        within your gates, Jerusalem.
3   Jerusalem restored!
        The city, one united whole!
4   Here the tribes ascend,
        the tribes of Our God.
    They come to praise Our God's Name,
        as God commanded Israel—
5   here, where the tribunals of justice are,
        the judgment seats of David's house.
6   Pray for peace within Jerusalem:
        "May those who love you prosper!
7   May peace be in your walls!
        May your citadels be always secure!"
8   For the sake of my family and friends,
        I say, "Peace be within you!"
9   For the sake of Adonai our God,
        I will seek your good.

1 I lift up my eyes to you,
    you who sit enthroned in the heavens!
2 As the eyes of a dog
    look to the hand of its owner—
as the eyes of attendants
    look to the hand of those they serve—
3 so our eyes look to you, Adonai,
    until you show us your mercy!
4 Have mercy on us, Adonai, have mercy!
    We have endured so much contempt.
5 We have endured far too much
    ridicule from the wealthy,
    too much contempt from the arrogant!

124

A Song of Ascents
By David

1 "If it had not been Adonai who was on our side"—
    let Israel now say—
2 "if it had not been Adonai who was on our side,
    when enemies attacked us,
3   they'd have swallowed us alive!
When their anger burned against us,
4   the flood would have swept us away,
the water would have drowned us,
5   the raging torrent would have engulfed us!"

6 Blessed be Adonai,
    who has not let us fall prey to their teeth!
7 We are free like a bird from the trap!
    The snare has been broken and we are free!
8 Our help is in the Name of Adonai,
    who made heaven and earth.

1 Those who trust in you, Adonai,
    are like Mount Zion,
  which cannot be moved
    but endures forever.
2 As mountains surround Jerusalem
    so you surround your people,
    both now and forever more.
3 For the scepter of corruption won't last
    over the land allotted to the upright,
  to spare the upright from the temptation
    to use their hands for evil.

4 Do good, Adonai, to the good,
    to those who are upright in their hearts!
5 But those who turn aside on their crooked roads, Adonai,
    you will lead them away with the evildoers!
  Peace be upon Israel!

1 When Our God brought us captives back to Zion,
   we thought we were dreaming!
2 Our mouths were filled with laughter then,
   our tongues with songs of joy.
 And from the nations we heard,
   "Their God has done great things for them."
3 Yes—Our God has done great things for us,
   and we are filled with joy.

4 Now set our captive hearts free, Adonai!
   Make them like streams in the driest desert!
5 Then those who now sow in tears
   will reap with shouts of joy;
6 those who go out weeping as they
   carry their seed for sowing,
 will come back with shouts of joy
   as they carry their harvest home.

127

A Song of Ascents
By Solomon

1 If Our God doesn't build the house,
   the builders work in vain;
 if Our God doesn't guard the city,
   the sentries watch in vain.
2 In vain you get up early and stay up late,
   sweating to make a living,
 because God loves us and provides for us
   even while we sleep.

3   Children are the heritage God gives us;
        our descendants are our rewards.
4   Having children when you are young
        is like equipping an archer with wonderful new arrows.
     Happy are those who have filled their quiver
        with such arrows!
     When they argue with their enemies at the city gate,
        no one will be able to make them feel ashamed.

128

A Song of Ascents

1   Happiness comes to those who revere Our God,
        and walk in God's ways!
2   You will eat what your hands have worked for;
        you will be blessed and prosperous.
3   You will be a fruitful vine
        in the heart of your house;
     your children will grow up around your table,
        spring up like olive trees.
4   This is how you will be blessed
        if you revere Our God.
5   May Our God bless you from Zion,
        and may you see the prosperity of Jerusalem
        all the days of your life!
6   May you live to see your children's children!
        Peace be on Israel!

¹ "They have oppressed me continually ever since I was a child"—
   let Israel now say—
² "they've oppressed me continually ever since I was a child,
      but they have never been victorious over me!
³ My back looks like a plowed field—
      the furrows are long and deep.
⁴ But the God of Justice has severed
      the cords of the tyrant!"

⁵ Let all who hate Zion be put to shame,
      be turned away.
⁶ Let them be like the grass on our flat clay housetops—
      it withers in the heat before you can pluck it,
⁷ so sparse that there's not a handful for the reaper,
      nothing for the gatherer to carry away.
⁸ Let no one who walks past them ever say,
      "The blessing of God be upon you!
      We bless you in the Name of Our God!"

130

¹ Out of the depths I cry to you, Adonai!
²   God, hear my voice!
   Let your ears be attentive
      to my voice, my cries for mercy!
³ If you kept track of our sins, Adonai,
      who could stand before you?
⁴ But with you is forgiveness,
      and for this we revere you.

    ⁵ So I wait for you, Adonai—
        my soul waits,
        and in your word I place my trust.
    ⁶ My soul longs for you, Adonai,
        more than sentinels long for the dawn,
        more than sentinels long for the dawn.
    ⁷ Israel, put your hope in Our God,
        for with Adonai is abundant love
        and the fullness of deliverance;
    ⁸ God will deliver Israel
        from all its failings.

131

A Song of Ascents
By David

    ¹ Adonai, my heart has no lofty ambitions,
        my eyes don't look too high.
    I am not concerned with great affairs
        or marvels beyond my scope.
    ² It's enough for me to keep my soul tranquil
        and quiet like a child in its mother's arms;
        my soul is as content as a nursing child.
    ³ Israel, rely on Our God like a child,
        now and forever!

1 O God, remember David
   and all his hardships!
2 Remember the oath he swore to you,
   his vow to the Strong One of Israel:
3 "I won't enter my house,
   I won't go to my bed—
4 I won't give sleep to my eyes
   or slumber to my eyelids
5 until I find a place for Our God,
   a dwelling for the Strong One of Israel!"
6 At Ephrata we heard of the ark;
   we found it on the plains of Yearim.
7 Let us go then, to the place of God's dwelling;
   let us kneel at Our God's footstool.
8 Arise, Adonai, to the place of your rest,
   you and the ark of your strength!
9 Your priests will be clothed with holiness;
   your faithful will sing for joy.

10 For the sake of David, your faithful one,
   don't reject your Anointed.
11 You swore an oath to David—
   don't go back on your word:
   "I will set your offspring
   on your throne!
12 If your children keep my Covenant
   and my laws that I teach them,
   their descendants will sit
   on your throne forever."
13 For you chose Zion, Adonai;
   you wanted to live there:
14 "This is where I'll rest forever,
   it is here that I wanted to sit.
15 I will greatly bless its crops
   and I will fill its poor people with bread.
16 I will clothe its priests with salvation
   and make its faithful sing for joy.

¹⁷ Here David's stock will flower;
   I will light a lamp for my anointed one.
¹⁸ I will clothe his enemies with shame
   but the crown on his head will shine."

133

A Song of Ascents
By David

1 See how good, how pleasant it is
   for God's people to live together as one!
2 It is like precious oil on Aaron's head
   running down on his beard,
   running down to the collar of his robes.
3 It is like the dew of Mount Hermon,
   falling on the hills of Zion.
For that is where Our God bestows the blessing—
   life that never ends.

134

A Song of Ascents

1 Come and bless Adonai,
   all you who serve Our God,
   ministering by night in God's house!
2 Lift up your hands in the sanctuary,
   and bless Adonai!
3 May you be blessed from Zion
   by the One who made heaven and earth!

1 Alleluia!
  Praise the Name of Our God—
    sing praise, you who serve the Most High,
2 who stand in the house of Our God,
    in the courts of God's house!
3 Alleluia! God is good!
    Sing praise to that wonderful Name!
4 For you, Adonai, chose us for yourself,
    chose Israel as your treasure.

5 I know how great you are, Adonai,
    that you are above all gods.
6 Your will is done in heaven and on earth,
    in the seas and all their depths.
7 You summon clouds from the ends of the earth;
    you send lightning with the rain;
    you bring the wind from your storehouses.
8 You struck down all the firstborn of Egypt,
    human and beast alike.
9 You sent signs and wonders into Egypt's midst,
    against Pharaoh and all the royal attendants.
10 You struck down nations in their greatness
    and killed rulers in their splendor—
11 like Sihon, ruler of the Amorites,
    and Og, ruler of Bashan,
    and all the dominions of Canaan.
12 You gave their land, their inheritance, to Israel,
    an inheritance for your people.

13 Adonai, your Name stands forever,
    your fame is told from one generation to the next.
14 For you do justice for your people;
    and you have compassion for your faithful.
15 The idols of the nations are silver and gold,
    the work of human hands.
16 They have mouths but they can't speak;
    they have eyes but they can't see.
17 They have ears but can't hear;
    there is never a breath on their lips.

18 Their makers will come to be like them,
   and so will all who trust in them!

19 House of Israel, bless Our God!
   Priests of the Temple, bless Our God!
20 Attendants of the Sanctuary, bless Our God!
   You who revere Adonai, bless Our God!
21 Blessings from Zion upon Our God,
   who dwells in Jerusalem!
   Alleluia!

136

1 Thank you Adonai, for you are good!
   Your love is everlasting!
2 Thank you, God of gods!
   Your love is everlasting!
3 Thank you, Sovereign of sovereigns,
   Your love is everlasting!
4 you alone perform such great marvels.
   Your love is everlasting!
5 Your wisdom made the heavens.
   Your love is everlasting!
6 You spread the land out over the waters.
   Your love is everlasting!
7 You made the great lights:
   Your love is everlasting!
8 the sun to govern the day,
   Your love is everlasting!
9 moon and stars to govern the night.
   Your love is everlasting!
10 You struck down the firstborn of Egypt,
   Your love is everlasting!
11 and brought Israel out.
   Your love is everlasting!
12 With mighty hand and outstretched arm,
   Your love is everlasting!
13 you split the Sea of Reeds,
   Your love is everlasting!

14 and led Israel through the middle,
Your love is everlasting!
15 and drowned Pharaoh and the armies of Egypt.
Your love is everlasting!
16 You led your people through the wilderness,
Your love is everlasting!
17 and struck down mighty rulers.
Your love is everlasting!
18 You cut down famous leaders,
Your love is everlasting!
19 like Sihon, ruler of the Amorites,
Your love is everlasting!
20 and Og, ruler of Bashan.
Your love is everlasting!
21 You gave their land as an inheritance,
Your love is everlasting!
22 an inheritance to Israel, your faithful one.
Your love is everlasting!
23 You remembered us when we were under the yoke,
Your love is everlasting!
24 and snatched us from our oppressors.
Your love is everlasting!

1 By the rivers of Babylon
     we sat and wept, remembering Zion.
2 On the willows there
     we hung up our harps.
3 For there our captors taunted us to sing our songs,
     our tormentors demanded songs of joy:
     "Sing us one of the songs of Zion!"
4 But how could we sing a song of Our God
     in a foreign land?

5 If I forget you, Jerusalem,
     may my right hand forget its skill!
6 May my tongue stick to the roof of my mouth
     if I ever forget you,
   if I ever stop considering Jerusalem
     my greatest joy.

7 Remember, Adonai, what the children of Edom did
     the day Jerusalem fell,
   when they said,
     "Tear it down!
     Tear it down to its foundations!"
8 Brood of Babylon, doomed to destruction,
     a blessing on those who will repay you
     for the evil you have done to us!
9 A blessing on those who will seize your infants
     and dash them against the rock!

By David

1   I thank you with all my heart;
     I sing your praise before the gods.
2   I bow down in front of your holy Temple
     and praise your Name
  because of your love and faithfulness,
     for you have put above everything else
     your Name and your word.
3   When I called, you answered me—
     you made me bold and strong of heart.
4   All the rulers of the earth will praise you, Adonai,
     when they hear the words of your mouth.
5   They will sing about what you have done, Adonai,
     and about your great glory.
6   Even though you are so high above,
     you care for the lowly
     and see arrogant people from far away.
7   Even when I'm surrounded by troubles,
     you keep me safe;
  you oppose the anger of my enemies,
     and save me with your right hand.
8   You will do everything
     you have promised me.
  Adonai, your love is eternal;
     don't abandon the work of your hands.

1 Adonai, you've searched me,
    and you know me.
2 You know if I am standing or sitting,
    you read my thoughts from far away.
3 Whether I walk or lie down, you are watching;
    you are intimate with all of my ways.
4 A word is not even on my tongue, Adonai,
    before you know what it is:
5 you hem me in, before and behind,
    shielding me with your hand.
6 Such knowledge is too wonderful for me,
    a height my mind cannot reach!

7 Where could I run from your Spirit?
    Where could I flee from your presence?
8 If I go up to the heavens, you're there;
    if I make my bed in Death, you're already there.
9 I could fly away with wings made of dawn,
    or make my home on the far side of the sea,
10 but even there your hand will guide me,
    your mighty hand holding me fast.
11 If I say, "The darkness will hide me,
    and night will be my only light,"
12 even darkness won't be dark to you;
    the night will shine like the day—
    darkness and light are the same to you.

13 You created my inmost being
    and stitched me together in my mother's womb.
14 For all these mysteries I thank you—
    for the wonder of myself,
  for the wonder of your works—
    my soul knows it well.
15 My frame was not hidden from you
    while I was being made in that secret place,
  knitted together in the depths of the earth;
16   your eyes saw my body even there.

All of my days
    were written in your book,
all of them planned
    before even the first of them came to be.
17 How precious your thoughts are to me, O God!
    How impossible to number them!
18 I could no more count them
    than I could count the sand.
But suppose I could?
    You would still be with me!

19 O God, if only you would destroy those degenerates!
    If only these reprobates would leave me alone!
20 They talk blasphemously about you;
    your enemies treat you as if you were nothing.
21 Don't I hate those who hate you, Adonai?
    Don't I loathe those who defy you?
22 I hate them with a total hatred,
    and regard them as my own enemies!
23 Examine me, O God, and know my heart,
    test me and know my thoughts—
24 see if there is misdeed within me,
    and guide me in the way that is eternal.

140

For the conductor
A psalm of David

1 Deliver me, Adonai, from these debased people;
   preserve me from the violent,
2 who plan evil things in their hearts,
   and start new wars every day.
3 They make their tongue as forked as a snake's,
   their lips drip poison like a viper's.
4 Guard me, Adonai, from the hands of the bloodthirsty,
      —— *Selah* ——
   protect me from violent people,
   who deliberately try to trip me.
5 The arrogant lay their traps for me,
   and they've spread out the mesh of their net,
   they have set traps for me just off the path.
6 I say, "You are my God, Adonai!
   Hear my cries for mercy!"
7 Adonai, my Sovereign, my strong deliverer—
   you shield my head in the day of battle.
8 Adonai, don't fulfill the desires of the corrupt!
   Don't let their plans succeed,
   or their arrogance will be intolerable!
9 Let the trouble their lips have caused
   fall on their own heads!
10 Let burning coals fall upon them!
   Let them be tossed into the fire,
   or into a pit of quicksand, and never get out!
11 Don't let a slanderer get a foothold in the land;
   let evil hunt down the violent and oppress *them*!

12 I know that Our God makes sure the poor have justice,
   and defends those in need.
13 I know that those who love justice will praise your Name,
   and the upright will dwell in your presence.

A psalm of David

1   I call out to you, Adonai! Come quickly!
     Hear my voice when I call to you.
2   My prayers rise like incense before you,
     my hands rise to heaven like smoke from the evening sacrifice.
3   Adonai, set a guard at my mouth
     and keep watch at the gate of my lips—
4   don't let my heart be seduced by evil
     or by the lure of easy corruption in the company of evildoers!
     Don't let me sample their delights!
5   Let the upright strike me in reproof
     for my own good,
  but never let me allow the corrupt
     to anoint my head with oil!
     Daily I counter their malice with prayer.
6   When their leaders are flung off the edge of a cliff,
     they will learn how mild my words have been.
7   As a plow breaks up the earth,
     so our bones are scattered at the mouth of Sheol.
8   But to you, Adonai, I turn my eyes.
     I take shelter in you: don't abandon me to death!
9   Keep me from the traps that are set for me,
     from the bait laid for me by evildoers.
10 Let the violent fall into their own net,
     while I go on my way.

142

A teaching psalm
By David, when he was in the cave
A prayer

1 With all my voice, I cry to you, Adonai!
    With all my voice I cry for mercy!
2 I pour out my distress before you,
    I tell you all my troubles.
3 When my spirit faints within me,
    it is you who knows my way.
   On the path I walk
    they have hidden a snare to entrap me.
4 Look—there is no one beside me now,
    no one who stands with me.
   I have no place of refuge,
    no one to care about my life.
5 I cry to you, Adonai;
    I have said, "You are my refuge,
    all I have in the land of the living."
6 Listen, then, to my cry,
    for I am in the depths of despair.
   Rescue me from those who pursue me,
    for they are stronger than I.
7 Set me free from this prison
    so that your Name may be praised.
   The just will assemble around me
    because of your goodness to me.

A psalm of David

1 Hear my prayer, Adonai,
    listen to my plea!
  In your faithfulness and justice
    answer me, give me relief!
2 Don't put your faithful one on trial,
    for no one who lives is innocent in your sight.
3 My enemy is pursuing me,
    grinding my life into the dirt.
  My enemy locks me in the deepest dungeon—
    I'm like those who died long ago.
4 I am totally dispirited,
    my heart is in deep despair.
5 I remember days gone by;
    I think about all you have done,
    and recall the works of your hands.
6 I lift up my hands to you in prayer;
    like dry ground, my soul thirsts for you!
                —— *Selah* ——
7 Hurry up and answer me, Adonai!
    I'm ready to give up!
  Don't hide your face from me,
    or I'll be like those who go down to the Pit.
8 In the morning bring me word of your constant love,
    for I lift up my heart to you.
    Show me the path I should tread.
9 Rescue me from my enemies, Adonai,
    for you are my hiding place.
10 Teach me to do your will,
    for you are my God.
  Let your nurturing Spirit guide me
    on a safe and level path.
11 You keep me alive for the sake of your Name, Adonai;
    in your justice, rescue me from trouble.
12 In your love, you silence my enemies and destroy all my foes
    because I am loyal to you!

1 Blessed are you, Adonai, my rock,
    who trains my arms for battle,
    my hands for the struggle—
2 my refuge and my fortress, my stronghold,
    my deliverer, my shield, in whom I trust—
    who subdues entire nations under me.

3 Adonai, what are we,
    that you should care for us?
What is humankind,
    that you should think of us?
4 We are like a mist,
    our days like a passing shadow.

5 Part your skies, Adonai, and come down,
    touch the mountains, and they will smoke;
6 pitch your lightning bolts and put them to flight,
    shoot your arrows, and rout them!
7 Reach out your hand from on high—
    deliver me and rescue me from raging waters,
    from the hands of neighboring peoples
8 who make spurious promises and treaties
    while their right hands are raised in perjury.

9 O God, I'll sing a new song to you;
    with a ten-stringed lyre I'll sing your praise:
10 you are the source of the victory rulers claim,
    you delivered David, your faithful one, from the deadly sword.
11 Deliver me once again!
    Rescue me from the hands of neighboring peoples,
who make spurious promises and treaties
    while their right hands are raised in perjury.

12 Then our sons will be like plants,
    well-nurtured in their youth,
and our daughters like the strong pillars
    that stand at the corners of the palace.
13 Then our barns will be full,
    with every kind of provision;

our sheep will be in the thousands
   and the tens of thousands in our fields.
14 Our chieftains will be firmly established;
   there will be no exile, no cry of distress in the streets.
15 Happy are the people for whom this is true;
   happy are the people whose God is Adonai!

145*

A psalm of praise
By David

1 I will extol you, my God, my Ruler,
   and I will bless your Name forever and ever!
2 Every day will I bless you,
   and I will praise your Name forever and ever!
3 Great you are, Adonai, and greatly to be praised;
   your greatness is unfathomable.

4 Generation after generation praises your works
   and proclaims your mighty deeds,
5 they'll speak of the splendor of your glorious majesty,
   and I will meditate on your wondrous acts.
6 They'll discourse of the power of your awesome deeds,
   and I will declare your greatness.
7 They'll celebrate the fame of your abundant goodness,
   and I will joyfully sing of your justice.

8 Adonai, you are gracious and compassionate,
   slow to anger and rich in love.
9 Adonai, you are good to all
   and compassionate toward all your creatures.
10 All your creatures will praise you, Adonai,
   and your holy people will bless you.
11 They will tell of the glory of your reign
   and speak of your strength.

---

* This psalm is an acrostic poem: the first letter of each verse begins with a subsequent letter of the Hebrew alphabet.

12 You make known to all humankind your mighty acts
and the glorious splendor of your reign.
13 Your reign is a reign for all the ages,
and your dominion endures from generation to generation.

14 You lift up those who are falling
and raise up those who are oppressed.
15 The eyes of all look to you in hope,
and you give them their food in due season.
16 You open your hand
and satisfy the desire of every living thing.
17 Adonai, you are just in all your ways
and loving toward all that you have created.
18 You are near to all who call upon you,
all who call upon you in truth.
19 You fulfill the desires of those who revere you;
you hear their cry and save them.
20 You watch over all who love you, Adonai,
but you'll destroy all who are corrupt.

21 My mouth will speak your praise, Adonai,
and may all creation bless your holy Name
forever and ever!

146

1 Alleluia!
Praise Adonai, my soul!
2 I will praise you all my life;
I will sing praise to my God while I live!

3 Do not trust in rulers,
in mortals in whom there is no salvation.
4 When their spirits depart, they return to the earth,
and on that day their plans perish.
5 Happy are those whose help is the God of Israel,
whose hope is in Adonai, their God,
6 who made heaven and earth,

the sea and all that is in it!

Adonai, you keep faith forever:
7   you secure justice for the oppressed,
you give food to the hungry,
      you set captives free,
8   you give sight to the blind,
      you raise up those who were bowed down,
      you love those who do justice,
9   you protect strangers,
      you sustain orphans and the bereaved—
      but you thwart the way of the corrupt.

10 Our God will reign forever—*your* God, Zion!—
      through all generations. Alleluia!

147

1   Alleluia!
      How good it is to praise our God!
      How pleasant and how fitting to sing God's praise!
2   Our God rebuilds Jerusalem,
      and gathers Israel's exiles.
3   God heals the brokenhearted,
      and binds up their wounds.
4   God knows the number of the stars
      and calls each one by name.
5   Great is Adonai, and mighty in power;
      there is no limit to God's wisdom.
6   Our God lifts up the oppressed,
      and casts the corrupt to the ground.

7   Sing to our God with thanksgiving,
      sing praise with the harp to our God—
8   who covers the heavens with clouds,
      who provides rain for the earth,
      who makes grass sprout on the mountains
      and herbs for the service of the people,*
9   who gives food to the cattle,

and to the young ravens when they cry.
10 God does not thrill to the strength of the horse,
    or revel in the fleetness of humans.
11 Our God delights in those who worship with reverence
    and put their hope in divine love.

12 Jerusalem, give glory to Adonai!
    Zion, praise your God!
13 For God strengthens the bars of your gates,
    and blesses your children within you.
14 God has granted peace within your borders,
    and fills you with the finest wheat.

15 God sends forth a command to the earth—
    swiftly runs the word!
16 God spreads snow like wool
    and scatters frost like ashes.
17 God hurls hail like pebbles—
    who can stand before God's freezing winds?
18 Then God sends a word and melts them;
    God lets the breeze blow and the waters run again.

19 God's words have been revealed to the chosen people,
    God's decrees and laws to Israel.
20 God has not done this with any other nation;
    They do not know God's law.
    Alleluia!

---

* This verse is found in the Greek version of the text, but is missing from the standard Hebrew version.

1   Alleluia!
Praise Our God from the heavens,
    praise God in the heights!
2   Praise God, all you angels,
    praise God, all you hosts!
3   Praise God, sun and moon,
    praise God, all you shining stars!
4   Praise God, you highest heavens,
    and you waters above the heavens!
5   Let them praise the Name of Our God,
    by whose command they were created.
6   God established them forever and ever
    and gave a decree which won't pass away.
7   Praise Our God from the earth,
    you sea creatures and ocean depths,
8   lightning and hail, snow and mist,
    and storm winds that fulfill God's word,
9   mountains and all hills,
    fruit trees and all cedars,
10   wild animals and all cattle,
    small animals and flying birds,
11   rulers of the earth, leaders of all nations,
    all the judges in the world,
12   young men and young women,
    old people and children—
13   let them all praise the Name of Our God
    whose Name alone is exalted,
14   whose majesty transcends heaven and earth,
    and who has raised up a Horn for God's people
to the praise of the faithful,
    the children of Israel, the people dear to God!
Alleluia!

1 Alleluia!
   Sing to Our God a new song!
   Sing praise in the assembly of the faithful.
2 Let Israel be glad in its Maker,
   let the children of Zion rejoice in their God.
3 Let them praise God's Name
   with festive dance,
let them sing praise
   with timbrel and harp.
4 For Our God loves the people,
   and crowns the lowly with salvation.
5 Let the faithful exult in this honor,
   let them sing for joy in their beds—
6   let the high praise of God be in their throats.
And let two-edged swords be in their hands
7   to execute vengeance on the nations
   and punishment on the peoples,
8 to bind their rulers with chains
   and their nobles with fetters of iron,
9 to carry out their sentence to the letter.
   This is the glory of all the faithful.
Alleluia!

1   Alleluia!
    We praise you, Adonai, in your sanctuary,
        we praise you in your mighty skies!
2   We praise you for your powerful deeds,
        we praise you for your overwhelming glory!
3   We praise you with the blast of the trumpet,
        we praise you with lyre and harp!
4   We praise you with timbrel and dance,
        we praise you with strings and flute!
5   We praise you with clashing cymbals,
        we praise you with resounding cymbals!
6   Let everything that has breath
        praise Our God!
    Alleluia!

job

1:1–2:13

O nce upon a time, in the land of uz, there lived a person named Job.* Job was honest and upright, revered God and turned away from evil. 2 Three daughters and seven sons blessed the household.

3 Job's holdings included seven thousand sheep, three thousand camels, five hundred yoke of oxen, five hundred donkeys, and a huge number of household workers. Job was considered the greatest of all the people of the East.

4 It was customary for Job's children to take turns holding great feasts in their homes, his three daughters as well as his sons. 5 Each time a cycle of feasting ended, Job would call his children together to purify them, rising early in the morning to offer burnt offerings for each of them. "Maybe they sinned and profaned God in their hearts," he reasoned. Job did this on a regular basis.

CR CR CR

---

* The name means "hated" or "persecuted."

⁶ One day, the heavenly court gathered to present themselves before Our God, and Satan* was among them. ⁷ Our God said to Satan, "Where have you been?"

Satan replied, "Here and there. Roaming around the world."

⁸ Our God said to Satan, "Have you noticed Job, my faithful one? There's no one on earth like him! He's who is unlike anyone else in the world, honest and upright, reveres God and turns away from evil!"

⁹ "Yes," Satan answered, "but Job doesn't revere God for no reason! ¹⁰ Haven't you put a hedge around him, his household, and everything he has, on every side? You've blessed the work of his hands so much that Job's livestock cover the countryside. ¹¹ But reach out your hand and strike everything he has, and Job will curse you to your face!"

¹² So Our God said to Satan, "Very well. Everything Job has is in your hand. Just don't lay a hand on Job himself." Then Satan left Our God's presence.

သ   သ   သ

¹³ One day when Job's daughters and sons were eating and drinking wine at the eldest brother's home, ¹⁴ a messenger came to Job and said, "Your oxen were plowing and your donkeys were feeding at their side, ¹⁵ when the Sabeans attacked and plundered them. They put your farmworkers to the sword, and I alone escaped to tell you!"

¹⁶ While the farmworker was still speaking, another messenger arrived and said, "Lightning struck the sheep and the shepherds. They're all dead, and I alone escaped to tell you!"

¹⁷ While the shepherd was still speaking, another messenger arrived and said, "Three columns of Chaldeans raided the camels and made off with them. The camel drivers were put to the sword, and I alone escaped to tell you!"

¹⁸ While the camel driver was still speaking, another messenger arrived and said, "Your daughters and sons were feasting and drinking wine at their eldest brother's home. ¹⁹ Suddenly a great wind came across the desert and struck the four corners of the house, and it collapsed on the young people. They're all dead, and I alone escaped to tell you!"

²⁰ When Job heard this, he got up, tore his robe and shaved his head. Then he prostrated himself on the ground in worship, and said,

---

* A common noun (literally, "the satan") which means "the adversary" or, in a legal context, "prosecuting attorney."

"Naked I came from my mother's womb,
and naked will I return.
It was Our God who gave,
and Our God who took away.
Blessed be the Name of Our God!"

²² Through all this, Job never sinned or ascribed any blame to God.

ℭ   ℭ   ℭ

2:1 Once again the heavenly court gathered to present themselves before Our God, and Satan was among them. ² Our God said to Satan, "Where have you been?"

Satan replied, "Here and there. Roaming around the world."

³ Our God said to Satan, "Have you noticed Job, my faithful one? There's no one on earth like him! He's who is unlike anyone else in the world, honest and upright, reveres God and turns away from evil! His integrity is intact—even though you incited me to ruin him without cause!"

⁴ Satan replied, "Skin for skin! A person will give away every possession just to stay alive. ⁵ But reach out your hand and strike Job's flesh and bone, and he'll curse you to your face."

⁶ So Our God said to Satan, "Very well. Job is in your hand. Just spare his life."

⁷ Then Satan left Our God's presence...

ℭ   ℭ   ℭ

...and afflicted Job with painful boils from the soles of his feet to the crown of his head. ⁸ Job would take a piece of broken pottery to scrape his skin with as he sat among the ashes.

⁹ Job's wife said to him, "So you're still holding onto your integrity? Curse God, and die!"

¹⁰ He replied, "Only foolish people talk like that. If we accept happiness from God, we should also accept adversity."

Through all this, Job never sinned with his words.

¹¹ When three of Job's friends*—Eliphaz of Teman, Bildad of Shuah,

---

* Each of the friends' names is meaningful. Eliphaz means either "my God is pure as gold" or "God makes me as gold"; Bildad may mean "the wearing out of the loved one"; and Zophar means "departing," in the sense of being near to death. Each character's name forms the attitude taken in that character's speeches.

and Zophar of Naamath—heard of his misfortune, they set out from their homes and agreed to go together to console and comfort their friend.

¹² When they saw Job from a distance, they didn't recognize their disfigured friend. They wept loudly for him, tore their robes and threw dust over their heads toward the sky. ¹³ Then they sat on the ground with Job for seven days and seven nights. No one spoke a word to him out of respect for his appalling grief.

*A*t last Job opened his mouth, and cursed the day he was born. ² Job said:

3 Let the day of my birth cease to be,
        and the night when they said, "It's a boy!"
4 On that day, God said, "Let there be darkness!"
        Let God above un-create it,
        let no light shine on it!
5 Let darkness and gloom claim it,
        let clouds make a shroud for it.
    Let the day be turned into the dead of night,
6   and let the night be abducted in terrifying darkness.
    Let it be dropped from the days of the year,
        and stand unnumbered among the months.
7 Yes, let that night be rendered childless—
        let no joyful cry break the silence.
8 Let powerful sorcerers curse this night
        by raising the sea monster from its sleep.
9 Let its morning stars grow dim;
        let it wait for the dawn in vain
        and never see the first light of day—
10 for it would not shut the door of the womb on me
        or hide all this suffering from my eyes.

11 Why didn't I die at birth?
        Why didn't I expire as I came from the womb?
12 Why was there a lap to hold me?
        Why were there breasts to nurse me?
13 All I want now is to rest in peace,
        wrapped in eternal sleep,

14 with the rulers and counselors of the earth
     who built great halls for themselves,
15 or with wealthy magnates
     who filled their homes with silver and gold.
16 Or why wasn't I buried quickly like a stillborn,
     like infants who never see the light?
17 There the wicked make no trouble;
     there the weary are at rest.
18 There, prisoners are unburdened,
     and no longer hear their overseer's shouts.
19 There the small and the great are equal,
     and the oppressed are free from their oppressor.

20 Why give light to those in misery?
     Why give life to embittered souls
21 who long for a death that doesn't come,
     who search for it more than for hidden treasures?
22 They're filled with joy
     and are glad when they reach the grave.
23 Why give light to one who is lost,
     whom God has hemmed in on all sides?
24 Sighing is my only food,
     and groaning pours out of me like water.
25 For what I feared most has come upon me,
     and what I dreaded has happened to me.
26 I have no peace, I have no quiet, I have no rest—
     only turmoil.

℞   ℞   ℞

4:1 Then Eliphaz of Teman replied:

2 Would you be offended if someone ventured a word to you?
     On the other hand, who can be silent?
3 Look, you have taught many people over the years,
     that you have strengthened weak hands.
4 Your words upheld those who stumble,
     and you strengthened faltering knees.
5 But now misfortune comes to you, and you get impatient;
     now trouble touches you, and you are dismayed.
6 Doesn't your piety give you confidence?
     Isn't your personal integrity your greatest hope?

7 Name me an innocent person who ever perished!
    Since when are the upright destroyed?
8 In my experience, it is those who plow evil and plant corruption
    who harvest the same.
9 God breathes on them, and they're annihilated;
    a blast of God's anger, and they're gone.
10 The lion roars, the lioness growls—and they're silenced;
    the young lion bares its fangs—and they're broken.
11 The aged lion perishes for lack of prey,
    and the cubs of the lioness are scattered.

12 Now, a word was brought to me in secret,
    a whisper graced my ear.
13 At night, in disturbing dreams,
    when the deepest of sleep prevails,
14 fear and trembling enveloped me,
    and terror shook my bones.
15 A spirit, a breath, brushed by my face,
    and all my hair stood on end.
16 Something stood before me,
    but I couldn't discern a form;
it stood there, in silence—
    and then I heard it say,
17 "Can mortals be judged blameless before God,
    or found pure before their Maker?
18 If God cannot trust even the most trustworthy servants,
    if the angels are charged with error,
19 what about those who live in houses of clay,
    whose foundations are made of dust,
    who are as vulnerable as a moth?
20 Between dawn and dusk they are shattered;
    they perish, and no one even notices.
21 If you pull up their tent-cord, don't they collapse?
    They die—and without wisdom."

5:1 Call out all you want, but will anyone answer you?
    To which of the holy ones will you make your case?
2 It's anger that kills the foolish,
    and resentment that slays the simpleton.
3 I personally witnessed a foolish couple putting down roots,
    when suddenly their household fell apart.

4   Now their children are far from safety,
        and they'll be crushed in court with no one to defend them.
5   Everything they've worked will be hungrily devoured—
        their harvest, even their thorns!—
        and people will thirst for their wealth.
6   Grief doesn't sprout from the soil,
        and sorrow doesn't spring up from the ground—
7   but humankind is born to trouble
        as surely as sparks fly upward!

8   If I were you, I'd appeal to God;
        I'd state my case before the Most High.
9   The works of God are great, beyond reckoning—
        miracles without number.
10 It is God who gives rain to the earth,
        and sends water out into the fields.
11 God rescues the lowly
        and lifts up the downcast to joyful heights;
12 and God thwarts the plans of the cunning
        so that their hands achieve no success.
13 God traps these "wise people" in their own devices,
        and makes fools of their shrewd counselors.
14 They're trapped in the darkness, even in daylight,
        and at noon they grope as if it were midnight.
15 God sees that they have swords in their mouths,
        and protects the needy from their treacherous hands.
16 So the poor have hope,
        and injustice shuts its mouth.

17 Look—happy is the person whom God rebukes,
        so don't reject Shaddai's discipline!
18 For God wounds, and God bandages;
        the hands that hurt are the hands that heal.
19 Six times God will deliver you from trouble,
        and evil will avoid you on the seventh as well.
20 In time of famine, God will save your life;
        and in mortal conflict, from the power of the sword.
21 You will be shielded from the lash of the tongue,
        and view the approaching plunderer fearlessly.
22 You will laugh at destruction and famine,
        and have no dread of the beasts of the wild.

²³ For you will have a covenant with the stones of the field,
   and the animals of the wilderness will be at peace with you.
²⁴ You will know that your dwelling place is secure,
   and when you inspect your flocks, you won't find any missing.
²⁵ You will witness the growth of your extended family,
   and your offspring will be as the grass in the meadows.
²⁶ You will approach the grave at a ripe old age,
   like a harvest gathered at just the right time.

²⁷ Look closely—we have examined all this, and it is true.
   Listen carefully—and know it for yourself.

C℞   C℞   C℞

6¹ Then Job replied:

² Oh, if only my grief could be measured,
   and all my calamity weighed!
³ They'd be heavier than all the grains of sand in all the seas—
   this is why my words seem rash.
⁴ For the lance of Shaddai impales me,
   and my spirit drinks its poison;
   the terrors of God surround me.
⁵ Tell me, does the wild ass bray when it has grass,
   or do the cattle moo over their fodder?
⁶ Can tasteless food be eaten without salt?
   Is there any flavor in slime of an egg white?
⁷ Yet I can't even touch even good food any more—
   food makes me ill just to look at it.

⁸ Oh that my prayers may be answered,
   and that God would grant me what I long for—
⁹ or that God would be willing to simply crush me,
   to reach out and cut me off entirely!
¹⁰ For then I'd have the consolation—
   the joy, even amid unspeakable pain—
   that I never denied the words of the Holy One.
¹¹ What strength is waiting for me,
   that I should have hope?
What prospects do I have,
   that I should tell myself to be patient?

12 Do I have the strength of a stone?
   Is my flesh tough as bronze?
13 No! I am now helpless,
   and deliverance has been driven from me!

14 When you're desperate, you need the devotion of your friends,
   lest you forsake your reverence for God.
15 Yet my closest friends are as fickle as intermittent streams,
   like wadis in the desert—
16 in winter they are dark with ice
   and covered in snow,
17 but after the thaw they vanish,
   and in the heat they're nothing but dry beds.
18 Caravans leave their routes to search for them,
   only to perish in the wilderness.
19 The caravans of Tema remember them
   and the convoys of Sheba depend on them—
20 but they trust in vain:
   they arrive there only to be disappointed.
21 And this is how it is with you and me,
   now that my condition fills you with fear.
22 Have I ever said, "Give me some money,"
   or, "I need you to bribe someone for me,"
23 or, "Save me from my creditors,"
   or, "Ransom me from my oppressors"?

24 Straighten me out, and I'll be quiet—
   make me understand what I've done wrong.
25 It isn't that the truth is too hard for me to hear—
   it's that you simply haven't proven your case.
26 Why do you consider your words as fact,
   and view the words of a desperate person
   as nothing but hot air?
27 Soon you'll be throwing dice with orphans as the prize,
   or selling off your friends!
28 Come now, look me in the eye—
   would I lie to your face?
29 Now back off, and be just with me!
   Back off—my integrity is intact.
30 Do you hear lies from my lips?
   Do you think my mouth doesn't know what malice tastes like?

7:1 Isn't a person's life in this world nothing but drudgery?
　　Aren't our days here like those of a hired hand?
2 Like a laborer vainly longing for shade
　　or a hired hand waiting for meager wages,
3 so I am assigned months of futility;
　　my only possessions are nights of misery.
4 When I go to bed, I wonder, "How long before I get up?"
　　—but the night drags on, as I toss and turn.
5 My skin is clothed with scabs and worms;
　　my flesh oozes pus from its cracks.
6 My days pass as swiftly as a weaver's shuttle,
　　and they come to an end without hope.

7 O God, remember that my life is just a breath,
　　and I will never experience joy again.
8 The eye that now sees me will look upon me no longer;
　　your eyes will search for me but I won't be there.
9 As the clouds fade and dissolve,
　　those who go down to Sheol never return.
10 They never come home again,
　　and those still there soon forget them.
11 That is why I refuse to stay silent—
　　my anguished spirit impels me to speak;
　　I will complain in the bitterness of my soul.

12 Am I the sea, or a sea monster,
　　that you have to put me under guard?
13 When I say, "My bed will comfort me,
　　my sofa will ease my complaint,"
14 you scare me with dreams;
　　you terrify me with visions,
15 so much so that I would rather be strangled to death,
　　than submit to such suffering!
16 I hate my life, and I don't want to live forever.
　　Leave me alone, for my days are meaningless!
17 What am I, that you make so much of me—
　　that you set your heart on me,
18 visiting me every morning
　　and testing me every moment?
19 How long will you stare at me,
　　and not let me alone long enough to swallow my spit?

²⁰ Perhaps I am a sinner—but what have I done to you,
  you Watcher of humankind?
Why have you made me your target?
  Why am I a burden to you?
²¹ Can't you pardon me of my sin;
  can't you overlook my transgression?
Shortly I will lie down in the dust;
  you'll search for me, but I will be no more!

CR   CR   CR

8:1 Then Bildad of Shuah replied:

² How long will you go on speaking like this?
  How long will you continue your long-winded rantings?
³ Does God pervert justice?
  Does Shaddai pervert the truth?
⁴ If your children sinned against God,
  they have paid for their wrongdoing.
⁵ And if they didn't sin, then if you look to God
  and plead with Shaddai—
⁶ if you are pure and just—
surely the Just Judge will immediately respond
  and restore what is rightfully yours.
⁷ Your former life will seem humble
  compared with your future prosperity!

⁸ Ask the generations long passed,
  and find out what their ancestors learned,
⁹ for we were only born yesterday, and we know nothing—
  our days on earth are only a shadow;
¹⁰ but the older ones will teach you, tell you,
  and their words will come from the heart.
¹¹ Can the papyrus grow in anything but marshland?
  Can reed grass survive without water?
¹² Even though green and at their peak,
  once they are cut they wither the fastest of all.
¹³ Such is the destiny of all who forget God,
  and the hope of the godless vanishes.
¹⁴ What they trust in is fragile;
  their faith is as flimsy as a spider's web.

15 They lean against their homes and they begin to sag;
    they grab at them but their houses do not stand.
16 They are lush plantings in the sunlight,
    their shoots spreading throughout the garden,
17 but their roots intertwine a pile of rocks
    they grasp for life among the stones.
18 Pluck them up, and the ground will disown them;
    it will say, "I never knew you."
19 Its only joy is in knowing
    that from its compost, new plants will grow.

20 Let it be known that God neither rejects the innocent
    nor lends a hand to the wicked!
21 Once again God will fill your mouth with laughter,
    and your lips with rejoicing.
22 Those who hate you will be clothed with shame,
    and the dwelling of the corrupt will cease to be.

ଔ   ଔ   ଔ

9:1 Then Job said:

2 I do know this to be true.
    But how can we be justified before God?
3 If I were to argue with God,
    I couldn't give a right answer once in a thousand times.
4 God is wise of heart and supremely powerful;
    who has challenged God and survived?
5 God moves mountains before they know what is happening,
    and throws them down when angry;
6 the Almighty shakes the earth and moves it from place to place,
    making its support columns tremble.
7 God commands, and the sun doesn't rise
    and the stars don't shine their light.
8 God alone stretches out the heavens,
    and treads on the waves of the seas.
9 God made the Bear and Orion,
    the Pleiades and the constellations of the south.
10 God's deeds are beyond understanding;
    God's wonders are numberless.
11 Were the Most High to approach me,
    I would not see anything;

were the Most High to pass me by,
    I would be unaware of any movement.
12 Were God to grab me by force, who could refuse?
    Who could ask, "What are you doing?"

13 God never relents when angry;
    the cohorts of Chaos remain vanquished.
14 How much less dare I reply,
    or choose to reason with God?
15 Even if I were innocent, I still could not answer;
    I could only beg the Judge for mercy.
16 If I called out and God answered,
    I still wouldn't believe God had heard me.
17 God could crush me with a hurricane,
    and, without reason, wound me over and over;
18 God could refuse to let me even catch my breath,
    and overwhelm me with misery.
19 If it were a matter of strength, I know that God is Strength;
    if a matter of justice, who will issue the summons?
20 If I were to justify myself, my own mouth would indict me;
    if I were innocent, it would declare me guilty.

21 But I *am* innocent,
    though I really don't care any more—
    so much do I loathe my life—
22 because it's the same either way!
    That's why I say,
    "God destroys the innocent and the guilty alike."
23 When a sudden disaster strikes,
    God laughs at the plight of the victims.
24 When a region is overrun by the wicked,
    God blindfolds the judges—
    and if it's not God doing so, then who?

25 My days run swifter than an athlete;
    they fly away and see nothing good.
26 They flash by like papyrus boats,
    like eagles diving on their prey.
27 Were I to say, "I'll drop my complaint,
    I'll change my sad expression and put a smile on my face,"
28 I would fear even greater suffering,
    because I know that you would not hold me innocent.

29 And since I'm already being judged guilty,
    then it doesn't matter *what* I do or say.
30 If I were to wash myself with soap
    and scrub my hands with lye,
31 you would still plunge me into a slime pit
    so that my own clothes would abhor me!
32 For you're not a human like me, that I could answer you;
    we can't confront one another in court,
33 nor is there a negotiator between us,
    to lay hands on us both.
34 There is no one to keep your rod from me,
    or remove your terrors which I fear so.

35 Nevertheless, I will speak out fearlessly!
    For I am not as others see me.
10:1 I loathe my very life—
    so I will give free rein to my complaints;
    I will speak from a bitter spirit.
2 I will say to God, "Don't condemn me.
    Just tell me why this onslaught against me.
3 Does it please you to assault me,
    to cheapen the good works of your hands,
    to encourage the wiles of the wicked?
4 Do you have eyes of flesh?
    Do you see as a mortal does?
5 Are your days like my days,
    are your years like mine,
6 that you have to search out my guilt,
    that you crave to know my sin?

7 "You know very well that I am not guilty,
    that there is no one to retrieve me from your grip.
8 Your hands formed me and fashioned me,
    yet you are intent on destroying your own.
9 Do you recall that you created me out of clay?
    Will you now return me to dust?
10 Haven't you already poured me out like milk,
    and curdled me like cheese?
11 You clothed me with skin and flesh;
    you pieced me together with bone and muscle.
12 Then you breathed life and love into me,
    and shaped my spirit with great care.

13 But now all this is hidden in your heart.
   It's all happening on purpose, isn't it?

14 "For if I should sin, you would be watching me,
   and you wouldn't absolve me of my wrongdoing.
15 If I am guilty,
      woe is me!
   But even when I am innocent,
      I'm unable to raise my head,
      so full of confusion and pain am I.
16 And if I get my spirits up, you stalk me like a lion,
   and add one more win to your scorecard.
17 You keep bringing new witnesses against me,
      and do so with increasing fury,
      wave upon wave, unrelenting.

18 "Why did you bring me out from the womb?
      I wish I had died unseen by human eyes,
19 never to become a person,
      to be carried from womb to grave.
20 Aren't my few days almost over?
      Let me alone! Allow me some small peace of mind,
21 before I move on to the place of no return,
      to the land of gloom and deep shadow,
22 the land of darkest night,
      of deep shadow and utter chaos,
      where darkness is the only light."

ᘓ   ᘓ   ᘓ

11:1 Then Zophar of Naamath spoke:

2 Should prattle go unanswered?
      Does verbosity prove a person right?
3 Should these lies of yours make people hold their peace?
      When you scoff, shouldn't someone shame you?
4 You say, "My arguments are flawless,
      and I am innocent in God's eyes."
5 If only God were to speak,
      to make a rebuttal and give you an answer!
6 If only the Most High were to give you the secrets of wisdom—
      for there are two sides to every story—

rest assured that God exacts of you
>   less than your guilt deserves!

7   Can you uncover the mystery of the divine?
>   Can you discover the limits of Shaddai?
8   They are as high as heaven—what can you do?
>   They are deeper than Sheol—what can you know?
9   Their measure is longer than the world,
>   and wider than the sea.
10 If God comes along and imprisons someone,
>   or summons someone to court, who can question it?

11 For won't the Almighty take note of deceitful people,
>   recognize iniquity, and take note of it?
12 Why, a fool can no more become wise,
>   than a wild donkey's foal can grow up into a human!
13 What you *can* do is to set your heart on the right path,
>   and reach out your arms to Almighty God,
14 reject the sin that rules your actions,
>   and remove any injustice in your household.

15 Then you'll be able to show your face without shame;
>   you will be able to stand tall fearlessly.
16 Your suffering will be a thing of the past;
>   you'll view it as water under the bridge.
17 And your life will be brighter than the noonday sun;
>   its gloom will turn into a bright dawn.
18 You'll possess renewed security, for now hope will reign;
>   you'll be able to take your rest in safety—
19 you'll lie down, and no one will make you afraid,
>   and you'll be sought out by others who seek your favor.

20 But the eyes of evildoers will grow dim;
>   freedom will elude them,
>   and their hope will be a dying gasp.

*t*hen Job replied:

2 Oh, I see that you people are the intelligent ones,
      that wisdom will die when you die!
3 Come on—I have knowledge as well as you,
      and I'm certainly not your inferior.
      Who doesn't know these things?
4 I have become a laughingstock to my friends—
      "He called to God, and did God ever answer him!"—
      a just and innocent laughingstock.
5 The prosperous, enjoying their ease,
      think that misfortune is a disgrace earned
      and prepared for those whose feet slip.
6 Yet the households of thieves are filled with abundance,
      and those who provoke God are secure
      while making gods of their violent ways.

7 But turn to the animals, and let them teach you;
      the birds of the air will tell you the truth.
8 Listen to the plants of the earth, and learn from them;
      let the fish of the sea become your teachers.
9 Who among all these does not know
      that the hand of Our God has done this?
10 In God's hand is the soul of every living thing;
      in God's hand is the breath of all humankind.

11 Doesn't the ear test the words it hears,
      just as the mouth tastes its food?
12 Wisdom comes with aging,
      and understanding with length of days.
13 In God are wisdom, strength,
      counsel and understanding.

14 When God tears down, it cannot be rebuilt;
      when God imprisons, it is forever.
15 The Most High restrains the waters, and a drought appears;
      when the waters are released, they overrun the earth.
16 With God are strength and wisdom;
      deceived and deceiver alike belong to God.

¹⁷ The Almighty strips mighty lawyers naked,
and makes fools out of judges.
¹⁸ God removes the shackles that rulers impose,
and trades their fine clothing for a loincloth.
¹⁹ The Most High humiliates the priests,
and overthrows the establishment.
²⁰ The Almighty silences trusted counselors,
and steals discernment from the aged.
²¹ God pours contempt on the exalted
and relieves the mighty of their strength.
²² The Most High uncovers the depth of the darkness,
and brings deep darkness to the light.
²³ The Almighty makes the nations mighty, and diminishes them,
and makes a people grow, only to bring them down.
²⁴ God takes understanding from the earth's great leaders,
and makes them wander the trackless waste,
²⁵ to grope in the darkest dark,
and stagger like those who are drunk.

13:1 Look, I have seen all these things;
my ear has heard it and I understand it thoroughly.
² I know what you know—
I am not your inferior!

³ It is to Shaddai alone that I would speak—
I intend to make my case before God.
⁴ You, however, aren't healers—you're quacks!
And you smear people with lies—you're spin-doctors!
⁵ If only you would shut up—
which, in your case, would be wisdom!
⁶ Listen closely to what I have to say;
pay special attention to my reasoning.

⁷ Will you tell lies in God's defense,
and speak words that are false?
⁸ Will you be biased in God's favor;
and plead a case for the Most High?
⁹ Will your reputations be acceptable in divine circles,
or will you dupe the Almighty
the way people dupe one another?
¹⁰ Won't God reprimand you
if you secretly show partiality—even in God's favor?

11 Surely God's splendor will sober you,
   and the divine dread overwhelm you.
12 Your statements are proverbs made of ashes;
   your defenses, defenses of clay.

13 Silence! Leave me alone to state my case,
   and bear the consequences.
14 I will put myself in jeopardy
   and take my life in my hands.
15 Even if the Almighty kills me,
   I will still hope in God.
   But I will also argue my case
   to God without flinching.
16 This is where I find salvation,
   for a godless person dare not do it this way!
17 Listen closely to my words;
   let your ears resonate with my comments.
18 At last my case is ready—
   I know that I'll be vindicated!
19 Who can challenge me in this?
   If any can, I'll accept death in silence.
20 O God, I only ask two things,
   then I will not hide from you:
21 remove your heavy hand from me;
   and don't let my fear of you terrorize me.
22 Then call, and I will answer you—
   or let me state my case first, then reply to me.

23 Tell me my sins and my crimes!
   What laws have I broken? Who have I offended?
24 Why do you hide your face from me,
   and treat me as your enemy?
25 Why are you bullying a leaf blown by the wind?
   Why are you pursuing some abandoned wheat chaff?
26 You're writing bitter accusations against me,
   and making me suffer for the faults of my youth.
27 You incarcerate me, and put me under continuous watch;
   you track my every move;
28 I waste away like rotting wood,
   like a moth-eaten dress.

14:1 One who is born of human parents
has a short life full of troubles.
2 It blossoms like a flower and quickly withers;
it flees like a shadow, and disappears.
3 Why do you now bring your gaze upon it,
and bring it into judgment with yourself?
4 Who can make the unclean clean?
No one!
5 You created humankind with numbered days;
our months are predetermined
because you set the bounds on our time.

6 Take your eyes off me, give me some space,
so that, like the day worker, we can complete our task.
7 Trees always have hope; once felled,
there is the chance of a new sprout with tender shoots.
8 Even with the root rotting underground
and a withered stump half alive,
9 yet it will bud at the scent of water,
and put out branches like a new plant.
10 But people die and decompose;
once dead, where are they?
11 As water evaporates from the sea,
and rivers go dry during drought,
12 so humans lie down and never rise again.
Until the heavens are no more,
they won't awake or be roused from their sleep.
13 If only you would hide me among the dead,
and conceal me until your rage cools down—
then set a time to remember me again!
14 When people die, will they ever live again?
All the days of my struggle I wait for my release.
15 Then you will call, and I will answer,
for you will want to see the work of your hands.

16 But now you number my steps,
and vigilantly observe my sins.
17 You gather all my transgressions together in a bag,
and glue my sins together to make a mound.
18 Just as the mountains eventually dissolve into dust,
and rocks move from one place to another,

¹⁹ and the waters erode the stones,
 and the rainstorm wipes out the land,
 so you wear down a person's hope!
²⁰ You are always against us, and so we pass on;
 you disfigure us, and then dismiss us.
²¹ If our children achieve honors, we don't know of it;
 if they're brought low by humiliation, we never see it.
²² We feel nothing but the pain of own bodies,
 and our souls mourn inside us.

    ೞ   ೞ   ೞ

15:1 Then Eliphaz of Teman spoke:

² Should wise people speak with transparent knowledge,
 and fill themselves with wind?
³ Should they reason with specious talk,
 or with terms that don't make sense?
⁴ You're throwing away all reverence,
 and disparaging the worship of God!
⁵ For your mouth is captured by your infamy,
 and you take on the language of the duplicitous.
⁶ It is your own mouth, not I, that condemns you;
 and your own lips testify against you.

⁷ Are you the first person ever born?
 Or were you created before the hills?
⁸ Do you participate in God's councils?
 Have you cornered the market on wisdom?
⁹ What do you know that we don't know?
 What do you understand that we don't understand?
¹⁰ We have venerable gray-haired people on our side,
 older than even your parents.
¹¹ Are the consolations of God too insignificant for you?
 Have our own words been too gentle?
¹² Why does your heart carry you away?
 Why do your eyes flash so
¹³ when you turn your spirit against God
 and spout such terrible words from your mouth?

14 How can human beings ever be pure?
   Those born of human parents,
   can they ever be called righteous?
15 If God puts no confidence in the angels
   and if the heavens are not clean in God's sight,
16 then how much less this corrupt abomination called humanity,
   that guzzles iniquity like water?

17 Now I will talk—it's your turn to listen.
   And what I have seen, that's what I'll declare—
18 what the sages have taught
   by passing on the traditions of their ancestors,
19 to whom alone the land was given,
   with no strangers involved.

20 The wicked live on in endless pain;
   their allotted time is compromised by anguish.
21 A dreadful sound is in their ears;
   denied prosperity, they will meet their end.
22 They dread the darkness,
   for fear of meeting a violent end.
23 They roam about seeking sustenance by begging,
   just out of reach of ruin.
24 Distress and anguish terrify them and finally subdue them,
   like a ruler prepared for a victorious encounter,
25 all because they raised a fist at God,
   and signaled their defiance of Shaddai,
26 rushing headlong, like a ram,
   and brandishing a massive shield.

27 They've covered their faces in luxury,
   their thighs are heavy with indolence;
28 they lived in vanquished cities,
   in houses no one would inhabit,
   dwellings already crumbling.
29 They will not become rich, nor will their wealth endure;
   even their crops will wither away.
30 They will not escape the darkness;
   the fires will consume what little they had,
   and they will disappear in a whisper.

31 So don't be deceived and put your trust in emptiness,
  or emptiness will be your reward.
32 Your branch will suffer a withering end,
  and your shoot will show no green.
33 You will shed your grapes before they ripen,
  and shed your bloom like the olive tree.
34 For the progeny of the godless is sterile,
  and the flame will consume the dwelling of the corrupt.
35 When you breed evil you bear sin,
  and give birth to a unhappy end.

ભ   ભ   ભ

16:1 Then Job replied:

2 I've heard all this many times!
  What sorry comforters you all are!
3 Will your flimsy statements never end?
  What is your motivation to have the last word?
4 Then again, I could speak as you do,
  if you sat where I sit.
I too could sermonize against you,
  and shake my head at all of you.
5 Or I could encourage you with my speech,
  and ease your grief with consoling words.

6 Even while I speak my grief carries on.
  When I am silent, does it leave me?
7 Now, God, you have worn me out
  and devastated my entire household.
8 My drawn features show your displeasure;
  they stand as a witness against me.
Even my starved body stands against me;
  its testimony I see daily.

9 Your anger has torn me in this grudge match;
  you gnash your teeth at me
  and glare at me like an angry opponent.
10 They stand with gaping jaws
  and slap me on the cheek in their contempt;
  they are united against me.

11 You abandon me to the godless,
　　and put me into the hands of the wicked.
12 Once I was at peace,
　　but you crushed me;
　you took me by the neck
　　only to dash me against a rock.
　I have become your target;
13　　your archers surround me.
　You mercilessly pierce me on all sides,
　　and my gall soils the ground.
14 You break me down like soldiers breaching a wall;
　　you run to make war upon me.
15 I cover myself with sackcloth,
　　and lie face down in the dirt.
16 My dirty face is streaked with tears,
　　and the shadow of death is in my eyes.
17 And all of this even though my hands harbor no violence
　　and my prayer is pure!

18 O earth, don't cover my blood,
　　and let my wail have no rest.
19 Yes, even now, my Witness is in heaven;
　　my Defender is on high.
20 My Intercessor is my friend,
　　though I shed a flood of tears to God.
21 May this be my plea before God
　　the way one friend makes a case for another.
22 For my years are numbered,
　　and I will soon make the trip of no return.
17:1 My spirit is broken;
　　the cemetery plot beckons me.
2 I am subjected to mockery;
　　it is everywhere I turn.

3 O God, give me your own guarantee;
　　no one else is willing to risk it.
4 For you've hidden understanding from their minds—
　　that's why they don't grasp what I'm saying.
5 They are like those who share the spoils with their friends,
　　while their children see no future.
6 I am now a byword to the people;
　　they use me for a spittoon.

7 My tears make my eyes grow dim;
   I am just a shadow of myself.
8 The upright are appalled at what they see,
   and the innocent are stirred to confront the unbeliever.
9 Even so, the righteous become set in their lifestyles,
   and grow strong in the conviction of their ways.

10 As for all of you, try me again—
   I don't see a wise person among you!
11 My time is long past, my hopes dissipated;
   the desire in my heart is dead.
12 You're pretending that night is day—
   you say, "Light is near" when there's nothing but darkness.
13 If all I can expect is Sheol as my domicile,
   if I spread my sheet in darkness,
14 if I say to the grave, "You are my mother and father,"
   and to the maggots, "You are my sister and brother,"
15 then where is hope?
   Can anyone see happiness for me?
16 Who will accompany me to Sheol?
   Who will go down into the dust with me?

ભ   ભ   ભ

18·1 Then Bildad of Shuah spoke:

2 When will you stop rattling on?
   Show some understanding, and then we can dialogue.
3 Why are you comparing to beasts,
   on a par with dumb animals?
4 Go ahead and tear yourself apart in your rage;
   but it won't turn the earth into a dust bowl,
   or make the hills move by themselves.

5 Yes, the light of the wicked will go out;
   no flame will glow in their hearth.
6 The light in their dwellings is dim,
   and the main lamp won't stay lit.
7 Their hurried steps are slowed,
   and their sly schemes backfire.

8   They rush headlong into the net;
        they stumble into the pit.
9   A snare grabs them by the heel;
        a trapdoor drops, and they are captured.
10 A noose brings them to a dead halt;
        thieves ambush them along the route.
11 Ever-present terror is at their heels;
        they never stay long in one place.
12 Their strength suffers for lack of nourishment,
        and disaster stalks their every step.
13 Their skin is diseased;
        death's firstborn lurks nearby.
14 They are kidnapped from their dwelling,
        and brought before the ruler of terrors.
15 Fire guts their tents,
        and brimstone is scattered over their dwellings.

16 Their roots below drown in the muck;
        their branches above wither in the heat.
17 Their memory perishes from the earth,
        and no one can recall their names in the marketplace.
18 They will be driven from light into darkness,
        driven into exile from the land.
19 They are without offspring among their peoples,
        making their absence absolute.
20 Those in the east are appalled at their fate,
        and in the west the news is met with terror.
21 Thus is the fortune of the household of the profane,
        the dwelling of all those who don't know God.

ଔ   ଔ   ଔ

19:1 Then Job replied:

2   Won't you ever back off with your torment,
        belittling me with your words?
3   This is the tenth time you've taken me to task,
        that you have insulted me.
4   Even if what you say is true,
        even if I am really wrong about myself,

5   it is still a fact that you deem yourselves better than I,
        my low state arguing against me.

6   I insist that God has wronged me,
        and has closed the net around me.
7   But when I shout, "Injustice!" I get no answer;
        if I cry for help I get none.
8   The Most High has cornered me in,
        clouded my future with darkness.
9   God has stripped me of my honor,
        and taken my crown from my head.
10 God breaks me down at every turn—and I am defeated;
        my hope is as worthless as an uprooted tree.
11 God's wrath is kindled against me,
        and I am treated as if I were a foe.
12 God's troops come together and move against me,
        building siegeworks all around.

13 All this has alienated my sisters and my brothers;
        my friends avoid me like the plague.
14 My relatives and acquaintances neglect me,
        and my guests have given up on me.
15 The household staff consider me a stranger—
        or should I say an "alien."
16 My personal attendant refuses to respond when I call,
        and I am reduced to begging.
17 Even my breath is unbearable to my spouse,
        loathsome to the members of my family.
18 Even children find me repulsive,
        to the point of mocking me.
19 My intimate friends recoil from me;
        those whom I especially loved are against me.
20 I am down to skin and bones—
        I am alive now only by the skin of my teeth.

21 Have pity on me, my friends, have pity on me!
        God's fist has floored me!
22 How dare you hound me as if you were God!
        Can't you be satisfied with just my flesh?
23 If only all this were on paper!
        What a book it would make!

²⁴ If only my words were engraved
     forever in granite!

²⁵ For I know that my Redeemer lives—
     my Vindicator, who at the end will stand on the earth;
²⁶ and after I awake, though this body has been destroyed,
     without my flesh I will see God.
²⁷ I will see God with my own eyes—God, and no other!
     How my heart yearns within me!

²⁸ And yet you still ask, "How will we persecute Job,
     now that we know that he's the root of the problem?"
²⁹ You yourselves should fear the sword—
     your anger will bring the sword's punishment.
     Then you'll know that there truly is a judgment!

ೞ   ೞ   ೞ

20¹ Then Zophar of Naamath spoke:

² I jump at the chance to reply:
     for what I hear disturbs me.
³ The reprimand that I hear insults me;
     my spirit understands that a reply is needed.

⁴ Don't you know that from long ago,
     as long as humans have inhabited the earth,
⁵ wicked triumph is short-lived,
     and godless joy is only momentary?
⁶ Though the pride of the godless is as high as the sky,
     with their heads in the clouds,
⁷ they will perish just as does their excrement;
     and those known to them will ask, "Where are they?"
⁸ They will evaporate forever like a dream;
     they will fade like a dream, gone forever;
     they will dissipate like a vision at night.
⁹ The eyes that beheld them will behold them no more;
     neither will their household ever see them again.
¹⁰ Their families will go begging for charity,
     and their children will be stuck with their debts.
¹¹ Bones that were full of youthful vigor
     they rest supine in the dust.

12 Because wickedness was so sweet in their mouth,
   they still hid it under their tongue;
13 loath to give it up,
   they continued to keep it in their mouth—
14 turning the food in their stomach
   into the venom of cobras.
15 They swallowed riches,
   but now they'll regurgitate them—
   God will empty their bellies.
16 They swallowed the poison of asps,
   and now the fang of the viper destroys them.
17 They will no longer look at their rivers of oil,
   streams of honey and butter.
18 They will give back the gain of their labors,
   no longer able to stomach it;
   they won't even be able to enjoy
   the wealth from all of their trading.

19 For they crushed the poor and oppressed;
   they stole a heritage they did not set up.
20 Because they had dealt actively in greed,
   its gain is their loss.
21 The plates were empty once they left the table;
   now there is nothing left.
22 When their wealth was at its highest,
   their ethic was at its lowest;
   the hand of everyone who suffers
   will come against them.
23 When they fill their belly,
   God will let loose a divine rage upon them,
   attacking them at dinner time.

24 If they escape the spear of iron,
   the bronze bow will do them in;
25 though the arrow is pulled from their body,
   its point will have pierced their very soul.
   Terrors will come upon them;
26   utter darkness waits for their treasures.
   A white hot flame will devour them
   and consume what is left in their tent.
27 The heavens will reveal their guilt,
   and the earth will rise up against them.

²⁸ Their household will be swept away
    in the day of God's wrath.
²⁹ This is God's allotment to the wicked;
    it is the heritage God has decreed for them.

21:1–31:41

Then Job replied:

² Listen, please listen to me,
    and let what I say be your consolation.
³ Just bear with me; hear me out,
    and then you can mock me, if you so desire.

⁴ Who do you think I'm complaining about? Other human beings?
    No—and why shouldn't I be impatient?
⁵ If you look at me, you'll be astonished
    and cover your mouth with your hands.
⁶ Even when *I* reflect on it, I'm horror-struck,
    and my flesh begins to crawl.

⁷ Why are the wicked kept alive,
    to grow old, and become mighty in power?
⁸ They witness their progeny's establishment;
    their offspring stand before them.
⁹ Their households are peaceful and safe from fear;
    the punishment of God doesn't frighten them.
¹⁰ Their bulls sire at breeding time;
    their cows calve without miscarriage.
¹¹ They themselves bring forth a flock of little ones,
    and their children dance.
¹² They sing to the tambourine and the lyre,
    and rejoice to the sound of the flute.
¹³ Their days are spent being wealthy,
    and they even go down to Sheol peacefully.
¹⁴ Yet these people say to God,
    "Go away! We aren't interested in your ways!
¹⁵ Who is this Shaddai who expects our obeisance?
    How does it benefit us if we pray to the Almighty?"

16 Let's face it, isn't their good fortune in their own hands,
   and doesn't the counsel of the wicked exclude God?
17 So I ask you—
   how often is the candle of the wicked extinguished?
   How often does disaster overcome them?
   How often does God's wrath overwhelm them?
18 Do they become straw in the wind,
   like chaff which the storm blows around?
19 You say that God stores their iniquity for the next generation;
   I say, "Let God repay them now,
   so they can know they're being punished!
20 Let them witness their own destruction;
   let them drink deep Shaddai's wrath!"
21 For what interest can they have in their households,
   once their time is up?

22 Since God judges the high-and-mighty,
   who'll presume to be God's teacher?
23 One person dies full of life,
   completely at ease and secure,
24 with a well-nourished body
   and bones rich with marrow.
25 And another person dies full of bitterness,
   who never ate from a full plate.
26 Both are buried in the same dirt,
   and the worms don't care which is which.

27 Now, I know what you are thinking,
   and how you feel about me.
28 For you ask, "Show us the house of the tycoon!"
   or, "Where is the household of the wicked person?"
29 Haven't you ever chatted with people
   who have traveled far and wide?
   Don't you accept their testimony?
30 They'd tell you that the wicked
   are spared catastrophe when it comes,
   and are saved on the day of wrath.
31 Who accuses them to their face for their wrongdoing?
   Who repays them for their evil deeds?
32 Even in the grave
   someone is watching over their tomb!

³³ The clods of the valley gently cover them.
All of humanity will follow them,
and countless throngs have preceded them.

³⁴ So tell me how you can console me with empty nothings!
Your arguments are still nothing but a pack of lies!

ભ   ભ   ભ

22:1 Then Eliphaz of Teman spoke:

² Can we humans benefit God in any way?
Can even a wise person be of any use?
³ Do you think Shaddai gets any pleasure if you are upright?
If your ways *were* blameless, what profit does God receive?

⁴ Do you think it's because of your reverence for God
that you're being punished?
⁵ Come now, isn't it really because of
the immensity of your wickedness,
and your endless iniquities?
⁶ You've demanded collateral from your closest relatives
for no reason,
and you've stripped poor people naked.
⁷ You've withheld water from the thirsty,
and food from the hungry.
⁸ And even though you were a powerful landowner,
frequently honored, and wealthy because of your holdings,
⁹ you have evicted widows, leaving them empty-handed,
and crushed the strength of orphans.
¹⁰ Because of all this you are now surrounded by snares;
small wonder that you wander around terrified,
¹¹ or why it is so dark that you cannot see,
or why a flood now covers you.

¹² Doesn't God, there in the highest heavens,
observe the stars in their dark realm?
¹³ Yet you say, "What does God know?
Can God judge us through the celestial dark?
¹⁴ Dark clouds prevent God from seeing clearly
as the Almighty crosses the heavenly vault."

15 Will you insist on following the ancient path
    which the corrupt have walked?
16 Their days ended prematurely,
    their foundations swept away by a flood.
17 They told God, "Leave us alone!"
    and, "What can Shaddai do to us?"
18 But it was God who filled their households with good things—
    so perhaps their opinion leaves something to be desired!
19 The just are gladdened at what they see;
    the innocent make fun of them,
20 saying, "Look at how power evaporates!
    All their wealth has been devoured by fire!"

21 Turn to God and you will be at peace,
    and reap the bounty of good will;
22 accept instruction from God's mouth,
    and plant God's word in your heart.
23 For if you return to Shaddai,
    you'll be restored.
If you remove corruption from your household,
24   if you give up your lust for gold,
and value the gold of Ophir
    no more than the pebbles in a stream,
25 then Shaddai will be your gold;
    God will be like the best silver to you.
26 Then you'll dwell in the embrace of Shaddai
    and lift up your face to God.
27 You will pray, and your prayers will be heard,
    and your vows will be fulfilled.
28 When you decide to do something, it will succeed,
    and your paths will be brightly lit.
29 When others are brought low, you'll say, "Lift them up!"
    and God will raise up the lowly.
30 God will liberate even someone who is not innocent—
    and they'll be delivered because your hands are clean.

ᛦ   ᛦ   ᛦ

23:1 Then Job replied:

2   I am still bitter in my complaint—
    God's hand is heavy, despite all my groaning.

3 If only I knew where to find the Almighty,
 so I could approach the Judgment Seat!
4 I would make my case to God,
 and expound my best arguments in my defense.
5 But I would also benefit by hearing the answers,
 and get a grip on what is behind all this.
6 Would God get on a high horse in debating with me?
 No, God would give me the chance to plead my cause!
7 There an upright person could make such a convincing case
 that I would be delivered forever from my Judge.
8 But if I go east, God isn't there;
 if I go west, I find nothing.
9 When God is working up north, I can see no one;
 when God turns south, I don't even catch a glimpse.

10 But the Most High knows my movements;
 and once I am tested, I will be as pure as refined gold.
11 I have always followed closely God's path;
 I have maintained a straight and narrow course.
12 I have treasured God's commands,
 and prized the divine words in my heart.
13 Who can dissuade the unchangeable divinity?
 Divine acts flow from divine desires.
14 For God will complete what is destined for me,
 like God's mandates for all of us.
15 That is why I am so afraid to be in the sight of God;
 when I think of it, I am horror-struck.
16 The Most High makes my heart sink,
 and makes my body shake in terror.
17 Even so, I'm not silenced by the darkness
 nor by the deep gloom that covers my face.

24:1 Why doesn't the Almighty One set up a schedule?
 Why do those closer to God wait in vain?
2 The villainous change boundary markers,
 and rustle sheep for their own pastures.
3 They steal the donkeys of the dispossessed;
 they take the ox of the widow through extortion.
4 They push the needy off the path
 and force the poor into hiding.

5 Like wild asses in the desert,
    the poor set forth on their task of foraging,
    searching the wilderness for bread for their children.
6 They cull what they can from the fields of the wicked;
    they glean the vineyards of the wealthy.
7 Lacking clothes, they lie naked at night,
    without protection from the cold.
8 The rain off the mountains drenches them;
    they seek shelter in the cleft of a rock.
9 Orphaned children have their property stolen,
    .and the poor lose their clothing through extortion.
10 They move from place to place naked; they have no clothes,
    and starve while working in the field.
11 They make oil among the olive vineyards of the wealthy;
    they crush grapes for wine yet die of thirst.
12 The groans of the dying rise from the cities,
    the pleas of the wounded fill the air.
    Yet God charges no one with any wrongdoing!

13 Roaming among the poor are those who rebel against the light;
    they neither know its way nor dwell in its paths.
14 In the dead of night they rise
    to murder the poor and the needy.
15 The eye of the adulterer also waits for the twilight,
    saying, "I won't be seen," and hiding in the darkness.
16 In the dark they burgle houses
    but shut themselves in during the daylight hours—
    for they don't know the light.
17 Their morning is the darkest of darkness;
    their companions the terrors of the night.

18 Yet they're nothing but foam on the water,
    and their portion of the land is cursed
    so that no one goes to their vineyards.
19 As drought and heat snatch away the melting snow,
    so Sheol snatches away transgressors.
20 Their own mother forgets them
    and the worm feasts on them—
    no more remembered than a broken tree.
21 They prey on the childless
    and wrong the defenseless.

²² But God drags away such powerful people
    by an even greater power—
and though they are well established,
    there are no assurances in life.
²³ Even if God allows them a little security,
    the eyes of the Almighty watch every step they take.
²⁴ For a while they're exalted, and then they're gone;
    they're brought low, and gathered up like dead branches,
    or cut off, like heads of grain.
²⁵ Isn't this the way things are?
    Who is there to disprove what I say,
    who can make a liar out of me?

ભ   ભ   ભ

25:¹ Then Bildad of Shuah replied:

² Authority and awe belong to God,
    who establishes peace in the heavens.
³ How many armies does God have?
    Upon whom does the Almighty's light not shine?
⁴ How, then, can we be justified before God?
    How can a human birth be considered clean?
⁵ If even the moon isn't bright in God's sight,
    and the stars aren't pure,
⁶ how much less are people, who are maggots,
    and mere mortals, who are worms?

ભ   ભ   ભ

26:¹ Then Job responded:

² How helpful you all are to the powerless!
    Isn't it wonderful that you aid the weak arm!
³ How wonderful that you counsel the witless,
    always ready with a helpful suggestion!
⁴ But who are you talking to, with these words of wisdom?
    Whose spirit spoke from your mouth?

⁵ The dead in Sheol tremble;
    the denizens of the deep are fearful.

6   Death itself stands stripped naked before God,
      and Perdition has no covering.

7   It is the Almighty who has spread the heavens over the void,
      and balanced the earth in its middle,

8   and creates clouds from all the water,
      though they never burst from the weight.

9   God covers the face of the full moon,
      by spreading clouds over it,

10   and has set boundaries for all the waters of the universe
      and separated light from darkness.

11   The pillars holding up the heavens tremble,
      and are awestruck at God's creative word.

12   God's power stills the oceans:
      God's wisdom vanquishes Chaos;

13   God's breath makes the heavens beautiful;
      God's hand governs the fleeing serpent.

14   All we observe are but the fringes of God's ways;
      how faint a whisper we hear!
    Who can understand
      the thunder of God's power?

27:1 Job continued his discourse:

2   I vow to the Most High, who has withheld my rights,
      and to the Almighty, who has embittered me,

3   that as long as I can take a breath,
      and God's Spirit is in my nostrils,

4   that my lips will never utter a lie
      and my tongue will not speak deceitfully.

5   I will never admit that you are right,
      and I will maintain my innocence till the day I die.

6   I am in the right and I cannot give it up;
      my conscience will be clear as long as I live.

7   Let my enemies be counted among the wicked;
      let those who are against me
      be numbered among the unjustified.

8   For what is the hope of the godless when they are cut off,
      when God takes away their life?

9   Will God listen to their pleas
      when disaster strikes?

10 Will they take delight in the Almighty?
   Will they call upon God at all times?
11 Let me tell you how God's power works,
   and I won't conceal God's ways.
12 Yet you have seen all this for yourselves—
   so why all these meaningless words?

13 This is the destiny the wicked receive from God,
   the inheritance the ruthless receive from Shaddai:
14 However many children they have,
   they'll all get the sword,
   and their descendants will all go hungry.
15 Those who survive will die during the plague,
   and their spouses won't mourn them.
16 Even if the wicked hoard silver like a mound of soil
   and store piles of clothes,
17 they may hoard it but the just will wear it;
   they may store it but the just will spend it.
18 The houses built by the wicked are as fragile as cobwebs,
   as temporary as a sentinel's shelter.
19 They may go to bed wealthy, but at their own peril—
   they awake to discover their riches gone.
20 Terrors sweep them away like a flood,
   and they disappear in a tempest in the night.
21 An east wind carries them off—they simply vanish
   and are swept away in the whirlwind.
22 It hurls itself against them without mercy
   as they flee its power in reckless flight.
23 It applauds them, mocking their vain struggles
   as they are whisked away from their homes.

28:1 You know that silver comes from a mine,
   and so is gold, before they are refined.
2 Iron is dug from the earth,
   and copper must be smelted from rocks.
3 You know that people can light up
   the darkest hole in search of ore.
4 We drive shafts into hillsides
   in remote and uninhabited regions;
   we dangle and sway on ropes, deep in the ground.
5 On its surface the earth produces bread,
   while underneath it's a violent cauldron of fire.

6   Its rocks are full of sapphires
        and its dust contains gold—
7   places unseen by birds of prey,
        even by the eyes of the falcon;
8   places unknown to wild animals,
        even to the noble lion.
9   We work over the flintiest rocks,
        and tear down mountains;
10 we cut channels through granite,
        in our quest for precious things.
11 We dam up streams in our drive
        to bring hidden treasure to sunlight.

12 But where does one find Wisdom?
        Where is the place of understanding?
13 We don't know how to get there!
        It is not to be found in the land of the living.
14 "It isn't here," says the abyss.
        "It isn't here, either," says the sea.
15 It can't be purchased with gold;
        it can't be had for any amount of silver.
16 It can't even be purchased with the tooled gold of Ophir,
        or precious onyx or sapphire.
17 There is no crystal, no gold equal to its value;
        there is nothing in fine jewels or gold equal to it.
18 Not even coral or jasper come close to its value.
        The price of Wisdom outbids pearls.
19 Ethiopia's topaz is not equal to it;
        it cannot be valued in pure gold.
20 Then where does one find wisdom?
        Where is the place of understanding?
21 It is hidden from the eyes of the living;
        it is hidden from the birds of the air.
22 Perdition and Death say,
        "Only a rumor of it has reached our ears."
23 Only God knows how to get there;
        for God is where it is.
24 For the Most High looks to the ends of the earth,
        and sees everything under heaven all at once.
25 When God gave wind its movement,
        and measured out the breadth and depth of the waters,

26 and made the rules for rain
   and designed paths for lightning,
27 God beheld Wisdom and named it,
   confirmed it and tested it.
28 Then the Most High said to us all:
   "Reverence for God—that is wisdom!
   And to shun all evil—that is understanding!"

29:1 Job continued:

2 If only I were back in the good old days,
   back when God looked after me;
3 back when the lamp of grace shone above my head,
   by which light I strode through the darkest times;
4 back when it was the spring of my life,
   when God's friendship permeated my household;
5 back when Shaddai was still with me,
   and my children still surrounded me;
6 back when my path was luxurious as butter,
   and the rocks issued a steady flow of oil!
7 When I stood at the city gate
   and took my seat in the square,
8 the young ones gathered there drew back
   and the ones advanced in years stood up out of respect;
9 the nobles held their tongues
   and put their hands on their mouths;
10 the elders were speechless,
   their tongues stuck to the roofs of their mouths.
11 The ears that heard me blessed me,
   and the eyes that saw me praised me;
12 for I was the person who came to the aid of the needy;
   I was the one who aided the orphans and the homeless.
13 Those at the brink of death blessed me;
   I made the hearts of widows and widowers sing for joy.
14 I dressed in righteousness;
   I wore justice like a robe and a turban.
15 I was eyes to the blind
   and feet to the lame.
16 I was a parent to the needy,
   and listened to the appeal of the stranger.
17 I broke the grasp of the wicked,
   and forced them to release their prey.

¹⁸ Then I would say to myself, "I will die in my own nest,
  and my days will be numerous as the grains of sand.
¹⁹ My roots reach down to the waters,
  and at night the dew refreshes my branches.
²⁰ My reputation is secured
  and my future is well prepared."
²¹ People listened to me, waited on me,
  were silent in anticipation of my counsel.
²² Once I spoke they dared not speak after me;
  my words dripped on them one by one.
²³ They waited for me as one waits for the rain;
  they drank in my words like a spring shower.
²⁴ If I smiled on them they were reassured;
  they studied my features for the faintest sign of approval.
²⁵ Like a tribal leader I chose for them their way of life;
  I lived like a sovereign among armed troops,
  or like one who comforted mourners.

30:1 But now those younger than me deride me—
  upstarts whose parents I wouldn't have let
  tend my sheepdogs!
² What few skills they had were useless to me—
  they had lost all their vigor.
³ Their lot was that of the hungry and homeless.
  They drifted into the desert as a last resort,
⁴ where they picked hibiscus leaves for food
  and broom tree roots for fuel.
⁵ They had been driven out of their community
  with a tumult accorded to thieves;
⁶ They dwelled in the gullies of the washes,
  in caves and among the rocks.
⁷ One could hear their moan from the bushes,
  from among the nettles where they gathered.
⁸ They were the offspring of the foolish and the base,
  born to be society's derelicts.

⁹ Yet now this brood mock me in song.
  I am an object of scorn to them.
¹⁰ They abhor me and keep their distance—
  except when they are spitting on me.
¹¹ But now that God has unstrung my bow and afflicted me,
  these people have dropped all restraint.

12 Now that I am vulnerable, this rabble attacks—
      they set traps for me and lay sieges against me.
13 They cut off my movements in anticipation of my end,
      for there is no one to stop them.
14 They come as through a broad breach;
      in a tumult they come on by waves.

15 Terror overwhelms me!
      My dignity is blown away by the wind,
      and my safety has evaporated like a cloud.
16 Now my soul is poured out within me;
      my life is now day after day of affliction.
17 My bones ache during the night;
      my guts seethe so that I cannot rest.
18 God seizes me, wrapping me up like a cloak,
      choking me like a tight collar.
19 God casts me into the muck,
      and I'm reduced to dust and ashes.
20 I wail to you, God, and you don't answer;
      I stand before you and you don't acknowledge it.
21 You are cruel to me!
      Your heavy and hostile hand presses down on me!
22 You lift me up to soar with the wind,
      to be tossed to and fro.
23 Now I know that you'll bring me down to death—
      and to the Gathering of all the living.

24 Who continues to bruise someone
      when they're broken and screaming for help?
25 In the past didn't I weep for the troubled?
      Didn't I grieve for the oppressed?
26 But when I expected good, evil came;
      when I waited for the light, darkness came.
27 I am seething inside, and I cannot rest;
      daily afflictions overwhelm me.
28 I roam about without the sun;
      I rise in the assembly and beg for help.
29 I am one with jackals,
      and a companion to the owls.
30 My sunburnt skin falls from my body;
      my fevered frame burns within.

³¹ My harp is tuned to funeral dirges,
    my flute to the sound of weeping.

31:1 I have made a vow with my eyes
    not to look lustfully at another.
² But what is our agreement with God above?
    What is our promised heritage from Shaddai, from on high?
³ Isn't it that the wicked will be the ones on whom calamity falls?
    Isn't it that disaster comes only to evildoers?
⁴ Doesn't God observe my behavior,
    and take note of my coming and going?

⁵ If I have consorted with liars,
    or moved about doing something deceitful,
⁶ I am willing to subject myself to the scales of justice;
    for then God will know that I am blameless.
⁷ If my steps have strayed from the straight and narrow,
    or if my eyes have caused my heart to wander,
    or if any stain blots my hands,
⁸ then let me plant that another may harvest—
    and let my crops be pulled up by the roots!

⁹ If I've ever lost my heart to another,
    or lurked about my neighbor's door,
¹⁰ or watched my spouse share in a household that is not mine,
    or watched my spouse sleep in a bed that is not mine—
¹¹ these would have been heinous acts
    serious enough to merit a court case,
¹² worthy of a punishing fire to burn until Destruction—
    worthy of "uprooting my harvest."

¹³ If I ever refused justice to my workers, women or men,
    when they had a complaint against me,
¹⁴ how could I justify myself when God stands up,
    when God holds court?
¹⁵ Didn't the One who made me in the womb also make them?
    Didn't the same One form us both in the womb?

¹⁶ If I have denied anything to the poor,
    or allowed the eyes of widow or widower to fail,
¹⁷ or ate my meal in peace
    while the orphan went without—

¹⁸ if I didn't act like a parent to them from my youth,
   like a benefactor, almost from my infancy;
¹⁹ or if I have let anyone freeze for lack of clothing,
   or ignored a homeless person—
²⁰ if their bodies didn't bless me wholeheartedly
   as they felt the warmth of my wool clothing;
²¹ or if I have struck the defenseless
   because I knew I had judges in my pocket;
²² then may my arm fall out of its socket,
   and my arm be broken at the elbow!
²³ For then the fear of God's punishment would overpower me;
   how could I defend my actions before the Almighty?

²⁴ If I had made a pact with gold,
   or made the finest gold my security;
²⁵ if I had gloated over the value of my wealth,
   or the abundance my hands managed to acquire;
²⁶ if I had beheld the shining sun
   or viewed the splendidly moving moon
²⁷ to the extent that they stole my heart
   and I blew them a secret kiss,
²⁸ these too would have been sins worthy of judgment,
   for I would have been denied God's supremacy.

²⁹ Have I ever been pleased to hear of my enemies' downfall,
   or rejoiced when my enemy turned to evil deeds?
³⁰ Never have I allowed my mouth to sin,
   to curse my enemies' life!
³¹ Haven't the members of my household said of me,
   "Is there anyone who hasn't eaten your food?"
³² I've always taken in wayfarers for a night
   rather than make them spend the night in the open.

³³ Have I ever hidden my sins as others do
   by keeping them close to my heart?
³⁴ Was I ever fearful of the gossip of nosy neighbors?
   Did I ever flee the scorn of other families,
   by becoming a recluse and never leaving home?

³⁵ Who then can arrange a hearing with God for me?
   Look—here's my signature on my defense!

Now let Shaddai answer me;
    get my accuser to draw up a bill of particulars!
³⁶ I would carry it around for all to see;
    wrap it around my head like a turban!
³⁷ I would give the Almighty a step-by-step account of my life;
    I would approach God as boldly as a ruler!

³⁸ If my land cries out against me,
    or its furrows weep together—
³⁹ if I ate its bounty without recompense,
    or gave its laborers reason to complain—
⁴⁰ let weeds flourish where once was wheat;
    let thistle take over the barley field!

⁴¹ Job's words are ended.

32:1–37:24*

So the three—Eliphaz, Bildad, and Zophar—ended of their criticism of Job, because they saw that in his view of things, Job was justified.

² Another individual, however—Elihu begot of Barachel the Buzite, of the clan of Ram—was furious. He was upset because Job considered himself to be in the right, rather than God. ³ Elihu was also upset with Job's three friends, because in not being able to refute Job, they were thereby condemning God.**

⁴ However, because Elihu was younger than the others he patiently heard them out. ⁵ When they failed to condemn Job, he lost his temper. ⁶ So Elihu begot of Barachel the Buzite, of the clan of Ram, spoke:

I am young, and you all are advanced in years.
    Because of this I hesitated to speak out.
⁷ I thought to myself, "Let the older ones speak out,
    for wisdom comes with age."

---

* This section is almost certainly a much later addition to the book of *Job*, and the character of Elihu is mentioned nowhere else in the work. Once again, however, the name is significant to the story: taken together, from the clan and family names to his own, the name translates roughly as "Once high, now despised; but God has blessed, and God is his"—Job's story in a nutshell.

**This rendering follows an ancient Hebrew scribal tradition. The standard text reads, "because even though they had not been able to refute Job, they still condemned him."

8   But it's the Spirit that lives within—the breath of Shaddai—
        that gives people understanding.
9   It isn't only the aged who are wise,
        nor does age guarantee our understanding to be right.
10 So I say, listen to me—
        allow me also to give you my opinion.
11 At one time I had great expectations of your discourse.
        I listened carefully to your arguments
        and to your choice of words.
12 I paid close attention to you—
        but not one of you has proved Job wrong!
        None of you has refuted his arguments!
13 So please don't say, "We have found wisdom," or,
        "Only God can punish Job, we can't."
14 I won't be using your arguments in reply to Job;
        besides, Job hasn't targeted his words against me.
15 He has, however, intimidated you,
        because you're now lost for an answer, unable to say a word.
16 So why should I wait any longer?
        You've thrown in the towel, and stand there without answers!
17 But I will give answers,
        and I will give my opinion.
18 For I am full of words;
        the spirit within me is compelling me.
19 The feeling within me is like unvented wine;
        just like a new wineskin, I'm ready to burst.
20 So I'll speak now, and get some relief;
        I will open my mouth and give you a reply.
21 I'll be completely impartial,
        and I won't use flattering phrases—
22 I don't even know how to flatter;
        and if I did, my Creator would silence me.

33:1 But now, Job, listen to my words,
        and pay attention to what I have to say.
2   Now I will open my mouth;
        my tongue and lips will form words.
3   And those words will come from an upright heart,
        and my lips will speak about what I know to be true.
4   The Spirit of God is what made me;
        the breath of Shaddai gives me life.

5   Disprove me if you can;
        set your arguments in order before me; state your case.
6   Like you, I stand before God;
        like you, I began as a piece of clay.
7   Consequently, nothing about me should alarm you;
        I will not lay a heavy hand on you.

8   But you said in my presence,
        as I listened intensely to your words,
9   "I am clean and without sin;
        I am innocent; there is no sin in me.
10 Yet God invents injustices against me
        and treats me as an enemy;
11 God shackles my feet
        and watches my every step!"
12 Let me be perfectly clear:
        you are wrong in what you say.
    God is greater than human beings.
13   So why do you complain that God isn't answerable to us?
14 God *does* speak to us, first one way, then a second way,
        yet no one notices it.

15 First God speaks in dreams, those visions of the night
        when deep sleep covers the land
        and all are slumbering in their beds.
16 At these times God speaks in our ears
        and terrifies us with admonitions,
17 to turn us away from wickedness
        and to keep us humble,
18 to save our souls from the deep pit,
        and our lives from acts of violence.

19 But God also speaks to us through pain,
        when we're in our beds and moaning about our bones,
20 pain so great that we loathe food,
        and have no appetite for sumptuous meals.
21 Our flesh can waste away so that we are unrecognizable,
        and the bones of our skeletons stick out.
22 Our souls approach the grave,
        and our lives the place of death.

²³ If there is a guardian angel—
    a mediator, one in a thousand—
    appointed for a person's rights and defense,
²⁴ the angel might say, mercifully,
    "Spare this one from the grave—
    I've found someone to pay the ransom!"
²⁵ And then your body becomes renewed with health;
    you'll be restored to your youthful vigor.
²⁶ Then you'll then pray and God will accept you—
    to come into God's joyful presence,
    and God will restore your integrity.
²⁷ At this point you will sing everyone your new song:
    "I was in the wrong by sinning,
    but God has mercifully punished me
²⁸ by delivering my soul from the pit,
    by restoring my life to light."
²⁹ God does all this to us—
    twice, maybe even three times—
³⁰ to turn us back from the pit
    and bring about enlightenment.

³¹ Job, pay attention, and listen to me—
    no, hold on to your words for now, and let me continue.
³² Then if you have anything to say, I'll be glad to hear it;
    speak out, for I want you to be justified.
³³ If you don't have anything to say, say nothing,
    and I will teach you wisdom.

34:1 Then Elihu continued:

² Listen to me, you wise people;
    lend me your ears, you learned ones!
³ For our ears taste words
    just as our tongues taste food.
⁴ Let us learn what is right;
    let us determine among ourselves what is good.
⁵ For Job said, "I am in the right,
    and God refuses to grant me justice;
⁶ my case is questioned and I am called a liar;
    my conscience is clear but my wounds are incurable."
⁷ Who among us is like Job,
    who slurps blasphemies like water;

8   who travels in the company of sinners
     and walks with the wicked?
9   For Job is on record as saying,
     "What good is it to delight in God?"
10   Now listen; hear me, all you with understanding:
     God is so far removed from evil and injustice
11   that we are compensated for our conduct,
     and rewarded for exactly how we live.
12   Truly, God cannot act in a wicked way;
     Shaddai cannot debase justice.
13   Who gave the Most High authority over the world?
     Who put God in charge of the earth?
14   If God were to decide
     to withdraw the divine Spirit-breath,
15   the flesh of all things would perish,
     and humankind would return to dust.

16   If you still understand, hear this!
     Listen to my words as I speak!
17   Could one who hates justice ever govern?
     Could you possibly condemn the Just and Mighty One,
18   who says to rulers, "You are worthless!"
     and to world leaders, "You are corrupt!"—
19   who is impartial to those of high degree,
     and doesn't distinguish between rich and poor;
     for all are made alike by God's own hand?
20   We all die in a moment, at midnight or at noon;
     social status has no value when our time comes.

21   For God is watching all our ways,
     all our actions.
22   There is no darkness so dense
     that the workers of injustice can hide in it.
23   God has no need to examine people twice
     when it is their time to face judgment.
24   God smashes the world's powerful without forethought,
     and sets others in their place;
25   God knows well their doings—
     then one fine night it all comes crashing down.
26   God strikes the mighty down for their wickedness
     in full view of all,

²⁷ for they strayed from the path,
     without regard for God's ways,
²⁸ so that the poor cried out to God against them
     and the wailing of the afflicted
     caught the Almighty's attention.
²⁹ So when God keeps quiet,
     who can find fault with that?
   When the Almighty remains hidden so that no one—
     neither nations nor individuals—
     can see the divine intention,
³⁰ it is to keep those who are godless from coming into power
     and ensnaring the people.

³¹ Now some might say to God,
     "I'm guilty, and I won't offend any more.
³² Help me understand what I don't know.
     And if I have done wrong, it will not happen again."
³³ Do you really think God should reward you on *your* terms,
     when you have refused to repent?
   You have to make that decision, not I—
     so tell me what you know.
³⁴ People who have understanding,
     who are wise and are listening to these words,
     will say to me:
³⁵ "Job is speaking without knowledge—
     his words don't make sense!
³⁶ Test him to the utmost,
     for his answers are those of a guilty person!"
³⁷ And to all his sins, he adds rebellion
     when he ignores our statements
     and hurls epithets at God.

35:1 Elihu continued:

² Do you really think it is right to say,
     "I am more just than God"?
³ Or to say to God, "What's the use of being innocent
     when I'm treated like a sinner?
     What do I gain by not sinning?"
⁴ I have an answer to your question—
     and to your three friends as well.

5 Look up to the heavens.
       Notice how high the clouds are above you
6 If you have sinned,
       how can you have hurt God?
   Even if your sins are many,
       what effect could they possibly have?
7 If you are upright, what does that give to God?
       How does God benefit from it?
8 Your wickedness affects only other people like you;
       and your justice helps only other human beings.

9 When oppression is rampant the masses cry out;
       they plead for relief from the tyranny of the mighty.
10 But no one asks, "Where is my God, my Creator,
       who gives songs in the night,
11 who teaches us more than the beasts of the earth,
       and makes us wiser than the birds in the sky?"
12 When such people cry out, God doesn't answer
       because of their rebellious arrogance—
13 God doesn't hear their empty plea;
       Shaddai pays no attention to it.
14 So how much less will you be heard
       when you say you don't see God,
   that your case is on the heavenly docket
       and you're waiting to be heard—
15 particularly if God doesn't answer when angry
       or give any response when people are arrogant!
16 So Job opens his mouth only for idle chatter,
       and his many words betray great ignorance.

36:1 Then Elihu continued:

2 Bear with me for just a while longer,
       and I will prove something to you;
       I have yet to speak on God's behalf.
3 I will reach out far afield
       to prove that God is just.
4 I give my word that I am not a liar;
       for one with perfect knowledge is at your side.

5 God is mighty, yet doesn't despise humankind;
       God is mighty in strength of understanding.

⁶ The Almighty doesn't preserve the life of the corrupt,
   but upholds the rights of the oppressed.
⁷ God's eyes are always on the upright—
   enthroning them with rulers and exalting them forever.
⁸ But if they find themselves trapped, or in chains,
   or held fast by ropes of affliction,
⁹ then the Most High counsels them on their misdeeds,
   on the arrogance of their ways,
¹⁰ and opens their ears to learning
   and commands them to give up evil.
¹¹ If they comply and serve,
   they live a life of prosperity,
   and years full of happiness.
¹² If they don't listen, they taste the sword,
   and die like all the unknowing.

¹³ To be godless in heart is to cherish anger;
   they don't plead for help when God shackles them;
¹⁴ they die young, and their lives are thrown away
   in pursuit of unrestrained profligacy.
¹⁵ Those who are suffering are delivered
   through that very suffering—
   pain is God's way of shouting to you.
¹⁶ God is entreating you from the jaws of distress,
   offering instead a place of unbounded freedom,
   with tables replete with rich fare.

¹⁷ Now you are saddled with the judgment due the wicked—
   judgment and justice have taken hold of you.
¹⁸ Beware lest you be tempted again by riches;
   don't be dismayed by the huge price to be paid.
¹⁹ Could all the wealth in the world, all the power,
   have saved you from your distress?
²⁰ Don't long for the night of retribution,
   of taking by force the things you had lost.
²¹ Beware lest you turn toward evil,
   which you seem to hate less than your affliction.

²² Think about God's magnificent power;
   What an excellent example for a teacher to give!
²³ Who has ever told God the right path to take,
   or accused God of wrongdoing?

24 Remember always to acclaim God's work—
    people have sung of it for ages;
25 all humankind has seen it,
    gazing on it from afar.
26 Keep in mind that God's greatness exceeds our knowledge;
    God's vastness is a mystery.
27 Think of how God collects droplets of water;
    distills its mist into rain,
28 which the skies spill onto the soil
    for the benefit of humankind.

29 Can anyone understand how God arranges the clouds,
    or explain thunder bouncing off the canopy?
30 Notice how God scatters the lightning around,
    and spreads the clouds around the tops of mountains.
31 With their assistance God nourishes the nations
    and provides them with an abundance of food.
32 God holds the lightning bolt until,
    upon command, it strikes its mark;
33 the thunder signals its approach,
    and even the cattle tell you it's coming.
37:1 Whenever I hear it, my heart trembles;
    it leaps out of its place.
2 Listen, listen—the thunder is God's voice;
    hear the rumbling that comes from God's mouth!
3 Across the whole heavens it rolls forth,
    and the lightning extends to the four corners of the earth,
4 followed by the roaring voice of God,
    a thundering, majestic voice.
God sends the unrestrained lightning bolts
    immediately followed by silence.
5 God's voice thunders wondrously,
    and performs great acts that we can't comprehend.
6 When God tells the snow, "Fall from the sky," or
    commands the rain to fall in torrents,
7 it makes everyone shut themselves indoors,
    so that all might know that this is God's work.
8 The wild animals take cover
    and hide in their dens.
9 From the southern canopy comes the hurricane,
    and from the north winds comes the cold.

10 God breathes, and there is ice;
    vast stretches of water freeze over.
11 God compresses waterdrops into clouds,
    and the clouds scatter the lightning.
12 At God's command they blow around
    over the face of the whole earth,
    doing whatever God directs them to do.
13 Whether the clouds are issuing a thunderous rebuke
    or watering the earth in an act of love,
    God causes it all.

14 Listen closely, Job;
    stop and reflect on God's wondrous works.
15 Can you describe how God controls these forces
    or how the clouds make the lightning flash?
16 Can you relate how the clouds are balanced—
    an act of wonder by the Person of perfect knowledge?
17 When your clothes are sticky with sweat,
    and the south wind stills the earth,
18 can you help God spread the heavenly canopy,
    or temper the steel-gray skies?
19 Tell us what to say to the Almighty;
    we need help because of the failing light.
20 Can my words carry the load with God?
    Do our words even reach those ears?

21 Now humankind doesn't see the light that is bright in the skies,
    even though the winds have swept them clear of clouds;
22 Out of the north there comes a golden splendor—
    it is God, arrayed in awesome majesty.
23 The Almighty is beyond our reach, overwhelming in power;
    there is no oppression in that greatest of power and justice.
24 Small wonder that the Most High is feared;
    those who are wise of heart stand in awe of God.

then Our God answered Job from the heart of the storm:

2   Who is this obscuring my plans
        with such ignorant words?
3   Hitch up your belt like the fighter you are;
        now *I* will ask the questions and *you* will answer *me*!

4   Where were you when I created the earth?
        If you know the answer, tell me!
5   Who decided its size? Do you know?
        Who stretched the measuring line across it?
6   Into what foundation
        were its pillars sunk?
    Who laid the cornerstone
7   while all the choruses of morning stars sang
        and the heavenly court shouted for joy?
8   And who held back the sea behind partitions
        when it burst forth from my womb,
9   when I created clouds as the earth's raiment
        and thick darkness as its swaddling clothes—
10   when I drew limits around the waters
        and locked the partitions in place
11   and said, "This far and no more;
        this is where your mighty waves stay"?

12   Have you ever in your life commanded the morning,
        or told the dawn that its assignment for the day
13   was to grasp the edges of the earth
        and shake out its wicked?
14   When the dawn lightens things to a clay red,
        like a garment died to a brighter color,
15   the wicked are denied the light,
        and their threatening arms are broken.

16   Have you traveled as far as the source of the sea,
        or walked in search of the Abyss?
17   Have you discovered the gates of death?
        Have you seen the gates of the Place of Darkness?
18   Do you comprehend the breadth of the earth?
        If so, address the following:

19 How does one get to the source of light?
    And where does darkness come from?
20 Could you walk them home?
    Do you know where they live?
21 If you do know, you were born when they were;
    so you must be very old!
22 Have you seen my warehouses of snow?
    Do you know where I store all the hail
23 that I keep in reserve for troubled times—
    for times of international conflict?
24 Which road do you take to the lightning fork?
    Where on the earth does the east wind finish its blowing?

25 Who lays down a channel for the downpour
    or prepares a path for the thunderbolt
26 so that rain can fall even on uninhabited land
    and deserts void of life,
27 enriching the wasted and desolate place
    and preparing the soil for plant life?
28 Does the rain have parents?
    Who begets dewdrops?
29 Whose womb gives life to ice
    or gives birth to skies filled with hoarfrost,
30 when waters become solid as stone
    and the face of the deep becomes hard as steel?

31 Can you harness the Pleiades,
    or untie the ropes of Orion?
32 Can you direct the morning star from season to season,
    or the Bear and its Cub?
33 Do you know the laws of the heavens?
    Can you fix their rule over the earth?

34 Can you boom out your voice at the clouds,
    and cause them to rain on command?
35 Can you send the lightning on its way?
    Does it report back to you, "Here we are?"
36 Who instills the ibis with its prophetic wisdom?
    Where does the rooster pick up its intuition?
37 Who classifies the clouds,
    and pours out the heavenly water jars

³⁸ until the soil is muddy,
and the dust has become solid?

³⁹ Do you stalk the prey for the lioness?
Do you provide food for her cubs,
⁴⁰ when they lie low in the den,
or crouch in a culvert?
⁴¹ Who provides the raven its nourishment
when its young cry out to God;
when they wander about without food?

39¹ Do you know in what season the mountain goats give birth?
Have you ever watched a red deer in labor?
² Do you know their gestation periods
and their time of birth,
³ when they crouch down to bring forth their young
and get rid of their labor pains?
⁴ Do you know how their young grow strong,
how they thrive in the open,
grow to maturity, then leave and never return?

⁵ Who freed the wild donkey,
and removed the bridle from its head?
⁶ I gave it the desert to roam in,
and the salt flats to dwell in.
⁷ It rejects the noisy city;
it has no driver to give it orders.
⁸ It ranges over mountains for a pasture,
and seeks out green places.

⁹ Is the wild ox willing to serve you,
to spend its nights at your manger?
¹⁰ Will it accept the harness for plowing,
to plow the soil for you?
¹¹ Will you rely on its massive strength,
or depend on it to do your heavy work?
¹² Will you trust it to return to its stall,
and haul the grain to the threshing floor?

¹³ The wings of the ostrich flutter joyfully
with elegant plumes and feathers.

¹⁴ Yet it lays its eggs on open ground,
  to be warmed there in the sand,
¹⁵ unmindful that a foot could smash them,
  or that a wild beast may trample them.
¹⁶ It treats its young cruelly and virtually disowns them;
  it doesn't care if all its labor was in vain.
¹⁷ For God has deprived it of wisdom
  and given it no share of common sense.
¹⁸ Yet, if challenged to a test of speed,
  it puts dust between the horse and its rider.

¹⁹ Was it you who gave the horse its strength,
  or gave its neck that beautiful mane?
²⁰ Did you teach it to leap like a locust?
  What makes its noble neighing so frightening?
²¹ It paws at the soil, rejoicing in its own strength,
  and rushes forth into danger.
²² It chuckles at fear, it isn't afraid;
  it defies weapons of destruction.
²³ The quiver, the sparkling spear and the javelin
  rattle upon its back.
²⁴ Twitching in anticipation, it takes off at a gallop;
  nothing can hold it back once the trumpet sounds.
²⁵ At each trumpet blast, it neighs an "Aha!"
  It smells the odor of struggle and strife,
  and listens to the tumult and the war cry.

²⁶ Are you and your wisdom the reason why the soaring hawk
  spreads its wings and heads south?
²⁷ Does the eagle fly aloft at your word
  to make its nest so high?
²⁸ It spends its nights amid rocks and cliffs,
  with the pinnacle of a peak as its stronghold.
²⁹ From this view it searches for its prey,
  with eyes that see from afar.
³⁰ Its feeds its young on blood;
  where carrion is found, there it is.

*40:1 Then Our God said to Job:

> 2   Do you still want to argue with Almighty God?
>   If you have something to say, speak up!

3 Then Job answered Our God:

> 4   "I am worthless; what can I say?
>   I'd better hold my hand over my mouth!
> 5   I spoke once, but I have no answer—
>   twice, but I'll say nothing more.

6 Then Our God again answered Job from the heart of the storm:

> 7   Hitch up your belt like the fighter you are;
>   now *I* will ask the questions and *you* will answer *me*!
>
> 8   Do you really question my justice,
>   and put me in the wrong so that you can be justified?
> 9   Do you have an arm as strong as mine?
>   Do you have a thundering voice like mine?
> 10 If so, take on your glory and splendor;
>   dress yourself with majesty and splendor.
> 11 Let your pent-up anger overflow;
>   look on the arrogant and humble them
> 12 look at the proud and put them down with a glance;
>   bring down the wicked where they stand.
> 13 Bury the lot of them where they fall;
>   imprison them in the world below.
> 14 Then I will be the first to acknowledge
>   that your own right hand can save you!
>
> 15 Now look at the hippopotamus, the great beast Behemoth—
>   which I made just as I made you;
>   it eats grass like an ox.
> 16 Notice the strength of its thighs,
>   the power of its stomach muscles;

---

* For the next two chapters, the verse numberings vary greatly between different ancient versions; our numbering follows most English versions.

¹⁷ its "tail" stiffens like a cedar;
       its loins bulge with vigor.
¹⁸ Its ribs are bars of bronze;
       its limbs are iron beams.
¹⁹ It is the crown jewel of my creation,
       created to be my plaything.
²⁰ Forbidding it from the mountain regions
       where all the wild animals make sport,
²¹ it lies under the lotus plants,
       hidden in the reeds and in the marshes;
²² the lotus plants give it shade,
       and the willows by the stream give it shelter.
²³ Notice that even if the river rages, it isn't frightened;
       the entire Jordan could pour down its gullet
       and it wouldn't bat an eyelash.
²⁴ Could anyone capture it when it is on watch?
       Can anyone put a ring through its nose?

41:1 Or the crocodile, that great Leviathan—
       can you catch it with a fishhook
       or put a bit in its mouth?
² Could you tie its nose with a rope
       or pierce its jaw with a gaff?
³ Will it beg you for mercy,
       or timidly ask your pardon?
⁴ Would it strike a bargain with you,
       becoming your lifelong servant?
⁵ Would you then make a pet of it,
       and lead it around on a leash to amuse the household?
⁶ Will traders bid for its hide,
       so it can be sold in shops the world over?
⁷ You could try to restrain it with barbs in its backside
       or harpoons in the head,
⁸ but once you lay a hand on it,
       you'll never forget the aftermath,
       or try it a second time!
⁹ Any hope to restrain this Leviathan would be futile;
       even the bravest tremble just at the sight of it.
¹⁰ It is relentless once aroused;
       this alone checks any challenges.
¹¹ Could anyone attack it with impunity?
       No one under the stars.

12 Let me describe its limbs,
   its strength and its graceful form—
13 who could strip its outer armor,
   or pierce its thick hide?
14 Who would dare face that door-sized gullet?
   Those rows of teeth are terrifying!
15 Rows of scales cover its back;
   they are tightly sealed into a single piece.
16 The seal is so tight
   that not even air comes between them.
17 They are joined in such a way
   that they clasp each other inseparably.
18 Its sneezes flash forth light;
   its eyes shine like the dawn.
19 Its mouth spews out flames;
   sparks of fire stream out.
20 Smoke erupts from its nostrils,
   just like a boiling pot on a kindling fire.
21 Its breath could light coals
   with the flame coming from its mouth.
22 The neck is strength itself;
   fear precedes its every move.
23 When it raises itself up, even the waves flee;
   all the waters fall back.
24 The folds of its flesh are joined,
   tightly bound up and immovable.
25 Its heart is as hard as granite,
   like the lower millstone.
26 A sword might strike, but won't pierce;
   nor will the spear, javelin, or dart.
27 Its tail considers iron as flimsy as straw,
   it smashes bronze as easily as rotten wood.
28 Arrows can't make it flee;
   stones from slingshots crumble into dust.
29 Clubs are like toothpicks to it;
   it laughs at the clatter of javelins.
30 Its underbelly is as sharp as pottery fragments,
   leaving a trail in the mud like a plow.
31 It churns the deep seas into a seething cauldron,
   making them smoke like an incense burner.
32 It leaves such a shining wake in the sea,
   that one would think the sea had a white shock of hair.

³³ Nowhere in or on the earth is there the like of it—
    a creature utterly without fear.
³⁴ It looks the most arrogant right in the eye,
    and rules over all beasts—even the proudest.

രു   രു   രു

42:1 Then Job answered God:

² I know that you can do all things:
    you have only to think something, and it is done.
³ "Who is this obscuring my plans
    with such ignorant words?" you asked
That was me. I've been spouting off
    about things I can't understand,
    about wonders beyond my experience and my knowledge.
⁴ "Listen now, and I will speak;
    I will ask the questions and *you* will answer *me*!" you said.
⁵ Formerly I knew you only by word of mouth,
    but now I see you with my own eyes.
⁶ And so I now take back all that I said,
    and repent in dust and ashes.

42:7-17

after Our God said all these things to Job, God turned to Eliphaz of Teman.

"I am very angry with you and your two friends," Our God said, "for not speaking truthfully about me as Job, my faithful one, did. ⁸ Therefore, I command you to take seven cattle and seven sheep, and go to Job, my faithful one, and offer up a burnt offering for yourselves, and ask Job, my faithful one, to pray for you. I will accept Job's prayer and not punish you as your folly deserves; for you have not spoken truthfully about me as Job, my faithful one, did."

⁹ So Eliphaz of Teman, Bildad of Shuah and Zophar of Naamath went and did what Almighty God told them to do, and Our God accepted Job's prayer.

¹⁰ After Job had prayed for his friends, Our God restored Job's prosperity, blessing him with twice as much as he had before. ¹¹ Then all his sisters and

brothers and everyone who had known him before visited Job and sat down and dined with him. They sympathized with him and comforted Job for all the evil Our God had heaped upon him. Each of them gave Job a piece of silver and a gold ring.

¹² Our God blessed Job's latter days even more than his former life: he came to own 14,000 sheep, 6,000 camels, 1,000 yoke of oxen, and 1,000 donkeys.

¹³ He also went on to have three daughters and seven sons. ¹⁴ He named the daughters Jemimah, Keziah, and Keren-happuch.* ¹⁵ In all the land there were no women as esteemed as the daughters of Job. And Job gave his daughters and sons equal shares of his inheritance.

¹⁶ After this Job lived on to the age of 140 years, and he saw his children and his children's up to the fourth generation. ¹⁷ And when Job died, he was old and full of days.

---

* Their names mean Dove, Cinnamon, and Horn of Beauty.

proverbs

The proverbs of solomon, begot of david, ruler of Israel:

2 for women and men to learn wisdom and self-discipline,
   and to understand words of enlightenment;
3 to acquire the disciplines of being equitable—
   rightness, justice, and fairness;
4 to instill competence in the uneducated,
   and knowledge and good sense to the young;
5 to help wise women and men increase their learning,
   and to give greater guidance to discerning hearts;
6 and to open the meaning of proverbs and parables,
   the sayings of sages, and their riddles.

7 When you stand in awe of Our God—
   that is when you begin to really understand.
   But to spurn wisdom and instruction
   is utter foolishness.

Listen, my children, to your father's lessons;
    don't reject your mother's instructions:
9 they will be a crown of grace for your head,
    a golden chain for your neck.

10 Children, when vicious people tempt you,
    don't give in.
11 When they say, "Come with us!
    we'll hide and wait for some unsuspecting fool,
    and kill them in a surprise attack—
12 we'll swallow them whole, like the grave,
    like the Pit, we can take them alive.
13 We'll steal any amount of expensive clothing;
    we will fill a house with what we loot!
14 Join up with us,
    and it will be one for all and all for one!"—
15 children, don't even associate with them,
    don't even cover the same ground they cover,
16 for their feet run to evil,
    and they're quick to shed blood.
17 Remember, the net is spread in vain
    when the bird is watching!
18 The blood to be had by these people is their own blood;
    they lie in wait to ambush themselves.
19 This is the destiny of any who gain through violence:
    in the end, the life they take is their own.

ଓ   ଓ   ଓ

20 Wisdom cries out in the streets;
    she raises her voice in the malls;
21 she cries out from the top of walls,
    on the roads leading in the city:
22 "How much longer, you ignorant people,
    will you love being ignorant?
How much longer, you mockers, will you keep mocking?
How much longer will fools sneer at understanding?

23 Listen closely to my warning,
   for I'll pour out my heart to you,
   and tell you what's on my mind.
24 Because I called and you chose not to listen,
   because I beckoned and you ignored me,
25 because you rejected all my advice
   and rejected all my counsels,
26 I, in turn, will laugh at your calamity;
   I will mock you when fear swallows you up—
27 when panic falls down upon you like a snowstorm,
   when terror engulfs you like a tornado,
   when distress and anguish knock you down.
28 At that time you will call upon me, but I won't answer;
   when you search for me, I'll be hiding.
29 Because you despised knowledge,
   didn't fear Almighty God,
30 ignored all my advice
   and turned up your nose at my cautions,
31 now you must eat the fruit of going your own way,
   and choke on your own choices.
32 When you turn away from me, you're choosing death,
   and your complacency will ruin you, you fool!
33 But you who listen to me will be at peace,
   have quiet, and fear no misfortune."

2:1 My children, if you heartily accept my words,
    and treasure my requirements,
2 incline your ear to Wisdom,
   and take her truth into your heart.
3 For if you yearn for insight
   and cry out for understanding,
4 if you search for it as you would for silver,
   and dig for it as you would for buried treasure,
5 you will understand what reverence for Our God is,
   and discover how to truly know God.
6 For Our God alone gives wisdom;
   from God's mouth comes knowledge and understanding.
7 The Most High stores up wisdom for the just,
   and shields those who walk in honor;
8 for the Almighty guards the path of justice
   and watches over the way of the holy ones.

⁹ Only then will you have an understanding of
    rightness, justice, and fairness—
    roads that lead to happiness.

¹⁰ When Wisdom enters your heart
    and knowledge delights you,
¹¹ good judgment will protect you,
    and understanding will guard you.
¹² She will protect you from the way of evil,
    from lying and debauched people,
¹³ from people who have abandoned honesty
    to roam paths of darkness,
¹⁴ who revel in evil
    and delight in the perverse,
¹⁵ whose roads are crooked
    and whose ways are devious.
¹⁶ You'll be delivered from seducers,
    from strangers with smooth words
¹⁷ who abandon their spouses and partners,
    and forsake God's covenant.
¹⁸ Their paths are deadly sinkholes,
    and their steps lead to Sheol.
¹⁹ Those who join up with them are lost;
    they lose the path of life.
²⁰ This way you'll walk the roads of good women and men
    and stay on the paths of the just—
²¹ because it is the upright who will inhabit the earth,
    and the upright will call it home;
²² while the wicked will be cut off from the land,
    the faithless uprooted from it.

ଔ   ଔ   ଔ

3:1 My children, don't ever forget these lessons,
    and keep these principles in your heart;
² they'll bring you length of days, years of life
    and above all, peace and prosperity:

³ Never let love and faithfulness abandon you—
    wear them like a necklace around your neck,
    inscribe them on the tablet of your heart.

4 Then you'll enjoy kindness and a good reputation
    from both God and people.

5 Trust Our God with all your heart,
    and don't rely on your own understanding;
6 acknowledge God in everything you do,
    and God will direct your paths.

7 Don't be wise in your own eyes;
    revere Our God and avoid evil.
8 This will provide health to your body,
    and enrichment to your bones.

9 Honor Our God with all that you have,
    and with the first and best part of what you create;
10 then your silos will be filled with wheat
    and your barrels filled with wine.

11 My children, don't despise God's reprimand
    or let it discourage you,
12 for God's discipline is a sign of divine love,
    the way a parent corrects a beloved child.

CR   CR   CR

13 Happy are you when you find Wisdom,
    when you develop discernment.
14 For she is more profitable than silver,
    and brings yields greater even than gold.
15 She is more precious than rubies;
    nothing you can conceivably desire
    can equal her value.
16 She holds long life in one hand,
    riches and honor in the other.
17 Her paths are pleasant ones,
    and all her roads lead to peace.
18 She is a tree of life for those who embrace her,
    and all who hold fast to her find happiness.
19 For it was through her that Our God laid the earth's foundation,
    through her that the heavens were set in place.

20 By God's knowledge the depths were deepened,
   and clouds dropped down dew.

21 My children, maintain sound wisdom and right judgment,
   and don't let them out of your sight,
22 for then they'll be the life of your soul,
   jewels to grace your neck.
23 Then your journey will be secure,
   and your feet won't stumble.
24 When you sit down, you won't be afraid;
   when you lie down, your sleep will be sweet.
25 So don't fear sudden disaster
   or the ruin that comes to corrupt individuals—
26 for Our God is your insurance,
   and will keep your feet from the snare.

27 Don't refuse a kindness to those who deserve it
   when it is in your power to do it.
28 Don't say to your neighbor,
   "Go away, I will give to you tomorrow,"
   if you can give today.
29 Don't plot to harm your neighbors
   when they live peacefully next to you.
30 Don't argue with people for no reason
   when they haven't harmed you.

31 Don't emulate violent people,
   and never copy their ways;
32 for Our God detests the corrupt,
   but confides in people who love honesty.
33 God curses the household of the wicked,
   but blesses the dwellings of those who do justice;
34 God mocks those who mock others,
   but shows favor to the humble.
35 For the wise will inherit honor,
   while fools will inherit nothing but disgrace.

4·1 Listen, my children, to a parent's lesson;
    listen closely, and gain insight.
2 I offer you sound teaching—
   don't squander it.

3 Once upon a time I too was a child in my parents' home—
       a sensitive child, and the darling of my mother.
4 My parents taught me well:
       "Keep these words in your heart," they said.
   "For your life's sake don't reject our principles.
5   Don't forget them, and never wander from our words.
   Grow in discernment!
       Grow in Wisdom!
6 Don't you give up on her,
       and she will never give up on you;
   if you love her,
       she will protect you.
7 Wisdom is supreme—so acquire Wisdom!
       Even if it costs you everything, get Understanding.
8 Acclaim her and she will exalt you;
       embrace her and she will honor you.
9 She will place a wreath of grace on your head,
       and grant you a garland of glory."

10 Listen, my children, take my words to heart,
        and you will have a long life.
11 We have taught you the way of wisdom,
        led you on the path of right.
12 If you walk, your steps won't falter;
        if you run, you won't stumble.
13 Hold on to Instruction, and don't let her go;
        nurture her, for she is your life.

14 Don't set your foot on the way of evil;
        don't walk the path the wicked walk.
15 Avoid it; don't take it;
        turn away from it; pass it by.
16 For they cannot rest unless they have done wrong;
        they cannot sleep without overpowering someone.
17 Wickedness is the bread they eat,
        wickedness is their cup of wine.
18 The way of the just is like the light of dawn,
        growing brighter as the day unfolds;
19 but the way of the wicked is like the dark of night—
        they never know what makes them stumble.

²⁰ My children, learn from my wisdom,
and concentrate on what words I say;
²¹ don't let them get out of your sight,
but keep them deep in your heart.
²² They'll give you life if you live by them;
they're good for your body and soul.
²³ Most of all, watch over your heart,
because it's the wellspring of life.
²⁴ Keep abusive language far from your mouth;
keep corruption far from your lips.
²⁵ Keep your eyes focused in front of you,
and always look straight ahead.
²⁶ Be confident of the road you take,
but stay clear of precarious pathways.
²⁷ Turn neither right nor left,
and guard your feet from evil.

ભ ભ ભ

5:1 My children, pay close attention to what I say;
concentrate on my wisdom,
² so that you'll acquire good judgment and understanding,
and know what to say, and when to speak.
³ Don't be like adulterers, like people who break faith
with those who trust them:
their lips drip honey
and their words are smoother than oil,
⁴ but their end is as bitter as wormwood,
sharp as a two-edged sword.
⁵ Their feet lead them down to death,
their steps take the road to the grave;
⁶ they ignore advice on the road to life;
and they wander, lost and uncomprehending.
⁷ So hear me well, my children, and listen closely;
don't wander from the words of my mouth:
⁸ keep your distance from these people;
don't even approach the door of their house,
⁹ or you'll surrender your integrity to others,
and your reputation to the merciless;
¹⁰ for then strangers will acquire your wealth,
and your labors will enrich someone else's household.

11 All you'll have in the end are your groans
        when your body and flesh are wasted,
12 and you say, "How I hated my lessons!
        How I hated to be corrected!
13 I wouldn't listen to the voice of my teachers,
        wouldn't pay attention to my instructors.
14 Now I'm all but ruined—
        and the whole neighborhood is watching!"
15 So drink water from your own tap,
        water that runs from your own faucet.
16 And don't let your river flow into the streets,
        or let just anyone drink from your streams;
17 let them be for yourself alone,
        and not for strangers.
18 May your fountain flow freely,
        to bless both you and your beloved—
    someone who loves you,
        and fills you with joy.
    May your affection always fill you with mutual bliss;
        may you always delight in your love for each other.
20 Why be infatuated, my children,
        with people who deceive those who trust them?
        Why embrace a false-hearted lover?

21 For our ways are always in Our God's sight,
        and God watches our paths.
22 Corrupt people are trapped by their own evil deeds,
        and they're caught in the nets of their own sin.
23 They die because of too little discipline—
        and too much foolishness.

03   03   03

6·1 My children, if you have accepted liability for a neighbor's debt,
        or guaranteed a stranger's bail;
2   if you have committed yourself verbally,
        and find yourself trapped by your own words;
3   do the following, my children, to free yourself,
        for you have come under the power of your neighbor:
    go and humble yourself,
        and plead with your neighbor!

4 Give up any thought of sleep—
     there is to be no closing of your eyelids—
5 and free yourself quickly, like a gazelle from a hunter's grasp,
     like a bird from the fowler's hand.

6 Study the ant, my lazy friend!
     Learn its ways, and be wise!
7 It doesn't have a boss,
     or anyone to give orders or supervise,
8 yet it readies its storehouse in summer,
     and gathers its food in the autumn.
9 Just how long, you idler, are you going to lie there?
     When will you get up?
10 A little sleep, a short nap,
     a little folding of the arms for rest,
11 and poverty sneaks upon you like a burglar,
     and scarcity like an armed robber.

12 The violent and the wicked
     are identified by their vicious words.
13 They wink, they tap their feet as a signal,
     they beckon with their fingers;
14 they're always scheming, their hearts are filled with deceit,
     and they're continuously sowing dissension.
15 They will suffer calamity quickly;
     they will be crushed beyond hope in an instant.

16 There are six things Our God hates—
     seven that are abominable to the Most High:
17 a proud look,
     a lying tongue,
     a hand that sheds innocent blood;
18 a heart that plots wicked conspiracies,
     feet that hasten to mischief,
19 a false witness who spews out lies,
     and a person who sows discord among sister and brothers.

                         CA   CA   CA

20 My children, keep your father's commandment,
     and don't reject your mother's teaching.

21 Wrap them around your heart;
    tie them around your neck.
22 They will guide you as you walk,
    they will watch over you as you sleep,
    they will talk to you when you're awake.
23 For these commandments are a lamp,
    these teachings are a light;
correction and discipline
    are the roads to life.
24 They'll keep you from sexual licentiousness,
    from the smooth line of the seducer.
25 Don't lust in your heart after physical beauty,
    and don't even make eye contact with them—
26 for a sex worker will take you for a loaf of bread,
    but an adulterer wants your very life.
27 Can you press fire to your breast
    without igniting your clothes?
28 Can you walk on hot coals
    without burning your feet?
29 That's what infidelity is like—
    you always get yourself burned.
30 We don't despise thieves
    who steal only because they're starving,
31 yet when they're caught, they pay sevenfold,
    even if it costs them everything they own.
32 But those who commit adultery are fools,
    and are only destroying themselves.
33 They can expect a violent reaction when they get home,
    and their shame will continue to dog their heels—
34 the offended spouse will be consumed with jealousy,
    and will show no mercy when taking revenge.
35 Nothing will be able to appease the one betrayed,
    not even a multitude of gifts.

7:1 My children, treasure my words,
    and honor my teachings;
2 Value them and you will have life.
    Keep them as the apple of your eye;
3 tie them around your fingers;
    inscribe them on the tablet of your heart.

4 Say to Wisdom, "You are my sister,"
     and call Understanding your close friend—
5 they'll will keep you from sexual enticements,
     from seducers with smooth words.
6 From the window of the house,
     they look out onto the street,
7 searching among the young and stupid
     for one more foolish than the rest.
8 The idiot then comes down the street, turns the corner,
     and heads straight for the house
9 just as night is falling, at twilight—
     or maybe in the dead of night.
10 Lo and behold, the seducer comes out,
     dressed to kill, cunning and smooth;
11 then bold, then brazen,
     and itching for action—
12 now in the street, now in the square,
     lurking on every corner.
13 The seducer grabs, and kisses,
     and holds in a bold embrace, saying,
14 "I made my offering today;
     I've fulfilled my vows,
15 so I came out to be with you.
     I just looked around, and there you were!
16 I've made my bed
     with the finest Egyptian linen.
17 I have lighted the incense
     and perfumed the room.
18 Come, let us drink deeply the cup of love,
     all night long, tasting the delights of sex.
19 My spouse is away right now—
     off on a long journey, 20 with plenty of money—
   so we'll be free to play
     at least until the full moon!"
21 The seducer's seductive words are persuasive,
     and the smooth talk wins over;
22 the fool follows obediently,
     like an ox led to the slaughter,
   or like a doe caught in a snare
23   until an arrow pierces its liver,

or like a bird flying into a net
　　unaware that its life is at stake.

24 And now, my children, listen to me;
　　listen closely to what I will say.
25 Don't let your heart be seduced,
　　don't wander down that road.
26 Seduction has brought down countless victims,
　　and killed an army of fools.
27 That house on the corner is an outpost of Sheol,
　　a road leading down to the chambers of death.

ᚱ　　　ᚱ　　　ᚱ

8:1 Doesn't Wisdom call?
　　Doesn't Understanding raise her voice?
2 On the hills along the road,
　　at the crossroads, she takes her stand;
3 beside the city gates of the town,
　　in the gates themselves, she cries out,
4 "Women and men, people everywhere, I'm calling out to you!
　　I cry out to all of humankind!
5 You who are simple, learn how to make sound judgments!
　　to the foolish among you, use your common sense!
6 Listen closely, for what I say is worth hearing,
　　and I will tell you what is right;
7 for my mouth will speak the truth,
　　and my lips hate to lie.
8 Everything I say is right;
　　none of it is twisted or crooked.
9 All of it is plain-spoken to those who understand,
　　clear to those seeking knowledge.
10 Accept my lessons in place of silver,
　　and knowledge in place of gold;
11 for wisdom outsparkles jewelry;
　　anything you desire cannot compare to her.
12 I, Wisdom, am the habitat of sound judgment,
　　the source of clear thinking.
13 To revere Our God is to abhor evil.
　　I despise pride and arrogance,
　　corrupt behavior and deceptive words.

¹⁴ I have good counsel and sound judgment,
   I have understanding and power as well.
¹⁵ Rulers reign because of me,
   and administrators issue just judgments.
¹⁶ Because of me governors govern well,
   and the noble apply justice.
¹⁷ I love those who love me;
   and those who seek me out zealously find me.
¹⁸ Riches and honor are with me
   enduring wealth and prosperity.
¹⁹ The gifts I distribute are better than gold, even fine gold;
   and my profits are better than fire-tried silver.
²⁰ I walk the upright way,
   the path of justice,
²¹ bestowing wealth on those who love me,
   and filling their treasuries.

²² "Our God gave birth to me at the beginning,
   before the first acts of creation.
²³ I have been from everlasting,
   in the beginning, before the world began.
²⁴ Before the deep seas, I was brought forth,
   before there were fountains or springs of water;
²⁵ before the mountains erupted up into place,
   before the hills, I was born—
²⁶ before God created the earth or its fields,
   or even the first clods of dirt.
²⁷ I was there when the Almighty created the heavens,
   and set the horizon just above the ocean,
²⁸ set the clouds in the sky,
   and established the springs of the deep,
²⁹ gave the seas their boundaries
   and set their limits at the shoreline.
   When the foundation of the earth was laid out,
³⁰ I was the skilled artisan standing next to the Almighty.
   I was God's delight day after day,
   rejoicing at being in God's presence continually,
³¹ rejoicing in the whole world
   and delighting in humankind.

32 "And so, my daughters and sons, hear me well:
   happy are you when you keep my ways!
33 Take my instruction seriously and grow wise;
   don't neglect my lessons.
34 Happy are you who listen to me,
   and keep watch at my door for me,
   waiting at my gates.
35 For you who find me find life,
   and earn the favor of Our God;
36 but you who lose me lose your own souls,
   for all who hate me love death."

 CR   CR   CR

9:1 Wisdom has built her house;
   she has set up her seven pillars.
2 She has prepared her food, decanted her wine,
   and set her table.
3 She has sent out her household staff to call
   from a spot overlooking the city.
4 "Whoever wants enlightenment, step this way!" she says,
   inviting all who lack common sense.
5 "Come, eat my bread and drink the wine
   which I have prepared for you.
6 Abandon your foolishness that you may live,
   and walk the path of understanding!"

7 Correct the mocker and you have an enemy;
   rebuke the wrongdoer and you court injury.
8 Censure the arrogant and you engender hatred;
   but correct the wise and you will be loved.
9 Instruct the wise, and they grow in wisdom;
   teach the just and they grow in understanding.

10 Reverence for Our God is the beginning of wisdom;
   and knowledge of the Holy One is understanding.
11 For through me your days are multiplied
   and years are added to your life span.

12 If you are wise, wisdom is your reward;
    but if you are arrogant, you alone suffer.

13 Fools are noisy, undisciplined,
    and completely without knowledge.
14 They sit in the doorway of their house
    as if on a judgment seat overlooking the city,
15 and call to passers-by
    as they walk down the street:
16 "Whoever wants enlightenment, step this way!" they say,
    inviting all who lack common sense.
17 "Stolen water is sweet,
    and bread eaten in secret is delicious!"
18 But these dupes don't know that the dead are there,
    that the guests of Folly are in the valleys of Sheol.

10:1–22:16

*t*he proverbs of Solomon:

Wise children gladden the heart of their father;
    foolish children sadden the heart of their mother.

2 Treasures of ill-gotten gain earn no interest;
    but uprightness saves one from death.

3 Our God doesn't let the just go hungry,
    but foils the craving of the wicked.

4 An idle hand leads to poverty;
    the hand of the industrious leads to wealth.

5 A child who gathers in summertime is using good judgment;
    a child who sleeps during harvest is a disgrace.

6 Blessings rest on the head of the just;
    violence covers the mouth of the wicked.

7 The memory of upright people will be blessed,
    but the reputation of the wicked will rot.

8 The wise person listens carefully to instructions,
    but a babbling fool is ruined already.

9   Those who walk with character walk with security;
        those who walk the crooked paths will be found out.

10 A sly wink causes grief;
        foolish prattle brings ruin.

11 The mouth of the upright is a fountain of life;
        the mouth of the wicked masks violence.

12 Hatred stirs up strife;
        but love covers all wrongs.

13 Wisdom is found on the lips of the discerning;
        a caning stick is appropriate for the back of a fool.

14 The wise store up their knowledge;
        the mouth of the fool invites ruin.

15 Wealth is a rich person's fortress;
        poverty is a poor person's ruin.

16 The salary of the just is life;
        the earnings of the wicked are destruction.

17 Those who heed their lessons are on life's path;
        those who reject reprimand lead others astray.

18 Those who conceal their hatred are liars,
        and those who spread slander are fools.

19 Many words make for many sins;
        few words make for sound judgment.

20 The just person's tongue is refined silver,
        but the heart of the wicked carries no value.

21 The just person's lips nourish many,
        but fools die wanting wisdom.

22 The blessings which come from Our God
        bring wealth, but none of the worries.

23 Fools do their mischief just for sport;
        but the delight of the discerning is to grow in wisdom.

24 The wicked see their worst fears come to pass,
        while the upright see their greatest desires fulfilled.

25 The storm passes through, and the wicked are swept away,
    but the just stand firm forever.

26 As vinegar to the teeth, and as smoke to the eyes,
    so are lazy workers to those who employ them.

27 Reverence for Our God prolongs life,
    but the years of the wicked are cut short.

28 The hope of the just is pure joy;
    the expectation of the wicked is frustration.

29 The way of Our God is a citadel to the honest,
    but ruination to evildoers.

30 The just can never be plucked up,
    but the wicked will never take root.

31 The mouth of the just speaks words of wisdom,
    but the debauched tongue will be torn out.

32 The lips of the upright know just what to say,
    but the lips of the wicked only know profanities.

11:1 Rigged scales are loathsome to Our God,
    but accurate weights are a delight.

2 Pride is always accompanied by disgrace,
    but with humility comes wisdom.

3 The integrity of the conscientious guides them;
    the treacherous are destroyed by their own treachery.

4 Wealth will have no value on the day of wrath,
    but righteousness will deliver from death.

5 The virtue of the honest guides them on the straight path,
    but the corrupt fall by their own corruption.

6 The righteousness of the upright saves them,
    but the unfaithful are caught in their own evil desires.

7 When the wicked die, hope dies too;
    the expectation of the godless perishes.

8 The upright escape hardship—
    the corrupt get it instead.

9 The godless are able to destroy lives with their words,
    but through knowledge, the upright are able to escape.

10 If the just prosper, the community rejoices;
    when the crooked are ruined, it celebrates.

11 The community is honored by the blessings of the honest,
    and degraded by the mouth of the corrupt.

12 Only the senseless belittle their neighbors;
    discerning persons hold their tongues.

13 Gossips reveal secrets as they make their rounds;
    the trustworthy keep secrets to themselves.

14 Without guidance, the people fail,
    but when there are many counselors, there is safety.

15 One who bails out a stranger will regret it,
    and those who refuse to take IOUs will benefit.

16 A gracious person earns respect,
    a ruthless person earns money, but nothing more.

17 Kind people benefit themselves,
    while cruel people do themselves injury.

18 The wages of the wicked are a deception,
    but the earnings of the upright are the real thing.

19 Truly upright people find life,
    but evil people pursue death.

20 Those with a debauched heart are scorned by the Most High,
    but God delights in those who walk blamelessly.

21 This is a certainty: evil will be punished,
    and the upright—and their children—will go free.

22 Physical attractivness without self-control
    is like a pig with a gold ring in its snout.

23 The desire of the just results in happiness,
    but for the devious, all they hope for is in vain.

24 One person gives generously, yet grows even wealthier,
    another is stingy, yet only grows poorer.

[25] The generous person will flourish,
and the one who refreshes others will be refreshed.

[26] The one who hoards grain reaps curses from the community,
but the one who is willing to sell hears blessings.

[27] Those who seek good find goodwill;
those who seek evil find that evil comes to them.

[28] Those who trust in their riches will fall,
but the just will flourish like green leaves.

[29] Those who bring trouble to their family will inherit only wind,
and the fool will serve the wise.

[30] The fruit of justice is a tree of life,
and those who teach others to act justly are wise.

[31] If the just receive their due here on earth,
how much more the evil one, the sinner!

12·[1] Those who love discipline love knowledge;
those who hate to be corrected are stupid.

[2] The good person wins favor from Our God,
but God condemns the treacherous.

[3] Evil cannot provide anyone a firm foundation,
but nothing can uproot the upright.

[4] When your spouse is of good character,
it's like you're wearing a crown;
when your spouse brings shame to the family,
it's like a cancer in the bones.

[5] The plans of the just are honest plans,
but the schemings of the corrupt are treacherous.

[6] The words of the wicked are a fatal ambush,
but speaking the truth boldly will save you.

[7] The wicked are overthrown and cease to be,
but the household of the upright stands firm.

[8] People are commended for their good judgment,
but those with depraved minds are contemptible.

9 It is better to be a nobody and financially secure
    than to be a "somebody" who can't afford bread.

10 Those who are upright treat their animals with compassion,
    but reprobates know nothing but cruelty.

11 Work hard, and you'll always have bread;
    chase pipe-dreams, and you're a fool.

12 Even the most powerful of the corrupt will come to ruin,
    while the plantings of the just always bear fruit.

13 The depraved are ensnared by the slips of their lips;
    the just are able to save themselves from grief.

14 The faithful enjoy the fruit of their words—
    each word they speak is productive.

15 Fools rely on fools when they consult themselves;
    the wise listen to advice.

16 The foolish cannot mask their frustration;
    prudent people ignore insults.

17 Truth-tellers provide honest evidence;
    false witnesses perjure themselves.

18 Sharp words cut like a sword,
    but the tongue of the wise brings healing.

19 Lips that speak truth speak forever;
    lying lips are ephemeral.

20 The heart of the schemer is a bitter heart;
    the heart of a peacemaker beats joyfully.

21 No harm comes to the upright;
    the wicked suffer troubles galore.

22 Lying lips are loathsome to Our God;
    those who are faithful are God's delight.

23 The discreet keep their knowledge in the background;
    the fools proclaim their folly.

24 The hand of the industrious will become the boss,
    while the idle hand will always remain an employee.

²⁵ Anxious people feel the weight of the world;
a single kind word can lighten the burden.

²⁶ The upright are a guide to their neighbors,
while the path of the wicked leads people astray.

²⁷ The slothful never make their quota;
the secret of success is diligence.

²⁸ The road of justice is where one finds life:
that path leads to immortality.

13:1 A wise child listens to discipline;
the senseless child doesn't take to reprimands.

² Those who do good eat well,
but the treacherous have only an appetite for violence.

³ Those who guard their mouth keep their life,
but those who talk too much go down to destruction.

⁴ While the idler yearns for the food not there,
the diligent have more than enough.

⁵ The just abhor lies,
but the wicked slander and defame.

⁶ Justice guards those whose lifestyle is honest;
the wicked find their downfall in vice.

⁷ One person pretends to be rich, but has nothing;
another pretends to be poor, but is wealthy.

⁸ Wealth has the power to ransom lives,
but the poor see no need to worry.

⁹ The light of the just shines brightly;
the lamp of the crooked will go out.

¹⁰ Contentions are driven by too much pride;
wisdom is developed by taking advice.

¹¹ Wealth hastily accumulated is hastily depleted:
fortunes are built little by little.

¹² Hope deferred makes for a sick heart,
but a desire fulfilled is a tree of life.

13 Those who despise the word court destruction;
 those who respect the commandments will be rewarded.

14 The teachings of the wise are a fountain of life,
 whereby one can avoid the snares of death.

15 Good sense merits favor,
 but the path of the faithless is their ruin.

16 The shrewd make sound judgments;
 fools make only foolishness.

17 A treacherous messenger creates havoc,
 but a faithful ambassador is a healer.

18 Poverty and disgrace are bred by rejecting discipline,
 but those who accept reprimands are honored.

19 Desire fulfilled is sweetness to the soul;
 fools who don't turn from evil find only frustration.

20 To walk with the wise is a wise thing to do;
 to accompany a fool is utter foolishness.

21 Misfortune dogs the heels of the sinner,
 but good fortune follows the upright.

22 Good parents leave an inheritance to their grandchildren,
 but the sinner's wealth eventually falls to the upright.

23 Even the fields of poor people can yield rich harvests—
 but then injustice snatches it away from them.

24 If you don't give correction, you hate your child;
 loving parents give their children structure and discipline.

25 The righteous eat to their heart's content,
 while the belly of the wicked goes empty.

14:1 Wisdom builds a household;
 folly tears it down brick by brick.

2 Those who walk conscientiously fear Our God,
 but those whose deeds are devious despise God.

3 The talk of fools bring them punishment,
 but the words of the wise bring them protection.

4 There is no grain where there are no oxen:
   it is their strength and labor that makes an abundant harvest.

5 A faithful witness does not lie;
   a false witness lives and breathes deceit.

6 Those who mock and jeer seek wisdom in vain,
   but knowledge comes easily to the understanding.

7 Avoid the fool or face peril;
   a void of knowledge inhabits that space.

8 The prudent are wise because they can discern the way;
   the folly of fools comes from delusion.

9 Fools jeer at the idea of making amends for wrongs,
   but the upright have a willing heart.

10 The heart suffers its own grief alone,
   neither can a stranger share its joy.

11 The household of the treacherous is doomed,
   but the tent of the honest will flourish.

12 There is a way which seems right to some,
   but its end is death.

13 Even when laughing the heart can be sad;
   joy can walk hand-in-hand with sorrow.

14 Deviates are rewarded with the fruit of their own ways,
   and the good with their worthy works.

15 The simple believe anything they're told;
   those of sound judgment weigh everything carefully.

16 Caution in the wise turns them away from evil;
   the fool sheds restraint and cares little.

17 Quick-tempered people do foolish things,
   though prudence is rarely valued.

18 The simple get folly as their inheritance;
   those of sound judgment are crowned with knowledge.

19 Evildoers will pay homage to those who do good,
   and corruption will bow down at the gates of justice.

20 The poor are detested even by their neighbors;
   the wealthy have friends to spare.

21 If you despise your neighbor, you sin;
   if you are kind to the needy, you'll be blessed.

22 Don't those who plot evil go astray?
   Thos who plan good reap kindness and loyalty.

23 When you work, you profit;
   when you talk, you lose.

24 The diadem of the wise is their wisdom.
   Folly is the garland of the fool.

25 The truthful witness saves a life;
   the liar betrays.

26 To revere Our God is to find a stronghold:
   as God's children we find a refuge.

27 Reverence for Our God is a life-giving spring
   which protects from the snares of death.

28 Rulers glory in the number of their people:
   without masses under their control, they're nothing.

29 Patient people demonstrate great understanding;
   a quick temper is the mark of a fool.

30 A peaceful heart gives life to the flesh,
   but envy rots the bones.

31 Those who oppress the poor blaspheme their Creator;
   to show kindness to the needy is to worship Our God.

32 The wicked are overthrown by their depravity;
   the just find refuge in their integrity.

33 Wisdom dwells in the hearts of the discerning;
   she cannot be found in fools' hearts.

34 Justice exalts a nation;
   inequity disgraces a whole people.

35 A wise employee enjoys the boss's favor,
   while worthless workers earn nothing but disrespect.

15:1 A mild reply deflects anger,
　　　but a harsh word stirs it up.

2　The tongue of the wise uses knowledge properly;
　　　the mouth of the fool vomits drivel.

3　The eyes of Our God are everywhere,
　　　watching both the wicked and the good.

4　The healing word is a tree of life;
　　　a deceitful tongue crushes the spirit.

5　Fools despise their parent's counsels,
　　　but those who follow guidance show sound judgment.

6　There are many treasures in the household of the just,
　　　but the income of the corrupt brings trouble.

7　The lips of the wise spread knowledge—
　　　unlike the hearts of fools.

8　Our God hates the offerings and sacrifices of the corrupt,
　　　but delights in even the humble prayers of the upright.

9　The path of the wicked is loathsome to Our God,
　　　but God loves those whose quest is justice.

10　Severe discipline awaits those who stray from the path,
　　　and those who reject punishment will die.

11　Sheol and Perdition lie open before the Almighty—
　　　how much more the hearts of humankind!

12　Cynics don't take to reprimand,
　　　so they avoid the wise.

13　A glad heart makes a happy face,
　　　but a sad heart breaks the spirit.

14　The discerning mind seeks insight,
　　　but the foolish mind feeds on folly.

15　All the days of the afflicted are sorrowful,
　　　but a joyful heart has a continual feast.

16　It is better to have little, yet with reverence for God,
　　　than to have great wealth, and great turmoil.

¹⁷ It is better to eat a plate of greens served with love
   than prime beef served with hatred.

¹⁸ The hot-headed person stirs up trouble;
   an even-tempered person soothes ruffled feathers.

¹⁹ The way of the goldbrick is strewn with potholes;
   the way of the conscientious is a smooth ride.

²⁰ Wise people have happy parents;
   foolish people despise mother and father.

²¹ Foolish pleasures are distractions to the fool,
   but the insightful person keeps a straight course.

²² Plans without advisors lead to trouble;
   more counsel brings more success.

²³ Apt replies bring joy everywhere—
   how good a word said in due season!

²⁴ The path of the wise leads up to life,
   that they may avoid "grave" consequences.

²⁵ The Most High dismantles the proud household,
   but saves the livelihood of widows and widowers.

²⁶ The schemes of the corrupt are revolting to the Most High,
   but the words of the pure please Our God.

²⁷ The greedy bring ruin upon their own households,
   but those who shun bribery will live.

²⁸ The prudent heart reflects on how to answer;
   the unthinking mouth pours out evil.

²⁹ God stands far from the wicked,
   but hears the prayers of the upright.

³⁰ A light in the eyes rejoices the heart,
   and good news brings health to the bones.

³¹ Those whose accept a loving correction
   will dwell with the wise.

³² Those who reject discipline hate themselves;
   those who accept corrections gain understanding.

³³ To revere Our God is a lesson in wisdom;
   humility precedes honor.

16:1 The plans of your heart are your own,
   but Our God decides the outcome.

² We may think our actions are innocent,
   but Our God weighs our motives.

³ Commit everything you do to Our God,
   and your plans will succeed.

⁴ Everything has its purpose in God's mind,
   even the vile for that day of destruction.

⁵ The arrogant are loathsome to Our God;
   know that they will not go unpunished.

⁶ Love and faithfulness atone for sin;
   reverence for Our God helps us avoid evil.

⁷ When our actions please the Almighty,
   Our God brings even our enemies to the peace table.

⁸ Better less with virtue,
   than injustice with more.

⁹ We plan;
   God directs.

¹⁰ The words of rulers are as powerful as oracles—
   and so their mouths must never betray justice.

¹¹ Our God controls the balances and scales,
   and made all the weights in the bag.

¹² Rulers are detestable when they do wrong,
   for their throne is established through justice.

¹³ Honest words should delight rulers—
   those who speak the truth are invaluable.

¹⁴ A ruler's wrath portends destruction;
   the wise step in to appease and pacify.

¹⁵ When a ruler's face brightens, it means life;
   the ruler's favors are clouds that bring rain to a parched land.

16 Better to have wisdom than gold,
   better discernment than silver.

17 The path of the just turns away from evil;
   those who watch where they go guard their lives.

18 Pride precedes Perdition,
   and a haughty spirit goes before a fall.

19 The best are humble among the meek;
   the worst share their booty with the proud.

20 To listen to the word is to prosper;
   to trust in Our God is to find happiness.

21 The wise of heart are called the most discerning;
   pleasant speakers are deemed the most persuasive.

22 Wisdom is the fountain of life to those who have it,
   while folly is a source of punisment to fools.

23 Enlightened speech flows from the wise mind,
   and makes words the more persuasive.

24 Pleasant words are like the honeycomb:
   sweet for the soul and healthy for the body.

25 People think they have the right road,
   but it's a road that leads to death.

26 It's a worker's appetite that does all the work!
   Hunger is a powerful motivator.

27 When worthless people plot evil,
   their words are scorching fires.

28 Troublemakers spread dissension,
   and gossips divide friends.

29 When the violent tempt their neighbors,
   they lead them down a dead-end street.

30 Beware of trickery from the eye-winker
   and mischief from those with pursed lips.

31 Gray hairs are crowns of glory
   gained through an honest life.

³² Better to be slow to anger than to do great exploits;
    better to be self-controlled than a conquering hero.

³³ You may roll the dice,
    but God decides the outcome.

17:1 Better a crust of bread in peace
    than a great feast with friction.

² When the child of the boss is worthless,
    the canny employee gets the job instead—
    and inherits the company just like a family member.

³ The crucible for silver, the furnace for gold,
    and Our God for testing hearts.

⁴ Evildoers listen to wicked lips,
    and liars rely on slanderous tongues.

⁵ Mockers of the poor insult the Creator;
    those who celebrate calamity will not go unpunished.

⁶ Grandchildren are the laurels of the elderly;
    children are the glory of their parents.

⁷ Eloquence from a fool? Absurd!
    Lies from a ruler? Obscene.

⁸ Bribes work like magic—
    they bring the giver success at every turn.

⁹ Forgive a friend's offence, and you foster love;
    but bring it up again, and you ruin the friendship.

¹⁰ A reprimand makes a deeper impression on a sensible person
    than a hundred blows on a fool.

¹¹ The wicked know nothing but their own rebellion—
    so a Messenger will visit them without mercy.

¹² Better to encounter a bear robbed of her cubs
    than the foolish in their folly.

¹³ When people return evil for good,
    evil doesn't leave their household.

¹⁴ Starting an argument is like opening the floodgates:
    shut it down before the quarrel gets out of hand.

15 Acquitting the guilty or condemning the innocent—
　　both are detestable to Our God.

16 Why give fools the means to buy wisdom,
　　when they don't even want it?*

17 Friends love you like a sister or brother—
　　they are born to give support during adversity.

18 Only fools guarantee others' loans
　　or accept responsibility for a neighbor's debts.

19 Those who love to argue love sin;
　　those who are haughty court destruction.

20 The deceitful don't find happiness;
　　the double-dealing tongue invites hardships.

21 To have a fool for a child brings nothing but grief;
　　there is no joy for parents whose children hate wisdom.

22 Glad hearts are good medicine,
　　but depressed spirits dry up the bones.

23 The evil accept bribes under cover
　　to pervert the course of justice.

24 Discerning people set their face toward wisdom,
　　but fools look to the ends of the earth and find nothing.

25 Foolish children are a grief to their fathers,
　　and bitterness to their mothers.

26 Punishing the innocent is bad,
　　but so is attacking an official just for telling the truth.

27 Those with intelligence know restraint,
　　and those with discernment keep tempers cool.

28 When fools hold their tongue, they can pass for wise;
　　when they shut their mouths, they can pass for clever.

18:1 Solitary people follow their own counsel;
　　they get upset with unsolicited advice.

---

* Or, in Mark Twain's words, "Never try to teach a pig to sing: it's a waste of time, and it annoys the pig."

2   Fools don't want to learn anything from others;
      they only want to hear their own opinions.

3   With wickedness comes contempt too,
      and with dishonor comes disgrace.

4   The words of one's mouth are deep waters—
      they can be a fountain of wisdom, or a dangerous flash flood.

5   It isn't good to show partiality to the corrupt,
      or to deprive the oppressed of justice.

6   The lips of fools court strife,
      and their mouths invite a caning.

7   The mouths of fools are their ruin,
      and their lips are traps for their lives.

8   The words of a gossip are tasty morsels—
      they slip right down into one's soul.

9   Those who are lazy in their work
      are little better than those who destroy.

10   The Name of Our God is a strong tower;
       the upright rush to it for security.

11   For the rich, wealth is a fortified city,
       or an unscalable wall—or so they think.

12   Prior to hardship a heart may be proud,
       but honor comes only after one has been humbled.

13   Give an answer before really hearing the question,
       and you'll suffer folly and shame.

14   A person may endure bad health,
       but who can bear a broken spirit?

15   A discerning heart always seeks to understand more,
       and the ears of the wise search for knowledge.

16   A gift can open all sorts of doors for you,
       even giving you access to powerful people.

17   The case that is stated first makes a lot of sense—
       until the second comes along.

18 The flip of a coin ends many a dispute,
   and keeps arguments from coming to blows.

19 Offended family members are an impregnable fortress;
   their contentions are like bars on a window.

20 It is the fruit of our mouth that fills our stomach;
   it is the yield of our lips that satisfies us.

21 Our tongue has the keys of both death and life,
   and we eat the fruit of everything we say.

22 Find a loving spouse and you find a treasure—
   and blessings from Almighty God.

23 The poor make their pleas softly;
   the rich shout their refusals.

24 There are companions who bring one to ruin,
   and there are friends who are closer than family.

19:1 Better to be poor and honest,
   than to be foolish and duplicitous.

2 Zeal without forethought isn't good;
   act too quickly and you'll lose your way.

3 People are ruined by their own foolishness,
   yet they shake their fists at God.

4 Become wealthy, and you make many new friends;
   become poor, and you lose the friends you have.

5 False witnesses will not go unpunished,
   and liars will never go free.

6 Powerful people attract sycophants—
   if you have something to give, everyone's your friend.

7 When you run out of money,
   even your family abandons you.
   Looking for reasons?
   Like your friends, they're nowhere to be found.

8 Those who find Wisdom nurture their own souls;
   and those who cherish Understanding find prosperity as well.

⁹ False witnesses will not go unpunished,
    and liars will meet their end.

¹⁰ For a fool to live in the lap of luxury
    is as unseemly as a laborer giving orders to the boss.

¹¹ Common sense makes a person slow to anger;
    it redounds to one's honor to overlook an offense.

¹² The ruler's wrath is like the roar of a lion;
    the ruler's favor is like dew on the grass.

¹³ Foolish children
    are the ruin of their parents.

A nagging spouse
    is like a dripping faucet.

¹⁴ Property and wealth may be inherited from parents,
    but a discerning spouse comes straight from God.

¹⁵ When laziness lulls one into drowsiness,
    hunger is not far behind.

¹⁶ Those who keep the commandments keep their soul,
    but those who despise the word are dead already.

¹⁷ Those who are kind to the poor are making loans to God,
    and God will repay them for their goodness.

¹⁸ Discipline your children while there is still hope;
    if you don't, you'll be a willing participant in their deaths.

¹⁹ Violent people need the stiffest sentences;
    let them off easy, and they'll be up for trial again in no time.

²⁰ Listen to advice and accept correction,
    and you'll be wise as time goes on.

²¹ We can plan anything we want in our hearts,
    but God's plan is the one that prevails.

²² Ambition is a valuable thing,
    but it is better to be poor than to be a liar.

²³ Reverence for Our God gives us life—
    we rest content, and evil doesn't touch us.

24 Some people are so lazy that they'll reach out for food
    but won't bring the fork back to their mouths!

25 Punish the arrogant, and the simple learn by example;
    reprimand the understanding, and they learn directly.

26 Those who evict their fathers and abandon their mothers
    are shameless and depraved children.

27 If you stop taking instructions, my child,
    you will stray from the words of knowledge.

28 Corrupt witnesses mock justice;
    the wicked gets drunk on inequity.

29 Penalties were designed for scoffers,
    and punishments for fools.

20:1 Wine mocks, liquor brawls,
    and those deceived by them are fools.

2 The wrath of rulers is like the roaring of a lion:
    those who provoke them seek a short life.

3 Honorable people are careful to avoid strife,
    but all fools are quick to argue.

4 It's plowing season, but sluggards would rather nap;
    no wonder they find no harvest!

5 The intentions of the heart are like deep waters,
    but the discerning are able to draw them out.

6 Many call themselves kind people—
    but when their faithfulness is needed, where are they?

7 Parents who love justice and whose walk is blameless
    endow their children with great happiness.

8 The ruler who sits on a throne of justice
    can scatter the corrupt with a glance.

9 Who can say, "I have made my heart pure,
    I am clean, I am sinless?"

10 One standard for some, a different standard for others—
    God hates dishonesty and double-dealing.

11 Even children at play demonstrate who they really are,
    by whether their conduct is honest and just.

12 The ear that hears and the eye that sees—
    Our God has made them both.

13 The quickest route to poverty is sleeping too much;
    keeping awake brings in plenty of food.

14 "Poor quality, poor quality!" the buyers wail—
    then they go off and boast about the bargain they got!

15 Perhaps you have gold, perhaps you have rubies,
    but the truly priceless jewels are wise lips.

16 When someone co-signs the loan of a stranger,
    or vouches for someone immoral, demand collateral!

17 Bread tastes sweet when gained through fraud,
    but you end up with a mouthful of sand.

18 Plans succeed when made with counsel—
    use wise guidance when much is at stake.

19 Gossipers who tell you other people's secrets
    will tell others your secrets as well—so beware!

20 Curse mother or father, and your lamp will be extinguished,
    and you will be plunged into deepest darkness.

21 Acquire property in haste,
    and suffer buyer's remorse.

22 Don't say, "I'll get you back for this wrong!"—
    wait for Our God to make it right.

23 One weight for friends, a different one for strangers—
    Our God detests dishonest scales!

24 It is God who guides our steps.
    How can we know the road by ourselves?

25 We're trapped when we rashly make a pledge
    and think about the cost only afterwards.

26 A wise ruler separates out the corrupt
    by making their own corruption recoil upon them.

²⁷ The lamp of Our God is the human spirit:
  it searches one's innermost parts.

²⁸ Kindness and loyalty stand guard over rulers
  when their judgment seats are anchored in justice.

²⁹ The glory of young people is their energy;
  the beauty of elders is their gray hair.

³⁰ The blows and wounds we get in life are good medicine;
  our calamities cleanse our very soul.

21:1 The ruler's heart is a stream of water in God's hand—
  who directs it at will.

² The doings of people are justified to themselves,
  but it is the Almighty who weighs the heart.

³ Doing what is right and being just
  please Our God more than sacrifice.

⁴ The lamp of the wicked—
  haughty eyes and proud hearts—is sinful.

⁵ The plans of the diligent eventuate in abundance;
  but those in haste create only want.

⁶ To acquire wealth through a lying tongue
  is a deadly chase of vanity.

⁷ The wicked are dragged away by their own violence
  and their refusal to do what is right.

⁸ The path of the corrupt is as filled with deceit
  as the conduct of the innocent is upright.

⁹ It is better to live in a corner of the attic
  than to dwell in a mansion with a belligerent spouse.

¹⁰ The souls of the wicked thrive on evil;
  their neighbors find no pity in their eyes.

¹¹ When the arrogant are punished, the simple are the wiser;
  the wise are enlightened as they acquire knowledge.

¹² The Just One studies the household of the devious
  and brings it down to the ground.

13 Those who refuse to hear the plea of the oppressed
   will themselves cry out and be ignored.

14 A gift given secretly allays anger,
   and a covert bribe pacifies great wrath.

15 When justice is done, the upright are overjoyed
   and the wicked are terrified.

16 Those who stray from the way of discernment
   will dwell in the gathering of the dead.

17 Lovers of pleasure will always be poor;
   those who love the fast lane leave their wealth there.

18 For there to be good people in the world, there have to be bad;
   for the upright to exist, there have to be deceivers.

19 It is better to live in a desert
   than to share a roof with a stubborn and irritable spouse.

20 Wise people keep a surplus of food and supplies,
   but fools devour everything they own.

21 Those who seek out virtue and kindness
   will gain life, prosperity, and honor as well.

22 One person with wisdom can storm a mighty citadel,
   and bring down the establishment they had so relied upon.

23 When we control our mouth and our tongue
   we keep ourselves out of trouble.

24 The proud and arrogant, the mockers,
   are always the ones with the least reason to mock.

25 Lazy people die craving for things that never come—
   and all because their hands refuse to work.

26 The corrupt spend the day wanting more, more, more,
   but the upright, freely and generously.

27 God hates the sacrifices that the wicked offer,
   particularly when they have evil motives.

28 The false witness will be lost to memory,
   but the testimony of the obedient will speak forever.

²⁹ The wicked wear their confidence outwardly;
the upright turn inward, and carefully choose their actions.

³⁰ There is no wisdom, no discernment, no advice,
that can prevail against Our God.

³¹ The horse stands ready for the day of conflict,
but success comes from the Most High.

22:1 A good name is better than great wealth,
the esteem of others, than gold and silver.

² The wealthy and the poor share a common bond:
Our God is the creator of us all.

³ The judicious foresee danger and take necessary measures;
the naive carry on and suffer the consequences.

⁴ The reward for humility and reverence for Our God
brings wealth, respect, and long life.

⁵ Snares and thorns lie in the path of the depraved,
but those who value their life avoid them.

⁶ Develop a child to its full potential,
and that training will last a lifetime.

⁷ The rich rule over the needy,
and the borrower serves the lender.

⁸ Calamity is the fruit of iniquity;
the reign of terror self-destructs.

⁹ A blessing comes to the generous
when they give of their bounty to the poor.

¹⁰ Drive out the contemptible and strife goes with them;
abuse and discord go too.

¹¹ Those who value loving hearts and nurturing words
will have powerful people as friends.

¹² The eyes of the Almighty mind all knowledge;
but God frustrates the words of the faithless.

¹³ The idler says, "I can't work today—there's a lion outside!"
or "I'll be killed in the streets!"

¹⁴ The mouth of the debauched is a deep pit;
   those with whom the Most High is angry will fall into it.

¹⁵ Folly is part of being a child;
   judicious discipline drives it away.

¹⁶ Those who oppress the poor to enrich themselves
   will end up as paupers, oppressed by those even richer.

22:17–24:22

Sayings of the Sages:

Hear my words
   and apply your heart to my teachings.
¹⁸ It will do you good you to hide them in your heart
   and have them ready on your lips.
¹⁹ Today I'm going to teach you—yes, you—
   so that you'll have complete trust in Our God.
²⁰ Haven't I already written thirty sayings
   of counsel and knowledge,
²¹ to teach you what is right and what is true,
   so you can give apt replies to those who question you?

²² Don't cheat the poor or take advantage of their poverty,
   or intimidate the needy in court.
²³ For Our God will defend their cause,
   oppressing those who oppress them.

²⁴ Don't befriend those with a short-fused temper,
   or become associates of angry people,
²⁵ lest you learn their ways
   and become caught up in a trap.

²⁶ Don't co-sign loans for others,
   or put up security for others' debts;
²⁷ for if you fall behind in payments
   you will lose even your bed!

²⁸ Never remove the ancient boundary stone
which your ancestors put in place.

²⁹ Have you ever met people
who are at the top of their craft?
They'll soon be working for the powerful and prominent,
and will never be found in a dead-end job.

23:1 When you sit down to eat at a lavish spread,
take special note of the food that you're offered:
² put a knife to your throat
if you are inclined to gluttony,
³ and don't crave their delicacies—
or you'll pay for it with indigestion!

⁴ Work hard, but not to be rich;
forgo thinking about it.
⁵ Wealth is illusory;
all of a sudden it has wings,
soaring as eagles up to the heavens.

⁶ Don't break bread with the stingy,
and don't crave their delicacies;
⁷ they're always thinking about
how much you're costing them!
"Eat and drink," they tell you,
but it's not in their hearts.
⁸ The tension will make you sick to your stomach,
and all your compliments will have been wasted.

⁹ Don't waste words on fools;
for they can't savor your wisdom.

¹⁰ Don't remove the ancient boundary stone
or usurp the fields of orphans,
¹¹ for their Redeemer is all-powerful
and will come to their defense.

¹² Accept instruction with all your heart;
lend your ears to words of knowledge.

¹³ Don't go lightly when disciplining children;
they won't die from a spanking.
¹⁴ If you give children firm discipline,
you save them from Sheol.

¹⁵ My child, if your heart is wise,
    my own heart will jump with joy;
¹⁶ my own soul will rejoice
    when your lips say what is right.

¹⁷ Don't open your heart to envy of those who sin,
    but be constant in reverence for Our God—
¹⁸ for you are part of what is to come,
    and your hope will not be cut off.

¹⁹ Listen closely, my children, and practice wisdom,
    and keep your heart on the right path.
²⁰ Don't spend your time with drinkers,
    nor with those who overindulge regularly.
²¹ For drunks and gluttons end up poor,
    and torpor dresses them in rags.

²² Listen to the father who begot you,
    and don't despise your mother when she is old.

²³ Once you have bought truth, never sell it,
    and hold tight to wisdom, and discipline, and discernment.

²⁴ The parents of the upright are happy indeed;
    they rejoice in having wise children.
²⁵ May you be the joy of your father,
    the gladness of her who bore you!

²⁶ My children, give me your hearts,
    and keep focused on my advice:
²⁷ sexual immorality is a bottomless pit,
    and adultery is a narrow well.
²⁸ Lust lurks in the shadows like a robber,
    and its victims are manifold.

²⁹ Who has troubles? Who has sorrows?
    Who has problems? Who is anxious?
    Who gets into fights? Whose eyes are bloodshot?
³⁰ Those who spend too much time with their liquor;
    who don't discriminate about what they drink.
³¹ Don't linger over the bouquet of the wine,
    or its sparkle, or its smoothness—
³² in the end it will bite like a snake
    and poison like an adder.

³³ You'll see strange things;
    your speech will be slurred;
³⁴ the room will spin like you're on a boat,
    and you'll be seasick and holding on for dear life.
³⁵ "They hit me," you'll say, "but it doesn't hurt."
    "They beat me, but I don't feel anything.
    When will I wake up?
        Maybe after another drink!"

24¹Don't envy the corrupt,
        don't even go near them—
² for their minds thrive on violence,
    and their lips talk trouble.

³ A household is built on wisdom;
    it is grounded on discernment.
⁴ Through learning its rooms are filled
    with riches: insight, ability, enlightenment.

⁵ The wise are more powerful than the strong;
    brains are better than brawn.
⁶ Battles are won through careful planning,
    and victory needs a multitude of counselors.

⁷ Wisdom is too delicate for a fool to appreciate;
    when weighty matters are discussed, it's best to keep quiet.

⁸ A person who plans evil even once
    will always be considered a schemer.
⁹ For plotting and folly are sin,
    and everyone hates the arrogant.

¹⁰ If you quake at the first sign of adversity,
    your strength is small indeed.

¹¹ Rescue the innocent who is about to be murdered,
    and hold back the members of a lynch mob.
¹² Maybe you'll say, "But we didn't know what they were doing!"
    Ah, but doesn't the One who weighs hearts see the truth?
    Doesn't the One who guards your life know what happened?
        Won't every soul get precisely what it deserves?

¹³ My children, you eat honey for its taste;
    you catch the drips of the honeycomb for its sweetness;

¹⁴ so too will be the knowledge of wisdom to your soul—
>> find it and only then will you have a future,
>> and your hope will be eternal.

¹⁵ Don't ambush the household of the upright like a burglar,
>> don't ravage their dwellings;

¹⁶ for the just fall seven times and come back,
>> but the corrupt are overwhelmed when calamity falls.

¹⁷ Don't celebrate when your foes collapse,
>> and don't let your heart leap when they stumble;

¹⁸ for Our God will be upset if you do,
>> and will restore good fortune to your enemy!

¹⁹ Don't let the corrupt provoke you,
>> do not be envious of the wicked:

²⁰ for they have no future,
>> and their lamps are to be extinguished.

²¹ Revere Our God, my children, and respect the government—
>> and don't throw your lot in with rebels!

²² For both may react without warning, destroying their enemies,
>> and who knows who might get caught in the crossfire?

24:23-34

More sayings of the wise:

>> Showing partiality in judgment is bad.

²⁴ Those who say to the guilty, "You are innocent,"
>> will be cursed by the people and abhorred by nations;

²⁵ but those who punish the treacherous will savor satisfaction,
>> and rich blessings will come to them.

²⁶ Those who give an honest reply
>> place a kiss on the lips.

²⁷ Prepare your fields and plant your crops,
>> and complete all the outdoor work first.
>> Only then should you build your house!

²⁸ Don't be frivolous about testifying against your neighbor,
>> and never deceive with your lips.

29 Never say, "I'll pay them back for what they did to me;
  I'll repay them for their deeds!"

30 I passed by the field of an idler,
  by the vineyard of a foolish farmer—
31 the land was overgrown with brambles,
  there were weeds everywhere,
  and its stone wall was falling down.
32 I mused as I gazed at it,
  and something I saw taught me this lesson:
33 "A little sleep, a little nap,
  a folding of the arms at rest,
34 and poverty will sneak upon you like a burglar,
  and deprivation like an armed bandit."

25:1–29:27

MORE proverbs of Solomon, as transcribed by Hezekiah, ruler of Judah:

2 It redounds to God's glory to keep some things concealed;
  rulers glory in searching things out.

3 Just as the heavens are high and the earth is deep,
  so too is the heart of the ruler unfathomable.

4 Refine the impurities from silver,
  and it comes out malleable for the smith;
5 remove corruption from a government,
  and justice will keep it securely established.

6 Don't try to act grand in the presence of the powerful,
  or grab the place of honor at a table—
7 it's better to be told, "Come sit up here,"
  than to be put down in front of someone important.

8 Don't reveal too quickly what your eyes have seen
  when up against an opponent in court—
you may need to use that trump card later
  when your neighbor presents damaging evidence!

9 When quarrelling with a neighbor,
   never disclose another's secret;
10 or someone, upon learning it, will reprimand you,
   to the loss of your reputation.

11 Words spoken at just the right time
   are like golden apples in a silver setting.

12 A wise admonition to an attentive ear
   is like gold ring or a gold brooch.

13 Like a cool snowfall during the heat of harvest
   are trustworthy messengers to those who send them:
   their faithful service refreshes the spirit.

14 Those who pledge a generous donation but then default
   are like clouds and wind with no rain following.

15 Patient persuasion can bring great change;
   soft words can even break bones.

16 When you find honey, eat only enough to sate;
   too much, and you'll get sick to your stomach.
17 Don't spend all your time at your neighbor's house;
   too much, and your friend will get sick of you!

18 Those who give false testimony about their neighbors
   wound them like war clubs, swords and arrows.

19 Trusting in a fickle person in times of trouble
   is like having an toothache or a sprained ankle.

20 Trying to spread cheer when a friend is depressed
   is like stealing someone's coat in winter
   or basting a wound with vinegar.

21 When your foes are hungry, feed them;
   when they are thirsty, give them water to drink.
22 In this way you heap live coals on their heads,
   and Our God will reward you.

23 As sure as the north wind produces rain,
   a back-biting tongue produces an angry face.

24 It is better to live in a corner of the attic
   than to dwell in a mansion with a belligerent spouse.

25 Good news from a distant country
is like cool water to one faint with thirst.

26 An upright person who is weak-willed before the corrupt
is like a muddied stream or a polluted fountain.

27 Eating too much honey is sickening.
So are people who seek honor for themselves.

28 A desolate city without walls
is like a person lacking self-control.

26:1 Like snow in summertime or rain during harvest time,
honoring a fool is out of place.

2 An undeserved curse never alights,
like a wandering sparrow, or a swallow in flight.

3 Riding crops for horses, bridles for donkeys,
and canes for the backs of fools.

4 Responding in kind to someone's foolishness
just makes you sink to their level.

5 But responding in kind to someone's foolishness
also lets you show them just how foolish they're being.

6 Using a fool as a messenger
is like cutting off your own feet or drinking poison.

7 To a fool, proverbs are about as useful
as wings on a flightless bird.

8 Giving honor to a fool
is like shooting oneself in the foot.

9 As a thorn pierces the hand of a drunk,
so also is a proverb on the mouth of a fool.

10 The one who hires a fool or a stranger
is like a sniper shooting at random.

11 Fools always repeat their folly
just as dogs always return to their vomit.

12 Do you know people who consider themselves wise?
There is more hope for fools than for them!

13 The idler shouts, "I cant work, there's a lion in the street!
There's a roaring lion outside!"

14 Like a door turning on its hinges,
    an idler turns over in bed.

15 The idler reaches for the platter of food,
    but is too lazy to eat it.
16 It is more likely that you'll hear, "I am wise!" from an idler
    than from seven people who can answer with discretion.

17 Those who meddle in other people's quarrels
    are like those who pick up a dog by the ears.

18 Like a child throwing rocks
    without thinking where they might land
19 is person who deceives a neighbor
    only to say, "Just kidding!"

20 No fuel, no fire;
    no gossip, no quarrels.

21 What bellows are to live coals and wood to fire,
    busybodies are to kindling discord.

22 Words of a gossip are like tasty hors d'oeuvres:
    they end up in the bowels of the body.

23 Smooth lips concealing a wicked heart
    are like a silver coating over a cheap clay pot.

24 Haters dissemble with their lips,
    with treachery just below the surface;
25 don't trust their smooth speech,
    for their hearts hide a sevenfold abomination.
26 They may disguise their guile with smiles,
    but their duplicity will be exposed before the congregation.

27 Those who create pitfalls will fall into their own pits.
    Those who start avalanches will be crushed under the rubble.

28 When you lie to someone, you're really crushing them;
    when you flatter someone, you ruin them.

27:1 Don't boast about tomorrow—
    you don't know what tomorrow will bring.

2 Let others praise you, not your own mouth—
    strangers, not your own lips.

3 Stones are heavy, sand is weighty;
   a fool's rage is heavier than both.

4 Anger is fierce as a fire, wrath relentless as a flood—
   but jealousy is something that no one can withstand.

5 An open reprimand is better
   than unexpressed love.

6 The wounds of a friend are trustworthy,
   and the kisses of an enemy are deceitful.

7 Fresh honey has no appeal for the sated,
   but even the bitter tastes sweet to the hungry.

8 Birds wander from their nest;
   we wander from our roots.

9 Perfume and incense gladden the spirit;
   so does heartfelt counsel from a friend.

10 Don't forget your friends, or those of your parents,
   and when disaster strikes, don't run to a relative:
   close friends are preferable to distant kin.

11 Be wise, my children, and gladden my heart—
   then I'll have a retort for those who mock me!

12 The thoughtful see danger and steer clear;
   the naive keep on walking, and suffer.

13 When someone cosigns the loan of a stranger,
   or vouches for someone immoral, demand collateral!

14 Bless someone in a loud voice early in the morning
   and they'll think you've cursed them!

15 What's the difference between a contentious spouse
   and a drip, drip, drip on a rainy day?
   Nothing!

16 Restraining your mate is like restraining the wind,
   or holding oil in your hand.

17 Iron sharpens iron,
   and friends sharpen friends.

18 Those who tend the fig tree will eat its fruit;
   workers who look after their employers will be honored.

19 Just as water reflects one's face,
   the heart reflects one's true self.

20 Like Sheol and the Abyss, always hungry,
   our eyes are never satisfied with they have.

21 The crucible tests silver; the furnace tests gold;
   praise tests the person.

22 Even pounding the foolish with mortar and pestle
   won't separate them from their folly.

23 Pay attention to your herds
   and tend your flocks—
24 for wealth, like political power,
   is fleeting indeed!
25 After the grass has died and the new growth appears,
   after the mountain meadows have yielded their harvest,
26 your lambs will still provide you with clothing,
   and your goats will bring you the price of a field;
27 the goats will provide enough milk for you,
   your household, and all of your workers.

28:1 The wicked flee even when no one pursues them;
   the upright are bold as lions.

2 When a nation transgresses, many vie for leadership;
   when the leadership is judicious, things are stable.

3 A poor person who oppresses those even poorer
   is like a downpour that washes away the crop.

4 People who abandon the law are always praising the corrupt;
   people who keep the law are always challenging them.

5 The evil don't understand justice;
   those who seek Our God know it thoroughly.

6 It is better to be poor and walk with integrity
   than to be wealthy and depraved.

7 The lawful are wise children;
   friends of the debauched dishonor their parents.

8   Those who grow rich on high interest and extortion
        accumulate it for another who will donate it to the needy.

9   If we close our ears from hearing the Law,
        even our worship is abominable.

10 Those who lead the upright down an evil road
        will fall headlong into their own pit;
        the innocent, however, will prosper.

11 The wealthy are wise in their own eyes;
        but the poor are perceptive, and can see right through them.

12 When the upright triumph, there is great joy;
        when the corrupt gain ascendancy, people hide.

13 Those who conceal their sins never prosper;
        those who confess and forsake them find mercy.

14 Those who are always reverent are blessed,
        but the hard of heart receive hardship.

15 Like a roaring lion or a voracious bear
        is a corrupt ruler of a poor people.

16 A leader who acts like a tyrant lacks good judgment.
        A leader who refuses ill-gotten gains will live a long life.

17 Those who have blood on their hands
        will forever be on the run. Shun them!

18 Those who walk uprightly will be kept safe;
        the crooked fall suddenly.

19 Those who till the land will have plenty of bread;
        those with worthless schemes will have plenty of poverty.

20 A faithful person is showered with blessings,
        but the get-rich-fast types will not go unpunished.

21 It's never good to judge by appearances—
        anyone who's hungry enough can be pushed to do wrong.

22 The greedy pursue wealth eagerly,
        unaware that poverty is waiting in the wings.

23 Those who reprimand are respected more in the end
        than those who use their tongues for flattery.

²⁴ Those who steal from their parents and say,
    "This really isn't stealing," are partners of the Destroyer.

²⁵ The greedy stir up strife,
    but those who trust in Our God will enjoy prosperity.

²⁶ One who trusts one's own mind trusts a fool;
    walking in wisdom is safer.

²⁷ Those who give to the poor will never want;
    those who close their eyes to them are cursed.

²⁸ When the wicked rise, others hide;
    when they fall, the upright flourish.

29.1 When the stiff-necked are repeat offenders,
    they will be broken suddenly and completely.

² When the upright rule, the citizens rejoice;
    when the corrupt are in power, they groan.

³ Those who love wisdom give joy to their parents;
    those who indulge in loose living squander their wealth.

⁴ Rulers give stability to the country through justice;
    those who impose unjust taxes ruin the country.

⁵ Those who flatter their neighbors
    set a snare around their own feet.

⁶ The corrupt are trapped by their transgressions;
    the upright sing for joy.

⁷ The just uphold the rights of the oppressed;
    the corrupt care only for themselves.

⁸ The arrogant create turmoil in the community,
    but the wise turn rage around.

⁹ When a wise person tries to argue with a fool,
    the latter either rages or mocks—and no one is satisfied.

¹⁰ Violent people hate the innocent,
    but the upright care for them.

¹¹ Fools vent their anger openly and loudly;
    the wise keep themselves under control.

12 When rulers listen to lies,
      all their officials become corrupt.

13 The common bond of the poor and the oppressor
      is the light Our God gives to the eyes of both.

14 When the ruler judges the poor with equity,
      the throne will always be secure.

15 Correction and reproof bring wisdom;
      children who get their own way bring shame to their parents.

16 When the corrupt are in charge, crime is on the increase;
      but the upright will see their downfall.

17 Discipline your children, and they will give you peace of mind
      and a heart full of joy.

18 Where there is no vision, the people are unrestrained;
      those who keep the Law find happiness.

19 To correct some people—
      the kind who never reply, even when they understand you—
      takes action, not just words!

20 Keep your eye on the person too ready to talk—
      even fools eventually learn to keep their mouth shut.

21 Mentor a young person from childhood,
      and end up with a beloved daughter or son.

22 An ill-tempered person stirs up discord,
      and the hothead causes much hardship.

23 Foolish pride brings humiliation,
      but the humble in spirit receive honor.

24 Companions of thieves are their own worst enemies:
      in a trial, anything they say just implicates themselves!

25 Worrying about what other people will say or do is a trap.
      Put your trust in God, and you'll be safe.

26 Many people look to their leaders to uphold their rights,
      but true justice comes from Our God.

27 The unjust are loathsome to the righteous,
      and the honorable are abominable to the corrupt.

the adages of Agur, begot of Jakeh the Massaite.

> I am weary, O God;
> I am weary, O God, and I faint.*
> ² Surely I am the most stupid of humans,
> lacking human understanding.
> ³ I have not learned wisdom,
> I have no knowledge of the Holy One.
> ⁴ Who has ascended to heaven and returned?
> Who holds the wind in the palm of a hand?
> Who has wrapped the heavenly waters in a cloak?
> Who has established all the ends of the earth?
> Who has done this? Give me a name!
> Or give me the name of the offspring, if you know!

> ⁵ Every word from God is tested and pure—
> they are a shield to those who take refuge in God.
> ⁶ Add no words to the divine revelation,
> lest you be reprimanded, and proven a liar.

> ⁷ Two things I request of you—
> don't deny them to me before I die:
> ⁸ take falsehoods and lies away from me;
> and give me neither poverty nor wealth.
> Give me only my portion of bread,
> ⁹ lest I be full, and say, "God? Who's that?"
> or be hungry, and steal,
> thus profaning the Name of my God.

> ¹⁰ Don't denounce underlings to their superiors,
> otherwise, they might curse you, and you'll pay for it.

> ¹¹ Some people curse their father
> and never bless their mother.
> ¹² Some people are pure in their own eyes,
> yet are still filthy.
> ¹³ Some people have haughty eyes—
> every glance exudes arrogance.

---

* This rendering comes from a different division of the Hebrew words; the Masoretic text reads, "Declaration to Ithiel, to Ithiel and Ucal."

14 Some people have swords instead of teeth
knives instead of a jaw:
they devour the poor from the earth,
the needy from among the people.

15 The leech has two offspring:
"Gimme! Gimme!"

There are three things—
no, four!—
that won't be satisfied,
that will never say, "Enough":
16 Sheol;
the childless couple;
the earth's insatiable lust for water;
and fire, which never cries, "Enough."

17 The eye that mocks its father,
that despises its mother,
will be pecked out by the ravens of the valley
and consumed by condors.

18 There are three things—
no, four!—
that are too wonderful for me,
that I just don't understand:
19 the way an eagle soars in the sky;
the way a snake glides over a rock;
the way a ship handles in mid-ocean;
and the way two people share intimacy.

20 This is how adulterers always respond:
after eating, they wipe their mouth and say,
"I haven't done anything wrong!"

21 There are three things—
no, four!—
that make the earth quake,
things it can't abide:
22 the minion who usurps the throne;
the fool who is full of food;
23 the person no one ever loved who gets married;
and the lover who supplants the spouse.

24 There are four things on earth that are tiny
   but exceedingly wise:
25 ants are not known for their strength,
   yet they gather in their food every summer;
26 badgers are not mighty,
   yet they make their houses in the rocks;
27 locusts have no leader,
   yet they capably march in ranks;
28 and lizards can be caught by hand,
   yet they are found living in palaces.

29 There are three things—
   no, four!—
   that have an impressive pace,
   that are imposing in their bearing:
30 the lion, that beast of beasts, which turns its back to no one;
31   the strutting rooster;
   the billy goat;
   and the ruler who feels impervious to revolt.

32 If you have been foolish enough to gloat or be presumptuous,
   cover your mouth with your hand;
33 for if you churn milk, you get butter;
   if you punch someone in the nose, you get blood;
   and if you stir up anger, you get strife.

31:1-31

*t*he adages of Lemuel, ruler of Massa, as taught by his mother:

2 Oh, my child! Oh, child of my womb!
   Oh, child of my prayers!
3 Don't spend all your energy on sex,
   or all your time on political intrigues.
4 These things are not for rulers, Lemuel—
   nor is imbibing wine and sipping whiskey,
5 for they make you forget what you have decreed,
   and make you neglect the rights of the oppressed.
6 Give whiskey to those near death,
   and wine to those whose hearts are bitter;

7   let people drink to deaden their pain,
      and not think of their misery.
8   But you, speak out for those who cannot speak,
      and for the rights of those abandoned by others.
9   Speak out, issue decrees,
      vindicate the rights of the homeless and the hungry.

10   What is worth more than a strong and loving wife?
      She is more precious than jewels;
11   Her husband's heart trusts in her,
      from which no little gain is drawn.
12   She brings good—not evil—
      to her house all the day of her life.
13   For she seeks out tools of her trade,
      and works with willing hands.
14   She is like the merchant ship
      which brings provisions from far off.
15   She rises before dawn
      to put into motions the working of the household.
16   After some consideration she buys a field
      and, with what she has earned, puts in a vineyard.
17   She is up to the demands of labor,
      and her limbs rise to meet the task.
18   She enjoys the success that comes with hard work,
      and her lamp burns late at night.
19   She works the spindle in one hand,
      while holding the distaff in the other.
20   She holds out a hand to the hungry,
      and opens her arms to the homeless.
21   She prepares her household for snowy weather,
      for they are all warmly clothed.
22   She makes her own quilts,
      and dresses in fine linen and purple.
23   Her husband is respected in the public square,
      and takes a seat among the elders.
24   She makes linen garments for the market,
      and delivers belts to the merchants.
25   Strength and honor are her mien;
      she rejoices in the future.
26   Her speaking displays her wisdom;
      words of kindness come from her tongue.

²⁷ She supervises the household well,
and does not sit idle.
²⁸ Her children rise up and bless her;
her husband, too, says, "Thank you,
²⁹ for there are many women who have done very well,
but you excel them all!"
³⁰ Charm deceives, and beauty flees;
but she who fears Our God is worthy of praise.
³¹ May she be filled with the fruit of her hands;
and may her works be extolled in the public square.

the song of songs

Solomon's song of songs.*

2   Oh, kiss me, touch me with your lips;
      your love tastes better than any wine.
3   You smell better than any perfume;
      even the sound of your name smells sweet—
      no wonder they all love you!
4   Come, take me; carry me off
      like some wild desert chieftain to his tent;
      take me!

---

* Although the original Hebrew text does not indicate who is speaking any of the parts, it is clear that in this piece there are two dialogues being carried on simultaneously—one is that of the primary voice, a woman, speaking with her lover; and the other is with the "daughters of Jerusalem," who fulfill here a role comparable to the chorus in a Greek drama. While we never insert headings into the text of any of our translations, we have adopted the convention here of using different typefaces and text placement to indicate the various speakers. The main typeface, as above, indicates that the speaker is a woman; the indented speeches are those spoken by a man; and those set in italics are spoken by the chorus. The title of the book means, simply, "Solomon's greatest song."

Oh, you are sweet; let us drink you!
You make us higher than any wine.

They are right to love you,
  every one of them!
5 Me? Do you think me dark, oh daughters of Jerusalem?
    Oh, I am; but I'm lovely, yes?
  Dark as the night inside a tent in Kedar;
    dark as the secrets inside Solomon's tents.
6 You wonder why I'm so dark? I'll tell you:
    it was my brothers—they thought I was loose
  and wild—they put me to work in the vineyards,
    hoping I would neglect my own vineyard.
  The sun turned me brown, like a grape;
    but, oh, the fire that burns inside me now!

7 Tell me, love, where do you take
    your sheep to graze?
  Do you have a shady place where you rest
    in the heat of the day?
  I want you; I don't want to spend all day
    wandering around among your friends,
    wearing all these clothes in the heat of the day.

8   Why, if you don't know, my pretty one,
        then come, follow the tracks of my sheep.
      Bring your goats to graze
        by this shepherd's tent.
9   Oh, you are a sweet one, and rare;
        you're like a little mare running wild
        with the Pharaoh's stallions.
10   You're so pretty, with your earrings
        dangling down your brown cheeks,
        and that delicate neck, with its jewels.
11   I'll make you earrings of gold,
        with silver studs for your sweet earlobes.

12 Ah, my royal shepherd—
    you've had your royal banquet,
  and now the whole tent smells of my fragrance.
    It's like perfume, yes?

¹³ And my sweet lover—
    he is a sachet of perfume,
      nestled between my breasts!
¹⁴ He smells better than a bouquet of henna
    gathered from the vineyards of En Gedi.

        ¹⁵ Oh, my darling, looking into your eyes—
          they're as pretty as a pair of little doves.

¹⁶ And you are pretty too, my lover,
    in this royal bower of grass and flowers,
    under the trees.

        ¹⁷ The beams of our house are these cedars;
          our only rafters these firs.

^{2:1} What need of houses, my sweet?
    I can live in the meadows of Sharon, like the saffron;
    like a lily, growing in her valley.

        ² Oh, you are a lily, you are—
          a lily among the thorns!

³ And you, sweetheart—you are as rare
    as an apple tree, in the middle of the forest.
  My little apple tree, can I lie in your shade?
    Can I eat just a little of this sweet fruit?
⁴ This will be our banquet hall,
    here in this green valley,
  and you shall be my roof:
    spread your love over me like a canopy.
⁵ I am weak with hunger; feed me—
    feed me your sweet apple,
    and these raisins, yes?
  Oh, I am dizzy—
⁶   give me your left arm for a pillow,
    and wrap the right one around me.

⁷ Oh daughters of Jerusalem, swear to me here—
    swear by the spirits of the fields,
    by the gazelle and the deer—
  that our desire not be disturbed
    till our fire we have quenched.

hERE comes my lover,
  running down the mountains like a gazelle,
⁹ leaping the hills like a stag
    in search of his doe.
  Look at him, standing out there
    staring in through the window lattices
    like the moon.
¹⁰ He is calling me: "Come, sweetheart,
    my pretty one, come out!
¹¹ Winter is over, the rains are gone,
¹²   the flowers are blooming.
  It's time for singing;
    let's walk out through the valleys
    and listen to the song of the dove.
¹³ The fig trees are setting fruit;
    and the air is full of the smell
    of grape blossoms.
  Arise and come, my pretty darling.
    come away with me!"

¹⁴ Oh, my little bird,
    out here among the rocks,
    on the mountainside,
  where no one can see us—
    let me see the beauty of your dark skin.
  Talk to me; let me hear
    the joy of your voice.
  Oh, it's sweet, your voice is,
    like the voice of the dove.
  And your skin—
    it is loveliness itself!

¹⁵ Oh, my sweet, here's a little fox
    for you to catch—catch him quick!
  He'll make mischief in your sweet
    vineyard, as it blooms!

16 My lover comes to me hungry,
   and I to him; hungry as the deer
   feeding among the lilies.
17 Feed then, my dear, feed till the dawn,
   when the sun comes chasing its shadow—
then, away with you, love; run,
   like a young stag, wild in the hills.

3:1–3:5

Oh, the nights are long in my empty bed;
   all night long in my dreams I look for you,
   my lover, my heart;
but when I wake,
   there's no one there.
2 I can't sleep with this fire;
   I'll get up and go walking,
out through the streets to the square,
   looking for the one I adore.

Ah, but I went looking,
   and found no one.
3 The sentries on their rounds
   found me, though.
I wanted to ask them,
   "Have you seen him, the one I love?"
4 But no sooner did I pass by them,
   than I found him at last, the one that I hungered for.
I put my arms around him, would not let go of him,
   till I had brought him home, to my mother's house;
   to the very room where she made me!

5 Oh daughters of Jerusalem, swear to me here—
   swear by the spirits of the fields,
   by the gazelle and the deer—
that our desire not be disturbed
   till our fire we have quenched.

Look! Who is this,
    coming up out of the desert
like the smoke that rises from the censer,
    smoke of incense and myrrh
made of the finest spices
    of the richest merchant.
7   It is Solomon, in his sedan,
    surrounded by sixty warriors,
Israel's finest, 8 battle-seasoned,
    each one wearing his own fine sword—
ready to meet whatever comes upon him
    in the night!
9   They say that Solomon's sedan
    was made by his own hands
    from the cedars of Lebanon.
10   Its pillars are made of silver,
    its base is of gold,
and swathed in the richest purple velvet—
but its interior is annointed with the love
    of Jerusalem's daughters.
11   Come out and see, now,
    you daughters of Zion;
come and see your Solomon now,
    crowned with the crown his mother
    has placed on his head,
the marriage crown, on this day,
    this day when his heart rejoices
    in me.

4:1   Ah, look at you, my pretty darling—
    look at your eyes, sweet as doves
    behind the veil that your hair makes,
    as it cascades from your head
    like a flock of young goats—
    black ones, bounding
    down off Mount Gilead.
2   And your teeth are sheep:
    white as the day they were born,

or newly shorn, and freshly washed,
    each with its perfect mate.
Not one of them is alone—
    why should we be?
3 And, ah, the lips of that lovely mouth—
    a ribbon of scarlet.
Your temples, behind that veil,
    glow like the halves
    of a freshly sliced pomegranate.
4 Your neck has the grace
    of David's Tower,
with its jewels hung round it
    like the shields of a thousand warriors.
5 And your breasts—
    like the twin fawns of a gazelle,
    hiding among the lilies.
6 All my nights, till the sun
    comes chasing its shadows,
let me play in these perfumed hills,
    these mountains scented with myrrh.
7 Beauty was named for you, my darling;
    your beauty is perfect.

8 Come with me out of Lebanon, my bride;
    come down from your heights,
    from your pinacle of grace;
where you live, with your she-lion,
    with mountain leopards for pets.
9 You have robbed me of my heart,
    my sister and bride;
stolen it, with one flash of your eyes
    and one flash of the skin
    beneath those jewels round your neck.
10 What a joy it is to love you,
    my sister-bride—the taste of your love
is sweeter than any wine; the scent of you
    is better than any spice.
11 You taste as if
    you had just eaten a honeycomb,
with the honey still dripping
    from your lips.

Honeyed milk
   is the taste of your tongue;*
the scent that fills your clothing
   brings back memories
   of the beauties of Lebanon.
12 You are a garden behind walls,
   my sister and bride,
a spring running clear
   that no one can drink from;
a fountain that flows
   behind a locked gate.
13 You are an orchard, planted
   with fine flowers and fruit:
with pomegranates, saffron,
   henna, and nard,
and with trees of spice: cinnamon
   and calamus, with aloes and myrrh.
15 Oh, what a garden you are,
   with a fountain of water
streaming down from Lebanon,
   a sweet running fountain—
   oh, how I thirst!

16 Winds of the south
   and winds of the north,
   wake up and blow now:
breathe through my garden,
   drive him mad with my fragrance,
   draw him into my garden;
let his tongue stop its talking,
   let it taste my choice fruits.

5.1 I enter your garden, my sister-bride,
   to gather myrrh and spice. I eat
of your honeycomb, and drink
   honeyed wine with sweet milk.

Eat, friends, and drink!
Sate yourselves, oh lovers.

---

* Milk and honey are ancient sexual euphemisms; when the Israelites were to enter "a land flowing with milk and honey," the peace and joy of such a land was depicted in terms of the full expression of physical love.

Asleep on my bed,
     my heart woke me to the sound
     of my sweetheart knocking:
"Open for me, my darling,
     my sister-lover, my sweetheart,
     my dove, my perfection.
My head is soaked with dew,
     with the damp of the night."
3 "Indeed," I thought, "I have taken off
     my nightgown—must I put it on again?
I have washed my feet—must I
     dirty them now?"
4 Ah, but when he thrust in
     his hand through the opening,
     fumbling in the dark for the latch—
then my heart pounded, and 5 I rose up
     to open for him, my hands dripping
     with myrrh as I reached for the door.
6 I opened to him then—
     only to wake and find him
     not there.
Oh, how my heart
     had risen to the sound
of his voice—I looked,
     and I cried out in the night,
but he was not there—
     I heard no answer
     anywhere.
7 Thus the sentries, making their rounds,
     found me wandering in the city.
They beat me and mocked me
     and stripped me of my cloak.
Laughing, they sent me on my way—
     oh, they are brave ones,
those guardians
     of the walls!

8 Oh, you daughters of Jerusalem,
     I swear to you—

if you find my lover tell him—

Tell him what?

Tell him I am dizzy with love!

> [9] *This shepherd of yours—tell us*
> *how is that he is so better than the others,*
> *that you, the most beautiful among women,*
> *should search for him in the night?*
> *Tell us, tell us—what does he have*
> *that makes you swear of your love?*

[10] Like the sun, he is, with his cheeks
all flushed with love.
You might search among ten thousand men;
but you would not find a one
that was like him.
[11] He is gold among the golden,
his hair, full of waves, shines like the raven.
[12] And his eyes, ah those eyes—
mild as milk, sweet as doves
bathing in a stream—they are like jewels.
[13] His cheeks are scented like a bouquet
of spice—my spice!—and to taste of his lips
it to drink nectar from lilies.
[14] His arms, all golden downed,
are as precious as topaz. His belly, so hard,
could be carved out of ivory—
ha! with a belly-button of sapphire!—
[15] or his legs, out of marble—
why, even the soles of his feet
are worth more than gold!
And his face, calm
as the cedars of Lebanon—
[16] and his mouth—what sweetness!
What can I say?
There is no part of him
that is not pretty,
this lover of mine,
this friend among friends,
oh daughters of Jerusalem !

6:1 *So where did he go, this lover of yours,*
oh, most beautiful among women?
Which way did he turn, this sweet shepherd?
We will seek him with you!

2 Ah but they did not know—
my lover had gone down
in his garden of spice,
down to gather the nectar of lilies.
3 I came to my lover hungering,
as he came to me; hungry as the deer
feeding among the lilies.

6:4–6:10

Oh my pretty one,
my little darling,
let them keep their Tirzah
and their Jerusalem—
you are beauty enough for me.
Every time I see you, my breath catches—
it's like stepping out of my tent
and seeing the stars, in a desert night.*

5 Don't look at me like that,
it makes me...too bold.
Ah, your hair, your hair
as it cascades from your head
is a flock of young goats—
black ones, bounding
down off Mount Gilead.
6 And your teeth are sheep:
white as the day they were born,
or newly shorn, and freshly washed,
each with its perfect mate.
Not one of them is alone—
why should we be?

---

* The majestic "army" referred to in other translations is properly "host," as in God of Hosts. The term can refer to a military host, a host of angels, or as here, the stars of heaven.

song of songs 6

⁷ Your temples, behind that veil,
   glow like the halves
   of a freshly sliced pomegranate.

⁸ Oh, I have known women,
   my heart.
There were wise ones,
   who could rule a country—
   of those, maybe sixty.
And beauties,
   in the bloom of their motherhood—
   say eighty.
And girls, in the flower of their youth—
   those, I couldn't count.
⁹ But of you, my little bird,
   there is only one;
and that one
   is perfection itself!
And, oh, those women, love—
   when they saw you?
The wise ones,
   and the mothers, and girls?
There's not a one of them did not
   sing your praises like a poet, saying,
¹⁰ "Who is this blessed one,
   blooming like the dawn,
radiant as the moon,
   pure as the fire of the sun,
as awesome and fearsome
   as the procession of the stars
   through the sky of night?"

6:11–7:10

I went down to the orchards of nut trees
   to see what was growing, fresh and green
in the valley. I only wanted to see
   if the vines were in bud, to smell
   the pomegranates in flower.

¹² I never guessed what I would find there:
   that I would be carried away by my passion,
carried off, as if I were flying
   on the chariot of Amminadab.

   *7:1 *Turn, turn, oh Shulammite,*
      turn, turn; turn before us,
      that we might gaze upon you.

And what is it that you love,
   what is it you hope to see,
as I dance before you, dancing
   the dance of Mahanaim?

> ² Even your feet are lovely,
>   dancing in their sandals,
>   like a ruler's daughter.
> Your graceful legs are precious jewels,
>   worked by the greatest craftsman of all.
> ³ Ah, and your navel is a chalice
>   that I will drink sweetened wine from!
> Your belly is golden, like wheat,
>   and scented of lillies.
> ⁴ Your breasts are
>   the twin fawns of a gazelle,
> ⁵ and your neck,
>   graceful as David's ivory Tower.
> But your eyes! Looking into them
>   is like looking into those pools of Heshbon,
>   outside the gates of Beth Rabbim.
> And your nose is as delicate
>   as those towers in Lebanon
>   that face out toward Damascus.
> ⁶ Mount Carmel itself
>   is no more elegant than your head,
> with its hair, weaving a tapestry
>   that would ensnare the proudest man.

---

* We have followed the verse numbering in the Hebrew text rather than the numbering found in many English translations, which has chapter 7 beginning at the next verse.

7   Oh, my pretty one, what a delight
                you are to look on,
              with all of your love-charms!
8   "Splendid as a palm tree,"
                I thought, when I first saw you—
                yes, with its well-rounded fruit!
9   "Let me climb this tree," I said,
                "and have a taste of these fruits."
              Oh, may they always be sweet
                as the fruit of the vine;
              the scent of your breath, fresh as apples,
                and your lips, like the sweetest wine.

10   I will drink the finest of wines
        from your lips, wine that flows gently
     from your mouth to mine, as we
        lie together, out of time.

7:11–8:5

I am yours, beloved,
        and you are my desire.
12   Come. Let's go out,
          into the country.
     We can spend the night
          in the little villages there.
13   Early in the morning
          we'll go into the vineyards,
             to see if the vines are budding.
     The flowers will be opening;
          the odor of pomegranate blossoms
          filling the air.
     There I will give you
          what you have waited for.
14   The scent of the mandrakes
          is breathing in the door. Come out;
     at the doorstep there awaits every pleasure
          that I have kept locked away
          for my lover.

8:1 If only you could appear like my brother—
   like one who had nursed at the breast of my mother.
Oh, then, when I found you outside,
   in the streets or the squares,
I could kiss you and hold you, and no one would
   whisper behind me.
2 Ah, then, I would take you by the hand,
   and bring you to the house
of my mother—she who has taught me all of her arts!—
   and there would give you spiced wine;
there you could drink down
   the nectar of my pomegranates,
3 with your left for my pillow,
   and your right arm around me.

4 Oh daughters of Jerusalem,
   swear to me here—
that our desire not be disturbed
   till our fire we have quenched.

5 *And who is here, coming up from the fields*
   of the gazelle and the deer—so weak
   with her love she must lean upon her dear?

8:5–8:14

beneath the apple tree, it was, my love,
   that I first wakened your desire—
was it there that
   your mother conceived you?
Or there that she brought you
   into the world?
6 Seal me around your heart, love,
   like the bracelets around your arm.
Love is stronger than death,
   and as unrelenting. I am jealous
of your love; my heart burns for you
   like the fire of God.

⁷   No water could ever
        put out this fire, love;
           no flood could wash it away.

If a rich man came to me, offering
  all of his gold and all his inheritance,
trying to buy my love—
  I would laugh in the face of that fool!

Not long ago, the sisters of my mother
  spoke this way:
⁸   "We have a young sister
  whose breasts are not yet budded.
What shall we do for our sister,
  toward the day when she is spoken for?
⁹   If she were a wall, we would
  build upon her towers of silver;
if she were a door, we would adorn
  her with panels of cedar."
But now I am that wall,
  and my breasts are like towers.
And for you, my sweetheart,
  I am She Who Brings Joy.
¹¹   Solomon had a vineyard in Baal Hamon, they say,
  and he leased out this vineyard to tenant farmers.
So fine was this vineyard, they say,
  that each one was to pay him
twenty-five pounds of silver
  for its use.
¹²   But my vineyard is mine alone to give,
  and the silver of its fruit I give to you alone,
  my Solomon.
Ah, but maybe just a little
  for those who tend the fruit, yes?

        ¹³   All you who tend my love's garden,
          hear me!
        Come forward;
           make yourselves known to me!

¹⁴ Shush, shush—
    come here, my love,
fast, like the gazelle—
    be like a young stag
on these mountains
    of spice.

Ruth

Long ago, when judges governed Israel, a famine swept over the land. So a family from the town of Bethlehem in Judah, a woman and man and their two children, emigrated to the region of Moab. ² The man was named Elimelech,* the woman's name was Naomi, and their two sons were named Mahlon and Chilon. They were Ephrathites, that is, from Bethlehem of Judah. They arrived in the land of Moab and settled there.

³ Soon afterward Elimelech died, leaving Naomi and the two sons to fend for themselves. ⁴ The two sons eventually married two Moabite women, whose names were Orpah and Ruth. They had lived in the land of Moab for about ten years ⁵ when both Mahlon and Chilon died.

Now that Naomi had lost both of her children as well as her husband, ⁶ she prepared to take her daughters-in-law and leave the land of Moab

---

* In *Ruth*, as in much of the Hebrew scriptures, the names are significant and serve as literary foreshadowings of what is to come. Elimelech means "God is my Ruler;" Naomi means "Joy" or "Delight;" and the sons' names mean either "Sickness" and "Consumption," or "Sterility" and "Small Vessel." Orpah means "The One Who Walks Away"—literally, "the one who turns the back of the neck;" and Ruth means, simply, "Beloved."

and return to her homeland, for she had heard that Our God had visited the people by providing an abundance of food.

⁷ So she and her two daughters-in-law left the house where they had been living, and she set out on the road to Judah. ⁸ But Naomi told each of her daughters-in-law, "Return to your mother's house. May the Most High care for you with the same kindness that you have cared for your dead and for me. ⁹ May the Most High give you security and true fulfillment, and lead you to new spouses." Then she kissed them both.

But they wept loudly ¹⁰ and said to her, "No, we want to go back with you to the land of your people!"

¹¹ But Naomi said to them. "Go back, my daughters. Why do you want to come with me? I have no more sons inside me that you can take as spouses. ¹² No, you must go back, my daughters. I am too old to marry again. Even if I told you that there was still hope for me, if I were to find a spouse and have children tonight, ¹³ would you be willing to wait until they are grown to marry them? Would you refuse to remarry for this far-off hope? No, if you did that, it would tear me apart, for the hand of the Most High has been raised against me."

¹⁴ And once more they wept loudly. Then Orpah kissed Naomi and returned to her people. But Ruth stayed by her side.

¹⁵ Naomi said to Ruth, "Look, your sister-in-law has returned to her people and to the god of her ancestors. You too must go. Follow your sister-in-law."

¹⁶ But Ruth said to her, "Please don't ask me to leave you and turn away from your company. I swear to you:

¹⁷   Where you go, I will go;
        where you lodge, I will lodge.
    Your people will be my people,
        and your God, my God.
    Where you die, I'll die there too
        and I will be buried there beside you.
    I swear—may Your God be my witness and judge—
        that not even death will keep us apart."

¹⁸ Seeing that Ruth was determined to accompany her, Naomi said no more. ¹⁹ And together they walked, until they came to Bethlehem.

When they arrived, the town was abuzz with gossip because of them. The townspeople said to each other, "Could this sad person be Naomi, our 'Joy'?"

²⁰ But she said to them, "Don't call me Naomi. Call me Mara, 'Bitterness,'

for Our God has afflicted me, and Shaddai* has brought bitter destruction on me. 21 I was filled to the brim when I departed, but Our God has brought me back empty. Why insist on calling me Naomi, since Our God has passed sentence upon me and Shaddai has brought me to ruin?"

22 And that is how Naomi left the land of Moab with Ruth the Moabite and returned to Bethlehem, arriving just as the barley harvest was beginning.

2:1-23

ⁿow Naomi had a relative on her husband's side from the clan of Elimelech. His name was Boaz,** and he was well-to-do.

2 One day Ruth the Moabite said to Naomi, "Let me go into the fields and be a gleaner, gathering the leftover grain behind anyone who will take pity on me."

And Naomi said, "Go ahead, my daughter."

3 So Ruth went out to the fields to follow the harvesters and gather the grain that they dropped. As providence would have it, she came to the part of the field that was owned by Boaz, of Elimelech's clan.

4 It so happened that Boaz had just returned from Bethlehem. He greeted the harvesters by calling out, "Our God be with you!"

They shouted back, "Our God bless you!"

5 Then Boaz turned to the supervisor in charge of the harvesters and asled, "Who does that woman work for?"

6 The supervisor of the harvesters replied, "She is the Moabite who returned from the land of Moab with Naomi. 7 She asked our permission to collect the grain that the workers dropped. She has been working steadily since early morning, with scarcely any rest."

8 Then Boaz said to Ruth, "Listen to my words, my child, and accept

---

* The word *Shaddai*, a name for God, sounds like *ashod*, which means destruction or ruin. The name Shaddai is usually translated "the Almighty," under the assumption that it derives either from the word *shadad*, which means "burly" or "powerful," or from *shadah*, which means "mountain"—hence "God of the mountains." There is growing opinion, however, that Shaddai may derive from the word *shad* or "breast"—thus *El Shaddai* may be a feminine image of God meaning "the Breasted God."

** Boaz may mean "strong one," but there are several opinions on this. *Gibbôr chayil*, "well-to-do," literally means "strong one of valor," and was a term used for any citizen ready for military service. The warrior connotations are not appropriate here, though, as it simply means one who had resources enough for equipment and provisions if called to military service. The emphasis is on wealth and independence.

my offer: don't collect your grain in anyone else's fields but mine; and don't leave here, stay with my binders. ⁹ Watch them closely, and whatever part of the field they are harvesting, follow behind them. I have ordered all my reapers not to bother you.* When you get thirsty, go to the water jars they bring with them and get a drink of water."

¹⁰ Ruth bowed down to the ground and said to Boaz, "How have I come to deserve your favor so much that you take care of me? I'm just a foreigner."

¹¹ Boaz replied, "I have heard how you have cared for your mother-in-law since your husband died, and how you left your own family and the land where you were born to come to live here among strangers. ¹² May Our God pay you in full for your loyalty! May you be richly rewarded by the Most High God of Israel, under whose wings you have come to find shelter!"

¹³ Ruth said, "May you find me deserving of your kindness. You have treated me gently and given me solace even though I am not one of your workers."

¹⁴ When noontime arrived, Boaz said to her, "Come here and share my bread and dip some of it in the wine." Ruth sat with the rest of the workers while Boaz prepared a bowl of roasted barley as a snack. She ate until she was no longer hungry and still had some left over. ¹⁵ Then she got up to continue her gathering.

Boaz ordered the binders, "Let her pick from among the bundles you have gathered, and do not hinder her. ¹⁶ In fact, go so far as to drop some grain from your bundles, and let her collect it without fear."

¹⁷ Ruth continued to gather in the field until evening. Then she winnowed what she had collected and had enough grain to fill a whole basket. ¹⁸ She picked up the basket and carried it into town.

When she arrived home, Ruth showed the basket to Naomi, and gave her the leftovers from her meal. ¹⁹ When she saw all this, Naomi asked, "Where did you gather today? Where have you been working? God bless whoever took care of you!"

Then Ruth told Naomi in whose fields she had been working: "The owner of the fields where I worked today is named Boaz."

²⁰ Then Naomi said, "May he receive blessings from Our God, who has not stopped showing tender love to both the living and the dead!"

---

* The reapers were male workers and the binders were female workers, which makes sense of Boaz's order that the reapers not bother or molest Ruth or the other binders.

"This Boaz," Naomi continued, "is a close relative of ours—he is our redeemer-trustee."*

²¹ Ruth the Moabite said, "He also told me, 'Follow my binders until they have finished with the harvest.'"

²² Naomi told her daughter-in-law, "This is very good news. It will be better to stay in his fields where you will be safe than to go to someone else's fields where you could be in danger."

²³ So Ruth stayed with Boaz's workers and worked as a gleaner until the harvest was complete. During this time, she continued to live with her mother-in-law.

3:1–4:22

One day, Naomi said to Ruth, "My daughter, it's my duty to ensure your security and fulfillment, and make sure you are provided for. ² And Boaz, whose workers you have been following, is our closest relative. Tonight he'll be winnowing grain on the threshing floor. ³ Wash up and put on perfume and dress in your finest clothes. Then go down to the threshing floor. But don't let him know you're there until he has finished eating and drinking.

⁴ "When he goes to sleep, watch to see where he lies down. Then go and 'uncover his feet' and lie down with him.** He'll tell you what to do next."

⁵ Ruth replied, "I will do as you tell me." ⁶ So she went down to the threshing floor just as her mother-in-law told her to do.

⁷ Boaz ate and drank until he was tipsy. Then he went to sleep against the bundles of grain. When Boaz was asleep, Ruth silently approached, laid down next to him, and "uncovered his feet." ⁸ In the middle of the night Boaz awoke and was startled to find a woman lying at his feet.

⁹ "Who's there?" Boaz asked.

She replied, "It's Ruth, your faithful one. Spread the corner of your cloak over me, for you are my family redeemer."

¹⁰ "May Our God bless you, my child," Boaz replied. "You have shown

---

* The word *gôel*, usually translated "kin," literally means "one with the right to redeem." Boaz can be asked to perform specific obligations—in this case, the protection of a small piece of land belonging to Elimelech and Naomi, which is now being held in trust. Being the *gôel* also obligates Boaz to marry Ruth to ensure that Elimelech's lineage continues.

** "Feet" is a common Hebrew euphemism for the genitals. When Ruth asks Boaz to cover her with the corner of his cloak in verse 9, she is asking him to marry her according to the laws of family succession.

yourself even more loyal to the family than you did before. You could have sought someone younger, whether rich or poor. ¹¹ Rest easy, my child, I am more than willing to do what you ask. Everyone knows that you are a person of great character and integrity.

¹² "But there is a problem: it is true that I am a close relative, but there is another who is even more closely related to you than I am. ¹³ Stay here tonight, and I'll go and talk to him in the morning. If he wishes to carry out his obligations as a redeemer-trustee, that is his right. If not, then as Our God lives, I will marry you! Now rest your head until morning."

¹⁴ So Ruth lay at his feet until the morning, but got up before dawn so that no one else would see that she had been there. Boaz thought it best that no one know she had been to the threshing floor.

Before she left, Boaz said, "Bring me your cloak and hold it out." When she did so, he poured out six measures of grain and lifted it for her to carry. Then Ruth went back to town.

¹⁶ When she returned home, Naomi asked, "So, how did it go with you, my daughter?"

Ruth told her all that had happened, ¹⁷ and added, "Boaz also gave me six measures of grain; he didn't want me to come home to you empty-handed."

Naomi advised her, "Let's wait and see what happens. Boaz won't rest until the matter is settled today."

4:1 In the meantime, Boaz went to the main gate of the town and waited there for the arrival of the relative he had mentioned. When that person arrived, Boaz called him by name and said, "Come and sit with me." When the relative sat down, ² Boaz stopped ten respected citizens in the town and asked them to sit there with them. ³ When they were all seated, Boaz addressed his relative:

"You may remember that piece of land that belonged to our relative Elimelech. Naomi is selling it now that she has returned from Moab. ⁴ I promised to discuss the matter with you and ask you to stake your claim on it in the presence of these august citizens. If you are willing to do your redemption duty in the family, then do so. Otherwise, please let me know, for you're the only other person with the right of redemption in the family—I'm in line after you."

The relative answered, "Yes, I will fulfill my family 'obligation.' "

⁵ Boaz continued, "If you accept this, you realize that on the day you buy the land from Naomi and Ruth the Moabite, you're also obligated to

marry Ruth, the Moabite who returned with Naomi, so as to perpetuate the name of our dead relative and keep it connected to the property."

At this the relative said, "Oh, then I can't redeem it. Such an obligation may cut into my already existing property. I cannot do it, you must take on the obligation yourself!"

⁶ In those times in Israel, it was the custom that when the redemption had been agreed to and the property contract had been ratified, one person should remove a sandal and hand it to the other party. This was the method for ratifying transactions in Israel.* ⁸ So when the relative said to Boaz, "Redeem it yourself," he took off his sandal and handed it to Boaz.

⁹ Then Boaz addressed the group who had gathered there: "You are the witnesses this day that I have bought all of Elimelech's property from Naomi, as well as the property of Chilion and Mahlon. ¹⁰ Further, I will marry Ruth the Moabite, Mahlon's widow, in order to keep the name of our dead relative connected with the property, so that his name will not be forgotten among our relatives or in the town records. You are my witnesses this day."

¹¹ Everyone who assembled at the gate, including the prominent citizens, said, "We are your witnesses!

> May Our God make Ruth,
> > who is about to come into your home,
> to be like Rachel and Leah,
> > the two who built up the family of Israel.
> ¹² May the children Our God gives to you
> > make your family like the family of Perez,
> > whom Tamar bore to Judah."

¹³ So Ruth and Boaz were married. And from their union, Our God enabled Ruth to conceive and she gave birth to a child.

¹⁴ Then the women of the village said to Naomi,

> "Praised be Our God,
> > who has not abandoned you
> > but provided you with yet another redeemer!
> ¹⁵ May the child's name be remembered through all of Israel—
> > and give you renewed life
> > and support you when you are old!

---

* It was customary for the individual acquiring property to set foot on the land to lay claim to it. This may have been the origin of the idea that the shoe was a symbol of power. By handing over the shoe, one is handing over the claim.

For your daughter-in-law,
    who loves you and has proven better
than seven of your own children could ever have been,
    has given birth to him."

¹⁶ Naomi took the child into her lap and she became his caretaker. ¹⁷ And Naomi's neighbors named the child, saying, "A son has been born to Naomi; we will call him Obed."*

And Obed begot Jesse—and Jesse begot David.

CR   CR   CR

¹⁸ Here, then, is the complete lineage of the Perez family:
    Perez begot Hezron;
¹⁹ Hezron begot Ram;
    Ram begot Amminadab;
²⁰ Amminadab begot Nahshon;
    Nahshon begot Salmon;
²¹ Salmon begot Boaz;
    Boaz begot Obed;
²² Obed begot Jesse;
    and Jesse begot David.

---

* Obed means "faithful one."

lamentations[*]

Aleph

1   O city,[**] how desolate you lie,
      you who once swarmed with crowds!
   Once great among the nations,
      how you mourn like a bereaved spouse!
   Once you ruled the territories in graciousness,
      now you toil in servitude.

beth

2   You weep bitterly in the night;
      tears run down your cheeks.
   Though many loved you,
      none comforts you.

---

* The Hebrew name of this book, *'êkah*, is an expletive, a cry of anguish, and was generally used as the first word of a Hebrew dirge, indicating wailing. A contemporary English equivalent might be to call the book "Aaugh!" The first four chapters are acrostic poems: the first word of each stanza begins with a subsequent letter of the Hebrew alphabet. Each of the five chapters is a separate poem; while each takes up the theme of exile, they have quite different perspectives and voices.

**Refers to Jerusalem. Throughout *Lamentations* (as is done traditionally), Jerusalem is given feminine imagery, and is referred to in the third person. We have changed those references into direct address, or made third-person references non-gender-specific, for the sake of inclusiveness.

Your friends—they all betrayed you;
    they have joined your enemies.

ghimel

3 Judah has gone into exile,
    after pain and bondage.
Dispersed among the nations
    you find no resting place.
Your oppressors overcame you
    while in your deep distress.

daleth

4 The roads to Zion weep—
    no pilgrims attend your sacred feasts.
Your gates are desolate;
    your priests cry out in pain;
your young people are grieving,
    and you are in bitter distress.

he

5 Your foes have become your oppressors,
    and it is your enemies who are at ease—
for Our God has made you suffer
    because of your many sins!
All of your children are gone into exile,
    prisoners of war in the hands of your enemies.

waw

6 All your radiance is gone,
    O child of Zion.
Your leaders are like deer
    unable to find pasture;
they race about without rest,
    pursued by the hunter.

zayin

7 In these days of turmoil and strife,
    you remember the treasures of bygone days,
before your people fell captive to the enemy,
    and none was left to come to your aid.
Your enemies looked on,
    laughing at your destruction.

heth

8 Jerusalem—greatly you have sinned;
    you are thrown away like a dirty rag.
Those who once revered you now hold you in disdain,
    now that they have seen your nakedness.
What could you do but cry out
    and turn your face away?

teth

9 Your clothes are soiled with your filth;
    you never thought about your future.
Your destruction was beyond belief;
    none was left to comfort you.
"Pay attention to my suffering, O God,
    for my enemy has triumphed!"

yod

10 The enemies stretched out their hands,
    seizing all your treasures.
You saw the nations
    plunder your sanctuary—
the very nations God had forbidden
    to enter your assembly!

kaph

11 All the people cried out
    and begged for bread.
They exchanged their treasures for food
    to regain their strength.
"Look, God—see for yourself!
    See the disdain they show me!"

lamed

12 "Is my misfortune nothing to you—
    you who walk past me?
Look around, do a search:
    is there anyone else who suffers my pain?
Anyone else inflicted with these torments
    which Our God has given to me
    on this day of divine anger?

mem

13 "God sent down fire from the skies
    and into my very bones.
The Most High laid a snare at my feet
    and turned me back.
God has made a desolation out of me;
    I am in pain all day long.

nun

14 "My own sins became my shackles,
    bound tightly by God's own hand.
Fastened around my neck,
    they drain me of all my strength.
The Most High left me in the hands
    of my conquerors; I am helpless.

samekh

15 "The Most High showed disdain
    to the warriors who guarded my walls.
Our God led armies against me,
    and vanquished my young soldiers.
The Most High stomped like grapes in a winepress
    the tender youth of Judah.

ayin

16 "This is why I am crying over my sad state,
    why tears pour from my eyes;
for anyone who could comfort me is now far away,
    and there is no one to restore my spirit.
My children have nothing
    because our enemy is victorious."

pe

17 Zion's hands reach out for help,
    but there is none to give comfort.
Our God has ordered that our neighbors
    are to become our enemies.
Jerusalem has became unclean,
    like a creature in their midst to be avoided.

tsadhe

18 "Our God acted justly,
    for I rebelled against the Law.
Listen, you nations,
    and look at my anguish:
all of my young women and men
    have been taken into captivity.

qoph

19 "I cried to my lovers,
    but they betrayed me.
My priests and elders
    perished in the city
while they sought out food
    to keep themselves alive.

resh

20 "O God, bear witness to my torment!
    My gut wrenches in anguish;
My heart is torn out
    because I recklessly rebelled.
In the street, the sword leaves mourners;
    in the house, pestilence and death.

shin

21 "Though many have heard my cry,
    no one comes to comfort me.
When my enemies heard of my plight,
    they were delighted at the work of your hand.
Quickly bring the day you have promised,
    when they will suffer as I do!

taw

22 "Let their evil deeds be exposed
    and do to them
what you have done to me
    because I rebelled against you!
My groaning is without end—
    my heart sinks into despair."

Qleph

1 How angry Our God is!
   Eternal night has descended on Zion!
Our God has cast out from the skies
   the light that shone on Israel,
and has forgotten the divine footstool
   on this day of anger!

beth

2 The Most High razed without warning
   the dwellings of Israel.
In anger, Our God toppled
   the towers of Judah.
The Most High laid to waste
   our nation and its rulers.

ghimel

3 Our God's rage
   cleaved the horn of Israel's pride.
The Most High withdrew protection
   as our enemies approached.
Our God blazed in the land of Jacob
   like a brush fire that burns out of control.

daleth

4 Like an enemy, God bent a bow;
   God's strong arm is ready.
Like a foe, God has killed
   all who were once held in delight.
The Most High poured out fury like fire
   over the tents of Zion.

he

5 Our God, like an enemy,
   has swallowed Israel up,
swallowing up all their palaces
   and laying their towers to ruin.
Our God brought to Judah
   eternal mourning and cries of anguish.

waw

6 God uprooted the tabernacle
      as if it were a garden
   and turned the Assembly
      into a ruin.
   Our God erased from Zion's memory
      the seasonal feasts and the Sabbath.
   Ruler and priest alike were condemned
      in Our God's fierce anger.

zayin

7 Our God rejected the altar
      and abandoned the sanctuary.
   The Most High gave the palaces of Zion
      over to the hands of the enemy.
   They shouted in triumph in the Temple
      as if it were a festival day.

heth

8 Our God was determined to destroy
      the walls of Zion.
   Our God measured out the walls
      and did not hesitate to destroy them,
   and forced the barricade and the wall to cry out
      as they toppled down in ruins.

teth

9 The Most High scattered the bars of the gates;
      now the gates themselves have sunk into the earth.
   Our leaders have been exiled among the nations
      and the Law is no more.
   Our prophets have received
      no vision from Our God.

yod

10 The Elders of Zion
      sit on the ground in silence,
   pouring dirt over their heads
      and wearing tattered rags.
   The youth of Jerusalem
      bow their heads in shame.

kaph

¹¹ I cannot see through my tears;
　　my gut wrenches in anguish.
My bile is poured out on the ground
　　all because of my people's wound.
Children and infants lie languishing
　　throughout the streets of the city.

lamed

¹² They cry out to their parents:
　　"Where can we find bread and wine?"
They fall in the streets,
　　weak from their wounds.
They gasp for their lives
　　in their parent's arms.

mem

¹³ What comfort can I give?
　　Who else has ever suffered your plight, O Jerusalem?
To what may I compare this
　　so that you might find comfort, O Zion?
Your wound yawns wider than the sea—
　　who can heal you?

nun

¹⁴ The visions the "prophets" told
　　were nothing but hot air.
They failed to convince you of your guilt,
　　so that you could avoid this misfortune.
The visions they foresaw for you were delusions—
　　bogus trickery!

samekh

¹⁵ All who pass by
　　snap their fingers at you.
They hiss at you and shake their head at you,
　　O Jerusalem.
They say: "Is this the city once known as beauty and perfection,
　　the joy of all the earth?"

pe

¹⁶ All your foes taunt you;
    they jeer at you and grind their teeth.
They say: "We have waited a long time for this day to come!
    Now we have lived to see it!"

ayin

¹⁷ Our God has carried out the plan;
    the Most High has made good on the age-old threat.
God destroyed you without mercy
    and let the enemy shout cries of victory over you.
Our God has filled your enemies with pride.

tsadhe

¹⁸ Call out to the Most High with all your heart
    on the wall of the holy place of Zion.
Let your tears flow day and night
    like a flood.
Do not allow yourself to rest—
    do not let your tears dry up.

qoph

¹⁹ Wake up!
    Cry out in the night!
Pour out your heart like water
    at the beginning of each hour.
Lift high your arms in supplication
    before the presence of Our God.
Cry out for the lives of your children,
    who languish hungry in the streets.

resh

²⁰ Look, O God, at the ones you torment!
    Who else have you ever treated this way?
Must parents consume their own children as food—
    the very ones they have held in their arms?
Must priest and prophet be murdered
    in the sanctuary of the Most High?

shin

21 Both young and old lie together
    in the dust of the streets.
All of my young women and men
    have fallen to the sword.
You slew them on the day of your wrath;
    you slaughtered them without mercy.

taw

22 You called up terrors against me from every side
    like a crowd assembled for a festival.
On the day of your anger no one escaped—
    not one person survived!
Children I held in my arms and raised
    have been destroyed by my enemies!

3:1-66

Aleph

1 I am the one who has known grief
    under the rod of Most High's anger.
2 I am the one who was led away—
    left to walk in the night, far away from the light.
3 The hand of God has been turned against me
    again and again, both day and night.

beth

4 God has torn away my skin and muscle
    and broken my bones.
5 God has surrounded and beseiged me
    with bitterness and calamity.
6 God has cast me out into the darkness
    like those long dead.

ghimel

7 God has walled me in—there is no escape—
    and has weighed me down with shackles.

8 Even when I call out for help,
  God ignores my plea.
9 God has obstructed my path with huge boulders
  and blocked my every step.

ᴅaleth

10 God lies in wait for me like a bear
   or like a lion prowling its prey,
11 forcing me into the briars—
   throwing me to the ground and leaving me in anguish.
12 The Most High has bent the bow;
   I am the target for God's arrows.

he

13 God has pierced my heart
   with shafts from the quiver.
14 Everybody laughs at me;
   I am the butt of their songs all day.
15 God has filled me with bitter herbs,
   and sated me with gall.

waw

16 God has broken my teeth on the rocks
   and trampled me into the dirt.
17 There is no peace in my life;
   I have forgotten what prosperity is.
18 "My light is gone!" I cry;
   the Most High is my only hope.

zayin

19 I remember my woes and wanderings—
   the wormwood and the gall.
20 Those memories are so clear to me,
   and they fill me with despair.
21 Yet it is because I remember all this
   that I have hope.

heth

22 Our God's favor is not exhausted,
   nor has God's compassion failed.

²³ They rise up anew each morning,
   so great is God's faithfulness
²⁴ "Our God is all I have," I cry.
   "So I will wait in patience."

teth

²⁵ The Most High is good to those who hope in God,
   to all who seek God's presence.
²⁶ It is good to wait patiently
   for Our God to set us free.
²⁷ It is good for anyone
   to bear a burden from youth.

yod

²⁸ Let those who bear such a burden, sit in silence—
   for Our God has laid it on them;
²⁹ or lie prostate on the ground—
   for there may yet be hope.
³⁰ Let them offer their cheek to those who would strike them;
   let them submit themselves to grave insult.

kaph

³¹ For Our God
   will not reject them forever.
³² God may punish now,
   but will show compassion and the fullness of love.
³³ God does not willingly torment
   or punish any human being.

lamed

³⁴ To tread underfoot
   prisoners anywhere on earth;
³⁵ to deny people their rights
   in opposition to the Most High;
³⁶ to twist justice in the courts—
   do you think Our God does not see?

mem

³⁷ Who can command—who has ever commanded—
   unless Our God has permitted it?
³⁸ Are not both good and evil
   from the Most High's mouth?

³⁹ Why should any among the living grumble
     when being punished for their sins?

nun

⁴⁰ Let us reflect on our path and examine it,
     then return to Our God.
⁴¹ Let us lift high our hearts and our hands
     to the God of heaven.
⁴² Let us say: "We have sinned and rebelled,
     and you have not forgiven us."

samekh

⁴³ You covered yourself with anger and hounded us,
     and slew us without mercy.
⁴⁴ You cloaked yourself in the clouds,
     far beyond the reach of our prayers.
⁴⁵ You treated us like scum and trash
     among the nations.

pe

⁴⁶ Our enemies laugh at us
     with open mouths.
⁴⁷ The snare and pit of the hunter lie ahead of us—
     devastation and ruin!
⁴⁸ Rivers of water run from my eyes
     because my people are destroyed.

ayin

⁴⁹ Tears flow continuously from my eyes,
     refusing all comfort—
⁵⁰ all of this while Our God
     watches from the heavens.
⁵¹ My spirit is grieved as I see
     the fate of children in my city.

tsadhe

⁵² Those who became my enemies without provocation
     chased and harangued me like a bird.
⁵³ They threw me in the grave alive to silence me
     and rolled a stone over the entrance.
⁵⁴ Waters rose to engulf me;
     they told me my time had come!

qoph

55 But I called your Name, O God,
  from the depths of the pit.
56 You heard me call: "Don't close your ears
  when I cry for mercy!"
57 You came to me when I called.
  "Fear not!" you said.

resh

58 O God, you took up my cause;
  you came to my rescue.
59 You bore witness to the injustices I endured
  and judged in my favor.
60 You saw how deeply vengeful they were;
  you saw all their schemes against me.

shin

61 You heard their sarcastic disdain, O God,
  and all their scheming,
62 the whispered rumors they told about me
  all day long.
63 See!—whether they sit or stand,
  I am the butt of their jokes.

taw

64 Pay them back for what they have done to me, O God!
  Give them what they deserve!
65 Show them how hard your heart can be,
  and let your curse fall on them.
66 Chase them down in anger and destroy them
  from under your skies, O God!

4:1-22

Aleph

1 The fine gold has faded,
  tarnished beyond recognition!
  The stones of the sanctuary are scattered;
  they lie on every street corner.

beth

2 Look—the dear children of Zion,
   once worth their weight in the finest gold,
now worth less than a clay pot—
   the kind made by any commoner.

ghimel

3 Even jackals offer their breasts
   to feed their young.
But my people have become as callous
   as an ostrich in the desert.

daleth

4 Infants who would nurse—
   their tongues cleave to the roof of their mouths.
Children begging for bread in the streets—
   no one offers them a crumb.

he

5 Those who dined on fine food
   sit starving in the streets.
Those reared in royal robes
   forage in trash heaps.

waw

6 The punishment inflicted on my people
   is harsher than that of Sodom,
whose demise took but an instant,
   with no hand outstretched to offer help.

zayin

7 Their rulers once shone brighter than snow,
   healthier than milk.
Their bodies were as rosy as coral;
   they glistened like lapis lazuli.

heth

8 Now their faces are covered with dirt;
   they wander the streets unrecognized.
Their withered skin is stretched against their bones,
   dry as kindling.

teth

9 The lucky ones perished by the sword—
  better than to die hungry,
 like those of us wasting away,
  without a scrap to eat.

yod

10 Even the most soft-hearted parents
  boiled their own children—
 yes, their own children were their food
  on the day my people were destroyed.

kaph

11 Our God erupted with rage
  and vented anger on the people.
 The Most High set a fire in Zion
  that consumed its very foundation.

lamed

12 The great rulers of the land couldn't believe it;
  no one in the world could believe
 that an enemy—any enemy—
  would ever enter the gates of Jerusalem.

mem

13 But it happened because of the sins of its prophets
  and the crimes of the priests,
 who stained the city walls
  with the blood of the upright.

nun

14 Now they grope through the streets,
  wandering aimlessly as if blind,
 their hands so defiled with blood
  that no one will even touch their garments.

samekh

15 "Away! Unclean!" people cried to them.
  "Get away! Don't touch us!"
 So they flee and roam the nations,
  with no place to call their home.

pe

16 It was Our God who scattered them;
  God no longer watches over them.
No pity for the priests—
  no honor for the elders!

ayin

17 Still, we looked in vain,
  hoping for some distant relief.
We watched day and night for a nation to come,
  a nation that could not rescue us anyway.

tsadhe

18 Our enemies watched our every move
  and stopped us on every street corner.
Our end was near, our days were numbered—
  it was all over for us.

qoph

19 Those who hounded us
  were swifter than the eagles in the sky.
They tracked us down over the hills;
  they ensnared us in the desert.

resh

20 Our God's anointed, our spirit, our breath,
  was caught in their traps,
even though we sought to live among the nations
  under the Most High's protection.

shin

21 Gloat while you can, children of Edom,
  dwellers in the land of Uz!
The cup will be passed to you in due course;
  you'll get drunk—and your nakedness will be exposed.

taw

22 Children of Zion—your punishment will end!
  Your exile will be extended no longer.
But you, Edom—you'll be punished for your offense,
  and your crime will be exposed.

Remember what happened to us, O God!
  Look—see how they deride us!
2 The land, our inheritance,
    is now in the hands of strangers—
    our homes belong to outsiders.
3 We wander like orphans without parents,
    and our parents grieve like widows and widowers.
4 We buy our own drinking water—
    water rightfully ours!
  We pay for it with the few sticks of kindling
    we have in our possession.
5 Shackles weigh down our necks—
    there is no relief.
  We are exhausted—
    they won't let us rest.
6 We humbled ourselves before Egypt and Assyria
    just to get food.
7 Our ancestors sinned,
    but they are long since gone.
  Now we are the ones who must bear
    the burden of their guilt.
8 Our lessers now rule us;
    no one can free us from their power.
9 We risk our lives to forage for food,
    fearing the sword in the desert.
10 Our skin burns like a furnace
    with the fever of starvation.
11 Women are violated in Zion—
    young women, in the towns of Judah!
12 Rulers are strung up by their hands;
    old people are slapped in the face.
13 Youth toil, grinding at the mill;
    children stagger under loads of wood.
14 Elders no longer meet at the city gate;
    young people no longer play their instruments.
15 Joy has disappeared from our hearts;
    our dancing has turned to mourning.
16 The laurel has fallen from our heads.
    Pity us—for we were sinners!

17 That's why our hearts are aching,
   that's why our eyes grow dim.
16 And that's why Zion has been destroyed,
   with jackals roaming freely in the streets.
19 O God, you rule forever;
   Your judgment seat lasts till the end of time.
20 Why have you utterly forgotten us,
   and abandoned us these many days?
21 Bring us back to you, O God;
   let us return.
   Bring us back to better days,
   like days now long past—
22 unless you have utterly rejected us
   in anger that is beyond all limits.

ecclesiastes

the sayings of qoheleth, begot of david,
and ruler in Jerusalem:

2 "Completely illusory!"
    says Qoheleth.*
"Completely illusory!
    Everything is just an illusion!"

3 What is humankind's benefit
    for all its labor under the sun?
4 One generation goes and another comes,
    but the world goes on forever.
5 The sun rises, then sets,
    then quickly gets ready to rise again.

---

* "Qoheleth," a feminine noun, means someone who calls a congregation to order, or serves as a lecturer or preacher. While it is clear that Qoheleth is a pseudonym for Solomon, some scholars feel it may have originally been an office filled by a woman; others feel the noun is feminine to indicate intensiveness, as in realizing an idea in its completeness. "Ecclesiastes," the Greek version of the term, simply means a member of an *ecclesia*, or assembly.

6 The wind blows first to the south, then to the north;
it swirls round and round, and then repeats its circuit.
7 All rivers empty into the sea, but the sea never fills up;
again and again the rivers go where they've always gone.
8 Everything is more wearisome
than words can possibly express—
even so, our eyes are never satisfied with what they see,
and our ears are never satisfied with what they hear.
9 What has been before will continue to be,
and what has been done before will continue to be done—
there's nothing new under the sun!
10 Can you think of anything about which we can say,
"Aha, this is new"?
No—already it has been here for ages,
long before our time.
11 Yet there is no remembrance of things past,
nor will there be any remembrance of things to come
by those who come even later.

12 I, Qoheleth, was ruler of Israel in Jerusalem. 13 I saw it as my duty—aided by Wisdom—to determine all that is accomplished under the sun. What a heavy task God has laid upon us! 14 So now I've seen all the works that have been done under the sun, and let me tell you: Everything is an illusion, like chasing the wind.

15 For what is crooked can't be straightened,
and what is lacking can't be counted.

16 I said to myself, "I have grown wiser than any of my forebears in Jerusalem. And I have expanded my mind immensely in wisdom and understanding." 17 But the more I studied wisdom—and the more I studied madness and foolishness as well—I realized that through it all, I was just chasing the wind.

18 In much wisdom there is much sorrow.
The more you know, the greater your grief.

2:1 So I said to myself, "All right, I'll give myself over to pleasure and see what is good."

Alas, I was to find that this too was illusory. 2 "Laughter is madness," I concluded, "and pleasure is useless."

3 I set out to enjoy wine, while still committed to wisdom. I set out to indulge in foolish things to understand what makes us happy, what is

good for us in that speck of time we are here under the heavens. ⁴ I took on great works; I built houses, and planted vineyards. ⁵ I created gardens and orchards for myself, with a variety of fruit trees. ⁶ I created ponds for watering stands of trees. ⁷ I had attendants galore—some of whom were "born into" my employ. I had herds of cattle and flocks of sheep larger than those of my ancestors in Jerusalem. ⁸ I amassed the treasures of rulers and provinces; I brought in singers—both women and men—and I gave myself over to sexual pleasure. ⁹ I became famous for accumulating more wealth than my ancestors in Jerusalem—and never forsook wisdom.

¹⁰ I denied myself nothing that my heart desired. I did not deprive myself of any pleasure. I rewarded myself by letting my heart rejoice in all my accomplishments. ¹¹ Then I reflected on what I had accomplished by my own hands, and the effort expended in doing it. And what did I find? It was all an illusion, like chasing the wind. I had accomplished nothing under the sun!

¹² I then turned my attention to wisdom, stupidity and folly. For instance, what can a ruler's successor do in office, other than what has already has been done?

¹³ Certainly I realized that wisdom outshines folly as light outshines dark. ¹⁴ The wise see ahead but the fool walks in the dark. Even so, I realized that the same fate awaits them both. ¹⁵ But then I asked myself the question, "If the fool and I both have the same fate, why have I striven for wisdom? Why bother?" Then the ironic conclusion came to me—this too is illusory. ¹⁶ For both the wise person and the fool will not be long remembered, for in the future they will have been forgotten. Whether wise or foolish, everyone dies!

¹⁷ Consequently I have come to hate life, and everything humankind does under the sun is grievous to me. Everything is an illusion, like chasing the wind.

¹⁸ I have come to abhor all my labor under the sun, the fruits of which I now must pass on to my successor. ¹⁹ Will this person be wise or foolish? Regardless, my successor will be in charge of all mighty things I created under the sun. This too is illusory. ²¹ For I, a person who has worked wisely, skillfully, and successfully, must leave it to someone who has not so much as lifted a finger—more illusion, another miscarriage of justice. ²² Why do I gain for all my sweat and struggle under the sun? ²³ What about the daily struggles, the strain of official duties, the anxiety in the dead of night? This too is illusory.

²⁴ In the end, there is nothing better for us than to eat and drink and find try to find solace in our work. This, I realized, is from the hand of

God, ²⁵ for who can eat and have enjoyment without God? ²⁶ God gives wisdom, knowledge and joy to those who are pleasing to the Most High; but the sinner gets to sweat at harvesting and storing and then giving it to the one pleasing to God.

This too is an illusion, like chasing the wind.

3:1–6:12

the**re** is a time for everything,
a season for every purpose under heaven:
² a season to be born and a season to die;
a season to plant and a season to harvest;
³ a season to hurt and a season to heal;
a season to tear down and a season to build up;
⁴ a season to cry and a season to laugh;
a season to mourn and a season to dance;
⁵ a season to scatter stones and a season gather them;
a season for holding close and a season for holding back;
⁶ a season to seek and a season to lose;
a season to keep and a season throw away;
⁷ a season to tear and a season to mend;
a season to be silent and a season to speak;
⁸ a season to love and a season to hate;
a season for hostilities and a season for peace.

ଓ଼   ଓ଼   ଓ଼

⁹ What do workers gain from their efforts? ¹⁰ I have reflected on this while learning all the kinds of work God gives to humankind. ¹¹ God has made everything in harmony with the divine; yet although the Almighty has imbued eternity in our soul, we are unable to grasp the totality of God's work from beginning to end.

¹² What I do know is that what is best for us is to be happy and enjoy life as long as we live. ¹³ And God's gift to us is to eat and drink and find fulfillment in our work.

¹⁴ I understand that whatever God does will endure for eternity; nothing can be added to it, nothing can be taken away. God makes it this way to keep reverence for the sacred alive in us.

¹⁵ That which is, has always been;
>
> that which is to be, has already been;
>
> and God calls the past back into existence.

¹⁶ Yet I notice that under the sun there is crime where justice should be, and the corrupt where the good should be. ¹⁷ I told myself that God will judge both the good and the corrupt at the appointed time for every issue and for every deed.

¹⁸ I told myself that God tests us to teach us that we're just like the animals. ¹⁹ For our fate and the fate of all living things are the same; as one dies, so dies the other. We all have the same breath, and we have no advantage over other forms of life. It's all an illusion. ²⁰ We all go to the same place. All forms of life are from dust, and return to dust. ²¹ Who knows whether our soul really goes up while an animal's soul goes down?

²² In short, I see there is nothing better than that we enjoy our work, for this is our destiny; who among us can see what will come after us?

4:1 Once more I reflected on all the oppression happening under the sun.

> I saw the tears of the oppressed;
>
> they have no one to comfort them.
>
> I saw the power of their oppressors,
>
> and they, too, have no one to comfort them.

² So I say that the dead, even though they are dead, are more fortunate than the living, even though they are still alive; ³ but more fortunate than both of these are the unborn, who have yet to experience all the corruption under the sun.

⁴ Then I saw that all labor, all skilled work, emerge from the envy one person feels for another. This too is an illusion, like chasing the wind.

> ⁵ Fools fold their arms,
>
> and suffer for lack of nourishment,
>
> ⁶ One handful of serenity
>
> is better than two of toil and frustration—
>
> and of chasing the wind.

⁷ Then I saw even greater illusion under the sun: ⁸ a solitary person, with no children, no sisters, no brothers. Yet there is no end of striving, no satisfaction with the wealth already accumulated: "For whom am I doing all this? For whom am I forgoing a life of pleasure?" This too is illusory. It's a miserable thing.

9   Two people are better than one,
        for they get a better return for their work.
10   For if one flags, the other gives support;
        but woe to the solitary person who falls
        and has no one to provide support.
11   And if two sleep together
        they keep each other warm;
        how can a person stay warm while alone?
12   One alone is easily overpowered;
        two provide protection for each other;
        and a rope of three strands is not easily broken.

13 A poor but wise teenager would be a better leader than a foolish ruler of riper years who can't accept advice; 14 such a teenager could have gone from prison to throne, or have been born a beggar only to reign in the same country. 15 I see a multitude of people under the sun following the youth, who is the ruler's successor. 16 There is no end to these people who are now subjects of the young sovereign. 17 Yet those who are to come later will not be happy with this ruler. Isn't that just as great an illusion, like chasing the wind?

ભ   ભ   ભ

* 5:1 When you go to the house of God, go carefully. And draw near to listen, rather than to offer the sacrifice of fools—they don't even know they're doing evil. 2 Don't be quick to speak, or impulsive in thought, to speak anything before God. God is in heaven while you are on earth, so let your words be as few as possible. 3 Just as nightmares come from being too anxious, being a fool comes from talking too much.

4 When you make a vow to God, fulfill it immediately. God is not pleased with fools; pay your pledges! 5 It is better not to make a vow than to make one and not fulfill it. 6 Don't let your words cause you to sin—don't say to the Messenger, "My vow was an mistake." Why make God angry with you and destroy the work of your hands? 7 Too many dreams and too many words—more illusion. So revere God!

8 Don't be surprised when you witness oppression of the poor in a province, or injustice, or the violation of their rights. That's because there's no

---

* In the Masoretic text, chapter 5 begins at verse 4:17 in our version, and there is a one-verse discrepancy throughout the chapter.

real accountability—one official watches over another, with even higher officials over them ⁹ And though you'll hear talk of the "common good," the ruler is the one who profits from all the fields.

¹⁰ Those who love money are never satisfied,
    those who love wealth feel they never have enough.

This too is illusion.

¹¹ When goods increase,
    consumers increase as well—
yet what use are things to their owners
    except as a feast for the eyes?

¹² Sweet sleep is the blessing of laborers,
    whether they're hungry or not;
but the richer the affluent become,
    the greater their insomnia!

¹³ Here's another grievous injustice I've seen under the sun: when the rich hoard their wealth—to their own detriment! ¹⁴ Or when people lose everything they have through some great misfortune, unable to leave even a crumb to their children.

¹⁵ Naked they come from their mother's womb,
    and naked they return.
As you come, so you go—
    and you can't take it with you!

¹⁶ This too is a grievous injustice—that they depart no better than they arrived. What do they gain in all their chasing the wind? ¹⁷ They eat their meals in darkness all of their days, in great frustration, ill-health and anger!

¹⁸ But then it finally dawned on me:

How good, how lovely it is to eat and drink
    and find satisfaction in everything we do under the sun
during the few days of life God gives us—
    to embrace everything that comes to us!

¹⁹ Regardless of how much wealth or possessions God gives us,
    we're also given the ability to find joy in what we have,
to accept whatever happens to us,
    and find fulfillment in our work—
    this is God's gift to us.

²⁰ If we embrace whatever comes,
    we never need to brood over the shortness of life,
    for God will keep our hearts filled with joy.

6:1 That's why another evil I see under the sun is so grievous, and places such a heavy burden on people. 2 To some God gives riches, wealth and honor—so much that there is nothing more for them to desire—yet God doesn't give them the chance to enjoy it, and it all goes to a stranger. This too is illusory, and a terrible injustice.

3 Let's say you have a hundred children and live to a ripe, old age—but if your soul doesn't take real satisfaction in the good things you're given, then a stillborn child who isn't accorded a proper burial is more fortunate than you! 4 It arrives in senseless darkness, and departs in that same darkness, without ever being given a name; 5 and though it never sees the sun and never tastes knowledge, it would be better off than someone 6 who lives for two thousand years yet never really savors all the good we are given. Both of them end their days in darkness.

> 7 We do everything we can to feed our appetite—
>   but if it never satisfies our soul,
> 8 what advantage do the wise have over the fools,
>   or those who know how to make money, over the poor?
> 9 Is the feasting of the eyes more important
>   than the soul's journey?

This too is illusory, like chasing the wind.

> 10 Whatever happens was planned long ago,
>   and it was known what would occur:
> humans can't contend
>   with One who is so much stronger!
> 11 You can talk all you want
>   but it still won't make any difference—
> how can it help you?
> 12 Who knows what is good for us in life,
>   in the few days of our meaningless life,
> which passes like a shadow?
> Who can tell us what will happen under the sun
>   when we're gone?

7:1-29

> **J**ust as a good name is better than expensive perfume,
>   so the deathday is better than the birthday.
> 2 It's better to go to a funeral home
>   than to a festival hall,

for all people come to the same end—
    let the living take this to heart!
3 Sorrow is better than laughter,
    and a sad face is good for the heart:
4 hearts grow wise in the house of mourning;
    they grow foolish in the house of merrymaking.

5 It is better to submit to the wise person's reprimand
    than to listen to the song of the fool.
6 For the laughter of fools is like
    the crackling of thorns in the fire under a cooking pot:
    it's all just illusion.

7 Doesn't oppression make fools of the wise?
    Don't bribes corrupt the heart?

8 The end of an argument is better than its beginning,
    and patience is better than pride.

9 Don't let your spirit become easily vexed,
    for anger lives in the heart of fools.

10 Never ask why the old days were better than the present;
    such a question doesn't come from wisdom.

11 Wisdom is as good as an inheritance:
    it profits those on whom the sun shines.
12 Just as money gives security, wisdom does the same;
    but knowledge has one further benefit:
    Wisdom saves the lives of those who treasure her.

13 Embrace those circumstances you can't control;
    for who can correct what God makes crooked?
14 Be full of joy in times of prosperity;
    in bad times consider this:
  one is the work of God; the other is too—
    and because of this, no one can discover the future.

15 In this fleeting life
    I have witnessed everything:
  just people perishing with all their justice;
    and the corrupt thriving with all their corruption.

16 Don't be too righteous—
    but don't be otherwise: why destroy yourself?
17 Don't be too wicked—
    but don't be naive, either: why risk an early death?
18 It is best to grasp the one
    and not release the other:
the person who reveres God
    will do justice to both.

19 Wisdom gives more strength to the wise
    than to ten rulers in a city.

20 There is not a just person alive
    who always does good and never sins.

21 Don't listen to everything people say,
    for you might hear your co-workers cursing you;
22 in your heart of hearts you know
    how many times you have cursed others.

23 All of these issues I tested with wisdom; I said, "I'll play the sage," but they were far from me— 24 well beyond my reach; deep, deep beyond discovering them. 25 So once more I focused my mind on the study of wisdom and justice, and on knowing that violence is foolishness and folly is madness. 26 And the greatest madness, more bitter than death? Sexual infidelity! Adulterers ensnare their partners with hearts like traps and hands like handcuffs. Let those who please God avoid them; let only sinners be their captives!

         ભ   ભ   ભ

27 This is what I, Qoheleth, have discovered, after thinking it all through and trying to find an explanation for everything: 28 though my soul searched, I found no explanation at all. I found one man among a thousand with an answer, but not a woman among them who would even try.* 29 In the end, all I found was that God made people to be upright— but they're always looking for explanations!

---

* The phrase "with an answer" is conjectural; the text says, simply, "I found one man among a thousand, and no woman among them all." Other versions insert "upright" before "man" and "woman," but this strikes us as even more implausible.

Who here is wise, and can explain the adage, "Wisdom gives a glow to the face, and makes it lose its hardness"?

² I can! It means you should obey the command of your ruler; since you took an oath before God, ³ don't act rashly and join evil cabals, for rulers do whatever they please, ⁴ and their word is preeminent. Who, then, can question them?

⁵ Those who keep the commandments will suffer no harm,
for the wise heart knows the proper time to take action,
and which action to take.

⁶ But even knowing the correct time and procedure can't change the fact that we all die, and that weighs heavily on the mind— ⁷ for who can know what is to come? Who can tell when it is to happen? ⁸ People don't have the power to keep body and spirit together; we don't control the day of our dying. Being a "conscientious objector" won't help in this war, nor can the rich buy their way out of it.

⁹ I reflected on all this; I took into account everything that happens under the sun, where people still tyrannize others and treat them unjustly. ¹⁰ For example, I see the corrupt carried in for the burial service, and Temple authorities honoring them; they are being praised in the very city they corrupted.

Here is another frustration: ¹¹ that the sentence upon criminals is not carried out immediately, which emboldens others to commit new crimes. ¹² Some people can commit a hundred new crimes while their first sentence is being appealed—and delayed! I know what they say, that it will go well for those who revere God when they stand in God's presence, ¹³ and that it will not go well for the corrupt, and their days won't be as long as their shadow, for they don't revere God. ¹⁴ Even so, this frustration occurs regularly on earth—that the just are treated as if they were corrupt, and the corrupt are treated as if there were just. It's completely senseless.

¹⁵ That's why I recommend that we enjoy ourselves, for there is nothing better under the sun for people other than to eat, drink, and be merry. Then we'll have joy along with our toil during the days of life God gives us under the sun.

CR CR CR

[16] When I undertook the pursuit of wisdom and of understanding what is done here on earth—going without sleep day and night— [17] I realized that humankind cannot grasp the totality of God's work done under the sun. No matter how hard they try to find meaning for it all, they never do. Even if the wise say they understand, they really don't.

9[1] But as I reflected on all this, I realized that the actions of the wise and the just are determined by God—even love and hate. We just don't know everything that awaits us. [2] But we all share the same fate—

> the upright and the corrupt,
>> the good and the bad,
> the clean and the unclean,
>> the pious and the irreligious.
> As with the good,
>> so with the sinner;
> as with those who take vows,
>> so with those who are afraid to take them.
> [3] One fate comes to all!

This is the worst thing that happens to humankind. Yes, the human heart is corrupt and filled with madness all our life—and then we die!

[4] At the same time, those who are still among the living at least have hope—after all, a live dog is better than a dead lion! [5] The living are conscious of living; the dead are conscious of nothing. They have no further reward, and even all memory of them will be forgotten. [6] Their loves, their hatreds and their envies have died with them. Never again will they take part in anything done under the sun.

[7] So go, eat your bread in merriment, and drink your wine with a merry heart, for God already judges your work. [8] Always wear white; don't spare the ointment on your hair. [9] Enjoy life with someone you love, all the illusory days of life allotted you under the sun—all these days of illusion. This is your lot in life; this is the work you are truly supposed to do under the sun.

[10] Whatever you choose to do, do with all the drive you have. There will be no sense of accomplishment, pride, learning, or wisdom in the grave. And the grave, after all, is where you are going.

[11] This too I have seen under the sun:

> The race is not won by the swift,
>> nor is the battle won by the brave;

bread is not won by the wise,
   nor wealth by the clever,
nor privilege by the experts—
   all are subject to time and fate.

¹² People are no more knowledgeable about their time than the fish in the fatal trap, or the bird in the snare. We too are snared in that fatal trap when our time comes.

¹³ I witnessed another event under the sun that deeply affected me. ¹⁴ A village with few inhabitants was attacked by a mighty ruler who surrounded it with siegeworks. ¹⁵ The city could have been saved through the wisdom of a poor but wise person who happened to live in the city, yet no one thought to consult the sage.

¹⁶ So I say: wisdom may be better than might, but the wisdom of sages is not valued and their words are not heard.

9:17–12:13

*T*he quiet words of the wise
   should be heeded over the shouts of a foolish ruler.

¹⁸ Wisdom is better than everything precious,
   but a single error can destroy much that is good.
10:1 Just as single dead fly can ruin precious ointment,
   a little folly can ruin great wisdom and honor.

² The heart of wise people leads them aright;
   the heart of fools leads them astray.

³ Even in simply walking down the road,
   fools demonstrate just how foolish they are.

⁴ When the wrath of the ruler erupts against you, don't lose hope;
   for calmness can pacify huge offenses.

⁵ There is an evil I have seen under the sun,
   as grave as a ruler's misjudgment:
⁶ fools placed in positions of power,
   while truly deserving people find no recognition.

7   It's like seeing peasants astride horses
        with royalty walking humbly alongside!

8   Dig a ditch, and you might fall in;
        knock down a wall, and a snake might bite you.
9   Quarry stones, and you can drop one on your foot;
        chop wood, and the ax could slip.
10 Let an ax get dull and forget to sharpen it,
        and you'll have to work harder to make it cut.
    Success in all these things
        depends on being prudent!
11 After all, if the snake bites before you weave your magic,
        what good is being an accomplished snake charmer?

12 Words from the mouths of the sages are pleasing,
        but fools' lips are their undoing.
13 They start out speaking foolishness,
        but end up wreaking disaster in their madness—
14   and they never stop talking!

    No one knows what is coming;
        who can tell what the future holds?

15 Fools find hard work so burdensome
        that they can't even find their way into town,
        much less find a job!

16 Woe to the land whose ruler is a weakling
        and whose ministers feast before noon!
17 Blessed is the land whose ruler is in control
        and whose ministers dine at a proper time,
        and for enrichment, not drunkenness!

18 Sagging rafters are caused by laziness;
        a leaky roof comes from idle hands.

19 A feast is for laughter,
        wine is for merriment in life—
        but money is the answer to everything!

20 Even in your thoughts, don't curse the ruler,
        even in your bedroom, don't curse the wealthy,

for a passing bird may deliver your words,
    and wings may tell all your secrets.

11:1 Cast your bread onto the waters,
    and you will receive it back at another time.
2 Share your portions with seven or eight others,
    for you never know what catastrophe will befall the earth.

3 When the clouds are full of rain,
    they empty it out on the earth.
When a tree falls, by the south wind or the north,
    it stays wherever it falls.
4 But worrying about the wind keeps you from sowing,
    and studying the clouds all day keeps you from reaping.
5 Just as you don't know how spirit enters into a child,
    knitting body to soul in a mother's womb,
so you can't foresee the actions of God,
    who brings all things to pass.
6 So then, sow your seed in the morning
    and keep busy in the evening,
for you don't know which of them will grow,
    this one or that one—or both!

7 Light is sweet;
    it is a pleasant thing to feast one's eyes on the sun!
8 People should enjoy all the years of their life,
    however many they may be,
remembering how long the darkness will be!
    The future is nothing but illusion.

9 Rejoice, women and men, while you are still young;
    may your hearts cheer you in the days of your youth.
Follow the desires of your heart
    and the vision of your eyes.
Keep in mind that God will call you
    to the judgment of all these things.
10 Unburden your heart,
    banish pain from your body,
    for youth and vigor are illusory.
12:1 Remember your Creator while you are still young,
    while still innocent,

before that time of life when you say,
    "There isn't pleasure anymore;"
2 before the sun dims, as well as the moon and the stars;
    before the clouds return once the rain stops;
3 before the day when the house guards tremble,
    and the mighty are bowed low,
and the millers stop for lack of help,
    for the day darkens at the windows;
4 and the front doors are shut;
    when the sound of milling is faint;
when the chirping of the birds vanishes,
    and the singers are silenced;
5 when you become afraid of heights,
    and dread walking in the streets;
when the almond trees bloom,
    the grasshoppers are sluggish with food,
    and you lose your appetite;
when you go to your eternal reward,
    and the mourners go about the streets;
6 before the silver cord—a sign of life—is snapped;
    or the golden bowl—a sign of life—is broken;
or the pitcher at the well—a sign of life—is smashed,
    as well as the pulley;
7 or before dust returns to the earth
    as it was at the beginning,
and before God rescinds
    the breath of life.

8 "Completely illusory!"
    says Qoheleth.
"Completely illusory!
    Everything is just an illusion!"

03   03   03

9 Qoheleth was both a sage and a teacher. After classifying, research-ing, and carefully editing many proverbs, Qoheleth went on to teach the people, 10 always striving to write with lucidity and honesty. 11 The words of the wise serve as goads; they are like long nails in prodding sticks given by one Shepherd.

¹² Daughters and sons, here is a final "proverb"—consider yourselves warned:

> Writing books is a long and arduous task,
>> and all the study that goes along with it is wearisome.

¹³ The last word summarizes all you have read:
>> revere God, and keep God's commandments—
>> that is humankind's only task.

> For God will call every creature to account
>> for every deed, every secret,
>> be it good or bad.

esther*

[**D**uring the second year of the reign
of Ahasuerus the Great,** on the first day of Nisan, a dream came to Mordecai, begot of Jair, begot of Shimei, begot of Kish, of the tribe of Benjamin—
³ a Jew living in Susa and holding high office in the imperial court. ⁴ He was

---

* The book of *Esther is* something of a hybrid—a Hebrew original with later Greek additions, some of
which duplicate the Hebrew text. We have interspersed the two versions so that the different texts
fall roughly in chronological order, but the verse numbering will not always be sequential; we have
set the Greek additions in brackets. Even a casual reading of the two versions will reveal significant
differences between them. One important difference is that the Hebrew account is famous for never
mentioning God, while the Greek text does; portions of the Greek additions, probably because of
their more overtly religious language, are used in the Roman Catholic liturgy, while the Hebrew
sections are not; and the Greek sections make explicit what is only implicit in the Hebrew story.
**This is a Latinized transliteration of the Hebrew version of the name of the Persian ruler Kshajarsha—
known to the Greeks as Xerxes—who lived 485-464 BCE. Other helpful introductory information:
Nisan begins on the first new moon after the March equinox; Mordecai is the Hebrew form of
Marduk, the creator god of Babylonian mythology who handed down tablets of sacred law on a holy
mountain—the name means "mighty warrior"; and Susa is the capital of Elam, which later became
winter residence of Persian rulers. In addition, the Babylonian captivity took place in 589 BCE. Given
the date of the events in the book, this would make Mordecai over 100 years old. What it may mean
here is that he is a descendant of one of the prisoners, though other interpreters do not think the
dates matter—that the writers of the book were playing fast and loose with the dates.

among the prisoners that Nebuchadnezzar the Great of Babylon had exiled from Jerusalem along with Jeconiah, ruler of Judah.

⁵ In the dream, there were shouts and clamors, thunder and earthquakes and chaos over the whole world. ⁶ Then two large dragons appeared, each ready for a fight, roaring fiercely. ⁷ When their voices thundered, every nation prepared to wage war against the nation of the Just.

⁸ A day of uncertainty and anguish, of sickness and agony, of oppression and tribulation, descended on the whole world. ⁹ The nation of the Just was sick with trepidation from the fear of the evils lurking in wait for them. They prepared for death as they cried out to God.

¹⁰ From their cry, as from a tiny spring, there grew a mighty river, a torrent of water. ¹¹ Dawn came, and the sun rose, and the lowly were raised up to devour the powerful.

¹² When he awoke from the dream—this vision of God's plan—Mordecai pondered the matter very seriously, attempting to discern the meaning of the dream.]

1:1–3:3, 13:1–6, 3:14–4:17, 13:7–14:19

*t*he following events took place during the time of Ahasuerus—the same Ahasuerus who ruled 127 provinces from India to Ethiopia—when he set up the imperial throne in the capital city of Susa.

³ During the third year of his reign, he gave a feast for all the government officials and members of the royal court as well as the governors of Persia and Media and all the nobles and administrators of the provinces. ⁴ So Ahasuerus put all the wealth of the empire on display for many days— 180 in all—with a great show of pomp and grandeur.

⁵ At the end of those six months, Ahasuerus gave a banquet for everyone in the capital city of Susa, both the mighty and the lowly. ⁶ The banquet lasted for seven days and was held in the courtyard of the royal gardens. The regal court was adorned with white and purple tapestries which hung by cords of fine linen and purple thread attached to silver rings on large marble pillars. Couches of gold and silver were placed on a mosaic floor of malachite, marble, mother of pearl, and turquoise. ⁷ Wine was served in golden goblets, each one unique in design. ⁸ The wine flowed freely, as was the style at an imperial banquet. The ruler gave strict orders, however, that no one was required to drink and that the waiters respect

the preferences of the guests. ⁹ Queen Vashti* also gave a banquet for the women in the court of Ahasuerus.

¹⁰ On the seventh day of the revels, Ahasuerus was drunk after a great deal of wine. He ordered Mehuman, Biztha, Harbona, Bigtha, Abagtha, Zethar, and Carkas, the seven eunuchs who attended to his every need, ¹¹ to bring Queen Vashti into his presence, crowned with the royal diadem, to put on "a show of her beauty"** for those present and for the government officials—she was very beautiful. ¹² But Queen Vashti rebuffed the eunuchs and refused to obey the order.

At this, Ahasuerus became irate and his rage boiled over. ¹³ So he consulted all his chief advisors, all experts in matters of law, since it was common to consult lawyers and jurists in such matters. ¹⁴ He called Carshena, Shethar, Admatha, Tarshish, Meres, Marsena, and Memucan, the seven governors of Persia and Media who had special access to the royal court and held the top offices of the empire. ¹⁵ "What does the law say about this?" Ahasuerus asked. "How do we deal with the matter of Vashti's disobedience of the order which I, Ahasuerus, delivered to her through the eunuchs?"

¹⁶ Memucan answered in the presence of the sovereign and all the governors, "Vashti has shown disrespect not only to you, Ahasuerus, but also to all the governors and peoples in all the provinces of your empire. ¹⁷ News of her conduct will spread to the women of the empire, and it will fan the flames of insolence among them toward their spouses—¹⁸ they could say, 'Look, Ahasuerus ordered Vashti to appear before him and she refused.' The spouses of all the governors of Persia and Media will hear of Vashti's behavior by the end of the day, and will start talking to the governors in the same manner. That will encourage anger and scorn all around.

¹⁹ "If it is your will, then, issue a royal decree to be fixed irreversibly into the laws of Persia and Media, which states that Vashti is never again to appear before Ahasuerus and that her position is to be given to another who is more worthy. ²⁰ Let this decree which you issue be proclaimed throughout the length and breadth of your empire, so that all women, whether aristocrat or commoner, will from now on submit to the authority of their husbands."

²¹ Ahasuerus was very impressed with the speech, so he and the gover-

---

* Unknown individual. The historian Herodotus lists Amestris as queen.
**Euphemism for a lewd sexual request. Ahasuerus' consultation of his legal staff in verse 13 was not at all common for such minor concerns, and the author is being deliberately sarcastic. At the same time, it shows how Vashti's refusal to allow herself to be denigrated actually challenged the very structure of Persian society.

nors did as Memucan advised. [22] He sent letters to all the provinces of the empire, each letter in the language and script of the province, declaring that every husband be proclaimed head of the house.

CR CR CR

[2:1] After a while, when Ahasuerus' anger abated, he thought of Vashti and her behavior and the sanctions he brought against her.

[2] The members of the imperial court approached Ahasuerus and said, "Why don't we seek out all the most beautiful women of the empire for the ruler? [3] You can appoint a committee representing all the provinces of the empire to bring all the most beautiful women to the palace at Susa, to the harem which is supervised by Hegai, our ruler's eunuch. [4] Let Hegai give them all the finery they need to adorn themselves, and let the one who pleases our sovereign most take Vashti's place in the palace." This advice pleased Ahasuerus very much, so he acted on it.*

[5] Now, in the palace of Susa there lived a Jew named Mordecai, begot of Jair, begot of Shimei, begot of Kish of the tribe of Benjamin, [6] who was taken captive in Jerusalem along with Jeconiah, ruler of Judah by Nebuchadnezzar, ruler of Babylon. [7] He was the guardian of Hadassah, who was also known as Esther.** [14] She was extremely beautiful. Esther was the daughter of Mordecai's cousin. After her parents died, Mordecai adopted her as his own child.

[8] After Ahasuerus' edict was issued, a great number of young women came to the palace at Susa and were placed under the supervision of Hegai, the chaperone. Esther was among them. [9] It was Esther who caught the ruler's attention; not only did he provide her with everything she wanted for her wardrobe and meals, he also gave her special attendants from his own court and transferred her personal attendants to the best part of the harem.

During this time, [10] Esther never revealed that she or her relatives were Jewish, because Mordecai warned her against doing so. [11] Mordecai paced

---

* Throughout *Esther*, Ahasuerus is easily swayed by the advice of others, whether for good or evil. Some commentators think the author's intent is to place blame on characters such as Haman later in the story. Others believe the tendency to be so easily influenced was typical of despots of the region.
** It was a common practice for Jews in exile to have both a Jewish name and a name from the culture where they lived. The name Esther is the Hebrew form of Ishtar, and means "beautiful as the moon." Ishtar was the Babylonian manifestation of the Great Goddess; her rites sought to find the balance between spirituality and sexuality. Each year the worshipers of Ishtar celebrated the sacrificial death of her son, a divine ruler, and her descent into the realm of the dead to resurrect him—culminating in the Day of Joy, when he was restored to life after three days.

in front of courtyard of the harem every day, trying to find out how she was and how she was being treated.

12 Each of the young women came before Ahasuerus in turn, after having spent twelve months in preparation, as the regulations for the women decreed. This preparatory period consisted of the following stages: six months with oil and myrrh, then six months with spices and lotions—all standard beauty treatments. 13 Each one was allowed to bring something of her own choosing from the harem before coming to Ahasuerus. 14 After appearing before Ahasuerus in the evening, the young woman was returned to a different harem in the morning, this one entrusted to Shaashgaz, the eunuch who was custodian of the ruler's concubines. The young women did not go back to Ahasuerus unless he was particularly pleased with her and called for her by name.

15 When it came time for Esther, daughter of Abihail, whose nephew Mordecai adopted her as his own daughter, to go to the palace, she did not bring anything with her beyond what had been given to her by Hegai, the royal eunuch and supervisor of the harem. Esther soon won the esteem of everyone who saw her. 16 She was brought to Ahasuerus at the palace in the tenth month, Tebeth, during the seventh year of his reign. 17 Ahasuerus liked Esther more than all the others—none of the others found as much favor with him. So he placed the crown on her head and proclaimed her to be queen in place of Vashti.

18 Then Ahasuerus gave a great feast in her honor for all the governors and government officials, proclaiming a holiday in all the provinces and making bounteous gifts with royal abandon.

19 Even after Esther had been transferred to the second harem along with the others, she continued to keep her heritage and her parentage secret, in respect of Mordecai's wishes, whose instructions she continued to follow in the same way she did when she was under his care.

20 During this time, Mordecai was a member of the Sovereign's Gate,* 21 and two rebels, Bigthan and Teresh, who were royal eunuchs belonging to the Guardians of the Threshold, hatched a plot to kill Ahasuerus. 22 Mordecai heard about the plot and informed Esther, who, on Mordecai's instruction, told Ahasuerus. 23 The matter was investigated and proven true, and the two schemers were sent to the gallows. The matter was then recorded in the Annals in the presence of Ahasuerus.

---

* The Sovereign's Gate was the term given to Ahasuerus' chancellery—both the royal administrative staff and the building where they worked.

[12:1 While residing at the imperial court with Bigthan and Teresh, two of the imperial eunuchs who guarded the palace, Mordecai learned of their evil scheme to assassinate Ahasuerus. Upon uncovering their plot, he warned the ruler about them. 2 Ahasuerus gave orders for the two eunuchs to be tortured. When they confessed, they were executed. 3 Then Ahasuerus had these events recorded in the palace history, and Mordecai kept his own account of them as well.

4 Ahasuerus appointed Mordecai to an office in the royal court and rewarded him with gifts.

5 But Haman, begot of Hammedatha the Agagite, who had the sovereign's favor, decided to get even with Mordecai on behalf of the two eunuchs.]

3:1 Not long after this happened, Ahasuerus selected Haman, begot of Hammedatha, from the land of Agag,* for promotion in rank and status above all the other members of the court and officers of the state, 2 and proclaimed that all the members of the Ruler's Gate must bow down and prostrate themselves before Haman.

Mordecai, however, refused to bow or prostrate himself. 3 The other members of the court asked him every day, "Why do you defy the imperial command?" 4 But Mordecai did not listen to them, so they reported the matter to Haman, hoping to see if Mordecai would continue this behavior, since they knew that he was Jewish.

5 When Haman saw for himself that Mordecai would not bow down and prostrate himself before him, he became enraged. 6 When he was told that Mordecai was Jewish, he was not content just to see Mordecai killed, but wanted to wipe out all of Mordecai's people throughout the empire of Ahasuerus.

7 So in the first month of the twelfth year of Ahasuerus' reign, the month of Nisan, they cast the *pur***—that is, the lot—in front of Haman to determine the day and the month in which extermination would begin. The lot fell to the twelfth month, Adar.

ભ   ભ   ભ

8 Haman then sought an audience with Ahasuerus. He said, "These are

---

* Unknown region. The name, however, refers to an Amalekite ruler conquered by Saul. The significance is that, as a Benjaminite, Saul is Mordecai's ancestor. This hints at a long-standing feud, and would provide additional motive for Haman's actions against Mordecai.
** An old Babylonian word. The ancients regularly cast lots to determine the will of the gods. The term is introduced to explain the Feast of Purim, which may have originally been a Babylonian festival.

a people who remain unassimilated into our ways, and they are scattered throughout the empire in all the provinces. Their laws are not like those of the other peoples and they disregard the imperial decrees. It is not in your interest, therefore, to tolerate them. ⁹ If the sovereign would order their destruction, I am willing to give 375 tons of silver to royal tax collectors to fill the royal treasury."

¹⁰ Ahasuerus removed his signet ring and handed it to Haman begot of Hammedatha the Agagite, oppressor of the Jewish people. ¹¹ "Keep your money!" Ahasuerus said, "You may deal with those people any way you want."

¹² On the thirteenth day of the first month, the royal scribes were summoned and copies were made of the orders given to Haman. Each copy was addressed to the governors and administrators of each of the provinces and written in the distinct language and script of the province. The edict was signed in the name of Ahasuerus and sealed with the imperial ring. ¹³ The letters were then sent by runners to every province in the empire, ordering the destruction, slaughter and annihilation of the Jewish people—old and young, women, men and children—together with the seizure of their property, on the thirteenth day of the twelfth month, which is Adar.

[13:1 The following letter was sent:

"The Great Ruler, Ahasuerus, to all the governors of the 127 provinces from India to Ethiopia, and to their subordinate district administrators:

² "Ever since I was placed in authority over many nations to govern the whole world, I was determined never to be carried away by the insolence of power, but rather to rule with moderation and clemency in order to assure for my subjects a life free from turbulence. I resolved to offer every person in my empire all the benefits of civilization as well as unhindered passage for all from one end to the other, and to restore the peace which all peoples desire.

³ "So, in consulting our advisors in how best to bring this about, I was informed by one of them, who is distinguished for his wisdom, confirmed in his loyalty and unshakable in his trustworthiness, and second in rank only to the sovereign—Haman by name— ⁴ that there is mingled among us a certain crude people who are opposed, by their own law, to every other people, and who defy the royal edicts in such a way as to obstruct that form of government which will assure the common good.

⁵ "Considering, therefore, that this people, so different from us, are in complete opposition to the rest of humanity by virtue of their barbaric sys-

tem of laws, of their hostility to our interests and of their propensity to commit the most unspeakable crimes—to the point of endangering the stability of the empire*—I therefore command that these people, including women and children, ⁶ who have been spoken about in letters written by Haman—who has been assigned to watch over our interests and who is like a second guardian to all of us—be destroyed, root and branch, by the swords of their enemies, without pity or mercy, on the fourteenth day of the twelfth month, Adar, of the current year, ⁷ so that all these past and present insurrectionists be sent to the underworld in a single day, and so that our government may continue to enjoy perpetual stability and peace."]

3:14 The text of this decree, which was to be proclaimed as law throughout the empire, was sent out to the myriad peoples so that each could prepare for the day. At the ruler's order, the couriers set out with great speed. The decree was first proclaimed in the palace of Susa.

¹⁵ So, as the ruler and Haman indulged themselves in food and drink, shock from the news spread throughout the city of Susa.

ଔ   ଔ   ଔ

4:1 When Mordecai heard about the decree, he ripped his tunic and put on sackcloth and ashes. Then, he paraded through the city, sounding loud and bitter shrieks, ² until he arrived at the front door of the Sovereign's Gate, though he was stopped there because no one was permitted to enter wearing sackcloth and ashes. ³ The same thing happened in every province—no sooner had the imperial decree been read than every Jewish person in the province began mourning, fasting, weeping and wailing, and many of them put on sackcloth and ashes.

⁴ When Esther's attendants told her what was happening, she was overwhelmed with grief. She sent out clothes for Mordecai to wear instead of sackcloth, but he refused to wear them. ⁵ Then Esther called Hathach, a eunuch assigned by the sovereign to attend her. She ordered him to go to Mordecai and ask him why he was behaving in this manner.

⁶ Hathach went out to Mordecai, who was still in the public square in front of the Sovereign's Gate. ⁷ Mordecai told him what happened to him, and about the bribe that Haman offered to the imperial treasury as payment for the destruction of the Jewish people. ⁸ Mordecai also gave the

---

* We hear in this edict the very words of the Nazis—or indeed those of any government which has sought to exterminate an entire people. Atrocity and genocide have always been excused or explained by the same arguments.

eunuch a copy of the decree of extermination which was proclaimed in Susa, and asked him to show it to Esther so that she might know everything that had happened. He also asked the eunuch to tell Esther to go to the sovereign and plead the case of their people before him. ["Remember your humbler origins," he said, "when I provided you with all you needed. Since Haman, who holds the second place in the empire, has asked the sovereign to kill us, implore Our God to speak to the sovereign on our behalf and save us from destruction!"]

9 Hathach returned to Esther and told her what Mordecai had said. 10 She returned the following message to Mordecai: 11 "All of the emperor's attendants and people of the provinces know that anyone who approaches the sovereign in the inner court without being summoned faces one punishment—death—unless the sovereign spares her life by pointing the golden scepter toward her. I have not been summoned to the sovereign for the last thirty days."

12 When Mordecai heard Esther's reply, he wrote back the following response: 13 "Don't fool yourself into thinking that, just because you are in the imperial palace, you will be the only Jewish person to escape. 14 If you insist on remaining silent at this time, vindication and liberation will come to our people through another source,* but both you and your family will surely die. Who's to say?—you may have come into the royal court for just this moment."

15 So Esther sent a message to Mordecai: 16 "Bring together all the Jewish people in Susa now and fast for me. Do not eat or drink, day and night, for three days. After that, I will go to the sovereign in defiance of the law. If I die, I die."

17 Mordecai went and carried out all of Esther's instructions.

[13.8 Then, recalling all the wonders of Our God, Mordecai offered this prayer:

9   My God, my God, Supreme Ruler of all things,
          everything is subjugated to you
      and none can withstand your power
          when you are determined to liberate Israel.
10   Yes, you created the heavens and the earth
          and all the wonders under the heavens.

---

* "Another source" is a circumlocution for God. One significance of the absence any mention of God in the Hebrew text is to emphasize that even though God is not present, God is still working behind the scenes.

¹¹ You are the God of All,
   and none can resist you, O God.
¹² You know all things;
   you know, O God—
you know that I am not motivated
   by impertinence, conceit or show
   when I refuse to bow down before proud Haman—
¹³ I would readily have kissed his feet
   for the safety of Israel.
¹⁴ But what I did, I did
   so that honor would not be given to any mere mortal
   above the Glory of God.
I refuse to bow before anyone but you, O God,
   and in refusing to bow, I will not act out of pride.
¹⁵ And now, my God, my sovereign,
   God of Sarah and Abraham,
I call on you to rescue your people!
   For there are those who seek our destruction
¹⁶ and plot to end your ancient people,
   whom you brought forth from the land of Egypt
   and called your own.
¹⁷ Hear my plea
   and have mercy on your chosen people.
Turn our tears into laughter
   that we may live to sing your Name, O God.
Do not let perish
   the mouths of those who praise you.
¹⁸ And, in the face of death, all of Israel cried out with all their strength.

14¹ Esther also sought strength in the Most High as she too looked death in the face. ² She took off her regal robes and put on mourning clothes. And instead of expensive oils, she covered her head with ashes and filth. She humbled herself severely and all traces of her former happiness and elegance were now defiled with tresses torn from her hair. ³ She called out to the Most High God of Israel with these words:

My God, our only Sovereign,
   come to my aid, for I am alone
and have no other relief but you,
⁴   for I am about to risk my own life.
⁵ I have been taught from my youth,
   in the heart of my family,

that you, O God,
   chose Israel from among the nations
and that you chose our ancestors
   from among all the peoples of ancient times,
to be your lot forever
   and that you have kept your promise to them.
6 But when we sinned against you,
   you gave us over to our enemies
7 since we paid homage to their gods.
   O God, you are just.
8 But, even now, they are not satisfied
   with the bitterness of our oppression.
They have placed themselves into the hands of their idols
9   and have sworn to destroy what you yourself decreed—
to obliterate our heritage,
   to silence those who sing your praises—
to extinguish your altar
   and the glory of your Temple—
10 and instead to open the mouths of the nonbelievers
   and sing songs of praise to worthless idols,
   and to worship forever a fleshly ruler.
11 Never hand over your power, O God,
   to illusory entities!
Never allow mere mortals
   to laugh at our destruction!
Turn their plans against them,
   and make them a byword,
   a warning those who would attack us.
12 Remember us, O God, and show yourself
   at this time of our need.
As for me, give me courage,
   Sovereign God of supreme power.
13 Give me a convincing tongue
   when I go in to face the lion,
and persuade him to hate our enemies
   so that they and all like them may be brought to their end.
14 As for our people, liberate us by your mighty hand
   and come to my aid, for I am alone
   and can rely on none but you, O God.
15 You know all things;
   you know how much I despise the favor
   these unbelievers heap on me,

that I hate the bed of these unbelievers,
  hate living in a foreign land.
¹⁶ You know that I am a prisoner here
  and that I hate the turban of my high position
that shackles my head
  when I appear in the imperial court—
I detest it as if it were a filthy rag,
  and I never wear it on my days of rest.
¹⁷ I have never eaten at Haman's table,
  nor taken pleasure in the imperial banquets,
  nor drunk the wine of oblation,
¹⁸ nor have I found any pleasure
  since the day I was placed in my position,
except in you, O God,
  the God of Sarah and Abraham.
¹⁹ O God, whose might surpasses all,
  save us from these criminals
  and free me from my fear.

15:1-15, 5:1–8:12, 16:1-24, 8:13–9:19

On the third day, after she finished praying, Esther removed her grieving clothes and adorned herself in her full grandeur. ² Now, in her splendor, she called on God who watches over all peoples and frees them.

Then she picked two attendants. ³ She leaned on one elegantly, ⁴ while the other accompanied her carrying her train. ⁵ Her face shone with perfect beauty and she looked happy, as if she had just fallen in love. But in her heart, she was frozen with fear. ⁶ When she had gone through the doors she stood face-to-face with Ahasuerus, who was seated on the throne and dressed in full imperial array with gold and precious jewels. He was a terrifying sight to behold.

⁷ Lifting a stern face, he looked at Esther in fierce anger. She faltered, turned pale and almost fainted, and had to lean her hand on her attendant's shoulder.

⁸ But God intervened, and Ahasuerus' heart grew soft. He rose from the throne and took her in his arms until she was once again able to stand. He soothed her with words of comfort, saying, ⁹ "What is it, Esther? I am your husband; you need not fear me. ¹⁰ Our law applies only to ordinary people. You will not die. Come here to me."

[11] He lifted his golden scepter and touched her on the neck. [12] Then he kissed her, saying, "Tell me what you want."

[13] "When I looked at you, my sovereign, I was overcome by your terrible majesty. [14] You are so great, and your face is filled with compassion."

[15] But while she was speaking, she fainted again. Ahasuerus grew concerned as all the attendants tried to revive her.]

[5:1] On the third day, Esther put on her royal garments and went to the courtyard of the palace, in front of the Imperial Court. Ahasuerus was sitting on the royal throne facing the entrance. [2] Ahasuerus was happy to see Esther and held out his royal scepter. Esther approached and touched the tip of the scepter.

[3] Ahasuerus said to her, "What is your desire, Queen Esther? What do you request of me? Whatever it is, I will give it to you—up to half of my empire."

[4] And Esther said, "This is a special day for me. If it pleases my sovereign, I would like you and Haman to be the guests of honor at a banquet I will prepare today."

[5] Ahasuerus said, "Summon Haman right now, so that we may do what Esther desires."

So they both came to the banquet that Esther had prepared. [6] While they were drinking wine, Ahasuerus said to Esther, "What do you desire, Esther? Anything you say will be given to you"

[7] So Esther said, "This is my request: [8] if I have found favor in the sight of my sovereign, let my sovereign and Haman return again to a second banquet that I will prepare for them. I will do tomorrow what I have done today."

[9] So Haman left the palace filled with joy. But when he caught sight of Mordecai in the courtyard, he burned with rage. [10] He restrained himself and went home, [11] calling his friends and wife Zeresh together. He told them of his riches and of the honor that the emperor had bestowed on him. [12] Haman said, "Esther did not invite anyone else to the banquet but me and the emperor, and I am invited again tomorrow. [13] But I can take no pleasure in this as long I see that Mordecai in the courtyard."

[14] Zosara said to Haman, "Build a gallows seventy-five feet high, and tomorrow morning ask the emperor to hang Mordecai there. Then proceed merrily with the emperor to the banquet."

Haman was pleased with the advice, and had a gallows built.

⁶¹ That same night, Ahasuerus could not sleep. He called for the record book, the Annals, to be brought and read to him. ² The texts told the story of how Mordecai had exposed the fiendish plot of Bigthan and Teresh, the two eunuchs who were Guardians of the Threshold who planned to assassinate Ahasuerus.

³ "How was Mordecai rewarded for this?" asked Ahasuerus.

"He received nothing," the attendant on duty said.

So Ahasuerus asked, "Who is on duty in the outer court right now?"

⁴ At that very moment, Haman entered into the inner court from the outer court to ask that Mordecai be hung on the gallows that he had just built. ⁵ So Ahasuerus' attendant answered, "Haman is in the outer court."

"Bring him here," Ahasuerus said.

⁶ After Haman entered the inner court, Ahasuerus asked, "What is the correct way to bestow an honor on an individual should the sovereign wish to do so?"

"Who else can Ahasuerus mean but me?" Haman thought. ⁷ So he replied, "If the sovereign wishes to bestow an honor on someone, ⁸ bring out your own imperial robes and one of your own horses adorned with the imperial diadem. ⁹ Hand these things over to one of your highest officials, who will clothe the person you wish to honor and lead that person on horseback through the streets of the city, proclaiming as they go, 'This is the way to treat someone the sovereign wishes to honor.' "

¹⁰ So Ahasuerus said, "Hurry, then, and take the robes and the horse and do everything you have said—to Mordecai, who works at the Ruler's Gate. Do not leave out anything you have suggested."

¹¹ So, taking the robes and the horse, Haman adorned Mordecai and led him on horseback through the streets of the city, proclaiming before them, "This is the way to treat someone the sovereign wishes to honor." ¹² After this, Mordecai returned to the Ruler's Gate, while Haman went home in shame, hiding his face in shame as he walked.

¹³ When he told the story to his wife Zeresh and all his friends, she told him, "Because of Mordecai, you just took a fall. Since he is Jewish, you will never get the upper hand again, and will continue to fall."

¹⁴ While they were still talking, Ahasuerus' eunuchs came to the door to escort Haman to a banquet that Esther had prepared.

⁷¹ Ahasuerus and Haman arrived at Esther's banquet. ² The next day, as they were drinking their wine, Ahasuerus said, "What do you desire, Esther? Anything you say will be given to you."

³ Esther replied, "My sovereign, if I have found favor in your eyes and if

it be your wish, I ask you to spare my life, and the lives of my people. That is what I desire most. ⁴ For we, my people and I, have been condemned to be destroyed, slain and turned into chattel—ourselves and our children. Had you merely intended to make us slaves, I would have said nothing. All this has been told to me by a reliable source. Our enemy brings shame upon the imperial court."

⁵ Ahasuerus said, "Who is this person who would dare do such a thing?"

⁶ Esther replied, "Our enemy is this scoundrel Haman."

Haman was terrified, and shrank in the presence of Ahasuerus and Esther.

⁷ Ahasuerus rose from the banquet table, enraged, and went into the garden. Haman began to beg for his life from Esther, for he knew that his very life was in danger.

⁸ When Ahasuerus returned from the garden, he saw that Haman had thrown himself on the couch to plead to Esther. He said, "Do you dare to attack my wife in our own house?"

At these words, Haman tried to sneak away. ⁹ Then Harbona, one of the eunuchs, said, "I have seen it myself. Haman has prepared a gallows for Mordecai—the very person who gave you true information. The gallows stands in front of Haman's house and is seventy-five feet high."

Ahasuerus declared, "That is where Haman will hang. ¹⁰ So Haman was hung on the gallows that he had built for Mordecai. Only then was Ahasuerus' anger abated.

 App App App

8:1 That very day, Ahasuerus presented Esther with Haman's house. Mordecai was brought in to see the ruler after Esther revealed that he was her uncle. ² Ahasuerus had taken the signet ring from Haman, and now gave it to Mordecai, and Esther placed Mordecai in charge of Haman's house.

³ Then she spoke to the ruler again. Showing him honor, she asked him to stop all of the violence that Haman had planned against the Jewish people. ⁴ Ahasuerus extended the golden scepter to Esther and she rose and stood before the emperor. ⁵ Esther said, "If it is your will, and if I have pleased you, issue a decree rescinding the letter that Haman wrote and sent, ordering the destruction of the Jewish people throughout the empire. ⁶ How can I watch my people be destroyed?"

⁷ Ahasuerus said to Esther, "I have given all of Haman's property to you and hung him on a tree because he acted against the Jewish people.

⁸ Now write a letter in my name ordering what you think best, and seal it with the royal seal. Whatever is written at my command and sealed with my ring can never be defied."

⁹ The scribes were summoned on the twenty-fourth day of the first month, Nisan, of that same year. All that was commanded with respect to the Jewish people was written in a letter to the administrators and governors of the provinces from India to Ethiopia—one hundred twenty-seven in all, each with its own culture and language. ¹⁰ The order was issued with the full authority of the emperor and sealed with the imperial seal, and then sent out by messengers.

In the letter Ahasuerus ordered that the Jewish community in each city be allowed to observe their own laws, defend themselves, and act as they wished against their enemies. ¹² This order was to take effect throughout the Persian Empire on the thirteenth day of Adar, the twelfth month.

[16:1 What follows is a copy of that letter:

"The Great Ruler, Ahasuerus, to all the governors of the 127 provinces from India to Ethiopia, and to their subordinate district administrators:

² "Many people become arrogant after they receive great honors from their benefactors. ³ They cannot bear the responsibility of prosperity, so they seek to cause injury to our subjects and plot against their own benefactors. ⁴ They are never grateful for what they have been given, but rather join in the boasts of evil people and assume that they will escape the wrath of God, who hates all injustice and knows all things. ⁵ As is often the case, those who are in entrusted with positions of authority are responsible for shedding innocent blood. ⁶ They are often persuaded by advisors to commit violent atrocities. Such advisors often lie and deceive to take advantage of their sovereign.

⁷ "We need not examine our histories to find evidence of such deceit. We need only look closely at this current matter. ⁸ In the future, we will take measures to ensure that the empire remains a peaceful and secure place for all. ⁹ We will do this by changing certain policies and by ensuring that in the future we judge prudently those things which are presented to us.

"Haman, begot of Hammedatha, a Macedonian—not a Persian, and therefore devoid of our kindliness—benefitted from being in our company, and enjoyed the status that we have among all the nations to the extent that he was called 'governor' of the empire and received more honor and praise than anyone else except the emperor.

¹² "But Haman could not restrain his arrogance and tried to deprive us of our empire and our life. This Haman deceived us and asked for the death of Mordecai, who once saved our life and who has always been our sup-

porter, and of Esther, the blameless partner of our empire, along with all of their people. ¹⁴ Haman thought that he could take advantage of us by trickery, and thereby allow the Macedonians to take over the Persian empire.

¹⁵ "But we have observed that the people who were condemned by this thrice-loathsome individual are not evildoers, but hold themselves to the most just law. ¹⁶ They are the children of the true God, who is all glory and power, and has preserved our empire in an excellent state from the time of our ancestors down to our own day.

¹⁷ "So, I strongly counsel you not to carry out the instructions in the letter sent by Haman begot of Hammedatha. ¹⁸ He has been executed at the gates of Susa with all his household—God, who rules over all things, has swiftly carried out this most deserved punishment.

¹⁹ "Post copies of this letter everywhere and allow the Jewish people to live peaceably by their own laws. ²⁰ Provide them reinforcements, so that on the thirteenth day of the twelfth month, Adar, they may defend themselves against anyone who attacks them at the time of persecution which Haman decreed. ²¹ God, who rules over all things, has commanded that this be a day of joy for the chosen people instead of the day of their destruction.

²² "You will observe this day with good cheer among all your commemorative festivals, ²³ so that now and henceforth, it may be remembered as a day of liberation for you and the loyal citizens of Persia—and that it serve as a warning to those who would plot against us.

²⁴ "Every city and province, without exception, that does not follow this order will be bitterly destroyed with spear and fire. And that place will be made impassable to all human beings and will be avoided by animals and birds for all time."]

8¹³ Copies of this decree were posted conspicuously throughout the empire, so that all Jews would be ready to fight against their enemies on that day. ¹⁴ The messengers set out on their horses to deliver the message as fast as they could. The decree was also published in Susa.

¹⁵ Mordecai left Ahasuerus' presence clothed in royal robes made from purple and white cotton and wearing a golden crown and a turban made from purple linen. ¹⁶ All of Susa shouted for joy when they saw Mordecai, and there was a great celebration in the Jewish community. ¹⁷ Throughout the provinces and in every city, wherever the decree was read, there was great rejoicing and celebration among the Jews there. Many people of the land became Jewish, because Jews were now feared.

⁹¹ On the thirteenth day of the month, Adar, the emperor's decree was to be promulgated. The day on which the enemies of the Jewish community had planned to destroy them, the opposite occurred: it was the Jews who destroyed their enemies. ² Throughout Ahasuerus' provinces, the Jews gathered to defend themselves against those who had planned to hurt them. People everywhere were afraid, and would not stand against the Jewish community. ³ The provincial governors, administrators and royal scribes paid honor to them because they were afraid of Mordecai. ⁴ The emperor's decree required that Mordecai's name be held in honor throughout the empire.

⁵ The Jewish people struck down their enemies with the sword and laid to waste all their enemies.* ⁶ In the city of Susa, they killed five hundred people, ⁷ including Pharsandatha, Dalphon, Aspatha, ⁸ Parathai, Adalia, Aridatha, ⁹ Parmashta, Arisai, Aridai and Vaizatha— ¹⁰ the ten children of Haman begot of Hammedatha, the enemy of the Jewish community. But they did not indulge themselves in plunder.

¹¹ That same day, the number of those killed was reported to the emperor. ¹² Ahasuerus said to Esther, "Your people have killed five hundred people in Susa alone. How many more can they be killing in the provinces? Tell me what you desire and I will grant it!"

¹³ Esther said, "Allow my people to do the same thing tomorrow. And hang the bodies of Haman's children in public view."

¹⁵ Ahasuerus permitted this to be done, and handed over the bodies of Haman's children to the Jewish community. They gathered together on the fourteenth day and killed three hundred people, but again took no plunder.

¹⁶ The other Jewish people in the empire gathered to defend themselves and fended off their enemies. They vanquished fifteen thousand of their enemies, but did not plunder their houses. ¹⁷ On the fourteenth day, they stopped their fighting and turned that day into a day of rest, celebrating it with gladness and joy. ¹⁸ The Jewish community in the capital city of Susa, did not stop fighting on the fourteenth day, but they did stop on the fifteenth day. ¹⁹ This is why the Jewish community in the countryside celebrates the feast on the fourteenth day of Adar—a time of giving gifts of food to one another[—while those who live in the cities celebrate the fifteenth day of Adar].

---

* Verse 5 is found in some versions of the text, but not in others.

Mordecai wrote down all these things in a scroll and sent copies to all the Jewish communities throughout the empire of Ahasuerus, both far and near, [21] telling them that they should keep the fourteenth and fifteenth day of Adar, [22] the days that they vanquished their enemies. They were to commemorate the entire month of Adar, for it was in that month when their lot had been changed from sorrow to joy. They were told to observe these days with celebrations and feasts, giving gifts of food to friends and to the poor. [23] And the Jewish community observed all that Mordecai had said.

[24] Mordecai wrote how Haman begot of Hammedatha, a Macedonian, tried to destroy the Jewish people, how he sent a decree and cast lots to determine the day that he would destroy them, [25] and how he had gone to the emperor to ask that Mordecai be hung from a gallows. But Haman fell into the very trap he had set for the Jewish community—both he and his children were hung on the gallows. [26] And so, from Mordecai's suggestion and because of the great suffering that they experienced, [27] the Jewish people established these days as the Feast of Purim—the festival of lots, from the word *pur*— [28] and agreed that all the Jewish people would celebrate these days down through the generations in every city and nation.

[29] Then Esther daughter of Abihail, together with Mordecai, made a written record of what they had done, and authorized the letter about Purim. [30] Mordecai sent copies of the decree concerning the peace and security of the Jewish people throughout the one hundred twenty-seven provinces of Ahasuerus' empire. [31] Mordecai and Esther made the declaration on their own responsibility, pledging their very lives to the plan. Esther established it as law forever and it was written down in the law books.

10[1] Then Ahasuerus imposed a tax on the entire empire, both land and sea. [2] Ahasuerus' power and wealth, as well as the glory of the empire, are recorded in the histories of the rulers of the Persians and the Medes. [3] Mordecai was next in rank to Ahasuerus in the empire and was honored among all people and among the Jewish community. He was loved by all because he worked for justice for all people.

---

* 114 BCE.

[⁴ Mordecai said, "All of this is God's doing. ⁵ I remember the dream I had about all these things, and all of it has been fulfilled. ⁶ There was the tiny well that became a river, and there was light and sun and plenty of water.

The river is Esther, whom Ahasuerus married. ⁷ The two dragons are Haman and myself. ⁸ The nations are all those who conspire to destroy the Jewish people. ⁹ And the single nation is my nation, Israel, who prayed to God and was saved. The Most High has saved the people and liberated us from these wrongdoers. Our God has shown great signs and wonders—the kind of wonders that no nation has ever seen before. ¹⁰ For this purpose, God created two distinct destinies: one for the people of God and one for the nations. ¹¹ Then came the day when God chose between these two destinies, and chose Israel over the nations. ¹² God remembered the people and vindicated the chosen ones. ¹³ So, every year, they will remember the month of Adar, and on the fourteenth and fifteenth day of that month, they will come together with joy and gladness before God for all generations.

ঔ ঔ ঔ

11¹ In the fourth year of the reign of Ptolemy and Cleopatra, Dositheus, who claimed to be a priest and Levite, together with his son Ptolemy, delivered the preceding letter about the feast of Purim in Egypt. The letter is authentic and has been translated by Lysimachus begot of Ptolemy, who lived in Jerusalem.]

daniel

Ín the third year of the reign of jehoiakim, ruler of Judah, there was an attack on Jerusalem from Nebuchadnezzar, the ruler of Babylon. ² God put Jehoiakim, ruler of Judah, into Nebuchadnezzar's hand—together with the remaining sacred vessels of the Temple of God. Nebuchadnezzar carried them off to the land of Shinar;* the people he offered to his gods, and the vessels he placed in his gods' temple treasury.

³ Nebuchadnezzar told Ashpenaz, the chief steward, to bring in some of the Israelite youth, from either the royal house or the nobility—⁴ young people without any physical defect, who were attractive, intelligent, quick learners, well-informed, and wise—and train them in the ways of the royal court and teach them the language and literature of the Chaldeans.** ⁵ The ruler assigned them daily rations of food and wine from the royal

---

* Another name for Babylon.
**Throughout *Daniel*, "Chaldean," literally someone from Chaldea, or Babylon, usually refers to a practitioner of the magical arts or an astrologer. In this case, it probably means that the Israelites were taught the literature of Babylon's ancient mystical traditions.

table, and after three years of training, they were to enter Nebuchadnez-zar's service.

⁶ Among these were young Judean nobles: Daniel, Hananiah, Mishael, and Azariah. ⁷ The chamberlain, however, changed their names: Daniel was renamed Belteshazzar, Hananiah was renamed Shadrach, Mishael was renamed Meshach, and Azariah was renamed Abednego.

⁸ But Daniel was determined not to be defiled with the non-kosher food or wine from the royal table, so he begged the chamberlain to spare him such a defilement. ⁹ Though God had inclined the chamberlain to be sympathetic to Daniel, ¹⁰ he nonetheless said, "I am afraid of my sovereign the ruler, who gave you the food and drink. If Nebuchadnezzar sees you looking pallid by comparison with the others of your age, my life will be in danger."

¹¹ Then Daniel said to the steward, whom the chamberlain had put in charge of Daniel, Hananiah, Mishael, and Azariah, ¹² "Please test us for ten days. Give us nothing but vegetables to eat and water to drink. ¹³ Then see how we look in comparison with the other young people who eat from the royal table, and treat us according to what you see." ¹⁴ The steward consented, and tested them for ten days.¹⁵ After ten days, they looked healthier and better off than any of the youths who ate from the royal table. ¹⁶ So the steward continued to take away the food and wine they were to receive, and gave them vegetables.

¹⁷ To these four youths God gave knowledge and proficiency in all literature and science; and Daniel was given the ability to understand all visions and dreams as well. ¹⁸ At the end of the time the ruler had specified for the preparation, the chamberlain brought them before Nebuchadnezzar. ¹⁹ When he had spoken with all of them, none was found equal to Daniel, Hananiah, Mishael and Azariah, and so they entered the royal service. ²⁰ In any question of wisdom and judgment which Nebuchadnezzar put to them, he found them ten times better than all the magicians and enchanters in the land.

²¹ Daniel remained there until Cyrus ascended the throne.

2:1-49

Ouring the second year of his reign, Nebuchadnezzar began to be troubled by dreams. They so disturbed him that he wasn't able to sleep. ² He gathered together the empire's greatest practitioners of the magical arts—magicians, enchanters, sorcerers and astrologers from Chaldea—

to interpret a dream for him. When each of them came before Nebuchadnezzar, ³ he said to them, "I have this recurring dream and am troubled because I don't understand its meaning."

⁴ The Chaldeans, answering Nebuchadnezzar in Aramaic, said, "Long live Nebuchadnezzar! Tell us your dream and we will interpret it for you."

⁵ Nebuchadnezzar answered them, "Here is my decision. If you can't tell me both my dream and its interpretation, I will have you dismembered limb by limb and your houses razed to the ground. ⁶ But if you do tell me my dream and its interpretation, I'll give you riches and honors beyond compare. Tell me, then, my dream and its interpretation."

⁷ They answered, "Let your majesty tell us the dream first, then we will interpret it for you."

⁸ Nebuchadnezzar retorted, "It's clear to me that you're trying to buy some time because I've proclaimed this firm decision of mine. ⁹ You have no intention of interpreting my dream—you just want to put me off with false interpretations until my crisis is past. Well, the only way I'll know that your interpretation is true if you can tell me what my dream was first."

¹⁰ The Chaldeans answered, "No one on earth can tell your majesty what you want to know! ¹¹ No ruler, no matter how great and powerful, has ever made such a demand upon a magician, enchanter or astrologer. What you ask of us cannot be known; only the gods can answer you, and they do not consort with mortals."

¹² At this, Nebuchadnezzar grew enraged and ordered that all of Babylon's scholars be put to death. ¹³ A decree of execution was issued for all the scholars in the land, and a search was made for Daniel and his companions.

¹⁴ When Arioch, the captain of the royal bodyguard, set out to execute all the scholars of Babylon, Daniel came to him in secret. He asked the captain, ¹⁵ "May I ask you, as the representative of the ruler, why Nebuchadnezzar is taking such aggressive action?"

Arioch explained the matter, ¹⁶ and Daniel begged to be allowed a chance to give Nebuchadnezzar an interpretation. ¹⁷ He then went home and told Hananiah, Mishael and Azariah, his companions, ¹⁸ to pray to God to let them know the secret of the dream so they would not be put to death with all the other scholars in Babylon. ¹⁹ And God revealed the secret to Daniel in a vision in the night.

In gratitude, Daniel praised God with these words:

²⁰ Blessed is God's Name from age to age,
for to God belongs wisdom and power!

²¹ God changes the seasons and the times;
    God deposes one ruler and sets up another;
God gives wisdom to the wise,
    and knowledge to those who have discernment.
²² God reveals all mysteries!
    God knows the things that dwell in the shadows;
    light has its dwelling with God.
²³ God of my ancestors, to you I give thanks and praise,
    for your have given me wisdom and power!
Now you have made known to me what we asked;
    you have given us the answer for the ruler.

²⁴ Daniel returned to Arioch, whom Nebuchadnezzar had charged to kill all the scholars of Babylon. Daniel approached Arioch, saying, "Don't execute the scholars; bring me before the ruler and I will interpret his dream."

Greatly disturbed by this, Arioch brought Daniel before Nebuchadnezzar, and said, ²⁵ "I have found one of the captives from Judea who claims he is able to interpret your dream."

²⁶ Nebuchadnezzar asked Daniel, who was also known as Belteshazzar, "Are you able to tell me what I saw in my dream and to interpret it for me?"

²⁷ Daniel answered, "No scholar or magician or enchanter or astrologer can tell your majesty the secret about which you ask. ²⁸ But there is a God in heaven who reveals what is hidden, and it is God who has revealed to Nebuchadnezzar what will happen at the end of this age.

"This is the dream and these are the visions that came into your head. ²⁹ The thoughts that came to you, your majesty, during your sleep, concerned the future, and the One who reveals secrets has made these things known to you. ³⁰ This has been revealed to me, not because I am wiser than anyone else, but so that you may know the correct interpretation and understand the thoughts that so trouble you.

³¹ "In your vision, O mighty ruler, you saw a statue. It was huge, glowed brilliantly, and you were terrified as you saw it standing there before you. ³² The head of the statue was pure gold, its chest and arms were silver, its belly and thighs bronze, ³³ its legs iron, and its feet partly iron and partly clay. ³⁴ While you looked at the statue, a stone—which was cut from a mountain without a hand being put to it—struck the statue on its feet of iron and clay, breaking them to pieces. ³⁵ The iron, clay, bronze, silver, and gold all crumbled at once, fine as the chaff on the threshing floor in summer, and the wind blew them away without leaving a trace. But the stone that struck the statue became a great mountain and filled the whole earth.

³⁶ "This was the dream; now the interpretation we will also tell in your presence. ³⁷ You, O mighty ruler, are the ruler of rulers; to you the God of heaven has given dominion and strength, power and glory; ³⁸ people, wild beasts, and birds of the air, wherever they may dwell, have been handed over to you, making you ruler over them all. You are the head of gold.

³⁹ "Another empire will take your place, inferior to yours as silver is to gold; then a third empire, of bronze, which will rule over the whole earth.

⁴⁰ "Then there will be a fourth empire, strong as iron; it will break in pieces and subdue all these others, just as iron breaks in pieces and crushes everything else. ⁴¹ The feet and toes you saw, partly of potter's clay and partly of iron, means that it will be a divided empire, but will still have some of the hardness of iron. Just as you saw the iron mixed with clay tile, ⁴² and the toes partly iron and partly clay, the empire will be partly strong and partly fragile. ⁴³ The iron mixed with clay tile means that they will seal their alliances by intermarriage, but they will not stay united, any more than iron mixes with clay.

⁴⁴ "In the lifetime of those rulers, the God of heaven will set up a reign that will never be destroyed or delivered up to another people; rather, it will break in pieces all these empires and put an end to them, and it will stand forever. ⁴⁵ That is the meaning of the stone you saw hewn from the mountain without a hand being put to it, which broke in pieces the clay, iron, bronze, silver, and gold.

"The great God has revealed to the ruler what will be the future; this is exactly what you dreamed, and its meaning is sure."

⁴⁶ When he heard these words, Nebuchadnezzar bowed down in homage to Daniel, and ordered that he be given grain and pleasant offerings. ⁴⁷ He said, "Your God is indeed the God of gods and Sovereign over rulers, and the revealer of secrets, since you have been able to reveal this secret!" ⁴⁸ Nebuchadnezzar promoted Daniel to a high position in the court and gave him many rich gifts. He gave Daniel authority over the whole province of Babylon and over all the scholars of Babylon. ⁴⁹ At Daniel's request, Nebuchadnezzar appointed Shadrach, Meshach, and Abednego to administer the province of Babylon while Daniel remained in the royal court.

3:1-29

𝒩ebuchadnezzar ordered a gold image to be built, ninety feet high and nine feet wide, and had it set up on the plain of Dura in Babylon.

² He then ordered all the nobility, governors, counselors, treasurers, judges, magistrates and all the provincial officials to assemble for the dedication of the image that Nebuchadnezzar had set up, ³ and the nobility, governors, counselors, treasurers, judges, magistrates and all the provincial officials took their place in front of the image. ⁴ Then the herald proclaimed in a loud voice, "This is the command for all peoples of every nation and tongue: as soon as you hear the sound of the royal orchestra, ⁵ you must fall down and worship the golden image that Nebuchadnezzar has set up. ⁶ Whoever does not fall down and worship will be immediately thrown into a blazing furnace." ⁷ When they heard the sound of the royal orchestra playing, all the peoples of every nation and tongue fell down and worshiped the statue that Nebuchadnezzar had set up.

⁸ But some of the Chaldeans came forward to inform upon those who were worshipping Our God. ⁹ They told Nebuchadnezzar, "Great Ruler, ¹⁰ you have decreed that everyone fall down and worship the image of gold at the sound of the orchestra, ¹¹ and that whoever does not do this will be thrown into a blazing furnace. ¹² But there are some who you have set over the affairs of Babylon—Shadrach, Meshach, and Abednego—who have ignored your order. Great Ruler, they neither serve your gods nor worship the image of gold that you set up!"

¹³ Nebuchadnezzar flew into a rage and summoned Shadrach, Meshach, and Abednego. When they were brought before the ruler, ¹⁴ Nebuchadnezzar asked them, "Is it true, Shadrach, Meshach, and Abednego, that you have refused to serve my gods or to worship the image of gold I set up? ¹⁵ Now, when you hear the royal orchestra play its music, if you are prepared to fall down and worship the image I have made, I'll give you another chance. But if you continue to refuse, I'll have you thrown into the blazing furnace immediately. No god will be able to rescue you from my hand."

¹⁶ Shadrach, Meshach, and Abednego replied to Nebuchadnezzar, "Great Ruler, we do not need to defend ourselves before you. If you throw us into the blazing furnace, ¹⁷ the God we serve is able to overcome the blaze and rescue us from your hand. ¹⁸ But even if God does not rescue us, we want you to know, Great Ruler, that we will not serve your gods or worship the image of gold that you set up."

¹⁹ Nebuchadnezzar fumed in anger at what Shadrach, Meshach, and Abednego had told him, and his attitude toward them changed. He ordered the furnace to be heated seven times hotter than usual ²⁰ and commanded several of the strongest soldiers in the army to tie up Shadrach, Meshach, and Abednego and throw them in the blazing furnace. ²¹ Wearing their trousers, shirts, headdresses and other clothes, they were tied up and thrown

into the furnace. ²² Because Nebuchadnezzar's order was so urgent and the fire was so hot, those who were carrying the three of them were killed as they approached the flames, ²³ and Shadrach, Meshach, and Abednego fell headlong into the blazing furnace.

ભ   ભ   ભ

* ²⁴ They walked straight into the flames, blessing and singing to Our God. ²⁵ In the middle of the fire, Azariah stood and prayed:

²⁶ Blessed are you, and worthy of praise,
     Our Sovereign, God of our forebears!
     Glory to your Name forever!
²⁷ For your justice is clear in everything you do—
     you always keep your promises,
     your ways are true, and all your judgments are right.
²⁸ In everything you have brought upon us,
     and upon Jerusalem, the holy city of our forebears,
   your sentence has been just,
     since it was because of our sins that you treated us this way—
     we got just what we deserved
²⁹ We sinned and betrayed you when we deserted you;
     we've done every kind of evil.
³⁰ We haven't listened to the requirements of your Law,
     we haven't observed them;
   we haven't done what you told us to do
     for our own good.
³¹ Therefore all the disasters you've heaped on us,
     everything you've done to us,
     have all been completey justified.
³² You've handed us over to our enemies,
     to a people who have no laws and no God,
     and to the world's worst ruler, and utterly unjust.
³³ So today our mouths are shut before you,
     and shame and dishonor cover us who worship and serve you.
³⁴ Please don't abandon us forever, for your Name's sake!
     Don't forsake your covenant with us!

---

* The following section, through verse 90, is part of the Apocrypha and is not found in the Masoretic text. As the New American Bible puts it, "These verses are inspired additions to the Aramaic text of Daniel, translated from the Greek form of the book. They were originally composed in Hebrew or Aramaic, which has not been preserved." In versions which do not include the Apocrypha, verse 91 in our version is numbered verse 24, and so on through the end of the chapter.

³⁵ Don't withold your mercy from us,
    for the sake of your beloved Abraham,
    or your servant Isaac,
    or your holy one Israel!
³⁶ You promised they'd have descendants as countless
    as the stars of heaven, as the grains of sand on the beach.
³⁷ Holy One, now we're the lowest of all the nations—
    now, today, we're despised the world over,
    because of our sins.
³⁸ Now we have no leader, no prophet, no ruler,
    no burnt offering, no sacrifice, no oblation, no incense,
no altar where we can offer you the firstfruits
³⁹   and turn your heart back to us.
So let our repentant soul, our humbled spirit,
    be as acceptable to you as burnt offerings
⁴⁰   of rams and bulls and thousands of fatted lambs.
Let this be our sacrifice to you today,
    and give us the ability to follow you with a whole heart,
    for those who trust you completely will never be disappointed.
⁴¹ We hereby put our whole heart into following you,
    into revering you and seeking your presence once again.
⁴² So please don't let us be disappointed, and treat us gently,
    because you yourself are gentle and so very merciful.
⁴³ Deliver us by your marvelous works—
    let your Name bring your the glory, Holy One!
⁴⁴ May confusion overtake those who mistreat your worshipers!
    May they be covered with shame,
    and all their power and strength broken!
⁴⁵ Let them learn that you alone are God, you alone are Sovereign,
    and glorious over the whole earth!

⁴⁶ Then the stewards who had thrown them into the fire continued to stoke the furnace with oil, tar, straw, and bundles of wood. ⁴⁷ The flames rose seventy-five feet above the furnace ⁴⁸ and went out of control, consuming the Chaldeans who were standing nearby.

⁴⁹ But the angel of Our God came down into the furnace, and stood beside Azariah and his friends. The angel drove the flames of fire away from them, ⁵⁰ and blew toward them in the heart of the furnace a breeze as cool as the air after a rain shower, so that the fire didn't touch them or hurt them in any way.

⁵¹ Then all three began to praise and bless God in song, while still in the furnace:

⁵² Bless you, our Sovereign, the God of our forebears!
    May you be praised and exalted above all forever!
Blessed is your holy and glorious Name!
    May you be praised and exalted above all forever!

⁵³ Bless you in the Temple of your glorious holiness!
    May you be praised and exalted above all forever!

⁵⁴ Bless you on your throne of your reign!
    May you be praised and exalted above all forever!

⁵⁵ Bless you, who sees the depths from your seat upon the cherubim!
    May you be praised and exalted above all forever!

⁵⁶ Bless you in the expanse of the heavens!
    May you be praised and exalted above all forever!

⁵⁷ Everything Our God has made, bless Our God!
    Praise and exalt God above all forever!

⁵⁸ Angels of Our God, bless Our God!
    Praise and exalt God above all forever!

⁵⁹ Heavens, bless Our God!
    Praise and exalt God above all forever!

⁶⁰ Waters above the heavens, bless Our God!
    Praise and exalt God above all forever!

⁶¹ Heavenly powers, bless Our God!
    Praise and exalt God above all forever!

⁶² Sun and moon, bless Our God!
    Praise and exalt God above all forever!

⁶³ Stars in the sky, bless Our God!
    Praise and exalt God above all forever!

⁶⁴ Rain and dew, bless Our God!
    Praise and exalt God above all forever!

⁶⁵ Wind, bless Our God!
    Praise and exalt God above all forever!

⁶⁶ Fire and heat, bless Our God!
    Praise and exalt God above all forever!

⁶⁷ *[Cold and chill, bless Our God!
    Praise and exalt God above all forever!

⁶⁸ Dew and rain, bless Our God!
    Praise and exalt God above all forever!]

⁶⁹ Frost and cold, bless Our God!
    Praise and exalt God above all forever!

---

* Verses 67 and 68 are close repeats of other verses, and are found in only two manuscripts; they are likely errors inserted by a tired copyist.

70 Ice and snow, bless Our God!
    Praise and exalt God above all forever!
71 Night and day, bless Our God!
    Praise and exalt God above all forever!
72 Light and darkness, bless Our God!
    Praise and exalt God above all forever!
73 Lightning and clouds, bless Our God!
    Praise and exalt God above all forever!

74 Let the earth bless Our God!
    Praise and exalt God above all forever!
75 Mountains and hills, bless Our God!
    Praise and exalt God above all forever!
76 Everything that grows on the earth, bless Our God!
    Praise and exalt God above all forever!
77 Springs of water, bless Our God!
    Praise and exalt God above all forever!
78 Seas and rivers, bless Our God!
    Praise and exalt God above all forever!
79 Dolphins and everything that lives in water, bless Our God!
    Praise and exalt God above all forever!
80 Birds in the sky, bless Our God!
    Praise and exalt God above all forever!
81 Animals wild or tame, bless Our God!
    Praise and exalt God above all forever!

82 All humankind, bless Our God!
    Praise and exalt God above all forever!
83 Israel, bless Our God!
    Praise and exalt God above all forever!
84 Priests, bless Our God!
    Praise and exalt God above all forever!
85 Worshipers, bless Our God!
    Praise and exalt God above all forever!
86 Spirits and souls of the upright, bless Our God!
    Praise and exalt God above all forever!
87 Holy people of humble heart, bless Our God!
    Praise and exalt God above all forever!

88 Hananiah, Azariah, and Mishael, bless Our God!
    Praise and exalt God above all forever!

For God has rescued us from Sheol,
and saved us from the hand of death—
saved us from the fiery furnace,
and delivered us from the blazing flames!
89 Give thanks for Our God's goodness,
for God's everlasting love!
90 Bless the God of gods, all who worship Our God!
Praise and give thanks to God
for such everlasting love!

GR   GR   GR

91 Then Nebuchadnezzar sprang to his feet in fear, saying to his court, "Didn't we throw these three into the fire?"

They answered, "Yes, your majesty."

92 "But," he continued, "I can see four people walking about in the flames, unbound and unharmed, and the fourth looks like a god!"

93 Nebuchadnezzar approached the opening of the furnace and called out, "Shadrach, Meshach, and Abednego, faithful ones of the Most High God, come out!" When Shadrach, Meshach, and Abednego came out of the fire, 94 all the nobility, governors, counselors, treasurers, judges, magistrates and all the provincial officials of the land gathered around them and saw that the fire had not harmed them. Not a hair on their heads had been singed, their clothing was untouched, and they didn't even smell of smoke.

95 Nebuchadnezzar then made this proclamation: "Praise the God of Shadrach, Meshach, and Abednego, who has sent an angel to save these faithful ones, who trusted in God and disobeyed my command! They were willing to be sent off to a fiery death rather than worship any god other than their own God. 96 I therefore decree that anyone, of any people, nation or tongue, who dares to utter blasphemy against the God of Shadrach, Meshach, and Abednego is to be dismembered limb by limb and their house is to be razed to the ground—for no other god can save like this!"

97 Then Nebuchadnezzar gave great riches and power to Shadrach, Meshach, and Abednego in Babylon.

Nebuchadnezzar the Great, to all peoples and nations of every language in the world:

May you have peace and abundance! 2 It is with pleasure that I recount here the wonders that the Most High God has worked for me.

3   How great are the signs of God;
        how mighty the wonders!
    God's reign lasts for all time,
        and God's rule endures
        from one generation to the next.

4 I, Nebuchadnezzar, was at home in my palace, prosperous and free of worry. 5 One day, as I was lying in bed, I had a dream that filled me with fear, and the fantasies and visions that filled my thoughts gave me no peace. 6 I issued an order to all the scholars of Babylon to come to me and interpret the dream for me. 7 When all the magicians, enchanters, astrologers and soothsayers came in, I told them of my dream, but they were unable to interpret it for me. 8 Finally, Daniel, whom I call Belteshazzar after the name of my god, Bel, came to me. In Daniel resides the spirit of the holy gods.

9 I told Daniel of my dream. I said, "Belteshazzar, I know that you possess the spirit of the holy gods and no secret is hidden from you. Listen to what I saw in my dream and interpret it for me."

10 This was the vision that came to me as I lay on my bed:

I looked into the night and saw before me a great tree, which grew up through the middle of the earth. 11 The tree grew larger and became stronger, until at last it reached up into the sky and could be seen from the farthest corners of the earth. 12 Its leaves were lush and it was filled with fruit, and it provided food for all who came near. In its shade, the wild beasts found shelter and birds built their nests in its branches, and from it all living creatures were nourished.

13 In the vision I saw as I lay in bed, a holy Watcher came down to me from heaven. 14 In a mighty voice it called out,

14   "Cut down this tree and cut off its branches,
        strip away its leaves and throw away its fruit;
    scatter the wild beasts from the shelter of its shade
        and the birds from its branches,

---

* In some versions, the first three verses of this section are verses 98-100 of chapter 3; the verse numbering for chapter 4 then begins, and continues to be three verses at variance through the end of the chapter.

15 but leave the stump with its roots in the ground,
   and wrap it in chains of iron and bronze
   and let the grass overtake it.
   Let him roll around in the morning dew
   and eat grass like the cattle;
16 he will lose his human mind
   and be given the mind of an animal
   until seven years have passed.
17 This is the decree pronounced by the Watchers
   the sentence pronounced by the holy ones.
   By this the living will know
   that the Most High rules over all earthly governments
   and places in positions of authority whomever God wants—
   even the lowliest of people."

18 This is the dream that I, Nebuchadnezzar the Great, had. Then I said, "Now, Belteshazzar, interpret it for me. Even though none of my own scholars was able to make any sense out of it, I know that you can do it because you possess the spirit of the holy gods."

19 Daniel, whom I call Belteshazzar, was silent for a moment, and hesitated to tell me the meaning. But I told him, "Don't let the dream or its interpretation alarm you."

Belteshazzar was greatly distressed. "Great Ruler," he said, "I only wish the dream was about those who hate you, and that its interpretation concerned your enemies! 20 The tree which you watched grow tall and strong, reaching high into the sky until it could be seen at the far corners of the earth, 21 a tree which gave food to all and in whose shade wild beasts lived and in whose branches the birds nested: 22 that tree, my ruler, is you. You have grown great and strong; your power has grown and reaches the sky, and your authority is known at the far corners of the earth.

23 "Also, my ruler, you saw a Watcher, a holy one, come down from the sky and saying, "Cut down this tree and destroy it, but leave the stump with its roots in the ground, and wrap it in chains of iron and bronze and let the grass overtake it; let him roll around in the morning dew and eat grass like the cattle; he will lose his human mind and be given the mind of an animal until seven years have passed.

24 "This is the interpretation, Great Ruler: it is a decree of the Most High God which affects my sovereign. 25 You will be exiled from human society and will live like the wild animals; you will feed on grass and roll around in the morning dew like the cattle. Seven years will pass until you have learned that the Most High rules over all earthly governments and places in positions of authority whomever God wants.

²⁶ " However, the command to leave the stump of the tree with its roots in the ground means that your realm will be kept for you until such time as you acknowledge the sovereignty of the Most High. ²⁷ I implore you to listen to me, Great Ruler: replace your sins with deeds of mercy, and be generous to the poor to make up for your wrongdoing. Then perhaps you will enjoy a long life of peace."

²⁸ All that Daniel foretold did in fact happen to Nebuchadnezzar the Great. ²⁹ Tweve months later, while walking on the parapets of the royal palace of Babylon, ³⁰ I cried out, "Babylon, how great you are! Was it not my power alone that built you to be a royal residence for my splendor and majesty?"

³¹ As these words fell from my lips, a voice came down from the skies: "Listen to my decree, Nebuchadnezzar the Great! Your dominion has passed out of your hands. ³² You are exiled from all peoples to eat grass like the cattle. Seven years will pass until you acknowledge that the Most High rules over all earthly governments and places in positions of authority whomever God wants." ³³ That same hour, I was deposed from the palace and went out to eat grass and roll around in the dew like the cattle, until my hair grew as long as eagles' feathers and my nails were like birds' claws.

³⁴ At the end of the seven years, I, Nebuchadnezzar, looked toward heaven and my senses returned to me. I blessed the Most High, praising and glorifying the Ever-living One:

> "God's rule last for all times,
>   and God's dominion endures through all generations.
> ³⁵   Those who live on the earth count for nothing;
>   God's will governs the powers of heaven
>   and those who live on the earth.
> No one can stand against the power of God
>   or say to God, "What are you doing?"

³⁶ In that moment, my senses returned to me, and my dominion, my royal majesty and splendor were returned to me. I once again ascended my throne and my power was increased. ³⁷ Now, I, Nebuchadnezzar, praise and exult and glorify the God of Heaven, whose deeds are right and whose ways are just, and who can bring low the arrogant!

5:1-31

Many years later, Belshazzar, ruler of Babylon, gave a great banquet for a thousand nobles, and drank with them. ² Under the influence of the wine, he sent for the gold and silver vessels which Nebuchadnezzar, his forebear, had looted from the Temple in Jerusalem, so that the royal family, the nobles and their families, and the entertainers might drink from them. ³ When the gold and silver vessels looted from the Temple of God in Jerusalem had been brought in, and while the royal family, the nobles and their families, and the entertainers ⁴ were drinking wine from them, they praised their gods of gold and silver, bronze and iron, wood and stone.

⁵ Suddenly, opposite the lampstand, the fingers of a human hand appeared, writing on the plaster of the palace wall. When Belshazzar saw the hand as it wrote, ⁶ the ruler went pale; his thoughts terrified him; his hips went slack and his knees began to knock.

⁷ He screamed for the enchanters, astrologers, and diviners to be brought in. When all the scholars of Babylon had assembled, he told them, "Whoever can read the writing on the wall and interpret it will be dressed in purple and wear a golden collar, and will be the third ranking official in the land." ⁸ All the scholars of Babylon came forward, but none of them could read the writing or understand its meaning. ⁹ At this, Belshazzar became like a ghost and all the nobles of the land fell into a state of confusion.

¹⁰ When the queen heard all the confusion, she came into the room and said, "Long live Belshazzar! There is no need to be so troubled or to be so afraid. ¹¹ There is someone in your land who possesses the spirit of the holy gods and was known in the time of your forbear to have keen insight and godlike wisdom. Nebuchadnezzar appointed him chief among all the magicians, enchanters, astrologers and diviners. ¹² This Daniel, who was called Belteshazzar, has extraordinary knowledge and insight, including gifts for interpreting dreams, explaining riddles and solving problems: this is the person who can interpret this message for you."

¹³ Then Daniel was brought before Belshazzar who asked, "Are you Daniel, the Jewish exile, whom my forebear brought from Judah? ¹⁴ I have heard that the spirit of God is in you, that you possess brilliant knowledge and extraordinary wisdom. ¹⁵ All the scholars of the land have been brought here to read this writing and tell me what it means, but they have all failed. ¹⁶ I have heard that you can interpret dreams and solve difficulties; if you are able to read the writing and tell me what it means, you will be clothed in purple, wear a gold collar around your neck, and be third in the government of the realm."

¹⁷ Daniel answered Belshazzar, "You may keep your gifts, or give your presents to someone else; but the writing I will read for you and tell you what it means. ¹⁸ Great Ruler, the Most High God gave dominion to your

forebear Nebuchadnezzar, with power, glory and honor, [19] and because of this power, all the nations of the earth trembled. Nebuchadnezzar put some to death at will and others he spared at will; some were promoted and others were brought down according to his whim.

[20] "But when he became arrogant and stubborn and insolent, he was overthrown and stripped of glory. [21] He was exiled from the company of people and his mind became like that of an animal; he had to live with the wild animals and eat grass like the cattle, and his body was drenched with the morning dew, until he acknowledged that the Most High rules over all earthly governments and places in positions of authority whomever God wants.

[22] "But even though you, the heir to the realm, knew all of this, you didn't change your ways. [23] You have rebelled against the God of heaven. You had the vessels of the Temple brought before you, so that you and the royal family, the nobles and their families, and the entertainers might drink wine from them; and you toasted your gods of silver and gold, bronze and iron, wood and stone, that neither see nor hear nor have intelligence. But the God in whose hand is your breath, and the whole course of your life, you did not honor. [24] That is why God sent the hand which wrote these things.

[25] "This is what the hand wrote: *Mene, Tekel,* and *Parsin.** [26] And this is the interpretation: 'Mene' means that God has numbered your days as ruler and put an end to your reign; [27] 'Tekel' means you have been weighed on the scales and found wanting; [28] and 'Peres' means your realm has been divided and given to the Medes and Persians."

[29] Upon hearing this, Belshazzar commanded that Daniel be dressed in purple and wear a golden collar around his neck, and a proclamation was made that Daniel was to rank third in authority in the land.

[30] That night, Belshazzar, the ruler of the Chaldeans, was slain, [31] and Darius the Mede took over the realm.** At the time of his accession, Darius was sixty-two years old.

---

* These words are puns. On their face, the three words are three different coins: the mina, the shekel, and the half-mina. But the root meanings of the three coins are "numbered," "weighed," and "divided." In addition, Peres, the singular of Parsin, can also mean Persia.

** In fact, it was Cyrus the Persian who conquered Babylon, having already taken Medea. The individual here called Darius the Mede may have been modeled on Darius the Great, a Persian ruler who came into power after Cyrus and his successor.

ᕅarius decided to appoint one hundred twenty nobles to be in charge of the realm. ² Three chief ministers appointed, and the nobles were to submit regular reports to them so that Darius's interests would be protected. And Daniel was one of these ministers.

³ Daniel's exceptional abilities outshone all the other ministers and nobles, and Darius wanted to place him in charge of the whole realm. ⁴ The other ministers and nobles grew jealous and began to look for some way to malign Daniel's administration of the realm, but they couldn't find any fault, since Daniel was completely responsible and trustworthy. Since they could find no carelessness or deceit in Daniel, ⁵ they said, "We'll never find any reason to accuse this Daniel—unless it has to do with the law of his God!"

⁶ The ministers and nobles conspired together and approached Darius, saying: "Long live Darius the Great! ⁷ We, the ministers of your realm, your administrators, nobles, advisors and governors, have come to an agreement, and we believe that you should issue a decree with the following prohibition: during the next thirty days, anyone who pays homage to any god or ruler other than you is to be thrown into the lions' den. ⁸ If you would sign this document, the edict will become inalterable, for the law of the Medes and the Persians can never be revoked." ⁹ So Darius signed the law.

¹⁰ Even after Daniel heard of the new law, he would go home, get on his knees and pray. The windows in the upstairs room faced Jerusalem, and it was there that he praised God as he had always done. ¹¹ Some nobles of Darius, ruler of Babylon, entered the upstairs room of Daniel's home and found him praying and pleading before God.

¹² The nobles then went to remind Darius of the prohibition: "Didn't you decree that no one is to address a petition to god or mortal for thirty days, except to you, on pain of being thrown into the lions' den?"

Darius replied, "The decree is absolute and irrevocable under Medean and Persian law."

¹³ To this the nobles replied, "Daniel, the Jewish exile, has paid no attention to you or to the decree you issued; three times a day Daniel offers prayers."

¹⁴ Darius was deeply grieved at this news and decided to save Daniel, racking his brain until sunset to find a way out. ¹⁵ But the officials insisted:

---

* In some versions, the numbering for chapter 6 begins one verse earlier, at 5:31, and continues to be one verse at variance through the end of the chapter.

"Keep in mind that under Medean and Persian law, every royal prohibition or decree is irrevocable."

[16] So Darius ordered Daniel to be brought and cast into the lions' den. To Daniel he said, "May your God, whom you worship so constantly, save you!" [17] To forestall any tampering, Darius sealed with the royal seals the stone that had been brought to block the opening of the den.

[18] Then Darius returned to the palace for the night. He refused to eat and dismissed the entertainers. Since sleep was impossible, [19] Darius rose very early the next morning and hurried to the lions' den. [20] Drawing near to the lions' den, Darius cried out to Daniel with anguish in his voice, "Daniel, servant of the living God! Has the God whom you worship so constantly been able to save you from the lions?"

[21] Daniel answered, "O Darius, ruler of Babylon, may you live forever! My God has sent an angel and closed the lions' mouths so that they have not hurt me. For I have been found innocent before the Most High. Nor have I ever done any harm to you, my ruler!"

[23] Darius joyfully ordered Daniel to be removed from the den, unhurt because he trusted in God; [24] then he ordered the officials who had accused Daniel, along with their spouses and children, to be cast into the lions' den. They had not reached the floor of the den before the lions overpowered them and crushed all their bones.

[25] Then Darius, ruler of Babylon, wrote this proclamation : "To the nations and peoples of every language, wherever they dwell on earth: May you always have peace and abundance! [26] I decree that throughout my realm the God of Daniel is to be revered and worshiped.

> For God is the living God, enduring forever,
>> whose realm will not be destroyed,
>> and whose dominion will be without end!
> [27] God is a deliverer and a savior,
>> working signs and wonders in heaven and on earth,
>> and delivering Daniel from the lions' power."

[28] Prosperity followed Daniel during Darius' reign, and that of Cyrus the Persian.

beginning in the first y   ar in Babylon,
Daniel had visions in his slee   rative of those
dreams.

² In the vision I saw during t!   inds of heaven
stirred up the great sea, ³ from   se beasts, each
one different from the others.   ut with eagles'
wings. While I watched, its wings were plucked; it was raised from the
ground to stand on two feet like a human, and given a human mind. ⁵ The
second was like a bear; it was standing on its hind legs, and in its teeth were
three ribs. It was given the order, "Get up! Eat your fill of flesh!' ⁶ After this,
I looked and saw another beast, like a leopard; on its back were four wings
like those of a bird, and it had four heads. To this beast was given the authority to rule.

⁷ After this in my night visions, I saw a fourth beast, different from all
others—terrifying, horrible, and of extraordinary strength. It had great iron
teeth which it used for devouring and crushing, and what was left it
trampled with its feet. And it had ten horns. ⁸ While I was looking at these
horns, I saw another, smaller horn sprouting among them, and three of the
original horns were torn away to make room for it. This horn had eyes like
a human, and a mouth that spoke arrogantly. As I watched,

> Thrones were set up, and the one who sat there
>> was the Ancient of Days,
> whose clothing was snow white,
>> with a head of hair as white as wool;
> whose throne was flames of fire,
>> with wheels of burning fire.
> ¹⁰   A stream of fire surged forth,
>> flowing from the Ancient One's presence,
> with tens of thousands ministering,
>> and hundreds of thousands standing in attendance.
> The court was convened,
>> and the books were opened.

¹¹ All the while, the horn kept making its arrogant boasts. Then, as I
watched, beast was killed and its body was thrown into the fire to be
burned up. ¹² Though the other beasts were thown out of power, they were
allowed to live a while longer.

¹³ I gazed into the visions of the night once again,

and I saw, coming on the clouds of heaven
  one who looked human,
  but somehow more than human.
This One came to the Ancient One
  and was led into the divine Presence.
14 Thus was conferred sovereignty,
  glory and dominion,
and all peoples, nations and languages
  became this One's subjects.
This sovereignty is an eternal Sovereignty
  which will never pass away,
  nor will this dominion ever be destroyed. |

15 I, Daniel, found my spirit troubled within me, and I was terrified by the visions going through my mind. 16 I approached one of those present and asked what all this meant, and it told me the meaning of these things: 17 "These four great beasts stand for four empires which will arise on the earth. 18 The ones receiving sovereignty are the holy people of the Most High, and the kindom will belong to them forever and ever."

19 But I wanted to make certain about the fourth beast, so very terrible and different from the others, devouring and crushing with its iron teeth and bronze claws, and trampling with its feet what was left. 20 I wanted to know about the ten horns on its head, and the other one that sprang up, before which three horns fell; about the horn with the eyes and the mouth that spoke arrogantly, which appeared greater than the other horns.

21 For as I watched, that horn made war against the holy ones and was victorious 22 until the Ancient One arrived; judgment was pronounced in favor of the holy ones of the Most High, and the time came when the holy ones possessed the realm. 23 The interpreter told me:

"The fourth beast will be
  a fourth empire on earth,
  different from all the others;
it will devour the whole earth,
  beat it down, and crush it.
24 The ten horns will be ten rulers
  rising out of that empire;
another will rise up after them,
  different from those before,
  who will lay low three rulers.

---

* Literally, "for a time, two times, and half a time."

²⁵ The fourth ruler will speak against the Most High
   and oppress the holy ones of the Most High,
   thinking to change the feast days and the Law.
They will be handed over to the fourth ruler
   for three-and-a-half years.*
²⁶ But when the court is convened,
   and the power of the fourth ruler is taken away
   by final and absolute destruction,
²⁷ then the self-rule and dominion and majesty
   of all the empires under the heavens
will be given to the holy people of the Most High,
   whose reign will be everlasting,
   and whom all dominions will serve and obey."

²⁸ The account of the vision ends here. As for myself, Daniel, my thoughts raced and I turned pale as a ghost, but I kept these things to myself.

ଞ୍ଜ ଞ୍ଜ ଞ୍ଜ

8¹ In the third year of the reign of Belshazzar, I, Daniel, had another vision following my earlier vision. ² In this vision, I was in Susa, the capital of the province of Elam, standing beside the Ulai River. ³ I looked up and saw a ram with two horns standing beside the river. Its horns were both very long, but the longer of the two was the second. ⁴ Suddenly the ram charged toward the west, then to the north and then to the south. No animal could withstand it, and nothing could escape its advances. It did what it pleased and grew more powerful.

⁵ While I thought about what I was seeing, a goat came from the west, hovering over the land without touching the ground. It had a very long horn between its eyes. ⁶ It approached the two-horned ram which I had seen beside the river and charged it headlong with great force. I saw it advance on the ram as its fury grew greater. ⁷ Then it struck the ram and broke off both its horns and the ram was powerless to resist. The goat threw the ram to the ground and trampled it, and there was no one who could rescue the ram.

⁸ The goat grew more powerful, but at the height of its power its long horn shattered, and in its place grew four long horns each pointing to the four quarters of heaven. ⁹ Out of one of the horns grew a smaller horn, which expanded in power toward the south and the east and toward the fairest of all lands as it grew. ¹⁰ It aspired to be as powerful as the armies of heaven, and it cast out of heaven some of the armies and even some of

the stars, and trampled them into the ground. ¹¹ It aspired to be as great as the Sovereign over the hosts of heaven, and suppressed the worship of the Most High and even tore down the Temple. ¹² The armies of heaven were delivered up and the small horn raised itself in blasphemy against the worship of Our God; it desecrated the daily sacrifice, and threw truth into the dirt. In everything it did, the horn succeeded.

¹³ I heard a holy one speaking. Someone asked, "How long will the time of this vision last? How long will the worship of the Most High be suppressed and the blasphemous destruction continue? How long will the Holy Place and its people be trampled underfoot?"

⁴ The answer came, "It will last 2300 evenings and mornings, then the Holy Place will be restored."

¹⁵ While I was watching this vision, I, Daniel, was trying to understand it. Suddenly one who looked human appeared before me, ¹⁶ and I heard a human voice calling across the Ulai, "Gabriel, tell him the meaning of this vision!"

¹⁷ Gabriel came over to me, and I fell down on my face in terror. But Gabriel said, "Understand this, mortal: the vision you see points to the time of the End." ¹⁸ As I heard these words, I continued to lie face down and fell into a trance. But the angel touched me and raised me to my feet. ¹⁹ "I will reveal to you everything that is to occur at the end of the time of chastisement, for the appointed time is coming.

"The two-horned ram that you saw represents the rulers of Medea and Persia, ²¹ the goat is the ruler of Greece, and the great horn on its forehead represents its first ruler. ²² As for the horn which was shattered and replaced by four other horns: four empires will rise out of that empire, but they will lack its power.

²³ "In the last days of those empires,
when their sins have reached their height,
a cunning and insolent ruler will arise.
²⁴ The ruler's power will grow though not through virtuous deeds,
and the schemer will spread destruction
and will be supremely successful.
The ruler will wreak havoc on the powerful
and on the holy people.
²⁵ Through lies and deception,
all of this ruler's plans will succeed,
and great destruction will beset all
when they least expect it.
The ruler will challenge the Sovereign of sovereigns
and be cast down, but not by human hands.

²⁶ All that has been revealed to you
concerning the things of the mornings and evenings
to come is true;
but you must keep all of this to yourself,
because the time is still to come."

²⁷ Then I, Daniel, lost consciousness and was sick for several days. When I awoke, I went on with the business of the ruler. But I was perplexed by what had been shown to me, and could not fathom its meaning.

ઝ   ઝ   ઝ

9:1 In the first year of the reign of Darius, begot of Ahasuerus (a Mede by birth, who was appointed ruler over the land of the Chaldeans), ² I, Daniel, was reading the scriptures and pondering the seventy years which, according to the prophet Jeremiah, were to be the length of time that Jerusalem was to be in ruins.

³ I turned to the Most High in sackcloth and ashes, with heartfelt prayers and petitions. ⁴ I prayed and made this confession to Our God: "O great and awesome God, you keep the Covenant and have kindness for those who love you and keep the commandments. ⁵ But we have sinned so much! We have sinned against you, we have done wrong, we have acted wickedly, we have turned away from your ordinances and your commandments and rebelled against you. ⁶ We haven't obeyed your emissaries, the prophets, who spoke in your Name to our rulers, our governors, our ancestors and all the people of the land. ⁷ Justice, O God, belongs to you. But to us belongs open shame today—to us, the people of Judah, the citizens of Jerusalem, the whole of Israel, near and far away, in every country to which you have dispersed us because of the treason we have committed against you. ⁸ O God, open shame belongs to us, to our rulers, to our governors, to our ancestors, because we have sinned against you.

⁹ "Mercy and pardon belong to you, O God. Yet we have sinned against you, ¹⁰ and have not listened to your voice, nor followed the laws you have given us through your faithful prophets. ¹¹ All Israel has broken your Law and refused to obey your command, and as a result, the just punishment that was foretold in the law of Moses, your faithful one, has come upon us, for we have sinned against you. ¹² You have made good on the warnings you gave to us and our leaders, and brought a greater disaster on Jerusalem than has ever taken place anywhere else in the world. ¹³ And even though this disaster was foretold by Moses, we didn't listen and did noth-

ing to please the Most High God. We have neither turned away from our evil ways nor remembered that you are true to your word. ¹⁴ The Most High has kept us under careful scrutiny and has now brought this disaster upon us. All that God has done has been just; yet even so we have refused to obey.

¹⁵ "And now, my God, whose mighty hand brought us out of the Land of Egypt—and in doing so, gave yourself a reputation that lives on to this day—we have sinned against you and have done what is wrong in your sight. ¹⁶ My God, by all your wonderful acts, we beg you to lift your fury and outrage from Jerusalem—your own city, your holy mountain. It is because of our crimes and the crimes of our ancestors that Jerusalem and your people have become a laughingstock to the nations. ¹⁷ Listen, my God, to the prayers and petitions of your faithful one, and look kindly upon your sanctuary which lies in ruin! ¹⁷ Turn to us and hear our call; open your eyes and see how we are in ruins, along with the city that bears your Name. Not because of our own virtue, but because we know of your great mercy, we lay our pleas before you. ¹⁹ My God, hear us! My God, forgive us! My God, listen and act! For the sake of your name, act swiftly and vindicate the people and city that bear your name."

²⁰ As I was speaking and praying, confessing my own crimes and the crimes of my people, Israel, and laying my pleas before the Almighty on behalf of the holy mountain, ²¹ the angel Gabriel, who had already appeared to me in a vision, flew near to me during the hour of the evening sacrifice.

²² Gabriel told me, "Daniel, I have come to illuminate your mind. ²³ When you began your pleas, a decree went out, and I have been sent to reveal it to you, for you are greatly beloved. Listen carefully to my words and pay attention to the vision.

²⁴ "Seventy 'sevens'* are decreed
    for your people and your holy city—
to put an end to rebellion,
    to put a seal on sin,
to make restitution for crimes,
    to bring about everlasting justice,
to fulfill visions and prophecy,
    and to anoint the Most Holy.

²⁵ Understand this well:
from the time the decree was issued
    for Jerusalem to be restored and rebuilt,

---

* Literally, "weeks," usually interpreted as seventy groups of seven years.

to the coming of an anointed one, a ruler,
   seven 'sevens' will pass;
then for sixty-two 'sevens,'
   its streets and squares will remain restored and rebuilt,
   but in times of trouble.

²⁶ After this time, the anointed one will be cut off,
   and then nothing will be left:
the people of an invading ruler will wreak destruction
   on both city and sanctuary,
and in the end there will be a great cataclysm,
   a war to the end, with inevitable desolation.

²⁷ The invading ruler will make a firm 'covenant' with the people
   for the space of one 'seven'—
but in the middle of that 'seven' will break the covenant
   and put a stop to all sacrifice and oblation.
The pinnacle will be an abomination that causes desolation,
   and it will remain until the end that is decreed
   is poured out on this tyrant."

10:1–12:13

DuRing the third year of Cyrus's reign in Persia, a vision came to Daniel, who was known as Belteshazzar—a true vision of a great war. He understood the vision only after it meaning was revealed to him in a second vision.

² During that time, I, Daniel, had been in mourning for three weeks. ³ I refused to eat fine foods and tasted no meat or wine—and didn't even bathe—until the three weeks had passed. ⁴ On the twenty-fourth day of the first month, I was standing on the banks of the Tigris and saw a person who was clothed in linen and wearing a belt of the finest gold from Ophir, whose body glowed like topaz and whose face shone like lightning, whose eyes were like flames and whose arms and feet gleamed like polished bronze, and whose single voice was like that of a multitude. ⁷ I alone saw the vision. Those around me didn't see it, but they grew so fearful that they ran away and hid. ⁸ I was left alone to gaze at this great vision, and all my strength left me, and I became deathly pale. ⁹ When I heard the sound of the voice, I fell face-down on the ground and lost consciousness.

¹⁰ Then I felt a hand touch me, and I was lifted onto my hands and

knees. ¹¹ The voice said, "Daniel, greatly beloved of God, listen to what I say to you and stand tall before me, for I was sent to you." When I heard these words, I stood up and trembled in fear. ¹² The voice went on, "Don't be afraid, Daniel. On the first day that you applied your mind to understanding and began to purify yourself before God, God heard your prayers, and I was sent to give you God's answer. ¹³ Persia's chieftain was able to hold me off for the past twenty-one days, but then Michael, one of our own chieftains, came to help me because the 'rulers' of Persia were detaining me. ¹⁴ I have come to you to reveal what will happen to your people in days to come, for this is also a vision of those days."

¹⁵ While the voice spoke to me, I cast my eyes to the ground and was unable to speak. ¹⁶ Suddenly, one who looked human touched my lips, and I was able to break my silence and speak to the one standing before me: "Please, I'm afraid of this vision and all my strength has left me. ¹⁷ How can I, humble before my God, presume to talk to one as glorious as you, since my strength has fled and my breath has left me?"

¹⁸ Again, the figure touched me and my strength was restored. ¹⁹ The figure said, "Do not be afraid, beloved of God, for there is nothing that can harm you. Take courage, stand up and be strong."

At these words, my strength returned and I said, "Then speak to me, for you have given me strength."

* ²⁰ᵃ The voice said, "Do you know why I have come to you? ²¹ᵃ It is to reveal to you what is written in the Book of Truth. **11**:¹ When Darius the Mede began his reign, I stood up to support and protect him. ²⁰ᵇ Soon I must return to fight with Persia's chieftain. When that fight is over, the chieftain of Greece will appear. ²¹ᵇ I have no allies on my side to back me up, except for Michael, your chieftain.

² "I will now tell you the truth about these matters. Three more rulers will reign in Persia, followed by a fourth whose wealth will exceed all the predecessors. When that wealth has grown greater than this ruler's power, this one will mobilize all the nations against the empire of Greece. ³ A great warrior will appear and will rule a vast empire. ⁴ But once the empire is established, it will be divided into four quarters under the heavens. These quarters will not pass to the leader's heirs, nor will their power ever equal that of this ruler, for these dominions will be uprooted and given to those other than the heirs.

⁵ "The ruler of the South will grow in strength, but will be surpassed in strength by one of the generals, and the general's authority will extended

---

* The verses in this paragraph have been rearranged for the sake of clarity.

further than the ruler's. ⁶ As time passes, the two rulers will enter into an alliance, and the agreement will be ratified with an arranged marriage: the ruler of the South's daughter will marry the ruler of the North. The marriage, however, won't last, and there will be no line of succession. The daughter and the ruler, together with their child and their entire entourage, will fall victim to subterfuge. ⁷ Then another shoot will spring from her family tree, and this one will be the heir to the ruler of the South. The heir will attack the defenses of the ruler of the North, capture the fortress and win a great victory. ⁸ All the wealth of the North—the statues of their gods, and their gold and silver vessels—will be carried off to Egypt. After this, the ruler of the South will cease attacks on the ruler of the North for a few years. ⁹ But the ruler of the North will attack the ruler of the South, and then return to the realm of the North.

¹⁰ "The heirs of the ruler of the North will build a large army and march against the South, and one of them will cross the land like an irresistible force. ¹¹ The ruler of the South will fly into a rage and will declare war on the ruler of the North, building a large army—but that army will be defeated. ¹² At the capture of the army, the triumphant ruler will be thrilled and will slaughter tens of thousands. Yet this tactical advantage will not last long. ¹³ The ruler of the North will build another large army, one even greater than the last, and after a few years, will advance these forces along with a large caravan of supplies.

¹⁴ "Many will rebel against the ruler of the South, but some of the rebels among your own people will give credence to a vision unwisely and will be brought to slaughter. ¹⁵ The ruler of the North will then invade and set up large siege ramps and capture a well-guarded city. The forces of the South will not be able to resist these advances, and even their best soldiers will not be able to withstand this force. ¹⁶ The invader will have complete advantage and there will be no opposition. The invader from the North will set up his rule over the fairest of all lands and control will be complete. ¹⁷ The invader will threaten to attack the entire realm of the South in full force, but will then make a treaty with the ruler of the South intending to overthrow the ruler of the South and give a child in marriage to the ruler. But the treaty will not last and its purpose will not be fulfilled. ¹⁸ Then the ruler of the South will send forces to the coastland and islands and will capture many prisoners. But a foreign commander will withstand the ruler of the North and put an end to the challenge, giving the ruler a taste of this one's own medicine. ¹⁹ The ruler of the North will be forced to retreat back into the realm of the North, and will there be defeated and deposed and never be seen again. ²⁰ The next in line will send out an officer with the

palace guards to extort taxes, but this one too will be humiliated though not publicly or in battle.

²¹ "The throne will be seized by a contemptible person who won't be given the title of the ruler, but will take advantage of a crisis to seize power through smooth talk and deception. When this person is firmly in control, ²² all the opposing forces will be conquered, even those of the High Priest of the Temple. ²³ This individual will enter into treaties, but will break every one, and even with only a few supporters, will continue to gain power. ²⁴ The traitor will ransack the most wealthy districts of the land, succeeding where those in the past had failed, plundering and pillaging and distributing all the spoils to followers, and plotting against the most fortified areas, but only for a time.

²⁵ "The villain will build up forces to lead a great army against the ruler of the South. But, because of treachery, the ruler of the South will not be able to resist: ²⁶ members of the royal court will prove themselves disloyal. The army will be swept away and many will be slaughtered in the battle. ²⁷ The two rulers will sit at the same table, but will lie to each other and neither one will succeed for the appointed time is still to come. ²⁸ Then the ruler of the North will return home carrying great spoils, and immediately upon returning to the North, will take action against the holy Covenant.

²⁹ "When the time is right, the ruler of the North will once again attack the South, but will not succeed as before. ³⁰ Ships will arrive from Kittim, and the North's forces will be held back. Retreating, the ruler of the North will lash out against the Covenant of Our God and will show favor to those who have forsaken it. ³¹ Soldiers will desecrate the sanctuary, and will abolish the regular worship. They will establish themselves in the sanctuary of Our God and set up an abomination there. ³² Through flattery, the ruler will corrupt many to forsake the Covenant, but those who are faithful to Our God will stand firm and take action. ³³ Wise leaders will guide the people, but for a while the people are destined to fall victim to sword and fire, captivity and pillage. ³⁴ And though the people will receive little help, there will be many on their side who will stand up as resistance fighters. ³⁵ Even some of these leaders will fall victim for a while, so that they will be tested, refined and purified; for the final outcome will happen in its own time.

³⁶ "The ruler will do as he pleases, exulting and praising himself above every god, and will utter great blasphemies against Our God. And he will have his way for a time until God gets fed up, for what has been prophesied must be fulfilled. ³⁷ Without thought to ancestral gods or to the goddess of fertility—without thought to any god whatsoever— ³⁸ he will place himself above them all and will pay homage to the god of security, a god unknown to his ancestors, with gold and silver and precious gifts. ³⁹ He will

use the people of a foreign god as defenders of his fortresses. Those who acknowledge him will receive great honors and authority over the people, and be rewarded with great estates of property.

⁴⁰ "As the end draws near, the ruler of the South will feign an attack against the ruler of the North, and the ruler of the North will attack in full force with chariots and cavalry and a fleet of ships. They will sweep over nations like a flood, ⁴¹ even through the fairest of all lands, and tens of thousands will be slaughtered. But the lands of Edom and Moab, and a large part of the land of the Ammonites, will escape the onslaught. ⁴² As country after country falls, not even Egypt will be able to withstand. ⁴³ All of the hidden gold and reserves in the treasury will be looted. Libyans and Cushites will be conquered. ⁴⁴ Then, upon hearing an alarming rumor from the east and North, the ruler will depart in anger to exterminate many. ⁴⁵ He will pitch camp between the sea and the holy mountain, the fairest of all mountains, and be brought down with no one to help.

12:1 "At that time, Michael,
    the great chieftain who stands guard over your people,
    will stand up;
and there will follow a time of great suffering
    the likes of which has never been known
    from the founding of the nation until that moment.
When that time comes, your people will be rescued,
    every one whose name is written in the Scroll;
² and those who lie sleeping in the dust will rise up,
    some to life everlasting
    and some to the reproach of eternal torment.
³ The wise will shine like the bright heavens,
    and leaders of justice like the stars forever more.

⁴ "But you, Daniel, must keep all of these things secret until the time of the End. Many will wander from the path of truth, and evil deeds will only increase."

⁵ When I looked, I, Daniel, saw two other figures standing beside the river— ⁶ one on this bank and one on the other. ⁷ To the figure robed in linen who hovered over the waters, I said, "How long do we have until these amazing events happen?" ⁷ The one robed in linen raised both hands to heaven, and swore by the One who lives forever: "It will be three-and-a-half years* before the one who crushes the spirit of the holy people will be brought to an end."

---

* Literally, "a time, two times, and half a time."

⁸ I heard this, but did not comprehend it, so I said, "Please, what will be the final outcome?" ⁹ The figure replied: "Go on your way, Daniel, for these words are to remain a secret and be sealed until the time of the End. ¹⁰ Many will purify themselves and be made strong, making themselves shine like light, but the wicked will continue in their corrupt ways. None of them will understand any of this, but those who are wise will understand.

¹¹ "From the time when the daily sacrifice is abolished and the abomination that causes desolation is set up, 1,290 days will pass. ¹² Happy are those who persevere and live to see the outcome after 1,335 days!

¹³ "But you, Daniel, must be on your way now; you will sleep, and at the end of the appointed time, you will rise again to receive your inheritance."

13:1-14:42*

In Babylon there lived a Judean named Joakim ² who had married Susanna, begot of Hilkiah, a woman of great beauty. She was devout to the Most High, ³ because her parents were worthy people who had instructed her in the Law of Moses. ⁴ Joakim was very rich and had a garden attached to his house. The Jewish people would often visit him because he was highly respected by them all.

⁵ That year, two elders were selected to act as judges. About such people God said, "Corruption has come to Babylon through the elders, who were judges posing as guides to the people." ⁶ These two, to whom all brought their cases, frequently met in the house of Joakim.

⁷ Every day around noon, after the visitors left, Susanna would go for a walk in her garden. ⁸ And every day, the two judges would watch her take that walk, and they began to lust for her. ⁹ They threw reason aside, making no effort to turn their eyes to heaven, forgetting its demands for virtue. ¹⁰ So each of them waited for an opportunity. Though both lusted after Susanna, neither told the other of this, ¹¹ for they were both ashamed of their urges. ¹² Day after day, they spied on Susanna ¹³ until one day they said to each other, "It's time for us to go home for the noonday meal." So they left and parted company, ¹⁴ but then doubled back and returned to the house. When they met, they asked each other the reason for coming back. At that,

---

* Chapters 14 and 15 are additions to Daniel found in the Apocrypha, and are not included in the Masoretic text.

they confided their secret thoughts to each other, and they conspired to wait for an occasion to find Susanna alone.

[15] One day, Susanna entered the garden accompanied only by two young attendants. She decided to bathe in the garden, for the day was very hot. [16] There was no one there except the two elders, spying on her from their hiding place. [17] "Bring me some oil and lotions," she said to the attendants, "and shut the garden doors while I bathe." [18] They did as she told them, and shut the garden doors, leaving by the side gate to bring what she had ordered, unaware that the two elders had hidden themselves inside the garden.

[19] As soon as the attendants left, the two elders got up and overtook her. [20] "Look," they said, "the garden doors are shut, and no one can see us. We want you, so you might as well give in! [21] If you refuse, we will testify against you that you dismissed your attendants because a young man was here with you."

[22] "I am trapped, whatever I do," Susanna groaned. "If I yield, it will result in my death. If I refuse, I cannot get away from you. [23] I choose to fall innocent into your power rather than to sin in the eyes of God!" [24] Then she began to scream as loudly as she could. The two elders began shouting too, accusing her, [25] and one of them ran to open the garden doors. [26] When the people in the house heard the shrieks from the garden, they rushed in by the side gate to see what had happened to her. [27] Once the two elders had told their story, the household was completely taken aback, for nothing of this sort had ever been said about Susanna.

[28] When the people came to her husband Joakim the next day, the corrupt elders also came, fully determined to put Susanna to death. They told those gathered there, [29] "Send for Susanna, begot of Hilkiah, who is married to Joakim." When Susanna was sent for, [30] she came accompanied by her parents, her children, and all her relatives. [32] Susanna, who was very beautiful, [33] had veiled herself in modesty. But the corrupt elders ordered her to remove the veil so that they could leer at her beauty. [33] All of her relatives were weeping, as were the onlookers.

[34] The two elders stood up, with all the people around them, and laid their hands on the woman's head. [35] Through her tears, she looked up to heaven, for she trusted in God wholeheartedly. [36] The two elders then testified, "While we were walking in the garden alone, this woman arrived with her two attendants. She shut the garden doors and then dismissed the attendants. [37] A young man who had been hiding came over and they lay down together. From the corner of the garden where we were, we saw this crime taking place and hurried toward them. [39] Though we saw them together, we couldn't catch the man, for he was too strong for us.

He opened the doors and ran out. ⁴⁰ But we did seize this one, and demanded to know who the young man was. ⁴¹ She refused to tell us. This is our testimony." The assembly believed them, since they were elders and judges of the people and they condemned Susanna to death.

⁴² But Susanna cried as loud as she could, "Eternal God, you know everything that has been hidden and everything before it happens. ⁴³ You know that they have lied about me. And now, do I have to die, even though I'm innocent of everything their malice has invented against me?"

⁴⁴ The Most High God heard her prayer. ⁴⁵ As she was being led away to the execution, God stirred up the Holy Spirit residing in a youth named Daniel, ⁴⁶ and he began to shout, "I will have no part in the death of this woman!"

⁴⁷ All the people turned to him and asked, "What is this you are saying?"

⁴⁸ He stood in their midst and continued, "Are you such fools, you Israelites? Do you condemn a woman of Israel without examination and without clear evidence? ⁴⁹ Return to the scene of the trial, for those two have borne false witness against her."

⁵⁰ So the people hurried back, and the elders mocked Daniel, saying, "Come and sit with us and bestow your insights on us, since God has given you the gifts reserved for old age!"

⁵¹ But he replied, "Separate these two far from each other, for I want to question them."

⁵² After they were separated, Daniel had one of them brought to him. "You have grown old in corruption," he said, "and now the sins of your youth overtake you— ⁵³ you with your unjust judgments, your condemnation of the innocent, and your acquittal of the guilty, despite the fact that God has said, 'The innocent and the just you will not put to death.' ⁵⁴ Now, then, since you saw her so clearly, tell me what tree you saw them lying under."

⁵⁵ "Under a clove tree," he replied.

Daniel said, "Aha! Your clever lie has cost you your head, for the angel of God has already received your sentence from God and will slash you in half!"

⁵⁶ He dismissed the judge, ordered the second one to be brought, and said, "Offspring of Canaan, not of Judah! Beauty has seduced you, lust has led your heart astray! ⁵⁷ This is how you have acted with the daughters of Israel, and in their fear they yielded to you. But here is a daughter of Judah who could not stomach your corruption! ⁵⁸ Now, then, tell me what tree you surprised them under?"

He replied, ⁵⁹ "Under an oak."

Daniel said, "Aha! Your lie springs back on your own head, for the angel of God is waiting with a sword to drive home and split you, and destroy the pair of you!"

⁶⁰ The whole assembly cried aloud, blessing the Most High who saves those who hope in God. ⁶¹ They rose up against the two elders, for by their own words Daniel had convicted them of perjury. According to the Law of Moses, they administered on them the punishment they had plotted to impose on their neighbor: ⁶² they put them to death.

The life of an innocent woman was spared that day. ⁶³ Hilkiah and his wife praised God for their daughter Susanna, and so did her husband Joakim and all her relatives, because she was found innocent of a shameful deed.

⁶⁴ From that day forward, Daniel was regarded as a great sage among the people.

CR   CR   CR

14.1 When Astyages the Great joined his ancestors, Cyrus of Persia aceeded to the throne. ² Daniel was a counselor to the ruler and was one of the most respected among the royal court.

³ The Babylonians had an idol they called Bel, and every day they would offer twelve baskets of fine flour, forty sheep and fifty gallons of wine to the idol. ⁴ The ruler would pay homage to the idol every day, but Daniel bowed down only to the Most High God.

⁵ The ruler asked Daniel, "Why don't you pay homage to Bel?"

Daniel replied, "Because I don't pay homage to idols made by human hands; I worship the living God, who created the heavens and the earth and is Sovereign over all peoples."

⁶ The ruler protested, "How can you say that Bel isn't alive? Don't you see how much food he eats every day?

⁷ Daniel just laughed and replied, Don't be fooled, your majesty, for this Bel is just clay inside and bronze outside. It has never eaten or drunk anything."

⁸ The king grew angry and called the priests of Bel, saying, "If you can't tell me who consumes all these offerings, I'll have you all killed. ⁹ But if you're able to prove that it is Bel who eats all this, I'll have Daniel executed for blasphemy against Bel."

Daniel replied, "Let it be as you say."

¹⁰ There were seventy priests of Bel in attendance, along with their

spouses and families. Then the ruler went to the temple of Bel accompanied by Daniel and the priests. [11] The priests told the ruler, "We're leaving now. Place the food in the temple with your own hands and seal the door with the royal seal. [12] If, in the morning when you return, you do not find that Bel has consumed all the food, then you may put us to death. But if Daniel's charges about us are proved false, then you must put him to death." [13] They weren't concerned about this because they had built a secret door underneath the altar and used it to enter the temple and consume all the food and drink.

[14] When the priests had gone, the ruler set out the food on Bel's altar, and Daniel ordered the attendants to bring in some ashes and sift them over the floor of the whole temple in the presence of the ruler. Then they both left the building and closed the door, placing the royal seal upon the door, and left for the night. [15] During the night, the priests, along with their spouses and families, came in as usual and ate and drank everything.

[16] When morning came, the ruler was up early and Daniel was with him. [17] The ruler said, "Are the seals intact?"

"They are intact, your majesty," Daniel replied.

[18] When the doors were opened, the ruler looked in and cried aloud, "How great you are, O Bel! In you there is no falsehood whatsoever!"

[18] But Daniel just laughed and held back the ruler from entering the room. "Just look at the floor," he said, "and judge for yourself whose footprints these are."

[20] The ruler replied, "I see footprints of all sizes here." [21] Enraged, the ruler had all the priests of Bel arrested, along with their spouses and families, and they revealed the secret door they had used to enter the temple and eat what was left on the altar. [22] The ruler had them all put to death, and handed Bel over to Daniel, who destroyed the idol.

[23] There was a huge serpent that the Babylonians worshiped. [24] The ruler said to Daniel, "Why don't you bow down to this one, for you can plainly see this is a living god."

Daniel responded, "I will only bow down before the Most High God, who alone is a living God. [26] But say the word, your majesty, and I will kill the serpent without staff or sword."

"I give you this authority," said the ruler.

[27] Then Daniel took some tar, some fat, and some hair, and boiled them together and formed them into cakes, which he then fed to the serpent. The snake swallowed them, and promptly exploded. Then Daniel said, "See the kind of things you people worship!"

²⁸ When they heard of this, the Babylonians became indignant and plotted against the ruler. "The ruler has become Jewish!" they cried. "The ruler has pulled down Bel, killed the serpent and put our priests to death!" ²⁹ They came to the ruler and demanded, "Turn Daniel over to us, or we will kill you and your family!" ³⁰ Because of their insistence, the ruler felt compelled to hand Daniel over.

³¹ They threw Daniel into a pit of lions, and he remained there for six days. ³² There were seven lions in the pit, and every day, two prisoners and two sheep had been fed to them. But now, to make sure the lions would eat Daniel, they were fed nothing.

³³ The prophet Habakkuk, who was in Judea, made a stew, broke bread into a basket, and was preparing to take the food to those who tended the fields, ³⁴ when the angel of the Most High called out, saying, "Habakkuk, carry the food you have to Babylon for Daniel, who is in the lion pit."

³⁵ "But I have never been to Babylon, and I don't even know where the lion pit is!" replied Habakkuk.

³⁶ So the angel picked Habakkuk up by his head, and carried him by the hair all the way to Babylon as fast as the wind, and set him down above the lion pit.

³⁷ Habakkuk called out, "Daniel, Daniel! Take this food that God has sent you."

³⁸ Daniel said, "You have remembered me, my God! You never abandon those who love you!" ³⁹ Daniel got up and ate, and at once the angel whisked Habukkuk home again.

⁴⁰ On the seventh day, the ruler went to the pit to mourn for Daniel. But looking inside the pit, the ruler saw Daniel sitting there, ⁴¹ and cried out, "You are truly wonderful, Most High God of Daniel, and there is no god but you alone." ⁴² The ruler lifted Daniel out of the pit and ordered into the pit those who tried to destroy Daniel—and they were all devoured before the ruler's very eyes.

ezra*

Ín the first year of the reign of Cyrus, the ruler of Persia, fulfilling the prophecy of Jeremiah, God inspired Cyrus to issue a proclamation throughout the empire, both in written word and by word of mouth: ² "Thus says Cyrus, ruler of Persia," it read, "the Most High, God of heaven, who has given to me all the nations of the earth, has ordered me to build a Temple in Jerusalem, in Judah. ³ Whoever among you is of God's people, may God be with you! You may go up to Jerusalem in Judah to build the Temple of your God, the God of Israel, the God who is in Jerusalem. ⁴ And every Jewish person, wherever they live, is to be assisted by the people of that place with silver, gold, goods and cattle, together with freewill offerings for the Temple of God in Jerusalem."

⁵ Then the heads of the families of Judah and Benjamin—together with the priests and the Levites and, in fact, everyone whom God inspired to do so—prepared to go and rebuild the House of God in Jerusalem. ⁶ All their

---

* In the Hebrew canon, the books of Ezra and Nehemiah were originally one volume. However, because the common chapter and verse numbering begins from scratch again with Nehemiah, we felt it best to present them as separate books.

neighbors gave them every assistance with silver, gold, goods and cattle, and with many precious gifts besides all their freewill offerings.

⁷ Cyrus himself brought out all the vessels which Nebuchadnezzar had taken from the House of God in Jerusalem and had placed in the temple of his god. ⁸ Cyrus the Great of Persia placed all these things in the care of Mithredath the treasurer, and instructed him to provide an inventory of them to Sheshbazzar, the governor of Judah.

⁹ The inventory included:

gold dishes	30
silver dishes	1,000
silver vessels	29
¹⁰ gold bowls	30
matching silver bowls	410
other items	1,000

¹¹ When everything was counted, there were 5,400 items of gold and silver. Sheshbazzar collected all of these things and brought them back from Babylon to Jerusalem along with the exiles who returned.

2:1 This is a list of those who came out of Babylon to return to Jerusalem and the villages of Judah, from where Nebuchadnezzar had taken their ancestors as captives into Babylon. ² Their leaders were: Zerubbabel, Jeshua, Nehemiah, Seraiah, Reelaiah, Nahamani, Mordechai, Bilshan, Mispar, Bigvai, Rehum and Baanah.

The numbers of the families that returned from exile were:

³ from Parosh	2,172
⁴ from Shephatiah	372
⁵ from Arah,	775
⁶ from Pahath-moab (in the line of Jeshua and Joab)	2,812
⁷ from Elam	1,254
⁸ from Zattu	945
⁹ from Zaccai	760
¹⁰ from Bani	642
¹¹ from Bebai	623
¹² from Azgad	1,222
¹³ from Adonikam	666
¹⁴ from Bigvai	2,056
¹⁵ from Adin	454
¹⁶ from Ater (in the line of Hezekiah)	98
¹⁷ from Bezai	323
¹⁸ from Jorah	112
¹⁹ from Hashum	223

²⁰ from Gibbar	95
²¹ from Bethlehem	123
²² from Netophah	56
²³ from Anathoth	128
²⁴ from Beth-azmaveth	42
²⁵ from Kiriath-jearim, Chephirah, and Be-eroth	743
²⁶ from Ramah and Geba	621
²⁷ from Michmas	122
²⁸ from Bethel and Ai	223
²⁹ from Nebo	52
³⁰ from Magbish	156
³¹ from another Elam	1,254
³² from Harim	320
³³ from Lod, Hadid and Ono	725
³⁴ from Jericho	345
³⁵ from Senaah	3,630

³⁶ The numbers of priests returning from exile were as follows:

from Jedaiah (in the line of Jeshua)	973
³⁷ from Immer	1,052
³⁸ from Pashhur	1,247
³⁹ from Harim	1,017

⁴⁰ The numbers of Levites returning from exile were as follows:

from Hodaviah (in the line of Jeshua and Kadmiel)	74
⁴¹ the cantors from the family of Asaph	128
⁴² the descendants of the doorkeepers (from the families of Shallum, Ater, Talmon, Akkub, Hatita, and Shobai	139

⁴³ These descendants of the Temple stewards were represented among the exiles:

Ziha, Hasupha, Tabbaoth, ⁴⁴ Keros, Siaha, Padon, ⁴⁵ Lebanah, Hagabah, Akkub, ⁴⁶ Hagab, Shamlai, Hanan, ⁴⁷ Giddel, Gahar, Reaiah, ⁴⁸ Rezin, Nekoda, Gazzam, ⁴⁹ Uzza, Paseah, Besai, ⁵⁰ Asnah, Meunim, Nephisim, ⁵¹ Bakbuk, Hakupha, Harhur, ⁵² Bazluth, Mehida, Harsha, ⁵³ Barkos, Sisera, Temah, ⁵⁴ Neziah, and Hatipha.

⁵⁵ Among the descendants of Solomon's officials, there were:

Sotai, Hassophereth, Peruda, ⁵⁶ Jaalah, Darkon, Giddel, ⁵⁷ Shephatiah, Hattil, Pochereth-haz-zebaim, and Ami.

⁵⁸ The number descendants of Temple stewards and officials from Solomon's court were 392.

⁵⁹ Another group of exiles returned to Jerusalem from the Persian cities of Tel-melah, Tel-harsha, Cherub, Addan and Immer at the same time, but

they had lost track of their ancestry, and could not prove they were true Israelites. ⁶⁰ These included the people of Delaiah, Tobiah, and Nekoda, who numbered together 652.

⁶¹ From the priesthood, the descendants of Habaiah, Hakkoz, and Barzillai—a priest who married into the family of Barzillai the Gileadite and took the family name—returned as well. ⁶² They had also lost track of their ancestry, so the leaders refused to allow them to continue as priests, ⁶³ nor were they permitted to eat the priest's share of the food from the sacrifices until the Urim and Thummim* were cast to determine whether they were actually descendants of priests.

⁶⁴ In all 42,360 returned to Judah, as well as 7,337 bonded workers, and 200 cantors, both women and men. They brought with them 736 horses, 245 mules, 435 camels, and 6,720 donkeys.

⁶⁸ When they reached the Temple of Our God in Jerusalem, many of the families made freewill offerings to raise the Temple on its former site. ⁶⁹ They gave as they were able, to the sum of 61,000 gold drachmas, 5,000 silver minas, and 100 priestly robes.

⁷⁰ The priests, Levites, cantors, doorkeepers, and Temple stewards settled in their own villages, along with other people. And all of Israel returned to their hometowns.

CR CR CR

3:1 When the seventh month arrived—the people having settled in their own villages—they assembled in Jerusalem as one body. ² Then Jeshua begot of Jozadak, together with the other priests, and Zerubbabel begot of Shealtiel, together with his family, began the building of the altar of the God of Israel so that they might make burnt offerings as was stipulated in the law of Moses, the godly one. ³ They built the altar first, for they lived in fear of the peoples who lived around them; and they made burnt offerings day and night. ⁴ They celebrated the feast of Booths as was prescribed, making the proper number of burnt offerings each day, ⁵ and in the same way they made burnt offerings for the Sabbaths, for the new moons, and for all the sacred festivals of Our God; and everyone made freewill burnt offerings to the Most High. ⁶ On the first day of the seventh month they began to make burnt offerings regularly, even though the foundations of the new Temple had not yet been laid.

---

* The words mean "lights" and "perfections." They were two objects, probably inscribed stones, which were originally fastened to the breastplate of the High Priest; they were used as oracles, and may have been cast like lots or runes.

⁷ Money was donated for the work of the stonemasons and carpenters; and food, drink and oil for the Sidonians and Tyrians who would bring cedars by sea from Lebanon to Joppa, as had been granted by Cyrus of Persia.

⁸ In the second month of the second year after they had arrived at the House of God in Jerusalem, Zerubbabel, begot of Shealtiel, and Jeshua, begot of Jozadak, began their work, together with the other priests and Levites who had returned to Jerusalem from their captivity. Levites twenty years and older were appointed to supervise the work on the house of God. ⁹ Jeshua and his family, and Kadmiel and his family, who were descendants of Hodaviah, together with the family of Henadad—all of whom were Levites—took charge together of the building of the Temple.

¹⁰ While the stoneworkers set the Temple's foundation, the priests in their robes with their trumpets, and the Levites—descendants of Asaph—with their cymbals, took up their places as was set down by David, ruler of Israel. Chanting antiphonally, they gave thanks to the Most High "who is good, whose love for Israel lasts forever."

The people joined in with shouts of praise to God, as the foundation of the House of Our God was being laid. ¹² Many of the older priests and Levites and heads of families who had seen the original Temple cried openly at seeing the new foundation being laid. And many more cried out for joy. ¹³ And the cries of joy and the cries of sorrow were so mingled that no one could distinguish between them, and the din of the cries could be heard from far away.

4:1–6:22

When hostile neighbors learned that the restored exiles were building a Temple to their God, the God of Israel, ² they approached Zerubbabel, Jeshua and the leaders of the families. "Let us build alongside you," they said, "for we too worship your God. In fact, we have made burnt offerings to your God ever since the days of Esarhaddon ruler of Assyria who brought us here."

³ But Zerubbabel, Jeshua and the leaders of the families replied, "You cannot share in the building of the Temple and the worshipping in it. We alone are to build it for the Most High, the God of Israel, just as Cyrus ruler of Persia ordered us."

⁴ Then the peoples living around them went about discouraging the people of Judah from continuing their work. ⁵ They tried fear. They bribed

court officials to intercede for them. This went on throughout the reign of Cyrus ruler of Persia and into the reign of Darius.

⁶ In the first year the reign of Xerxes, they brought written charges against the Judeans and the people of Jerusalem. ⁷ And when Artaxerxes was the ruler of Persia, Bishlam, Mithradath, and Tabeel and those connected with them decided to send a letter to the ruler. The letter was written in Aramaic, then translated. ⁸ Rehum, the commanding officer, and Shimshai, the secretary, were the authors of the letter to Artaxerxes the ruler about the situation in Jerusalem; it read as follows:

⁹ "From Rehum the commanding officer, Shimshai the secretary, together with their associates—the judges, magistrates, and governors of the citizens of Tripolis, Persia, Erech and Babylon, the Elamites in Susa, ¹⁰ and the other deported nationals whom the famous and noble Ashurbanipal deported and settled in the cities of Samaria and in other parts of the province of Trans-Euphrates,

¹¹ * "To Artaxerxes the ruler, from his servants, residing in the province of Trans-Euphrates: Greetings.

¹² "We wish it to be known that the Judeans who left there to come here have arrived in Jerusalem. They are rebuilding that rebellious and treacherous city. They are repairing its walls and rebuilding the foundation of its Temple. ¹³ We wish to warn the ruler that if they do rebuild the city and repair the walls, they will pay neither tribute, nor duty, nor taxes; and in the end your revenue will suffer.

¹⁴ "Now, because we use the ruler's salt, it would be in poor taste for us to witness your dishonor; so we are sending this letter for your information. ¹⁵ We suggest that you conduct a search of the archives of your predecessors. You will substantiate our claim that this city is a rebellious city, forever troublesome to rulers and provinces, with a history of being a cesspool of sedition. It was for these reasons that it was laid to waste. ¹⁶ Let it be known to your eminence that if the city is rebuilt and its walls repaired, you will lose possession of the Province of Trans-Euphrates."

¹⁷ Artaxerxes answered:

"To Rehum the commanding officer, Shimshai the secretary, and your associates residing in Samaria and in other parts of the Province of Trans-Euphrates: Greetings.

¹⁸ "Your letter to me has now been translated and read in my presence. ¹⁹ I ordered the search of the archives concerning that city, and learned it

---

* The Hebrew inserts the following note here: "This is a copy of the letter they sent him."

has a long history of opposition to rulers from times long past, and that rebellion and sedition are part and parcel of its history. 20 Jerusalem had powerful rulers who ruled formerly throughout the Province of Trans-Euphrates with tribute, taxes and tolls collected.

21 "Therefore, issue orders to the workers to stop; this city is not to be rebuilt until a decree to that effect is issued by me. 22 Make certain that this notice is carried out without delay. Why should more harm come to us?"

23 When the letter from Artaxerxes the ruler was read to Rehum and Shimshai and their associates, they hastened to the Judeans in Jerusalem and forcefully put a stop to their work. 24 So the work on the house of God in Jerusalem came to a halt, and was at a standstill until the second year of the reign of Darius ruler of Persia.

ભ ભ ભ

5:1 The prophet Haggai, and the prophet Zechariah begot of Iddo, prophesied to the Judeans in Judah and Jerusalem, upbraiding them in the name of the God of Israel. 2 Then Zerubbabel, begot of Shealtiel and Jeshua, begot of Jozadak, with the prophets of God at their sides, set out to rebuild the House of God in Jerusalem.

3 Tattenai, governor of the Province of Trans-Euphrates, as well as Shethar-bozenai and other emissaries, came to them and asked, "Who gave you permission to build this temple and complete its structure?" 4 They asked also for the names of those working on the structure. 5 But the elders of the Judeans were watched by the eye of God, and they did not desist from their rebuilding until report of their work reached Darius and an official response was made.

6 The following is a copy of a letter to Darius the ruler from Tattenai, governor of the Province of Trans-Euphrates, Shethar-bozenai and his colleagues, the inspectors in the province of Trans-Euphrates. 7 This is the report that was sent:

"To Darius the ruler: Cordial greetings.

8"We wish that it be known to you, your majesty, that we went to the province of Judah where we found the Temple of the great God under construction, with walls of hewn stone and the roof beams already set in the walls. The work is being carried out with diligence, and moves rapidly under the direction of the elders. We asked them by whose authority they were building and finishing this structure. 10 We asked also their names, so we might provide you with a list of those supervising the work.

11 "This was their reply: 'We serve the God of heaven and earth, and we

are rebuilding this house which was first constructed many years ago. It was built and completed by a great ruler of Israel. ¹² But because our ancestors angered the God of heaven, God handed them over to Nebuchadnezzar the Chaldean, of Babylon, who destroyed this Temple and deported our people to Babylon.

¹³ "However, Cyrus the ruler of Babylon, in the first year of his reign, decreed that this house of God should be rebuilt. ¹⁴ Moreover, he removed from the temple in Babylon the gold and silver vessels of the house of God, which Nebuchadnezzar had taken from the Temple in Jerusalem to the temple in Babylon. He handed them over to a person named Sheshbazzar, whom he had appointed governor, ¹⁵ telling him, 'Take these vessels to Jerusalem and restore them to the Temple there, and let the house of God be rebuilt to its original size.' ¹⁶ Then this Sheshbazzar came and laid the foundation of the House of God in Jerusalem. From that day to this the rebuilding continues and is still not finished.'

¹⁷ "Therefore, now, if it is pleasing to you, let a search be made in the archives of Babylon to see if Cyrus the ruler did in fact issue such a decree to rebuild this house of God in Jerusalem. Then let the ruler send us his decision in this matter."

6:1 Darius the ruler ordered a search be made in the archives where treasures were stored in Babylon. ² But it was in Ecbatana, the capital of the province of Media, that a scroll was found on which the following was written:

"Memorandum:

³ "In the first year of the reign of Cyrus, the ruler issued a decree concerning the House of God in Jerusalem: Let the House be rebuilt as a place where burnt offerings are made. It is to be ninety feet high and ninety feet wide, ⁴ with three courses of large stones and one course of timber. The cost is to be paid from the national treasury. ⁵ And the gold and silver vessels of the house of God, which Nebuchadnezzar took from the Temple in Jerusalem and brought to Babylon, are to be returned. They are to be taken back to the Temple in Jerusalem, with each to be returned to its original place in the house of God."

⁶ Then Darius issued this decree:

"Now, Tattenai, governor of the Province of Trans-Euphrates, Shethar-bozenai and your colleagues, the inspectors in the province of Trans-Euphrates, you are to keep away from that place. ⁷ Let the governor of the Jewish people and their elders rebuild the house of God on its site. ⁸ And I decree futher that you are to do for the elders of these people, with regard to the construction of this house of God, as follows: their expenses are to be repaid to these people, in full and immediately, from the royal treasury out of the taxes levied on the province of Trans-Euphrates, so that their work not be brought to a standstill. ⁹ Whatever may be needed—be it young bulls, rams, or sheep for the burnt offerings to the God of heaven, or wheat, salt, wine or oil, as the priests in Jerusalem require—let it be delivered to them daily, without fail, ¹⁰ so that they may offer burnt offerings pleasing to the God of heaven, and pray for the life of the ruler and of his children.

¹¹ "Furthermore, I decree that any person who tampers with this edict will have a beam taken from the house where this person lives. Then this person will be impaled upon it. Then their house shall be reduced to rubble. ¹² May the God whose Name dwells there depose any ruler or people who lifts a finger to change this decree, or any who would destroy this Temple in Jerusalem. I, Darius of Persia, have decreed. Let it be done without delay."

¹³ Then Tattenai, governor of the province of Trans-Euphrates, and Shethar-bozenai and their colleagues, carried out to the letter these instructions which Darius had sent them. ¹⁴ The elders of the Jewish people went on with their work, and the work progressed well. With the exhortation of Haggai and Zechariah begot of Iddo, they finished the rebuilding as commanded by the God of Israel and by the decrees of Cyrus, Artaxerxes, and Darius, the rulers of Persia. The house was completed on the third day of the month of Adar, in the sixth year of the reign of Darius.

¹⁶ Then the Israelites, priests, Levites, and all the exiles who had returned celebrated the dedication of the House of God with loud rejoicing. ¹⁷ At its dedication they offered 100 bulls, 200 rams, and 400 lambs, and as a sin offering for all Israel, twelve male goats, one for each tribe of Israel. ¹⁸ They installed the priests in their groups and the Levites in their divisions for the service of God in Jerusalem, as was laid out in the book of Moses.

¹⁹ On the fourteenth day of the first month, the returned exiles observed the Passover. ²⁰ The priests and Levites, one and all, had purified themselves. All were ritually clean, and they killed the Passover lamb for all the returned exiles, for their fellow priests, and for themselves. ²¹ It was eaten by the people of Israel who had returned from exile, and by those who had joined them and separated themselves from the unclean practices of their Gentile neighbors, seeking the Most High, the God of Israel. ²² They observed the feast of Unleavened Bread for seven days joyfully, for the Most High had given them much cause for rejoicing, changing the disposition of the ruler of Assyria toward them, so that he supported them in the work of the house of God, the God of Israel.

It was following this, in the reign of Artaxerxes the ruler, that Ezra came up from Babylon. He was begot of Seraiah, begot of Azariah, begot of Hilkiah, ² begot of Shallum, begot of Zadok, begot of Ahitub, ³ begot of Amariah, begot of Azariah, begot of Meraioth, ⁴ begot of Zerahiah, begot of Uzzi, begot of Bukki, ⁵ begot of Abishua, begot of Phinehas, begot of Eleazar, begot of Aaron the chief priest. ⁶ Ezra was a scribe, an expert on the law of Moses which the Most High God had given to Israel. Artaxerxes granted Ezra whatever he wished, for the hand of the Most High was on him.

⁷ Ezra left Babylon with certain other Israelites, Levites, Temple cantors, doorkeepers, and Temple stewards, in the seventh year of the reign of Artaxerxes the ruler. ⁸ They reached Jerusalem in the fifth month of the seventh year of the ruler: ⁹ on the first day of the first month they began their journey; and on the first day of the fifth month they arrived in Jerusalem; and God's grace was with Ezra. ¹⁰ He had devoted himself to the study of the Law of the Most High and its observance, and to the teaching the statutes and ordinances in Israel.

¹¹ This is a copy of a letter which Artaxerxes the ruler gave to Ezra the priest and scribe, student of the matters of the commandments and statutes which the Most High had laid down for Israel:

¹² "Artaxerxes, ruler of rulers, to Ezra the priest and scribe, learned in the Law of the God of heaven: Greetings.

¹³ "It is my decree that any of the people of Israel or their priests or Levites in my country who wish to go to Jerusalem may go with you. ¹⁴ For you are sent by the ruler and the ruler's seven counselors to see how things stand in Judah and Jerusalem concerning the Law of your God, with which you are entrusted. ¹⁵You are to deliver the gold and silver which the ruler and the counselors freely offer to the God of Israel who dwells in Jerusalem, ¹⁶ along with any gold and silver that you might acquire from the province of Babylon, and with any freewill offerings of the people and the priests for the Temple of their God. ¹⁷ With these you will buy bulls, rams and lambs, along with the proper grain offerings and drink offerings, and offer them on the altar of the Temple of your God in Jerusalem.

¹⁸ "And if any of the gold and silver is left over it may be put to use as you and your colleagues see fit, all to be carried out according to the will of your God. ¹⁹ The vessels given to you for the service of the house are to be handed over before your God, the God of Jerusalem. ²⁰ Anything else

needed for the house of Your God, which you are responsible for providing, draw out of the ruler's treasury.

21 "I, Artaxerxes the ruler, hereby command that all the treasuries in the Province of Trans-Euphrates, are to promptly provide to Ezra the scribe, learned in the Law of the God of heaven, whatever he may ask of you, 20 up to 3.75 tons of silver, 600 bushels of wheat, 600 gallons of wine, 600 gallons of oil, and an unlimited supply of salt. 23 Let it be done zealously, whatever the God of heaven requires for the house of God, or the wrath of God will fall on the realm of the ruler and on his children. 24 Let it be known also that no one shall impose tribute, custom fees or tolls on any of the priests, Levites, musicians, doorkeepers, Temple stewards, or any other of the house of God.

25 "You, Ezra, in accordance with the wisdom which God has given you, are to appoint judges and magistrates to minister justice among those of your people residing in Trans-Euphrates who know the Laws of your God; and those who do not are to be instructed in the Law. 26 Those who will not obey the Law of Your God and the law of the ruler are to be firmly judged, whether by death, or by banishment, or by imprisonment, or by the confiscation of their property."

ଓ ଓ ଓ

27 * Bessed be with the Most High, the God of our ancestors, who softened the heart of the ruler to honor the house of Our God in Jerusalem as he did, 28 and who has made the ruler, the ruler's counselors and other officials well-disposed to me! Because the hand of Our God, the Most High, was on me, I took courage and called together the leaders of Israel to travel with me.

8:1 These are the heads of the families of Israel, and those registered with them, who left Babylon with me during the reign of Artaxerxes the ruler:

> 2 of the line of Phinehas, Gershom;
> of the line Ithamar, Daniel;
> of the line of David, Hattush 3 begot of Shecaniah;
> of the line of Parosh, Zechariah, along with 150 others registered in that clan;
> 4 of the line of Pahath-moab, Eliehoenai begot of Zerahiah, along with 200 others registered in that clan;

---

* At this point the narrative switches to the first person, with Ezra narrating the rest of the story.

⁵ of the line of Zattu, Shecaniah begot of Jahaziel, along with 300 others registered in that clan;

⁶ of the line of Adin, Ebed begot of Jonathan, along with 50 others registered in that clan;

⁷ of the line of Elam, Jeshaiah begot of Athaliah, along with 50 others registered in that clan;

⁸ of the line of Shephatiah, Zebadiah begot of Michael, 80 others registered in that clan;

⁹ of the line of Joab, Obadiah begot of Jehiel, along with 280 others registered in that clan;

¹⁰ of the line of Bani, Shelomith begot of Josiphiah, along with 160 others;

¹¹ of the line of Bebai, Zechariah begot of Bebai, along with 28 others;

¹² of the line of Azgad, Johanan begot of Hakkatan, along with 110 others

¹³ of the line of Adonikam, the last line, Eliphelet, Jeiel, and Shemaiah, along with 60 others; and

¹⁴ of the line of Bigvai, Uthai begot of Zabbud, along with 70 others.

¹⁵ I gathered all of them by the river that flows toward Ahava. We camped there for three days. Studying the lists of the people and priests, I saw that there were no Levites. ¹⁶ So I called together Eliezer, Ariel, Shemaiah, Elnathan, Jarib, Elnathan, Nathan, Zechariah and Meshullam, leaders all; and Joiarib and Elnathan, who were known for their wisdom. ¹⁷ I sent them to Iddo, leader of a settlement in Casiphia. They carried my message to Iddo and his colleagues, the Temple stewards at Casiphia, asking them to send us ministers for the House of God. ¹⁸ God's grace being upon us they sent us Sherebiah—who was known for his discretion—of the line of Mahli, begot of Levi, begot of Israel, together with eighteen of his offspring and kin; ¹⁹ and Hashabiah and Jeshaiah begot of Merari, together with twenty of his offspring and kin. ²⁰ They sent, as well, 220 Temple stewards, listed by name, of the order created by David and his officials to aid the Levites.

²¹ There, beside the Ahava river, I proclaimed a fast, so that we all might humble ourselves before Our God, asking for a safe journey for us and our children and all our possessions. ²² I would have been ashamed to ask Artaxerxes for a troop of cavalry to protect us from the enemy along the way, for I had told the ruler that God's gracious hand protects those who seek it, and God's wrath turns against all who turn away. ²³ So we fasted and prayed to our God for protection, and God heard our prayers.

²⁴ Then I selected twelve of the leading priests: Sherebiah, Hashabiah and ten of their kin with them. ²⁵ I weighed out to them the silver and gold and

vessels which hsd been donated to the house of Our God by the ruler and his counselors and officers, and by all the Israelites with me. ²⁶ I weighed out to them twenty-five tons of silver, nearly four tons of gold, ²⁷ twenty gold bowls weighing about nineteen pounds, and two fine articles of polished bronze as precious as gold. ²⁸ I said to them, "You are holy to Our God, and the vessels are holy. The silver and the gold are a freewill offering to Our God, the God of your ancestors. ²⁹ Guard them and keep them safe until you weigh them in Jerusalem before the high priest and the Levites, and the heads of families in Israel, in the house of Our God." ³⁰ So the priests and the Levites accepted the consignment of silver and gold and vessels, to be delivered to the house of God in Jerusalem.

³¹ We left the river Ahava for Jerusalem on the twelth day of the first month. God's hand was with us, and protected us from being ambushed by our enemies while we were on the road. ³² When we arrived in Jerusalem we rested for three days. ³³ On the fourth day the silver and gold and the vessels were weighed and handed over in the house of our God to Meremoth the priest, begot of Uriah, and Eleazar, begot of Phinehas, and with them the Levites Jozebad, begot of Jeshua, and Noadiah, begot of Binnui. ³⁴ Everything was counted and weighed and recorded.

³⁵ At this time, all these exiles who had returned from Babylon made burnt offerings of twelve bulls for all Israel, ninety-six rams, and seventy-seven lambs, with twelve male goats as a purification offering. These were made as a whole offering to Our God. ³⁶ They also delivered the ruler's orders to the ruler's satraps and the governors in the province of Trans-Euphrates, who in turn supported the people and the house of God.

9:1 When all this business was done, the leaders came to me, saying: "The Israelite people, even the priests and Levites, have not separated themselves from those among them from other lands, with their abominable practices—the Canaanites, Hittites, Perizzites, and Jebusites; the Ammonites, Moabites, Egyptians, and Amorites. ² They have intermarried until the holy race has become mixed with the people around it; and it is the unfaithfulness, above all, of the officials and the leaders that has led to this."

³ When I heard this, I ripped my tunic and my cloak. I tore hair from my head and from my beard, and then, overcome with anguish, sat still. ⁴ All who trembled at the words of the God of Israel, because of the faithlessness of the returned exiles, gathered around me while I sat staring until the evening burnt offering.

⁵ At the evening offering I stood, torn tunic and cloak obvious to all, and threw myself on the ground with arms outstretched, praying, ⁶ "I am debased, O God, I am ashamed, my God, to raise my face to you. Our sins

rise over our heads; our guilt is so immense it reaches to high heaven. [7] From the times of our ancestors to the present day our guilt is deep. Because of our iniquities we, our rulers, and our priests were handed over to the rulers of foreign lands, to be killed, to be captured, plundered and to be humiliated, to this very day. [8] And here, now, for a brief moment, the light of our God's grace has shone upon us, giving us a foothold in this holy place. Our God has given light to our eyes once more, given us a chance to renew our lives out of our slavery. [9] Yes, we are slaves; yet our God has not abandoned us to our slavery, but has secured for us the favor of the ruler of Persia, who gives us means of renewal, and encouragement to repair our house of God, to rebuild its ruins—giving us a defending wall in Judah and Jerusalem.

[10] "Now, O God, after all this, what are we to say? We have abandoned your commandments, [11] given to us through your servants, the prophets. You said to us, 'The land you move into is a defiled land, inhabited by heathen people with unclean practices. Their impure ways pollute it from end to end. [12] Therefore, do not give your children into marriage with their children. Do not enter into treaties of friendship with them, ever. Only then will you grow strong and eat of the bounty of the land. Only then will you leave it to your children as an everlasting inheritance.'

[13] "After all that has happened to us because of our wicked ways and immense guilt—though you, O God, punished us less than we deserved, and allow us to survive as we do now—[14] should we disobey your commandments once again, and intermarry once again with people who take part in such abominable practices? Surely you would be so angry with us that you would destroy us and leave us without survivors! [15] O Most High God of Israel, you are just. As it is, we are survivors, a mere remnant. We stand before you in our guilt, though no one can face you in such a state as this!"

10[1] While Ezra prayed and confessed, prostrate and tearful before the House of God, a great throng of Israelites gathered around him—women, children, and men—and they too wept bitterly. [2] Shecaniah, begot of Jehiel, of the family of Elam, told Ezra, "We have been unfaithful to God by marrying the foreign people of the land. But there is yet hope for Israel. [3] Let us now make a covenant with Our God to disown our foreign spouses and children, according to your advice and the advice of those who live in reverence of our God's commands. And let the Law take its course. [4] Take action as you see fit, according to your duty; we will follow you. Be strong, and do what must be done!" [5] Then Ezra rose, and made the leading priests, the Levites, and all the Israelites swear that they would do as had been proposed. And so they swore.

⁶ Then Ezra left the house of God and went to the room of Jehohanan begot of Eliashib. He fasted there, eating no food and drinking no water, mourning even more for the lack of faith of the exiles.

⁷ A proclamation was issued througout Judah and Jerusalem for all the returned exiles to assemble in Jerusalem. ⁸ Any who failed to appear within three days would forfeit all property, by orders of the elders and officials, and would be expelled from the assembly of the exiles.

⁹ Within three days, all the residents of Judah and Benjamin gathered in Jerusalem. It was the twentieth day of the ninth month. They all sat in the open space in front of the house of God, deeply distressed over these matters—and by the heavy rain. Ezra, standing before them, said, "You have gone against the law by marrying foreigners, and have deepened Israel's guilt. ¹¹ Now confess to Our God, the God of our ancestors, and do God's will. Separate yourselves from the natives around you, and from your foreign spouses."

¹² The whole assembly responded as one, "You are right. We will do as you say, ¹³ but our numbers are great and it is the rainy season. We can't stay here in the open. And this is not a task of one or two day's duration. This is a serious matter. ¹⁴ Let our leaders speak for us, and let those of us who have married foreigners present ourselves in a scheduled manner, along with the elders and judges of each town, until God's fierce anger at what we have done is turned away from us." ¹⁵ Only Jonathan, begot of Asahel, and Jahzeiah, begot of Tikvah, spoke against this, and Meshullam and Shabbethai the Levite.

¹⁶ The returned exiles did what had been proposed. Ezra the priest selected family heads, one from each family division, each designated by name. They sat down to study the issue on the first day of the tenth month, ¹⁷ and by the first day of the first month they had examined all these intermarriages.

¹⁸ Among the members of priestly families who had married foreigners were: Maaseiah, Eliezer, Jarib and Gedaliah, of the line of Jeshua begot of Jozadak, and his kin. ¹⁹ They pledged themselves to dismiss their spouses, and to offer a ram from the flock as a sin-offering for the offense.

²⁰ Of the line of Immer: Hanani and Zebadiah.

²¹ Of the line of Harim: Maaseiah, Elijah, Shemaiah, Jehiel and Uzziah.

²² Of the line of Pashhur: Elioenai, Maaseiah, Ishmael, Nethanel, Jozabad and Elasah.

²³ Of the Levites: Jozabad, Shimei, Kelaiah—that is, Kelita—Pethahiah, Judah and Eliezer.

²⁴ Of the cantors: Eliashib and Zaccur.

Of the doorkeepers: Shallum, Telem and Uri.

25 And of Israel:

Of the line of Parosh: Ramiah, Izziah, Malchijah, Mijamin, Eleazar, Malchijah and Benaiah.

26 Of the line of Elam: Mattaniah, Zechariah, Jehiel, Abdi, Jeremoth and Elijah.

27 Of the line of Zattu: Elioenai, Eliashib, Mattaniah, Jeremoth, Zabad and Aziza.

28 Of the line of Bebai: Jehohanan, Hananiah, Zabbai and Athlai.

29 Of the line of Bigvai: Meshullam, Malluch, Jedaiah, Jashub, Sheal and Jeremoth.

30 Of the line of Pahath-moab: Adna, Chelal, Benaiah, Maaseiah, Mattaniah, Bezalel, Binnui and Manasseh.

31 Of the line of Harim: Eliezer, Isshijah, Malchijah, Shemaiah, Shimeon, 32 Benjamin, Malluch and Shemariah.

33 Of the line of Hashum: Mattenai, Mattattah, Zabad, Eliphelet, Jeremai, Manasseh and Shimei.

34 Of the line of Bani: Maadai, Amram and Uel, 35 Benaiah, Bedeiah and Cheluhi, 36 Vaniah, Meremoth, Eliashib, 37 Mattaniah, Mattenai and Jaasau.

38 Of the line of Binnui: Shimei, 39 Shelemiah, Nathan and Adaiah.

40 Of the line of Zaccai: Shashai and Sharai, 41 Azarel, Shelemiah and Shemariah, 42 Shallum, Amariah and Joseph.

43 Of the line of Nebo: Jeiel, Mattithiah, Zabad, Zebina, Jaddai, Joel and Benaiah.

44 All these had married foreigners, and they dismissed them and their children.

nehemiah

1:1–7:73a

the words of nehemiah begot of hacaliah.

In the month of Chislev in the twentieth year of the reign of Artaterxes, when I was in the capital city of Susa, it happened ² that Hanani, one of my brothers, came there with other Judeans. I asked them about Jerusalem, and about the Jewish remnant, the survivors of the exile. ³ They told me, "The survivors of the captivity who returned to the province are in serious straits, and are humbled. The wall is in ruin and its gates are burned down."

⁴ When I heard this, I sat down and cried, and mourned for days, fasting and praying to the heavenly God. ⁵ I prayed, "Adonai, God of heaven, great and awesome God, you keep your covenant of love with us who love you and obey your commandments. ⁶ Let your ears be attentive and your eyes open to the prayer that I, your servant, offer night and day for your people, the women and men of Israel. I confess the sins which we Israelites have committed against you. I have sinned, and my family has sinned. We have acted dispicably toward you. We disobeyed the commandments, and the decrees and laws, which you gave to your servant Moses.

⁸ "Do not forget the word which you gave to your servant Moses: 'If you

do not keep faith, I will scatter you among the nations, 9 but if you return to me and observe my commands and live by them, I will find you where you wander under foreign skies in the farthest corners of the earth and gather you to the place which I have chosen as a dwelling place for my name.

10 "They are your servants; your people, whom you redeemed by the strength of your mighty hand. Adonai, lend your ear to my prayer, and to the prayers of your own who take joy in honoring your Name. Give me success today by granting me favor in the eyes of the ruler."

At this time, I was the ruler's cupbearer. 2:1 It was in the month of Nisan, in the twentieth year of Artaxerxes' reign. When it came time for the ruler's wine, it was I who brought to him. Now, I had never been sad in the ruler's presence before, so he now asked, 2"Why do you look so ill, and yet are not ill? You must be sad of heart."

I was very afraid, 3 but I answered, "May the ruler live forever! Should I not be sad? The city where my ancestors are buried lies in ruins, with its gates burned to the ground?"

4 Artaxerxes asked me, "What is your wish?"

I silently prayed to the God of heaven, 5 then said aloud, "If it pleases your majesty, and if I have found favor with you, let me go to Judah, to the city where my ancestors rest, so that I may rebuild it."

6 The ruler, sitting with his consort at his side, asked, "How long is the journey, and when would you return?"

And so I saw that he would let me go. I told him when I might return, and 7 then said to him, "If it pleases you, give me letters for the governors in the province of Trans-Euphrates for my safe conduct to Judah, 8 and also a letter to Asaph, the keeper of the ruler's forest, instructing him to provide me with timber to make the the gates of the citadel near the Temple, and for the city wall, as well as the house I'll be living in." The ruler granted my requests, for God's gracious hand was on me.

9 Eventually I came to the governors of Trans-Euphrates and showed them the ruler's letters of safe passage. Artaxerxes had sent with me officers of the army and the cavalry. When Sanballat the Horonite, and Tobiah, an Ammonite official heard of this, they were angry that someone would come to promote the interests of the Israelites.

11 When I arrived in Jerusalem, I waited three days, 12 then went out after nightfall with a few others, telling no one what my God put in my heart to do for Jerusalem. We only took one mount, which I rode; 13 we went out by the Valley Gate past the Jackal's Spring to the Dung Gate. I inspected the

walls of Jerusalem and saw where they were broken down, and the gates burnt. [14] Then I went on to the Fountain Gate and to the Ruler's Pool, where there was no room for my mount to pass through. [15] So I went up the valley by night, inspecting the city wall. Then I reentered the city through the Valley Gate, and returned [16] without the city officials knowing where I had been and what I had been doing, for I had not yet spoken of this to the Jewish people, the priests, the nobles, the officials or any of those who would be responsible for the work.

[17] Now I said to them, "See what the trouble we are in! Jerusalem lies in ruins, its gates burned to the ground. Come, let us rebuild the wall of Jerusalem, and rid ourselves of derision."* [18] I told them of how the gracious hand of God had come upon me, and of what the ruler had told me. They responded willingly, "Then let us begin work!" And they set forth working toward the good of all.

[19] But when Sanballat the Horonite, Tobiah the Ammonite and Geshem the Arab heard of this, they jeered at us and asked contemptuously, "What is this you are doing? Is this a rebellion against the ruler?"

[20] But I replied, "The God of heaven will give us success. We, God's servants, are beginning the rebuilding. But you have no claim, nor any traditional right in Jerusalem."

3:1 Eliashib the high priest and the other priests began work rebuilding the Sheep Gate. They consecrated it and set up the gates. They carried their work all the way to the Tower of the Hundred and the Tower of Hananel. [2] Workers from Jericho built side by side with Eliashib; and next to them, Zaccur, begot of Imri.

[3] Those of the line of Hassenaah rebuilt the Fish Gate. They erected its beams and set up its gates with their bolts and bars in place. [4] At their side worked Meremoth, begot of Uriah, begot of Hakkoz, making repairs; and next to them Meshullam, begot of Berechiah, begot of Meshezabel; and next to them Zadok, begot of Baana. [5] Next in line were workers from the line of Tekoa, doing repair work; but their nobles refused to do any strenuous labor, even for Our God.

[6] The Old Gate was repaired by Joiada begot of Paseah, with Meshul–lam begot of Besodeiah. They laid its foundations and set up its gates with its bolts and bars in place. [7] Next to them worked Melatiah the Gibeonite and Jadon the Meronothite, workers from Gibeon and Mizpah, doing the repair work under the auspices of the governor of the province of Trans-Euphrates. [8] At their sides worked Uzziel, begot of Harhaiah, a goldsmith,

---

* Rebuilding the wall and gates first had a two-fold purpose: to keep out looters and marauding bands; and to shield the city, still in ruins, from the eyes and mockery of outsiders.

and Hananiah, of the perfumers' guild, both doing repair work. They reconstructed Jerusalem's walls as far as the Broad Wall. ⁹ Next to them worked Rephaiah, begot of Hur, ruler of half the district of Jerusalem—making repairs. ¹⁰ Then there was Jedaiah, begot of Harumaph, making repairs opposite his own house; and after him Hattush, begot of Hashabniah. ¹¹ Malchijah, begot of Harim, and Hasshub, begot of Pahath-moab, repaired another section which included the Tower of the Ovens. ¹² After them was Shallum, begot of Hallohesh, ruler of half the district of Jerusalem, doing repairs with his daughters working by his side.

¹³ The Valley Gate was repaired by Hanun and the residents of Zanoah. They rebuilt it and set up its gates with its bolts and bars in place, and repaired the fifteen hundred feet of the wall that reached to the Dung Gate.

¹⁴ The Dung Gate was repaired by Malchijah, begot of Rechab, governor of the district of Beth-hac-cherem. He rebuilt it and set up its gates with its bolts and bars in place.

¹⁵ The Fountain Gate was repaired by Shallum begot of Col-hozeh, governor of the district of Mizpah. He rebuilt it and put a new roof over it and set up its gates with its bolts and bars in place, and then he rebuilt the wall of the Pool of Shelah next to the ruler's garden and as far as the steps leading down from the City of David. ¹⁶ Beyond Shallum, Nehemiah begot of Azbuk, governor of half the district of Beth-zur, did repair work across from the tombs of David, and as far as the artificial pool and the House of Warriors. ¹⁷ Next to Nehemiah worked the Levites under Rehum, begot of Bani; and beside them, Hashabiah—governor of half the district of Keilah—worked on the behalf of his district. ¹⁸ Next to Hashabiah worked members of his clan: Binnui, begot of Henadad, ruler of the second half of the district of Keilah. ¹⁹ Next to Binnui was Ezer, begot of Jeshua, governor of Mizpah, who repaired a section opposite the point where the ascent meets the rampart. ²⁰ After Ezer was Baruch, begot of Zabbai, repairing a section from the rampart to the door of Eliashib the high priest. ²¹ Beside him Meremoth, begot of Uriah, begot of Hakkoz, repaired a section from the door of Eliashib's house to the end of the house.

²² The priests of the neighborhood of Jerusalem made the repairs next to Meremoth's. ²³ Beyond them were Benjamin and Hassub, doing repairs opposite their own house; and next Azariah, begot of Maaseiah, begot of Ananiah, did the repair work beside his house. ²⁴ After Azariah, Binnui, begot of Henadad, repaired a section from the house of Azariah as far as the rampart and the corner. ²⁵ Palal, begot of Uzai, worked opposite the rampart and the tower projecting from the upper palace near the court of the guard. After Palal was Pedaiah, begot of Parosh, ²⁶ and the Temple stewards who lived on Ophel hill, and they worked toward the east to a

point opposite the Water Gate and the projecting tower. ²⁷ Then came workers from Tekoa, who repaired a second section from the great projecting tower to the wall of Ophel.

²⁸ Above the Horse Gate the priests repaired the parts of the wall that were opposite their own houses. ²⁹ Zadok, begot of Immer, repaired the wall opposite his own house; ³⁰ and next to Zadok, Hananiah, begot of Shelemiah, and Hanun, sixth child of Zalaph, repaired another section. After them, Meshullam begot of Berechiah did the repairs opposite his quarters. ³¹ Next to Berechiah, Malchijah, a goldsmith, did the repair work as far as the house of the Temple stewards; and the merchants, opposite the Mustering Gate, as far as the roof-chamber at the corner. ³² The goldsmiths and the merchants did the repairs between the roof-chamber at the corner and the Sheep Gate.

ଓ୫   ଓ୫   ଓ୫

4:1 When news of the rebuilding of the wall reached Sanballat, he was infuriated. He ridiculed the Jewish workers, ² saying to his colleagues and soldiers from the Samarian army, "What are these feeble Jewish people up to? Are they restoring their wall? Will they make burnt offerings and finish their work in a day? Can they reuse the stones out of the rubble heap, that burned heap?"

³ Tobiah the Ammonite, standing at his side, said, "Whatever it is they are building, a fox climbing up that wall would bring it down."

⁴ See, O God, how despised we are! Turn their taunts back onto their own heads. Let them become slaves in a land of captivity. ⁵ Do not let their guilt be overlooked or let their sin be blotted from the record, for they have thrown insults in the faces of the builders.

⁶ So we rebuilt the wall until it was unbroken and reached up to half its original height, because the people put their hearts into their work.

⁷ But when Sanballat and Tobiah and the Arabs and Ammonites and Ashdodites saw that the new work in Jerusalem was progressing and the breaches were being closed, they were so furious ⁸ they plotted together to come into Jerusalem, stir up trouble and spoil our work. ⁹ But we prayed to God, and posted a guard day and night to counter the threat.

¹⁰ In Judah people were saying, "The laborers' strength has failed, and there is such a wealth of rubble that we will never be able to rebuild the walls." ¹¹ Our enemies said, "Before they know what is happening, we will be upon them, killing them, and putting an end to their work."

¹² When the Jews living nearby came into the city, they warned us a dozen

times that our foes would attack us regardless of what we did. [13] So I posted people at the lowest places at the bottom of the wall and in places to observe the open spaces. [14] Then I addressed the authorities, the magistrates and the people: "Don't fear these people. Think of Our God, the great and awesome, and fight for your sisters and brothers, your daughters and sons, your wives and husbands and your homes." [15] When our enemies learned that their plot was known to us, and that God had foiled it, we were able to return to the wall and to our tasks.

[16] From then on, only half of the workers I supervised worked on the wall, while the other half stood guard with their spears, shields and bows, wearing armor. And the leaders posted themselves beside the people of Judah [17] who worked on the wall. [18] Each of the workers carried a sword at his side while working, and the sentry stood at my side with a trumpet. [19] I said to the authorities and officials and to all the people, "The work is extensive and is widely spread out along the wall, and so are we. [20] Where you hear the trumpet sound, join us there, and Our God will fight for us!" [21] So with half the workers on guard we continued the work from daylight to starlight. [22] I said to the people, "Keep all the workers and helpers inside the city of Jerusalem. We will have guard duty in the night and work in the day." [23] Neither I nor my kin, nor my workers and bodyguard ever took off our clothes. All kept their spears at the ready.

CR   CR   CR

[5:1] Now it happened that the common folk, both women and men, raised a hue and cry against their Jewish sisters and brothers. [2] Some said, "We and our daughters and sons are so numerous that we must have grain in order to stay alive!"

[3] Others said, "We're mortgaging our fields, vineyards and homes to buy enough grain during this famine!"

[4] Still others complained that they had to borrow money against their fields and vineyards to pay the ruler's tax. [5] "But our needs are the same as anyone's," they complained. "Our children are as good as yours, yet we must sell our daughters and sons into slavery. Some of our daughters have already been sold into prostitution. But we can do nothing about it; our fields and vineyards are owned by others."

[6] I was enraged when I heard these complaints and stories. [7] After some thought, I approached the officials and said, "I charge you with exacting usurious interest rates to your Jewish sisters and brothers." Then I called together an assembly to deal with them, [8] saying, "We have done every-

thing we can to bring back our Jewish sisters and brothers who were sold into slavery in foreign lands. Yet now you are now selling your own flesh and blood, who now must be brought back by us!" They were silent and had nothing to say.

⁹ I continued, "It is wrong for you to do this! You should be living in respect of God's ways, so that you are above reproach in the eyes of the nations of our enemies. ¹⁰ My kin and I, and the workers under me, are lending these people money and grain. Stop this usury immediately! Return their fields, their vineyards, their olive groves and their houses, as well as all the usurious profits you've made, whether in money, in grain, in new wine, or in olive oil—and do it today."

¹² "We will give them back," they promised, "we will exact nothing more. We will obey your word."

Then, after summoning the priests, I put the offenders under oath to do as they promised. ¹³ And then I shook out the folds of my robe, saying, "And so may God shake out everyone from house and property who doesn't keep this promise. May they be shaken out like this and emptied!"

The assembly answered, "Amen" and praised Our God. Everyone kept the promise.

¹⁴ From the twentieth year of Artaxerxes' reign, when I was appointed governor in Judah, until his thirty-third year—a twelve-year period—neither I nor my kin drew the governor's allowance for food. ¹⁵ The governors before me had placed a heavy burden on the people, taking from them food and wine, as well as forty shekels of silver. Their staff, as well, behaved like tyrants over the people.

But I, who stand in awe of God, did nothing of this. ¹⁶ I spent myself in building the wall. I acquired no property; and all my own staff worked alongside the rest. ¹⁷ At my table I fed 150 people—officials, guests, diplomats, workers, magistrates, even visitors from other countries. ¹⁸ In one day the food that was served in my household included an ox and six prime sheep, as well as poultry; and every ten days a new supply of wine was provided as well. But never did I demand the food allowance that was allotted the governor, because of the heavy demands placed on the shoulders of the common people.

O God, remember me with favor for all the good I have done for these people.

6:1 When it was finally reported to Sanballat and Tobiah and Geshem the Arab and the rest of our enemies that the wall was built without a gap remaining in it—at this time I hadn't set the gates yet— **2** Sanballat and Geshem invited me to confer with them in one of the villages on the plain of Ono.

I knew that they intended me harm, **3** so I sent messengers to them, replying, "My work here on this great project makes it impossible for me to respond to your request. My work will come to a standstill if I leave it to come to you." **4** Four times they sent me similar messages, and four times I sent the same reply.

5 On the fifth occasion Sanballat sent the message by a servant carrying an unsealed letter. **6** It read, "It is common knowledge among the nations— and Geshem says it is true—that you and the Jewish people are plotting to rebel, and that this is the reason behind your rebuilding the wall. Furthermore, it is reported that you intend to become their ruler, **7** and that you have even picked out prophets to proclaim in Jerusalem, 'There is a ruler in Judah!' Now all this will be reported to the ruler in these exact words. So, do come, and let us sit down and confer."

8 I sent him this reply, "Nothing close to what you say has ever happened, nor is it planned. You are inventing facts out of your mind." **9** They were trying to intimidate us, with the thought that we would relax our defenses, become discouraged and give up the work. But, O God— strengthen me in my work!

10 One day when I went to the house of Shemaiah, begot of Delaiah, begot of Mehetabel, who was a shut-in. He said, "Let us all meet in the House of God, in the Temple. And let us shut the doors, for they will come to murder you. Tonight, in fact, they will come."

11 But I said, "Should a person like myself run away? Would a person like myself run into the Temple to save my own life? I will not do any of it!" **12** I realized that God had not sent these words to Shemaiah, but that this prophecy was intended to harm me, and Tobiah and Sanballat had bribed him to say it— **13** Shemaiah had been bribed to frighten me into commiting a sin, which would give me a bad name and discredit me.

14 O God, remember Tobiah and Sanballat for what they have done, as well as the prophet Noadiah and all the other prophets who have tried to intimidate me.

15 On the twenty-fifth day of the month of Elul, the wall was finished. It took fifty-two days to complete it. **16** When our enemies heard of it and all the surrounding nations saw it, they they were afraid, and knew that they had lost face, and they saw that it was with God's help that this work had beern done.

¹⁷ In those days the authorities in Judah kept in touch with Tobiah by letters, ¹⁸ for many Judeans were in cahoots with him, because he was married to the daughter of Shecaniah, begot of Arah, and his son Jehohanan was married to the daughter of Meshullam, begot of Berechiah. ¹⁹ So they were always praised him in my presence and reported my response to him. Tobiah himself tried to intimidate me with letters as well.

7:1 When the wall was rebuilt and the gates had been set in their places, with the gatekeepers, the singers and the Levites appointed, ² I put my brother Hanani in charge of Jerusalem, and Hananiah the governor of the Citadel, for he was faithful, and respected God more than most. ³ I said to them, "The entrances to Jerusalem must not be left open until the heat of the day. They must be shut and barred before the gatekeepers take their rest. Appoint guards from among the people, with some on sentry duty and others watching from their homes."

ᘓ   ᘓ   ᘓ

⁴ The city was large and spacious, but it had few inhabitants and it lacked new houses. ⁵ Then God inspired me to assemble the authorities, the officials and the people in order to register them by families. I found the genealogical records of the families who had returned in the first group. What was recorded there follows:

⁶ Out of all the captives which Nebuchadnezzar the ruler of Babylon took into exile, these are the people of the province who returned from exile and captivity to Jerusalem and to their towns in Judah. The leaders of their return were ⁷ Zerubbabel, Jeshua, Nehemiah, Azariah, Raamiah, Nahamani, Mordecai, Bilshan, Mispereth, Bigvai, Nehum and Baanah.

The numbers of the Israelite families:

⁸ the descendants of Parosh	2,172
⁹ from Shephatiah	372
¹⁰ from Arah	652
¹¹ from Pahath-moab (in the line of Jeshua and Joab)	2,818
¹² from Elam	1,254
¹³ from Zattu	845
¹⁴ from Zaccai	760
¹⁵ from Binnui	648
¹⁶ from Bebai	628

[17] from Azgad	2,322
[18] from Adonikam	667
[19] from Bigvai	2,067
[20] from Adin	655
[21] from Ater (in the line of Hezekiah)	98
[22] from Hashum	328
[23] from Bezai	324
[24] from Hariph	112
[25] from Gibeon	95
[26] the people of Bethlehem and Netophah	188
[27] from Anathoth	128
[28] from Beth-azmaveth	42
[29] from Kiriath-jearim, Chephirah and Beeroth	743
[30] from Ramah and Geba	621
[31] from Michmas	122
[32] from Bethel and Ai	123
[33] from Nebo	52
[34] from the other Elam	1,254
[35] from Harim	320
[36] from Jericho	345
[37] from Lod, Hadid, and Ono	721
[38] from Senaah	3,930

[39] The priests:

the descendants of Jedaiah (in the line of Jeshua)	973
[40] from Immer	1,052
[41] from Pashhur	1,247
[42] from Harim	1,017

[43] The Levites were the descendants of Jeshua, in the line of Kadmiel through the line of Hodaviah, and numbered 74.

[44] The cantors were the descendants of Asaph, and numbered 148.

[45] The doorkeepers were descended from Shallum, Ater, Talmon Akkub, Hatita and Shobai, and numbered 138.

[46] The Temple stewards included descendants of Ziha, Hasupha, Tabbaoth, [47] Keros, Sia, Padon, [48] Lebana, Hagaba, Shalmai, [49] Hanan, Giddel, Gahar, [50] Reaiah, Rezin, Nekoda, [51] Gazzam, Uzza, Paseah, [52] Besai, Meunim, Nephussim, [53] Bakbuk, Hakupha, Harhur, [54] Bazluth, Mehida, Harsha, [55] Barkos, Sisera, Temah, [56] Neziah and Hatipha. [57] The descendants of the attendants of Solomon, Sotai, Sophereth, Perida, [58] Jaala, Darkon, Giddel, [59] Shephatiah, Hattil, Pochereth-haz-zebaim and Amon. [60] The number of all the Temple stewards and the descendants of the attendants of Solomon came to 392.

⁶¹ The following also came up from the towns of Tel-melah, Tel-harsha, Cherub, Addon and Immer, but could not show that their families were descended from Israel: ⁶² the descendants of Delaiah, Tobiah and Nekoda—numbering, in all, 642.

⁶³ And from among the priests there were descendants of Hobaiah, Hakkoz and Barzillai (who married a daughter of Barzillai the Gileadite and took that name). ⁶⁴ These people searched for their family records but could not find them, and so they were excluded from the priesthood as unclean. ⁶⁵ The governor therefore ordered them not eat of the most sacred food until a priest who knew how to use the Urim and Thummin should come.

⁶⁶ The count of those listed came to 42,360, ⁶⁷ not counting their male and female indentured workers, of whom there were 7,337. They also had 245 women and men cantors. ⁶⁸ There were 736 horses, 245 mules, ⁶⁹ 435 camels and 6,720 donkeys.

⁷⁰ Some of the family leaders donated to the work. The governor gave to the treasury 1,000 drachmas of gold, 50 bowls and 530 priestly garments. ⁷¹ Some of the family leaders donated to the treasury for the work 20,000 drachmas of gold and 2,200 minas of silver. ⁷² The total given by all the other people came to 20,000 drachmas of gold, 2,000 minas of silver and 67 priestly garments.

⁷³ The priests and Levites, along with some of the people, settled in Jerusalem and the surrounding area. The doorkeepers, the cantors, the Temple servants and the rest of the Israelites settled in their own towns.

7:73b–13:31*

When the seventh month came and the Israelites had settled in their various towns, ⁸·¹ all the people came together in the broad expanse before the Water Gate. They asked Ezra the scribe to bring the Book of the Law of Moses which God had given to Israel.

² On the first day of the seventh month, Ezra the scribe brought out the Book of the Law ³ before all the assembled people, women and men, and children old enough to understand the reading. ³ Ezra read the book aloud from early morning till noon while facing the broad expanse before the Water Gate, in the presence of the women and men and children. All listened attentively to the Book of the Law.

---

* This section is written in the third person.

⁴ He stood on a wooden platform made for the purpose, and beside him on his right stood Mattithiah, Shema, Anaiah, Uriah, Hilkiah, and Maaseiah. On his left stood Pedaiah, Mishael, Malchijah, Hashum, Hashbaddanah, Zechariah and Meshullam. ⁵ Ezra, standing on the raised platform, opened the book in the presence of all the people. When he opened the book all stood up.

⁶ When Ezra blessed the Most High, the great God, all the people raised their hands with the response, "Amen, Amen"; then they bowed their heads and worshipped Our God lying face down on the ground. ⁷ The Levites Jeshua, Bani, Sherebiah, Jamin, Akkub, Shabbethai, Hodiah, Maaseiah, Kelita, Azariah, Jozabab, Hanan and Pelaiah, instructed the people in the Law as the assembled stood there. ⁸ Reading from the Book of the Law, they interpreted it and gave it meaning so that the people understood it.

⁹ Then Nehemiah the governor and Ezra the priest and scribe, along with the Levites, instructed the people, saying to all of them, "This day is holy to the Most High, your God. Do not mourn. Do not weep"—for the people all had been weeping as they listened to the words of the Law.

¹⁰ Nehemiah continued, "Go now and enjoy rich food and sweet wine, and be certain that you send a share to those who cannot provide for themselves, for this day is holy to Our God. Let no one be sad, for Our God's joy is your strength." ¹¹ The Levites continued to quiet the crowd, saying, "Be calm. Today is holy; let there be no sorrow." ¹² So every one of them went to eat and drink, and to send a portion of their food to the hungry, and to rejoice. For they understood the words that had been given to them.

¹³ On the second day, the heads of all the families, as well as the priests and Levites, came together around Ezra the scribe to study the law. ¹⁴ They learned from studying the Law, which the Most High God had given them through Moses, that they should live in booths during the festival of the seventh month. ¹⁵ Then they issued this proclamation throughout Jerusalem and all the towns: "Go into the hills to gather olive branches, wild olive branches, branches of myrtle or palm, or any other kind, to make booths according to the instructions in the Law. ¹⁶ So the people went and gathered branches and made booths for themselves on their roofs, or in their courtyards, in the precincts of the House of God, in the square before the Water Gate and the square before the Ephraim Gate. ¹⁷ The whole community of those who had returned from the exile made booths and lived in them—a thing which the Israelites had not done since the days of Joshua begot of Nun.

And there was much rejoicing ¹⁸ as, day after day, the Book of the Law of God was read from the first day to the last. They all celebrated the feast for seven days, and on the eighth day, in accordance with the law, they held a solemn assembly, as it was commanded.

9:1 On the twenty-fourth day of the same month the Israelites, clothed in sackcloth with ashes on their heads, assembled for a fast. 2 Those of Israelite descent separated themselves from the foreigners. They stood alone and confessed their sins and the sins of their ancestors. 3 Then, as they stood where they were, the book of the Law of the Most High God their God was read for a quarter of the day. And another quarter of the day was dedicated to confessing sins and worshipping their Most High God.

4 On the steps assigned to the Levites stood Jeshua, Binnui, Kadmiel, Shebaniah, Bunni, Sherebiah, Bani, and Kenani, and they cried out to the Most High their God. 5 Then the Levites Jeshua, Kadmiel, Bani, Hashabniah, Sherebiah, Hodiah, Shebaniah, and Pethahiah, said, "Stand up and bless your Most High God in these words: 'From everlasting to everlasting may your glorious Name be blessed and exalted, above all blessing and praise.' "

6 And Ezra said, "You alone are the Most High; you created the heavens, the highest heavens with all their hosts, the earth and all that is on it, the oceans and all that is in them. You give life to all of these, and the heavenly hosts worship you. 7 You are the Most High, the God who selected Sarai and Abram, who brought them out of Ur from the Chaldeans, and renamed them Sarah and Abraham. 8 Finding faith in them, you made a covenant with them to give to all their descendants the land of the Canaanites, Hittites, Amorites and Perizzites, the Jebusites and the Girgashites; and you fulfilled your promise, for you are just.

9 "You witnessed the misery of your ancestors in Egypt and heard their cry at the Sea of Reeds. 10 You worked miracles and wonders against Pharaoh, against all the servants of the royal court, for you knew how arrogantly they treated our ancestors; you made glory for yourself that lives today. 11 You divided the sea before them, and they passed through on dry land; but you hurled their pursuers into the depths, like a stone into turbulent waters. 12 You guided them by day with a pillar of cloud, and with a pillar of fire by night to light the way ahead.

13 "You descended onto Mount Sinai and spoke of heaven; you gave them laws that are right and just, wise statutes and commandments. 14 You instructed them of the sanctity of the Sabbath; you gave them commandments, laws and statutes. 15 You gave them heavenly bread to ease their hunger and drew water out of the rocks for their thirst; you sent them to possess the land which had you solemnly promised.

¹⁶ "But our ancestors were arrogant; they were stubborn; they scorned your commandments. ¹⁷ Not listening, they forgot all the miracles you had done for them. They were stubborn and made up their minds to return to their slavery in Egypt. But you, Our God, are a forgiving God, gracious and compassionate and slow to anger, who overflows with love and kindness. And you did not abandon them.

¹⁸ "They made an image of a calf for themselves, saying, 'This is our God who delivered us out of Egypt,' and committing other gross blasphemies. ¹⁹ But you in your compasion did not abandon them in the wilderness; the pillar of cloud leading them by day did not vanish, nor did the pillar of fire leading them by night fail to light the way. ²⁰ You gave your good Spirit to instruct them; you did not withhold your manna, and you gave them water to drink. ²¹ You sustained them for forty years; even in the desert they lacked for nothing; their clothing didn't wear out; their feet did not swell up.

²² "You gave them rulers and their people as spoils of war. Your people took the land of Sihon, ruler of Heshbon, and of Og, ruler of Bashan. ²³ You made their ancestors as numerous as the stars of the sky, and gave them the land you had promised their descendants to enter and possess. ²⁴ When their ancestors entered the land to possess it, you put down the Canaanite inhabitants living there, and placed in their hands the rulers and the people to do with what they pleased. ²⁵ They captured fortified cities and fertile land, possessing well-stocked houses with rock-lined cisterns and vineyards, olive groves, large orchards. They ate, had their fill, and grew fat; they delighted in your great goodness.

²⁶ "But they grew defiant; they rebelled, and turned against your Law; they murdered your prophets who came to warn them against disobedience; they were guilty of all manner of blasphemy. ²⁷ You punished them through the oppression of their enemies; and when they were oppressed, they turned to you. You, compassionate in your heaven, heard them and sent saviors to free them from the hands of their enemies. ²⁸ Again, after a brief respite, they did evil; and again you left them to their enemies, who broke them. And so once more, they turned to youand once more you heard them from heaven. Many times, in your compassion, you saved them.

²⁹ "You warned them to return to your ways; they were arrogant and flaunted your commandments. They disobeyed the very ordinances which give life. They turned their back stubbornly and held their heads proudly; they refused to obey. ³⁰ Your patience endured for years; your spirit admonished them through the prophets. Still, they did not listen; so you put them in the hands of other peoples.

[31] "But in your mercy you did not abandon them or put an end to them; for you are a most merciful and gracious God.

[32] "Now, O great and Mighty One, O God who inspires awe and who faithfully keeps faith—do not regard as nothing the hardships we have endured: our rulers, our governors, our priests, our prophets, our ancestors, and all our people from the time of the Assyrian rulers, up to the present moment.

[33] "You have always been just in all that has happened; you have kept faith with us while we went about doing evil. [34] Our rulers, our governors, our priests and our ancestors, did not keep your Law; they ignored your commandments, and your warnings. [35] Even in their own realm, enjoying your great prosperity and the spacious and rich land you gave them, they neither served you nor renounced their ways.

[36] "And now, today, we are slaves—enslaved in our own land, which you gave to our ancestors so that we might have fruit to eat and good things to enjoy. [37] But all its produce now goes to the that rulers you have set over us because of our sins. They have power as well over our bodies and our livestock, to do with as they please.

"Seeing our great distress, [38] we write this binding declaration, with our officials, our Levites and our priests affixing their names under seal.

10[1] "Those affixing their names under seal are:

Nehemiah the governor, begot of Hacaliah, Zedekiah, [2] Seraiah, Azariah, Jeremiah, [3] Pashhur, Amariah, Malchijah, [4] Hattush, Shebaniah, Malluch, [5] Harim, Meremoth, Obadiah, [6] Daniel, Ginnethon, Baruch, [7] Meshullam, Abiah, Mijamin, [8] Maaziah, Bilgai, Shemaiah; these are the priests.

[9] "The Levites:

Jeshua, begot of Azaniah, Binnui of the line of Henadad, and Kadmiel, [10] and their kin: Shebaniah, Hodaviah, Kelita, Pelaiah, Hanan, [11] Mica, Rehob, Hashabiah, [12] Zaccur, Sherabiah, Shebaniah, [13] Hodiah, Bani, Beninu.

[14] "The leaders of the people:

Parosh, Pahath-moab, Elam, Zattu, Bani, [15] Bunni, Azgad, Bebai, [16] Adonijah, Bigvai, Adin, [17] Ater, Hezekiah, Azzur, [18] Hodiah, Hashum, Bezai, [19] Hariph, Anathoh, Nebai, [20] Magpiash, Meshullam, Hezir, [21] Meshezabel, Zadok, Jaddua, [22] Pelatiah, Hanan, Anaiah, [23] Hoshea, Hananiah, Hasshub, [24] Hallohesh, Pilha, Shobek, [25] Rehum, Hashabnah, Maaseiah, [26] Ahiah, Hanan, Anan, [27] Malluch, Harim, Baanah.

[28] "The rest of the people, the priests, the Levites, the doorkeepers, the

cantors, the Temple stewards, their spouses, their daughters and their sons, all who were of an age of understanding, all who for the Law's sake kept themselves separate from the foreign peoples—²⁹ these all now join their sisters and brothers and leaders and bind themselves with a curse and an oath in swearing to obey God's Law given by Moses, God's servant. They are to observe and fulfill all the commandments of the Most High God, God's rules and statutes.

³⁰ "We will not let our daughters marry any foreigners nor will we let any of our sons marry foreign women. ³¹ If on the Sabbath the foreigners bring their grain or merchandise to sale we will not buy from them on the Sabbath or on any holy day. We will let the land lie fallow every seventh year and release debtors from their obligation to pay.

³² "We assume the obligation of paying one third of a shekel annually for the service of the house of Our God: ³³ for the rows of the bread of Presence, the regular grain offering, the regular whole-offering, the Sabbaths, the new moons, the appointed seasons, the holy gifts, and the purification offerings to make expiation on Israel's behalf, and for all else that needs to be done in the House of Our God. ³⁴ We, the priests, the Levites, and the people, will cast lots for the wood offerings, so that it may be brought into the house of Our God by each family in turn, at appointed, yearly times, to burn on the altar of the Most High God, Our God, as prescribed by law.

³⁵ "We take it upon ourselves to bring, every year, the firstfruits of our land and the firstfruits of every fruit tree to the house of Our God. ³⁶ We also undertake to bring to the House of Our God, to the priests ministering in the House of Our God, the firstborn of our children and our cattle, the firstborn of our herds and of our flocks, as prescribed by the Law. We undertake to bring to the priests the first kneading of our dough, the firstfruits of every tree, of the new wine and of the oil, to the storage rooms in the House of Our God.

"We undertake to bring to the Levites the tithes from our land, for it is the Levites who collect the tithes in all our farming villages. ³⁸ A priest a descendeant of Aaron, shall accompany the Levites when they collect the tithes. The Levites are to bring us one tenth of the tithes to the house of our God, to the appropriate rooms in the storehouse. ³⁹ For the Israelites and the Levites must bring the contributions of grain, new wine and oil to the rooms where the vessels of the sanctuary are kept, and where ministering priests, the doorkeepers, and the cantors stay. We will no longer neglect the House of Our God."

11.1 Then the leaders of the people settled in Jerusalem. The rest of the people cast lots to bring one in every ten to live in Jerusalem, the Holy City, while the other nine settled in other towns. 2 The people blessed those who volunteered to live in Jerusalem.

3 These are the provincial leaders who settled in Jerusalem. But in the towns of Judah other Israelites, priests, Levites, Temple servants, and descendants of Solomon's servants lived on their own property, in various towns. 4 Other people from both Judah and Benjamin lived in Jerusalem.

From Judah:

Athaiah begot of Uzziah, begot of Zechariah, begot of Amariah, begot of Shephatiah, begot of Mahalalel of the line of Perez; 5 and Maaseiah begot of Baruch, begot of Col-hozeh, begot of Hazaiah, begot of Adaiah, begot of Joiarib, begot of Zechariah of the Shelanite family. 6 The descendants of Perez living in Jerusalem numbered 468.

7 From Benjamin:

Sallu begot of Meshullam, begot of Joed, begot of Pedaiah, begot of Kolaiah, begot of Maaseiah, begot of Ithiel, begot of Jeshaiah, 8 and his kin Gabbai, and Sallai, numbering 928 in all. 9 Joel begot of Zichri commanded them, and Judah begot of Hassenuah was the second in charge in the city.

10 From the priests:

Jedaiah begot of Joiarib; Jakin; 11 Seraiah begot of Hilkiah, begot of Meshullam, begot of Zadok, begot of Meraioth, begot of Ahitub, supervisor of the house of God, 12 and their associates responsible for the work in the Temple, 822 in all. Adaiah begot of Jeroham, begot of Pelaliah, begot of Amzi, begot of Zechariah, begot of Pashhur, begot of Malchijah, 13 and his kin, heads of families, 242 in all. And Amashai begot of Azarel, begot of Ahzai, begot of Meshillemoth, begot of Immer, 14 and his able-bodied kin, 128 in all. Their commander was Zabdiel begot of Haggadol.

15 From the Levites:

Shemaiah begot of Hasshub begot of Azrikam begot of Hashabiah begot of Bunni; 16 and Shabbethai and Jozabad of the leaders of the Levites, who were in charge of the outside work of the house of Our God. 17 Mattaniah begot of Micah, begot of Zabdi, begot of Asaph, who led the prayer of thanksgiving, and Bakbukiah who was second in rank among his kin; and Abda begot of Shammua, begot of

Galal begot of Jeduthun. [18] The Levites in the holy city numbered 284 in all.

[19] The doorkeepers:

Akkub, Talmon and their kin, 172 in all. [20] The rest of the Israelites lived in all the towns of Judah on their inherited property. [21] The Temple servants lived on Ophel Hill. Ziha and Gishpa were their leaders.

[22] The Levite's overseer in Jerusalem was Uzzi, begot of Bani, begot of Hashabiah, begot of Mattaniah, begot of Mica of the line of Asaph. Uzzi, a descendant of Asaph, was a member of the clan responsible for the chanting of the service. [23] The cantors were under the ruler's orders, which determined their daily schedule. [24] Pethahiah begot of Meshezabel, of the line of Zerah begot of Judah, was the ruler's advisor on all matters pertaining to the people.

[25] As for the villages surrounded by their fields: some of the families lived in Kiriath-arba and its villages, in Dibon and its villages, and in Jekabzeel and its villages, [26] in Jeshua, Moladah, and Beth-pelet, [27] in Hazar-shual and in Beersheba and its villages, [28] in Ziklag and in Meconah and its villages, [29] in Enrimmon, Zorah and Jarmuth, [30] in Zanoah, Adullam and their villages, in Lachish and its fields, and in Azekah and its villages. They occupied the country from Beersheba to the valley of Hinnom.

[31] The Benjaminites lived in Geba, Michmash, Aija and Bethel with its villages, [32] in Anathoth, Nob and Ananiah, [33] in Hazor, Ramah and Gittaim, [34] in Hadid, Zeboim and Neballat, [35] in Lod, Ono, and the Valley of Artisans. [36] Some of the divisions of the Levites in Judah were attached to Benjamin.

12.1 Following is a list of priests and Levites who returned with Zerubbabel begot of Shealtiel and with Jeshua:

Seraiah, Jeremiah, Ezra, [2] Amariah, Malluch, Hattush, [3] Shecaniah, Harim, Meremoth, [4] Iddo, Ginnethoi, Abijah, [5] Mijamin, Maadiah, Bilgah, [6] Shemaiah, Joiarib, Jedaiah, [7] Sallu, Amok, Hilkiah, Jedaiah.

These were the leaders of the priests and their kin in the days of Jeshua.

[8] The Levites were:

Jeshua, Binnui, Kadmiel, Sherebiah, Judah, as well as Mattaniah, who, with his kinsfolk was responsible for the songs of thanksgiving. [9] Bakbukiah and Unni and their kin formed an alternate choir. [10] Jeshua begot Joiakim, Joaikim begot Eliashib, Eliashib begot Joiada, [11] Joiada begot Johanan, and Johanan begot Jaddua.

[12] The following priests were heads of families in the days of Joiakim:

Meraiah was head of Seraiah's family; Hananaiah was head of Jeremiah's family; [13] Meshullam was head of Ezra's family; Jehohanan was head of Amariah's family; [14] Jonathan was head of

Malluchi's family; Joseph was head of Shebaniah's family; 15 Adna was head of Harim's family; Kelkai was head of Meremoth's family; 16 Zechariah was head of Iddo's family Meshullam was head of Ginnethon's family; 17 Zichri was head of Abijah's family; Moadiah's was head of Miniamin's family; Piltai was head of Moadiah's family; 18 Shammua was head of Bilgah's family; Jehonathan was head of Shemaiah's family; 19 Mattenai was head of Joiarib's family; Uzzi was head of Jedaiah's family; 20 Kallai was head of Sallai's family; Eber was head of Amok's family; 21 Hashabiah was head of Hilkiah's family; Nethanel was head of Jedaiah's family.

22 The heads of Levite families in the days of Eliashib were Joiada, Johanan, and Jaddua. They were recorded down to the reign of Darius the Persian. 23 The heads of the families of Levites were recorded in the annals only down to the days of Johanan grandchild of Eliashib. 24 And the leaders of the Levites were Hashabiah, Sherebiah, Jeshua, Binnui, Kadmiel, with their kin, who stood opposite them to give praise and thanksgiving as required by David, God's own.

25 The gatekeepers were Mattaniah, Bakbukiah, Obadiah, Meshullam, Talmon and Akkub. They guarded the storerooms at the gates. 26 They served in the days of Joiakim begot of Jeshua, begot of Jozadak, and in the days of Nehemiah the governor, and Ezra the scribe and priest.

CR   CR   CR

27 * At the dedication of the wall in Jerusalem, the Levites were called together from where they dwelled and brought to Jerusalem to celebrate the dedication with joyful songs of thanksgiving and with music of cymbals, harps and lyres. 28 The cantors of the Levites were also brought from the region around Jerusalem—from the hamlets of the Netophathites, 29 from Beth-gilgal, and from the areas of Geba and Azmaveth. The cantors had built dwellings for themselves around Jerusalem. 30 Once the priests and Levites had purified themselves, they purified the people, the gates and the wall.

31 Then I assembled the leaders of Judah on the city wall, and organized two large choirs to give thanks. One proceeded to the right, toward the Dung Gate. 32 Hoshaiah and half of the leaders of Judah followed them, 33 along with Azariah, Ezra, Meshullam, 34 Judah, Benjamin, Shemaiah, and Jeremiah, 35 followed by some priests with trumpets, as well as Zechariah,

---

* Here the text reverts to first-person narrative.

begot of Jonathan, begot of Shemaiah, begot of Mattaniah, begot of Micaiah, begot of Zaccur, begot of Asaph, ³⁶ and Asaph's kin Shemaiah, Azarel, Milalai, Gilalai, Maai, Nethanel, Judah and Hanani, with musical instruments prescribed by David, God's own. Ezra led the procession.

³⁷ At the Fountain Gate they continued forward up the steps of the City of David on the ascent to the city wall, past the house of David, and on to the Water Gate on the east.

³⁸ The second choir went in the opposite direction. I followed them on top of the wall, along with half of the people-past the Tower of the Ovens to the Broad Wall ³⁹ over the Gate of Ephraim, over the Jeshanah Gate, over the Fish Gate, passing the Tower of Hananel, the Tower of the Hundred to as far as the Sheep Gate. We stopped at the Gate of the Guard.

⁴⁰ The two choirs took their places in the house of God, as did I, with half the officials with me, ⁴¹ and with the priests Eliakim, Maaseiah, Miniamin, Micaiah, Elioenai, Zechariah and Hananiah with their trumpets—⁴² and also Maaseiah, Shemaiah, Eleazar, Uzzi, Jehohanan, Malchijah, Elam, and Ezer. The cantors were directed by Jezrahiah. ⁴³ And on that day they offered great sacrifices and rejoiced, and God gave them great joy. All the children, women and men rejoiced, and the sound of celebration in Jerusalem could be heard for miles around.

⁴⁴ On that day appointments were given to those in charge of the storerooms for contributions, firstfruits, and tithes. The fields surrounding the towns were to provide the portions required by the Law for the priests and the Levites. And all Judah rejoiced in the ministry of the priests and Levites, ⁴⁵ for they celebrated the services of their God and the services of purification, as did the cantors and the doorkeepers according to the rules set down by David and David's heir Solomon. ⁴⁶ Long ago in the days of David, it was Asaph who served as leader of the cantors and director of the praise of thanksgiving to God. ⁴⁷ So in the days of Zerubbabel and of Nehemiah, all Israel provided the daily portions for the cantors and the doorkeepers. They also set aside the due portion for the other Levites, and the Levites set aside the portion for the descendants of Aaron.

13:1 On that day, at the public reading from the Book of Moses, it was revealed that no Ammonite or Moabite could ever enter the assembly of God, ² because they had not welcomed the Israelites with food and water. Rather, they hired Balaam to curse them—which curse, in fact, God made a blessing. ³ When the gathered people heard the Law, they expelled all foreigners from Israel.

⁴ But before this could happen, the priest Eliashib—who had been appointed overseer of the storerooms, and who was related to Tobiah by

marriage—⁵ had provided for Tobiah's use a large room which had formerly held the grain-offerings, the frankincense, the Temple vessels, the tithes of grain, and ther new wine and oil set aside for the Levites, the cantors and the doorkeepers, and also the contributions for the priests.

⁶ I was not in Jerusalem while all this took place; I was visiting the ruler Artaxerxes—it was the thirty-second year of the rerign of the ruler in Babylon. Some time later, however, with the ruler's permission, ⁷ I returned to Jerusalem and learned of this wickedness which Eliashib had done, in providing Tobiah with a room in the House of God. ⁸ I was enraged, and threw all of Tobiah's belongings out of the room. ¹⁰ I gave orders that the room be purified, and then returned to their proper place the vessels of the house of God, and the grain offerings and frankincense.

¹⁰ I also learned that the portions of food assigned to the Levites had not been delivered to them, so that the Levites and cantors responsible for the service had had to return to their fields. ¹¹ I reprimanded the officials, demanding, "Why is the house of God deserted?" I regathered the Levites and cantors and restored them to their proper places. ¹² Then all Judah brought in their tithes of grain, new wine and oil to the storerooms. ¹³ I assigned to the priest Shelemiah, and the scribe Zadok, and the Levite Pedaiah, the guardianship of the storeroom; and as their assistant I appointed Hanan, begot of Zaccur, begot of Mattaniah. These people were trustworthy, and would be scrupulous in distributing the supplies to their colleagues.

¹⁴ Oh God, remember me for this and for what I have faithfully done for the house of my God and its liturgy.

¹⁵ It was at around that same time that I saw workers in Judah treading winepresses on the Sabbath, and harvesting their grain and loading it on donkeys, with wine, grapes, figs and other produce, and bringing it to Jerusalem. I warned them against selling food on the Sabbath. ¹⁶ Tyrians living in Jerusalem would also bring fish and other merchandise to sell on the Sabbath. ¹⁷ I berated the authorities of Judah, "How do you dare to profane the Sabbath this way! ¹⁸ This is what your ancestors did; and God brought ruin on us and on this city. What you are doing—this profaning of the Sabbath—will only bring more wrath down on Israel."

¹⁹ So when shadows of evening settled on the gates of Jerusalem, just before the Sabbath, I had the gates shut, and kept shut until the Sabbath was over. I placed my own workers at the gates to see to it that no merchandise entered the city on the Sabbath. ²⁰ Once or twice after that the merchants and traders spent the night outside the walls of Jerusalem. ²¹ But I warned them, "Why do you camp outside our walls? Do not do this any more, or I will punish you." This put an end to their coming on the

Sabbath. ²² I commanded the Levites to purify themselves, and take over the guard duty at the gates to keep the Sabbath holy.

O God, remember me for this as well, and show your mercy to me in your great love.

²³ It was also in those days that I saw Judeans marrying Gentiles from Ashdod, Ammon and Moab. ²⁴ Half of their children spoke the language of Ashdod or some other tongue, and not the language of Judah. ²⁵ I scolded them and cursed them; I beat some of them and pulled out their hair, and made them take an oath in God's name, saying to them, "You shall not give your children in marriage to their children. Nor will you to take their children in marriage to your children, nor for yourselves. ²⁶ Don't you remember that it was this sort of marriages that made Solomon sin? There was no ruler like him among all nations; he was God's beloved, and God made him ruler over all Israel—but even he fell into sin through such marriages. ²⁷ Shall we all now act as wickedly as you, and betray Our God, by marrying foreigners?"

²⁸ One of the heirs of Jehoiada, begot of Eliashib the high priest, was related to Sanballat the Horonite through such a marriage—I drove him from my presence.

²⁹ Remember them, O God—they have defiled your priestly office and the covenant of the priesthood and of the Levites.

³⁰ So I purified the priests and the Levites of everything foreign, and assigned to them the duties of their office. I also arranged for the delivery of the wood at prearranged times, and for the firstfruits.

O God, remember me with favor.

1 chronicles

eve and adam → seth → enosh → ² Kenan → Mahalalel → Jared → ³ Enoch → Methuselah → Lamech → Noah.

⁴ The line of Noah: Shem, Ham, and Japheth.

⁵ The line of Japheth: Gomer, Magog, Madai, Javan, Tubal, Meshech, and Tiras.

⁶ The line of Gomer: Ashkenaz, Riphath, and Togarmah.
The line of Javan: Elishah, Tarshish, the Kittim, and the Rodanim.

⁸ The line of Ham: Cush, Egypt, Put, and Canaan.

⁹ The line of Cush: Seba, Havilah, Sabta, Raama, and Sabtecha.
The line of Raama: Sheba and Dedon.

¹⁰ From the line of Cush came Nimrod, who became a powerful chieftain over the whole earth.

¹¹ The line of Egypt: the Lydians, the Amanites, the Lehabites, the Naphthites, ¹² the Parthrusites, the Casluhites, and the Caphtorites, the ancestors of the Philistines.

¹³ The line of Canaan: Sidon, the firstborn, then Heth, ¹⁴ the Jebusites, the Amorites, the Girgashites, ¹⁶ the Arvadites, the Zemarites, and the Hamathites.

¹⁷ The line of Shem: Elam, Asshur, Arphaxad, Lud, and Aram.
The line of Aram: Uz, Hul, Gether, and Mash.
¹⁸ The line of Arphaxad: Shelah.
The line of Shelah: Eber. ¹⁹ Eber had two children: The firstborn was named Peleg—"Earthquake"—because the earth was divided during this time; the second was Joktan.
²⁰ The line of Joktan: Almodad, Sheleph, Azarmoth, Jerah, ²¹ Hadoram, Uzal, Diklah, ²² Obal, Abimael, Sheba, ²³ Ophir, Havilah and Jobab. All of these were the children of Joktan.

ᐉᖇ   ᐉᖇ   ᐉᖇ

²⁴ Shem → Arphaxad → Shelah → ²⁵ Eber → Peleg → Reu → ²⁶ Serug → Nahor → Terah → ²⁷ Abram, who came to be known as Abraham.

²⁸ The line of Abraham: Isaac and Ishmael.

²⁹ The line of Ishmael, in order of birth: Nebaioth, the firstborn, then Kedar, Adbeel, Mibsam, ³⁰ Mishma, Dumah, Massa, Hadad, Teman, ³¹ Jetur, Naphish, and Kedemah. These were the children of Ishmael.
³² The line of Keturah, of Abraham's harem: Zimran, Jokshan, Medan, Midian, Ishbak and Shuah. The line of Jokshan: Sheba and Dedan. ³³ The line of Midian: Ephah, Epher, Enoch, Abida, Eldaah. All of these were Keturah's descendants.

³⁴ Sarah and Abraham were Isaac's parents, and Rebecca and Issac were the parents of Esau and Israel.
³⁵ The line of Esau: Eliphaz, Reuel, Jerush, Jaalam, and Korah.
³⁶ The line of Eliphaz: Teman, Omar, Zephi, Gatam, Kenaz, Timna, and Amalek.
³⁷ The line of Reuel: Nahath, Zerah, Shammah, and Mizzah.

³⁸ The line of the Seir: Lotan, Shobal, Zibeon, Anah, Sishon, Ezer, and Dishan.

³⁹ The line of Lotan: Hori and Homam. Lotan had a sister named Timna.
⁴⁰ The line of Shobal: Alvan, Manahath, Ebal, Sephi, and Onam.

⁴¹ The line of Zibeon: Aiah and Anah.

The line of Anah: Dishon.

The line of Dishon: Hamran, Eshban, Ithran, and Cheran.

⁴² The line of Ezer: Bilhan, Zaavan and Akan.

The line of Dishan: Uz and Aran.

⁴³ These are the ones who ruled over Edom before there were any rulers established in Israel: Bela begot of Beor, who was from the city of Dinhabah. ⁴⁴ After his death, he was succeeded by Jobab begot of Zerah of Bozrah. ⁴⁵ When Jobab died, he was succeeded by Husham from Teman. ⁴⁶ When Husham died, he was succeeded by Hadad begot of Bedad, who defeated the Midianites in the Moabite homeland. He was from Avith. ⁴⁷ When Hadad died, he was succeeded by Samlah of Masrekah. ⁴⁸ When Samlah died, he was succeeded by Saul of Rehoboth on the River. ⁴⁹ When Saul died, he was succeeded by Baal-hanan begot of Akbor. ⁵⁰ When Baal-hanan died, he was succeeded by Hadad of Pai. Hadad was married to Mehetabel, whose mother was Matred of the tribe of Mezahab. ⁵¹ After Hadad died, the chieftains of Edom were Timna, Aliah, Jetheth, ⁵² Oholi-bamah, Elah, Pinon, Kenaz, ⁵³ Teman, Mibzar, ⁵⁴ Magdiel, and Iram. These were the chieftains of Edom.

ର   ର   ର

2:1 The line of Leah, Rachel, and Israel: Reuben, Simon, Levi, Judah, Issachar, Zebulun, ² Dan, Joseph, Benjamin, Naphtali, Gad, and Asher.

³ The line of Judah: Er, Onan, and Shelah. Their mother was Bathshua of Canaan. Er, the firstborn of the line of Judah, provoked God, so God killed him. ⁴ Then Tamar, who was Judah's daughter-in law, bore him Perez and Jerah, so Judah had five sons in all.

⁵ The line of Perez: Hezron and Hamul.

⁶ The line of Zerah: Zimri, Ethan, Heman, Calcol, and Darda, five in all.

⁷ The line of Zimri: Carmi.

The line of Carmi: Achar, who brought a curse on Israel by violating the sacred ban.*

---

* Literally, "by violating *cherem*." The word often referred to a sacred object or ritual item; it was something that had been dedicated irrevocably to God—sometimes by completely destroying it, as with something placed on an altar. In this case it probably means touching or stealing a sacred object, but the concept included anything that was taboo (to borrow the Polynesian term), including a ruler's "harem"—the Arabic form of the same word.

⁸ The line of Ethan: Azariah.

⁹ The line of Hezron: Jerahmeel, Ram, and Caleb.

¹⁰ The line of Ram: Amminadab.

The line of Amminadab: Nahshon, leader of Judah.

¹¹ The line of Nahshon: Salma.

The line of Salma: Boaz.

¹² The line of Boaz: Obed.

The line of Obed: Jesse

¹³ The line of Jesse: Eliab, the eldest; Abinadab, the second in line of succession; Shimea, the third in line of succession; ¹⁴ Nethanel, the fourth in line of succession; Raddai, the fifth in line of succession; ¹⁵ Ozem, the sixth in line of succession; David, the seventh in line of succession. ¹⁶ Their sisters were Zeruiah and Abigail.

The line of Zeruiah: Abishai, Joab, and Asahel, three in all.

¹⁷ Abigail was the mother of Amasa, whose father was Jether the Ishmaelite.

Azubah and Caleb, whose father was Hezron, were Jeritoth's parents.

¹⁸ Azubah's children were Jesher, Shobab, and Ardon.

¹⁹ When Azubah died, Caleb married Ephrath. From her came Hur.

²⁰ Hur begot Uri. Uri begot Bezalel.

²¹ When Hezron was sixty years old, he married Machir's daughter, whose father was Gilead. She gave birth to Segub.

²² Segub begot Jair, who ruled over twenty-three villages in Gilead. ²³ He conquered the villages of Geshur, Aram Havvoth-jair, and Kenath, as well as the surrounding villages, a total of sixty places.

All of these were the descendants of Machir, whose father was Gilead.

²⁴ After Hezron died, Caleb married Ephrathah. They were the parents of Ashhur, who founded Tekoa.

²⁵ The line of Jerahmeel, the firstborn of Hezron whose mother was Ahijah: Ram, who was firstborn, Bunah, Oren, and Ozem. ²⁶ Jerahmeel had another spouse, whose name was Atarah. She was the mother of Onam.

²⁷ The line of Ram, firstborn of Jerahmeel: Maaz, Jamin and Eker.

²⁸ The line of Onam: Shammai and Jada.

The line of Shammai: Nadab and Abishur.

²⁹ Abishur was married to Abihail, who was the mother of Ahban and Molid.

³⁰ The line of Nadab: Seled and Ephraim.

Seled died with no heirs.

³¹ The line of Ephraim: Ishi.

The line of Ishi: Sheshan.

The line of Sheshan: Ahlai.

³² The line of Jada, whose brother was Shammai: Jether, who died childless, and Jonathan.

³³ The line of Jonathan: Peleth and Zaza.

These were all the descendants of Jerahmeel.

³⁴ Sheshan had daughters but no sons. One of the attendants of his house was named Jarha the Egyptian, who married ³⁵ Sheshan's daughter. Their child was Attai.

³⁶ Attai → Nathan → Zabad → ³⁷ Ephlal → Obed → ³⁸ Jeru → Azariah → ³⁹ Helez → Eleasah → ⁴⁰ Eleasah → Sismai → Shallum → ⁴¹ Jekamiah → Elishama.

⁴² The line of Caleb, whose brother was Jerahmeel:

Mesha was the firstborn. Mesha → Ziph → Mareshah → Hebron.

⁴³ The line of Hebron: Korah, Tappauah, Rekem, and Shema. ⁴⁴ Shema → Raham → Jorkeam. Rekem → Shammai → ⁴⁵ Maon → Beth-Zur.

⁴⁶ Caleb's attendant Ephah was the mother of Haran, Moza, and Gazez. Haron begot Gazez.

⁴⁷ The line of Jadai: Regem, Jotham, Geshan, Pelet, Ephah, and Shaaph.

⁴⁸ Caleb's attendant Maacah was the mother of Sheber and Tirhanah. ⁴⁹ She gave birth to Shaaph, who begot Madmannah, and to Sheva, who begot Macbenah and Gibea.

Caleb's daughter was Acsah.

⁵⁰ These were the descendants of Caleb.

The line of Hur, firstborn of Ephrathah: Shobal, who begot Kiriath Jerim; ⁵¹ Salma, who begot Bethlehem; and Hareph, who begot Beth Gader.

⁵² The line of Shobal, who begot Kiriath Jearim: Haroeh, half the Manahathites ⁵³ and the tribes of Kiriath Jearim—the Ithrites, Puthites, Shumathites and Mishraites. From these tribes came the Zorathites and Eshtaolites.

⁵⁴ The line of Salma: Bethlehem, the Netophathites, Atroth Beth Joab, half of the Manahathites, the Zorites, ⁵⁵ and the tribes of the Sopherites who lived who lived at Jabez—the Tirathites, the Shimeathites, and the Sucathites. These are the Kenites who descended from Hammath, who established the house of Recab.

3:1 The line of David—children born at Hebron: Amnon, the firstborn, whose mother was Ahinoam from Jezreel; Daniel, the second, whose mother was Abigail from Carmel; ² Absalom, the third, whose mother was Maacah daughter of Talmai who ruled over Geshur; Adonijah, the fourth, whose mother was Haggith; ³ Shephatiah, the fifth, whose mother was Abital; Ithream, the sixth, whose mother was Egleah. ⁴ These six were born at Hebron, where David ruled for seven years and six months.

David reigned in Jerusalem for thirty-three years. ⁵ David's children born in Jerusalem: Shimea, Shobab, Nathan, and Solomon. Bathsheba, daughter of Ammiel, was the mother of all four. ⁶⁻⁸ There were nine others: Ibhar, Elishama, Eliphelet, Nogah, Nepheg, Japhia, Elishama, Eliada, and Eliphelet. ⁹ Including their sister, Tamar, these were all David's children— not counting the children that David had sired illegitimately.

¹⁰ Solomon → Rehoboam → Abijah → Asa → Jehoshaphat → ¹¹ Joram → Ahaziah → Joash → Amaziah → Azariah → Jotham → ¹³ Ahaz → Hezekiah → Manasseh → ¹⁴ Amon → Josiah.

¹⁵ The line of Josiah: Johanan, the firstborn; Jehoiakim, the second; Zedekiah, the third; and Shallum, the fourth.

¹⁶ The line of Jehoiakim: Jeconiah and Zedekiah.

¹⁷ The line of Jeconiah, the prisoner: Shealtiel, ¹⁸ Malchiram, Pedaiah, Shenazzar, Jekamiah, Hoshama, and Nedabiah.

¹⁹ The line of Pedaiah: Zerubbabel and Shimei.

The line of Zerubbabel: Meshullam, Hananiah, and Shelomith, their sister. ²⁰ There were five others: Hashubah, Ohel, Berechiah, Hasadiah, and Jushab-hesed.

²¹ The line of Hananiah: Pelatiah and Isaiah. Isaiah begot Rephaiah, Rephaiah begot Arnan, Arnan begot Obadiah, Obadiah begot Shecaniah.

²² The line of Shecaniah: Shemaiah, Hattush, Igal, Bariah, Neariah, and Shaphat, a total of six.

²³ The line of Neariah: Elioenai, Hezekiah and Azrikam, a total of three.

²⁴ The line of Elioenai: Hodaiah, Eliashib, Pelaiah, Akkub, Johanan, Delaiah, and Anani, a total of seven.

4:1 The line of Judah: Perez, Hezron, Carmi, Hur, and Shobal. 2 Shobal begot
Reaiah, Reaiah begot Jahath, and Jahath begot Ahumai and Lahad; all
of these made up the tribe of the Zorathites.

3-4 The line of Etam: Jezreel; Ishma; Idbash; Penuel, the founder of Gedor;
Ezer, the founder of Hushah; and their sister, Hazelelponi.

The line of Hur: Ephrathah, the firstborn, founded Bethlehem; 5 Ashhur,
who founded Tekoa, had two spouses: Helah and Naarah; 6 Naarah was
the mother of Ahuzzam, Hepher, Temeni and Haahashtari—this was
the line of Naarah.

7 The line of Helah: Zereth, Jezoar, Ethnan and Koz. 8 Koz begot Anub and
Zobebah, and was the ancestor of the tribes of Aharhel, begot of Harum.

9 Jabez—that is, "Pain"— was held in higher esteem than all his siblings.
His mother called him "Pain" because her labor was very painful.
10 Jabez prayed to the God of Israel, "If only you would bless me and
give me vast territories! Let your hand guide me, don't let any harm
come to me, and let me be free from pain!" And God answered Jabez's
prayer.

11 Kelub, brother of Shuah, begot Mehir, who begot Eshton. 12 Eshton begot
Beth-rapha, Paseah, and Tehinnah; Tehinnah begot Irnahash. These
were the warriors of Rechah.

13 The line of Kenaz: Othniel and Seraiah.
The line of Othniel: Hathath and Meonothai. 14 Meonothai begot Ophrah.
Seraiah begot Joab, who founded Ge-harashim—"Artisan Valley"—for
they were artisans by trade.

15 The line of Caleb, begot of Jephunneh: Iru, Elah, and Naam.
The line of Elah: Kenaz.

16 The line of Jehallelel: Ziph and Ziphah, Tiria and Asarel.

The line of Ezra: Jether, Mered, Epher, and Jalon.

17-18 The line of Bithaiah, daughter of Pharaoh, who was married to Mered:
Miriam, Shammai, and Ishbah,who founded Eshtemoa. Mered had another spouse from the house of Judah. From her came Jered, who

founded Gedor; Heber, who founded Soco; and Jekuthiel, who founded Zanoah.

¹⁹ The line of Mered and Hodiah, whose sister was Naham: Daliah, who begot Keilah the Garmite; and Eshtemoa the Maacathite.

²⁰ The line of Shimon: Amnon, Rinnah, Ben-hanan and Tilon.

The line of Ishi: Zpheth and Benzoheth.

²¹ The line of Shelah begot of Judah: Er, who founded Lecah; Laadah, who founded Mareshah, the tribes of the guild of linen workers at Asbea; ²² Jokim; the inhabitants of Kozeba; Joash; and Saraph, who had an argument with Moab and returned to Bethlehem*—or so say the ancient records. ²³ They were potters, and those who lived at Netaim and Gederah were at the service of the ruler.

²⁴ The line of Simeon: Nemuel, Jamin, Jarib, Zerah, Saul. ²⁵ Saul begot Shallum. Shallum begot Mibsam. Mibsam begot Mishma.
²⁶ The line of Mishma: Hammuel. Hammuel begot Zaccur. Zaccur begot Shemei.

²⁷ Shemei had six daughters and sixteen sons, but everyone else in his family had only a few children. So the tribe, as a whole, did not grow in the same way as the tribe of Judah. ²⁸ They settled in Beersheba, Moladah, Hazar-shual, ²⁹ Bilhah, Ezem, Tolad, ³⁰ Bethuel, Hormah, Ziklag, ³¹ Beth-marcaboth, Hazar-susim, Beth-biri, and Shaaraim. They lived in these villages until the time of David's rule. ³² They had settlements in Etam, Ain, Rimmon, Tochen and Ashan, five villages in all. ³³ They also had encampments around these villages and as far as Baalath. These were all the places where they lived.

Their family register lists the following names: ³⁴ Meshobab, Jamlech, Joshah begot of Amaziah, ³⁵ Joel, Jehu begot of Joshibiah, who was begot of Seraiah, who was begot of Asiel, ³⁶ Elioenai, Jaakobah, Jeshohaiah, Asaiah, Adiel, Jesimiel, Benaiah, ³⁷ Ziza begot of Shiphi, who was begot of Allon, who was begot of Jedaiah, who was begot of Shimri, who was begot of Shemaiah.

³⁸ All of these names are recorded as leaders of their tribes, and their descendants grew in such great numbers ³⁹ that they went to the outskirts of Gedor, east of the valley, to pasture their flocks, ⁴⁰ for there the land was spacious and quiet and peaceful. Before they came, the land

---

* This could also be rendered, "who ruled in Moab and Jashubi Lechem."

was occupied by the Hamites. ⁴¹During the rule of Hezekiah of Judah, those whose names are listed above came into the land and attacked the tribes of Ham and the Meunites whom they found there. They wiped them off the land* so that no trace of them could be found to this day. Then they took possession of the land, for it provided rich pastures for their flocks.

⁴² From their members, 500 Simeonites invaded the hill-country of Seir, led by Pelatiah, Neariah, Rephaiah, and Uzziel, who were the children of Ishi. They destroyed all the remaining Amalekites, and they live there to this day.

5:1 The line of Reuben, the firstborn of Leah and Israel—Reuben was in fact the firstborn, but because he committed incest with one of his father's spouses, his status as heir was transferred to the children of Joseph, another of Israel's sons. Because of this, Reuben could not be registered as the one holding the birthright. ² And while Judah was the most noteworthy of his brothers because a great leader came from his lineage, Joseph was still the firstborn. ³ The line of Reuben, firstborn of Leah and Israel: Enoch, Pallu, Hezron, and Carmi.

⁴ The line of Joel: Joel begot Shemaiah; Shemaiah begot Gog; Gog begot Shimei; ⁵ Shimei begot Micah; Micah begot Reaia; Reaia begot Baal; ⁶ Baal begot Beerah, who was carried off into exile by the ruler Tiglath-pileser of Assyria; he was the leader of the Reubenites. ⁷ His kin, listed family by family, as registered in their tribal records: Jeiel the chief, Zechariah, ⁸ Bela begot of Azaz, Azaz begot of Shema, and Shema begot of Joel. They lived in Aroer, and their lands extended as far as Nebo and Baal-meon. ⁹ Extending to the east, they occupied lands as far as the edge of the desert which stretches from the river Euphrates, for they had large numbers of cattle in Gilead. ¹⁰ During Saul's rule, they fought the Hagarites, whom they conquered, and occupied their encampments throughout the territory east of Gilead.

¹¹ In the adjoining land were the Gadites, who occupied the area of Bashan as far as Salcah: ¹² Joel the chief; Shapham, the second in command; then Jaanai and Shappat in Bashan. ¹³ The other members of their tribe belonged to the families of Michael, Meshullam, Sheba, Jorai, Jachan, Zia, and Heber, a total of seven. ¹⁴ All of these were of the house of Abihail begot of Huri, who was begot of Gilead, who was begot of Michael, who was begot of Jeshishai, who was begot of Jahdo, who was

---

* Or, "subjected them to the sacred ban"; literally, "*cherem*-ized them."

begot of Buz. [15] Ahi begot of Addiel, who was begot of Guni, was the leader of that family, [16] and they settled in Gilead, Bashan and its villages, as well as the pastureland of Sharon as far as it stretched. [17] These family records were compiled during the time that Jotham ruled in Judah and Jeroboam ruled in Israel.

[18] The tribes of Reuben and Gad and the half-tribe of Manasseh had forty-four thousand seven hundred and sixty ready for active duty: warriors armed with shields and swords, archers, and battle-ready soldiers. [19] They fought the Hagarites, Jetur, Nephish, and Nodab. [20] They were helped in their fight because they prayed to God for help in battle. God listened to them because of their faith, and the Hagarites and all their other enemies surrendered to them. [21] They drove away their enemies' cattle, 50,000 camels, 250,000 sheep and 2,000 donkeys, and took 100,000 captives. [22] Many of the Hagarites were killed, because the war was of God's making, and the victors occupied the land until the exile.

[23] The half-tribe of Manasseh settled in the land between Bashan and Baal-hermon, also known as Senir or Mount Hermon, and they settled there in great numbers. [24] The chiefs of their families were: Epher, Ishi, Eliel, Azriel, Jeremiah, Hodaviah and Jahdiel, individuals of superior ability and reputation. [25] But they sinned against the God of their ancestors by turning promiscuously toward the worship of the idols of the people they had destroyed before them. [26] So the God of Israel raised up the ruler Pul of Assyria—that is, Tiglath-pileser the Great of Assyria—and the Assyrian armies defeated Reuben, Gad and the half-tribe of Manasseh. They took them to Halah, Habor, Hara, and the river Gozan, where they live to this day.

[6:1] The line of Levi: Gershom, Qohath, and Merari.
[2] The line of Qohath: Amram, Izhar, Hebron, and Uzziel.
[3] The line of Amram: Aaron, Moses, and Miriam.
The line of Aaron: Nadab, Abihu, Eleazar, and Ithamar.
[4] Eleazar → Phinehas → [5] Abishua → Bukki → [6] Uzzi → Zerahiah → Meraioth → [7] Amariah → [8] Ahitub → Zadok → [9] Ahimaaz → Azariah → [10] Johanan → Azariah, the priest who served in the Temple which Solomon built in Jerusalem → [11] Azariah → Amariah → [12] Ahitub → Zadok → [13] Shallum → Hilkiah → [14] Azariah → Seraiah → [15] Jehozadak, who was captured and led away when God send Judah and Jerusalem into exile under Nebuchadnezzar.

[16] The line of Levi: Gershom, Qohath, and Merari.

17 The line of Gershom: Libni and Shimei.
18 The line of Qohath: Amram, Izhar, Hebron and Uzziel.
19 The line of Merari: Mahli and Mushi.

The tribes of Levi, family by family:

20 Gershom → Libni → Jahath → 21 Zimmah → Joah → Iddo → Zerah → Jeaterai.

22 Qohath → Amminadab → Korah → 23 Assir → Elkanah → Elbiasaph → Assir → 24 Tahath → Uriel → Uzziah → Saul.
25 The line of Elkanah: Amasai and Ahimoth. 26 Ahimoth → Elkana → Zophai → 27 Nahath → Eliab → Jeroham → Elkanah.
28 The line of Samuel: Joel, the firstborn, and Abiah, the second.

29 Merari → Mahli → Libni → Shimei → Shimei → 30 Uzza → Shimea → Haggiah → Asaiah.

31 These were the ones that David appointed to be in charge of the music in the House of God when the Ark was there. 32 They performed their musical duties in front of the Meeting Tent before Solomon built the Temple of Our God in Jerusalem. Each took a turn in performing the duties laid out for them. 33 The following individuals served, along with their many descendants:

From the Qohathites, Heman the musician, begot of Joel, who was begot of Samuel, 34 who was begot of Elkanah, who was begot of Jeroham, who was begot of Eliel, who was begot to Toah, 35 who was begot of Zuph, who was begot of Elkanah, who was begot of Mahath, who was begot of Amasai, 36 who was begot of Elkanah, who was begot of Joel, who was begot of Azariah, who was begot of Zephaniah, 37 who was begot of Tahath, who was begot of Assir, who was begot of Ebiasaph, who was begot of Korah, 38 who was begot of Izhar, who was begot of Qohath, who was begot of Levi, who was begot of Israel;

39 standing to Heman's right, his colleague Asaph, begot of Berechiah, who was begot of Shimea, 40 who was begot of Michael, who was begot of Maaseiah, who was begot of Malchiah, 41 who was begot of Ethni, who was begot of Zerah, who was begot of Adaiah, 42 who was begot of Ethan, who was begot of Zimmah, who was begot of Shimei, 43 who was begot of Jahath, who was begot of Gershom, who was begot of Levi;

44 and standing to Heman's left, their colleague of the line of Merari:

Ethan begot of Kishi, who was begot of Adbi, who was begot of Malluch, ⁴⁵ who was begot of Hashabiah, who was begot of Amaziah, who was begot of Hilkiah, ⁴⁶ who was begot of Amzi, who was begot of Bani, who was begot of Shemer, ⁴⁷ who was begot of Mahli, who was begot of Mushi, who was begot of Merari, who was begot of Levi.

⁴⁸ The Levites were dedicated to the service of the Tabernacle, the House of Our God. ⁴⁹ But it was Aaron and his descendants who made whole burnt offerings on the altar of sacrifice and the altar of incense, to fulfill all the duties connected with the most sacred gifts to atone for Israel's sins as Moses, God's faithful messenger, had commanded.

⁵⁰ Aaron → Eleazar → Phinehas → ⁵¹ Abishua → Bukki → Uzzi → ⁵² Zerahiah → Meraioth → Amariah → ⁵³ Ahitub → Zadok → Ahimaaz.

⁵⁴ The following are the settlements of encampments in the areas assigned to the descendants of Aaron, to the family of Qohath, for great responsibility had been given to them: ⁵⁵ they were given Hebron in Judah, along with all the pasture lands surrounding it, ⁵⁶ but to Caleb begot of Jephunneh was given the open country belonging to the villages and encampments. ⁵⁷ The line of Aaron was given Hebron, the city of Refuge; Libnah; Jattir; Estemoa; ⁵⁸ Hilen; Debir; ⁵⁹ Ashan; and Beth-Shemesh, together with the pasturelands surrounding each one.

⁶⁰ The tribe of Benjamin was given Geba, Alemeth and Anathoth, as well as the surrounding pasture lands, making it thirteen towns held by this family.

⁶¹ For the remaining families of the line of Qohath, ten towns were set aside from the half-tribe of Manasseh. ⁶² The descendants of Gershom were given thirteen villages taken from the tribe of Issachar, the tribe of Asher, the tribe of Naphtali and the tribe of Manasseh in Bashan. ⁶³ The line of Merari and their families were given twelve towns taken from the tribe of Reuben, the tribe of Gad, and the tribe of Zebulun. ⁶⁴ The line of Israel gave these towns along with their pasturelands to the Levites. ⁶⁵ The towns mentioned above from the tribes of Judah, Simeon, and Benjamin were assigned by lot.

⁶⁶ A few of the families of Qohath had cities allotted to them. ⁶⁷ They were given the following cities of refuge: Shechem, in the hill country of Ephraim; Gezer; ⁶⁸ Jokmeam, Beth-horon, ⁶⁹ Aijalon, and Gathrimmon, as well as the pastureland for each of the cities. ⁷⁰ The lands of the half-tribe of Manasseh, Aner, and Beleam, as well as their pasture lands, were given to the remaining families of Qohath.

⁷¹ The descendants of Gershom received from the half-tribe of Manasseh:

Golan in Bashan, and Ashtaroth, along with the pasture lands. 72 From the tribe of Issachar: Kedesh, Daberath, 73 Ramoth and Anem, each with its pasturelands. 74 From the tribe of Asher: Mashal, Abdon, 75 Hukok and Rehob, each with its pasture lands. 76 From the tribe of Naphtali: Kedesh in Galilee, Hammon, and Kiriathaim, each with its pasture lands.

77 To the remnant of the descendants of Merari were given from the tribe of Zebulun: Rimmon and Tabor, each with its pasturelands. 78 On the east bank of the Jordan, opposite Jericho, from the tribe of Reuben: Bezer-in-the-desert, Jahaz, 79 Kedemoth, and Mephaath, each with its pasture-lands. 80 From the tribe of Gad: Ramoth in Gilead, Mahanaim, 81 Heshbon, and Jazer, each with its pasturelands.

7:1 The line of Issachar: Tola, Pua, Jashub, and Shimron, a total of four.

2 The line of Tola: Uzzi, Rephaiah, Jeriel, Jahmai, Jibsam, and Samuel—all able-bodied, and the heads of their families, and all descended from the line of Tola, according to their family records. They numbered 22,600 during the time of David.

3 The line of Uzzi: Izrahiah.

The line of Izrahiah: Michael, Obadiah, Joel, and Isshiah, and all five of them were leaders. 4 In addition, there were bands of warriors whose families numbered 36,000, according to the tribal lists, for their families were very large. 5 The other warriors of the line of Issachar were all able-bodied and numbered 87,000. Every one of them has been accounted for.

6 The line of Benjamin: Bela, Becher, and Jediael, three in all.

7 The line of Bela: Ezbon, Uzzi, Uzziel, Jerimoth, and Ira, five in all. They were the heads of their families, and able-bodied. The number recorded is 20,034.

8 The line of Becher: Zemira, Joach, Eliezer, Elioenai, Omri, Jeremoth, Abijah, Anathoth, and Alemeth; all of these were the descendants of Becher, 9 and according to their tribal lists they were all the heads of their families and able-bodied. They numbered 20,200.

10 The line of Jediael: Bilhan.

The line of Bilhan: Jeush, Benjamin, Ehud, Kenaanah, Zethan, Tarshish, and Ahishahar. 11 All of these were descendants of Jediael, leaders of families and able-bodied. They numbered 17,200, all fit for active duty.

12 The line of Dan: Hushim, and the descendants of Aher.

¹³ The line of Naphtali: Jahziel, Guni, Jezer, and Shallum; these were the descendants of Bilhag.

¹⁴ The line of Manasseh: Asriel, whose mother was Aramean; she also gave birth to Machir, who begot Gilead. ¹⁵ Machir married Maacah. Their second child was named Zelophehad, who had daughters. ¹⁶ Maacah, who was the spouse of Machir, had a son whom she named Peresh. Peresh's brother was named Sheresh whose descendants were Ulam and Rakem. ¹⁷ The descendant of Ulam: Beda. These were all descendants of Gilead begot of Machir, begot of Manasseh. ¹⁸ His sister Hammoleketh was the mother of Ishhod, Abiezer, and Mahlah.

¹⁹ The line of Shemida: Ahian, Shechem, Likhi and Aniam.

²⁰ The line of Ephraim: Shuthelah, who begot Bered, who begot Tahath, who begot Eladah, who begot Tahath, ²¹ who begot Zabad, who begot Zuthelah. Two other of Ephraim's offspring, Ezer and Elead, were killed by the Gittites who lived on the land when they came in to steal their cattle. ²² Ephraim mourned for them a long time, and relatives came to comfort him. ²³ Then he and his wife and relations and she gave birth to another child, who was named Beriah—"Misfortune"—because there had been misfortune in the family. ²⁴ Ephraim's daughter was Sheerah, who build Lower and Upper Beth-horon as well as Uzzen-sheerah.

²⁵ The line of Ephraim: Rephah → Resheph → Telah → Tahan → ²⁶ Lada → Ammihud → Elishama → ²⁷ Nun → Joshua.

²⁸ Their lands and settlements were Bethel and its surrounding villages, Naaran to the east, Gezer and its villages to the west, and from Shechem and its villages all the way down to Ayyah and its villages. ²⁹ Along Manasseh's borders were Beth-shean, Taanach, Megiddo, and Dor, with all their villages. In all of these places lived the descendants of Joseph begot of Israel.

³⁰ The line of Asher: Imnah, Ishvah, Ishvi and Beriah, and their sister Serah.

³¹ The line of Beriah: Heber, and Malchiel, who begot Birzavith; ³² Heber begot Japhlet, Shomer, Hotham, and Shua.

³³ The line of Japhlet: Pasach, Bimhal, and Ashvath; these were the children of Japhlet.

³⁴ The line of Shomer: Ahi, Rohgah, Jehubbah, and Aram.

³⁵ The line of Hotham: Zophah, Imna, Shelesh, and Amal.

³⁶ The line of Zophah: Suah, Harnepher, Shual, Beri, Imrah, ³⁷ Bezer, Hod, Shamma, Shilshah, Ithran, and Beera.

³⁸ The line of Jether: Jephunneh, Pispah, and Ara.

³⁹ The line of Ulla: Arah, Hanniel, and Rezia.

⁴⁰ All these descendants of Asher were heads of families, selected for their abilities and great leadership qualities. They were enrolled in the army, who totaled 26,000 in number.

8:1 The line of Benjamin: Bela, the eldest; Ashbel, the second; Ararah, the third; ⁴ Nohah, the fourth; and Rapha, the fifth.

³ The line of Bela: Addar; Gera, who begot Ehud; ⁴ then Abishua, Naaman, Ahoah, ⁵ Gera, Shephuphan, and Huram.

⁶ This was the line of Ehud, all of whom were heads of families living in Geba, but were later moved to Manahath: ⁷ Naaman, Ahihud, and Gera, who was the one who moved them. Gera begot Uzza and Ahihud.

⁸ Following the death of his spouses, Hushim and Baara, Shaharaim moved to Moab ⁹ and married Hodesh, who gave birth to Jobab, Zibia, Mesha, Macham, ¹⁰ Jeuz, Sachiah, and Mirmah. They were all heads of families. ¹¹ With Hushim he had begotten Abitub and Elpaal.

¹² The line of Elpaal: Eber; Misham; Shamed, who built Ono and Lod along with the surrounding villages; ¹³ Beriah and Shema, who were heads of families living in Aijalon after chasing away the inhabitants of Gath. ¹⁴ Ahio, Shashak, Jeremoth, ¹⁵ Zebadiah, Arad, Eder, ¹⁶ Michael, Ishpah, and Joha were the children of Beriah. ¹⁷ Zebadiah, Meshullam, Hizki, Heber, ¹⁸ Ishmerai, Izliah, and Jobab were the children of Elpaal. ¹⁹ Jakim, Zichri, Zabdi, ²⁰ Elienai, Zillethai, Eliel, ²¹ Adaiah, Beraiah, and Shimrath were the children of Shimei. ²² Ishpan, Eber, Eliel, ²³ Abdon, Zichri, Hanan, ²⁴ Hananiah, Elam, Antothiah, ²⁵ Iphedeiah, and Penuel were the children of Shashrak. ²⁶ Shamsherai, Shehariah, Athaliah, ²⁷ Jaareshiah, Elijah, and Zichri were the children of Jeroham.

²⁸ All of these were written in the tribal records as heads of families and great leaders living in Jerusalem.

²⁹ Jehiel, the founder of Gibeon, lived in Gibeon and was married to Maacah. ³⁰ Their eldest child was named Abdon, followed by Zur, Kish, Baal, Nadab, ³¹ Gedor, Ahio, Zecher, and Mikloth.

³² Mikloth begot Shimeah, and they lived near their relatives in Jerusalem.

³³ Ner begot Kish. Kish begot Saul. Saul begot Jonathan, Malchishua, Abinadab, and Eshbaal. ³⁴ Jonathan begot Meribbaal, who begot Micah.

³⁵ The line of Micah: Pithon, Melech, Tarea, and Ahaz.

³⁶ Ahaz begot Jehoaddah, who begot Alemeth, Azmoth, and Zimri. Zimri begot Moza, ³⁷ who begot Binea, who begot Raphah, who begot Elasah,

who begot Azel. [38] There were six heirs in the line of Azel: Azrikam, Bocheru, Ishmael, Shearaih, Obadiah, and Hanan—all children of Azel.
[39] The line of Eshek: Ulam, the eldest; Jeush, the second; and Eliphelet, the third. [40] Ulam's offspring were all capable archers who had many offspring themselves, a total of 150.
All of these were the descendants of Benjamin.

CR   CR   CR

[9:1] All of Israel was recorded in the census of the book of the rulers of Israel, but Judah was carried off into Babylon because of their sins. [2] The first group to occupy their ancestral land were lay Israelites, priests, Levites, and temple doorkeepers. [3] Jerusalem was occupied partly by Judahites, partly by Benjaminites, and partly people from Ephraim and Manasseh.

[4] The Judahites: Uthrai begot of Ammihud, begot of Omri, begot of Imri, begot of Bani of the line of Perez in the family of Judah.
[5] The Shelantites: Asaiah the eldest and all his children.
[6] The line of Zerah: Jeuel and 690 of their relatives.

[7] The Benjaminites: Sallu begot of Meshullam, begot of Hodaviah, begot of Hassenuah; [8] Ibneiah begot of Jeroham; Elah begot of Uzzi, begot of Micri; Meshullam begot of Shephatiah, begot of Reuel, begot of Ibnijah, [9] along with all their relatives who have been recorded in the tribal records, numbering 956, all of whom were heads of families.

[10] The priests: Jedaiah; Jehoiarib; Jachin; [11] Azariah begot of Hilkiah, begot of Meshullam, begot of Zadok, begot of Meraioth, begot of Ahitub the official in charge of the house of God; [12] Adaiah begot of Jeroham, begot of Pashhur, begot of Malchiah; Maasai begot of Adiel, begot of Jahzerah, begot of Meshullam, begot of Meshillemith, begot of Immer; [13] as well as all their workers. They were all heads of families numbering one thousand seven hundred and sixty. They all possessed great character, and were responsible for the work connected with the service in the house of Our God.

[14] The Levites: Shemaiah begot of Hasshub, begot of Azrikam, begot of Hashabiah, a descendant of Merari; [15] Bakabakkar; Heresh; Galal; Mattaniah begot of Mica, begot of Zichri, begot of Asaph; [16] Obadiah begot of Shemaiah, begot of Galal, begot of Juduthun; and Berechiah

begot of Asa, begot of Elkanah, who lived in the villages of the Netophamthites.

¹⁷ The doorkeepers were Shallum, Akkub, Talmon, and Ahiman. Shallum was their leader. ¹⁸ Until then, they had all been doorkeepers in the houses of Levites at the Ruler's Gate on the east side. ¹⁹ Shallum begot of Kore, begot of Ebiasaph, begot of Korah, as well as all of the relatives of the Korahite households, served as guards of the threshhold of the Tabernacle. Their ancestors were in charge of guarding the entrances to the encampment of Our God. ²⁰ Phinehas begot of Eleazar was their supervisor in the past, because Our God was with him. ²¹ Zecharaiah begot of Meshelemiah was the doorkeeper for the Tent of Meeting.

²² Those chosen to be the doorkeepers numbered 2,012 in all, as recorded in their town registries. David and Samuel the prophet had installed them because they were trustworthy. ²³ They and their offspring, each in turn, had charge of guarding the entrances to the house of Our God, the Tent of Meeting. ²⁴ The doorkeepers were placed at the four quarters: east, west, north and south. ²⁵ Their relatives from the villages were to be on duty with them for seven days at a time, each taking a turn. ²⁶ The four main doorkeepers were picked for their trustworthiness. They were all Levites and in charge of rooms and the stores in the house of God. ²⁷ They always stayed in the precincts of the house of God, for it was their duty to keep guard and they were in charge of the key to open the gates every morning.

²⁸ Some of them were in charge of the vessels used in the service of the Temple. They were to keep an inventory of them as they were brought in and taken out. ²⁹ Some of them were to maintain the furniture and all the sacred vessels, the floor, the wine, the incense and the spices. ³⁰ Some of the priests mixed the oils for the perfumes. ³¹ Mattithiah the Levite, the eldest of Shallum the Korahite, was in charge of the preparation of wafers because he was trustworthy. ³² Some of the other Korahites were in charge of setting out the rows of the Bread of Presence every Sabbath.

³³ Those who were musicians, heads of Levite families, were lodged in rooms set aside for them, because they were called on to perform at many times during the day and night.

³⁴ All of the above were heads of Levite families, leaders according to the family records, and they lived in Jerusalem.

³⁵ Jehiel, the founder of Gibeon, lived in Gibeon. He was married to Maacha. ³⁶ Their children were Abdon, the eldest; then Zur, Kish, Baal, Ner, Nadab, ³⁷ Gedor, Ahio, Zechariah, and Mikloth.

³⁸ Mikloth begot Shimeam and they lived near Jerusalem with all their relatives.

³⁹ Ner begot Kish, and Kish begot Saul. Saul begot Jonathan, Malchi-shua, Abiadab and Eshbaal. ⁴⁰ Jonathan begot Meribaal. Meribaal begot Micah. ⁴¹ Micah begot Pithon, Melech, Tahrea and Ahaz. ⁴² Ahaz begot Jarah. Jarah begot Alemeth, Azmaveth and Zimri. Zimri begot Moza. ⁴³ Moza begot Binea. Binea begot Rephaiah. Rephaiah begot Eleasah. And Elesah begot Azel. ⁴³ Azel had six children, who were named Azrikam, Bokeru, Ishmael, Shearaiah, Obadiah, and Hanan. These were children of Azel

10:1–14:17

When the Philistines attacked Israel, the Israelites fled from them, but were massacred at Mount Gilboa.

² The Philistines pressed hard against the ranks where Saul fought, and they killed Jonathan, Abinadab, and Malchi-shua, all of Saul's heirs. ³ Suddenly, the fighting grew heavier for Saul: archers caught him off guard, and he was wounded and fell, pierced with an arrow.

⁴ Saul shouted to his shield-bearer, "Draw your sword and run me through! I don't want these unbelievers to gloat over me!" But fear overtook the shield-bearer, who refused to obey the order. ⁵ So Saul took his own sword and ran himself through with it. Upon seeing that Saul was dead, the shield-bearer ran himself through with his own sword, and died beside Saul.

⁶ And that is how Saul died, along with all his heirs and his dynasty with him. ⁷ And when the Israelites in the valley saw that all of Israel's warriors had scattered and that Saul and all his heirs were dead, they left their villages and fled, and the Philistines came in and occupied the villages.

⁸ The next day, the Philistines came out to loot the corpses, they found Saul and his heirs lying on the ground of Mount Gilboa. ⁹ They stripped him, took his head and all his armor, and carried them back to the land of the Philistines to proclaim this great victory for their gods and their people. ¹⁰ They displayed the armor in the temple of their lesser gods, and prominently displayed Saul's head in the temple of Dagon, their chief god.

¹¹ When the residents of Gideon heard all that the Philistines had done to Saul, ¹² they sent out all their warriors to retrieve the bodies. They took the bodies of Saul and his heirs and brought them to Jabeth. There they buried the bodies under the oak tree of Jabesh, and they fasted for seven days.

¹³ Saul was slain because he was unfaithful to Our God: He did not keep God's work and had even questioned and consulted a necromancer, ¹⁴ without ever bothering to consult Our God. So God put Saul to death and transferred the throne to David begot of Jesse.

11.¹ All the tribes of Israel gathered at Hebron behind David. "Look," they said, "we are your own relatives. ² In the past years, when Saul had been our ruler, it was really you who led Israel on to victory. It was you to whom Our God spoke and said, 'You are to be the shepherd of my people Israel, you are to be their leader.' " ³ Then the elders of Israel came to David at Hebron, and David made a covenant with them in the presence of Our God. There they anointed David to rule over Israel, just as God had spoken through Samuel.

⁴ David and all of Israel went to Jerusalem, which until then had been called Jebus, where the inhabitants of the region, the Jebusites, lived. ⁵ The citizens of Jebus declared, "You'll never get in here!"

But David conquered the stronghold of Zion—now called the City of David— ⁶ declaring, "The first person to kill a Jebusite will be made a commander-in-chief!" The first one to do so was Joab, begot of Zeruiah, so he was given command of the forces.

⁷ David took up residence in the fortress, which is why it became known as the City of David: ⁸ he built the rest of the city around it. David started at the Millo and included its neighborhood inside the walls, while Joab rebuilt the remainder of the city. ⁹ David's power continued to grow, for Adonai Sabaoth* was with him.

¹⁰ The following are the individuals who commanded David's warriors, who gave their full strength to support his government and, with the rest of Israel, joined in extending his reign over the whole land, as promised by Our God.

¹¹ First in the ranks was Jashobeam the Hachmonite, leader of the Thirty, David's chieftains; Jashobeam wielded a battle-ax against three hundred and killed them in a single assault.

¹² Next came Eleazar the Ahohite, begot of Dodo, one of the Three, the warriors ¹³ who were with David at Pas-dammin when the Philistines prepared to fight there. Their armies fled from the Philistines through a field of barley, ¹⁴ but they stood their ground in the middle of the field and defeated the Philistines. And out of this, Our God brought a great victory.

---

* *Sabaoth* means "hosts" or "armies," reflecting the idea that God was the power behind both the angelic forces and, in this case particularly, the armies of Israel.

¹⁵ These three of the thirty went to see David at the rock near the Cave of Adullam when a regiment of Philistines was encamped in the Valley of the Rephaim. ¹⁶ David was in the fortress, and there was a Philistine garrison in Bethlehem.

¹⁷ "If only someone would bring me a drink of water from the well which stands at the gates of Bethlehem!" David sighed. ¹⁸ At these words, the Three forced their way through the Philistine camp, drew water from the well that stands at the gate of Bethlehem, and brought it back through the encampments to give it to David.

But David refused to drink it, and instead poured it out as a drink-offering to Our God. ¹⁹ "O God, keep me from doing this! Am I to drink the blood of these warriors? They risked their own lives to bring this water to me!" So David did not drink. Such were the deeds of these warriors.

²⁰ Abishai, Joab's brother, was placed in charge of the Three. He had wielded a spear against three hundred soldiers and killed them all, thus becoming as famous as the Three. ²¹ Twice he received military honors along with the Three and became their captain, even though he was not one of their original members.

²² Benaiah begot of Jehoiada was a warrior from Kabzeel. Through his many exploits, he struck down the two greatest warriors of Moab and on one snowy day, went down and killed a lion in its den. ²³ He also killed an Egyptian, a giant who was seven-and-a-half feet tall. The Egyptian carried a spear the size of a weaver's rod, but Benaiah took him down with a club; he then took the spear from the giant's hands and killed him with his own weapon. ²⁴ Such were the deeds of Benaiah begot of Jehoida, winning him a reputation among the Thirty. ²⁵ He was more famous than the Thirty, but was no match for the Three. He was in charge of David's bodyguard.

²⁶ The great warriors: Ashel, the brother of Joab; Elhanan, begot of Dodo from Bethlehem; ²⁷ Shammoth from Harod; Helez the Pelonite; ²⁸ Ira, begot of Ikkesh, from Tekoa; Abiezer from Anathoth; ²⁹ Sibbecai from Hushah; Ilai from Ahoh; ³⁰ Maharai from Netophah; Heled begot of Baanah from Netophah; ³¹ Ithai, begot of Ribai, from Gibeah of Benjamin; Benaiah from Pirathon; ³² Hurai, from the rivers of Gaash; Abiel from Beth-ha-arabah; ³³ Azmaveth from Baharum; Eliahba from Shaalbon; ³⁴ Bene-hashem from Gizon; Jonathan begot of Shagee, from Harar; ³⁵ Ahiam begot of Sacar from Harar; Eliphelet begot of Ur; ³⁶ Hepher from Mecherah; Ahijah the Pelonite; ³⁷ Aezro from Carmel; Naarai begot of Ezbai; ³⁸ Joel the brother of Nathan; Mibhar begot of Hagri; ³⁹ Zelek the Ammonite; Naharai from Beeroth, the shield-bearer for Joab begot of Zeruiah; ⁴⁰ Ira from Jattir; Gareb from Jattir; ⁴¹ Uriah the Hittite; Zabad begot of Ahlai; ⁴² Adina begot of Shiza the

Reubenite, leader of the Reubenites and an officer over the Thirty; ⁴³ Hanan begot of Maacah; Joshaphat the Mithnite; ⁴⁴ Uzzia from Ashteroth; Shama and Jeiel, begot of Hotham the Aroerite; ⁴⁵Jediael begot of Shimri and Joah his brother, the Tizite; ⁴⁶ Eliel the Mahavite; Jeribai and Joshaviah, begot of Elnaam; Ithmah the Moabite; ⁴⁷ and Eliel, Obed and Jaasiel from Zoba.

12⁴ The following are the soldiers who rallied to David's side at Ziklag when he was still exiled from the house of Saul begot of Kish. They were among the bravest in battle, ² all of them expert archers who could sling stones with either their left or their right arm. They were Benjaminites, relatives of Saul.

³ The most prominent among them were Ahiezer and Joash, begot of Shemaah of Gibeah; Jeziel and Pelet, from Beth-azmoth; Berakah and Jehu from Anathoth; ⁴ Ismaiah the Gibeonite, a warrior among the Thirty and a leader among them; Jeremiah, Jahaziel, Johanan, and Jozabad from Gederah; ⁵ Eluzia, Jerimoth, Bealiah, Shemariah, and Shephathiah the Haripite; ⁶ Elkanah, Isshiah, Azarel, Joezer, and Jashobeam, all Korahites; ⁷ and Joelah and Zebadiah begot of Jeroham from Gedor.

⁸ Some Gadites also rallied around David at the desert fortress. They were brave and well trained for battle: all were experts with heavy shield and spear, and were as fierce as lions and swift as gazelles on the mountain. ⁹ Ezer was their leader, Obadiah the second in command, Eliab the third, ¹⁰ Mishmannah the fourth, Jeremiah the fifth, ¹¹ Attai the sixth, and Eliel the seventh, ¹² Johanan the eighth, Elzabad the ninth, ¹³ Jeremiah the tenth, and Machbanai the eleventh. ¹³ They were the leaders of the Gadites in the army, the least of them a match for a hundred and the greatest of them a match for a thousand. ¹⁵ These were the soldiers who in the first month crossed over the Jordan, which had already flooded all its banks, and cleared the valleys to the east and west.

¹⁶ Some of the Benjaminites and Judahites came to David at the fortress. ¹⁷ David sought them out and said, "If you come as friends to help me, then you are welcome to join me; but if you come to betray me to my enemies, even though I am innocent of any violent crime, then may the God of our ancestors see your intent and judge you!"

¹⁸ At that, the Spirit came over Amassai, the leader of the Thirty, and he said, "We are on your side, David! We are with you, begot of Jesse! May abundant success come to you and to all who help you, for your God is your helper!"

So David welcomed them and attached some of them to the columns of his raiding parties.

¹⁹ There were some soldiers from Manasseh who defected to David's army when he and the Philistines went to war against Saul, though he did not in fact take the side of the Philistines. The leaders of the Philistines dismissed him, fearing that they might lose their heads if David decided to betray them to Saul; they knew that David had sworn allegiance to Saul in the past. ²⁰ The deserters who joined up with David when he went to Ziklage were Adnah, Jozabad, Jediael, Michael, Jozabad, Elihu, and Zillethai—and each of these commanded a thousand soldiers each in Manasseh. ²¹ They stood bravely with David against the raiders, for they were all good fighters. And David gave them command of his forces. ²² Day by day, more warriors joined David until he had gathered an immense army.

²³ Here are the numbers of the armed soldiers who joined David at Hebron and declared their loyalty to him over Saul, just as Our God had said:

²⁴ the Judahites, bearing shields and spears: 6,800 ready for active duty;

²⁵ the Simeonite warriors ready for active duty: 7,100;

²⁶ the Levites: 4,600, ²⁷ with Jehoida, the leader of the house of Aaron, commanding an additional 3,300, ²⁸ and Zadok, a brave warrior, bringing twenty-two officers from his own tribe;

²⁹ the Benjaminites, Saul's own relatives: 3,000, though most of them had remained loyal to the house of Saul until that time;

³⁰ the Ephraimites, brave warriors and famous in their own clans: 20,800;

³¹ from the half-tribe of Manasseh: 18,000, who had been appointed to come to make David their ruler;

³² the Issacharites, who were skilled at discerning the signs of the times to discover what course Israel should follow: 200 leaders, with all of their relatives under their command;

³³ the Zebulunites: 50,000 soldiers, all of whom were battle-ready and skilled with every conceivable weapon, bold and single-minded in their loyalty to David;

³⁴ the Naphtalites: 10,000 officers and 37,000 soldiers, all equipped with heavy shields and spears;

³⁵ the Danites: 28,600 battle-ready soldiers;

³⁶ the Asherite troops, experienced warriors prepared for battle: 40,000;

³⁷ and from the east side of the Jordan, the Reubenites, the Gadites, and the half-tribe of Manasseh: 120,000, armed with every kind of weapon.

³⁸ These brave soldiers, who were all ready for war, came to Hebron determined to make David ruler over all Israel. All the rest of Israel shared in

this conviction. ³⁹ The troops spent three days in Hebron with David, eating and drinking with the provisions their families had sent with them. ⁴⁰ And neighbors from far away as Issachar, Zebulun and Naphtali, brought food on donkeys, camels, mules, and oxen. Their gifts included supplies of grain, fig cakes, raisin cakes, wine and oil, and many oxen and sheep, for this was a time of great celebration in Israel.

13:1 David met with his officers—the commanders of thousands as well as the commanders of hundreds—and consulted with them on whatever concerns they had. ² Then he said to the assembled Israelites, "If you approve, and if Our God leads the way, let us send a message to all our families who have stayed behind in all the districts of Israel, and to the priests and Levites in the cities and villages where they have pasturelands, and ask them to join forces with us. ³ Let us reclaim the Ark of Our God, for while Saul reigned, we never ministered before it as we should have." ⁴ All the nation approved and those assembled resolved to do all this.

⁵ So David brought together the tribes of Israel, from as far south as the Shihor River in Egypt to as far north as Lebo-hamath, in order to take the Ark of God from Kiriath-jearim. ⁶ David went with all of Israel to Baalah, to Kiriath-jearim in Judah, to reclaim the Ark of God, upon which Our God sat enthroned upon the cherubim, the very Ark which bore God's Name.

⁷ They placed the Ark in a new cart and transported it from the house of Abinadab, with Uzza and Ahio guiding the cart. ⁸ David and all of Israel danced for joy before Our God, with all their strength and with the sound of singing, accompanied by lyres, lutes, tambourines, cymbals and trumpets.

⁹ When they came to the threshing-gate of Kidon, the oxen stumbled, and Uzza reached out to steady the Ark. ¹⁰ God was angry with Uzza and struck him down because he dared place his hand on the Ark. And Uzza died there before God. ¹¹ David became confused and angry because God's wrath fell upon Uzza, so he called the place Perez-uzza—"Outbreak against Uzza"—and to this day that place still bears that name. ¹² David was afraid of God that day, and said, "How can the Ark of God remain with me?"

¹³ So he decided not to take the Ark with him to Jerusalem, but took it instead to the house of Obed-edom, ¹⁴ where it stayed for three months. During that time, God blessed the family of Obed-edom and all that they had increased.

14:1 Hiram, the ruler of Tyre, sent messengers to David, who brought with them cedar logs, masons, and carpenters, and they built him a house. ² By now, David was sure that God had confirmed that he was ruler of Israel, and that God had raised up his government for the sake of the people of Israel.

³ David married several more times while he lived in Jerusalem, and had more children. ⁴ These are the names of the children of David born in Jerusalem: Shammua, Shobab, Nathan, Solomon, ⁵ Ibhar, Elishua, Elpelet, ⁶ Nogah, Nepheg, Japhia, ⁷ Elishama, Beeliada, and Eliphelet.

⁸ When the Philistines found out that David had been anointed ruler over all of Israel, they sent all their forces to capture him. David heard about their plan, and went out to face them.

⁹ So when the Philistines raided the valley of Rephaim, ¹⁰ David asked God, "If I attack the Philistines, will you deliver them into my hands?"

God answered, "Go ahead. I will deliver them into your hands."

¹¹ So David attacked the Philistines and defeated them at Baal-perazim. "God used me to break through my enemies' defenses," David said, "the same way that a river breaks through its banks." That is why the place is called Baal-perazim—"God's Breakthrough." ¹² The Philistines abandoned their gods there, and David ordered that the idols be burned.

¹³ The Philistines again tried to raid the valley, and David again prayed to God.

¹⁴ God told David, "This time you must attack them from behind. Go around them without making contact with them and surprise them on the opposite side of the aspens. ¹⁵ As soon as you hear a rustling sound in the tops of the trees, attack them immediately, for God will go out before you to defeat the Philistine army."

¹⁶ David obeyed God's commands, and the Philistine army was driven away, all the way from Gibeon to Gezer. ¹⁷ David's reputation spread quickly, and Our God made all the nations fear him.

15:1–29:30

After David had built his house in the City of David, he prepared a place for the Ark of God, pitching a tent for it. ² Then David said, "Only the Levites will carry the Ark of God, since Our God had chosen them to carry it and to minister before God forever."

³ David brought all of Israel together at Jerusalem to witness the Ark

being brought up and placed in the tent he had prepared. 4 He also alled together the descendants of Aaron and the Levites:

5 from the descendants of Qohath, Uriel their leader with 120 of his relatives;

6 from the descendants of Merari, Asaiah their leader and 220 relatives;

7 from the descendants of Gershom, Joel their leader and 130 relatives;

8 from the descendants of Elizaphan, Shemaiah their leader and 200 relatives;

9 from the descendants of Hebron, Eliel their leader and 80 relatives;

10 and from the descendants of Uzziel, Amminadab their leader and 112 relatives.

11 David called Zadok and Abiathar, the priests, together with the Levites Uriel, Asaiah, Joel, Shamaiah, Eliel and Amminabad, 12 and said to them, "You are the leaders of the Levite families. Purify yourselves, you and all your relatives, and bring the Ark of God to the place I have prepared for it. 13 It is because you were not present the first time we tried to bring up the Ark that God's anger broke out on us. We forgot to seek out God's guidance as we should have done."

14 The priests and the Levites purified themselves and prepared to bring in the Ark of the God of Israel. 15 The Levites carried the Ark of God, bearing it on poles, the way Moses had commanded on God's instructions.

16 David ordered the leaders of the Levites to appoint as musicians those of their relatives who were skilled in making joyful sounds on their instruments—lutes, lyres, and cymbals. 17 The Levites appointed Heman begot of Joel, and from his relatives, Asaph begot of Berechiah; from the family of Merari, Ethan begot of Kushaiah, 18 together with their relatives twice removed, Zechariah, Jaaziel, Shemiramoth, Jeiel, Unni, Elab, Benaiah, Maaseiah, Mattithiah, Eliphelehu, and Mikneiah, and the doorkeepers Obed-edom and Jeiel.

19 They assigned Heman, Asaph, and Ethan to sound the bronze cymbals; 20 Zechariah, Jaaziel, Shemira-moth, Jehiel, Unni, Eliab, Maaseiah, and Benaiah were assigned to play the lute; 21 and Mattithiah, Eliphelehu, Mikneiah, Obed-edom, Jeiel, and Azaziah were assigned to play the lyres. 22 Kenaniah, an officer among the Levites, was conductor in charge of the music because of his proficiency.

23 Berechiah and Elkanah were doorkeepers for the Ark, 24 while the priests Shebaniah, Joshaphat, Nethanel, Amasai, Zechariah, Benaiah, and Eliezer sounded the trumpets before the Ark of God. Obed-edom and Jehiah were also doorkeepers for the Ark.

25 Then David, along with the elders of Israel and the commanders of

units of 1,000 soldiers, went to retrieve the Ark of the Covenant of Our God with great joy from the house of Obed-edom. ²⁶ Because God had helped the Levites who carried the Ark of the Covenant of Our God, they sacrificed seven bulls and seven rams.

²⁷ David and all the Levites who carried the Ark, along with the musicians led by Kenaniah the conductor, wore robes of fine linen, and David wore a linen ephod. ²⁸ All Israel accompanied the Ark of the Covenant of Our God, shouting loudly and blowing horns and trumphets, clashing cymbals and playing on lutes and lyres. ²⁹ As the Ark of the Covenant of Our God entered Jerusalem, Saul's daughter Michal looked down from the window and saw David dancing and being joyful. In her heart, she hated him.

16¹ When they finished bringing in the Ark of God, they placed it inside the tent David had set up for it, and presented whole burnt offerings and peace offerings to Our God.

² Once the sacrifices were done, David blessed the people in the name of Our God, ³ and distributed a loaf of bread, a portion of meat, and a raisin cake to each Israelite.

⁴ David appointed certain Levites to minister before the Ark of Our God, to celebrate and give thanks and praise to the Most High, the God of Israel. ⁵ Their leader was Asaph; the second in rank was Zechariah, followed by Jaaziel, Shemiramoth, Jehiel, Mattithiah, Eliab, Benaiah, Obed-edom, and Jeiel playing their lutes and lyres. Asaph sounded the cymbals, ⁶ and Benaiah and Jahaziel were the priests who blew the trumpets at regular intervals before the Ark of the Covenant of Our God.

⁷ It was then that David first composed this psalm of thanks to Our God, and dedicated it to Asaph and his family:

⁸ Give thanks to Our God,
    and call on God's Name;
    proclaim God's deeds among the nations!
⁹ Sing to God, sing praise,
    and tell of all God's marvels!
¹⁰ Glory in God's holy Name;
    let the hearts that seek Our God rejoice!
¹¹ Turn to Our God, to God's strength,
    and seek God's presence constantly.
¹² Remember the marvels God has done,
    the wonders performed and the judgments pronounced,

13 you descendants of Sarah and Abraham,
   God's faithful ones,
  you children of Leah, Rachel and Jacob,
   God's chosen.

14 Adonai is our God,
   whose authority covers all the earth.
15 God remembers the Covenant forever,
   the promise God made for a thousand generations,
16 the pact made with Sarah and Abraham,
   the oath to Rebecca and Isaac,
17 the decree confirmed to Leah, Rachel and Jacob,
   an everlasting covenant for Israel:
18 "I give you the land of Canaan
   as the portion you will inherit."

19 There they were fewer in number,
   no more than a handful, strangers in that land.
20 They roamed from nation to nation,
   from one country to another,
21 yet God let no one oppress them,
   and punished rulers on their behalf.
22 "Don't touch my anointed ones!" God said,
   "Don't harm my prophets!"

23 Sing to Our God, all the earth!
   Proclaim God's salvation day after day!
24 Declare God's glory among the nations,
   God's marvels to every people!
25 Our God is great, most worthy of praise;
   Our God is to be revered above all gods.
26 The gods of the nations are all good-for-nothings,
   but Our God created the universe!
27 In God's presence are splendor and majesty,
   in God's sanctuary, power and beauty.
28 Pay honor to Our God, you tribes of the people,
   pay tribute to the God of glory and power!
29 Pay honor to the glorious Name of Our God;
   bring out the offering, and carry it into God's courts.
  Worship Our God
   in the splendor of holiness!

³⁰ Tremble in God's presence, all the earth!
   The world stands firm and unshakable:
³¹ Let the heavens be glad, let the earth rejoice,
   Say among the nations, "Our God reigns supreme!"
³² Let the sea roar and all that it holds!
   Let the fields exult and all that is in them!
³³ Let all the trees of the forest sing for joy,
      at the presence of Our God,
   for God is coming,
      coming to rule the earth!

³⁴ Give thanks for Our God's goodness;
   God's love endures forever!
³⁵ Cry out, "Save us, God our Savior,
      and gather us from among the nations,
   that we may give thanks to your holy Name
      and glory in your praise!"
³⁶ Blessed be Our God, the God of Israel,
      from everlasting to everlasting!
   Let all the people say,
      "Amen! Alleluia!"

³⁷ David left Asaph and his relatives to attend to the Ark of the Covenant of Our God, and they performed their duties before the Ark as was required of them. ³⁸ David left Obed-edom begot of Jeduthun and Hosah as door-keepers. Obed-edom and his relatives numbered sixty-eight. ³⁹ David left Zadok to be the High Priest and his relatives to be the priests for the Tabernacle of Our God at the shrine of Gibeon. ⁴⁰ They were to make an offering to Our God every morning and evening on the altar of burnt offerings, as prescribed by the Law given to them by the God of Israel. ⁴¹David left Heman and Jeduthun and the others chosen by name to give thanks to Our God, "whose mercy endures forever." ⁴² They played trumpets and cymbals and the other instruments used in sacred songs. The descendants of Jeduthun kept the gate.

⁴³ And all the people went home, and David returned home to bless his household.

ଓଃ   ଓଃ   ଓଃ

17^{:1} Once David was settled in his house, he called in the prophet Nathan and said, "Here I am living in a cedar house, while the Ark of the Covenant of Our God lives in a tent."

² Nathan answered, "Do whatever you want, for God is with you."

³ But that night, God spoke to Nathan: ⁴ "Tell my faithful one David, 'Our God says this: It is not your place to build a house for me. ⁵ Until now, I have never lived in a house. From the day I brought the children of Israel out of Egypt, I have lived in a tent, moving from one dwelling place to another. ⁶ Wherever I moved with the people of Israel, did I ask any of the judges whom I appointed as shepherds of Israel why they hadn't built a cedar house for me?'

⁷ "So tell this to David: 'Our God, the God of Hosts, says this: I took you from the pastures and from following the flock, and placed you over my people Israel. ⁸ I have been with you wherever you have gone, and have cleared away all your enemies before you. I will bring you fame greater than the greatest rulers of the earth. ⁹ I will make a place for my people Israel; I will plant them to live on their own land. They will never have anything to fear again, and evildoers will never wear them down as they did before, ¹⁰ during the time that I appointed judges over my people Israel. And I will restrain all your enemies.

" 'I will make you great, and through me you will build up your royal house. ¹¹ When your life is over and you join your ancestors, I will set up one of your own descendants to succeed you, and his rule will be set firm. ¹² It is this one who will build me a house, the one whose reign I will make last forever. ¹³ I will be like a loving parent to your heir, and your heir will be like my own child. I will never withdraw my love as I withdrew it from your predecessor. ¹⁴ I will set your heir over my house and over my reign for all time, and his throne will last forever.' "

¹⁵ Nathan recounted to David all that God had revealed to him the night before.

¹⁶ Then David went into the presence of Our God, and stood there and said, "Who am I, my God, and what is my family that you have brought me this far? ¹⁷ As if this were not enough, my God, you have spoken about the future of my house. And now you look upon me as the most exalted of human beings.

¹⁸ "What more can I say to you about the honor you have given to me? You yourself know me. ¹⁹ For the sake of your faithful one, my God, and in accordance with your purpose, you have done this great thing and revealed all the great things still to come.

²⁰ "There is no one like you, my God. You alone are God, and everything we have gives witness to you. ²¹ And your people Israel—who can be com-

pared to them? Is there any other nation on earth whom you, my God, rescued from slavery and made into your own people? You have made yourself known through your great and awesome deeds, driving away the nations to make way for your people whom you rescued from Egypt. ²² You have made Israel to be your own people forever, and you have become their God.

²³ "But now, my God, let what you have decreed for your faithful one and his house last for all time and fulfill what you have promised. ²⁴ Let it last so that your Name may be great forever, so that all people will say, "The God of Hosts, the God of Israel, is Israel's God!" Let the house of your faithful one, David, be established before you. ²⁵ You, my God, revealed your intentions to me, to build up the house of your faithful one. So I am able to pray before you. ²⁶ My God, you are holy, and you have made these great promises to your faithful one. ²⁷ So now bless the house of your faithful one, so that it may continue always before you. You have blessed it and you will keep it forever."

ଓ   ଓ   ଓ

18:1 Soon after this prayer, David attacked the Philistines, and captured Gath and its villages. ² Then he defeated the Moabites, and they became subject to him and paid him tribute. ³ David also defeated Hadadezer of Zobah-hamath, who was about to set up a victory monument by the river Euphrates. ⁴ David captured 1,000 chariots from him, as well as 7,000 cavalry and 20,000 foot soldiers. He cut the hamstrings of all the chariot horses, except for 100 which he kept for himself. ⁵ When the Arameans of Damascus came to help Hadadezer, ruler of Zobah, David defeated an army of 22,000 ⁶ and stationed garrisons among the Arameans. They became David's subjects and also paid him tribute.

In short, Our God gave David victory wherever he went. ⁷ David took the gold shields carried by Hadadezer's attendants and brought them to Jerusalem. ⁸ He also looted a great deal of bronze from Hadadezer's cities, Tibhath and Kun. From these items, Solomon made the bronze Sea, the pillars, and the bronze vessels.

⁹ When Tou, ruler of Hamath, heard that David defeated the entire army of Hadadezer of Zobah, ¹⁰ he send his heir, Hadoram, to David to congratulate him on the triumph over Hadadezer, for Hadadezer had been at war with Tou. Hadoram brought vessels of gold, silver and bronze. ¹¹ David dedicated all of these things to Our God, along with all the silver and gold that was looted from the nations Edom and Moab, from the Ammonites and Philistines and from Amalek.

¹² Abishai begot of Zeruiah killed 18,000 Edomites in the Valley of Salt. ¹³ He placed troops all through Edom, and all the Edomites became subject to David. God gave David victory wherever he went.

¹⁴ David ruled over all Israel and kept law and order among all the people. ¹⁵ Joab begot of Zeruiah was in charge of the army; Jehoshaphat begot of Ahilud was secretary of state, ¹⁶ Zadok and Abiathar begot of Ahimelech, begot of Ahitub, were priests; Shavsah was adjutant-general; ¹⁷ Benaiah begot of Jehoiada was in charge of the Kerethite and Pelethite guards; and David's oldest children were his attendants.

19·1 Some time afterward, Nahash, ruler of the Ammonites, died and was succeeded by his heir. ² David said, "I must maintain the same loyal friendship with Hanun begot of Nahash as his father showed me." So David sent out an envoy to grieve with Hanun over his father's death.

When David's envoys crossed over the borders into the land of the Ammonites to grieve with Hanun, ³ the other Ammonite leaders said to Hanun, "Do you really think David intends to pay homage to your father when he sends envoys to grieve with you? All of these envoys are spies who are being sent to determine your weaknesses so that they can conquer you." ⁴ So Hanun seized David's messengers, had them shaved, and cut off the bottom half of their tunics before sending them on their way. ⁵ When David heard how they were treated, he ordered a party to go and meet them, for they were too humiliated to return. He instructed them to wait in Jericho and not to return until their beards had grown back.

⁶ When the Ammonites realized they had offended David, Hanun and the Ammonites sent a thousand pieces of silver to hire chariots and cavalry from Aram-naharaim, Maacah, and Aramzobah. ⁷ They hired 30,000 chariots, and the ruler of Maacah and all their people came and encamped before Medeba, while the Ammonites came from their cities and prepared for battle.

⁸ When David heard this, he sent out Joab with all the warriors. ⁹ The Ammonites took their position at the city gate, while their allies took their positions in the surrounding country. ¹⁰ When Joab saw that he was outflanked at the front and the rear, he detailed some select troops and ordered them up to the Aramean lines. ¹¹ The rest of the forces were placed under Abishai, Joab's brother, who took up the position facing the Ammonite forces at the city gate. ¹² "If the Arameans are too strong for me," he said, "You must come to my aid. If the Ammonites are too strong for you, I will come to your aid. ¹³ Take courage! Let us fight valiantly for our people and for the cities of Our God. And may God's will be done."

¹⁴ Joab and his troops engaged the Arameans in close combat and put them to flight. ¹⁵ When the Ammonites saw them fleeing, they too fled before Abishai and withdrew from the city. Then Joab returned to Jerusalem.

¹⁶ The Aramaeans, pondering this defeat by the forces of Israel, sent messengers to call other Aramaean forces from the Great Bend of the Euphrates. Shophach, the commander of Hadadezer's army, commanded their forces. ¹⁷ David caught wind of their movements and immediately called together all the forces of Israel. They crossed over the Jordan and advanced against the oncoming troops, taking up the battle position. The Aramaeans also took up position facing David and engaged him. ¹⁸ But Israel put them to flight, and David killed 7,000 Aramaeans in chariots and 40,000 infantry, killing Shophach, the commander of the army. ¹⁹ When Hadadezer's legions saw that Israel had defeated them, they made a peace treaty and became David's subjects.

The Aramaeans never again came to the aid of the Ammonites.

20:1 At the turn of the year, when rulers usually go into battle, Joab led the army out and plundered the land of the Ammonites, while David remained in Jerusalem. Joab came upon Rabbah and laid siege to the town. After defeating them, he razed it to the ground.

² David took the crown from Milcom's head and discovered that it weighed about seventy-five pounds, made of solid gold and inlaid with precious stones; it was then placed on David's head. He also removed a vast amount of loot from the city.

³ He brought out the inhabitants and forced them to work with saws and iron picks and axes. David did this to all the Ammonite towns, then returned with his army to Jerusalem.

⁴ Some time later, war broke out with the Philistines in Gezer. It was at that time that Sibbechai of Hushah killed Sippai, who descended from the Rephaim, and the Philistines were conquered and submitted to David.

⁵ In another campaign against the Philistines, Elhanan begot of Jair killed Lahmi, the brother of Goliath of Gath, whose spear was the size of a weaver's beam. ⁶ On another campaign in Gath, there appeared a giant with six fingers on each hand and six toes on each foot, a total of twenty-four. He too was descended from the Rephaim. ⁷ When he attacked Israel, Jonathan begot of Shimea—David's brother—killed him. ⁸ These giants were all descendants of the Rephaim in Gath, and all of them fell to the sword of David and his armies.

21:1 Then Satan rose up against Israel, and incited David to take a census of the people. ² David ordered Joab and all the officers of the army to count all of Israel from Beersheba to Dan, and report the number back to him.

³ Joab answered, "Even if Our God increases the people a hundredfold, wouldn't you still be ruler and all peoples your subjects? Why should you want to do this? It will only bring guilt upon Israel." ⁴ But David dismissed Joab's plea. So Joab went out to the countryside taking the tally. He returned to Jerusalem ⁵ and reported the number he had counted to David: those able to bear arms numbered 1,100,000 in Israel and 470,000 in Judah. ⁶ Joab did not count Levi and Benjamin, so deeply was he disturbed by David's order.

⁷ God was also angry with the order and proceeded to punish Israel.

⁸ David said to God, "I have acted like a corrupt politician. I pray that you remove my guilt! I have been such a fool."

⁹ So God said to Gad, David's seer, ¹⁰ "Tell this to David: 'Our God says this: I offer you three options. Choose the one you want me to carry out against you.' "

¹¹ Gad came to David and said, "Our God says this, 'Take your choice: ¹² three years of famine; three months of being chased by your enemies, their swords closing in hot pursuit; or three days of God's own sword bringing pestilence throughout the land, and Our God's angel wreaking havoc throughout the land of Israel.' Determine what your answer will be now, and I will take it back to the One who sent me."

¹³ David said to Gad, "This situation is very desperate. But I place myself into God's hands, whose mercy is great. Don't let me fall into the hands of mortals."

¹⁴ So God sent a pestilence throughout Israel, and seventy thousand Israelites died. ¹⁵ God sent an angel to Jerusalem to destroy it. But as the angel was destroying the city, God saw and took back the evil, calling back the destroying angel who was then standing at the threshing-floor of Ornan the Jebusite. "Enough!" God said. "Withdraw your hand!"

¹⁶ When David looked up and saw the angel standing between earth and heaven with sword outstretched over Jerusalem, both he and the elders donned sackcloth and fell down to the ground. ¹⁷ David said to God, "I'm the one who ordered the census, I'm the one who sinned! I, the shepherd, committed this wrong. But these poor sheep, what have they done to deserve all this? My God, let your mighty arm fall on me and my family, and put an end to this reign of terror against the people."

¹⁸ The angel of God, speaking through the lips of Gad, commanded David to go to the threshing-floor of Ornan the Jebusite and set up an altar there. ¹⁹ David proceeded to do what Gad had spoken in the name of Our God.

²⁰ While Ornan was busy threshing the wheat, he turned and saw the angel; so did his four children who were working with him, but they ran and hid. ²¹ When David came, Ornan rose up from the threshing-floor and approached him, falling prostrate before David.

²² David said to Ornan, "Allow me to have your threshing-floor so that I can build an altar to Our God. I will buy it from you at full price so that this plague upon our people will end."

²³ Onrnan answered, "Take it and do with it as you see fit. See, I have oxen for burnt offerings, threshing sledges which can be used as fuel, and wheat for the grain offering. I give it all to you."

But David answered, ²⁴ "No, I'll pay the full price. I'm not going to offer to Our God what belongs to you, or give a burnt offering which has cost me nothing." ²⁵ So David paid Ornan fifteen pounds of gold for the place, ²⁶ and built an altar to Our God there. He offered burnt sacrifices and peace offerings, calling out to Our God, who answered him with fire from the heavens that came and consumed the whole offering. ²⁷ Then, at Our God's command, the angel sheathed its sword.

²⁸ David then realized that Our God answered his prayer at the threshing-floor of Ornan the Jebusite where he offered the sacrifice. ²⁹ The Tabernacle of Our God and the altar of burnt offerings which Moses made in the wilderness were at that time housed at the shrine at Gibeon, ³⁰ but David was not able to go there to seek guidance because he was so frightened by the sword of Our God's angel.

22:¹ Then David said, "The House of Our God is to be built here, as well as the altar of burnt offerings for Israel."

² David ordered all the foreign residents of the land to come together and made them all stone cutters to build a house for Our God. ³ He brought out iron from the storehouses to make nails and hinges for the doors, and he brought out more bronze than could be weighed ⁴ and a limitless supply of cedar wood. The residents of Sidon and Tyre also brought David a great supply of cedar.

⁵ Then David said, "My child Solomon is still very young, and the house that must be built for Our God must be exceedingly magnificent; it must be known and talked about in every land. So, I must make some provision for its construction myself." So David set abut making provisions before he died.

⁶ He called Solomon and commissioned him to build the house for Our God, the God of Israel. ⁷ "Solomon, my child," David said, "it has always been my dream to build a house for the Name of Adonai my God. ⁸ But

God forbade me to do this, saying, 'You have shed too much blood in my sight and waged great wars. Because of this, you are not to build a house for my Name. ⁹ But you will have a child who will be known as one of peace. I will give your child peace from all the surrounding enemies. Your child's name will be Solomon—"Peaceful One"—and I will give peace to all of Israel during Solomon's reign. ¹⁰ Solomon is to the one who is to build a house for my Name. Solomon will be my child and I will be Solomon's parent, and I will establish his throne over Israel forever.'

¹¹ "Now, my child, may Our God be with you! May you prosper and build the house of Our God to fulfill what God has promised. ¹² May God grant you wisdom and understanding, so that when you receive authority in Israel, you may keep the Law of Our God. ¹³ You will succeed only if you are careful to observe the decrees and ordinances that Our God handed down through Moses for all of Israel. So be strong and stand firm, and don't be afraid or discouraged.

¹⁴ "At great cost, I have collected for the house of Our God 3,700 tons of gold and 37,000 tons of silver, and such great quantities of bronze and iron that we cannot even weigh it, as well as timber and stone. You may add to the stock as you see fit. ¹⁵ Besides these materials, you have at your disposal a large labor force of stone cutters, sculptors and carpenters, and every kind of artisan ¹⁶ who works with gold and silver, bronze and iron. So be about your work, and may God be with you!"

¹⁷ David ordered all the officers of Israel to help Solomon: ¹⁸ "Is not Our God with you? Won't God give you peace on all your borders? God has delivered into my power those who inhabited the land. The land will be subdued before Our God and the people. ¹⁹ So devote your heart and soul to seeking guidance from Our God, and get to building this sanctuary so that the Ark of the Covenant of Our God and God's holy vessels may be brought into the house built for God's Name."

ଓଃ   ଓଃ   ଓଃ

23¹ David was now very old and burdened with years, and he appointed Solomon to rule over Israel. ² David assembled all the officers of Israel, together with the priests and the Levites. ³ Levites who were thirty-three years old or older were counted, and their number was 38,000. ⁴ Of these, 24,000 were responsible for maintaining and ministering in the house of Our God; 6,000 were assigned to work as officers and magistrates; ⁵ 4,000 were to be door-keepers; and 4,000 were to sing the praises of Our God on musical instruments which David had produced for the praise of Our God.

⁶ David organized them in divisions, named after Gershon, Qohath, and Merari, the children of Levi.

⁷ The line of Gershon: Laadan and Shimei.

⁸ The line of Laadan: Jehiel the chief, Zetham and Joel, three in all. ⁹ These were the heads of families grouped under Laadan.

¹⁰ The line of Shimei: Jahath, Ziza, Jeush, and Beriah. ¹¹ Jahath was chief, with Ziza the second; and since the clans of Jeush and Beriah numbered so few, they were grouped together as a single family.

¹² The line of Qohath: Amram, Izhar, Hebron, and Uzziel, four in all.

¹³ The line of Amram: Aaron and Moses. Aaron was set apart forever, along with all his descendants, to dedicate the most holy gifts and burn sacrifices before Our God, to minister to Our God and give blessings in the Name of the Most High forever. ¹⁴ But the descendants of Moses, God's chosen, were to be counted among the tribe of Levi.

¹⁵ The line of Moses: Gershom and Eliezer.

¹⁶ The line of Gershon: Shubael the chief.

¹⁷ The line of Eliezer: Rehabiah the chief. Eliezer had no other descendants, but Rehabiah had many.

¹⁸ The line of Izhar: Shelomith the chief.

¹⁹ The line of Hebron: Jeriah the chief, Amariah the second, Jahaziel the third, and Jekameam the fourth.

²⁰ The line of Uzziel: Micah the chief, Isshiah the second.

²¹ The line of Merari: Mahli and Mushi.
The line of Mahli: Eleazar and Kish. ²² Eleazar died without an heir, having several daughters. The children of Kish married them.

²³ The line of Mushi: Mahli, Eder, and Jerimoth—three in all.

²⁴ These were the Levites as grouped by family—the heads of families as they were registered under their family names, and all family members twenty years old or older who ministered in the house of Our God. ²⁵ As David said, "Because Our God, the God of Israel, has given the people peace and has made a dwelling in Jerusalem forever, ²⁶ the Levites will no longer have to carry around the Tabernacle or any of the vessels for its service."

²⁷ According to David's final instructions, all Levites from age twenty and up were counted. ²⁸ Their duty was to help the descendants of Aaron in the service of the house of Our God. They were responsible for the care of the

courts and the rooms, and for keeping all sacred objects clean, as well as giving general service to the house of Our God. ²⁹ They were to maintain the rows of the Bread of Presence, the flour for the grain offerings, unleavened wafers, cakes baked on the griddle, and anything that needed to be weighed or measured. ³⁰ They were to be on duty at all times, each morning and evening, standing and giving thanks and praise to God, ³¹ and serving as ministers whenever burnt offerings were presented to God, as well as on Sabbaths, new moons, and at the appointed seasons. They were to minister before Our God regularly, in the prescribed numbers and manner. ³² The Levites were to have charge of the Tent of Meeting and of the sanctuary, but Aaron's descendants, their relatives, were given charge of the service of worship in the house of Our God.

24·1 The divisions of the line of Aaron:

Aaron had four children: Nadab and Abihu, Eleazar and Ithamar. ² Nahab and Abihu died before Aaron did, leaving no descendants, so Eleazar and Ithamar held the office of priest.

³ David, along with Zadok of the line of Eleazar, and with Ahimelech of the line of Ithamar, organized them into divisions to discharge the duties of their office. ⁴ The heads of families proved to be more numerous in the line of Eleazar than in that of Ithamar, so that sixteen families were grouped under the head of Eleazar and eight under the head of Ithamar. ⁵ David divided them impartially by drawing lots among them, for there were officers of the sanctuary and officers of God in the lineages of both Eleazar and Ithamar.

⁶ Shemaiah the scribe, a Levite begot of Nethanel, wrote down the names in the presence of David and the following officials: Zadok the priest, Ahimelech begot of Abiathar, and the heads of families of the priests and the Levites—one priestly family being taken from the line of Eleazar and one from the line of Ithamar.

⁷ The first lot fell to Jehoiarib, the second to Jedaiah, ⁸ the third to Harim, the fourth to Seorim, ⁹ the fifth to Malchijah, the sixth to Mijamin, ¹⁰ the seventh to Hakkoz, the eighth to Abijah, ¹¹ the ninth to Jeshua, the tenth to Shecaniah, ¹² the eleventh to Eliashib, the twelfth to Jakim, ¹³ the thirteenth to Huppah, the fourteenth to Ishbaal, ¹⁴ the fifteenth to Bilgah, the sixteenth to Immer, ¹⁵ the seventeenth to Hezir, the eighteenth to Happizzez, ¹⁶ the nineteenth to Pethahiah, the twentieth to Jehezkel, ¹⁷ the twenty-first to Jachin, the twenty-second to Gamul, ¹⁸ the twenty-third to Delaiah, and the twenty-fourth to Maaziah. ¹⁹ This was the rotation of their duty to perform the services when they entered the house

of Our God, according to the rule prescribed for them by their forebear, Aaron, who had received his instructions directly from Our God, the God of Israel.

20 As for the rest of the Levites:

From the children of Amram: Shubael. From the children of Shebael: Jehdeiah.

21 From the children of Rehabiah: Isshiah the firstborn.

22 From the children of Izhar: Shelomoth. From the children of Shelomoth: Jahath.

23 From the children of Hebron: Jeriah the firstborn, Amariah the second, Jahaziel the third, and Jekameam the fourth.

24 From the children of Uzziel: Micah. From the children of Micah: Shamir. 25 Michah's sibling: Isshiah. From the children of Isshiah: Zechariah.

26 From the children of Merari: Mahli and Mushi. From the children of Jaaziah: Beno, 27 Shoham, Zaccur, and Ibri. 28 From the children of Mahli: Eleazar, who had no descendants.

29 From Kish: the only descendant of Kish, Jerahmeel.

30 From the descendants of Mushi: Mahli, Eder, and Jerimoth.

These were the Levites by families. 31 They too cast lots, just as their relatives the descendants of Aaron had done, in the presence of David, Zadok, Ahimelech, and the heads of the priestly and levitical families. Each was treated equally, whether they were heads of families or the youngest siblings.

25:1 David and the chief officers assigned special duties to the descendants of Asaph, Heman, and Jeduthun, who were set apart as ministers, prophesying* to the accompaniment of lyres, lutes, and cymbals. The list of those who performed this work in the temple are as follows:

From the line of Asaph: Zaccur, Joseph, Nethaniah and Asharelah; these were under the supervision of Asaph, who prophesied under David.

3 From the line of Jeduthun: Gedaliah, Izri, Isaiah, Shimei, Hashabiah, and Mattithiah; these six were under Jeduthun's supervision, who prophesied to the accompaniment of the lyre, giving thanks and praise to Our God.

4 From the line of Heman: Bukkiah, Mattaniah, Uzziel, Shebuel, Jerimoth, Hananiah, Hanani, Eliathah, Giddalti, Romamti-ezer, Joshbekashah, Mallothi, Hothir, and Mahazioth; 5 these were the descendants of

---

* Prophecy, throughout the Hebrew scriptures, was more about speaking the thoughts and words of God—here in the form of sacred song—than about predicting the future: a forth-telling rather than a foretelling.

Heman, David's seer, and they were given to him in fulfillment of God's promises to lift up a trumpet of praise. God gave Heman fourteen sons and three daughters.

6 All of them were under the supervision of the heads of their families, for providing music in the house of Our God. They all participated in the services of the Temple playing cymbals, lutes, and lyres. In turn, Asaph, Jeduthun, and Heman were themselves accountable to David. 7 Along with their relatives, all of whom were skillful and well-trained musicians in Our God's service, they numbered 288. 8 They cast lots to determine their duties, young and old, maestro and apprentice alike.

9 The first lot fell to Joseph, along with his siblings and children, twelve in all. The second to Gedaliah, along with his siblings and children, twelve in all. 10 The third to Zaccur, along with his siblings and children, twelve in all. 11 The fourth to Izri, along with his children and siblings, twelve in all. 12 The fifth to Nethaniah, along with his children and siblings, twelve in all. 13 The sixth to Bukkiah, along with his children and siblings twelve in all. 14 The seventh to Asarelah, along with his children and siblings, twelve in all. 15 The eighth to Isaiah, along with his children and siblings, twelve in all. 16 The ninth to Mattaniah, along with his children and siblings, twelve in all. 17 The tenth to Shimei, along with his children and siblings, twelve in all. 18 The eleventh to Azarel, along with his children and siblings, twelve in all. 19 The twelfth to Hashabiah, along with his children and siblings, twelve in all. 20 The thirteenth to Shubael, along with his children and siblings, twelve in all. 21 The fourteenth to Mattithiah, along with his children and siblings, twelve in all. 22 The fifteenth to Jeremoth, along with his children and siblings, twelve in all. 23 The sixteenth to Hananiah, along with his children and siblings, twelve in all. 24 The seventeenth to Joshbekashah, along with his children and siblings, twelve in all. 25 The eighteenth to Hanani, along with his children and siblings, twelve in all. 26 The nineteenth to Mallothi, along with his children and siblings, twelve in all. 27 The twentieth to Eliathah, along with his children and siblings, twelve in all. 28 The twenty-first to Hothir, along with his children and siblings, twelve in all. 29 The twenty-second to Giddalti, along with his children and siblings, twelve in all. 30 The twenty-third to Mahazioth, along with his children and siblings, twelve in all. 31 The twenty-fourth to Romamti-ezer, along with his children and siblings, twelve in all.

26:1 The doorkeepers were organized in this manner:

The children of Qorach: Meshelemiah begot of Kore, begot of Ebiasaph. 2 The children of Meshelemiah: Zechariah, the eldest, Jediael, the second, Zebadiah, the third, Jathniel, the fourth, ³ Elam, the fifth, Jehohanan, the sixth, Eliehoenia, the seventh.

⁴ The children of Obed-edom: Shemaiah, the eldest, Jehozabad, the second, Joah, the third, Sacar, the fourth, Nethanel, the fifth, ⁵ Ammiel, the sixth, Issachar, the seventh; Peulthai, the eighth. God had truly blessed Obed-edom with such a brood.

⁶ The children of Shemaiah were all tribal leaders and proved themselves to be gifted individuals. ⁷ Their names were Othni, Repha-el, Obed, and Elzabad. Their cousins, Elihu and Semachiah, were also gifted individuals. ⁸ All of these descendants of Obed-edom, as well as their children and cousins—sixty-two in all—were gifted individuals. ⁹ Meshele-miah's eighteen children and their cousins were also gifted leaders. ¹⁰ Hosah, of the line of Merari, appointed Shimri as the leader among all the siblings, even though he was not the oldest. ¹¹ The names of the other children were: Hilkiah, the second; Tebaliah, the third; and Zechariah, the fourth. Hosah's children and cousins numbered thirteen in all.

¹² The divisions of the doorkeepers were named after their leaders. Like all the other Levites, they were responsible for ministering at the Temple, just as their ancestors had done. ¹³ Within each family, lots were cast to determine their station at each gate, young and old alike.

¹⁴ The lot for the eastern gate fell to Shelemiah. Then lots were cast for the northern gate, which fell to Zechariah, a learned sage. ¹⁵ The lot for the southern gate fell to Obed-edom, and the lot for the storehouse fell to his children. The lots for the western gate and the Shalleketh gate on the upper road fell to Shuppim and Hosah.

A company of doorkeepers were assigned to each door every day: ¹⁷ there were six Levites at the eastern gate, four at the northern gate, four at the southern gate, and two at the storehouse. ¹⁸ As for the western gate, there were four stationed at the road and two in the court itself.

¹⁹ These were the divisions of the doorkeepers, who were descendants of Korah and Merari.

²⁰ Other Levites were placed in charge of the Temple treasuries and the storehouses for gifts offered to Our God. ²¹ They were members of the family of Ladan, from the tribe of Gershon. They were Jehieli, ²² the children of Jeheili, Zetham and Joel. They were placed in charge of the treasuries of the Temple of Our God.

²³ Also among them were the following Amramites, Izharites Hebronites,

and Uzzielites: 24 Shubael, a descendant of Gershom begot of Moses, was the officer in charge of the treasuries, 25 whose descendents through Eliezer were Rehabiah, Jeshaiah, and Joram, his children. 26 Shelomith and his relatives were in charge of the storehouses of gifts dedicated by David and by the heads of tribes who were the commanders of thousands and commanders of hundreds, and all the other army commanders. 27 They dedicated some of the plunder taken in battle toward the building of the Temple of the Most High. 28 Also included in the treasury were the offerings from Samuel the prophet, from Saul begot of Kish, from Abner begot of Ner, and from Joab begot of Zeruiah. All of their offerings were placed in the care of Shelomith and his family.

29 From the family of Izhar: Kenaniah and his children were given duties away from the Temple as officials and judges over Israel.

30 From the family of Hebron: Hashabiah and his cousins—seventeen hundred in all—who were all able-bodied, were responsible for the work of Our God and the service of David in the regions west of the Jordan. 31 According to the genealogical records, Jeriah was the leader of the family of Hebron. In the fortieth year of David's reign, a search of the records was made, and talented individuals among the Hebronites were found at Jazer in Gilead. 32 Jeriah had twenty-seven hundred relatives, all of whom were able leaders of their families. David placed them in charge of all the affairs concerning God and the state among the Reubenites, the Gadites and the half-tribe of Manasseh.

27:1 These are the citizens of Israel, the heads of households, the commanders of thousands and hundreds of soldiers as well as their officers, who served the ruler in all matters concerning the divisions that came and went, month by month, throughout the year. Each division numbered 24,000:

2 Jashobeam, begot of Zabdiel, commanded the division during the first month. There were 24,000 soldiers in this division. 3 His ancestor was Perez, and he was the commander-in-chief of the division of the first month.

4 Dodai the Ahohite commanded the division of the second month; Mikloth was the chief officer of this division. There were 24,000 soldiers in this division.

5 Benaiah, begot of the priest Jehoiada, was the commander during the third month. There were 24,000 soldiers in this division. 6 This was this same Benaiah who was a mighty warrior and member of the Thirty. Benaiah's offspring, Ammizabad, was in charge of this division of 24,000.

⁷ Asahel, who was Joab's brother, was the commander during the fourth month, and his offspring, Zebadiah followed after him. There were 24,000 in this division.

⁸ Shamhuth the Izrahite was the commander during the fifth month. There were 24,000 soldiers in this division.

⁹ The commander for the sixth month was Ira begot of Ikkesh the Tekorite. There were 24,000 soldiers in this division.

¹⁰ The commander for the seventh month was Helez the Pelonite of the Ephraimites. In this division there were 24,000.

¹¹ The commander for the eighth month was Sibbecai of Hushah, a Zerahite. There were 24,000 members of this division.

¹² Abiezer of Anathoth, the Benjaminite, was the commander for the ninth month. There were 24,000 members of this division.

¹³ Maharai of Netophah of the Zerahites was the commander of the tenth month. There were 24,000 members of this division.

¹⁴ Benaiah of Pirathon, from Ephraim, was commander for the eleventh month. There were 24,000 members of this division.

¹⁵ Heldai the Netophathite of Othniel was the commander of the division for the twelfth month. There were 24,000 members of this division.

¹⁶ These were the chief officers of the families of Israel:
> for the Reubenites, Eliezer begot of Zichri; for the Simeonites, Shephatiah begot of Maacah;
> ¹⁷ for the Levites, Hashabiah begot of Kemuel;
> for the Aaronites, Zadok;
> ¹⁸ for the Judeans, Elihu, one of David's brothers;
> for the Issacharites, Omri begot of Michael;
> ¹⁹ for the Zebulunites, Ishmaiah begot of Obadiah;
> for the Naphtalites, Herimoth begot of Azriel;
> ²⁰ for the Ephraimites, Hoshea begot of Azazia;
> for the half-tribe of Manasseh, Joel begot of Pedaiah;
> ²¹ for the half-tribe of Manasseh in Gad, Iddo begot of Zechariah;
> for the Benjaminites, Jaasiel begot of Abner;
> ²² for Dan, Azarel begot of Jeroham.

These were the leaders of the families of Israel. ²³ David did not take into account those below twenty years of age because Our God had promised to make Israel as numerous as the stars in the sky. ²⁴ Joab begot of Zeruiah began to count those under twenty, but could not finish; God's wrath came upon Israel for this, and the number was not entered into the census of the Annals of David.

²⁵ Azmaveth begot of Adiel was minister of David's treasuries.

Jonathan begot of Uzziah was minister of the treasuries in the country, in the cities in the villages and in the fortresses.

²⁶ Chelub begot of Ezri was minister of all field workers and tillers of the soil.

²⁷ Shimei the Ramathite was minister of vineyards.

Zabdi the Shiphmite was minister of the harvest from the vineyards as well as the wine cellars.

²⁸ Baal-hanan the Gederite was minister of the olive and fig trees in Shephelah.

Joash was minister of the oil supply.

²⁹ Shitrai the Sharonite was minister of the cattle herds in Sharon.

Shaphat begot of Adlai was minister of the cattle herds that roamed in the valleys.

³⁰ Obil the Ishmaelite was minister of the camels.

Jehdeiah the Meranothite was minister of the donkeys.

³¹ All of these were the ministers of David's property.

³² Jonathan, David's uncle, was an advisor and scribe, one who possessed keen understanding and knowledge. Jehiel begot of Hachmoni instructed David's children. ³³ Ahithophel was David's advisor, and Hushai the Archite was David's friend. ³⁴ After Ahithophel came Jehoiada begot of Benaiah, and Abiathar. Joab was in charge of David's army.

಄   ಄   ಄

28:1 David called together all the officials of Israel to Jerusalem—all the heads of families, the officers of the divisions that served David, the commanders of the thousands, the commanders of the hundreds, the ministers of property and cattle held by David and his family, together with all palace officials, heroes and all warriors.

² When all had assembled, David rose to his feet and said, "Hear me, my friends and people. I intended to build a house of rest for the Ark of the Covenant, a place to serve as the footstool for Our God. I even went so far as to draw up plans for the building. ³ But God said to me, 'Do not build a house in my Name, for you are a warrior and have shed much blood.' ⁴ Yet

Our God, the God of Israel, chose me from all other members of my tribe to rule over Israel forever. God chose Judah as leader of Israel, and from all of Judah, my household, and from the members of my household, God took delight in making me ruler over all Israel. ⁵ And of all my children—for God has given me many—Our God has chosen Solomon to sit upon the throne of Israel. ⁶ God said to me, 'Solomon is the one who will build my house and my courts, for I have chosen him as my own, and I will be a parent to him. I will secure his rule forever—provided he keeps all my commandments and ordinances, just as he does today.'

⁸ "So now, in the sight of all Israel, in the assembly of Our God and in the hearing of the Most High, I adjure you to observe and search out the commands Our God has given, so that you may possess this good land and leave it after you for your children and for generations yet to come.

⁹ "And hear this, Solomon, my child: seek out the God of your ancestors and serve the Most High faithfully and with devotion in your heart. For God searches every thought and understands every plan and intention. If you seek God, you will find God; but if you forsake God, God will forsake you. ¹⁰ Now listen closely, for Our God has chosen you to build a Temple as a sanctuary, so be strong and take action."

¹¹ Then David handed Solomon the plans for the vestibule of the Temple, as well as all its houses and treasuries, its upper rooms and inner chambers, as well as the room which would hold the Ark. ¹² It was the plan for every detail David had in mind for the courts of the house of Our God, even to the last vessel used in the service of the Most High and the treasuries to hold gifts offered to Our God, ¹³ as well as the division of the priests and the Levites and a description of the work they would do in service of the house of God; all the vessels for service in the Temple; ¹⁴ the weight of the gold to be used in all the vessels in each service; the weight of the silver vessels for each service; ¹⁵ the weight of the golden lampstands and their lamps as well as the silver lampstands and their lamps, according to how each would be used in the service; ¹⁶ the weight of gold for each table for the rows of the Bread of Presence, and the weight of the silver for the silver tables; ¹⁷ the weight of the pure gold to be used for the forks, the basins and the cups as well as the golden bowls; ¹⁸ the weight of the refined gold for the altar of incense; and the plan for the golden chariot of the cherubim whose wings covered the Ark of the Covenant.

¹⁹ "All this is written down at the direction of Our God," David said. "God has revealed this plan to me to its last detail."

²⁰ David also told Solomon, "Be strong and take courage in all you do.

Don't be afraid or be overwhelmed, for the Most High God, my God, is with you. God will not fail you or abandon you until you have finished all the work of the house of Our God. ²¹ The divisions of the priests and the Levites are ready for all the services of the Temple of God, and the officials and all the people will do as you command."

29:1 Then David spoke to the whole assembly: "My child Solomon, whom God has chosen, is young and inexperienced, and the task before him is daunting; for the house of Our God will not be for the service of mortals, but for the service of the Most High God.

² "So I have acquired, so far as I was able, the gold for the golden objects, the silver for the silver objects, the bronze for the bronze objects, the iron for the things made of iron, and the wood for the things made of wood, that will be used in the house of Our God, as well as great quantities of onyx for the settings, turquoise, colored stones, and all sorts of precious stones and marble in abundance. ³ In addition to all these things that I have assembled for the house of Our God, I have a treasure of my own gold and silver. Because of my devotion to building this Temple, I give these things over to the house of God: ⁴ 110 tons of gold—gold from Ophir!—and 260 tons of refined silver for overlay on the walls of the house ⁵ as well as for all the work to be done by the artisans, gold for the objects of gold and silver for the objects of silver.

"Now, who will offer themselves to the service of Our God?"

⁶ Then the leaders of the ancestral houses made their freewill offering, as did the heads of families, the commanders of the thousands and the hundreds, and the officers. ⁷ They gave 190 tons and 185 pounds of gold, 375 tons of silver, 675 tons of bronze, and 3,750 tons of iron—all for the service of the house of Our God. ⁸ Those who possessed precious stones also gave them to the treasury of the House of Our God, turning them over to the care of Jehiel the Gershonite. ⁹ Then the people rejoiced because of their willing generosity, for they had offered their gifts to Our God freely and with a single mind. And David rejoiced with them.

¹⁰ Then David praised Our God before the assembly, saying,

"Blessed are you, Adonai, God of our ancestor Israel,
	forever and ever!
¹¹ With you, Adonai, are the greatness, power,
	glory, victory, and majesty.
Everything in the heavens and on the earth
	belongs to you.

Yours is the kindom, O God,
and you are exalted as head over all.

¹² Riches and honor come from you,
and you rule over all.
You hold power and might in your hands,
and it is in your hand to make great and give strength to all.

¹³ And now, my God, we give thanks to you
and praise your glorious Name!"

¹⁴ "But who am I, and what is my people, that we should be worthy to make this freewill offering? For all things come from you, and of your own works we have given to you. ¹⁵ For we are strangers and wanderers before you, as were our ancestors. Our days on earth are as fleeting as a shadow, without hope. ¹⁶ Adonai, our God, all this abundance that we have given to build a house to your holy Name comes from your hands and is all your own.

¹⁷ "I know, my God, that you search the heart, and take pleasure in those whose hearts are pure. So it is with a pure heart that I offer you these things. And now I see your people, who are here before you, offering their abundance joyfully to you. ¹⁸ My God—the God of Sarah and Abraham, Rebecca and Isaac, Leah, Rachel, and Jacob—keep forever the purposes and thoughts in the hearts of your people, and direct their hearts to you.

¹⁹ "Grant that Solomon may have a single mind that he may keep your commandments, your decrees and your statutes, performing all of them faithfully, and that he may build the house of Our God for which I have made provision."

²⁰ Then David addressed the whole assembly, saying, "Give praise to Adonai, your God!" And all the assembly praised Our God, the God of their ancestors, and bowed their heads and fell to the ground before Our God and before David.

²¹ The next day, they offered sacrifices and burnt offerings to God: a thousand bulls, a thousand rams, a thousand lambs, with their libations, and sacrifices in abundance for all of Israel. ²² Then they ate and drank before Our God with great joy.

They once again declared Solomon to be David's successor, anointing him as the sovereign appointed by Our God, and they anointed Zadok as priest. ²³ Then Solomon sat on the throne, succeeding David as sovereign of Israel.

Solomon prospered, and all of Israel obeyed him. ²⁴ All the leaders and heroes, as well as all of David's other children, pledged their allegiance to

Solomon. ²⁵ Our God exalted Solomon in the sight of all of Israel, and bestowed upon him reign more splended than any ruler in Israel had ever seen before.

ଔ ଔ ଔ

²⁶ Thus David begot of Jesse reigned over all of Israel. ²⁷ David reigned over Israel for forty years, seven in Hebron and thirty-three in Jerusalem. ²⁸ He died at a ripe old age, having lived many days blessed with wealth and honor, and Solomon succeeded him.

²⁹ The acts of David, from the first to the last, are written in the records of the prophet Samuel, and in the records of the prophet Nathan, and in the records of the prophet Gad, ³⁰ with accounts of his rule and power, and the events that occurred in Israel and all the nations of the earth.

2 chronicles

Solomon, begot of david, had secured
a firm hold on the realm. The Most High God was with Solomon, and
brought fame and high regard to the nation.

² Solomon now addressed all of Israel: those in positions of great power
and those of lesser power as well, and the foremost among the women and
men of Israel, heads of all the families. ³ He led all those assembled out to
the sacred mound at Gibeon, to Our God's Tent of Meeting, which had been
built by Moses, the godly one, in the wilderness.

⁴ Now, David had brought the Ark of God from Kiriath-jearim to a site
he had prepared for it—even erecting a tent for it there—in Jerusalem.
⁵ However, the bronze altar which had been made by Bezalel, begot of Uri,
begot of Hur, was at Gibeon, in front of the Tent of Meeting of the Most
High. So Solomon and those with him went there.

⁶ Solomon went in to the bronze altar before Our God in the Tent of Meeting and offered a thousand burnt offerings on it.

⁷ That night God came to Solomon and said, "What can I give you? Tell
me."

⁸ Solomon answered, "You showed constant and unfailing love to David, my forebear, and you have made me the ruler after him. ⁹ Now, Most High God, confirm your promise to David. You have made me ruler over a people whose numbers are like the dust of the earth; grant me the wisdom to know how I should come and go in their eyes—for how else can I lead this great people of yours?"

¹⁰ Our God said to Solomon, "Since you have not asked for wealth or for possessions; for honor or for the lives of your foes; nor even for a long life for yourself; since this is what is in your heart, I will grant it. Wisdom and understanding will be yours. And I will give you as well what you have not asked for—wealth, possessions and honor such as no ruler has had before you nor any that will come after you."

¹³ Solomon then left the Tent of Meeting at the sacred mound at Gibeon, and returned to Jerusalem, and to the business of reigning over Israel. ¹⁴ He gathered together chariots and horses—1400 chariots and 12,000 horses. They were located both in Jerusalem and in towns dedicated to the chariot trade. ¹⁵ He made gold and silver in Jerusalem as common as stones, and planted cedars there as plentifully as the sycamores that grew in the foothills. ¹⁶ Solomon's agents imported horses at a fair price from Egypt and Kue. ¹⁷ They were imported from Egypt, and then exported—chariots for 600 silver shekels apiece, horses for 150 silver shekels—to the rulers of the Hittites and the rulers of the Arameans.

☙ ☙ ☙

2:1 Solomon resolved to build two houses—a Temple for the Name of Our God, and royal palace. ² He gathered 70,000 laborers and 80,000 stonecutters, as well as 3600 overseers.

³ He sent a message to Hiram of Tyre which read:

"You once dealt with David my father, sending him cedar with which to build his house. ⁴ I am now preparing to build a house for the Name of Our God, which will be dedicated to the Most High. It will be used for the offering of fragrant incense to God's presence; for the offerings of consecrated bread; and for burnt offerings every morning and evening, on the Sabbaths and the new moons, and at the festivals of the Most High God. This is Israel's obligation for all time.

⁵ "The house that I build will be great, for Our God is greater that any other god. ⁶ But who can build a house for the Almighty, which heaven itself, even the highest heavens, can never contain? Who am I to build such a house, except as a place where offerings might be made in the presence of Our God?

⁷ "So I ask now that you send to me an artisan skilled in the working of silver, gold, bronze and iron, with tapestries in purple, crimson and cerulean blue. This artisan should be a skilled engraver as well, and be able to work with my own skilled workers here in Judah and Jerusalem, who were provided by David, my father.

⁸ "Send me also Lebanese cedar, pine, and juniper, for your woodcutters are experts in cutting the trees of Lebanon. Those whom I am sending will work with them ⁹ to provide me with an ample supply of timber, for the house that I will build will be both vast and beautiful.

¹⁰ "For your workers who will cut this timber, I will provide 125,000 bushels of wheat, 125,000 bushels of barley, 115,000 gallons of wine, and 15,000 gallons of olive oil."

¹¹ Hiram of Tyre responded with this letter:

"It is because of God's love for your people that you have been made ruler over them." ¹² The ruler continued, "Blessed by the Most High God, the God of Israel, who made heaven and earth. The Most High God gave David a wise child, endowed with intelligence and understanding, who will build a house for the Almighty and a house for his own royal household.

¹³ "I am sending to you Huram-Abi, who is both wise and a skilled artisan. ¹⁴ He was of a Danite mother and a Tyrian father. Huram-abi is skilled in the working of gold and silver, bronze and iron, stone and wood, as well as purple, crimson and cerulean blue tapestries and fine linen. The artisan is also well experienced in engraving of all kinds, and can execute any design that might be asked of him. He will work well with your own skilled workers, those fine artisans trained in David's time.

¹⁵ "As for the wheat and barley, and the wine and olive oil that you have promised—send it as you have arranged. ¹⁶ We will cut for you in Lebanon as much timber as you may need, and float it as rafts down to Joppa where you can take it to Jerusalem."

¹⁷ Then Solomon took a census of all resident aliens in Israel, not unlike the census David had taken. It was found there were 153,600. Solomon conscripted 70,000 as laborers, 80,000 as stonecutters, and 3,600 as overseers to supervise the work.

3·1 Then Solomon began the work of the house of Our God in Jerusalem on Mount Moriah, on the site where God had appeared to David his father—the threshing floor of Ornan the Jebusite, which David subsequently consecrated to God. ² Work was begun on the second month of the fourth year of Solomon's reign.

³ The dimensions which Solomon laid down for the house of God were ninety feet in length, using the "old cubit" as the standard of measurement, and thirty feet in width. ⁴ The portico in front of the house ran the width of the building, thirty feet, and was thirty feet high.* Its interior was overlaid with pure gold. ⁵ The main area was paneled with pine, again covered in gold, which in turn was engraved with palms and a chain pattern. ⁶ He adorned the entire structure with precious stones. The gold was gold from Parvaim; ⁷ with it also the beams, the threshholds, the walls and the doors of the building were covered; and cherubim were carved on the walls.

⁸ Solomon then built the Holy of Holies. Its length corresponded with the width of the house, thirty feet. It was covered with gold weighing twenty-three tons. ⁹ The ornamental nails were also made of gold, each weighing one and a quarter pounds. Its upper chambers also were dressed with gold.

¹⁰ Within the Holy of Holies were two cherubim, carved and covered with gold leaf. ¹¹ Their outstretched wings spanned thirty feet—each wing was nearly eight feet long, so that they touched in the center of the room and ¹² extended outward to the outer walls. ¹³ So the wings of the cherubim spread thirty feet, and they stood on their feet facing the main area. ¹⁴ Solomon made the veil of fabrics of violet, cerulean blue, and crimson, together with fine linen with cherubim embroidered upon it.

¹⁵ In front of the building were placed two pillars, fifty-two feet high, and on top of each pillar was a capital nearly eight feet high. ¹⁶ The top of each pillar was encircled with chain, and from these there were hung one hundred carved pomegranates. ¹⁷ These pillars were set up in front of the building, one on the right and one on the left. The one on the right bore the name Yakin, and the one on the left, Boaz.**

4:1 Solomon made a bronze altar, thirty feet square and fifteen feet high. ² Then he made the ceremonial basin known as "the sea" out of molten metal, round with a diameter of fifteen feet, and a height of nearly eight feet. One would need a cord forty-five feet in length to measure its circumference. ³ Below the sea, and encircling it, were panels measuring one-and-a-half feet long on which was a frieze of bulls, ten to each panel, in two rows; the panels were cast at the same time as the sea. ⁴ The sea was then placed on twelve carved bulls; three faced to the north, three to the west,

---

* The Hebrew text reads "180 feet high"; thirty feet is the figure found in Syriac manuscripts.
**While both were common Hebrew names, and the pillars were perhaps dedicated in honor or memory of prominent members of the community, the names' meanings are fitting words to be engraved before a temple: Yakin means "God establishes," and Boaz means "strength."

three to the south, and three to the east, with their hindquarters facing inward and the sea resting on their backs. 5 The sea was a hand's width in thickness, with its rim like a cup and its shape like a lily. It held nearly 17,500 gallons of water. 6 He also had made ten smaller basins for washing, placing five on the left side and five on the right side. These were to be used to rinse everything that would be used used for the burnt offerings; but the sea was for the priests to wash in.

7 He made ten golden lampstands according to specifications; these were set up in the house, five on the south side and five on the north side. 8 He also made ten tables and placed them in the house, with five on the right side and five on the left side; and also there were one hundred gold sprinkling bowls. 9 Next were built the court of the priests and the great courtyard, the doors of the courtyard. The doors were plated with bronze. 10 The sea was placed at the right side, at the southeast corner of the house.

11 Huran-abi personally made the pots, the scoops, and the bowls. With these Huram-abi completed the work he was to do for Solomon on the house of God: 12 the two pillars, the two capitals of the pillars, the two works of filigree to decorate the capitals, 13 and the 400 pomegranates for the filigree—two rows of pomegranates for each set of filigree, to cover the capitals on the pillars. 14 He made the ten stands and the basins for each stand, 15 the sea and the twelve bulls supporting it, 16 the pots, the scoops, the meat hooks and all related accessories.

All these items made by Huram-abi for Solomon the ruler for the house of Our God were of burnished bronze. 17 They were cast in clay molds on the Jordan plains, between Succoth and Zeredah. 18 They were made in such vast quantity that the weight of the bronze that was used is unknown.

19 So it was that Solomon made all the furnishings for the house of God: the golden altar, the table for the consecrated bread, 20 the lampstands of pure gold with their lamps burning before the inner sanctuary as was prescribed, 21 the flowers, the lamps, the tongs of pure gold, 22 the snuffers, the bowls, the incense containers, and the censers of pure gold. And the doors of the house of Our God, the inner doors to the Holy of Holies, and the doors of the main hall, were all made of gold.

5:1 When all the work undertaken by Solomon for the house of Our God was finished, he brought in the things which David had dedicated to the Temple—the silver, the gold, the vessels—and put them in the treasury of the house of Our God.

2 Then Solomon summoned the elders of Israel, the heads of the tribes and the leaders of the ancestral families, to Jerusalem, in order to bring the

Ark of the Covenant of Our God up from Zion, the City of David. ³ All the Israelites assembled around Solomon during the festival of the seventh month. ⁴ All the elders of Israel came, with the Levites carrying the Ark, ⁵ and brought it up; the Levites, who were the priests, brought up the Tent of Meeting and all the furnishings of the Tent. ⁶ So the entire assembly of Israel with Solomon their ruler stood before the Ark, and so many sheep and oxen were sacrificed that their number is unknown.

⁷ The priests brought in the Ark of the Covenant of Our God to its place in the inner sanctuary of the house, the Holy of Holies, beneath the wings of the cherubim. ⁸ The cherubim spread their wings over the setting of the Ark and made a covering over the Ark and its carrying poles. ⁹ These poles were so long that their ends could be seen from in front of the inner sanctuary, but not from outside; they are there to this day. ¹⁰ The only thing in the Ark are the two tablets Moses placed in it at Horeb, when Our God made a covenant with the Israelites after they had come out of Egypt.

¹¹ After the priests had come out of the Holy of Holies—all the priests there, without regard for divisions, had purified themselves—¹² the levitical cantors, Asaph, Heman, and Jeduthun, and their heirs and their kinfolk, all dressed in fine linen, stood with cymbals, harps and lyres to the east of the altar with 120 priests with trumpets. ¹³ It was the duty of these trumpeters and singers that they should be heard in a single voice praising and giving thanks to Our God, and so this chant was raised, to the sound of the trumpets and cymbals, and harps and lyres: "Give thanks to Our God, who is good, and whose mercy endures forever."

Then the building was filled with a cloud of God's glory. ¹⁴ The priests could not continue to minister because of the cloud, for the glory of Our God filled the house of Our God.

଎ ଎ ଎

6:1 Then Solomon spoke:

> "O Most High God, you have chosen to dwell in a dark cloud.
> ²   And I have built you a house, the house of God—
>   a place for you to dwell in forever and ever."

³ While the whole assembly of Israel stood before him, Solomon blessed them, saying:

⁴ "Blessed be the Most High God of Israel who has given by hand what was promised by mouth to David: ⁵ 'From the day I brought my people out of Egypt, I did not choose that any city or any tribe of Israel should build a house for my Name; nor did I choose anyone to be the leader of my

people Israel. ⁶ But now I have chosen Jerusalem as a dwelling place for my name, and I have chosen David to rule over my people Israel.' "

⁷ Solomon continued, "David wished to build a house for the Name of Our God, the God of Israel; ⁸ but Our Sovereign said to David, 'It is good that you wish to build a house for my Name. ⁹ Nonetheless, it will not be you who builds this house, but your heir who will be born of you, who will build this house for my Name.' ¹⁰ Our God has now fulfilled what was promised: I have succeeded David and have taken my place on the judgment seat of Israel, as God promised. And now I have built the house for the Name of Our God of Israel; ¹¹ and I there placed the Ark containing the covenant of the Most High which God made with Israel."

¹² Then Solomon, before the entire assembly of Israel, stood in front of the altar of the Most High with his hands raised. ¹³ A bronze platform had been made, eight feet square and five feet high, which was placed in the middle of the outer court. He now mounted this, kneeling down before the assembly, with hands spread out toward heaven, ¹⁴ and said, "Most High God of Israel, there is no God like you in heaven or on earth—you who keep your covenant with your people and show them constant love when they walk wholeheartedly in your way. ¹⁵ You kept your promise to your servant David. You made your promises then with your mouth, and you have fulfilled them today with your hand.

¹⁶ "Therefore, Sovereign God, keep again your promise to your servant David, when you said, 'Your lineage will always sit upon the judgment seat of Israel, so long as your heirs walk in my ways and keep my laws as you have.' ¹⁷ O Most High God of Israel, let this promise made to your servant David be now confirmed.

¹⁸ "But can God really dwell among mortals here in earth? For even heaven itself, the highest heaven, cannot contain you; how much less this house I have built! ¹⁹ Listen to the prayers and my pleas for mercy, O God. Hear my cry and the prayer I place before you, ²⁰ that your eyes watch over this house day and night, this place where you have said that you would plant your name. ²¹ Hear me, your servant, when I pray, and your people Israel when they pray, for this place. Hear from your dwelling place in heaven; and when you hear, forgive.

²² "When a person wrongs a neighbor and must take an oath, and comes to take the oath before your altar in this house, ²³ listen from heaven and act on it: judge between your faithful. Punish those who offend and hold them to account for their actions. Vindicate the innocent and reward them according to their innocence.

²⁴ "Should your people Israel suffer defeat for having sinned against you, and should they return to you praising your Name, praying and ap-

pealing to you in this house, ²⁵ hear them from heaven, forgive the sin of your people Israel and bring them back to the land that you gave them and their ancestors. ²⁶ When the sky is closed up and there is no rain because your people have sinned against you, and then they pray in this place, praising your Name and confessing their sin, ²⁷ hear from heaven and forgive the sin of your people Israel. In this way you teach us correct action. Restore rain to our land which you gave us to possess. ²⁸ When famine comes to the land, or plague, or blight or mildew, or locusts or caterpillars, or when enemies lay siege to our cities, or disaster or sickness comes, ²⁹ and when a prayer or plea is made by one of us, your people Israel—each of us in our pain and our sorrow, spreading our arms and hands toward this house— ²⁹ then hear us from your dwelling place in heaven and forgive us. You know our hearts—reward us in the light of our actions; for only you know the hearts of us all. ³¹ And we will live in awe of you and in obedience to you throughout our lives in the land that you gave to our ancestors.

³² "Then there are the foreigners, who are not of your people Israel, but have come from afar because of your great Name, your mighty hand and your outstretched arm, who come from distant places because of your great fame. When they come and pray in this house ³³ hear them from heaven where you dwell and grant all they ask, that all people of the earth may know your Name, and, like your people Israel, worship you, and learn that this house which I have built bears your Name.

³⁴ "When your people go to war against their enemies, wherever you send them, and when they pray to you toward this city which you have chosen and toward this house which I have built for your Name, ³⁵ then hear their prayers and pleas and uphold their cause.

³⁶ "If your people sin against you—is there anyone who doesn't?—and if you grow angry with them and give them into the hands of some enemy who leads them away as prisoners to some place far or near; ³⁷ and if they then have a change of heart in their captivity, repenting and pleading with you, saying, 'We have sinned, we have been perverse and wicked,' ³⁸ and if they turn back to you with an open heart, there in their place of exile, and pray toward the land that you gave to their ancestors, toward your chosen city and this house which I have built for your Name; ³⁹ then hear them from heaven, from your dwelling place: hear their prayers and their pleas; and uphold their cause. Forgive your people their sins against you.

⁴⁰ "Now, O God, let your ears be attentive and your eyes be open to the prayer offered in this place.

⁴¹   'Arise, O Sovereign God,
        and come to your resting place,

you and your mighty Ark.
  May your priests be clothed in salvation;
    may your faithful rejoice in your grace.
42 Do not turn away, O Most High, from your anointed one;
    remember the great love that was promised
    to David, your servant.' "

7:1 As Solomon completed this prayer, fire came down from heaven and consumed the burnt offerings and the sacrifices; and the glory of Our God filled the house. 2 The priests could not enter the house, for the glory of Our God filled it. 3 All the Israelites witnessed this fire descending with the glory of Our God on the house, and bowed down where they stood on the paved court and gave thanks to God, saying,

  "Our God's love is good;
    it is steadfast, and endures forever."

4 Solomon and all the people presented burnt offerings before Our God. 5 Solomon offered a sacrifice of 22,000 oxen and 120,000 sheep. And so he and all the people dedicated the house of God. 6 The priests stood in their places, as did the Levites with the musical instruments which David the ruler had made for the praise of Our God, and which were used whenever he sang in prayer, "God's steadfast love endures forever." Opposite them, the priests sounded the trumpets, while all the Israelites stood.

7 Solomon then consecrated the middle part of the courtyard in front of the house of Our God. There he presented the burnt offerings and the fat of the peace offerings—the bronze altar which Solomon had made could not accommodate the burnt offerings, the grain offerings and the fat portions.

8 Solomon then held a festival which lasted seven days, and all Israel celebrated with him, with great contingents coming from places that ranged all the way from Hamath Pass to the River of Egypt. 9 On the eighth day they held a solemn ceremony, for they had celebrated the dedication of the altar for seven days and the festival for seven days. 10 On the twenty-third day of the seventh month, Solomon sent the people home with joy and gladness in their hearts for the goodness that God had shown to David, to Solomon and to all of Israel, God's people.

ର   ର   ର

11 After Solomon had completed the house of Our God and the royal house as well, and had successfully carried out all that had been planned, 12 the Most High came to him at night:

"I have heard your prayers, and I have chosen this place for myself as a house for sacrifice. When I shut up the skies and the rain stops—or send locusts to consume the land—or send pestilence among my people— 14 if, then, these people whom I have named my own should humble themselves and pray, and, seeking my face, turn from their wicked ways—I will hear them from heaven, and I will forgive their sins, and will restore their land. 15 My eyes will be open and my ears will be attentive to the prayer that is offered in this place. 16 I have chosen this house and made it holy, so that my Name may live there for all time and my eyes and my heart will live there forever.

17 "For your part, if you walk before me as David did, and do all that I command, and keep my statutes and my ordinances, I will establish the throne of your reign for you and for your children, as I promised to David when I said, 'You will never want for a descendant to rule Israel.' 19 But if you should turn from me, and abandon the statutes and commandments that I have set before you, or if you should wander, and serve and worship other gods, 20 I will rip you from this land which I have given to you; I will abandon this house which I have consecrated to my Name, and I will make it an expression of scorn, of ridicule, among all peoples. 21 This house of beauty will be in ruins. Passers-by will be appalled at what they see, and will ask, 'Why has the Most High God so utterly destroyed it?' 22 The answer will be, 'Because they turned their backs on the Most High God of their ancestors, who delivered them from Egypt, and they took up with other gods, bowing down and scraping before them. That is why Their God has brought this misfortune upon them.' "

଼ଃ ଼ଃ ଼ଃ

8:1 The building of the house of Our God and of Solomon's royal palace took twenty years. 2 Afterward, Solomon rebuilt the towns which Hiram had given to him, and settled Israelites in them. 3 He then captured Hamath-zobah; 4 after that, he built up Tadnor in the wilderness, and built garrison towns in Hamath. 5 He rebuilt Upper Beth-horon and Lower Beth-horon as garrison towns, with walls and barred gates; 6 as well as fortifying Baalath and all the garrison towns that he held, and all the towns used for quartering cavalry and chariots; and all through his domain, from Jerusalem to Lebanon, he built and strengthened the land.

7 All that remained of the Hittites, Amorites, Perizzites, Hivites, and Jebusites—those who were not Israelites, 8 but descendants remaining on the land of those that had dwelt there before, whom the Israelites had not exterminated—these were taken by Solomon and used for forced labor, as

they are yet to this day. ⁹ No Israelites were used for forced labor; they made up the common soldiery and the officers, and the commanders of chariots and calvary. ¹⁰ These were Solomon's chief officers—250 of them kept order among the people.

¹¹ Solomon brought his wife, Pharaoh's daughter, up from the City of David to the palace he had just completed building for her, saying, "No one should live in the palace that David, ruler of Israel, had built, for the presence of the Ark of Our God there has made it sacred ground."

¹² Solomon made sacrifice of burnt offerings to Our God on the altar which he had built in front of the vestibule, ¹³ which was the daily require-ment for offerings commanded by Moses for the sabbaths, the new moons and the three annual feasts: the pilgrim-feasts of Unleavened Bread, of Weeks, and of Tabernacles. ¹⁴ Following the precepts that David had laid down, Solomon appointed the divisions of priests for their duties, and the Levites who offered praise and assisted the priests as the day required; like-wise he appointed the doorkeepers for each gate according to the manner of David, God's chosen. ¹⁵ In no way did they vary from the instructions which David had given concerning the priests and the Levites, the trea-sury, and all other such matters.

¹⁶ All the work Solomon planned, from the laying of the foundation of the house of Our God, to its completion, was now finished.

❧ ❧ ❧

¹⁷ Solomon then journeyed to Ezion-geber and to Eloth on the Edom coast. Hiram sent him ships with Lebanese captains and crews, experienced in seafaring, who transported Solomon's servants to Ophir, where they bought for him seventeen tons of gold.

9:10 The ministers of Hiram and of Solomon, who had brought gold from Ophir, had brought also juniper wood and precious stones. ¹¹ The wood, Solomon used to make steps for the house of Our God; but also for lyres and lutes for the musicians, and such instruments had never been heard before in the land of Judah.*

9:1 When the Queen of Sheba** learned of Solomon's fame, she came to

---

* These two verses are clearly out of place where they fall in the Hebrew text, in the middle of the Queen of Sheba's visit; we have moved them here, where the context is more appropriate.

**Sheba was a country on the southern tip of the Arabian peninsula, comprising present-day Yemen. Its people colonized Ethiopia and were known for their wealth and commercial prosperity. Tradition holds that the Queen of Sheba was of African descent.

Jerusalem to test the ruler with subtle questions. She arrived in Jerusalem with a huge retinue, camels laden with spices, large quantities of gold and precious stones. When she came to Solomon, she talked with him about all that was on her mind. ² Solomon answered each of her questions; there were none to which he could find no answer.

³ When she had seen the wisdom of Solomon, the house of worship, ⁴ the food of his tables, the accommodations of the ministers, the attendants and cup-bearers in their livery and the burnt offerings offered in the house of Our God, she was utterly overwhelmed. ⁵ She said to Solomon, "The things that have been said of you in my homeland—the tales of your wisdom and wonders of your deeds—are true, ⁶ but I could not believe them until I came here and saw them with my own eyes. Not half of the greatness of your wisdom has been told; you are beyond all that I heard. ⁷ How fortunate your people are! How fortunate are those who serve under you every day and hear your counsel! ⁸ Blessed be the Most High who delights in your wisdom and has placed you on the judgment seat as ruler in the name of your Almighty God. It is for the sake of God's love for Israel, and because God wishes your nation to endure forever, that you have been made their ruler, to establish justice and righteousness."

⁹ She then presented him with four-and-a-half tons of gold, great quantities of spices, and precious stones. There have never been such spices as those that the Queen of Sheba gave to Solomon.

¹² Solomon gave to Sheba's ruler all that she desired, whatever she asked for and more—more than she had brought to Israel. Then she left with her retinue and returned to her own country.

೧ ೧ ೧

¹³ The gold that came into Solomon's treasury in a year amounted to twenty-five tons, ¹⁴ which does not count the duties levied on merchants and traders who imported goods. All the rulers of Arabia and the regional governors also brought gold and silver to Solomon.

¹⁵ Solomon had 200 shields made of hammered gold, seven-and-a-half pounds of gold went into each shield. ¹⁶ The ruler also made 300 smaller shields of hammered gold, with half as much gold being used for each of them. Solomon had them displayed in the Hall of the Forest of Lebanon.

¹⁷ He also made a great ivory throne, overlaid with pure gold, ¹⁸ with six steps leading up to it, and a footstool, all made of gold. On each side of the throne were two armrests, with a lion standing beside each; these also were made of gold. ¹⁹ Twelve lions stood on the steps, one on each side of each step. Nothing like it had ever been made for any other ruler. ²⁰ All of

Solomon's drinking cups were gold, and all the furnishings in the Hall of the Forest of Lebanon were of pure gold; nothing was made of silver, because silver was considered of no value in Solomon's days. ²¹ The ruler had a fleet of trading ships, crewed by Hiram's sailors. Every three years it returned laden with gold, silver, ivory, and apes and peacocks.

²² Thus Solomon surpassed all the rulers of the world in wealth and wisdom, ²³ and all the rulers of the world sought audience to hear the wisdom God put in his heart. ²⁴ Each of them brought gifts: articles of silver and gold, garments, weaponry, perfumes and spices, horses and mules, and so on, year after year. ²⁵ Solomon had 4,000 stalls for horses and chariots, but he had 12,000 horses. He kept these both in Jerusalem, and in the outlying towns that were devoted to the chariot trade.

²⁶ Solomon reigned over all the rulers from the Euphrates to the land of the Philistines and down to the border of Egypt. ²⁷ He made silver as common as stone in Jerusalem, and cedars were planted as thickly as the sycamores that grew in the foothills. ²⁸ Solomon's horses were brought from Egypt, and from many other nations as well.

²⁹ The rest of the story of Solomon's reign, from first to last, is recorded in the history of Nathan the prophet, in the prophecy of Ahijah of Shiloh, and in the visions of Iddo the seer concerning Jeroboam begot of Nebat. ³⁰ Solomon ruled in Jerusalem over all of Israel for forty years. Then Solomon went to sleep with his ancestors, and was buried in the city of David.

Rehoboam, begot of Solomon, succeeded him.

Rehoboan went to Sechem, and all of Israel went there to make him ruler. ² When Jeroboam, begot of Nebat, heard this in Egypt—Jeroboam had fled to Egypt to escape Solomon*—he returned from Egypt. ³ Jeroboam and all the people came to Rehoboam and said, ⁴ "Solomon put a heavy load on us. If you lighten the heavy load and the hard labor, we will serve you."

⁵ Rehoboam replied, "Give me three days and then come back."

⁶ After the people left, Rehoboam turned to the elders who had served

---

* As recounted in 1 Kings, Jeroboam was a member of Solomon's court who, according to the prophet Ahijah, would take ten of the twelve tribes away from Solomon because Solomon had become an apostate, worshipping other deities. Jeroboam led a revolt, and when Solomon tried to kill him, he fled to Egypt.

Solomon when he was alive, asking "What do you advise me to say to these people?"

⁷ They counseled him, "If you are kind to them, and speak wisely to them and treat them fairly, they will serve you forever."

⁸ But Rehoboam rejected the elders' advice "to be kind and fair" and turned instead to the companions that he had grown up with, who were now attendants at the court, and asked, ⁹ "What do you advise me to say to these people who ask me to lighten their burden?"

¹⁰ They said, "Say this to those people who ask you lighten the load which Solomon placed on them: 'My little finger is thicker than Solomon's waist. ¹¹ Solomon put a heavy burden on you. I will make it heavier. Solomon beat you with whips; I will scourge with scorpions.' "

¹² Jeroboam and the people all returned to Rehoboam, as he had told them, on the third day. Rehoboam spoke harshly to them; he rejected the elders' advice ¹⁴ and said instead, "My father placed a heavy burden on you. I will make it heavier. Solomon beat you with whips; I will scourge you with scorpions."

¹⁵ Rehoboam would not listen to the people, for it had been ordained so by Our God so that the promise might be fulfilled which the Almighty had spoken through the mouth Ahijah of Shiloh to Jeroboam, begot of Nebat.

¹⁶ When the assembly of Israelites saw that Rehoboam would not listen to them, they answered,

> "What share do we have in David,
>   what part in Jesse's offspring?
> To your tents, O Israel!
>   See to your own house, O David!"

Then all the assembled Israelites went home. ¹⁷ But Rehoboam still governed the Israelites who lived in the towns of Judah.

¹⁸ Rehoboam the ruler sent out Hadorum, who was the overseer in charge of forced labor; but the Israelites stoned him to death. Rehoboam quickly mounted his chariot and fled to Jerusalem.

¹⁹ And so it is: Israel has been in rebellion against the house of David from that day on.

ᔥ   ᔥ   ᔥ

11:1 In Jerusalem, Rehoboam mustered the house of Judah and the house of Benjamin, raising a total of 180,000 chosen soldiers to fight the house of Israel and restore his sovereignty.

² But the word of Our God came to the prophet Shemaiah: ³ "Say to

Rehoboam, begot of Solomon, ruler of Judah, and to all the Israelites in Judah and Benjamin, ⁴ 'This is the word of Our God: You are not to take up arms against your own kin. Return to your homes, for this which has happened is my doing.'" They heard the word of Our God and turned back from their campaign against Jeroboam.

⁵ Rehoboam took up residence in Jerusalem, and fortified many of the towns in Judah, ⁶ including Bethlehem, Etam, Tekoa, ⁷ Beth-zur, Soco, Adullam, ⁸ Gath, Mareshah, Ziph, ⁹ Adoraim, Lachish, Azekah, ¹⁰ Zorah, Aijalon, and Hebron. ¹¹ He fortified their defenses and stationed commanders in them, and provisioned them well with with food, olive oil and wine. ¹² He stored shields and spears there and made them very strong, and so held Benjamin and Judah firmly under his control.

¹³ The priests and Levites throughout Israel presented their allegiance to Rehoboam from all their territories. ¹⁴ The Levites had left their pastures and property and had come to Judah and Jerusalem because Jeroboam and his heirs had rejected them as priests of Our God. ¹⁵ Jeroboam had appointed new priests at the sacred mounds—priests to the goat and calf idols he had made. ¹⁶ People from all the tribes of Israel—those who were wholeheartedly devoted to the worship of the Most High God of Israel—followed the Levites to Jerusalem to offer sacrifice to the Most High God, the God of their ancestors. ¹⁷ For three years their numbers grew, adding strength to the realm of Judah, for during this time Rehoboam, begot of Solomon, lived faithfully by the examples of David and Solomon.

¹⁸ Rehoboam married Mahalath, whose father was Jedrimoth begot of David, and whose mother was Abihail daughter of Eliab, begot of Jesse. ¹⁹ They had three sons—Jeush, Shemariah and Azham. ²⁰ After Mahalath, Jeroboam married Maacah, granddaughter of Absalom; and four children were born to them: Abijah, Attai, Ziza, and Shelomith. ²¹ Of all whom he married, Rehoboam loved Maacah the most. In the end, Rehoboam had eighteen wives and sixty concubines, who bore him twenty-eight sons and sixty daughters.

²² Rehoboam chose Abijah, begot of Maacah, to be first among his siblings, and began preparing him to be the next ruler. ²³ Rehoboam dealt wisely with his sons; he saw to it that they were well-married, and distributed them throughout the regions of Benjamin and Judah, establishing them as govenors in the fortified towns, which he made certain were well provisioned.

12:1 When in time Rehoboam became firmly established in his realm, he began to abandon the Law of the Most High, and all of Israel with him. ² In the fifth year of Rehoboam's rule, Our God—reacting to this disloyalty—saw to it that Shishak, ruler of Egypt, attacked Jerusalem ³ with 12,000 chariots and 60,000 calvary. Shishak brought with him also vast numbers of Libyans, Sukkites and Cushites. ⁴ They captured the fortified towns of Judah and advanced as far as Jerusalem.

⁵ There Shemaiah the prophet came to Rehoboam and the Judean leaders, who had gathered in Jerusalem to face Shishak saying, "This is the word of Our God: You have abandoned me; therefore I abandon you to Shishak."

⁶ The ruler and the Judean leaders humbled themselves saying, "Our God is just."

⁷ When the Most High saw that they had so humbled themselves, the word of Our God came again to Shemiah: "In that they have humbled themselves I will not destroy them utterly, but will give them some measure of relief. My wrath will not be poured out on Jerusalem through Shishak. ⁸ Yet still, they will become Shishak's subjects, so that they will learn to know the difference between serving me and serving other nations."

⁹ So it was: Shishak's army conquered Jerusalem, and carried away the treasures of the house of Our God and the treasures of the house of Rehoboam. They took everything of value—even the gold shields which Solomon had made. ¹⁰ Rehoboam replaced them with shields of bronze, and put them in the care of officers of the escort who watched the doors of the house of Rehoboam. ¹¹ When the ruler would go to the house of Our God, the guards would accompany him bearing their shields, and afterwards would return them to the guard room.

¹² Because Rehoboam humbled himself, the wrath of Our God was assuaged. The destruction was turned aside, and life was good once again in Judah.

¹³ And so it was that Rehoboam established his power in Jerusalem, and such was his reign. For seventeen years he reigned in Jerusalem, taking power when he was forty-one years of age, in the city which Our God chose to honor from among all the tribes of Israel. Rehoboam's mother was Naamah, an Ammonite. ¹⁴ Rehoboam did evil in that he did not make it his practice to follow the way of Our God.

¹⁵ The events of Rehoboam's life, from beginning to end, are written in

the Annals of Shemaiah the prophet and of Eddo the seer. There were continual struggles between Rehoboam and Jeroboam. Rehoboam went to sleep with his ancestors and is buried in the city of David.

Rehoboam was succeeded by his heir Abijah.

CR CR CR

13₁ Abijah became ruler of Judah after eighteen years of Jeroboam's rule. His reign in Jerusalem lasted three years. ² Maacah, daughter of Uriel of Gibeah, was his mother.

³ War broke our between Abijah and Jeroboam, ³ and Abijah went into battle with a hand-picked force of 400,000 brave warriors, against Jeroboam's hardy force, 800,000 strong. ⁴ Abijah, standing on the face of Mount Zemaraim—which in the foothills of Ephraim—cried out:

"Jeroboam and all Israel, hear me out! ⁵ Don't you know that the Most High God of Israel gave eternal sovereignty to David and David's children by a covenant of salt? ⁶ Yet Jeroboam, begot of Nebat—who served under Solomon, heir of David—rebelled against Rehoboam. ⁷ Certain worthless scoundrels joined with him in his rebellion against Solomon's heir Rehoboam when the young ruler was inexperienced and not yet come into his power.

⁸ "Now you think to defeat the sovereignty of Our God which belongs to David's heirs, you and your great mob, with your golden calves which Jeroboam made to be your gods. ⁹ Didn't you expel the priests of Our God, the descendants of Aaron and the Levites, and ordain priests of your own like they do in other lands? Anyone among you who comes to you for ordination with a young bull and seven rams can be consecrated as a priest— to a god who is no god!

¹⁰ "As for us, the Most High is Our God, whom we have not abandoned. Our priests are descendants of Aaron, serving Our God with the Levites who assist them. ¹¹ Morning and evening they proffer burnt offerings and fragrant incense to Our God and set out the consecrated bread in rows on a pure table. They tend the gold lampstand each day so that the lamps may burn each night. For we keep the laws of the Most High, Our God, which you have abandoned. ¹² You see that God, our leader, is at our head. The priests with their trumpets will sound the battle cry against you. Children of Israel, do not fight against the Most High, the God of your ancestors! You will not succeed!"

¹³ Jeroboam had sent a detachment of troops around to ambush Abijah from the rear, while the main body of troops remained facing Judah.

¹⁴ Judah found itself suddenly in battle in both front and behind. They cried out for God's help, and the priests sounded the trumpets. ¹⁵ Then Judah raised its battle cry in response, and God scattered Jeroboam and all the Israelites before Abijah and Judah. ¹⁶ The Israelites fled before Judah and God delivered them into their hands. ¹⁷ At the hands of Abijah's army that day there was a bloodbath: 500,000 were killed. ¹⁸ And so the Israelites were subdued at that time; and the Judeans prevailed because they had relied on the Most High God of their ancestors. ¹⁹ Abijah pursued Jeroboam and captured the cities of Bethel, Jeshanah and Ephron and their villages. ²⁰ Jeroboam never regained power in Abijah's time, for God struck him down and he died.

²¹ But Abijah grew in his power. He took fourteen wives and had by them twenty-two sons and sixteen daughters. The rest of the tale of Abijah's life, the events and the deeds, are recorded in the annoations of the prophet Iddo.

14:1 Abijah went to sleep with his ancestors and is buried in the city of David.

Abijah's heir was Asa, who succeeded him.

℞   ℞   ℞

For the first ten years of Asa's rule, there was peace in the land. ² Asa did what was pleasing in Our God's eyes ³ He did away with the foreign altars and the sacred mounds, smashed the sacred pillars and cut down the Asherah groves.* ⁴ He commanded that Judah return to Our God, the God of their ancestors, and observe the laws and the statutes. ⁵ Asa destroyed the shrines and incense altars in every town in Judah, and the realm was once more at peace. ⁶ He fortified the cities in those years, while the land was at peace. All during those years there was no war, for the Most High God granted peace to the land.

⁷ Asa said, "Let us rebuild these cities and fortify them; wall them around with towers, and barred gates. This land still belongs to us, for we have turned to Our God Most High; we sought God, and so we have been given peace on every side." And so they built, and they prospered.

⁸ Asa had an army from Judah of 300,000, equipped with large shields and spears, and 280,000 archers from Benjamin, with bucklers, and all were

---

* These are the places of worship dedicated to the Great Goddess, Asherah, and her consort, the bull-god El—both ancient Canaanite deities. The sacred groves represented the birthplace of all things; the sacred pillars, the male element.

fine soldiers. ⁹ And then came Zerah the Ethiopian, invading with a force of 1,000,000 soldiers and 300 chariots. They had reached as far as Mareshah ¹⁰ before Asa met them, taking up a position in the valley of Zephathah at Mareshah. ¹¹ The ruler called to the Most High God and said, "O God, you defend the weak as easily as the strong. Help us, O Most High God, for we turn to you, and we face this horde in your Name. O God, you are Our God, let no mortals stand against you."

¹² It was as he prayed; the Sovereign God defeated the Ethiopians before Asa and the Judeans. The Ethiopians fled, ¹³ with Asa and his army pursuing as far as Gerar until not one of them remained alive, for they had faced the wrath of the Most High and the army of the Most High. The people of Judah collected rich plunder, ¹⁴ moving on to conquer all the cities in the region of Gerar—for the people of these towns were struck by Our God with great terror, and had no will to fight—and plundering wherever they went. ¹⁵ Likewise they attacked the camps of the shepherds and herders, gathering up great flocks of sheep, goats, and the camels, ¹⁶ before returning to Jerusalem.

15:1 The Spirit of God came upon Azariah, begot of Obed. ² Obed went out to meet Asa and said, "Hear me, O Ruler, and all you of Judah and Benjamin! The Most High God is with you when you are with God. If you seek God, God will be found, but if you abandon God, God will abandon you. ³ For many years Israel did not worship the true God, and there were no priests to teach the law, and they were lawless. ⁴ But when in their distress they sought out the Almighty, the God of Israel, they found God Almighty. ⁵ In those days it was not safe anywhere, for great turmoil filled the land and all its inhabitants. ⁶ Ruin was everywhere. Nations struggled against nations; cities against cities; and God tormented them with every kind of affliction. ⁷ But you, now—be strong, and have courage! Your work will have its own reward."

⁸ When Asa heard these words of prophecy from Asariah, begot of Obed, he was moved to destroy the detestable idols throughout all of Judah and Benjamin, and in the towns he had captured in the hill country of Ephraim. He repaired the altar of the Most High God that stood before the vestibule of the house of Our God. ⁹ Then the ruler gathered all the people of Judah and Benjamin, and those who had come from Ephraim, Manaseh and Simeon, settling among them—for a large number of Israelites had come to Asa when they knew that Our God was with him.

¹⁰ They gathered at Jerusalem in the third month of the fifteenth year of Asa's reign. ¹¹ They sacrificed to the Most High God that day 700 cattle and 7,000 sheep from booty they had brought back, ¹² and they made a sacred pact that they would seek Our God, the God of their ancestors, with heart

and soul, ¹³ and that any who would not seek Our God, the God of Israel, would be executed, young or old, women and men alike. ¹⁴ They swore their oath God with loud cries, and with the sound of trumpets and horns. ¹⁵ All Judah rejoiced at this oath, taken so wholeheartedly; for they had sought God with great eagerness, and they had found God, and for this, they had been given peace on every side.

¹⁶ Asa even deposed Maacah, his ruling queen mother, because she had made an obscene Asherah pole. Asa cut it down, broke it up and burned it in the Wadi Kidron. ¹⁷ Although the sacred mounds were not removed in Israel, Asa remained faithful throughout his life. ¹⁸ He gave to the house of God votive offerings of his own, of silver, gold and sacred vessels, as well as much that Abijah had left.

There was no more war until the thirty-fifth year of Asa's reign.

16¹ In the thirty-sixth year of the reign of Asa, Baasha the ruler of Israel invaded Judah and fortified Ramah to prevent anyone leaving or entering the realm of Asa of Judah. ² Asa took gold and silver from the treasuries of the house of Our God and from his own house as well, and sent them to Ben-hadad, ruler of Aram, in Damascus, with this message: ³ "Let there be an alliance between us, as there was between our families in former times. I am sending you gold and silver; and I ask in return that you end your alliance with Baasha of Israel, so he will have to withdraw from Judah."

⁴ Ben-hadad accepted this proposal from Asa of Judah, giving orders to the commanders of his army to move against the cities of Israel. They conquered Ijon, Dan, Abel-mayim, and all the store cities of Naphtali.

⁵ When Baasha heard of this turn of events, he gave up the fortification work at Ramah; ⁶ and Asa brought forces from all Judea to remove the timber and stone which Baasha had brought to Ramah, and used them instead to fortify Geba and Mizpah.

⁷ At this time Hanani the seer came to Asa of Judah and said, "Because you relied on Ben-hadad and not on the Most High your God, the army of Baasha has escaped. Look at the Ethiopians and the Libyans—didn't they field a massive army, with huge numbers of chariots and calvary? Yet you relied on Our God, and they were delivered into your power. The eyes of Our God look this way and that through the world, looking to encourage those who are faithful. You have acted foolishly on this occasion. From now on you will have wars."

¹⁰ Asa was angered at this, and had the seer imprisoned, for he was in a rage; and in his rage, he treated others of his people brutally.

¹¹ The history of Asa's reign, from its beginning to its end, is recorded in

the books of the Rulers of Judah and Israel. ¹² In the thirty-ninth year of his reign he came down with a serious foot disease. Even in sickness Asa did not seek God's help, but instead sought the help of physicians. ¹³ Asa went to sleep with his ancestors in the forty first year of his reign, and was buried in a tomb that was hewn out of the hillside for him in the City of David. Asa was laid in a bier that was filled with spices and perfumes, and a great fire was lighted in his honor.

◌૨ ◌૨ ◌૨

17:1 Jehoshaphat succeeded his father Asa as ruler, and strengthened Judah's position against Israel. ² Jehoshaphat stationed battalions in all the fortified cities of Judah, establishing garrisons not only in Judah but in the towns of Ephraim that Asa captured.

³ Our God was with Jehoshaphat, for he followed the example set by Asa in his earlier days, and did not consult the Baals. ⁴ He sought the God of his ancestors, and followed God's commandments rather than the practices of Israel. ⁵ So Our God made the kingdom secure, and all Judah paid honor to him. ⁶ Jehoshaphat's heart was strong in the service of Our God; and once more removed the sacred mounds and the Asherah groves from Judah.

⁷ In the third year of his reign the ruler sent the officials Ben-hayil, Obadiah, Zechariah, Nethanel and Micaiah to teach in the towns of Judah. ⁸ With them were the Levites Shemaiah, Nethaniah, Zebadiah, Asahel, Shemiramoth, Jehonathan, Adonijah, Tobiah, and Tob-adonijah; and with them, the priests Elishama and Jehoram. ⁹ They taught in Judah, having with them the Book of the Law of Our God, and traveled through all the cities of Judah, teaching everywhere.

¹⁰ The fear of Our God descended on all the rulers of the countries surrounding Judah, and they made no wars against Jehoshaphat. ¹¹ Some of the Philistines brought gifts of silver as a peace sign; the Arabs brought 7,700 rams and 7,700 goats. ¹² Jehoshaphat grew in power, building more fortresses and garrison towns in Judah ¹³ and stockpiling provisions in the store cities. Great works were begun in the cities of Judah, and a fine army of the most highly trained soldiers was kept in Jerusalem. ¹⁴ Following is a listing of their chief commanders and their numbers, in the order of their ancestral houses: From Judah, there were three commanders who had units of 1,000 soldiers: Adnah, with 300,000; ¹⁵ Jehohanan, with 280,000; ¹⁶ and Amasiah, begot of Zichri, who volunteered to be in Our God's service, with 200,000. ¹⁷ From Benjamin: Eliada, with 200,000 archers, and ¹⁸ Jehozabad, with 180,000 regular soldiers.

[19] These were the troops serving the ruler in Jerusalem; beside these were the many that were kept in the fortified cities throughout the rest of Judah.

18[1] Jehoshaphat had great wealth, and was well regarded; and he had arranged an alliance with Ahab,* sealed with a marriage.

[2] After some years, Jehoshaphat went to visit Ahab in Samaria. The father-in-law slaughtered many sheep and cattle for his guest and entourage. Making use of the geniality of the occasion, Ahab pressed Jehoshaphet to take up arms with him against Ramoth-gilead. [3] Ahab ruler of Israel asked Jehoshaphat ruler of Juda, "Will you come with me against Ramoth-gilead?"

Jehoshaphat replied, "You and I are one. My people and your people are one as well. We will be with you in this war." [4] "But first," he counseled, "let us ask God's will."

[5] So Ahab brought together the prophets, 400 in number, and asked, "Shall we go to war against Ramoth-gilead, or shall we keep the peace?"

"Attack!" was the response. "God will deliver them into your hands."

[6] Jehoshaphat asked, "Is there no other prophet of Our God here to give us counsel?"

[7] "There is yet one more," the Israelite ruler replied, "Micaiah begot of Imlah is his name, but I hate him, because he never prophesies anything good for me—it is always bad news. "

Jehoshaphat replied, "A ruler should not say such things!"

[8] Ahab told a minister close by, "Bring Micaiah begot of Imlah immediately."

[9] So the rulers of Israel and of Judah were seated on their judgment seats in full regalia at the threshing floor near the entry gate of Samaria, with all the prophets were prophesying before them. [10] One of them, Zedekiah, begot of Kenaanah, seizing two pieces of iron and holding them to his head as horns, said, "Thus says Our God: With horns like these you shall gore the Aramaeans and destroy them."

[11] The other prophets spoke in the same vein: "Attack Ramoth-gilead and you shall prevail," they said, "for the Sovereign One will deliver it into the ruler's hands."

[12] The minister who had been sent to get Micaiah advised the prophet, "See here! All the prophets speak as one, and they speak favorably. See that what you say agrees with what they say."

---

* Ahab succeeded Baasha as ruler of Israel. During this period, the region of Samaria served as the headquarters for the Israel, while Jerusalem continued to be the seat of power in Judah.

¹³ But Micaiah responded, "As the Most High lives, what God says is what I will say, and nothing else."

¹⁴ When Micaiah arrived, the ruler asked, "Micaiah, should we attack Ramoth-gilead, or should we keep the peace?"

"Attack and it will be delivered into your hands," replied the prophet.

¹⁵ "How often must I entreat you," Ahab said, "to tell me nothing but the truth in the name of Our God?

¹⁶ Then Micaiah said,

> "I saw all Israel scattered on the mountains
>   like sheep without a shepherd;
> and Our God said, 'They have no leader.
>   Let each one go home in peace.' "

¹⁷ The ruler of Israel said to Jehoshaphat, "Didn't I tell you that he would never foretell anything positive for me, nothing but disaster?"

¹⁸ Micaiah continued, "Listen to the word of Our God! I saw the Sovereign One sitting on the judgment seat, with the whole assembly of heaven present, half on the right and half on the left of the throne. ¹⁹ Our God said, 'Who will lure Ahab, ruler of Israel, to attack Ramoth-gilead, and fall at their feet?'

"Some answered one way and others answered the other, ²⁰ until a spirit came forward and, standing before the Almighty, said, 'I will do it.'

"Our God asked, 'How?'

²¹ "'I will go out and become a lying spirit in the mouths of all the prophets,' it said.

"God said, 'You are the one, and you will succeed. Go and do it.'

²² "And so you see: God has put a lying spirit in the mouths of all these your prophets; God has decreed disaster for you."

²³ Then Zedakiah, begot of Kenaanah, came forward and struck Micaiah in the face, asking, "Which way did the spirit of Our God go when it left me to go to you?"

²⁴ Micaiah responded, "You will learn that on the day you flee to an inner room to hide."

²⁵ The ruler of Israel ordered Micaiah arrested in the custody of Amon the governor of the city and, of Joash, the ruler's heir, saying, ²⁶ "Tell them I said 'Throw this Micaiah in prison and give him nothing but bread and water until I return in peace.' "

²⁷ Micaiah declared, "If you do return in peace, Our God had not spoken through me." And turning to those around them, he cried, "All you who hear—remember my words!"

²⁸ Ahab of Israel and Jehoshaphat of Judah marched on Ramoth-gilead.
²⁹ The ruler of Israel said to Jehoshaphat, "I will go into battle disguised,
but you wear your full attire." ³⁰ The ruler of Aram ordered the commanders of the charioteers that they were not to fight with any but the ruler of
Israel.

³¹ When the commanders saw Jehoshaphat, they thought he was the
ruler of Israel. They wheeled for an attack, but Jehoshaphat cried out to
God, and the Almighty assisted him, drawing the charioteers away; ³² for
the chariot commanders saw that this wasn't the ruler of Israel, and broke
off their attack.

But an archer, shooting into the Israelite ranks, hit the Ahab by chance
between the scales of his armor. Ahab said to the driver, "I am hit; turn
around and take me out of the line." ³⁴ The fighting grew fiercer as the day
drew on. The ruler of Israel stood in his chariot, propped up to face the
battle until the evening came; but as the sun set, he died.

19:1 When Jehoshaphat of Judah returned to the safety of home and
Jerusalem, ² Jehu the seer, begot of Hanani, came out and to meet him, saying, "Is it right to assist the wicked and befriend those who hate Our God?
What you have done will bring God's wrath down upon you. ³ Yet God
will find some good in you, for you did tear down the Asherah groves. And
have set your heart on seeking God."

⁴ After a stay in Jerusalem, Jehoshaphat went out among the people, from
Beersheba to the hill country of Ephraim, calling them back to the ways of
the Most High, the God of their ancestors. ⁵ The ruler appointed judges
throughout the country, in each of the fortified cities of Judah. He charged
them, "Think well how you act; you are not judging for the sake of any
human, but for the sake of the Most High God, who will be with you in
every verdict you give. ⁷ Now, stand in awe of Our God. Think carefully of
what you do; the Sovereign One will tolerate no fraud, nor partiality. Take
no bribes."

⁸ In Jerusalem, Jehoshaphat appointed certain priests and Levites and
heads of the families of Israel to sit as judges in matters regarding the Law
of Our God and to settle disputes in Jerusalem.

⁹ He instructed them, "Do your duties always in reverence for Our God,
and in faith and with all your heart. ¹⁰ In any case that comes before you
from your sisters and brothers in their towns—whether it be an issue of
bloodshed, or violation of the Law or the commandments, or any statutes
or regulations—you must teach them, so that they commit no offenses

against Our God, and so that the wrath of Our God does not strike you and your kin. Do as I say, you will be innocent.

¹¹ "Amariah, the chief priest, is your authority in all religious matters. Zebadiah, begot of Ishmael, the leader of the tribe of Judah, is your authority in all matters of the state. The scribes and the Levites will serve as your officials. Have courage. Be strong. And may Our God judge with you!"

ରେ ରେ ରେ

20·1 It happened that some time later, the Moabites and the Ammonites, along with some of the Meunites, staged an attack against Jehoshaphat. ² Messengers came telling him, "A large army is coming from beyond the Dead Sea, from Edom. They have already reached Hazazon-tamar"—that is, En-gedi.

³ Jehoshaphat was afraid; he turned to the Most High, and proclaimed a fast for all Judah. ⁴ The Judeans gathered to ask Our God for help, coming in from every town in Judah to seek God.

⁵ Jehoshaphat stood up before the assembly of Judah and Jerusalem in the house of Our God in front of the new courtyard, ⁶ and prayed, "O Most High God of our ancestors, are you not the God in heaven? Do you not rule all the nations of the earth? So much power and strength are in your hands that no one can resist you. ⁷ You, O God, drove out those who lived in this land in favor of your people. You gave it to us who are descendants of your beloved Abraham. ⁸ We who dwell here built a sanctuary to your Name, saying, ⁹ 'If disaster occurs—war, floods, pestilence, famine—we will stand in your presence before this house and before you, for your Name dwells in this house. We will cry out to in our grief, and you will hear us and save us.' ¹⁰ When the Israelites came out of Egypt we did not invade the Ammonites, or the Moabites, or the hill-country people of Seir. Instead we passed by them without destroying them. ¹¹ See how they repay us: they come to expel us from the possession you gave us, our heritage. ¹² O God Most High pass judgment on them. We are helpless against this invading horde; we don't know what to do, and so we look to you!"

¹³ All the Judeans stood there before the Almighty with their children, their spouses, and even their infants. ¹⁴ Then suddenly the Spirit of Our God came over Jahaziel, begot of Zechariah, begot of Benaiah, begot of Jeiel, begot of Mattaniah, a Levite and descendent of Asaph. ¹⁵ Jahaziel said, "Hear me, Judah and all you inhabitants of Jerusalem; and you also, Jehoshaphat. This is what Our God says to you: Do not be afraid of this vast horde. This is not your battle. It is God's. ¹⁶ March down against them tomorrow. They will be approaching up through the Pass of Zia. You will

find them at the end of the wadi which opens onto the wilderness of Jeruel. ¹⁷ You will not have to fight this battle. Take up your positions and stand firm for you will witness the deliverance Our God has in store for you, Judah and Jerusalem. Don't fear. Don't lose heart. Go out tomorrow to face them, and Our God will be with you."

¹⁸ Jehoshaphat prostrated himself, and all Judah and the residents of Jerusalem fell down before the Sovereign One in worship. ¹⁹ Then Levites of the lineage of Kohath and Korah stood up and praised the Most High God of Israel, chanting with a great voice.

²⁰ They all rose early the next day and went out into the wilderness of Tekoa. While they prepared, Jehoshaphat stood before them and said, "Listen to me, Judah and all you residents of Jerusalem. Have faith in your God and your faith will be supported; have faith in God's prophets." ²¹ Consulting with those gathered, he arranged for cantors to march out at the head of the army, chanting to God and praising the splendor of God's holiness as they sang, "Give thanks to Our God, for God's love endures forever."

²² Even as they were chanting their praise and joy, the Most High was setting a trap for these Ammonites and Moabites and the troops from the hills of Seir that were invading Judah, to their own destruction. ²³ For they quarreled among themselves, and the Ammonites and Moabites turned on those from the hills of Seir and utterly annihilated them; and then, when they had done with that, in the rage of battle, they turned on each other. ²⁴ The Judeans, arriving at the overlook at the head of the wilderness valley, looked down expecting to see the multitude, and saw instead nothing but corpses; not one living soldier.

²⁵ When Jehoshaphat and the rest came down to the battlefield they found not only equipment, clothing, and precious items, but an abundance of cattle. They gathered up the booty until they could carry no more, and in the end it took them three days to take it all. ²⁶ On the fourth day they all gathered in the valley of Berakah. It goes by this name to this day, for here they praised Our God. ²⁷ Then, led by Jehoshaphat, the Judeans and residents of Jerusalem returned to the city in triumph, for the Most High God had given them reason to rejoice over their enemies. ²⁸ The triumphal procession into Jerusalem was accompanied by lutes, lyres and trumpets, and ended at the house of Our God. ²⁹ The dread of God fell on the rulers of every nation when they heard that God fought against Israel's foes; ³⁰ and the realm lived in peace, for the Almighty gave Jehoshaphat safety on all sides.

³¹ Jehoshaphat ruled over Judah from Jerusalem for twenty-five years, beginning at the age of thirty-five. Jehoshaphat's mother was Azubah, daughter of Shilhi. ³² Jehoshaphat did not deviate at all from the ways of

his father Asa: do what is right in the eyes of the Sovereign One. ³³ But the sacred mounds still remained, because the people had still had not turned their hearts to the God of their ancestors. ³⁴ The rest of the details of Jehoshaphat's reign, from beginning to end, are found in the history of Jehu, begot of Hanani. It can be found in the book of the Rulers of Israel.

³⁵ In his later years Jehoshaphat of Judah made alliance with Ahaziah, ruler of Israel, who did evil things. ³⁶ They joined in an enterprise of building ships for trade with Tarshish. After these ships had been built at Ezion-geber, ³⁷ Eliezer, begot of Dodavahu of Mareshah, denounced Jehoshaphat with the prophecy, "Because of your alliance with Ahaziah, God will destroy your work." The ships broke up and never made the voyage to Tarshish.

21:1 Jehoshaphat went to sleep with his ancestors and was buried with them in the City of David.

જી   જી   જી

Jehoshaphat was succeeded by Jehoram. ² The heirs of Jehoshaphat of Judah included Azariah, Jehiel, Zechariah, Azariahu, Michael, Shephatiah and Jehoram. ³ Jehoshaphat gave them many gifts of silver, gold and precious things, and established them in the fortified cities throughout Judah. Jehoram, being firstborn, was made ruler.

⁴ When Jehoram was firmly established on the throne, he murdered all his brothers, and various officials of Israel as well. ⁵ Jehoram, who was thirty-three years old at the time of his investiture, ruled in Jerusalem for eight years.

⁶ Jehoram followed the ways of the rulers of Israel, after Ahab, and in fact married Ahab's daughter. His actions were evil in the eyes of the Most High God. ⁷ But God did not destroy the house of David for the sake of the covenant which had been made with David and David's heirs, that their light would shine forever.

⁸ During the reign of Jehoram, Edom revolted against Judah and set up its own monarchy. ⁹ Jehoram, with the commanders of the army and all the chariots, attacked them in the night, but the Edomites encircled them, and they fled. ¹⁰ To this day, Edom remains independent of Judah.

Libnah revolted at the same time because Jehoram had abandoned the Almighty One, the God of their ancestors. ¹¹ He built shrines in the hill country of Judah, and led the inhabitants of Jerusalem into idolatry—and so led Judah astray.

¹² The ruler received a letter from Elijah the prophet which read, "This

is the word of Our God, the God of David your ancestor: You have not followed the example of Jehoshaphat, your forebear, and Asa, the ruler of Judah, [13] but have followed the example of the rulers of Israel and have led astray Judah and the inhabitants of Jerusalem, just as the house of Ahab did. You have murdered your siblings, your own family, who were better than yourself. [14] Our God will strike your people, your children, your spouses and all your possessions. [15] You yourself will suffer from such a disease of the bowels that they will finally come out of you, bit by bit."

Our God stirred up the hostility of the Philistines against Jehoram, as well as that of the Arabs who dwell near the Ethiopians. [17] They invaded Judah, carrying off all the possessions they could find in the ruler's household. They took the wives and the children, leaving only the youngest, Jehoahaz.** [18] Then Our God struck the ruler with an incurable disease of the bowels. [19] It continued for two years when the disease caused his bowels to come out of him, and the ruler died in great pain. The people built no great fire in his honor, as they had done for those who went before him.

[20] Jehoram was thirty-two years old when he ascended the throne, and ruled for eight years. No one mourned him; he was buried in the city of David, but not in the tombs of the rulers.

෬ ෬ ෬

22[1] The citizens of Jerusalem made Ahaziah, Jehoram's youngest, the new ruler; for the Arab raiders who had attacked the ruler's household had killed all the older heirs. Thus, Ahaziah, begot of Jehoram became ruler of Judah. [2] He was twenty-two* at the time, and ruled in Jerusalem for one year. Athaliah, the granddaughter of Omri, was the mother of the ruler.

[3] Ahaziah also took up the practices of Ahab, and Athaliah encouraged him to do so. [4] The new ruler did what was evil in the eyes of the Most High, as the house of Ahab had done, for they were his counselors, to the point of ruin. [5] Following their advice, he made an alliance with Jehoram, begot of Ahab of Israel, to take up arms against Hazael, ruler of Aram, at Ramoth-gilead. But Jehoram was wounded by the Arameans, [6] and so he returned to Jezreel to recover from the wounds he recieved at Ramoth in the battle with Hazael of Aram.

Ahaziah, begot of Jehoram of Judah, went down to Jezreel to visit the wounded Jehoram, begot of Ahab. [7] It was through this visit that God

---

* The Hebrew says "forty-two," but this is probably a copyist's error; the Septuagint and Syriac manuscripts agree with 2 Kings 8:26, that he was indeed twenty-two.
**He is called Ahaziah in 22:1.

brought down Ahaziah. Ahaziah went out with Jehoram to do battle with Jehu begot of Nimshi, whom God had anointed to end the house of Ahab. ⁸ Jehu was taking vengeance against the house of Ahab, and coming upon Jehoram and his retinue, he killed them all. ⁹ Ahaziah fled, wounded, into Samaria, but Jehu sent out trackers who found him where he was hiding. They brought him back to Jehu, who had him executed. But they gave him burial, for they said, "He was descended from Jehoshaphat who faithfully sought Our God."

Now the house of Ahaziah was left with no one who could rule. ¹⁰ When Athaliah, mother of Ahaziah, learned of his death, she proceeded to kill all the remaining heirs of the house of Judah. ¹¹ But Jehosheba, the daughter of Jehoram of Judah, took Ahaziah's heir Joash and secreted him away from the other children who were about to be murdered, hiding the child and its nurse in a bedroom. In this way Jehosheba, the daughter of Jehoram and wife of Jehoiada, a priest—she was Ahaziah's sister—hid Joash from Athaliah and saved the child's life. ¹² Joash remained hidden with them at the house of God for six years, while Athaliah ruled the country.

23:1 In the seventh year, this Jehoiada took courage and made a pact with the commanders of the units of a hundred. These were Azariah, begot of Jeroham; Ishmael, begot, of Jehohanan; Azariah, begot of Obed; Maaseiah, begot of Adaiah; and Elishaphat, begot of Zichri. ² They traveled throughout Judah and summoned the Levites from all the towns of Judah and the heads of the Israelite families to come together in Jerusalem. ³ The whole assembly made a pact with the ruler in the house of God.

Jehoiada said to them, "Here is the heir of the ruler! He is to be the ruler, as Our God promised of the heirs of David. ⁴ This is what must be done: one third of you priests and Levites, when you come to serve on the Sabbath, are to guard at the threshold gates, ⁵ a second third are to be at the residence of the ruler, and the last third are to be at the Foundation Gate. All the people are to be in the courts of the house of Our God. ⁶ No one is to enter the house of Our God except the priests and the Levites on duty. They may enter for they are consecrated. But all the people are to observe the prescription of Our God. ⁷ The Levites will place themselves around the ruler, each with weapons in hand. Anyone who attempts to enter the house of Our God is to be killed. You must escort the ruler as he comes or goes."

⁸ The Levites and all the Judeans did as Jehoiada the priest had ordered. Each leader brought their coterie, both those coming on duty on the sabbath and those going off, for Jehoiada the priest had been adamant in his orders. ⁹ Then Jehoiada brought out the spears that had been David's, and

the shields, large and small, which were stored in the house of Our God
¹⁰ and set all the people as guards, each holding a weapon, from the north
end to the south end of the house of Our God, around the altar and around
the building. ¹¹ Then Jehoiada brought out the young heir and crowned
him, giving him a copy of the covenant and proclaiming him the new ruler.
Jehoiada and those assisting him anointed the young sovereign to shouts
of "Long live Joash!"

¹² When Athaliah heard the tumult of the people running and cheering
the ruler, she came into the house of Our God where the people were,
¹³ and found the ruler standing by the pillar at the entrance. The commanders and the trumpeters were at the ruler's side as all the people of
the nation rejoiced and blew horns, and singers with musical instruments
led the rejoicing.

Athaliah tore her garments and screamed, "Treason! Treason!"

¹⁴ Jehoiada had already warned the commanders, "Do not kill her in
the house of Our God." He now told them, "Take her outside. And kill
any of her followers as well." ¹⁵ They grabbed at Athaliah, and she fled
through the gates of the stable yard of the ruler's residence, but there they
caught her and with their swords, made an end of her.

¹⁶ Jehoiada the priest made a covenant between himself and people on
the one hand and the ruler on the other that they should be the people of
the Most High God. ¹⁷ Then the people went to the temple of Baal and tore
it down. They smashed the altars and idols, and killed Mattan the priest of
Baal in front of his altars.

¹⁸ Jehoiada restored the order of responsibility for the house of Our God
among the priests and Levites, according to that which David had originally established. Each was to bring whole offerings to Our God as prescribed in the Law of Moses, with singing and rejoicing, as had been passed
down from David. ¹⁹ He stationed door-keepers at the gates of the house of
Our God to prevent any from entering who were unclean. ²⁰ Then, with the
commanders, the nobles, the governors, and all the people of the land gathering around, they escorted the new ruler down from the house of Our
God. They brought him in procession into the ruler's residence through
the Upper Gate and seated this new ruler on the judgment seat. ²¹ All the
people of the land rejoiced; and the city had peace after the execution of
Athaliah.

24 ¹ Joash was crowned at seven years years of age, and ruled in Jerusalem for forty years. Joash's mother, Zibiah, was from Beersheba. ² The
young ruler did everything that was pleasing in the eyes of Our God

throughout the life of Jehoiada the priest. ³ The priest chose two wives for Joash and they provided the ruler with many children.

⁴ Some time later Joash, having decided to renovate the house of Our God, ⁵ called together the priests and Levites and said to them, "Go without delay through the towns of Judah and collect from all the Israelites the annual tax that is required for the maintenance of the house of Our God."

But the Levites did not act quickly enough. ⁶ The ruler summoned Jehoiada the chief priest, and demanded, "Why have you not required the Levites to gather from Judah and Jerusalem the tax which Moses, the servant of Our God, levied on all of Israel for the Tent of the Testimony?" ⁷ What had happened was that the children of the evil Athaliah had broken into the house of Our God and had taken all of its sacred items for use in the temple of Baal.

⁸ The ruler ordered that a chest be made and placed outside the gate of the house of Our God. ⁹ A proclamation was issued throughout Judah and Jerusalem that the people were to bring to the Most High God the tax which Moses the godly one had imposed on Israel in the wilderness. ¹⁰ So the leaders and the people gladly brought their taxes and filled the chest with them. ¹¹ Whenever the chest was full, the Levites would bring it in to the ruler's officials. The ruler's secretary and the chief priest's deputy would empty it, and the chest would be replaced. They did this day by day, and soon a large amount of money was collected. ¹² Joash and Jehoiada then gave the money to those in charge of the work in the house of God. They in turn hired the masons and carpenters to carry out the renovations, as well as iron workers and coppersmiths. ¹³ The workers carried out their tasks diligently and work moved along splendidly, and in time the house of God was restored to its original design and reinforced. ¹⁴ When the work was done there was money left over, and this they brought to Joash and Jehoiada, and it was used to make vessels for the house of Our God, both for the service and the burnt offerings: saucers and other objects of gold and silver. Throughout the lifetime of Jehoiada, burnt offerings were presented regularly in the house of Our God.

¹⁵ Jehoiada lived a long and full life. He died at the age of one hundred and thirty years, ¹⁶ and was buried with the rulers in the City of David. It was a reward for the good work which he had done for Israel in the service of God.

¹⁷ After the death of Jehoiada, the leading subjects of Judah came to do homage to Joash, who now fell under their influence. ¹⁸ They abandoned the house of Our God, the God of their ancestors, and worshipped sacred pillars and idols.

The rage of Our God turned on Judah and Jerusalem because of what they had done. [19] The Almighty sent prophets to call them back to the one true God, but the prophets were ignored and their words fell on deaf ears. [20] Then the spirit of Our God came to Zechariah, begot of Jehoiada, the priest. Zechariah stood up before the people and said, "This is the Word of Our God: Why do you disobey the commands of Our God and bring yourselves nothing but grief? You have abandoned Our God; now the Almighty will abandon you."

[21] But they conspired against the prophet, and by the ruler's own command, they stoned Zechariah to death in the court of the house of Our God: [22] Joash, forgetting the kindness and loyalty which Jehoiada had shown, murdered his heir. Zechariah's dying words were, "May Our God see this and punish you."

[23] At the end of that same year, the Arameans took up arms against Joash. They invaded Judah and Jerusalem, killing all the leaders of the people; they sent all their plunder back to the ruler in Damascus. [24] Though they attacked with only a small force, they overcame a great army, because Judah had abandoned the Most High God, the God of their ancestors. So the Arameans executed God's just punishment upon Joash.

[25] Joash was severely wounded. After the Arameans withdrew, his own servants conspired against Joash to avenge the death of Zechariah, the heir of Jehoiada the priest; and they killed him in his bed. Joash was buried in the city of David, but not in the tombs of the rulers. [26] The conspirators were Zabad, begot of Shimeath, an Ammonite woman, and Jehozabad, begot of Shimrith, a Moabite woman.

[27] The account of Joash's heirs, the many prophecies against him, and the account of the restoration of the house of God are recorded in the books of the Rulers. Joash was succeeded by his heir, Amaziah.

℞   ℞   ℞

25[1] Amaziah was twenty-five years old when he ascended the throne; he reigned in Jerusalem for twenty-nine years. Amaziah's mother was Jehoaddan, from Jerusalem. [2] The ruler did everything that was pleasing in the eyes of Our God, though not wholeheartedly. [3] Once the realm was well in control, Amaziah executed those who assassinated Joash, the former ruler. [4] But Amaziah spared their children, in obedience to what is written in the Law, in the Book of Moses: "Parents are not to be put to death for their children, nor children for their parents; each may be put to death only for their own sins."

[5] Amaziah assembled all the Judeans and ordered them by their ancestral families, with commanders of the thousands and the hundreds for all

Judah and Benjamin. The ruler drafted those twenty years old and older, and found there were 300,000 eligible for military service, able to handle spear and shield. ⁶ Amaziah also hired 100,000 warriors from Israel, which cost nearly four tons of silver.

⁷ But a holy person came to the ruler and said, "O ruler, the Israelite troops must not march with you, Our God is not with Israel, not with any Ephraimites! ⁸ Let Judah go alone; be decisive and fight courageously, or the Most High God will bring you down before the enemy. God has the power to give you victory or bring you down in defeat."

⁹ Amaziah said to the holy person, "But what about the four tons of silver I already paid to the Israelite army?"

The holy person replied, "God can give you more that that."

¹⁰ So Amaziah sent home the fighters who had come from Ephraim, but they were insulted; they were furious with Judah, and went home in a rage.

¹¹ Finding courage in this exchange, Amaziah led the army out into the Valley of Salt, where they killed 10,000 troops of Seir. ¹² The Judeans captured another 10,000, who they threw from the top a cliff; they were all dashed to pieces. ¹³ Meanwhile the hired warriors who were sent home having no part in this battle raided the towns of Judah all the way from Samaria to Beth-horon. They killed 3,000 people and carried off great quantities of plunder.

¹⁴ Amaziah, returning triumphant over the Edomites, brought with him the gods of the people of Seir. They set them up and worshipped them, and made burnt offerings. The Most High God was enraged with Amaziah for this, and sent a prophet who said, "Why do you worship these gods who could not save their own people from your hands?"

¹⁶ Amaziah interrupted him, asking, "Have we appointed you to be counselor to the ruler? Silence! Do you know that you risk your life?"

The prophet did stop, but not without these words: "I know that God has determined to destroy you, because you did this thing, and now will not hear what I say."

¹⁷ Amaziah of Judah, taking counsel, sent emissaries to Jehoash, begot of Jehoahaz, begot of Jehu, the ruler of Israel, issuing a challenge. ¹⁸ Jehoash of Israel replied to Amaziah of Judah: "The thistle of Lebanon sent a message to a cedar in Lebanon saying, 'Give your daughter in marriage to my heir.' But a wild beast in Lebanon trampled the thistle as it passed. You say to yourself, 'I have defeated Edom.' It makes you arrogant and full of pride. I say, 'Stay at home!' Why go looking for trouble and bring ruin upon yourself, and on Judah as well?"

¹⁹ Amaziah, however, would not hear him, for God had determined that Judah should fall to Israel for worshipping the gods of Edom. ²¹ So Jehoash of Israel marched out against them, and they met at Beth-shemesh in Judah. ²² The Judeans were routed by the Israelites, and the troops fled. ²³ Jehoash of Israel captured Amaziah of Judah, begot of Joash, begot of Jehoahaz, at Beth-shemesh. Jehoash brought Amaziah back to Jerusalem, where he demolished the city walls from the Gate of Ephraim to the Corner Gate, a distance of four hundred cubits. ²⁴ Jehoash took all the gold and silver and all the vessels found in the house of God that had been in the care of Obed-edom, as well as the treasures of the royal residence. He then returned to Samaria, taking the hostages with him.

²⁵ Amaziah begot of Joash, ruler of Judah, outlived Jehoash begot of Jehoahaz, ruler of Israel by fifteen years. ²⁶ The rest of the history Amaziah's life, from first to last, is to be found in the books of the Rulers of Judah and Israel. ²⁷ From the time Amaziah rejected the Most High God, there was plotting against him in Jerusalem. Eventually he fled to Lachish, but he was followed there and assassinated. ²⁷ His body was returned to Jerusalem tied on the back of a horse, and he was buried with his ancestors in the city of David.

ଓ ଓ ଓ

26:1 All the people of Judah choose the sixteen-year-old heir, Uzziah, to succeed Amaziah. ² It was Uzziah who rebuilt the city of Elath, which was restored to Judah after the death of Amaziah .

³ Uzziah, who was sixteen when he took the throne, reigned for fifty-two years. Uzziah's mother was Jecoliah from Jerusalem. ⁴ Uzziah did what was right in the eyes of Our God, just as Amaziah did in his early years, ⁵ and sought the counsel of the Most High God diring the lifetime of Zechariah. Zechariah instructed the ruler in the fear of Our God, ⁵ and as long as Uzziah sought God's counsel, God gave him prosperity.

⁶ Uzziah went to war against the Philistines and broke down the walls of Gath, Jabnet, and Ashdod, and built towns in the region of Ashdod and among the Philistines. ⁷ God helped Uzziah against the Philistines, as well as against the Arabs who lived in Gur-baal, and against the Muenites. ⁸ The Ammonites paid tribute to the ruler, and Uzziah's fame spread to the area of Egypt, and Uzziah grew very powerful.

⁹ The ruler built towers in Jerusalem at the Corner Gate, at the Valley Gate, and at the escarpment, and fortified them. ¹⁰ He built other towers in the wilderness, and cisterns for the large cattle herds both in the foothills

and on the plain. Uzziah established farmers and vinedressers in the hill country and in the fertile lands, for he loved the earth.

¹¹ Uzziah kept a standing army ready to campaign. It was organized in divisions as described by the scribe Jeiel and Maasiah the registrar, under the supervision of Hananiah, one of Uzziah's commanders. ¹² The total number of commanders from the heads of the ancestral families was 2,600. ¹³ Under them was a corps of 307,500 soldiers. It was a highly trained force, well prepared to support the ruler against any enemy. ¹⁴ Uzziah provided them with shields, spears, helmets, armor, bows and slings. ¹⁵ In Jerusalem, Uzziah had built engines of war, mounted on the towers and on the corner defenses, which were designed by engineers not only to hurl large stones, but to shoot arrows as well. The ruler's fame spread wide and far, for Uzziah was especially gifted as well as very powerful.

¹⁶ But when Uzziah became powerful, his pride became even greater, and this led to his downfall. He offended the Most High God by entering the Temple of Our God to burn incense on the incense altar. ¹⁷ Azariah the priest, with eighty other courageous priests, followed Uzziah ¹⁸ and confronted him, saying, "It is not for you, Uzziah, to burn incense to Our God, but for the Aaronite priests who have been consecrated for this office. Leave the sanctuary: you have been unfaithful, and you will not be honored by the Most High God." ¹⁹ The ruler, holding a censer and about to burn incense, was enraged. And while he was raging at the priests, standing at the incense altar in the house of Our God, he broke out with leprosy on his forehead as they watched.

²⁰ While Azariah, the chief priest, and the other priests stared at Uzziah, they saw his forehead turning leprous. They rushed the ruler out of the house of Our God, and he no longer opposed them, for he was struck by Our God with disease. ²¹ Uzziah the ruler remained a leper until the day he died. He lived in the royal residence as a leper, relieved of his duties and excluded from the house of Our God. His heir Jotham supervised the household and served as regent.

²² All of the details of Uzziah's reign, from first to last, are recorded by the prophet Isaiah, begot of Amoz. ²³ Uzziah went to sleep with his ancestors and was buried, not with them, but in a field adjoining the royal tombs, for they said, "Uzziah is a leper."

The heir Jotham succeeded Uzziah.

☙ ☙ ☙

27:1 Jothan, the twenty-five year old heir, assumed the judgment seat and reigned for sixteen years. Jothan's mother was Jerushah, daughter of

Zadok. [2] Jothan did what right in the eyes of Our God, as Uzziah did, but unlike Uzziah, Jothan did not enter the Temple of Our God. But the people continued their ways of corruption. [3] The ruler rebuilt the upper Gate of the house of Our God and did considerable construction work on the wall at Ophel Hill. [4] He also built cities on the Judean hills and forts and towers on the wooded hills.

[5] Jothan went to war against the ruler of the Ammonite and was victorious. He extracted from the Ammonites tribute of nearly four tons of silver, 62,000 bushels of wheat, and 62,000 bushels of barley, and required of them the same in the second year, and the third. [6] Jothan grew strong, living a life that was resolutely obedient before the Most High God.

[7] The rest of the life of the ruler, the wars and policies, are recorded in the books of the Rulers of Israel and Judah. [8] The ruler assumed the throne at the age of twenty-five and reigned in Jerusalem sixteen years. [9] Jothan went to sleep with his ancestors and was buried in the city of David, and was succeeded by his heir, Ahaz.

*a*haz, who was twenty years old when he assumed the throne, reigned in Jerusalem for sixteen years. The ruler did not do what was right in the eyes of Our God like his ancestor David, but followed rather in the footsteps of the rulers of Israel. Ahaz cast idols for worshiping the Baals, [3] and made burnt offerings in the Valley of Ben-hinnom. He made his heirs pass through fire in the tradition of the abominable nations whom the Most High God dispossessed in favor of the Israelites. [4] The ruler offered sacrifices and incense on the hilltops and under every spreading tree.

[5] The Most High his God delivered Ahaz into the hands of the ruler of Aram. The Arameans defeated Ahaz, taking great numbers of captives, whom they carried off to Damascus. Ahaz suffered similarly at the hands of the ruler of Israel—a defeat with huge casualties. [6] The victorious ruler, Pekah, begot of Remallah, killed 120,000 Judeans in one day. These were seasoned troops, but they had abandoned the Most High, the God of their ancestors. [7] Zichri, an Ephraimite warrior, killed Maaseiah, Ahaz's heir; Azrikam, the administrator of the royal residence; and Elhanah, the ruler's second-in-command. [8] The Israelites captured 200,000 Judean women and children, and took vast plunder back to Samaria.

[9] In Samaria was a prophet of God named Obed. Obed went out to meet the army returning to Samaria, saying to them, "You are victorious because

the Sovereign One, the God of your ancestors, was angry with Judah. But the rage of your massacre towers up to heaven. [10] And now do you propose to reduce these Judeans, women and children, to slavery? Aren't you also guilty of sins against Our Most High God? [11] Listen to me! Send back these women and children you have carried away from your sisters and brothers. God's burning anger hangs over you."

[13] Some of the Ephraimite leaders—Azariah, begot of Jehohanan, Berechiah, begot of Meshillemoth, Hezekiah, begot of Shallum, and Amasa, begot of Hadlai—met the victorious warriors in protest, [13] and said to them, "Don't bring these women and children into our country, it will only add to our sins and our guilt. We have guilt enough as it is, for God's anger is a fierce anger." [14] So the fighters turned over the captives and spoils to the officials and the whole assembly. [15] The captives were placed in the care of members of the community chosen by the assembly, who found clothing from among the spoils for the naked captives. They clothed them and gave them shoes, and food and drink, and anointed them. Those who were old or weak were put on donkeys, and then all were taken to their kin in Jericho, the city of palm trees. Then they returned to Samaria.

[16] It was at this time that Ahaz of Judah sent to the ruler of Assyria for help. [17] The Edomites had attacked and defeated Judah once again and carried off prisoners. [18] The Philistines had raided towns in the foothills and in the Negev of Judah, capturing and occupying the cities of Bethshemesh, Aijalon, and Gederoth, Soco, Timnah, and Gimzo with their outlying villages. [19] Our God had broken Judah to subjection because of Ahaz of Judah; for Ahaz had behaved without restraint in Judah, and had been utterly faithless to God. [20] But Tiglath-pileser, the ruler of Assyria, came to Ahaz not in aid but to oppress him further. [21] Ahaz stripped the house of Our God, the royal residence, and the houses of the officials to gather tribute for Tiglath-pileser—but little good it did him in the end. [22] The more Ahaz was pressed, the more faithless he became. [23] He made burnt offerings to the gods of the Damascenes who had defeated him, reasoning, "The gods of the rulers of Aram helped them. If I sacrifice to them, they will help me." But they brought only downfall, for Ahaz and for the entire nation.

[24] Then Ahaz gathered up the furnishings of the house of God, broke them up, and locked the doors of the house of Our God. He set up altars on every street corner of Jerusalem, [5] and set up sacred mounds in every town of Judah to make burnt offerings to various gods. He provoked the anger of the Most High God, the God of his ancestors.

[26] Other doings, and all the events of the reign of Ahaz, from the beginning to the end, are recorded in the books of the Rulers of Judah and Israel. [27] Ahaz went to sleep with his ancestors and was buried in the city of Jerusa-

lem, but not with the other rulers of Judah. Ahaz was succeeded by his heir Hezekiah.

⁍ ⁍ ⁍

29:1 Hezekiah, who was twenty-five years old upon assuming the judgment seat, reigned in Jerusalem for twenty-nine years. Hezekiah's mother was Abijah, daughter of Zechariah. 2 Hezekiah did what was right in the eyes of Our God, doing as David his ancestor had done.

3 In the first month of the first year of his reign, Hezekiah repaired the doors of the house of Our God. 4 The ruler summoned the priests and the Levites and assembled them in the square on the east side 5 to address them: "Listen to me, you Levites! Consecrate yourselves now and consecrate the house of Our God, the God of our ancestors. Remove the filth in the sanctuary. 6 For our predecessors did what was wrong in the eyes of Our God. They abandoned Our God, they turned their faces away from the place that Our God called home. They turned their backs on our Creator. 7 They shut the doors of the vestibule and extinguished the lamps; they offered no incense and no burnt offerings in the sanctuary to the God of Israel. 8 So the wrath of the Most High God has fallen on Judah and Jerusalem. God has made us an object of wondrous derision, as you can see for yourselves. 9 This is why our soldiers fell by the sword, why our daughters, sons and spouses are now held captives. 10 I now intend to make a covenant with Our God, the God of Israel, so that God's fierce anger will turn from us. 11 No more negligence, my compeers, for the Sovereign One has chosen you to serve and to stand in the divine presence, to offer incense and burnt offerings."

12 The Levites set to work. Among them were, from the family of Kohath, Mathan begot of Amasai, and Joel begot of Azariah; from the family of Merari, Kish begot of Abdi, and Azariah begot of Jehallelel; from the family of Gershon, Joah begot of Zimmah, and Eden begot of Joah; 13 from the family of Elizaphan, Shimri and Jeiel; from the family of Asaph, Zechariah and Mattaniah; 14 from the family of Heman, Jehiel and Shimei; and from the family of Jeduthun, Shemaniah and Uzziel. 15 They assembled their relatives and consecrated themselves. 16 Then they entered the house of Our God to consecrate it. They moved all that had been defiled from the temple into the courtyard, and then carried it out to the Kidron Valley. 17 They began their work of sanctification on the first day of the first month, and they entered the Vestibule on the eighth day of the month. They took eight more days to sanctify the house of Our God, and on the sixteenth day of the first month they were done.

¹⁸ Then they said to Hezekaih the ruler, "We have purified the entire house of Our God, the altar of burnt offerings and its utensils, the table that holds the consecrated bread, and all its utensils. ¹⁹ We have cleaned and consecrated all the items which Ahaz the ruler removed during the time of his apostasy. They are now in place before the altar of Our God."

²⁰ Early the next morning, Hezekiah assembled the officials of the city and went up to the house of Our God. ²¹ They brought seven bulls, seven rams and seven lambs as a sin offering for the realm, for the sanctuary and for Judah. The ruler ordered the priests, descendants of Aaron, to offer these on the altar of Our God. ²² When the bulls were slaughtered, the priests took the blood and threw it against the altar. The rams were slaughtered and their blood was thrown at the altar. The lambs were slaughtered and their blood was thrown against the altar. ²³ The goats for the sin offering were brought before the ruler and the assembly, who laid their hands on them. ²⁴ The priests slaughtered them and presented their blood on the altar as a sin offering to atone for all Israel. It was Hezekiah's command that the burnt offerings and the sin offerings were made were for all of Israel.

²⁵ Hezekiah positioned the Levites in the house of Our God with cymbals, harps and lyres, in accordance with the regulations of David, of Gad the ruler's seer and Nathan the prophet. This rule had come from God, down through the prophets. ²⁶ The Levites stood with the instruments of David and the priests with the trumpets. ²⁷ Then Hezekiah gave the order to sacrifice the burnt offering on the altar, and when the offering began, the singing to Our God began as well, accompanied by the horns and the instruments of David, ruler of Israel. ²⁸ The assembly prostrated itself in worship; the singers sang; the trumpeters played; all this was done until the burnt offering was consumed. ²⁹ When the offering had been consumed, the ruler and the assembly fell to their knees and worshipped. ³⁰ Hezekiah and the officials told the Levites to sing the praises of Our God in the words of David and of Asaph the seer. They praised the Almighty with joy and bowed their heads in worship.

³¹ Hezekiah said, "Now that you have dedicated yourselves to Our God, come forward with your sacrifice and your offerings of thanksgiving to the house of Our God. The assembly came forward with their sacrifices and thank offerings. Those of a willing spirit brought burnt offerings. ³² The number of burnt offerings brought forward by the assembly was 70 bulls, 100 rams, 200 lambs. All these were burnt offerings made to Our God. ³³ The number of consecrated burnt offerings were 600 bulls and 3,000 sheep and goats. ³⁴ However, there too few priests to skin the burnt offerings, so the Levites helped them until the work was finished and the priests had

consecrated themselves—for the Levites were more conscientious about consecrating themselves than the priests had been. ³⁵ Burnt offerings were in abundance as well as the fatty parts of the burnt offering and the drink offerings of the burnt offerings. And so the ministry of the house of Our God was restored. Hezekiah and all the people rejoiced over what God re-established for the people—and the suddeness with which it come about.

30¹ Hezekiah sent word to all Israel and Judah and also wrote letters to Ephraim and Manasseh, inviting them to come to the house of Our God to celebrate the Passover of Our God, the God of Israel. ² The ruler, the officials and the whole assembly in Jerusalem had agreed to celebrate Passover in the second month— ³ they were not able to keep it in its proper time, because not enough of the priests had not consecrated themselves, and the people had not assembled in Jerusalem. ⁴ This arrangement was agreed upon, ⁵ and a proclamation was published throughout Israel, from Beersheba to Dan, calling the people to come to Jerusalem to celebrate the Passover of Our God, the God of Israel.

Never before had so many celebrated Passover in the prescribed manner. ⁶ Messengers went throughout Israel and Judah with letters from Hezekiah and his officials which said, "Women and men of Israel, return to Our God, the God of Sarah and Abraham, Rebecca and Isaac, and Leah, Rachel and Jacob, that the Most High God may again be present to the remnant of you who have escaped from the hands of Assyria. ⁷ Do not be like your ancestors and your families who refused to be faithful to the God of their mothers and fathers until God made them an object of horror, as you have seen. ⁸ Do not be stubborn like those before you. Give yourselves to Our God and come to God's eternally consecrated sanctuary. Serve the Most High, so that the divine fire of anger will be abated. ⁹ When you return to Our God, your relatives and your children will receive mercy from their captors and will return to their homeland. The Almighty is gracious and merciful, and will not turn away from you if you return again to enter the divine presence."

¹⁰ The messengers went from city to city thoroughout the land of Manasseh and the land of Ephraim, as far as Zabulun, but they were greeted with scorn and ridicule. ¹¹ Only a few of people of Asher, Manasseh, and Zabulun humbled themselves to come to Jerusalem.

¹² But in Judah, on the other hand, the power of God moved the Judeans as one to obey what Hezekiah and the officials had decreed, and so to follow the word of Our God. ¹³ A throng of people streamed into Jerusalem to celebrate the Festival of Unleavened Bread in the second month. ¹⁴ They began by removing the foreign altars in Jerusalem and all the altars for

burning incense and threw them into the Kidron Valley. ¹⁵ They slaughtered the Passover lamb on the fourteenth day of the second month. The priests and the Levites were humbled; they consecrated themselves so that they could bring burnt offerings into the house of Our God. ¹⁶ They took up their proper places as decreed in the Law of Moses, the godly one, and the priests threw the blood on the altar that was handed to them by the Levites. ¹⁷ Because many in the crowd had not consecrated themselves, the Levites had to slaughter Passover lambs for all who were unclean so that the Passover feast would be consecrated to God. ¹⁸ Many of the people, especially those from Ephraim, Manasseh, Issachar, and Zebulun, had not purified themselves; and yet they ate the Passover feast despite the usual proscriptions, for Hezekiah prayed for them, "May Our God, who is good, pardon those ¹⁹ who seek God wholeheartedly, the God of our ancestors, even if they have not kept the rules of purification of the sanctuary."

²⁰ Our God listen to Hezekiah's prayer, and the people were healed.

²¹ The Israelites who had gathered in Jerusalem celebrated the Feast of Unleavened Bread for seven days with great rejoicing, and the Levites and the priests praised Our God through each day. ²² Hezekiah encouraged all the Levites who showed good understanding of the service of Our God. So the people ate the food of the festival for seven days, offering sacrifices of well-being and of thanks to the Most High God, the God of their ancestors. ²³ Then the whole assembly agreed to keep the festival for another week, and they did with a joyful spirit. ²⁴ For Hezekiah of Judah provided for them 1,000 bulls and 7,000 sheep; and the officials provided another 1,000 bulls and 10,000 sheep; and the priests consecrated themselves in great numbers. ²⁵ The whole assembly of Judah rejoiced, with their priests and Levites; and those who had come out of Israel, together with devout Gentiles and foreigners living in Israel as well as those living in Judah.

²⁶ Jerusalem was a city of joy; since the time of Solomon, begot of David, ruler of Israel, there had been nothing like this. ²⁷ Finally the priests and Levites stood to bless the people; and their voices were heard; their prayers reached God's holy dwelling in heaven.

31 ¹ When the festival ended the Israelites present went out to the towns and cities of Judah, smashing the sacred pillars and cutting down the Asherah groves. They tore down the sacred mounds and altars throughout all Judah and Benjamin, as well as in Ephraim and Manasseh. When all were destroyed, the Israelites returned to their own towns and homesteads.

² Hezekiah installed the priests, group by group, assigning the priests and Levites their duties—for burnt offerings or peace offerings, to serve or

to give thanks or to chant praise at the gates of the house of Our God.
³ Hezekiah set aside a portion of his own wealth for the morning and evening sacrifices, the sabbaths, the new moons and the solemn feasts, as was required by the Law of Our God. ⁴ The ruler required that the citizens of Jerusalem give their due share to the priests and Levites, so that they would be able to devote themselves entirely to the Law of Our God. ⁵ Once Hezekiah issued this order, the Israelites contributed generously from their first fruits of their grain, new wine, oil and honey, and all the produce of the land. They gave a full tithe of everything. ⁶ The Israelites and Judeans dwelling in the towns of Judah also gave a tenth of their cattle and sheep, and a tenth of all their crops as offerings dedicated to the Most High God. They stacked the crops that were offerings in mounds. ⁷ They began to build these mounds in the third month and finished in the seventh month.

⁸ When Hezekiah and the officials saw the mounds of crops they praised God and God's people Israel. ⁹ The ruler questioned the priests and the Levites about the mounds, ¹⁰ and Azariah the chief priest, from the family of Zadok, replied, "From the time the people started to bring in their donation to the house of Our God, they have had plenty to eat and plenty to spare. For Our God has blessed them. These piles are the leftovers!"

¹¹ Hezekiah ordered that storerooms be prepared in the house of Our God. When they were ready ¹² the people faithfully brought in their contributions, their tithes, and their dedicated gifts.

Conaniah the Levite was the overseer. His brother, Shimei, was the deputy. ¹³ Jehiel, Azaziah, Nahath, Asahel, Jerimoth, Jozabad, Eliel, Ismachiah, Mahath and Benaiah were selected by Hezekiah and Azariah, the primary overseer of the house of Our God, to assist Conaniah and his brother Shimei. ¹⁴ Kore, begot of Imnah the Levite—the keeper of the east gate—was in charge of the freewill offerings, and apportioned the most holy offerings made to Our God. ¹⁵ Eden, Miniamin, Jeshua, Shemaiah, Amariah and Shecaniah faithfully assisted Kore in the towns of the priests by distributing to their kindred, young and old alike, by their priestly divisions. ¹⁶ Over and above this, they distributed to males three years and older whose names were listed in the genealogical records—the ones who would one day enter the house of Our God to participate in the daily service according to their division, as their office required.

¹⁷ The priests were registered in the genealogy by families. The Levites twenty years and older were registered by their office in their divisions. ¹⁸ The priests were registered with all their dependants: their wives, their daughters, their sons, the whole company of them. They had to keep themselves consecrated because of their permanent status. ¹⁹ As for those priests, begot of Aaron, living in the farmlands and in the villages, there were those

designed by name to distribute to every male among the priests and to everyone among the Levites who was registered.

²⁰ Hezekiah, who did what was good and right and faithful in the eyes of the Most High his God, set up this system throughout Judah. ²¹ Whatever the ruler did in the service of the house of God, and in accordance with the Law and the commandments, was carried out wholeheartedly in the name of God. And Hezekaih prospered.

ભ ભ ભ

32·¹ After these events and these acts of faithfulness, Sennacherib, ruler of Assyria, invaded Judah. He besieged the fortified cities with the intent to take them for his own. ² When Hezekiah realized that Sennacherib was intent upon capturing Jerusalem, ³ he consulted with officials and officers about the possibility blocking the springs outside the city. They supported the idea. ⁴ They gathered a large body of people who went out and blocked all the springs and streams flowing through the area. "Why should the Assyrian ruler find plenty of water here," they said. ⁵ Then Hezekiah worked to strengthen the defenses: the broken parts of the wall were repaired, towers were built on it and a second wall outside the first. He strengthened the Millo—a weak point in the original city, the "City of David"—and store up quantity of weapons and shields.

⁶ The ruler appointed military commanders over the people, assembled them in the square by the city gate, and exhorted them saying, ⁷ "Be brave! Be strong! Be fearless! Don't panic when Sennacherib and his army appear on the horizon. We have much more than they do. ⁸ The Assyrians only have arms of flesh at their sides, but we have the Most High God at our side to fight our battles." All the people were encouraged by the words of Hezekiah the ruler of Judah.

⁹ Meanwhile, Sennacherib of Assyria and his high command were camped at Lachish. Sennacherib sent envoys to Jerusalem with a message to Hezekiah of Judea, and to all the Judeans, saying, ¹⁰ "These are the words of Sennacherib, the ruler of Assyria: What gives you the confidence to remain in Jerusalem while it is beseiged? ¹¹ When Hezekiah says, 'The Most High God will save us from Sennacherib,' you are being duped by your ruler. You will all die of hunger and thirst. ¹² Didn't Hezekiah tear down the shrines and altars and tell you, the people of Judah and Israel, that you must worship at one altar only and make your offerings on it? ¹³ Don't you know what I, and my ancestors, have done to the people of other nations? Did the gods of other countries save their lands for them? ¹⁴ Not one of the gods of these nations, which my ancestors destroyed, was able to save their

people from me. Can your god save you? ¹⁵ How, then, can you let Hezekiah dupe you like this? How can you trust in your ruler, for no god of any nation has been able to save its people from me or my ancestors. And far less will your god save you!"

¹⁶ Sennacherib's envoys carried on in this vein, ranting ever more against the Most High God and God's servant Hezekiah. ¹⁷ Sennacherib wrote yet another letter insulting the Almighty: "If the gods of other nations could not save their people from me, neither can your Hezekiah's God save your people from me." ¹⁸ The envoys shouted these things loudly in Hebrew at the people on the walls in an attempt to frighten them—hoping that this would make capturing the city easy for them. ¹⁹ They spoke as though the God of Jerusalem was like the gods of other peoples of the world—something made by human hands.

²⁰ Then Hezekiah, the ruler, and Isaiah the prophet, begot of Amos, cried out to heaven in prayer, ²⁰ and Almighty God sent an angel who cut down every warrior and commander and officer in the camp of the ruler of Assyria. Sennacherib returned home in disgrace, and when he entered the Assyrian temple there, some of his own children were cut down with swords.

²² And so Our God saved Hezekiah and the people of Jerusalem from the tyranny of Sennacherib, ruler of Assyria, and from all their enemies. Peace reigned on every side. ²³ Many brought offerings to Our God in Jerusalem and expensive gifts to Hezekiah, ruler of Judah. And from that time on Hezekiah was regarded with high esteem by all nations.

²⁴ In those days Hezekiah fell mortally ill. The ruler prayed to God, who said, "I will heal you," and gave him a miraculous sign.* ²⁵ But, being proud, the ruler was not grateful for this kindness; so the wrath of God came upon Hezekiah, and on Jerusalem and Judah. ²⁶ Then the ruler repented of his pride and submitted, as did the people of Jerusalem, and God's wrath never fell on them again in Hezekiah's time.

²⁷ Hezekiah, growing in wealth and honors, built treasuries for silver, gold, precious stones, spices, shields and various costly items. ²⁸ There were storehouses for the grain harvest, oil and new wine; and stalls for all breeds of cattle as well as flocks of sheep. ²⁹ The ruler built villages and amassed huge flocks and herds, and God gave him vast possessions. ³⁰ It was Hezekiah who blocked the upper outlet of the waters of Gihon, directing

---

* This is the sign described in 2 Kings 20, in which the sun's shadow reverses direction. News of the phenomenon was apparently widespread enough that it caused envoys to be sent from Babylon, verse 31, to inquire about it. Their visit reawakened Hezekiah's arrogance and ingratitude, which provoked God's rejection.

them down and to the west of the city of David. Indeed, he excelled in every endeavor he attempted.

³¹ It happened that the ruler of Babylon sent envoys to Hezekiah to ask about the miraculous sign that had been heard of in the country; after their visit, God abandoned him. God's deserting Hezekiah, as it happened, was a test, and a means of discovering the secrets of his heart.

³² The rest of the events of Hezekiah's reign and his good works are recorded in the prophecies of Isaiah, begot of Amos, in the books of the Rulers of Judah and Israel. ³³ Hezekiah went to sleep with his ancestors and was buried on the slope leading the graves of the descendants of David. All of Judah and people of Jerusalem honored the ruler.

Hezekiah was succeeded by his heir, Manasseh.

ର ର ର

33^{:1} Manasseh, who was twelve years old at the time of his acension to the throne, reigned for fifty-five years. ² Manasseh did not do what was right in the eyes of Our God, in that he took up the abominable practices of the peoples whom Our God had dispossessed in favor of the Israelites. ³ Manasseh rebuilt the altars which Hezekiah had destroyed, and set up altars to the Baals, made Asherah groves and worshipped all the heavenly bodies. ⁴ He built altars in the house of Our God, the very place in which the Most High God had said, "My Name will live forever in Jerusalem." ⁵ Manasseh built altars for the heavenly bodies in both courts of the house of Our God; ⁶ and made his heirs pass through the fires in the valley of Benhinnom. He practiced soothsaying, divination and sorcery, and consulted mediums and spritists.

The ruler was evil in the sight of Our God and provoked God's wrath. Manasseh commissioned a carving of an idol, and set it up in the house of Our God—the very house of which God had said to David and Solomon, "In this house and in Jerusalem, the city I chose out of all the tribes of Israel, I will give my Name for all time. I will never again depossess Israel of the land I gave their ancestors—so long as they carefully observe all that I commanded through Moses, all the law, the statutes and the rules." ⁹ But Manasseh led Judah and the inhabitants of Jerusalem astray, until they gave rise to more evil than the nations—which God had destroyed in front of the Israelites—had ever done.

¹⁰ Our God spoke to Manasseh and the people, but when they would not hear hear, ¹¹ Our God brought against them the commanders of the army of Assyria. They captured Manasseh, put him in shackles, and took him to Babylon.

¹² Manasseh, in his wretched state, begged for God's favor and humbled himself before God and his ancestors. ¹³ God listened to Manasseh's petitions, and accepting his supplication, brought the ruler back to Jerusalem and to the judgment seat. Then Manasseh knew that the Most High was in fact the true God.

¹⁴ After this, the ruler built an outer wall for the city of David west of Gihon, in the valley, out as far as the Fish Gate. It enclosed Ophel and rose to a great height. He also installed commanders in all the fortified cities of Judah. ¹⁵ Manasseh removed the foreign gods, and the sculptures which he had commissioned, from the house of Our God. He also removed the altars set up on the mountain of the house of Our God and threw them out of the city. ¹⁶ The ruler repaired the altar of Our God and sacrificed peace offerings and thank offerings on it; and ordered the Judeans to serve the Most High, the God of Israel. ¹⁷ The people still sacrificed at the sacred mounds, but now only to the Most High, the God of Israel.

¹⁸ The rest of the acts of Manasseh, the prayers to God, and the words of the seers who spoke to the ruler in the name of Our God, the God of Israel, are recorded in the books of the Rulers of Israel. ¹⁹ Manasseh's prayer and God's answering of it, all the sins of unfaithfulness, and the places where, before his conversion, the ruler built shrines, created Asherah groves, and carved idols, are recorded in the Chronicles of the Seers.

²⁰ Manasseh went to sleep with his ancestors and was buried in the family's garden tomb.

Manasseh's heir Amon succeeded him to the judgment seat.

²¹ Amon, who was twenty-two years old at the time of Manasseh's death, reigned in Jerusalem for two years. ²² The ruler did not do what was right in the eyes of Our God, following in Manasseh's earlier ways. Amon worshipped and made sacrifice to the images that Manasseh made. ²³ Amon did not repent before the Most High God as Manasseh had, for his guilt was much greater. ²⁴ Amon was assasinated in the royal residence in a conspiracy among his officials. ²⁵ But the people of the land killed the conspirators and made Josiah, Amon's heir, their new ruler.

CR   CR   CR

34¹ Josiah was eight years old when he succeeded Amon to the throne. He reigned in Jerusalem for thirty-one years. ² Josiah did what was right in the eyes of Our God, following in the footsteps of David his ancestor, deviating neither to the right nor to the left. ³ After eight years on the throne, while still a youth, the ruler sought guidance from the God of his ancestor David.

And in the twelfth year of his reign Josiah began to purge Judah of its shrines and Asherah groves, the carved idols and the cast idols. ⁴ The ruler watched as the workers pulled down the altars of the Baals, as well as the incense altars which stood above the altars. They smashed the Asherah groves, the idols and the graven images, ground them into dust, then scattered the dust on the graves of those who had sacrificed to them. ⁵ Josiah burned the bones of their priests on their altars and purged Judah and Jerusalem. ⁶ He did the same in the towns of Manasseh, Ephraim and Simeon, and as far as Naphtali, and in the ruins beyond. ⁷ Josiah demolished the shrines and the Asherah groves, ground the idols into powder, and tore down the incense altars throughout the land of Israel. Then the ruler returned to Jerusalem.*

⁸ In the eighteenth year of his reign, Josiah felt the need to purify the land and the house of Our God. He delegated Shaphan, begot of Azaliah, and Maaseiah, the governor of the city, as well as Joah, begot of Hoahaz, his secretary, to see to the repair of the house of Our God. ⁹ They delivered to the high priest Hilkiah money that had been recieved for the house of Our God—money which the Levites who were the doorkeepers had collected from Manasseh, Ephraim, and all of Israel, as well as from Benjamin and from the people of Jerusalem. ¹⁰ This money was given to those who would oversee the work on the house of Our God, for repairs and renovations. ¹¹ They hired carpenters and masons who bought hewn stone and timber for the beams and rafters, because the rulers of Judah had allowed the building to fall deeply into disrepair. ¹² The builders carried out their work faithfully under the supervision of Jahath and Obadiah, Levites of the line of Merari, along with Zechariah and Meshullam, of the family of Kohath. Other Levites, who happened to be skilled musicians, ¹³ supervised the laborers and coordinated the workers of each trade. Some of the Levites served as secretaries, bookkeepers, and doorkeepers.

¹⁴ When they were fetching the money which had been collected for the house of Our God, the high priest Hilkiah stumbled upon a Scroll of the Law which had been given through Moses.** ¹⁵ Hilkiah told Shaphan the secretary, "I have have found the Book of the Law in the house of Our

---

* It is noteworthy that through the reigns of four rulers, the writer emphasizes how the rulers keep tearing down these ancient sacred places—yet they always seem to reappear. Clearly, the people themselves kept coming to rebuild them as soon as the ruler's workers were gone.
** Probably the book of Deuteronomy.

God."

¹⁶ He gave it to Shaphan, who took it to Josiah and reported, "Your officials are carrying on with the work you have given them. ¹⁷ They have taken the money in the house of Our God and given it to the skilled workers and laborers." ¹⁸ Shaphan the secretary told Josiah about the scroll which the priest Hilkiah had given him. He then read it to Josiah.

¹⁹ When the ruler heard what was written in the Book of the Law he tore his clothes in grief. ²⁰ Josiah ordered Hilkiah, Ahikam, begot of Shaphan, Abdon, begot of Micah, Shaphan the secretary, and Asaiah, the ruler's attendant: ²¹ "Go and consult Our God for me, and for all of us who remain in Israel and Judah, about the contents of this book which has been found. Great must be the wrath that Our God pours down upon us because our ancestors did not observe the commands of Our God and do all that is written in this book."

²² Hilkiah and the rest went to Huldah the prophet, wife of Shallum, begot of Tikvah, begot of Hasrah, the keeper of the wardrobe, and consulted her at her home, which was in the Second Quarter in Jerusalem.

²³ "This is the word of the Most High God, the God of Israel," she answered: "Tell the one who sent you to me ²⁴ this is what Our God says: 'I am about to bring on this place and its people disaster—all the curses written in the scroll which was read in the presence of the ruler of Judah. ²⁵ They have forsaken me; made burnt offerings to their gods, provoking my anger with all their idols which they created with their own hands; this is why my wrath will be poured out on this place and will not be quenched.

²⁶ " 'Tell the ruler of Judah who sent you to inquire of Your God that this is what Your God, the God of Israel, says: You have listened to my words ²⁷ and have shown a willing heart. You have humbled yourself before Your God and have heard what I said about this place and its inhabitants. You have humbled yourself and torn your clothes and wept in my presence. Because of this, I have heard you. This is the word of Your God. ²⁸ Because of this, I will gather you to your ancestors, and you will come to your grave in peace. You will not live see all the disaster that I will bring on this place and its inhabitants.' "

They took her answer back to Josiah the ruler.

²⁹ At the ruler's summons, all the elders of Judah and Jerusalem assembled. ³⁰ Josiah went up to the house of Our God with all the people of Judah and the people of Jerusalem, the priests, the Levites—the entire population, high and low. There Josiah read the entire text of the Scroll of the Covenant which had been found in the house of Our God. ³¹ Then, standing by the pillar, the ruler entered into a covenant before the Most High, to obey and keep the commandments, the decrees, the statutes with

heart and soul, and so to carry out the terms of the covenant as they were written in the scroll. ³² He then compelled all who were present to swear by an oath to keep the covenant of God, the God of their ancestors. ³³ Josiah removed all the abominable idols from all the lands of the Israelites, and made everyone who lived in Israel serve the Most High God, their God. As long as Josiah lived, they were steadfast in following the Most High God, the God of their ancestors.

35:1 Josiah celebrated the Passover to Our God in Jerusalem. The Passover lamb was slaughtered on the fourteenth day of the first month. ² The ruler reestablished the priests in their offices and made it possible for them to carry out their duties of the house of Our God. ³ Josiah said to the Levites—who were consecrated to Our God and were responsible for the instruction of all Israel—"Put the sacred Ark in the house that Solomon, begot of David ruler of Israel, built. You are no longer to carry it on your shoulders. You are to serve the Most High God and God's people Israel. ⁴ Prepare yourselves according to your ancestral houses, according to your divisions, following the written instructions of Solomon, begot of David. ⁵ Take up your places in the Holy Place, representing the family groups of the laity with one division of the Levites for each ancestral group. ⁶ Slaughter the Passover lamb, consecrate yourselves, and in the name of your sisters and brothers, prepare yourselves to fulfill the word of Our God as it was commanded through Moses."

⁷ Josiah donated to the people 30,000 lambs and kids from his own flock, and 3,000 bulls, as Passover offerings. ⁸ The officials donated willingly to the people as well as to the priests and the Levites. Hilkiah, Zechariah and Jehiel, the chief officials of the house of God, donated on behalf of the priests 2,600 small livestock plus 500 bulls for the Passover. ⁹ Conaniah, his brothers Shemaiah and Nethanel, and Hashabiah, Jeiel and Jozabad, the Levite chiefs, donated 5,000 small livestock and 500 bulls on behalf of the Levites.

¹⁰ When the services were arranged with the priests in their places and the Levites in their divisions according to the ruler's command, ¹¹ the Levites slaughtered the Passover lambs, and the priests flung the blood against the altar while the Levites skinned the victims. They set aside that which was for the burnt offerings and gave it to the various groups of the families of the people to offer to Our God, as prescribed in the Book of Moses. They did this with the cattle as well. ¹³ Then they roasted the Passover animals over the fire according to custom, and boiled the holy offerings in pots, caldrons and pans, and served them quickly to the people.

¹⁴ After this, they prepared the Passover for themselves and for the priests. The priests, descendants of Aaron, had been busy sacrificing the

burnt offerings and the fatty portions until nightfall; this is why the Levites made the necessary preparations for themselves and for the priests. ¹⁵ The cantors, begot of Asaph, were in their proper places as prescribed by David, as were Asaph, Heman, and the ruler's seer, Jeduthun. The gatekeepers, too, kept their places—for their kin, the Levites, made their preparations for them.

¹⁶ So the service of Our God was carried out that day, to keep the Passover and sacrifice the burnt offerings, as Josiah the ruler directed. ¹⁷ The Israelites present celebrated the Passover at that time, followed by the pilgrim feast of Unleavened Bread for the next seven days. ¹⁸ Passover had not been celebrated like this in Israel since the days of Samuel the prophet. None of the rulers of Israel had ever celebrated such a Passover as Josiah did—with priests and with the Levites and with all the inhabitants of Israel and Judah, and with the inhabitants of Jerusalem as well. ¹⁹ This Passover was celebrated in the eighteenth year of Josiah's reign.

²⁰ Some time after Josiah had put the house of Our God in order, Necho, ruler of Egypt, marched up from Egypt to attack Carchemish on the Euphrates.

Josiah marched out against the Egyptians ²¹ and Necho sent envoys, and said, "What disagreement is there between us today, Ruler of Judah? My disagreement is not with you, but with another sovereign. God has commanded me to make haste. Don't stand in my way—God is at my side, and will destroy you if you do."

²² Josiah would not to be dissuaded from fighting, and ignored Necho's words, which came from God. Disguising himself, he pushed forward to join battle in the valley of Megiddo.

²³ Josiah was soon wounded by archers and told those with him, "Take me away, I am seriously wounded." ²⁴ They lifted the ruler out of the chariot, put him in another to rush him to Jerusalem. Josiah died there and was buried among the tombs of his ancestors. All Jerusalem and Judah mourned for Josiah. ²⁵ Jeremiah composed laments for Josiah. And to this day the singers, women and men, commemorate Josiah with laments. This has become a custom in Israel; they are recorded in the book of Lamentations.

²⁶ Other events of Josiah's reign, including all his works of devotion, as defined by the Law of Our God— ²⁷ and his life's work, first to last, is recorded in the books of the Rulers of Israel and Judah.

36:1 The country people took Josiah's heir, Jehoahaz, and made him ruler in Jerusalem in place of Josiah. ² The twenty-three year old Jehoahaz assumed the judgment seat in Jerusalem and reigned three months. ³ Then Necho, ruler of Egypt, removed him from the judgment seat and imposed on Judah a levy of 100 talents of silver and one talent of gold. ⁴ The Egyptian ruler put Eliakim, brother of Jehoahaz, on the judgment seat as ruler of Judah and Jerusalem, and renamed him Jehoiakim. Jehoahaz was taken to Egypt.

⁵ Jehoiakim, who was twenty-three years old at the time of his accession to the throne, reigned for eleven years. He did not do what was right in the eyes of Our God. ⁶ Nebuchadnezzar, ruler of Babylon, took Jehoiakim prisoner, and putting him in chains, took him off to Babylon. ⁷ Nebuchadnezzar carried off to Babylon as well some of the furnishings of the house of Our God and put them in his royal residence there. ⁸ Other events of Jehoiakim's reign, including his abominable activities and all that was found against him, are recorded in the books of the Rulers of Israel and Judah. Jehoiakim's heir, Jehoiachin, succeeded him.

⁹ Jehoiachin, who was eighteen years old at the time of his succession, reigned in Jerusalem for three months and ten days. The ruler did not do what right in the eyes of Our God. ¹⁰ In the spring of the year, Nebuchadnezzar had Jehoiachin brought the Babylon—along with more treasures from the house of Our God—and made Jehoiachin's uncle ruler over Judah and Jerusalem.

¹¹ Zedekiah, who was twenty-one at the time of he was placed on the judgment seat, reigned in Jerusalem for eleven years. ¹² Zedekiah did not do what was right in the eyes of Our God. The ruler spurned the counsel of the prophet Jeremiah, who spoke in the name of God. ¹³ He also rebelled against the ruler Nebuchadnezzar, who had required that Zedekiah swear an oath of allegiance before God. The young ruler was stiff-necked and hard-hearted in his refusal to return to Our God, the God of Israel.

¹⁴ All the leaders of the priests and the people were unfaithful as well, worshiping the abominable idols of other nations. They defiled the house which had been consecrated in the Name of Our God in Jerusalem.
¹⁵ The Most High God, the God of their ancestors, warned them time

and time again through messengers, for God had compassion for the people and desired to spare the house of worship. ¹⁶ Yet the people mocked the messengers, despised the word, and ridiculed the prophets until at last the rage of Our God became so great there was no remedy.

¹⁷ God brought down on them the ruler of the Babylonians, who put their young defenders to the sword in the sanctuary. Neither male nor female, young nor old were spared. God handed all them over to Nebuchadnezzar, ¹⁸ who carried them off to Babylon along with all the furnishings, large and small, of the house of Our God, all of its treasures, as well as the treasuries of the officials and the ruler. ¹⁹ They set fire to house of God, razed the walls of the city of Jerusalem, and burned all the stately residences and their furnishings. Everything was destroyed; nothing was left.

²⁰ Nebuchadnezzar took the remnant into exile in Babylon—those who escaped the sword—to be slaves. They remained the slaves of the Babylonians until the Persians came to power, ²¹ fulfilling the prophecy of Jeremiah: "Until the land has fulfilled its Sabbaths, it will lie desolate; it rest, untended, until the seventy years have passed."

ଊ   ଊ   ଊ

²² In the first year of the ruler Cyrus of Persia, the Most High God—fulfilling the word spoken through Jeremiah—inspired the ruler to issue a proclamation in writing throughout the land. It was written, "This is the proclamation of Cyrus, ruler of Persia: the Most High God of heaven gave me all the realms of the world, and God has appointed me to build a temple for God in Jerusalem in Judah. ²³ Whoever among you belongs to God's people, may the Most High God be with you! You can go home again."

tobit

this is the story of tobit, from the tribe of Naphtali. Tobit* was begot of Tobiel; Tobiel was begot of Ananiel; Ananiel, of Aduel; Aduel, of Gabael; and Gabael, of Asiel.

² During the reign of Shalmaneser, ruler of Assyria,** Tobit was taken captive from Thisbe, which is south of Kedesh Naphtali in upper Galilee: above and to the west of Hazor, and to the north of Phogor.

❧   ❧   ❧

³ I am Tobit. All my life, I have walked the path of truth and justice. I have freely shared the blessings of my fortune with my family and my people, who, like me, are exiles in Nineveh of Assyria.

⁴ When I was young and still living in the land of Israel, my entire tribe, the descendants of Naphtali, abandoned both the house of David and

---

* Greek form of the Hebrew name Tobiah (Tôbiyyah). The name means "Our God is good." Following this introduction to the book, the narrative changes to the first person, until 3:7.
**Shalmaneser V ruled from 726 to 722 The tribe of Naphtali was taken captive under Tiglath-pileser in 734.

Jerusalem—the city chosen from among all the tribes as the place for all of Israel to come and offer sacrifice. There the Temple—God's own dwelling place—had been built and consecrated for all future generations. ⁵ But the tribe of Naphtali sacrificed to the calf that had been set up by Jeroboam of Israel, in Dan, and on every hilltop in Galilee.

⁶ I alone made the pilgrimage to Jerusalem for the festivals, as the Law commands all of Israel to do for all time. I would travel to Jerusalem as quickly as I could with the firstfruits of my crops and the firstborn of my flocks, a tenth of my cattle and the first shearlings among my sheep. ⁷ I would give these to the priests, the descendants of Aaron, who attended the altar there. To them—the descendants of Levi who led the worship in Jerusalem—I also gave one-tenth of my grain, wine, olive oil, pomegranates, figs, and other fruits that I had produced.

I set aside a second tenth of my wealth for six years, and then distributed it in Jerusalem.* ⁸ I gave a third tenth of my produce to the orphaned, to those who were bereaved, and to the immigrants now living in Israel. I would bring the gift to them every third year, and we would eat it according to the mandates concerning such things which are laid down in the Law of Moses, as well as the instructions of my mother, Deborah—for Tobiel died and left me fatherless. ⁹ After I had grown, and married one of my own tribe, my wife and I had a son whom we named Tobiah.

¹⁰ After I was exiled to Assyria and became a refugee in Nineveh, I saw that all of my relatives began to eat the food that the foreigners ate. ¹¹ I didn't defile myself by eating this food.

¹² Because I remained devoted to God with all of my heart, ¹³ the Most High showed favor to me, keeping me in good standing with Shalmaneser, for whom I became a purveyor. ¹⁴ Until the time of Shalmaneser's death, I would go to Media to buy his supplies for him there. Whenever I went to Media, I would entrust Gabael, whose brother was Gabri, with bags of silver weighing 970 pounds in all. ¹⁵ But after Shalmaneser died, his heir Sennacherib ruled, and then the road to Media became so dangerous to travel that I no longer went there.

¹⁶ In the days of Shalmaneser, I performed many acts of kindness for my relatives, members of my own tribe. ¹⁷ I gave food to those who were starv-

---

* The second tithe was to be converted to money and used for rejoicing each year except the seventh year, or Sabbath year. The third tithe was to go to the poor, according to Dt. 18:3-5. This was the most idealistic tithe in terms of people actually observing it. Its significance in the story is to demonstrate how closely Tobit observed the Law.

ing, and clothing to those who needed it. If I saw the dead body of one of my own people discarded behind the walls of Nineveh, I rushed to bury it.*

¹⁸ I also buried those whom Sennacherib executed. These included many whom he had killed on his way when he fled in haste from Judea, during the time that the Ruler of the Heavens passed judgment upon him for his many blasphemies. In his rage, Sennacherib massacred many Israelites. But I would later remove the bodies in secret and bury them, so that when he went back to look for those he had slaughtered, he never found them.

¹⁹ Then one of the Ninevites informed Sennacherib about my activities, and he sent his people to search me out and kill me. I was afraid and ran away. ²⁰ They seized all my property—there was nothing left for me to return to except my wife Anna and my son Tobiah.**

²¹ But within forty days of that time, two of Sennacherib's own children killed him and fled to the mountains of Ararat. Sennacherib's next in line, Esarhaddon, took the throne, and he appointed Ahikar, who was begot of my brother Hanael, over the royal treasury. Ahikar, who had authority over the entire administration, ²² spoke on my behalf, so that I was allowed to return to Nineveh. He had been both chief cupbearer and the keeper of the signet, as well as being in charge of the treasury, during the time of Sennacherib; so Esarhaddon reappointed him. He was a close relative—my nephew, in fact.

2:1 So it was during the reign of Esarhaddon that I returned home and was greeted by my wife Anna and my son Tobiah. On our festival of Pentecost, the Feast of Weeks, a fine dinner was prepared for me, and I sat down to eat. ² The table was set, and when many different dishes were placed before me, I said to Tobiah, my son, "Go out and try to find someone who is poor and hungry among our relatives exiled here in Nineveh. If that person is a true worshipper of God, bring her or him back, so that we may share this meal. I'll wait to begin the dinner until you return, Tobiah."

³ Tobiah went out to look for some poor relatives of ours. He returned, exclaiming, "Father!"

I answered, "What is it, my child?"

---

* Giving the dead a proper burial is one of the obligations of all Israelites. That none of the other Israelites buried the dead points to the degree to which Israel had abandoned its spiritual obligation. Tobit is presented as a contrast as one who is faithful to the Law.

**Tobit's goodness was no protection from misfortune. The mystery of why just people suffer is one of the major themes of the book.

He answered, "One of our people has been strangled! The body lies in the marketplace."

⁴ Leaving my dinner untouched, I went out quickly, and removed the body from the street and put it in a room, so that I might bury it after sunset. ⁵ Returning to my own quarters, I washed myself and ate my food in sorrow. ⁶ I remembered the words of the prophet Amos concerning Bethel,

> "Your feasts will be turned into wailing,
>   and all your songs into dirges."

And I wept.

⁷ Then at sunset I went out, dug a grave, and buried the body. ⁸ The neighbors mocked me, saying to each other, "Will he never learn! Once before Tobit was hunted down for execution because of this very thing; yet now that he has escaped, here he is again, burying the dead."

⁹ That same night I bathed, and went into the courtyard and lay down by the courtyard wall. Because of the heat, I left my face uncovered. ¹⁰ I didn't know that there were birds perched on the wall above me, until their hot droppings fell into my eyes. And their droppings caused cataracts to form.

I went to the doctors for a cure, but the more they anointed my eyes with various salves, the worse the cataracts became, until I could no longer see at all. For four years I was deprived of eyesight, and all my kin were grieved at my condition. Ahikar, however, took care of me for four years, until he left for Elymais.

¹¹ My wife Anna then went to work; she took in people's wool, to spin and weave into cloth; ¹² when she sent back the goods to the owners, they would pay her. On the seventh day of the month of Dystros* she finished the cloth and delivered it to the owners. They paid her a full salary, and gave her as well a young goat for the table.

¹³ On entering the house, the goat began to bleat. I called to my wife and said, "Where did this goat come from? Perhaps it was stolen! Give it back to its owners. We have no right to eat stolen food."

¹⁴ But she said to me, "It was given to me as a bonus over and above my wages."

But I wouldn't believe her, and told her to give it back to its owners. I became very angry with her over this.

---

* Late January or early February.

So she responded, "Where are your charitable deeds now? Where are your virtuous acts? See! Your true character is finally showing itself!

3.1 Grief-stricken in spirit, I groaned and wept aloud. Then with sobs I began to pray:

2 "O God, you are just,
    and all your works are just.
All your ways are grace and truth,
    and you are the Judge of the world.
3 Therefore, O God, remember me,
    seek me out.
Do not punish me for my sins,
    or for my heedless faults
    or for those of my ancestors.
For we have sinned against you
4   and broken your commandments;
and you have given us over to plundering,
    to captivity, and to death,
to be the talk, the laughingstock, and the scorn
    of the nations among whom you have scattered us.
5 All your decrees are true,
    and you deal with me as I deserve
because of my faults
    and those of my ancestors,
since we have neither kept your commandments
    nor walked in truth before you.

6 So now, do with me as you will,
    take my life from me if you please;
all I want is to be delivered from earth
    and become earth again.
For death is better for me than life;
    I have been reviled without cause,
    and my despair is beyond measure.
O God, send forth your command
    to deliver me from this affliction.
Let me go away to my everlasting home;
    do not turn your face from me, O God.
For it is better to die than to continue living
    in the face of trouble that knows no pity;
    I am weary of hearing myself insulted."

CR CR CR

⁷ * On the same day, it the town of Ecbatana in Media, it so happened that Raguel's daughter Sarah also had to listen to abuse from one of her father's attendants.

⁸ For she had been married to seven husbands, but the Asmodeus,** the worst of the demons, killed them off before any of them could have intercourse with her. So the attendant said to her, "You're the one who strangles your husbands! Look at you! You've already been married seven times, but you've had no joy with any of your husbands. ⁹ Why do you beat us? Because your husbands are dead? Then why not join them? May we never see a daughter or son of yours!"

¹⁰ She was deeply grieved in spirit. She went in tears to an upstairs room in her parents' house with the intention of hanging herself. But she reconsidered, saying to herself, "No! People would level this insult against my parents: 'You had only one beloved daughter, and she hung herself out of grief!' And thus would I cause my parents in their old age to go down to Sheol laden with sorrow. It is far better for me not to hang myself, but to beg God to let me die, so that I need no longer live to hear such insults."

¹¹ Then she spread her hands, and facing the window, poured out her prayer.

> "Blessed are you, God of mercy!
>> Blessed is your Name for all ages!
>> May your creation praise you at all times!
> ¹² Now, my God, I turn my face to you;
>> I raise my eyes toward you.
> Command that I be released from this earth
>> so I will not have to listen to these insults any more.
> My God, you know that I am innocent
>> of any promiscuity.
> ¹⁵ I have neither soiled my honor
>> nor the honor of my family here in exile.
> I am my parents' only child—
>> they have no other to survive them

---

* At this point the narrative changes to the third person, which continues through the end of the book.

**Demons—and angels who are featured characters in stories—did not appear until late in Hebrew literature. Asmodeus, whose name means "Destroyer," is in fact the destroying angel of God, but is here depicted as the most evil of demons.

or any near relative or any other kin
　　with whom I may marry.
I have already lost seven husbands.
　　Why should I continue to live?
But if it does not please you to take my life, my God,
　　then at least take mercy on me,
　　for I can no longer bear these insults."

ᘓ　　　ᘓ　　　ᘓ

¹⁶ At the same moment, the prayer of these two suppliants was heard in the glorious presence of God, ¹⁷ who sent the angel Raphael to heal them both: to remove the cataracts from Tobit's eyes so that he might once again see the sunlight that God created; and to bring together Sarah the daughter of Raguel and Tobiah the son of Tobit, and join them in marriage—and to free her from her oppressor, the demon Asmodeus. Because of the kinship laws, Tobiah was the next in line to ask for her hand in marriage.

At the exact moment that Tobit returned from the courtyard into his house, Sarah came down from her upper room.

4:1–11:18

that same day, Tobit remembered the money he had entrusted to Gabael at Rages in Media. ² He said to himself, "Now that I have prayed to die, why don't I call in Tobiah and tell him about the money?"

³ So he called in Tobiah, who came to him. Tobit said, "Listen to what I have to tell you, and after I die, give me a proper burial:

"Respect your mother all the days of her life and never forsake her. Try to please her and don't cause her grief in anything. ⁴ Remember her, my child, for she endured great pain when you were still in her womb. When she dies, bury her next to me in the same grave.

⁵ "Remain faithful to God throughout your life, my child—reject sin and obey all of Our God's commandments. Live a life of justice and don't involve yourself in evil schemes. ⁶ Be honest and you will always succeed.

⁷ "Be generous toward all who are faithful to Our God. If you are miserly toward the poor, God will be miserly toward you. ⁸ Give according to your abundance: if you have more, you should give more; if you have only a little, give what you are able. ⁹ By doing this, you will be setting aside treasures for yourself for a later day—you will be rewarded when

you are in need. Giving to the poor is a sure protection for you at your hour of death and will keep you away from the Abyss—¹¹ indeed, it is this kind of offering that most pleases Our God.

¹² "Stay on guard against licentiousness. Marry someone from your own lineage, but most of all, do not marry a foreigner who isn't from our tribe—for we are the descendants of prophets. Always remember that Noah, Abraham, Isaac and Jacob married from among their own tribe. They all had many descendants and their posterity will inherit the earth. ¹³ So remain loyal to your own people, and don't be too proud to marry from among them. This kind of pride can only lead to anxiety and self-destruction, in the same way that laziness leads to poverty and starvation.

¹⁴ "Pay your workers the wages they have earned at the end of each day—never keep their pay overnight. If you serve God in this way, God will reward you with many blessings.

"Keep on guard in everything that you do, and be self-disciplined in all your conduct. ¹⁵ Do nothing to anyone that you would not want done to you. Don't overindulge in wine or make a habit out of drinking too much.

¹⁶ "Give food to the hungry and clothes to those who need them. Whatever you have left in surplus, give it to the poor—and always give gladly.

¹⁷ "Whenever one of the people of God dies, prepare food for their family; but never do this when someone evil dies.

¹⁸ "Seek counsel from the sages and never reject sensible advice.

¹⁹ "Seize every opportunity you have to praise the Name of Our God. Pray to God to bring you abundance and success in all your endeavors. All of the other nations lack understanding: they may or may not receive sage counsel according to the will of Our God.

²⁰ "To conclude, my child, I have entrusted 670 pounds of silver to my friend Gabael, begot of Gabri, who lives in Rages of Media. ²¹ You have nothing to fear because of our current poverty. If you obey God and stay clear of sin, you will be rewarded with great wealth."

5:1 Then Tobiah answered Tobit: "I'll do everything you told me. ² But how can I get the money back from Gabael? I don't know him and he doesn't know me. What kind of proof can I show so that he will recognize and trust me, and give me the silver? In fact, I don't even know the way to Media or even which road to take."

³ Tobit replied, "I have a contract signed by both Gabael and myself. I tore it in half and each of us took a part. His half remains with the silver. Twenty years have passed since that time. Now, find a reliable guide to

accompany you to Media and back. We will pay the guide when you have returned. But now you must get the money that I entrusted to Gabael."

஘   ஘   ஘

⁴ Tobiah went looking for a guide to go with him, one who knew the way to Media. No sooner had he left the house than he met Raphael. Tobiah did not recognize Raphael to be the messenger of God, for the angel appeared to him as a youth. ⁵ He asked Raphael, "Where do you come from?"

"From Israel," replied the angel. "I am a member of your tribe and have come here seeking work."

So Tobiah asked the youth, "Do you know the way to Media?"

⁶ "I do," replied Raphael. "I have been there many times, and know all the best roads. I have often stayed with our relative Gabael who lives in Rages. It takes two days to travel from Ecbatana to Rages, because it is in the mountains while Ecbatana is in the middle of the plains."

⁷ So Tobiah replied, "Wait right here. I am going speak to my father. I do need a guide and I will pay you a good wage for your services."

⁸ Then Raphael answered, "I will wait for you here, but not for long."

⁹ Tobiah ran to tell Tobit, "I have found one of our own, who is able to be my guide."

Tobit said, "Bring him to me so that I can find out about his tribe and family and whether we can trust him to go with you."

¹⁰ So Tobiah went outside and called Raphael: "Come in, my father wants to meet you."

When Raphael entered the house, Tobit greeted him, and Raphael replied, "Joyful blessings to you!"

But Tobit replied, "Where can I find joy any more? I have lost my eyesight and can no longer see the light in the sky. I am like the dead who live in the darkness, never seeing the light. I am alive, but I might as well be dead. I hear people's voices, but I cannot see them."

But the youth answered, "Take courage, the time of God's healing draws near for you."

Then Tobit said to the youth, " Tobiah wishes to go to Media. Can you go with him and guide him there? I will pay you for your services."

Raphael answered, "I can travel with him, and I know all the roads. I have gone to Media many times, so I know the way across the plains and through the mountain passes."

¹¹ Then Tobit said to Raphael, "Tell me who your family is and to which tribe you belong."

¹² Raphael replied, "Why do you need to know my tribe?"*

And Tobit answered, "I want to make sure whose family you belong to and what your name is."

¹³ Raphael replied, "I am Azariah, begot of Hananiah the elder, one of your relatives."

¹⁴ Then Tobit said to him, "Welcome, and God's peace upon you, my friend! Please don't resent me for my questions. I wanted to make sure of your ancestry. As it happens, we are related and you are of very noble lineage. I knew Hananiah and Nathaniah, the two children of Shemaiah. They used to accompany me to Jerusalem, and worshipped with me there. They were not led astray as were so many in our tribe. You come from a good family and from good stock."

¹⁵ Then Tobit went on, "I will pay you minimum wage, as well as cover all the expenses for both you and Tobiah. ¹⁶ If you complete the journey, I promise to pay you even more than the standard wage." Raphael answered, "You have nothing to fear. I will go with Tobiah. We will leave you in good health and return to you in good health, for the roads are safe."

¹⁷ Then Tobit said to Raphael, "God bless you, my friend."

Then Tobit called Tobiah and said, "Get your provisions ready for the journey and prepare to leave with our cousin. May Our God keep you safe and return you in good health to me. And may the angel of God accompany you and keep you safe."

When he was ready to leave, Tobiah kissed his mother and father goodbye. Tobit said to him, "Have a safe journey."

¹⁷ But Tobiah's mother began to cry and said, "Why do we have to send our only child away like this? He's our only means of support. Who will care for us now? ¹⁸ Is that money of yours so important that you are willing to risk your own child's life to get it back? ¹⁹ Why can't you be content to live on what Our God has given us?"

²⁰ "Don't worry," replied Tobit, "he leaves us in good health and will return to us in good health. ²¹ So don't worry about them. A good angel will go with Tobiah. He will have a successful journey and return to us in good health." At those words, Anna dried her tears.

---

* Raphael's caginess recalls the conversation Jacob had with the angel with whom he wrestled during the encounter at Peniel.

6:1 So Tobiah left with Raphael, ² and their dog followed them out of the house and traveled with them. They walked until dusk and set up camp on the banks of the Tigris.

³ Tobiah went down to the river to wash his feet when suddenly a large fish leaped from the water and tried to swallow his foot. ⁴ Tobiah screamed in panic, but Raphael said to him, "Hold on to that fish!" So Tobiah reached down and grabbed the fish and pulled it to the shore.

⁵ Raphael then said to him, "Cut open the fish and remove its heart and liver, as well as the gall—these things make great medicine." ⁶ After he cut the fish, Tobiah gathered the liver, heart and gall. He then roasted part of the fish for his dinner and saved the rest to be salted.

The two travelers then continued on their way to Media. ⁷ As they drew near the town, Tobiah began to question Raphael: "What possible medicinal value do fish guts have?"

⁸ Raphael replied, "The heart and liver can be burned in the presence of someone who is oppressed by a demon. The smoke they produce will drive the demon away. ⁹ The gall can be used as a salve to cure cataracts. When you rub the gall over the eyes, where the white films have formed, and then blow gently on the white films, they will fall away. The person will be able to see again."

¹⁰ Once they reached Media and were approbaching Ecbatana, ¹¹ Raphael said to the youth, "Tobiah!"

"Yes?" Tobiah replied.

"Tonight we are going to stay in the house of Edna and Raguel. They are your relatives and have a daughter named Sarah. ¹² They have no other children except for Sarah. You are their nearest relative and it is most fitting that you be the one to marry her. It is also fitting that you be the one to inherit the family fortune. Sarah is also wise, brave and beautiful, and her parents are good people. ¹³ It is fitting that you and Sarah be married. So tonight I will speak to her parents and ask that they permit you to marry her. Then, after we return from Rages, we will celebrate the wedding. Her parents cannot refuse to let her marry you. They know that, according to the Law of Moses, you are the only one eligible to marry her and to inherit the family fortune. I will discuss the matter tonight and will arrange the engagement to Sarah. Then, when we return from Rages, she will accompany you back to your house."

¹⁴ Then Tobiah answered Raphael, "Azariah, there is a rumor going

around that she has already been married seven times, and that each of her spouses died on their wedding night. People have said that it was a demon who killed them. ¹⁵ The demon never harms her, but will kill anyone who comes near her. I am my parent's only child. If I die, they will be so grief-stricken that they themselves will die. Then there will be no one left to bury them."

¹⁶ But Raphael said, "Remember the advice that your father gave to you: to marry someone from your own tribe. Now, listen to what I tell you and fret no more about this demon. Marry Sarah. I know that you will be married to her this very night. ¹⁷ When you enter the bridal chambers, take some of the liver and heart from the fish and place it on the embers of the fire there. ¹⁸ They will give off an odor that will drive the demon away, never to be seen again. Before the two of you go, both of you must stand up and pray that the Most High God will give you mercy and protect you. You have nothing to fear. You and Sarah were meant to be together from the beginning of time. She will be liberated from her oppressor and the two of you will be together. You and Sarah will have many children who will give you much love. So don't be afraid."

Now that Tobiah understood that Sarah was a near relative on his father's side, his heart melted and he longed to marry her.

7:1 When they arrived in Ecbatana, Tobiah said to Raphael, "Azariah, take me to see Raguel right away." So Raphael led Tobiah to the house of Raguel, whom they found seated by the courtyard gate. They greeted him first.

Raguel said to them, "Greetings to both of you. Good health to you, and welcome!" Then he brought them into his house.

² Once they had entered, he said to his wife, Edna, "See how much this youth looks like my cousin Tobit!"

³ Edna questioned them: "Who is your family?"

They answered, "We are descendants of Naphtali and have been living in exile in Nineveh of Assyria."

⁴ Edna questioned them further: "Do you know our cousin, Tobit?"

"Yes, we know him very well," they said.

"And how is he?" she asked.

⁵ "He is alive and healthy," they said. Then Tobiah added, "In fact, Tobit is my father!"

⁶ At these words, Raguel ran to Tobiah and embraced him, shedding tears of joy. ⁷ But when he learned of Tobit's blindness, he said, "Bless you,

my child! Your father is noble and kind! How terrible that someone so full of justice and charity should lose his sight!" He continued to weep and to embrace his cousin Tobiah. ⁸ Edna also wept with him, as did their daughter, Sarah.

⁹ Afterwards, Raguel slaughtered a ram from the flock and gave them the warmest of receptions. When they had bathed and sat down to eat, Tobiah said to Raphael, "Azariah, ask Raguel to let me marry my kinswoman Sarah."

¹⁰ Raguel overheard the words; so he said to the boy, "Eat, drink and be merry tonight, for no one is more entitled to marry my daughter Sarah than you. ¹⁰ Besides, not even I have the right to give her to anyone but you, because you are my closest relative.

¹¹ "But I will explain the situation to you very frankly. I have given her in marriage seven times, each time with kin of ours, and each one died on the very night they approached her. But now, eat and drink. I am sure Our God will look after you both."

Tobiah answered, "I will eat or drink nothing until you have come to a decision about me."

¹² Raguel said to him, "I will do it. You and Sarah will be married according to the decree of the Book of Moses. Your marriage to her has been decided in heaven. Take your kin; from now on, you are her love, and she is your beloved. She is with you today and ever after. And tonight, may the God of heaven prosper you both. May the Most High grant you mercy and peace."

¹³ Then Raguel called Sarah to come stand next to him. Raguel took her hands and joined them with Tobiah's, with these words: "Take each other according to the Law. According to the decree written in the Book of Moses, the two of you are now married. Bring her back safely to your parents. And may the God of heaven grant both of you peace and prosperity." He then turned to her mother and asked her to bring a scroll so that he might draw up a marriage contract stating that Sarah and Tobiah were married according to the decree of the Mosaic Law.

¹⁴ Her mother brought the scroll, and he drew up the contract, to which they affixed their seals. ¹⁵ Then they began to eat and drink.

¹⁶ Raguel called Edna and told her, "Prepare the spare room and bring Sarah there." Edna went and prepared the room. She then led Sarah into the room and began to weep. But when she had wiped away her tears, she said, "Don't be afraid, my daughter, I'm certain that this time the Most High God will bring you happiness to overcome your sorrow. So don't be afraid." Then Edna left the room.

8:1 When the banquet was done, they wanted to retire, so they led Tobiah from the banquet table to the bedroom. 2 It was then that Tobiah remembered Raphael's instructions. He went to his bag and removed the fish's heart and liver and laid them on embers with plenty of incense. 3 The smell of the burning fish guts so repulsed the demon that it fled through the air to the farthest reaches of Egypt. Raphael chased the demon there and bound it hand and foot. Then Raphael returned.

4 Later, after her parents had left and shut the door to the room, Tobiah arose from the bed and said to Sarah, "My love, get up. Let us pray and beg God to have mercy on us and to grant us deliverance." 5 She got up and they started to pray and beg that deliverance might be theirs. Tobiah began with these words:

> "Blessed are you, O God of our ancestors;
>> praised be your name forever and ever.
> Let the heavens and all your creation
>> praise you forever.
> It was you who created Adam and Eve
>> to be each other's help and support,
>> and from these two the human race was born.
> 6 It was you who said,
>> "It is not good that people should be alone;
>> let us make helpmates for them.
> 7 And so I do not take her out of lust;
>> I do it in singleness of heart.
> Be kind enough to have pity on both of us,
>> and bring us to old age together."

8 Together, they said, "Amen, Amen!" 9 Then they went to bed, and were together until morning.

In the meantime, Raguel arose and sent some workers to dig a grave. 10 He told them, "There is a good chance that this one will die too and we will become a joke among our peers." 11 When the workers finished the grave, Raguel left the house and called to his wife, 12 "Send one of your attendants over to see if he's still alive. If he's dead, I want to bury him in secret."

13 So they called the attendant, who lit a lamp and opened the bedroom door a crack, where she found them both fast asleep. 14 The attendant came out of the bedroom and told the parents that nothing was wrong. 15 They both praised God saying,

"Blessed are you, Most High God,
  with every blessing pure and true.
May your people praise you
  and bless your Name forever.
¹⁶ I praise you for the happiness
  that you have brought to me.
You have shown your infinite compassion
  and dispelled our worst fears.
¹⁷ Praise you for looking with kindness on these two,
  who are the only children of their parents.
Show them your mercy, O God, and keep them safe
  so they may live out their lives together
  in happiness and love."

¹⁸ Then they told the workers to fill up the grave before dawn.

¹⁹ After they prayed, Edna baked many loaves of bread and Raguel went out to the flocks and brought in two steers and four rams and ordered the attendants to slaughter the animals and begin preparations for the feast.

²⁰ In the morning, he called in Tobiah and vowed, "You must stay here for a fortnight. We will eat and drink together. Your presence will bring cheer to my daughter, especially after this long suffering. ²¹ Then you may claim half of everything I own and return to your parents in safety. The other half will belong to the two of you when Edna and I die. Never doubt the love we have for you—you are as much our son as Sarah is our daughter. Of that you can be certain."

9:1 Tobiah called Raphael over and said, ²"Azariah, take four of the attendants and two camels with you and travel the rest of the way to Rages. Go to Gabael's house and give him the half of the contract he made with my father. When you get the money, bring him with you to the wedding celebration. ³ I'd go myself, but you witnessed the oath Raguel made, and I need to stay here to fulfill the terms of the agreement. ⁴ You know that my parents must be counting the days until I return, and if I delay even one more day, I will bring them to grief."

⁵ So Raphael left with the four attendants and two camels and went to Rages in Media and went to the house of Gabael. Raphael presented Gabael with the contract and informed him that Tobit's son Tobiah had just gotten married, and invited him to the wedding feast. Gabael got up and counted all the bags of money, each one with its seal intact, and loaded them on the camels.

⁶ The next morning, they both rose early and went to the wedding feast.

When they arrived at Raguel's house, they saw Tobiah reclining at the table. He sprang to his feet to greet Gabael, who wept and said these words of blessing:

"Good and noble child of good and noble parents! You are a reflection of your parents' justice and charity. May the Most High bless you and Sarah, and grant Sarah's parents blessings too! Praised be God, for I see in Tobiah the image of my cousin, Tobit."

≔ ≔ ≔

10:1 As the days went by, Tobit would keep count of how long Tobiah would need before returning home. Days became weeks, and still Tobiah did not return. ² Tobit mused to himself, "Is it possible that something has detained him? What if Gabael has died and there is no one there to give him the money?" ³ And he began to fret.

⁴ Anna kept saying to him, "My child is dead!" She began to weep, saying, ⁵ "Why me? Why me? My child! My child—the light of my eye! I should have never let you go!"

⁶ But Tobit admonished her, "Be quiet. Don't speak like that. He will return safely. I would guess that he has been delayed by some unexpected circumstances. But remember, the person who accompanied him is trustworthy and is from our own tribe. So don't grieve, he will return soon."

⁷ She answered, "You be quiet yourself! Don't lie to me! My child is dead!"

Every morning, Anna would rush outside to watch the road where Tobiah had departed and refused to answer anyone's call. And when evening came, she would return to the house and cry all night, getting no sleep at all.

≔ ≔ ≔

After the fourteen days of the wedding celebration which Raguel had sworn to observe for Sarah had passed, Tobiah came to him and said, "I must return now. I am sure that my mother and father think that they will never see me again. Please, father, let me go so that I may see my own parents again. I have already explained how they were when I left them."

⁸ But Raguel replied, "Stay with us, my child. I will send out messengers to your parents to let them know that you are well."

⁹ But Tobiah protested, "No. Please let me go back to my parents."

¹⁰ So Raguel promptly said goodbye to Sarah and gave half of all the

family estate to them, including attendants, oxen, sheep, donkeys, camels, clothes, money and many other goods. ¹¹ When they were ready to leave, Raguel embraced Tobiah, saying, "Goodbye, my child. Stay safe on your way. May the Most High bless you and Sarah—and may I see grandchildren before I die!"

¹² Then he kissed Sarah and said, "My daughter, love your mother-in-law and father-in-law since they are as much your parents as your mother and I." He then bade them farewell and let them go.

Then Edna said to Tobiah, "My child, may the Most High bring you back to us safely, and may I live long enough to see grandchildren from you and Sarah before I die. In the sight of the Most High, I entrust Sarah to you. Do nothing to bring her grief as long as she lives. Now, go in peace, my child. And remember that, just as Sarah is now your beloved, I am now your mother. May all of us find blessings all the days of our lives." Then she kissed them both and saw them safely on their journey.

¹³ Tobiah departed from the house of Edna and Raguel filled with joy and praising the Most High, who rules the heavens and the earth, for making the journey such a success. Finally, he blessed Edna and Raguel saying, "The Most High has commanded me to love you all the days of my life."

^{11:1} As they approached Kaserin, on the outskirts of Nineveh, Raphael said, ² "Remember how your parents were when we left them. ³ We should go ahead of the caravan, and prepare the house while the rest are still on their way."

⁴ As they went on ahead, Raphael said, "Make sure you have the gall ready." And the dog cavorted behind them.

⁵ In the meantime, Anna sat staring at the road by which Tobiah was to return. ⁶ When she saw him coming, she ran to her husband and cried, "Tobit, our child is coming, and so is his travelling companion!"

⁷ Raphael said to Tobiah before they reached Tobit, "I give you my word that your father's eyes will be opened. ⁸ Smear the fish gall on them. This medicine will make the cataracts shrink and peel off from his eyes; then your father will again be able to see the light of day."

⁹ By then, Anna had come running, and threw her arms around Tobiah's neck. "Now I can die," she said, "I have seen you again." And she sobbed aloud.

¹⁰ Tobit got up and stumbled out through the courtyard gate. ¹¹ Tobiah went up to him with the fish gall in his hand, and holding him firmly, blew into his eyes. "Courage, father," he said. ¹² Next he smeared the

medicine on Tobit's eyes, which made them smart. [13] Then, beginning at the corners of Tobit's eyes, Tobiah used both hands to peel off the cataracts.

[14] When Tobit saw his son, he threw his arms around him and wept. He exclaimed, "I can see you, son, the light of my eyes!" Then he cried,

> "Blessed be God,
>> and praised be the great Name of God
>> and blessed be all the holy angels of God!
> May God's holy Name be praised
>> throughout all ages,
> [15] because it was God who scourged me,
>> and it is God who has had mercy on me.
> Behold, I now see my son Tobiah!"

And Tobit continued to praise God in this way at the top of his lungs.

Tobiah told his father that the journey had been successful, that he had the money and that he had married Sarah, the daughter of Edna and Raguel, and that she was on her way, fast approaching the gates of Nineveh.

[16] Tobit was ecstatic, and rushed out to greet his new daughter-in-law at the city gate, praising God all the way. When the people of Nineveh saw him running excitedly through the streets with no guide, they were all dumbfounded. [17] Tobit told them of how God had been merciful and restored his sight.

When Tobit met Sarah at the gate, he threw his arms around her, saying, "My daughter, come with me! Welcome. Praise to God who has brought you here to us. Blessings on your parents, blessings on Tobiah and blessings on you. Now, come into your new home and be welcome. May you have blessings and joy. Come, now!"

On that day, there was great rejoicing in the Jewish community at Nineveh. [18] Ahikar and his nephew Nadab were also there to share in Tobit's excitement. Together, they made merry and celebrated a great feast in honor of Sarah and Tobiah for seven days, during which time many gifts were given to them.

12:1–14:15

When the wedding feast was over, Tobit called his son Tobiah and said, "See to it that you give what is due to your travelling companion, plus a bonus."

² Tobiah responded, "How much of a bonus should we give? Would it really harm us very much if we gave our friend half of everything we brought back? ³ He has done well in leading me back to you safely, he freed Sarah from her oppressor, he got the money for me, and he healed you. How much more can I give him for all the good things he has done for us?"

⁴ Tobit said, "Yes, he deserves half of everything you brought back."

⁵ So Tobiah called Raphael and said, "Take half of what you brought back in payment for all you have done, and go in peace."

⁶ Then Raphael took Tobit and Tobiah aside and said to them,

> "Bless and praise God before all the living
>   for all the favors bestowed upon you!
> Bless and extol the holy Name!
>   Proclaim before all mortals the deeds of God as they deserve,
>   and never tire of giving thanks!
> It is right to keep the secret of a ruler,
>   yet it is better to reveal and publish the works of God—
>   who is worthy of your thanks.
> Do what is good,
>   and no evil can befall you.
> Prayers with fasting and charity with right conduct
>   are better than riches with iniquity.
> It is better to practice charitable giving
>   than to hoard up gold.
> Charity saves from death and purges every kind of sin.
>   Those who give alms have their fill of days.
> Those who commit sin and do evil
>   bring harm on themselves.

¹¹ "I will now tell you the whole truth. I will hide nothing from you. I have already said to you, 'It is right to keep the secret of a ruler, yet better to reveal and publish the works of God—who is worthy of our thanks.' I can now tell you, Tobit, that when you and Sarah prayed, it was I who presented and read the record of your prayer before the glory of Our God. I did the same thing when you used to bury the dead. When you did not hesitate to get up and leave your dinner in order to go and bury the dead, I was sent to put you to the test. But God also commissioned me to heal you, as well as your daughter-in-law Sarah. I am Raphael, one of the seven angels who enter and minister before the glory of Our God."

¹⁶ Tobit and Tobiah were struck with awe, and fell down prostrate before Raphael. Raphael said to them, "Do not be afraid. Praise God at all times! ¹⁸ For my own part, during all my time with you, I never acted on

my own behalf; I was carrying out the will of God—sing praises and bless God each and every day! [19] Through all the time you have observed me, you have never seen me eat or drink anything. Everything that happened with me was a vision.

[20] "So now, rise from the ground and praise Our God. I will now return to the One who sent me; write down all these things that have happened to you." At these words, Raphael vanished.

Tobit and Tobiah stood up and could no longer see Raphael. They continued to bless and sing the praises of the Most High, thanking God continually for all the great things that had happened since the angel appeared to them.

꩜   ꩜   ꩜

13[1] Then Tobit said,

    "Bless Our God, the Eternal One
        whose reign endures for all times!
[2]   God brings to us both pain and mercy;
        God leads us to the pits of Sheol
    and then rescues us from the great Abyss—
        there is nothing that can escape God's hand.
[3]   Praise God before all nations, O children of Israel.
        God has scattered you among the peoples,
[4]   but has demonstrated great power even there.
    Glorify God before all living creatures,
        praise the One who is our ruler and parent forever.

[5]   God will punish you for your sins
        but will show you mercy again and again.
    God will gather you from among the nations
        among whom you are scattered.
[6]   If you trust in God with your whole heart and soul
        and act justly before our Creator,
    then the Most High will seek you out
        and will no longer hide from you.
    See the wonders God has worked for you,
        and thank God at the top of your lungs.
    Praise the God of Justice
        and glorify the Ruler of the ages.

Here in the land of my exile, I thank God
  and sing of God's power and majesty to a nation of sinners:
"Repent, you evildoers,
  and act with justice before Our God.
Perhaps God will look on you with kindness
  and will show you mercy."
7 As for me, I lift up my voice to the Most High
  and my soul revels in the Ruler of the Heavens.
8 Let all people declare God's majesty
  and praise the Most High in Jerusalem.

9 O Jerusalem, holy city,
  God punished you for your evil deeds,
but God will once again show mercy
  on the children of the Just.
10 Praise the goodness of the Most High
  and bless the Ruler of all ages.
May the Tabernacle of the Most High be rebuilt
  and may God bring happiness to all us who are exiles
and show love to those of us who are suffering,
  for all generations and all times.
11 Jerusalem—a light shining forth to the ends of the earth—
  nations will flock to you from far away;
people from the furthest corners of the earth
  will seek refuge in you,
  and will bring gifts to the Ruler of the Heavens.
The name of Jerusalem
  will endure for all times.
12 Let those who curse you be cursed,
  as well as those who attack your walls,
or overturn your towers,
  or set your houses on fire!
But let those who bless you be blessed!

13 Go, then, and rejoice for the children of the Just,
  for they will be gathered together
  and will praise the Ruler of the ages.
14 Happy are those who love you,
  and happy are those who rejoice in your blessings.
Happy are those who grieve with you
  through your many sufferings,

for they will one day rejoice with you
and witness your glory forever.
15 My soul praises Our God, Our Ruler,
16 who will rebuild Jerusalem as a dwelling place for all time.
I will be happy if a small remnant of my descendants survive
to see your glory and praise the Ruler of the heavens.

Jerusalem, you will be rebuilt with sapphire and emerald,
and your walls will be precious stones.
Your towers, Jerusalem, will be golden,
and your streets paved with rubies and the stones of Ophir.
17 Your gates will sing joyful praises
and all your inhabitants will cry, "Alleluia!
Blessed be the God of Israel!'
And the blessed will bless the Name of Our God forever."

14:1 Thus ends the song of Tobit.

ᘓ   ᘓ   ᘓ

Tobit died peacefully at the age of one hundred twelve, and was buried with great honor in Nineveh. 2 He went blind at the age of sixty-two,
and after his cure lived a prosperous life doing good works and praising
God at all times. 3 When he was ready to die, he gave Tobiah these instructions:

4 "Gather your family and flee to Media. I believe that the judgment of
Nineveh, which Our God revealed through Nahum, is about to be fulfilled.
All that was prophesied about Nineveh and Assyria is about to take place.
Their words will prove true, and it will all happen at the appointed time.
It will be safer for you in Media rather than in Assyria or Babylon. I am
certain that everything God has said will come about—not a single word
of the prophecies will be lost. All your relatives, inhabitants of the land of
Israel, will be scattered and taken as captives from the promised land. All
of Israel will be destroyed—even Samaria and Jerusalem. The Temple of
God will be razed to the ground and will lie in ruins for a time.

5 "But after a time, God will have mercy on the people and will lead
them back to the land of Israel. Then they will rebuild the Temple—
though it will not be as grand as the first one, at least not until God's appointed time. But at the appointed time, all of Israel will return and
rebuild Jerusalem in all its grandeur. And there, the Temple of Our God
will be rebuilt, just as the prophets of Israel have foretold. 6 Then all the

nations will turn back to the Most High and worship the true God. They will abandon their idols—those things which led them astray—and will praise the eternal God in a spirit of justice. All the remnant of Israel who are delivered from captivity at that time will be gathered together. They will return to Jerusalem and live in safety forever in the land of Sarah and Abraham; and it will be their land for all times. Those who love God with all their hearts will sing for joy, but those who do evil and act unjustly will perish from the face of the earth.

8 "So now, my children, I charge you with this request: resolve to serve God and do what is pleasing in the sight of the Most High. 9 Teach your children to act justly and to do good works, to remember God at all times and to praise the Most High with all their hearts and all their strength. Now, leave Nineveh—don't stay here! 10 The day you bury your mother beside me, leave. Don't even stay another night in the walls of this city. I see so much corruption here—so many lies going about. The people here have no conscience. Remember what Nadab did to Ahikar, the very person who raised him: how Nadab tried to kill Ahikar and hid the still-live body in a tomb. But God repaid Nadab for this shameful deed: Ahikar came out to the light of day and Nadab was cast into eternal night. It was because Ahikar did good deeds that he escaped the trap that Nadab had set. Nadab was caught in his own trap and perished. So, always remember my children, the consequences of good deeds—and the consequences of evil deeds. Works of evil bring death."

Then he said, "My spirit is about to leave me."

They laid Tobit on his bed and there he died. He received an honorable funeral.

12 When Tobiah's mother died, he buried her beside Tobit. Then Tobiah and Sarah and all their children left for Media and settled in Ecbatana. There they lived with Edna and Raguel. 13 Tobiah demonstrated great love for his in-laws in their old age. When they died, they were buried in Ecbatana in Media. Tobiah inherited both Raguel's estate as well as the estate of his own parents. 14 He died with great dignity at the age of one hundred seventeen.

15 Before Tobiah died, he heard of the destruction of Nineveh and saw the captives that Cyaxares, ruler of Media, led in procession into Media. Tobiah praised God for what had befallen the people of Nineveh and Assyria. And for the rest of his life, he praised God for the fate of Nineveh.

judith

Ít all began during the twelfth year of
the reign of Nebuchadnezzar, who ruled over the Assyrians from the capital city of Nineveh.* At the same time, Arphaxad ruled over the Medes in Ecbatana. ² Arphaxad built fortifications around the city, with stones five feet thick and nine feet long. The walls surrounding the city were 105 feet high and 90 feet wide. ³ The guard towers that were built at the city gates were 150 feet high and 90 feet wide at the base. ⁴ The gates were 105 feet high and 60 feet wide—large enough for an army to march through with its battalions in formation.

⁵ So, in his twelfth year, Nebuchadnezzar declared war on Arphaxad in the vast plateau surrounding the city of Rages. ⁶ The mountain folk joined in alliance with Arphaxad, as did the river-dwellers who lived along the

---

* Nebuchadnezzar ruled over the Babylonians from 605-562 BCE. The author of *Judith*, however, places Nebuchadnezzar as ruler of Assyria in Nineveh in the post-exilic period, after the rebuilding the the Temple in 512. Further, Nineveh was destroyed in 612 by Nabopolasser, Nebuchadnezzar's father. This way of playing with historical figures gives the story a fictitious rather than historical tone. The author wishes to create a composite figure of all the oppressors of Israel—"every age has its Caesar," as it were. In doing so, the author contrasts an archetype of the nations who oppress Israel with an archetype of Israel—Judith, whose name means "Jewess."

Tigris, Euphrates, and Hydaspes, and those who lived on the plateau which was ruled by Arioch of Elymais. Many other nations became allies with the Chaldeans.

⁷ Then Nebuchadnezzar sent out a call to arms to the inhabitants of Persia, as well as to the western regions of Cilicia, Damascus, Lebanon, Antilebanon, and those who lived along the coast, ⁸ as well as the peoples of Carmel, Gilead, northern Galilee, and the plateau of Esdraelon, ⁹ and those living in Samaria and its villages. The order was also given to the people who lived on the other side of the Jordan, to Jerusalem and Bethany in the west, Chelous and Kadesh in the south, and even down along the Nile, the river of Egypt: Tahpanhes and Ramses, the whole land of Goshen, ¹⁰ and beyond to Tanis and Memphis—even to the borders of Ethiopia.

¹¹ But everyone who lived in these regions ignored Nebuchadnezzar's call and refused to align with him. They did not think that Nebuchadnezzar had any chance of victory, so they were not afraid to ignore the call. All the messengers returned to Nebuchadnezzar empty-handed and in shame.

¹² Nebuchadnezzar became enraged at the whole region, and swore vengeance on the territories of Cilicia, Damascus, and Syria. He swore to destroy all the inhabitants of Moab, Ammon, and Judea, as well as everyone in Egypt—everyone between the two great seas.*

¹³ Five years later, in the seventeenth year of his reign, Nebuchadnezzar led the army against Arphaxad. Nebuchadnezzar defeated Arphaxad in battle, vanquishing the whole army along with the cavalry and charioteers. ¹⁴ After occupying all of the villages, Nebuchadnezzar advanced toward Ecbatana, captured its towers, plundered its markets, and turned this once glorious place into a ruin. ¹⁵ Arphaxad was captured in the mountains near Rages and was killed. After Arphaxad's death, ¹⁶ Nebuchadnezzar and the entire army returned to Nineveh with the spoils of war. They feasted for 120 days.

2:1 In the eighteenth year of Nebuchadnezzar's rule, on the twenty-second day of the first month of the year, the palace was abuzz with talk that Nebuchadnezzar was about to make good on the threats he made against all the nations. ² Nebuchadnezzar called in all the chief advisors and administrators, and presented to them his secret plan calling for the total destruction of all the countries that had ignored his call to arms. ³ They

---

* The seas referred to here are not identified. In the context of the passage, it seems to be the Mediterranean and the Red Sea, but some people have taken it to mean the land between the Mediterranean and the Persian Gulf.

decided to kill everyone who had refused to comply with the order he had issued.

⁴ After the entire plan was laid out, Nebuchadnezzar called in Holofernes, the chief general of the entire army and second only to Nebuchadnezzar in authority, and said:

⁵ "I, Nebuchadnezzar the Great, sovereign* of the entire world, command you to raise an army of the strongest and fiercest soldiers in the land. I want 120,000 foot soldiers, and 12,000 cavalry ⁶ to march against the western regions who disobeyed my orders. ⁷ Tell these nations to prepare their offerings of earth and water to demonstrate their unconditional surrender to me.** They will know the full force of my rage as they watch my troops sweep across the face of the whole earth as one body, plundering as they go. ⁸ I will fill the river beds and mountain passes with the bodies of my enemies until they are filled to the brim. ⁹ I will take all who survive as my prisoners and scatter them over the face of the earth.

¹⁰ "Now, Holofernes, go ahead of me and conquer their lands. If they surrender to you, you must occupy their villages until I can come and take my vengeance upon them personally. ¹¹ If they fight, show them no mercy: kill them all and loot their entire region. ¹² I swear to you by my own life and the power of my empire that I will do everything I have said.

¹³ "And a word of warning to you: don't attempt to betray me or disobey my orders. You must carry out everything exactly as I have planned it, and without delay."

¹⁴ So Holofernes departed and summoned all the commanders, generals, and officers in the Assyrian army. ¹⁵ He called all the soldiers and hand-picked the troops, exactly as the sovereign ruler had told him to do: 120,000 foot soldiers, together with 12,000 archers on horseback. ¹⁶ Holofernes trained them to march together in the great campaign. ¹⁷ He gathered a large number of donkeys and camels to use for transportation, and countless sheep, oxen and goats for food—¹⁸ as well as sufficient rations for the army and a large sum of gold and silver from the palace treasury.

¹⁹ Then the entire army set out ahead of Nebuchadnezzar to the lands of the west to sweep over the face of the earth with their chariots and cavalry and foot soldiers. ²⁰ A teeming mob followed them like a swarm of locusts, or a dust cloud in the desert. There were so many they could not be counted.

²¹ They marched for three days from Nineveh toward the plateau of Bectileth, near the mountain north of upper Cilicia. ²² From there, Holo-

---

* The word is *Kyrios*, indicating that Nebuchadnezzar is challenging God.
**"Have earth and water ready for me" is a Persian expression referring to the military practice of using the resources of conquered lands as a source of provisions for their armies.

fernes led the whole army, infantry, cavalry and chariots, and marched toward the hill country. ²³ They pillaged Put and Lud, and plundered the Rassisites and the Ishmaelites who roamed along the borders of the desert south of the land of Cheloeon. ²⁴ They followed the Euphrates and swept through Mesopotamia, destroying as they went all the fortified villages along the Abron River as far as the sea. ²⁵ They conquered the land of Cilicia and butchered all who resisted. Then they arrived at the border on the south of Japheth, facing the Arabian desert. ²⁶ There they ambushed the Midianites, burnt their tents and stole their sheepfolds. ²⁷ They proceeded down the plateau of Damascus during the wheat harvest, burning their fields, destroying their flocks and herds, pillaging their villages, despoiling their land and putting their young people to death.

²⁸ All the people along the seacoast came to dread Holofernes and the army, and were panic-stricken and trembled in fear. All the peoples in the towns of Tyre, Sur, Ocina, Jamnia, Azotus, and Ashkelon were terrified.

3:1 All the peoples in these lands sent delegations to Nebuchadnezzar to sue for peace, saying, ² "We, the loyal subjects of Nebuchadnezzar the Great, submit* to you. You may do whatever you want with us. ³ All of our buildings, our land, our wheat fields, our flocks and herds, as well as our encampments, are yours for the taking. Do with them as you please. ⁴ Our villages and all their inhabitants are chattel to do with as you please."

⁵ The messengers came to Holofernes and delivered the message.

⁶ Then Holofernes led the army down the seacoast and stationed occupation troops in all their fortified cities and chose a number of compliant city officials to serve as their representatives. ⁷ The townspeople and those who lived in the surrounding villages welcomed the occupation force with parades of garlands and dancers with tambourines. ⁸ Even so, Holofernes destroyed their temples and razed their sacred grounds, since he had been ordered to destroy all the gods of the lands so that all the nations would worship Nebuchadnezzar alone—so that people of all tribes and tongues would call Nebuchadnezzar "god."

⁹ As Holofernes approached Esdraelon near Dothan, which faces the mountain ridges of Judah, ¹⁰ the army set up camp between Geba and Scythopolis and remained there an entire month in order to regroup and restock their provisions.

---

* Literally, "to lie down," with strong sexual connotation. A sharp contrast is drawn here between the cowardice of the nations and the courageous resistance of the Israelites.

4:1 When the people of Israel living in Judah heard tales of how Holofernes, chief general of Nebuchadnezzar the Great's forces, had disposed of the other nations, plundering their temples and destroying them, they trembled in fear at word of his approach. ² They shook in fear for the fate of Jerusalem and the Temple of the Most High, their God. ³ It was only recently that they had returned from exile. The people of Judah had only recently joined forces and reconsecrated the Temple, replacing the sacred vessels and altar, after it had been defiled.

⁴ They sent messengers to every district of Samaria, as well as Kona, Bethhoron and Jericho. ⁵ They quickly secured the mountain tops and built ramparts around the villages on them. And they stored up food to prepare for the war—fortunately, they had just brought in the harvest.

⁶ Then the High Priest Joakim, who lived in Jerusalem at the time, wrote to the people of Bethulia* and Betomesthaim, ⁷ ordering them to establish a foothold overlooking the mountain passes, through with Israel could be invaded. From there, it would be easy to stop anyone who tried to enter, for the path was narrow—only wide enough for two to pass at a time.

⁸ The Israelites carried out the orders passed on to them by the High Priest Joakim and the Council of Elders of Israel which met in Jerusalem. ⁹ All Israelites loyal to God prayed zealously and submitted themselves to God in sackcloth and ashes. ¹⁰ Entire families, along with their livestock—as well as every resident alien, hired hand and indentured worker—wore sackcloth around their waists. ¹¹ And all Israelites—women, men and children—living in Jerusalem fell down before the Temple, covered with sackcloth and ashes. ¹² They even covered the altar with sackcloth as they cried out with one voice with ardent pleas to the God of Israel not the allow their children to be taken as prisoners or their families to be enslaved. They pleaded with God not to allow the towns where they had settled to be leveled or the Sanctuary which had just been rededicated to be defiled and desecrated for the perverse amusement of these foreigners.

¹³ The Most High heard their prayers and looked with mercy on their affliction. People throughout Judea and Jerusalem fasted for many days before the Sanctuary of God Almighty. ¹⁴ The High Priest Joakim and all who stood before the sanctuary of the Most High worshipped God with sackcloth around their waists as they made their daily burnt offerings, votive offerings and freewill offerings of the people. ¹⁵ With ashes on their

---

* No city by this name is known. It is thought to be a fictitious city. It is an Armageddon-type setting where the forces of God stand against the forces of evil.

turbans, they cried out to the Most High with all their strength to look with favor on the House of Israel.

℞ ℞ ℞

5:1 Holofernes, the Assyrian commander, got reports that the people of Israel had prepared for war and had barricaded the mountain passes, secured the mountaintops and set up ramparts on the uplands.

² Enraged, he summoned all the tribal leaders of Moab, as well as the commanders of Ammon and the governors of the coastlands ³ and said to them, "You're all Canaanites. Tell me about these people who live in the mountain regions. What cities do they inhabit? How great are their forces? What is the source of their strength? Who is their ruler, and who leads their armies? ⁴ Why have they alone, among all you western peoples, refused to surrender to me?"

⁵ Then Achior, leader of the Ammonites, spoke: "If it please my sovereign to listen to what your humble subject says, I will tell you all the relevant facts about these mountain dwellers who live near your encampment. I'll tell you the truth.

⁶ "These people are the descendants of the Chaldeans. ⁷ At one time, their ancestors drove them out of that land—out of the presence of the gods of Chaldea— ⁸ because they abandoned the ways of their ancestors and refused to worship the gods of Chaldea, worshipping instead the God of heaven.

"They drifted until they settled in Mesopotamia, where they remained for a long time. ⁹ Then their god ordered them to leave that place and migrate to the land of Canaan. Here they established themselves and began to prosper in silver and gold and large herds of livestock. ¹⁰ But when famine swept through the land of Canaan, they migrated to Egypt and lived there for as long as there was food. There they grew to such great numbers that their people could not be counted. ¹¹ So the Pharaoh turned against them. They were made into indentured workers and forced to make bricks. ¹² But they cried out to their god, who heard them and sent incurable plagues over the land of Egypt. So the Egyptians drove them out of their presence. ¹³ Then their god dried up the Red Sea* before them ¹⁴ and led them along the way to Sinai and Kadesh-barnea.

"They drove out the people who lived in the southern part of Canaan, ¹⁵ conquered the land of the Amorites, vanquished the Heshbonites, then

---

* This is the only place in the Hebrew scriptures where the body of water crossed in the Exodus is actually called the Red Sea, despite it being translated that way in many English versions. In general it is called the Sea of Reeds, or simply "the Sea."

they crossed the Jordan and laid claim to the mountain country there. [16] They then drove out the Canaanites, the Perizzites, the Jebusites, the Shechemites, and all the Girgashites, and took up residence there.

[17] "As long as they did not sin against their god, they prospered, for theirs is a god who hates injustice. [18] But when they rejected the statutes their god had given them, they lost many battles, and were led away as prisoners into a foreign land. The temple of their god was torn down and their towns were occupied by their enemies. [19] But since they returned to the ways of their god, they have come together from the many places where they were scattered. They occupy Jerusalem, where their holy place is, and have re-settled in the mountain country, which was uninhabited.

[20] "So, my sovereign, these people have one weakness: if in any way they are sinning against their god, even unwittingly, and we can be sure of their guilt, we can march up and defeat them. [21] But if these people carry no guilt, then I beg my sovereign to pass them by—their god will defend them and we will be the laughingstock of the nations!"

[22] When Achior finished his report, everyone in the vicinity of the council tent began to protest. Holofernes' officers, along with all the inhabitants of the seacoast and Moab, demanded that Achior be hacked to bits. [23] They declared, "We're not afraid of these Israelites! They're a nation with no strength or power to make war. [24] So onward, great Holofernes—your immense army will swallow them whole!"

[6:1] When the ruckus around the council tent subsided, Holofernes, commander of the Assyrian army, said to Achior in front of all the foreign dignitaries, [2] "Who do you think you are, Achior, you and your Ephraimite soldiers, to speak to us as you have today and tell us that we should not go to war against Israel because their god will defend them? What god is there but Nebuchadnezzar? Nebuchadnezzar's forces will wipe them off the face of the earth. Their god will not save them. [3] We will attack them as one body—they cannot resist the strength of our cavalry. [4] We will overpower them. Their mountains will flow with their own blood, and their fields will be piled high with their dead. Not even a footprint will be left after we attack them. So says Nebuchadnezzar the Great, sovereign of the whole earth! Our sovereign has spoken—and his are never empty words!

[5] "But you, Achior—you're nothing but an Ammonite mercenary, and what you say is treason. You will not see my face again until I take my revenge on this brood from Egypt. [6] Then all you'll see are the swords of my soldiers and the spears of my commanders coming at you; they'll pierce your side and you'll die with these Israelites. [7] My people will take you into the hill country and leave you in one of the mountain passes near a village; [8] you won't die until it is time for you to die with them.

⁹ "So, Achior, why do you look so glum? Don't you truly believe that this puny village can stand against me? I have spoken, and it will happen just as I have said."

¹⁰ Then Holofernes ordered his attendants to seize Achior, take him away to Bethulia, and turn him over to the Israelites living there. ¹¹ They took him out of the camp and led him across the plateau toward the mountain country until they reached the springs below Bethulia.

¹² When the soldiers guarding the town caught sight of them, they gathered their weapons and ran out of the town to the mountaintops. All the slingshooters pelted them with stones to prevent them from approaching further. ¹³ The entourage managed to find shelter at the foot of the slope. There they tied Achior hand and foot and left him lying at the base of the mountain. Then they returned to their leader.

¹⁴ The Israelites came out of the town and found Achior. They untied him and took him to Bethulia, where they brought him before the town elders— ¹⁵ in those days they were Uzziah begot of Micah of the tribe of Simeon, Chabris begot of Gothoniel, and Charmis begot of Melchiel. ¹⁶ They called the elders of the town together, and all the young people in the village ran to the elders. They sat Achior in the middle of the crowd, and Uzziah interrogated him. ¹⁷ Achior answered all their questions and told them everything that was said in Holofernes' tent and what he had said in the midst of the Assyrian commanders. He told the council how Holofernes bragged about what he would do to Israel.

¹⁸ Then the people fell down and worshipped God, crying out, ¹⁹ "Sovereign God in heaven, witness the arrogance of this people who think nothing of humiliating our people! Look kindly on those who are dedicated to you!"

²⁰ Then they praised Achior for his testimony. ²¹ When the council dispersed, Uzziah took Achior home and gave a banquet there for the elders. That night they prayed to the God of Israel for help.

7:1 The next day, Holofernes ordered the whole army and all their allies to break camp and march against Bethulia. They were ordered to occupy the mountain passes and engage the Israelites in fighting. ² All their warriors marched off that day, with fighting forces numbering 170,000 infantry and 12,000 cavalry—not counting the provisions or the baggage carriers. It was a vast army. ³ They established their camp in the valley near Bethulia, near the spring, and deployed their front lines in a formation which stretched from Dothan to Balbaim in width, and from Bethulia to Cyamon in depth, facing Esdraelon.

⁴ When the Israelites saw the huge army, they shook with fear and said, "They will strip the entire land! Not even the mountain peaks or the river valleys will be able to withstand their onslaught!" ⁵ But in spite of their fear, they took up their weapons, kindled the fires on their watchtowers, and remained on guard through the night.

⁶ The next day, Holofernes led the cavalry across the plateau in full view of the Israelites in Bethulia. ⁷ They reconnoitered all the approaches to the village, and searched out the springs which provided water. Holofernes captured the springs and set guards to watch over them. He then returned to the base camp.

⁸ Then the commanders of the Edomite soldiers, the leaders of Moab, and the commanders from the coastal villages came to Holofernes and said, ⁹ "If you listen to us, my sovereign, your army will suffer no losses. ¹⁰ These Israelites don't rely on the length of their spears to defend themselves, but on the height of their mountains. It isn't easy to reach the tops of their mountains. ¹¹ So, my sovereign, don't fight them in regular formation. We guarantee that not one soldier will fall. ¹² Just remain in your camp and keep all the soldiers in your army with you. We'll guard the spring of water at the foot of the mountains— ¹³ this is where the people of Bethulia get their water. They'll be weakened by their own thirst and will surrender their village willingly. ¹⁴ They and all their families will waste away in famine, and will be lying around in the streets before even a single sword reaches them. ¹⁵ In this way, you'll avenge yourself, because they rebelled against you and did not surrender to you willingly."

¹⁶ Holofernes was pleased at these words, and called all the officers and gave them orders to carry out what they had said. ¹⁷ The Ammonite army moved forward together with 5,000 Assyrians. They set up camp in the valley and stood guard around the water supply and well that the Israelites used. ¹⁸ Then the Edomites and Ammonites marched up into the mountainous regions opposite Dothan and set up camp there. Then they sent out a contingent to the south and east, toward Egrebel, near Chusi beside the Mochmur Valley. The remainder of the Assyrian forces remained encamped on the plateau.

Even spread this wide, their numbers covered the whole face of the land. Their tents and supply caravans spread out innumerably and together they were a vast throng. ¹⁹ The Israelites cried out to the Most High God, because their courage had vanished at the sight of all the enemies that surrounded them, from whom they could not escape.

²⁰ The whole Assyrian army, with the full array of infantry, chariots, and cavalry, held the blockade for thirty-four days until the village water supplies were depleted. ²¹ Their wells began to dry up, and as each day passed, they had less and less water to drink. At that point, all water was rationed. ²² The young people in the village became restless and women and men collapsed from thirst. They fell down in the streets and in the gateways of the village, no longer having any strength.

²³ Then all the people, women, men and children, gathered around Uzziah and the village elders and pleaded in a loud voice, ²⁴ "Let God be the judge between you and us! You have done a grave injustice by not surrendering peacefully to the Assyrians. ²⁵ No one can help us now! God has handed us over to them, and we are weak and are dying of thirst. ²⁶ Send word to them now, and surrender the whole village to them to take as plunder for the armies of Holofernes and all the assembled forces. ²⁷ We'll be better off as their prisoners. We may be their slaves, but at least we'll be alive.* Then we won't have to watch our own children die before our eyes and our spouses draw their last breath. ²⁸ We implore you, by heaven and earth, by our God, the Sovereign One of ages past, who punishes us for our sins and the sins of our ancestors—do as we have asked today!" ²⁹ Then a great wail arose throughout the assembly and they cried out to the Most High in a loud voice.

³⁰ But Uzziah assured them, "Courage, my sisters and brothers! Let's wait for five more days to see if our Sovereign God will show mercy on us. ³¹ If these five days pass and nothing happens, I will do as you say."

³² Then Uzziah dismissed the people. Some went to their assigned posts on the walls and towers of the village, while others went home. Throughout the whole village, they were utterly despondent.

j

** J**uðíth had been kept informed about what was happening. She was the daughter of Merari begot of Ox, begot of Joseph, begot of Oziel, begot of Elkiah, begot of Ananias, begot of Gideon, begot of Raphaim, begot of Ahitub, begot of Elijah, begot of Hilkiah, begot of Eliab, begot of Nathanael, begot of Salamiel, begot of Sarasadai, begot of Israel.

² Judith had been married to Manasseh, who came from her own tribe and family. ³ Manasseh died during the barley harvest as he was supervising the

---

* This echoes the complaint of the Israelites against Moses in Exodus 14:12.

workers who were binding the sheaves in the field. The heat was too much for him to bear, and he died of sunstroke in his bed in Bethulia. They buried Manasseh in the ancestral burial site in the fields between Dothan and Balamon.

⁴ Judith maintained her bereavement for three years and four months. ⁵ She build a small tent on the roof of her house and lived there, wearing sackcloth. ⁶ She fasted every day, except for those times when fasting is forbidden—the day before the Sabbath and the Sabbath itself, the day before the festival of the New Moon and the festival of the New Moon itself, as well as all the festivals and days of celebration observed throughout Israel.

⁷ Judith was very beautiful. Her husband Manasseh left her an estate of silver and gold, attendants, livestock, and fields. She ran the entire estate. ⁸ No one ever spoke a harsh word about her because she was very devout.

⁹ Judith heard the harsh words that the people, out of their weakness for lack of water, were speaking against their leader, and she heard all that Uzziah said to them, and how he promised them under oath to surrender the town to the Assyrians after five days. ¹⁰ She sent her attendant, who managed the affairs of her estate, to invite the village elders, Uzziah, Chabris, and Charmis, to her home.

¹¹ When they arrived, she said to them, "Listen to me. You are supposed to be the leaders of the people here in Bethulia. But what you said to the people today was wrong. You should never have sworn before God that you would surrender the village to our enemies if Our God did not come to our aid in five days. What gives you the right to put God to the test as you have done today? ¹² Who do you think you are to put yourself in God's place in dealing with human affairs? ¹³ It is the Almighty God that you are putting to the test! Will you never learn? ¹⁴ You can never fathom the depths of the human heart or know what anyone is thinking. Yet you dare to read God's mind and interpret divine matters!

"No, my friends, you must not goad the anger of Our God. ¹⁵ Even we are not rescued in five days, God still has power to protect us at will, or even to destroy us in the presence of our enemies. ¹⁶ Do not try to force God's hand or demand guarantees in this matter! God can't be threatened like a human being, or won over by pleading like a mere mortal. ¹⁷ So, while we wait for deliverance, we must continue to call upon God to help us. If God wills it, our voices will be heard.

¹⁸ "Throughout recent memory, and down to the present day, none of our tribes or families or villages has worshipped gods made by human hands, even though our ancestors did long ago. ¹⁹ That is why our ances-

tors were delivered over to sword and plunder, and why they suffered so greatly at the hands of our enemies.

²⁰ "But we claim no other god but the Most High, and we trust that Our God will never betray us or any of our people. ²¹ For if we fall, all of Judea will fall and our Sanctuary will be plundered. Then we will pay for this blasphemy with our own blood. ²² Our loved ones will be slaughtered, our land will be seized and our inheritance will be laid to waste. God will do this in the sight of the nations so that wherever we are taken in bondage, our captors will hold us in scorn and contempt. ²³ Our surrender will not win our enemy's favor—Our God will see that we are put to shame.

²⁴ "And so, my friends, we must stand as an example of courage for our whole people. Their very lives rest upon what we do here—as do the Temple and its altar. ²⁵ In the face of everything, we must continue to give thanks to Our God, who tests us in the same way that our ancestors were tested. ²⁶ Remember what God did to Abraham? How God tested Isaac? Remember what happened to Jacob in upper Mesopotamia while he was tending the sheep of his uncle, Laban? ²⁷ God is not testing our devotion as severely as they were tested. God has not sent this test to us out of vengeance, but as a warning to us, who are near Our God's heart."

²⁸ Then Uzziah spoke: "Everything you have said comes from a pure heart. None of us can doubt your words. ²⁹ This is not the first time you have shown your wisdom. Ever since you were born, people recognized that you possessed keen understanding and that your heart was pure. ³⁰ But the people were so thirsty that they forced our hand in the matter. They made us promise to do this and the oath we made is binding. ³¹ We know of your unwavering devotion. Pray for us that God will send rain to fill our wells. Then we will no longer be weak from thirst."

³² Judith said to them, "Listen to me. What I am about to do will be retold for generations by our descendants. ³³ Tonight, meet me at the village gate so that you can allow me and my attendant to exit. Before the day comes when you have promised to surrender the village, God will deliver Israel by my hand. ³⁴ But you must not ask what I am planning to do. I will explain everything to you when it is over."

³⁵ Uzziah and the rest of the elders said to her, "Go in peace. May Our God guide you to take vengeance on our enemies." They left Judith's tent on the rooftop and returned to their posts.

⁹ᐟ¹ Judith threw herself to the ground and covered her head with ashes. She disrobed as far as the sackcloth under her clothes. At the time of day when incense was being offered in the Temple of God, Judith cried out to the Our God in a loud voice, saying,

2 "Adonai! God of my ancestor Simeon!
    You handed Simeon a sword
to take vengeance on a band of foreigners
    who dared to lay their hands on a young woman.
They stripped her naked and shamed her,
    raped her and defiled her.
Even though you had forbidden this,
    they did it anyway.
3 So you duped their leaders and allowed them to be killed
    on the very bed where they committed their brutal crime.
You slaughtered them all—
    subordinates along with their rulers,
    and rulers on their very thrones.
4 You handed over their families to be oppressed,
    and their children taken prisoner.
All the booty was divided up by your beloved children
    whose hearts burn with passion for you,
    eager to do your will.
They were enraged at the crime
    committed against one of their own
    and called upon you for help.

O God, listen to me,
    in the same way you listened to them!
5 You are the Creator of all that has passed,
    as well as what will happen now
    and what the future will bring.
6 Your purpose is always true
    and your designs are always manifest.
You have planned everything in advance
    and your judgment is all-knowing.

7 Look now at these Assyrians
    who stand before us in vast numbers,
who boast of the might of their cavalry,
    who trust in the shield and spear and bow and sling.
They do not know that you are Sovereign—
    that you crush warfare.
    You alone are Sovereign!
8 Crush them with your great strength;
    bring down their power in your anger.

They intend to defile your own Sanctuary
   and violate the tabernacle where your Name resides,
   to hack off the horns of the altar with their swords.
9 Witness their pride
   and send your anger upon their heads.

I am only one widow,
   but give me the strength to do as I have planned.
10 Give me guile so that I may strike down
   the subordinate with the ruler
   and the rulers with their subordinates.
Let the strength of a woman
   break their pride.
11 Your power does not depend on numbers
   nor your might on armies.
You are the God of the downcast,
   the Liberator of the oppressed,
the Defender of the weak,
   the Protector of the forgotten,
   the Savior of the despairing.

12 I cry to you, please, God of my ancestors,
   God of the heritage of Israel!
Sovereign of heaven and earth,
   Creator of the seas,
Ruler of all creation—
   hear my prayer!
13 Let lies be my weapons
   to maim and kill those who plan to do injury
against your Covenant,
   against your holy Temple,
against Mt. Zion,
   against the house that belongs to your children.
14 Show that you alone are Sovereign
   of every nation and every tribe—
that you are God, God All-Powerful, God Almighty,
   and that the people of Israel have no protection but you."

ଔ   ଔ   ଔ

10:1 When Judith finished crying out to the God of Israel, 2 she arose from
the ground where she had been praying. She summoned her attendant and

went to the house below, where she celebrated her Sabbaths and festival days. ³ She removed the sackcloth she had been wearing and took off her bereavement garments. She bathed her body and anointed herself with fragrant oils. She combed her hair, placed a turban upon her head, and dressed herself in the festival clothing that she used to wear when her husband Manasseh was still alive. ⁴ She put sandals on her feet, and decorated herself with anklets, bracelets, rings, earrings, and other jewelry. She decorated herself in this way so that she would capture the attention of all the men who might see her.

⁵ She gave her attendant a skin of wine and a flask of oil, a bag filled with roasted grain, dried fig cakes, and bread baked according to the Law. Then she wrapped up her dishes and gave them to the attendant to carry.

⁶ The two women proceeded to the village gate of Bethulia. There they found Uzziah waiting with the village elders, Chabris and Charmis. ⁷ When they saw how she had transformed her appearance and dressed differently, they were overwhelmed at her beauty. They said, ⁸ "May the God of Israel bless you and bring you success in your plans, so that the people of Israel may glory and Jerusalem exult!"

⁹ Judith prayed to receive God's blessing, then said, "Order the village gate to be opened for me so that I may go and accomplish all you have charged me with." So they ordered the guards to open the gates for her.

¹⁰ When the gates were opened, Judith went out, followed by her attendant. The guards of the village watched her until she had gone down the mountain and passed through the valley. Then they lost sight of her.

¹¹ As the two women passed through the valley, they were met by an Assyrian patrol ¹² and were taken prisoner. They asked Judith, "Who are your people, and what village do you come from? Where are you going?"

Judith replied, "I am a Hebrew, but I am escaping from them because they are about to be handed over to you. ¹³ I am on my way to see Holofernes, the commander of your army, to deliver some useful information. I will show him a way to capture all the mountain country without having a single soldier captured or killed."

¹⁴ The soldiers could not help but be taken in by her beauty as they listened to what she said. They told her, ¹⁵ "You saved your life by coming here to see our commander. A few of us will take you to his tent and hand you over to him. ¹⁶ When you meet Holofernes, you will have nothing to fear. As long as you tell him what you have told us, you will be treated well."

[17] They chose from their ranks a hundred soldiers to go with Judith and her attendant, and brought them to Holofernes' tent. [18] There was a great commotion throughout the entire camp, and her arrival was reported from tent to tent. They gathered about her as she stood outside of Holofernes' tent waiting for the soldiers to tell him about her. [19] They were awed by her beauty and began to wonder about what kind of people the Israelites were. They said to one another, "Who can hate these people who are able to produce such a beauty among them? It is not wise to leave any of their soldiers alive—if we let them go, they will seduce the whole world!"

[20] Then Holofernes' guards and stewards came out and led her into the tent. [21] Holofernes was reclining on his bed under a canopy that was woven with strands of purple and gold thread, and decorated with emeralds and other precious stones. [22] When they announced her presence, Holofernes came to the front of the tent, with silver lamps carried before him. [23] When Holofernes and his stewards caught sight of Judith, their jaws dropped at the sight of her beauty. She bowed down to the ground in front of Holofernes, but the stewards lifted her up.

11[1] Holofernes said, "Take courage! You have nothing to fear from me. I have never harmed anyone who sided with Nebuchadnezzar, ruler of the earth. [2] Indeed, if your nation of mountain dwellers had not rebelled against me, I would not have raised a single spear against them. They brought this on their own heads. [3] Now tell me, why have you run away from them and come over to our side? Whatever the reason, you are safe now, so take courage! Your life will continue on after tonight. [4] No one will hurt you. Everyone will treat you well—as they would any of the subjects of my sovereign, Nebuchadnezzar."

Then Judith said to Holofernes, [5] "If you would permit me, a humble subordinate, to speak to you, my liege, I will speak no lie to my sovereign this night. [6] If you follow the words of your humble subordinate, God will work through you and you will be successful. [7] I swear by the life of Nebuchadnezzar, sovereign of the whole earth, and by the power of the one who has sent you to subdue every living thing! For you have brought not only human beings, but also the animals of the field and livestock and the birds of the air into the realm of Nebuchadnezzar. [8] Word of your wisdom and skill has spread through the whole world, and we have heard that you are the greatest in all the empire, the most intelligent and the most adept in military strategy.

[9] "We also know what Achior said in your council chamber. The people of Bethulia spared his life and he told them everything. [10] I must tell you,

my sovereign, don't disregard what he said to you. Take it seriously, for it is true. Our nation cannot be punished or defeated by the sword as long as they have not sinned against their God.

¹¹ "But still, you will not be thwarted in your purpose, for death will overtake them. A great blasphemy has risen up among them by which they will provoke the anger of their God. ¹² Since their food supply is almost exhausted and their water has almost given out, they have decided to kill all their livestock and eat those things which are expressly forbidden for them to eat according to the Law of God. ¹³ They have decided to eat the firstfruits of grain and the offerings of oil and wine, which have been consecrated and set aside for the priests who attend to the presence of God in Jerusalem. It is not lawful even to touch these things.

¹⁴ "Since even the people of Jerusalem have been doing this, the people of Bethulia have sent a messenger to Jerusalem to ask the Council of Elders to permit them to do this too. ¹⁵ When the messengers return, and they act upon the permission, they will be handed over to you to be destroyed.

¹⁶ "So when I, your subordinate, learned of this, I ran away from them. God has sent me to accomplish through you things that will astound the whole world when they are retold. ¹⁷ I am a very devout person and worship the God of heaven night and day. So, my sovereign, I will remain with you. But every night I will go into the valley to pray to God. God will tell me when they have committed their sacrilege. ¹⁸ Then I will come and tell you so that you can ride out with your whole army and not one of them will be able to stand against you. ¹⁹ Then I will guide you through the Judean countryside and escort you into Jerusalem. There I will place a crown on your head. You will rout the people of Jerusalem like sheep without a shepherd, and not even a dog would dare growl at you. God has said all of this to me, and I was sent to tell you."

²⁰ Holofernes was pleased at her words, as were all in attendance. They were astonished at her and said, ²¹ "No other woman on the face of the earth is so beautiful or speaks so skillfully!"

Then Holofernes said to her, ²² "God has done well to send you ahead of your people, to bring us victory and destroy those who have insulted my sovereign. ²³ You are not only beautiful, you are also articulate. If you do as you have said, your god will be my god. You will live in Nebuchadnezzar's palace and your name will be known throughout the world."

12:1 Holofernes then commanded the stewards to take Judith to the banquet room, and ordered them to set a table for her out of his own provisions, with some of his own wine to drink.

² But Judith said, "I cannot eat any of those things without committing

an offense against God. I will have enough with these things that I have brought with me."

³ Holofernes said, "If your supply runs out, where can we get you more of the same? None of your people is here with us."

⁴ Judith replied, "As surely as you live, I will not use up all the supplies I have with me before the Most High carries out by my hand what has been determined."

⁵ Then Holofernes' stewards brought her into the tent and she slept until midnight. Just before the morning watch, she got up ⁶ and sent a message to Holofernes, "Please order the guards to allow your subordinate to go out and pray." ⁷ So Holofernes ordered the guards to let her go. She remained in the camp for three days, and each night went out to the valley of Bethulia where she bathed in the spring at the camp. ⁸ After bathing, she prayed to the Most High God of Israel to guide her way for the victory of her people. ⁹ Then she returned and stayed in her tent until she ate her food in the evening.

¹⁰ On the fourth day, Holofernes held a banquet for the stewards only, and did not invite any of the soldiers. ¹¹ He said to Bagoas, the eunuch in charge of his personal affairs, "Go and persuade this Hebrew woman in your care to come here to eat and drink with us. ¹² It would be a disgrace to let such a woman go without getting to 'know' her better. If I do not try to seduce her, I will become a laughingstock."

¹³ So Bagoas left Holofernes and went to Judith and said, "Come with me, pretty woman. I will take you to my sovereign to be honored in his presence. Come drink with us and enjoy yourself as would an Assyrian woman in the palace of Nebuchadnezzar."

¹⁴ Judith replied, "Who am I to refuse my sovereign? Whatever his pleasure, I will do at once. It will be a joy I will remember up until the day of my death." ¹⁵ So Judith dressed herself in all the finest clothes. She sent her attendant ahead of her to spread out in front of Holofernes the lambskins that Bagoas had given to her to use as cushions.

¹⁶ Then Judith entered the tent and reclined. Holofernes' heart was filled with lust for her and he could barely control his own passions. He had been waiting for this opportunity since the first day he saw her. ¹⁷ Holofernes said, "Drink with us and be merry!"

¹⁸ Judith said, "I will gladly drink, my sovereign, because today is the greatest day in my whole life." ¹⁹ She then took what her attendant had prepared and ate and drank in his presence. ²⁰ Holofernes was so excited that he guzzled a great amount of wine, more than he had ever drunk in his life.

13·1 When evening came, Holofernes' attendants withdrew from the tent. Bagoas closed the tent from the outside and shut out the attendants from Holofernes' presence. Then they all went to bed, weary since the banquet had lasted so long. ² So Judith was alone in the tent, with Holofernes stretched out in front of her dead drunk.

³ Judith had told her attendant to wait outside of the bedchamber for her, just as she had done every other day, for she had told everyone that she would be going out for prayers. She had told this to Bagoas, too. ⁴ So all the guests had left the banquet and not one, great or small, was left in Holofernes' presence.

Judith stood beside the bed and prayed,

> "Adonai, my God, source of all strength,
>   guide the work of my hands
>   for the greater glory of Jerusalem.
> ⁵   Now is the time to rescue your heritage
>   and help me carry out the plan
>   to crush the enemies who march against you."

⁶ When she finished, she went up to the bedpost beside Holofernes' head and took his sword. ⁷ Then she crept up to him and took hold of him by the hair. Raising her hand above her head, she prayed, "Give me strength today, Most High God of Israel!" ⁸ Then she struck his neck twice with all her might and cut off his head. ⁹ Next she rolled his body off the bed and pulled down the canopy from the posts. Then she went outside and gave Holofernes' head to her attendant, ¹⁰ who stuffed it in the food bag.

The two of them departed from the camp, just as they had done each night for prayer. They passed through the camp, circled around the valley and went up the mountain to the gates of Bethulia. ¹¹ As they approached the gates, Judith called out to the sentries, "Open up! Open the gates! The Most High, our God, is with us! The Most High still reigns with power in Israel against our enemies, and has shown that power today!"

¹² When the villagers heard her voice, they hurried to the town gates and called out the village elders. Everyone, small and great, ran together. No one believed that she would ever return. ¹³ They opened the gate and welcomed them.

¹⁴ Then Judith said in a loud voice, "Praise God! Give Our God praise! Praise our God who has not held back mercy from the house of Israel! God has destroyed our enemies by my hand this very night."

¹⁵ Then she pulled Holofernes' head out of the bag and showed it to them, saying, "Look here! This is the head of Holofernes, the commander

of the Assyrian army. And here is the canopy where he was lying dead drunk. The Most High has vanquished him by the hand of a woman! [16] He let himself be seduced by my beauty, to his own destruction. He committed no sin with me to defile and shame me, for God protected me all the way."

[17] Everyone was astounded and bowed down to worship God, saying with one voice, "Blessed are you, Our God! You have humiliated the enemies of your people today."

[18] Then Uzziah said to her,

> "O daughter, you are truly blessed by the Most High God
>   above all other women on the earth;
> and blessed be the Most High God—
>   who made the heavens and the earth—
> who guided your hand
>   when you cut off the head
>   of leader of our enemy.
> [19] Your faith in God
>   will be remembered in the hearts
>   of all who celebrate the power of Our God.
> [20] May God grant you a perpetual remembrance
>   and reward you with many blessings
> since you did not think of your own life
>   when our nation was on the verge of destruction!
> Instead, you fended off our desolation
>   by walking in the path of justice before Our God!"

And the people said, "Amen! Amen!"

14[1] Then Judith said to them, "Listen to me, my friends. Take this head and hang it over the village walls. [2] When morning comes, and the sun is up, let every able-bodied warrior take up arms and march out of the village. Appoint a leader over them as if you meant to march down to the plateau, and act as if you are preparing to march down to the Assyrian encampment. Only don't go down. [3] When they see you, they will take up arms and rush back to their headquarters to alert their officers. They will rush into Holofernes' tent, but will not find him alive. They will panic and will flee before you. [4] At that moment, you, and all who live on the borders of Israel, must pursue them and mow them down in their tracks. [5] But before you do all of this, bring Achior the Ammonite to me so that he can look at the one who insulted the house of Israel and sent him to us as if to death."

⁶ They called Achior from the house of Uzziah. When he arrived, he saw the head of Holofernes in the hand of one of the warriors among the people. At the sight, he fainted in his tracks. ⁷ When the people revived Achior, he threw himself at Judith's feet, praising her, saying, "Blessed are you in the tents of Judah! Throughout the nations those who hear your name will tremble in fear! ⁸ Now tell me how you accomplished these things."

Judith recounted the events of the past days to Achior in front of the entire village. She told everything from the moment she left to the moment before she returned. ⁹ When she finished her tale, the people made a joyful sound which created a din throughout the village. ¹⁰ When Achior saw what the God of Israel had done, he turned to God in faith. He was circumcised and joined the house of Israel, remaining there to this day.

¹¹ As dawn broke, they hung Holofernes' head over the wall. Then they armed themselves and marched out in formation to the mountain passes. ¹² When the Assyrians saw them, they sent word back to their officers. ¹³ They came to Holofernes' tent and said to the eunuch in charge of personal affairs, "Wake up our leader! These impudent upstarts have the audacity to come down from their mountain and attack us. It will be their destruction!"

¹⁴ So Bagoas went into the tent and knocked on the entry pillar of the bedchamber—he assumed that Holofernes had been sleeping with Judith. ¹⁵ When no one answered, Bagoas entered the bedchamber and found Holofernes lying dead on the floor with his head missing. ¹⁶ He screamed loudly and wept and groaned and tore his clothes. ¹⁷ Then he went to the tent were Judith had been staying. When he didn't find her there, he rushed out into the encampment shouting, ¹⁸ "These peasants have tricked us! One Hebrew woman has brought disgrace upon the house of Nebuchadnezzar the Great! Look—Holofernes lies in his own blood, and his head is missing!"

¹⁹ When the leaders of the Assyrian army heard this, they tore their clothes and began to panic. Their loud cries and shouts were heard throughout the camp.

15¹ When the soldiers who were still in their tents heard the news, they were dumbfounded. ² Filled with panic and terror, they did not wait for one another. As one body, they rushed out of their tents and ran away down every highway and mountain pass. ³ The soldiers who had encamped in the mountains around Bethulia also turned tail and ran.

Then the Israelites, every warrior among them, descended upon them. ⁴ Uzziah sent warriors to the towns of Betomasthaim, Bebai, Choba, and

Kola, and throughout the land of Israel, to tell them what had happened and to urge them to descend on the enemy and destroy them. ⁵ As soon as the Israelites heard the news, they descended upon the Assyrians as one body and cut them down as far as Choba. Even those from Jerusalem and the rest of the mountain region took part in this, for they had been told of all that had happened. Gileadites and Galileans outflanked the retreating armies and slaughtered them even up through Damascus and beyond its borders.

⁶ The rest of the people of Bethulia fell upon the Assyrian camp and plundered it of its riches. ⁷ When the Israelite warriors returned from the slaughter, they took whatever remained. Even the towns and villages in the mountain regions and the plateau got a great amount of booty, since there was a vast quantity.

⁸ Joakim the High Priest and the council of elders of Israel, who were in Jerusalem, came out to see for themselves the great things that God had done in the land of Israel and to see Judith themselves and to praise her.

⁹ When they came to her house, they blessed her in one voice, saying,

> "You are the glory of Jerusalem!
>   You are the pride of Israel!
>   You are the most esteemed of our people!
> ¹⁰ What you have done by your own hand,
>   you have done for all of Israel,
>   and God has blessed your mighty deeds.
> May you continue to be blessed by the Most High
>   for as long as you live!"

And all the people said, "Amen!"

¹¹ The villagers plundered the camp for thirty days. They gave Holofernes' tent to Judith along with the silver plates, the bed, the bowls, and all the furniture. She took them and packed them onto her mules, and hitched up her carts and piled everything in the carts.

¹² All the women of Israel came out to see her, singing her praises, and some of them performed a dance in her honor. ¹³ Judith distributed ivy-covered branches to the women who were with her, and she and those who were with her crowned themselves with olive wreaths. Then she went out in front of all the people in the dance, leading all the women while the men of Israel followed behind—brandishing their weapons, wearing garlands, and singing songs of praise.

[14] Judith began to sing this song of thanksgiving before all of Israel, and the people joined in.*

16[1] She sang:

> "Take up the tambourine and break into song for Our God;
> > praise the Most High with drums and cymbals!
>
> Raise to God a new psalm;
> > cry out for joy and call upon God's Name.
>
> [2] For the Most High is a God who crushes armies,
> > who lives among the people in a tent,
> > who rescued me from the hands of my pursuers!

> [3] The Assyrians descended from the northern mountains
> > bringing innumerable warriors,
>
> whose numbers filled all the river valleys
> > and whose cavalry covered the mountains.
>
> [4] They bragged that they would level my land,
> > put my young people to the sword,
>
> dash my infants to the ground,
> > take all of my children prisoner,
> > and carry off all our young women.
>
> [5] But Almighty God thwarted them
> > by the hand of a woman!
>
> [6] Their own champion was not slain by young soldiers,
> > nor did children of Titans bring him down.
>
> It was Judith, daughter of Merari,
> > who vanquished him with her beauty.
>
> [7] She put away her grieving clothes
> > so that the oppressed of Israel could be raised up.
>
> She anointed herself with fragrant oils
> [8] and placed a turban on her head
> > and donned a linen gown to seduce him.
>
> [9] Her sandal enthralled his eye;
> > her beauty entranced his very soul—
> > and then the sword severed his neck!

> [10] The Persians shook with fear at her courage;
> > the Medes were daunted at her daring.
>
> [11] Then my oppressed people cried out;
> > my weak people raised their voices and the enemy quaked.
> > They made a great clamor and the enemy ran away.

---

* This recalls Miriam's leading the women in song in Exodus 15:20.

¹² The children of the oppressed ran them down
  and wounded them like children of fugitives.
  They were vanquished before the army of the Most High.

¹³ I will sing a new song to my God:
  Adonai, you are great and strong!
  Your strength is marvelous;
  you are invincible.

¹⁴ Let all of your creatures worship you;
  as a result of your words, they came to be.
  You breathed into them and they lived.
  None can resist your voice.

¹⁵ The mountains shake to their foundations; the seas tremble,
  and rocks melt like wax at your glance.
  But you show mercy
  on those who revere you.

¹⁶ Even the most fragrant sacrifice is a small thing to you,
  and the fat of a single burnt offering is but a trifle.
  But worshipping you in reverence
  is the greatest gift of all.

¹⁷ Pity the nation that marches against my people!
  Almighty God will punish them on the day of judgment!
  The Most High will send fire and worms to devour their flesh
  and they will wail in anguish forever!"

℞   ℞   ℞

¹⁸ When the people arrived in Jerusalem, they worshipped God. Once they had purified themselves, they presented their burnt offerings and free-will offerings and gifts. ¹⁹ Judith offered to God all the possessions of Holofernes that the people had given to her, as well as the canopy which she herself had taken from the bed. ²⁰ The people in Jerusalem continued to feast before the Sanctuary for three months, and all that time Judith remained with them.

²¹ After this, they returned home to their own villages and families. Judith returned to Bethulia and lived on her estate there. For the rest of her life, she was honored throughout the country. ²² Many wanted to marry her, but she never remarried after the death of her husband Manasseh.

²³ Her legend continued to spread, and she lived to a ripe old age, living until the age of 105. She died in Bethulia and was buried in the cave next

to her husband Manasseh. ²⁴ All the House of Israel mourned for seven days at her passing. Before she died, she distributed all her possessions to the relatives of her husband Manasseh and to her own relatives. And for the rest of her life, and for a long time afterward, no one ever again threatened Israel.

1 maccabees

1:1–64

Ít came about that alexander the ma-
cedonian—heir to the throne of Philip, who came from the land of Kittam*
—had conquered Darius, ruler of Persia and Media, and placed himself on
the throne, having already made himself the ruler of Greece. ² He fought
many battles and captured many strong cities, putting their leaders to
death. ³ He advanced to the edges of the world, plundering the treasures
of many nations. The entire earth stood silent before him and he became
vain and contemptuous. ⁴ He build a mighty army and conquered entire
regions, nations, and rulers, all of whom paid tribute to him. ⁵ But when
the conquests were done, he became ill and knew that he would die soon.
⁶ So he brought together his most trusted generals, each of whom had accompanied him throughout his youth, and divided the empire among them
while he was still alive. ⁷ Then, having reigned twelve years, Alexander
died.

⁸ So these generals began their rule, each in their own realm. ⁹ Each one
wore a crown, and after they died, their descendants did the same for many
years. And through their rule, they unleashed countless evils over the

---

* Usually refers to Cyprus, whose capital was Kiti, but can also refer to the rest of the Aegean area.

earth. ¹⁰ From their trunk sprang a vile branch whose name was Antiochus Epiphanes, begot of Antiochus, ruler of Syria. Once a hostage at Rome, he became ruler in the 137th year of the Selucid era.

¹¹ In those days, there appeared in Israel certain people who questioned the Law. They seduced many with their words. "Let's go and make an alliance with the Gentiles all around us," they said. "Since we separated from them, many evils have come upon us."

¹² The proposal met with the enthusiasm of many of the citizens. ¹³ Some from among the people went eagerly to their ruler, who authorized them to practice the ways of the Gentiles. ¹⁴ They built a gymnasium in Jerusalem according to the Gentile custom; ¹⁵ the men even covered their circumcision,* abandoning the holy Covenant. They allied themselves with the Gentiles and sold themselves to the ways of wrongdoing.

¹⁶ Once Antoichus was confident that his rule was well-established, he then wanted to rule over the land of Egypt, thus acquiring both realms. ¹⁷ He brought together a great army and invaded Egypt with chariots and elephants, cavalry and fleets. ¹⁸ He fought Ptolemy of Egypt in a great battle, and Ptolemy's army fled in defeat, leaving many wounded. ¹⁹ Then they captured the great citadels of Egypt and plundered the entire land.

²⁰ Antiochus returned from the conquering of Egypt in the 143rd year. He turned his attention toward Israel, and brought his mighty army against Jerusalem. ²¹ There, he arrogantly entered the Holy of Holies and plundered the golden altar, the lampstand for the light, and all the utensils. ²² He took the table for the Bread of Presence, the cups used for the drink-offerings, the bowls, the golden censers, the curtain, the crowns, and the gold decoration on the front to the Temple—everything became plunder. ²³ He took the silver and gold and the precious vessels and the hidden treasures. ²⁴ And taking all these things, he returned to his own land.

> He shed innocent blood
>   and spoke arrogant words;
> ²⁵ all the villages of Israel mourned
> ²⁶   the leaders and elders wailed.
> Young people grew weak,
>   their courage failed
>   and their beauty faded.

---

* In Greek tradition, athletes exercised naked; Jewish men who were pro-Hellenization wanted to downplay their difference as much as possible, and so would "uncircumsize" themselves with a device they wore as a sheath.

²⁷ Every married couple sang a dirge
    and newlyweds wailed in their wedding chamber.
²⁸ The very land shook for its inhabitance
    and all the House of Jacob was clothed in shame.

୭ଅ   ୭ଅ   ୭ଅ

²⁹ Two years later, Antiochus send an emissary to the cities of Judea to collect tribute. This emissary came to Jerusalem with a large army. ³⁰ He spoke soothing words of deceit to them, and when they believed him, he turned on the city and struck it hard, killing many of the people of Israel. ³¹ He plundered the city, burned it down, and razed the houses and walls. ³² He made prisoners of many and seized the livestock.

³³ Then they built a wall around the City of David with large towers, and made it their citadel. ³⁴ They established those who rebelled against the Law in the positions of power. ³⁵ They stored arms and provisions in the citadel, and all the spoils that had been plundered. So this fortress hung as a grave threat over Jerusalem.

³⁶ The citadel lies in wait to ambush the Temple;
    it stands as a perpetual threat to all of Israel.
³⁷ Throughout the Temple, they spilled innocent blood,
    and even defiled the Holy of Holies.
³⁸ The people of Jerusalem fled in fear,
    and the city fell into the hands of foreigners.
Jerusalem was a stranger to its children;
    its children forgot the holy city.
³⁹ The sanctuary was as barren as the desert;
    all the festivals became dirges.
Each Sabbath became a time of shame;
    the city's honor became an object of ridicule.
⁴⁰ Jerusalem's shame was as great as its former glory;
    its pride was turned into anguish.

⁴¹ Then Antiochus Epiphanes issued a proclamation to all his subjects that they were to become a single nation, and all people were to renounce the customs of their homeland. ⁴² The Gentiles conformed to the royal decree, ⁴³ and many of the Israelites were in favor of converting; they sacrificed to idols and profaned the Sabbath.

⁴⁴ The ruler sent letters by messenger to Jerusalem and the villages of Judah commanding them to follow customs which were alien to the land.

⁴⁵ They were forbidden to make burnt offerings, or sacrifices or drink offerings in the Sanctuary; and were commanded to treat the Sabbath and the festivals like any other day; ⁴⁶ and to defile the sanctuary and the holy things it contained ⁴⁷ by sacrificing pigs and other unclean animals; ⁴⁸ and to end the practice of circumcision. ⁴⁹ They were required by this decree to do all that was unclean and profane, so that they would forget the Law and abandon its ordinances. The ruler added, ⁵⁰ "Whoever does not obey my word will be put to death!"

⁵¹ He issued this order throughout his realm, appointed inspectors over the people, and ordered each town of Judah to offer sacrifices to the gods. ⁵² Many of the Israelites, those who abandoned the Law, joined forces with these inspectors. They defiled the land with their evil deeds, ⁵³ and their conduct forced Israel into hiding.

⁵⁴ On the fifteenth day of the month of Chislev, in the 145th year, Antiochus Epiphanes erected the Abomination of Desolation—the altar of Baal Shamen—over the altar of burnt offerings in Jerusalem, and similar altars in the surrounding cities of Judah. ⁵⁵ They also burned incense at the doors of the houses and in the streets. ⁵⁶ Any scroll of the Law which they found, they tore up and burned. ⁵⁷ Whoever was found with a scroll of the Covenant, and whoever was seen to observe the Law, was condemned to death by royal decree. ⁵⁸ Month after month, those who remained in the villages were faced with acts of violence against them.

⁵⁹ On the twenty-fifth day of the month, the recreants offered sacrifices on this altar built over the place dedicated to burnt offerings. ⁶⁰ By royal decree, mothers who had their babies circumcised were put to death, ⁶¹ along with their families and those who performed the circumcision; the infants were hung from their mother's neck.

⁶² But many in Israel were determined, and resolved in their hearts not to eat anything unclean; ⁶³ they preferred death to the defilement of unclean food or the profaning of the holy Covenant; and they did die. ⁶⁴ Terrible affliction was upon Israel.

2:1–70

*A*t that time, Mattathias begot of John, whose ancestor was Simeon—a priest from the family of Joarib—moved from Jerusalem and settled in Modein. ² He had five children: John, who was known as Gaddi; ³ Simon, known as Thassi; 4 Judas, nicknamed Maccabeus; 5 Eleazar, nicknamed Avaran; and Jonathan, who was called Apphus.*

6 When Mattathias saw the many evils being committed in Judah and Jerusalem, 7 he said,

> Why me? Why was I born to see these things—
>> to witness the destruction of the Temple and the Holy City?
> To live in its midst while it is in the hands of our enemies?
>> To watch while foreigners parade around in the sanctuary?
> 8 The Temple is like a person defiled,
> 9   its glorious vessels plundered.
> Our own children have been killed in our streets;
>> our young ones have fallen to the sword of our enemies.
> 10 Is there any nation that hasn't occupied us,
>> and taken away all our possessions?
> 11 All our finery have been stripped clean;
>> we are captives without freedom.
> 12 See—our Holy Place, our splendor, and our honor
>> have all been laid to waste.
> The nations have profaned them.
> 13   Why should we go on living?

14 Then Mattathias and his children tore their clothes, put on sackcloth and began to mourn.

15 The officers of Antiochus Epiphanes in charge of enforcing the apostasy came to the city of Modein to organize the sacrifices.

16 Many Israelites supported them, but Mattathias and his family drew apart. 17 Then the officers addressed Mattathias, "You are a leader, an honorable and great citizen in this city. 18 Come now, be the first to obey the royal command, as all the Gentiles and the leaders of Judah and the survivors in Jerusalem have done. Then you and your family will be numbered among the ruler's Friends,** and you will be enriched with silver and gold and many gifts."

---

* The names here are significant. Matthias, or Mattituyahû, means "gift of God." Maccabeus, the nickname given to Judas—that is, Judah—has multiple meanings: "Designated by God," "Hammerer," or "Hammerhead." His other sons' nicknames are, respectively, "Fortunate," "Burning," "Awake," and "Favorite."

** A technical term of honor for a member of the ruler's inner circle or the society's nobility, with several subdivisions; the Friends had liberal access to the ruler, and the ruler often gave them special responsibilities. The practice was common in the Hellenic system, but originated in the royal courts of Persia.

¹⁹ But Mattathias answered resoundingly, "Although all the Gentiles in the realm of Antiochus may obey him, forsaking the religion of their ancestors and consenting to the royal orders, ²⁰ still I and my family will keep to the Covenant of our ancestors. ²¹ God forbid that we should forsake the laws and commandments! ²² We will not obey the words of Antiochus nor depart from our religion in the slightest degree."

²³ As Mattathias finished saying these words, a certain Judean came forward in the sight of all to offer sacrifice in Modein according to the royal decree. ²⁴ When Mattathias saw him, he was filled with zeal; his heart and just fury were aroused, and Mattathias sprang forth and killed the idolator upon the altar. ²⁵ Then, turning on the royal messenger who was forcing them to sacrifice, Mattathias killed him as well, and then tore down the altar. ²⁶ Thus he demonstrated zeal for the Law, just as Phinehas did with Aimri, begot of Salu.

²⁷ Then Mattathias ran through the city shouting, "Let everyone who is zealous for the Law and who stands for the Covenant follow after me!" ²⁸ Then he fled to the mountains with his family, leaving all their possessions behind in the city.

²⁹ Many who sought to live according to righteousness and religious custom went into the wilderness to settle there. ³⁰ Entire families went, taking their livestock, because of the oppression and suffering being inflicted upon them. ³¹ It was reported to the royal officers of the troops that occupied Jerusalem, the City of David, that there were many who had disobeyed the royal order and had gone into hiding in the wilderness. ³² A large company of soldiers went out after them, and caught up with them there. The soldiers set up camp opposite them, preparing to attack them on the Sabbath. ³³ They called out, "Enough of this, you rebels! Surrender now and obey the ruler's decrees, and you will live."

³⁴ But they replied, "No, we will never surrender, nor will we obey the royal command and scorn the Sabbath." ³⁵ The soldiers attacked them, ³⁶ but they did nothing to resist; they didn't even throw stones or block the entrances of the caves where they were hiding. ³⁷ They called out, "Let us die innocent! Heaven and earth are our witnesses that you kill us unjustly!" ³⁸ The soldiers attacked and everyone died—women, men, children and all the livestock. A thousand died that day.

³⁹ When Mattathias and his friends heard of this they were deeply grieved. Talking among themselves with their neighbors, they said, ⁴⁰ "If we do what our people have done—refusing to fight the Gentiles to save our lives and preserve our Law—they will wipe us off the face of the earth." ⁴¹ Coming to a decision, they let it be known to those with them, "We will

resist anyone who attacks us on the Sabbath. We will not die as our people have died in their caves!"

⁴² They were joined by a company of Hasideans,* mighty Israelite warriors who were willing to give up their lives to defend the Law. ⁴³ Soon all those who were fleeing the persecutions joined them as reinforcements. ⁴⁴ They formed an army and turned their rage on those who abandoned the Law, striking them down. The survivors fled to the Gentiles for safety. ⁴⁵ Then Mattathias and the fighters tore down the altars ⁴⁶ and forcibly circumcised all the males within the borders of Israel who had not been circumcised. ⁴⁷ They hunted down the lawbreakers, and their campaign was a success: ⁴⁸ they rescued the Law from the hands of the Gentiles and their rulers, and never let the sinners gain any advantage.

⁴⁹ When the day of Mattathias' death approached, he called his sons together and said to them, "Arrogant and scornful people are everywhere. These are times of violence and rage. ⁵⁰ Now, my children, demonstrate your zeal for the Law and sacrifice your lives for the Covenant of our ancestors.

⁵¹ Remember the great deeds of our ancestors,
    each in their own generation,
and you too will achieve great honors
    and perpetual remembrance.
⁵² Abraham was tested and found worthy,
    and justified by faith.
⁵³ When tested, Joseph kept the Law
    and so became the ruler of Egypt.
⁵⁴ Phinehas, our ancestor,
    received the covenant of perpetual priesthood
    as a reward for his burning zeal.
⁵⁵ Joshua became a judge over Israel
    for carrying out the assigned task.
⁵⁶ Caleb inherited the land
    for giving witness before the assembled people.
⁵⁷ David was given the throne of everlasting rule
    as a reward for a generous heart
⁵⁸ Elijah was taken directly to heaven
    for demonstrating consuming zeal for the Law.

---

* "Pious ones" dedicated to strict observance of the Law. They were forerunners of both the Pharisees and the Essenes, as well as the modern-day Hasidim.

⁵⁹ Hananiah, Azariah and Mishael were saved from the flame,
for their loyalty.
⁶⁰ Daniel was rescued from the lions' jaws
for being pure of heart.
⁶¹ So remember: generation after generation,
none who trust in God will fail in their strength.
⁶² Do not fear the words of the sinner Antiochus—
for all his bluster, he will end up with dust and worms.
⁶³ Today exalted,
tomorrow he will be gone—
he will have returned to dust
and his schemes will have been for nothing.
⁶⁴ So, my children, take courage, be strong, and keep the Law,
and by it will you be glorified.

⁶⁵ "Here is your brother Simeon, who possesses sound judgment. Listen to him all of your lives; I choose Simeon to take my place as your guardian. ⁶⁶ Judas Maccabeus has been a mighty warrior from youth—he will be the leader of the army and fight the battles against the Gentiles. ⁶⁷ Call on everyone who obeys the Law to rally around you, and avenge the evils that have been committed against your people. ⁶⁸ Pay the Gentiles what is due them for what they do—and always keep the Law and its statutes."

⁶⁹ Then Mattathias gave them a final blessing and was taken to the place of his ancestors. ⁷⁰ He died in the 146th year and was buried in the ancestral tomb at Modein. All of Israel mourned his death with great wailing.

3:1–9:22

*t*hen Judas, known as Maccabeus, took Mattathias' place of command. ² All the family and all who had joined with Mattathias helped him gladly as they fought for Israel.

³ Judas brought glory to the people,
standing like a giant in armor
with his sword at his side
he defended the entire camp.
⁴ Like a mighty lion,
like a young lion roaring for prey
⁵ Judas stalked all who broke the Law
and burned all who oppressed the people.

6 The lawless trembled in fear at the sight of Judas
    and evildoers were put to disorder
    as liberation flowed from his hand.
7 He made the lives of rulers miserable
    and brought great joy to the tents of Israel—
    "We will praise the deeds of Judas forever!"
8 Judas marched through Judea
    and destroyed the evildoers in the land
    and averted God's wrath from Israel.
9 Judas was known from the ends of the earth
    As he gathered together those who were perishing.

10 The governor of Samaria, Apollonius, now assembled a large number of Gentiles into an army, including a contingent from Samaria, to attack the people of Israel. 11 When Judas learned of Apollonius' movements, he went out to meet this army and defeated them, killing Apollonius. Many were wounded and fell, the rest fled. 12 Among the spoils, Judas found Apollonius' own sword, which he took, and used it in battle for the rest of his life.

13 When Seron, commander of the Syrian forces, learned that Judas had gathered large a force, and had a loyal group of warriors who always accompanied him in battle, he said, 14 "I will establish my name and win fame in the realm by making war with this Judas and his companions who disobey the royal commands." 15 Once again, a great army of evildoers joined in to take vengeance on Israel.

16 When they approached the ascent of Beth-Horon, Judas took a small band out to meet the army. 17 But when they saw the size of the army, they said to Judas, "How can we, just a handful of soldiers, fight against such a large army so much stronger than we are? Besides, we are weak because we have not eaten today"

18 Judas answered, "It is easy for a large army to be waylaid by a smaller army. In the sight of Heaven, there is no difference between victory by many or by few. 19 Victory depends not on the size of the force, but on the strength that comes from Heaven. 20 They attack us with evil words and deeds, and seek to destroy our families and our inheritance. 21 But we fight for our lives and our Law. 22 God will crush them before us—have no fear of them."

23 Having made this speech, Judas charged against Seron's army without warning, and they fell beneath him. 24 They pursued the remaining soldiers down the mountain of Beth-Horon and out across the plain. Eight hundred of them were killed, and the rest retreated to the land of the Philistines.

²⁵ When news of this spread, the family of Judas came to be feared through all the nations, who recoiled in terror. ²⁶ Word of them soon reached the ruler, for the battles of Judas became the stuff of tales among the Gentiles.

²⁷ When Antiochus heard these reports, he became enraged and called together all the forces in the realm and amassed a strong army to send against the Israelites. He went to the royal treasuries to give each soldier a year's pay and ordered them to be ready when they were called to duty. ²⁸ But he found that the royal treasuries were nearly empty and that the revenues from the land were dwindling ²⁹ because of the strife and troubles that he had caused through outlawing customs and ways of life which had been observed from time beyond memory. ³⁰ Antiochus feared—since it had happened before—that funds were so low that he wouldn't be able to cover his military expenses, which included paying bounties more generous than any previous ruler had offered. ³¹ He was perplexed about what to do, but decided to go to Persia to collect revenues from those regions in order to replenish the treasury.

³² Antiochus left Lysias, a distinguished person of royal blood, in charge of the affairs of the land between the Euphrates and the Egyptian border. ³³ Lysias was also charged with the care of the heir to the throne until Antiochus' return. ³⁴ Lysias was also given control of half of the military forces—with elephants—and given explicit orders about all that was to be done. He was given commands in particular about the people of Judea and Jerusalem— ³⁵ he was to send forces against them and wipe out and destroy the strength of Israel; they were to destroy all trace that these people had even existed. ³⁶ Then he was to give the land to others, settling them there and distributing the land into lots. ³⁷ Antiochus then took his army and left the capital city of Antioch. In the one hundred forty-seventh year, they crossed the Euphrates and entered into the northern territories.

³⁸ Lysias chose as generals Ptolemy, begot of Dorymenes, and Nicanor and Gorgias. They were all able commanders, well known as "Friends of Antiochus." ³⁹ They were given 40,000 infantry and 7,000 cavalry to march against the land of Judah, and conquer it as Antiochus had commanded. ⁴⁰ They set out with their entire force; arriving near Emmaus, they set up camp on the plain. ⁴¹ Slave traders from the region heard of their arrival, and brought great quantities of gold and silver, along with iron shackles, so that they might buy Israelite captives. The army was joined there also by forces from Idumea and Philistia.

⁴² Judaa and his brothers saw that the troubles were escalating, and that the armies had set up camp in their territory. They heard the report that Antiochus had commanded that all the people be destroyed. ⁴³ They said to each other, "We must gather the remnant of our people together to fight for our people and our Temple." ⁴⁴ So the people came together to prepare for battle, and to pray for God's favor:

⁴⁵ Jerusalem was as barren as the desert;
    the people could not come or go.
The sanctuary was defiled by foreigners
    and the Gentiles camped in the city's citadel.
There was no joy in the tents of Israel,
    No flute or harp was played.

⁴⁶ The people marched to Mizpah, opposite Jerusalem, because they once had a place of prayer there. ⁴⁷ That day, they fasted and put on sackcloth. They sprinkled ashes over their heads and ripped their clothes. ⁴⁸ In such a situation the Gentiles would have consulted idols, but the Israelites went to the scrolls of the Law to search for God's guidance. ⁴⁹ They brought out the priestly vestments, and their firstfruits and tithes, and they gathered some Nazirites* who had just completed their vow. ⁵⁰ Then they cried out to Heaven, saying:

"What will we do with these things?
    Where will we keep them?
⁵¹ Your Temple has been conquered and desecrated
    and your priests mourn in humiliation.
⁵² And now the Gentiles have gathered to destroy us—
    you know how they plot against us.
⁵³ How are we to withstand their onslaught
    unless you come to our aid?

⁵⁴ Then they blew their trumpets and shouted loudly.

⁵⁵ After this, Judas organized the people in divisions of thousands, hundreds, fifties, and tens, and selected leaders for each group. ⁵⁶ Anyone who was building a house, or who was about to get married, or who was planting a vineyard, or was weak was excused from duty, according to the Law. ⁵⁷ Then the army marched out and set up camp south of Emmaus.

---

* "Nezîr" means "one set apart" or "one of high rank." A Nazirite is one who has pronounced a certain kind of vow as a voluntary act of devotion. The vow included avoiding alcoholic beverages or eating unclean food, and keeping the hair unshorn during the time of the vow. When the time of the vow had passed, the hair was cut off and burned. Having just completed their vow, the Nazirites would have been ritually pure, and would have been able to rededicate the Temple. John the Baptist was likely a Nazirite.

⁵⁸ Judas told the troops, "Take up your arms and stand your ground. Early in the morning, be prepared to fight these Gentiles, who threaten our people and our Temple. ⁵⁹ Better that we die in battle than see the destruction of our people and Temple. But what God wills, God will accomplish here."

4·¹ Gorgias took 5,000 foot soldiers and 1,000 handpicked cavalry and moved out by night, guided by Jewish deserters from the citadel. ² Their intention was to stage a sneak attack the Jewish camp, ³ but Judas had caught wind of their plan, and moved his troops into position to attack the royal army at Emmaus ⁴ while Gorgias' entire division was separated from the camp. ⁵ And Gorgias, entering the Jewish camp that night, found no one there. So he then went looking for them in the hills, thinking, "We have them on the run!"

⁶ At daybreak, Judas was on the plain with three thousand soldiers, but were not as well armed as they would like to have been. ⁷ When they saw the Gentile camp, strong and well-defended, with cavalry and soldiers well-trained in war, they quailed. ⁸ But Judas said to them, "Don't fear their numbers or be afraid when they charge. ⁹ Recall how our ancestors were saved at the Sea of Reeds when the forces of Pharaoh pursued them. ¹⁰ So, let us cry to Heaven to see whether God will favor us and remember the Covenant with our ancestors, and crush this army before us today. ¹¹ Then all the Gentiles will know that there is a God who liberates Israel from their oppression."

¹² When the Gentiles saw the Israelite army arrayed against them, they came out of their camp to do battle. ¹³ Then Judas' soldiers blew their trumpets and charged, ¹⁴ and the battle was on. It was a rout, with the Gentiles soon fleeing across the plain, and those not quick enough were soon victims of the sword. The Israelites pursued them to Gazara and on to the plain of Idumea and the towns of Azotos and Jamnia. ¹⁵ Three thousand of the enemy fell. ¹⁶ When Judas and his forces turned back from the chase, Judas said to his people, ¹⁷ "Don't be greedy for plunder—there is a battle yet to be fought! ¹⁸ Gorgias and his army are nearby in the hills. Now is the time to stand against our enemies. Later there will be time for spoils"

¹⁹ No sooner had Judas said these words than Gorgias' detachment appeared from the hills. ²⁰ But once they saw that a rout had taken place—indeed, the rising smoke told them of their burning camp—²¹ they were more than disheartened; and when they saw Judas' army ready for battle on the plain, ²² they turned and fled into the land of the Philistines. ²³ Judas' army then turned to plunder the camp, and found great riches of gold and silver, as well as blue and purple weavings, and riches of all kinds.

²⁴ Returning home, they sang hymns of praise to Heaven: "Give thanks to Our God, who is good, and whose mercy endures forever." ²⁵ So it was that God saved Israel on that day.

²⁶ The Gentiles who had escaped reported what had happened to Lysias. ²⁷ When Lysias heard the news, he was greatly disturbed and confused, for the attack against Israel had not gone as he had planned, far less as Antiochus had ordered.

๛ ๛ ๛

²⁸ The following year, Lysias gathered 60,000 handpicked soldiers and 50,000 cavalry to bring against Israel. ²⁹ They marched into Idumea and set up camp in Beth-zur, where Judas met them with 10,000 soldiers.

³⁰ When Judas saw the size of the enemy forces, he prayed:

> Blessed are you,
>   the Liberator of Israel,
> who crushed the attack of a mighty warrior
>   by the hand of your faithful one David.
> You gave the Philistines' camp
>   into the hands of Jonathan, begot of Saul,
>   and the attendant who carried his armor.
> ³¹ As you did against their enemies, hem in this army
>   and let their troops and cavalry slink home in shame.
> ³² Let them be filled with fear;
>   let their confidence in their numbers melt away,
>   and let them quiver in the face of destruction.
> ³³ Strike them down with the swords
>   of those who revere you
> and let all who know your Name
>   sing your praises in hymns.

³⁴ Then both sides charged each other. In the battle that ensued, Lysias' army lost 5,000 soldiers. When Lysias saw his own troops break and run, and saw the courage of Judas' troops had—how ready they were to live or to die with honor—he retreated to Antioch. ³⁵ From there, he hired mercenaries to attack again with an even larger army.

³⁶ Judas Maccabeus and his followers decided, "Now that our enemies have been crushed, let us go up and purify the sanctuary and rededicate it." ³⁷ So the whole army assembled and went up Mount Zion. ³⁸ They saw

the sanctuary in ruins, the altar desecrated, and the gates burned. In the courtyard, bushes grew up between the stones as they would on the hillsides, and the priests' chambers were destroyed. [39] They tore their clothes and let out a great wail. Covering themselves with ashes [40] they fell on the ground. Then, when the trumpet sounded, they cried out to Heaven.

Then Judas sent fighters to attack the citadel, while he and those with him rededicated the Temple. [42] Blameless priests who were devoted to the Law were recruited to perform the task. [43] They cleansed the Sanctuary and removed the stones that had been defiled, taking them to an unclean place. [44] Then they debated then about what to do with the altar of burnt offerings, which had been desecrated. [45] In the end they decided to tear it down so that it would not stand before them as an everlasting disgrace because the Gentiles had defiled it. [46] They took the altar apart and placed the stones in a convenient place on the Temple hill until a prophet might come along who would tell them what to do with them. [47] Then they took uncut stones, as the Law dictates, and built a new altar like the old one. [48] They rebuilt the Sanctuary and the inner parts of the Temple and consecrated the outer courts. [49] They cast new sacred vessels and brought the lampstand, and the showtable into the Temple. [50] Then they offered incense on the altar and lit the lamps on the lampstand, so that the Temple was illuminated. [51] They placed bread on the table and hung up the tapestries. And so they finished this work which they had undertaken.

[52] Early in the morning of the twenty-fifth day of the ninth month—that is, the month of Chislev—in the 148th year, [53] they rose to offer sacrifice according to the Law on the new altar of burnt offerings which had been made. [54] On the very anniversary of the day on which the Gentiles had defiled it, it was reconsecrated with songs, and the sound of harps, flutes and cymbals. [55] All the people prostrated themselves and worshipped and gave Heaven praise for their success.

[56] For eight days they celebrated the dedication of the altar and joyfully offered burnt offerings and sacrifices of deliverance and praise. [57] They ornamented the facade of the Temple with gold crowns and shields; they repaired the gateways, and the priests' chambers, and fitted them with new doors. [58] There was great joy among the people now that the disgrace of the Gentiles was washed away. [59] Then Judas and his followers and the entire congregation of Israel decreed that the days of the dedication of the altar should be observed with joy and gladness on the anniversary every year for eight days, beginning on the twenty-fifth day of the month of Chislev.

[60] Then they built fortifications around Mount Zion with high walls and watchtowers, so that the Gentiles would not trample them down again.

⁶¹ Judas placed a garrison there to guard it, so that the people would have a stronghold that faced Idumea.

5:1 When the nations around them heard that the Israelites had rebuilt their altar and rededicated their Temple, they became enraged. ² They decided among themselves to destroy all the Jews living in their villages, and so began a killing rampage among the Jewish communities.

³ The descendents of Esau who lived in Idumea had besieging Israel, so Judas attacked them at Akrabattene, defeated them, and sacked their village. ⁴ He also attacked the people of Baean, who were a constant threat to Israel because they would ambush them on the highways. ⁵ Judas trapped them in their forts and then set up camp surrounding them. Vowing their complete destruction, the Israelite forces burned down their fortifications with everyone inside. ⁶ Then they turned on the Ammonites, whose leader was Timothy, who commanded a large band with many followers. ⁷ They fought many engagements, and in the end Judas and his army destroyed them. ⁸ They took Jazar and the surrounding villages as well before returning to Judea.

⁹ The Gentiles gathered their forces in Gilead to attack the Israelites who lived among them. ¹⁰ But the Israelites fled to the fortress at Dathema and sent Judas and his brothers a letter which read, "The Gentiles are surrounding us and intend to kill us all. ¹¹ They have enough forces to take the fortress where we are hiding, and their army is led by Timothy. ¹² Hurry and save us from their hands—many of us have already fallen. ¹³ Those of us who were in the land of Tob have been massacred; our families have been enslaved, our property taken, and 1,000 of our people killed there."

¹⁴ While the letter was being read, messengers arrived from Galilee, their garments torn, bearing similar reports. ¹⁵ They said that the armies of Ptolemais, Tyre, Sidion and Galilee had all joined forces to destroy Israel. ¹⁶ When Judas and the people heard the reports, they called together a great council to determine what should be done for their people who were under siege from the enemies of Israel.

¹⁷ Then Judas said to his brother Simon, "Choose your best fighters and go save our people in Galilee. Jonathan and I will go to Gilead." ¹⁸ Judas left behind Joseph, begot of Zechariah, and Azariah, one of the leaders of the people, to guard Judea. He ordered them, ¹⁹ "Take charge of the people, but do not go to battle yourselves until we return." ²⁰ Three thousand soldiers were sent with Simon to Galilee, and 8,000 went with Judas to Gilead.

²¹ Simon fought many battles against the Gentiles in Galilee, defeating them soundly. ²² They chased them all the way to the gates of Ptolemais,

killing 3,000 and gathering plunder as they went. ²³ Then they gathered up the Jewish community living in Galilee and Arbatta, with all their families and possessions, and led them rejoicing back to Judea.

²⁴ Judas Maccabeus and Jonathan crossed the Jordan and traveled three days into the wilderness. ²⁵ They came upon a group of Nabateans, who met with them peaceably and provided information of what had happened to the Jewish community in Gilead. ²⁶ "Many of them are besieged in the fortresses of Bozrah, Bosor, Alema, Chaspho, Maked and Carnaim"—all large and strong cities— ²⁷ "while others are besieged in the smaller villages in Gilead. The enemy is prepared to attack the fortresses tomorrow and capture and kill all these people in a single day."

²⁸ When they heard this, Judas and the Israelite forces quickly turned back to the wilderness road to Bozrah, where they took the town, put all the enemy soldiers to the sword, and looted and burned down the city. ²⁹ That night, they left that place and marched all the way to the fortress of Dathema.

³⁰ Arriving at dawn, they sent scouts ahead who saw a large army—so large their numbers could not be counted—preparing their ladders and battering rams to attack the city and kill the Jews living there. ³¹ Judas saw that the battle had begun and that the cries of the town had reached up to Heaven. ³² Amid trumpeting and shouting, he cried out to his troops, "Today, we fight for our people!"

³³ The Israelites then divided into three companies, and attacked the Gentiles from behind, sounding the trumpets and crying out to Heaven as they attacked. ³⁴ When Timothy's army realized that Maccabeus was upon them, they broke ranks and fled in terror, and were utterly defeated. Over eight thousand of them died that day.

³⁵ Next, Judas turned the army toward Maapha, and took that city, killing all the enemy soldiers there, plundering the city and burning it to the ground. ³⁶ Then they marched on to Chaspho, Maked and Bosar, and the surrounding villages, and conquered them all.

³⁷ Following these defeats, Timothy gathered another army and encamped opposite Raphon, on the other side of the river. ³⁸ Judas sent spies into the camp and they reported back, "All the Gentiles have joined Timothy's ranks, and they have amassed a very large force. ³⁹ They've hired Arab mercenaries to help them, and they're all camped across the river, waiting to fight you." So Judas went out to meet them.

⁴⁰ As Judas and the army drew near the river, Timothy said to his officers, "If they cross over to us first, we won't be able to turn back the attack and we will be defeated. ⁴¹ But if they hesitate, and set up their camp on the other side of the river, we'll cross over and defeat them."

⁴² As Judas approached the river bank, he stationed officers along it and commanded them, "Don't let anyone set up camp. Make sure everyone is ready for battle." ⁴³ Then Judas charged across the river at the head of the whole Israelite army. The Gentile forces broke ranks, threw down their arms and fled to the temple at Carnaim. ⁴⁴ Judas conquered the village and burned the pagan temple to the ground, together with all who were inside. So Carnaim was conquered, with the enemy offering no resistance.

⁴⁵ Then Judas called all the Israelites in Gilead together, the great and the small, families and their possessions, and led this large company back to the Judea. ⁴⁶ As they were returning, they approached Ephron, a large fortified town on the road, so large they could neither go around it on the right nor on the left, but only go through it. ⁴⁷ But the people in the town shut themselves inside and blockaded the gate with stones.

⁴⁸ Judas sent a friendly message to the townspeople saying, "Let us pass through your territory so that we can get back to our own land. We will not harm you. All we want to do is pass through." But the townspeople refused to open the gates, ⁴⁹ so Judas ordered his troops to set up camp where they were. ⁵⁰ They set up camp, and then Judas led an attack against the town all that day and through the night until it fell into their hands. ⁵¹ Every male in the town was killed, and they razed and plundered the town. Then they passed through the town over the bodies of the dead.

⁵² They crossed over the Jordan and onto the vast plain of Beth-shan. ⁵³ Along the way, Judas walked with the stragglers and encouraged them until they reached Judea. ⁵⁴ Then, with great joy, they went up to Mount Zion and made burnt offerings to thank God that they had returned in safety and not one of them had been killed.

⁵⁵ Now, while Judas and Jonathan were in Gilead and their brother Simon was in Galilee fighting against Ptolemais, ⁵⁶ Joseph, begot of Zechariah, and Azariah—the commanders of the forces left to protect Judea—had heard of the valiant deeds and heroic battles that were being fought. ⁵⁷ They had said to one another, "Let's make a name for ourselves. We too will go to war against the Gentiles around us."

⁵⁸ They had issued orders to the soldiers who were with them and attacked Jamnia, ⁵⁹ but Gorgias and the Gentile army had come out of the town and met them in battle. ⁶⁰ Joseph and Azariah and their troops were utterly defeated, and pursued all the way back to the borders of Judea; 2,000 Israelites died that day. ⁶¹ Thus the people suffered a major defeat because these two wanted to be heroes and didn't listen to what Judas had told them. ⁶² Joseph and Azariah were not cut from the same cloth as those whom God had chosen to bring deliverance to the people of Israel.

⁶³ Judas and his brothers were greatly esteemed throughout Israel, and among the Gentiles as well, wherever their name was spoken. ⁶⁴ People flocked around them and praised them.

⁶⁵ Then Judas and his followers went to war against the descendants of Esau in the south. They attacked Hebron and its surrounding villages, tearing down its fortifications and destroying its surrounding towers. ⁶⁶ Then they marched to the land of the Philistines and passed through Marisa. ⁶⁷ It was on this day that some priests who had wished to show themselves heroes died in battle—they were unprepared for war. ⁶⁸ Judas then turned aside to Azotus in Philstia, where he destroyed their altars, burned their graven images, and plundered their villages before returning to Judea.

CR CR CR

⁶:¹ Now Antiochus Epiphanes, ruler of Syria, was making his way across the inland provinces. He heard that in Persia there was a city called Elymais, famous for its wealth in silver and gold ² and the riches of its temple, containing gold helmets, breastplates and weapons left there by Alexander, begot of Philip, ruler of Macedon, the first ruler of the Greeks. ³ So Antiochus went there to capture and pillage the city. But he could not, because his plan had become known to the people of the city, ⁴ and they were prepared to withstand him in battle. So he was forced to retreat, and in great dismay withdrew, intending to return to Babylon.

⁵ While Antiochus was still in Persia, a messenger brought news that the armies he had sent into the land of Judea had been put to flight; ⁶ that Lysias had gone at first with a strong army and been driven back by the Israelites; that the Israelites had grown strong because of the arms, supplies and abundant wealth they had taken from the armies they had destroyed; ⁷ that they had pulled down the Abomination which had been built over the altar in Jerusalem; and that they had surrounded the sanctuary with high walls, as it had been before, and his own city of Beth-zur, as well.

⁸ When Antiochus heard this news, he was struck with fear and was deeply shaken. Sickened with grief over all his failed plans, he took to his bed. ¹⁰ There he remained for many days, overwhelmed with sorrow; and he knew he was dying.

¹⁰ So the ruler called in all his Friends and said to them, "I cannot find sleep, and my heart is sunken with anxiety. ¹¹ How could such troubles have come over me? Why do such floods of sorrow overwhelm me— ¹² I, who was so generous, so beloved when I was at the height of my power?

But I now recall the evils I did in Jerusalem, when I carried away all the vessels of gold and silver that were there, and for no cause gave orders that the inhabitants of Judea be destroyed. [13] I know that this is why these evils have overtaken me. Now I am dying, in bitter grief, in a foreign land."

[14] Then Antiochus called for Philip, one of his Friends, and made him crown regent over the entire realm. [15] To Philip were given the crown and the robe and the signet ring, and he was instructed to raise Antiochus' heir to take his place as ruler. [16] And then Antiochus died in the year 149.

[17] When Lysias heard that the ruler was dead, he made Antiochus' heir—also named Antiochus—the ruler in the place of his father. Lysias had raised the child and now gave him the name Eupator.

[18] Meanwhile, the troops in the citadel continued to blockade Israel around the Temple area, causing trouble for the people and lending support to the Gentiles against Israel. [19] Judas made up his mind to destroy them, and gathered all the people to prepare to attack them. [20] They came together and attacked the citadel in the year 150, and built huge siege towers and battering rams.

[21] But some of the garrison escaped, and were joined by a group of apostate Israelites.* [22] These made their way to the new ruler and said to him, "How long do we have to wait for you to do what is right, and avenge our peoples? [23] We were more than happy to serve your father, to live by the royal commands. [24] And for our loyalty, we are now besieged in the citadel, and our own people have become our enemies. They have put everyone they have caught to death and they have plundered all our property. [25] Nor have they been content to attack us; they have also attacked beyond their own borders. [26] See for yourself— now they are attacking the citadel in Jerusalem and want to destroy it. And they have built fortifications around Beth-zur. [27] If you do not act now to stop them, they will do even worse things, and you will be unable to stop them."

[28] The ruler** was greatly angered by these words. He summoned all his Friends, the generals of the armies, and everyone in authority. [29] He brought in mercenary armies from other lands and from the islands in the sea. [30] The forces numbered 100,000 foot soldiers, 20,000 cavalry, and 32 war elephants. [31] They marched through Idumea and set up camp opposite to Beth-zur. For eight days they fought, while building battering rams and

---

* Members of the Jewish community who favored adopting Hellenizing influences.
**The actual ruler, Antiochus Eupator, was still very young. The real decisions were being made by the crown regent, Lysias.

war towers. But the defenders of the city fought bravely, and made forays out to burn all these things.

³² Judas marched the army away from the citadel and set up camp at Beth-zechariah, opposite to the enemy forces. ³³ Early the next morning, the ruler led his army on a long march to Beth-zechariah, and the troops made ready for battle. ³⁴ They gave the elephants wine made from grapes and mulberries to stir them up for the fight. ³⁵ Then they distributed them among the phalanxes; around each of them were placed 1,000 foot soldiers clothed in heavy armor, with brass helmets on their heads. ³⁶ Five hundred cavalry riders were picked and assigned to each animal—they were to stay with the elephant at all times, following wherever it went. ³⁷ A large wooden tower was placed on the back of each elephant, held fast with a special harness, and three soldiers fought from there, as well as the Indian elephant driver. ³⁸ The remaining cavalry was positioned at both flanks of the army, giving them freedom to attack, while they themselves were protected by the phalanxes. ³⁹ When the sun shone on the gold and bronze shields, it looked as if the hillsides were ablaze like a burning torch.

⁴⁰ Part of the royal army was placed in the high hills, while the rest were spread out across the plain. They advanced steadily and in good order. ⁴¹ Everyone who heard the clamor made by the marching army with their armor clanking trembled in fear, for they were very large and strong. ⁴² But Judas and his fighters advanced on them, and 600 soldiers in the royal army quickly fell.

⁴³ Eleazar, who was also known as Avaran, saw that one of the elephants was equipped with royal armor, and was taller than all the others, he presumed that the ruler was riding it. ⁴⁴ For the sake of his people, Eleazar earned everlasting remembrance—⁴⁵ he gave his own life by bravely hacking and slashing right and left into the midst of the enemy who parted before his fury. ⁴⁶ Reaching the elephant, he darted beneath it and stabbed it from below, killing it. But the elephant fell and crushed him. ⁴⁷ However, when the Judean forces realized the strength and determination of the royal army, they retreated.

⁴⁸ The royal army pressed on to Jerusalem, where they set up camp outside the gates. ⁴⁹ They made a treaty with the people of Beth-zur, who had run out of provisions—it was the sabbatical year* for the land—and could not withstand a siege, and evacuated the town. ⁵⁰ Then they set up camp in front of the Temple and remained there for many days. ⁵¹ They set up siege

---

* The Law required that the land lie fallow every seventh year. So without the land being sowed or harvested, a famine was imminent.

towers, battering rams, catapults to launch fire and rocks, and other weapons to shoot arrows. ⁵² The Judean resistance also built weapons of war to match those of the royal army, and fought back for many days. ⁵³ But they had no food in storage, because it was the seventh year and those who had fled to Jerusalem from the Gentile territories had used up what was already stored. ⁵⁴ There were only a few left to guard the Temple, the rest having dispersed and gone home because the famine proved to be too much for them to endure.

⁵⁵ But now Lysias heard that Philip—whom Antiochus had appointed before he died to train the younger Antiochus for the throne—had returned from Persia and Media ⁵⁶ with the forces that had accompanied the late ruler, and now was trying to seize control of the government. ⁵⁷ Lysias gave orders to withdraw, saying to the young ruler, and the commanders and troops, "We are growing weaker every day. Our rations are being depleted and the place we are fighting is well fortified. Besides that, there are stirrings in our own government which require our immediate attention. ⁵⁸ So, let us make a treaty with these people, and make peace with them and with their entire nation. ⁵⁹ We will agree to let them live by their own law, as they did before. It was our attempt to abolish their laws that began this whole trouble in the first place."

⁶⁰ The ruler and the commanders agreed with this recommendation, and Lysias sent a messenger to the Judeans to offer terms of peace. ⁶¹ The ruler and the commanders swore an oath, and the Judeans evacuated the fortress. ⁶² But when the ruler entered Mount Zion and saw how strong a fortress it actually was, he broke the oath and ordered his army to tear down the walls. ⁶³ Then they hurried off to Antioch, where they found Philip in control of the city. They fought against him and took the city by force of arms.

ʘ ʘ ʘ

7:1In the 151st year, Demetrius, begot of Seleucus, left Rome and sailed with a few soldiers, landing in a town by the sea. There he set himself up as ruler. ² Just as he was entering into the royal palace of his ancestors, his soldiers captured young Antiochus and Lysias and brought them to him. ³ When Demetrius heard of this, he ordered, "Get them out of my sight!" ⁴ So they killed them, and Demetrius ascended to rule the realm.

⁵ Then the Israelites who had rebelled against both the Law and piety came to him, led by Alcimus, who wanted to be high priest. ⁶ They brought to the ruler all sorts of accusations against their own people: "Judas and

his family have defeated all your allies and driven us from our own land. ⁷ Send someone you trust to see for certain the degree of destruction that Judas has brought upon us and upon your realm. Let your messenger punish them and all who have helped them."

⁸ So Demetrius chose Bacchides, one of his Friends, who was governor of the province west of the Euphrates. Bacchides was known well throughout the realm, and was very loyal to the ruler. ⁹ Demetrius sent him, along with the apostate Alcimus, whom he had appointed high priest, and commanded them to take vengeance upon the Israelites. ¹⁰ So they gathered forces and marched into the land of Judah. When they arrived, they sent a messenger to Judas speaking peaceful but treacherous words. ¹¹ Judas was not taken in, for he saw the large force which they had brought.

¹² But a group of scribes approached Bacchides and Alcimus to seek terms of peace. ¹³ The Hasideans were the first group among the Israelites to seek a treaty with them. ¹⁴ They reasoned, "A priest of Aaron's line has come with them. What have we to fear?"

¹⁵ Alcimus spoke soothing words and swore to them, "We will not harm you or your allies," ¹⁶ and so they trusted him. But then he took sixty of them prisoner and executed them in one day, as it says in the scripture,

> ¹⁷ "The flesh of your faithful ones and their blood
>   have been scattered throughout Jerusalem
>   with no one left to bury the dead."

¹⁸ Afterwards, fear of Alcimus and Bacchides grew and the people said, "They don't even know the meaning of truth or justice, for they have broken the oath which they have sworn."

¹⁹ Bacchides withdrew the forces from Jerusalem and set up camp at Bethzaith. From there, he ordered the arrest of the faithful Jewish people, as well as some of the apostates who had joined forces with him. He had them killed and threw their bodies into a deep pit. ²⁰ Then Bacchides appointed Alcimus to take charge of the province, and leaving him a force of soldiers to help, he returned to Demetrius.

²¹ Alcimus strove to be recognized as high priest, and was joined in this struggle with every miscreant in the land. ²² They gained control of the Judea and caused great upheaval throughout the province. ²³ But Judas heard of the trouble that Alcimus and those who joined with him had done in Israel, which was even worse than that committed by the Gentiles.

²⁴ Judas moved around the borders of Judea taking revenge on the traitors and preventing them from fleeing into the wilderness. ²⁵ When Alcimus saw that Judas and the Judean forces were gaining strength, he realized

that he could not stand against them long. He returned to Demetrius, accusing them of high treason.

²⁶ So Demetrius sent Nicanor, a general of great renown and a bitter enemy of Israel, with orders to destroy the people of Judea. ²⁷ Nicanor marched on Jerusalem with a large force and sent lies of peace to Judas, saying, ²⁸ "Let there be no war between the two of us. I will meet to you peacefully with only a few soldiers."

²⁹ Nicanor came to Judas and they met each other without violence. But in the background, Judas' enemies were waiting to seize him. ³⁰ When Judas saw that Nicanor had come to trap him, he retreated and would not come out to meet him again. ³¹ When Nicanor saw that his ruse had failed, he brought his forces against Judas at Capharsalama. ³² Five hundred of Nicanor's soldiers fell here in battle; then the rest retreated to Jerusalem.

³³ Following this, Nicanor went up to Mount Zion. A few of the priests in the sanctuary and some of the elders came out in peace to show the offering they were making on behalf of the ruler. ³⁴ But Nicanor mocked them and ridiculed them. He spat on them and showed them his disdain. ³⁵ Raging, he swore an oath, "If Judas and his rebels are not handed over to me at once, then when I return victorious over them, I will burn this temple to the ground once." Then he stormed out of the Temple.

³⁶ The priests returned to the sanctuary, stood before the altar and wept, ³⁷ "You have chosen this Temple to bear your Name, to be a house of prayer and petition for your people. ³⁸ Take vengeance on this Nicanor and his army, so that they may all meet their end by the sword. Remember their blasphemies and do not let them live."

³⁹ Nicanor left Jerusalem to set up headquarters at Beth-horon, and the royal forces joined him there. ⁴⁰ Judas set up camp at Adasa with 3,000 soldiers. Here Judas prayed,

⁴¹   "When those whom the tyrant sent blasphemed,
      you sent your angel to kill 185,000.
⁴²   So also crush this army that stands against us today,
      and let the world know the evil words
   Nicanor spoke against your holy place.
   Judge him according to his crimes."

⁴³ The two armies met in battle on the thirteenth day of Adar. Nicanor's army was demolished, and he was among the first to fall in the battle. ⁴⁴ When the royal forces saw that Nicanor was dead, they threw down their weapons and fled. ⁴⁵ The Judeans pursued them from Adasa to near Gazara, a day's journey, blowing trumpets behind them as signals. ⁴⁶ All the people from the surrounding villages of Judea came out and closed them in. Once

they were trapped, the entire enemy army was killed—not one was left alive.

⁴⁷ The Judean forces collected the spoils and booty; and cut off Nicanor's head, and the right arm which he had so arrogantly lifted up. They brought these to Jerusalem and put them on display. ⁴⁸ The people rejoiced mightily, and the day was observed as a great festival. ⁴⁹ It was decreed that this day would be remembered every year on the thirteenth day of Adar. And so—for a very brief time—the land of Judea was at peace.

⋅⋅⋅ ⋅⋅⋅ ⋅⋅⋅

⁸:¹ The fame of the Romans as a military power had reached Judas' ears. They were strong and built a strong bond of friendship with all their allies. ² Judas heard tales of brave deeds in their war with the Gauls, and how they defeated them and forced them to pay tribute. ³ They had done the same in Spain in order to gain control of the gold and silver mines there. ⁴ They accomplished this through their great planning and patience, even though the place was so far away from their home. They had conquered the rulers of distant lands who had opposed them, and those who did not wish to oppose them paid tribute. ⁵ They fought and conquered Perseus and Philip, the rulers of Macedonia, and other rulers who challenged them as well. They conquered Antiochus the Great, ruler of Asia, who fought against them with one hundred twenty elephants as well as cavalry, chariots and a large infantry. ⁶ They defeated Antiochus, took him prisoner and forced his successors to pay heavy tribute, to give hostages, and to surrender control of some of their best provinces—⁸ India, Media and Lydia among them. They took these and turned them over to the control of Eumenes.

⁹ The Greeks laid plans to come and destroy them, ¹⁰ but the Romans learned of these plans and sent in a general to attack the Greeks. Many of the Greeks fell in battle and the Romans took many prisoners whom they put under subjection, plundered their possessions, occupied their lands, tore down their fortresses and kept them enslaved—as they are yet to this day. ¹¹ They fought and subjected all the remaining realms and islands that opposed them. ¹² But those who became their allies and relied on them for protection they counted as friends. They conquered rulers near and far until all who heard their name trembled in fear. ¹³ They set up rulers and disposed of rulers as they chose; and they had become a glorious power.

¹⁴ Yet for all their greatness, not one of them had ever tried to place themselves ahead of the others by wearing a crown and royal robes. ¹⁵ They had established a Senate, and every day 320 senators assembled there to delib-

erate on matters concerning the people, and on good government. ¹⁶ Each year, they entrusted one individual to control their whole empire, and they would obey that individual. Among them, there was no spite or resentfulness for each other's positions.

¹⁷ So Judas chose Eupolemus, begot of John, whose ancestor was Accos, and Jason, begot of Eleazar, and sent them to Rome to establish a treaty of friendship and alliance. ¹⁸ Judas saw clearly that the oppression of the Syrians was enslaving the people. ¹⁹ So, the two emissaries made the long journey to Rome.

When they arrived, they entered the Senate chamber and stated their case: ²⁰ "Judas, who is called Maccabeus, his brothers and the people of Judea have sent us to you to make a treaty of alliance and peace so that we will be known among you as allies and friends."

²¹ The proposal was accepted with pleasure and ²² the Romans wrote the following message on bronze tablets and sent it to Jerusalem so that it would be a perpetual reminder of peace and friendship:

²³ "May all go well for the Romans and for the Jewish people on land and sea! May they never have enemies, and may they be free of war! ²⁴ But, if war is declared against Rome or any of our allies anywhere, ²⁵ the Jewish people will come to our aid with wholehearted support, as the situation requires. ²⁶ The Jewish people may not give food, money, arms or ships to any who fight against Rome or our allies. ²⁷ In the same manner, if war is declared against the Jewish people, we Romans will give the Jewish people our assistance, as the situation demands. ²⁸ Their attackers will not receive any aid from Rome in the form of food, weapons, money or ships. And the Romans will keep their obligations to the Jewish people without deceit.

²⁹ "These are the terms of the treaty that Rome makes with the Jewish people. ³⁰ If, in the future, both parties agree to add or delete any part of this treaty, they are free to do so, and what they add or delete will be ratified.

³¹ "We have written the following letter to Demetrius concerning the oppression of the Jewish people: 'Why have you treated our friends and allies, the Jewish people, so bitterly? ³² If they come to us again for help against you, we will defend their rights and fight you on land and sea.' "

9·1 When Demetrius heard that Nicanor and the army had been defeated, he sent Bacchides and Alcimus back to Judea, this time with the Syrian wing of the army. ² They traveled the road leading to Galilee and set up camp against Mesaloth in Arbela. They captured the city and killed many people. ³ In the first month of the year 152, they set up their headquarters outside Jerusalem. ⁴ From there, they marched for Berea with 20,000 infantry and 2,000 cavalry.

⁵ Judas had set up headquarters in Elasa with 3,000 handpicked soldiers. ⁶ When they saw the size of the enemy forces, they were seized with fear. Many left the camp under cover of darkness until there were only eight hundred left.

⁷ When Judas realized that many of the soldiers had deserted just as the battle was about to begin, his heart sank. There was not enough time to gather a new army. ⁸ Though he was troubled, he said to those who remained, "Now is time to take up arms and fight our enemies. We may still possess the strength to defeat them."

⁹ But the remaining soldiers tried to talk Judas out of going into battle: "We aren't strong enough now. Now is the time to retreat and save our lives. Then we can return with reinforcements enough to defeat them. Right now, there are not enough of us."

¹⁰ Judas replied, "It will never be said that I ran from battle. If it is our time to die, then let us die bravely for the sake of our people. We must leave no question about our honor among the people."

¹¹ Bacchides' army marched out of their encampment and set up their battle lines for the fight. They divided their cavalry into two squadrons, while the slingers and archers moved to the front, along with their strongest warriors. ¹² Bacchides took the right side. Flanked on both sides by the cavalry, the infantry phalanx advanced to the sound of trumpets. Judas' forces also sounded their trumpets. ¹³ The earth shook from the thunder of the armies, and the battle raged on from morning until evening.

¹⁴ When Judas saw that Bacchides and the main forces of the army were on the right flank, he gathered his bravest fighters to him and attacked there. ¹⁵ The right wing crumbled and then fled, and he chased them all the way to Mount Azotus. ¹⁶ When those on the left saw that the right flank had been defeated, they wheeled and attacked Judas' forces from the rear.

¹⁷ The battle became desperate and many on both sides were wounded and killed. ¹⁸ Then Judas, too, fell, and all his forces scattered.

¹⁹ Jonathan and Simon took Judas' body and buried it in the tomb of their ancestors at Modein. Their they wept for their fallen brother. ²⁰ All of Israel mourned for many days, saying,

²¹ "How could this have happened?
Our great warrior, the savior of Israel, has fallen."

²² All the tales of Judas—tales of battles, of brave deeds and of valor—have never been fully recorded, so great is their number.

After Judas died, the apostates began to reappear, emerging from all parts of Judea. ²⁴ There was a great famine at this time and the whole country sided with them. ²⁵ Bacchides deliberately assigned some of these renegades to rule the country, ²⁶ and they hunted down anyone who had allied themselves with Judas and brought them before Bacchides, who subjected them to torture and humiliation. ²⁷ It was a time of great tribulation in Israel—far worse than any other time since prophets had ceased appearing among them.

²⁸ Judas' old allies gathered and approached Jonathan, and said, ²⁹ "Since Judas died, no other leader has emerged challenge our enemies, Bacchides and those of our own people who oppose us. ³⁰ Today, we choose you as the successor of Judas to carry on as our leader and commander, and to lead us into battle." ³¹ Jonathan accepted the mantle of leadership that day and took the place of his brother Judas.

³² When Bacchides learned of this, he tried to have Jonathan killed. ³³ But Jonathan and Simon, and all who were with them caught news of this threat and fled into the wilderness of Tekoa. There they set up camp at the oasis at Asphar.* ³⁵ Jonathan sent his brother John, who was one of the leaders of the people, to ask the Nabateans, their allies, if they would store for them the great amount of baggage they were carrying. ³⁶ But the Jambrites of Medeba waylaid John, taking him and everything he had.

³⁷ Later, Jonathan and Simon found out that the Jambrites were preparing to celebrate an important wedding, with a grand procession from the town of Nadabath, the home of the bride, who was the daughter of an important Canaanite leader. ³⁸ Thinking about the death of their brother Judas, John, Jonathan and Simon ³⁹ took their troops up into the hills and hid. They watched the commotion down below them, as the bride's party made their way, loaded down with all the bride's dowry, and the groom's party came out to meet them, heavily armed, and with great fanfare and music. ⁴⁰ Jonathan's troops ambushed them, killing many and wounding more; the rest fled into the hills, while Jonathan and his fighters gathered up the plunder. ⁴¹ So this wedding celebration was turned into mourning, and their joyful music into dirges. ⁴² But Jonathan and Simon had revenge for their brother's death before returning to the marshes along the Jordan.

⁴³ Bacchides heard the reports of this and moved a large contingent of troops to the banks of the Jordan, on the Sabbath. ⁴⁴ When Jonathan saw the advancing army, he said to his fighters, "Rise up and fight for your

---

* Verse 34 is a duplicate of verse 43, probably due to a scribal error. We have kept the second occurrence only, since it is more appropriate to the context there.

lives! We have never been in a situation like this. ⁴⁵ Look! The battle lines are forming in front us and behind us are the waters of the Jordan. Surrounding us on both sides is nothing but marsh and thicket. There is no way out of here. ⁴⁶ Cry out to God to rescue us from our enemies!"

⁴⁷ The battle began, and Jonathan made his way through the melee to Bacchides, ready to kill him, but Bacchides evaded him and moved to the rear of his army. ⁴⁸ Finally Jonathan and the rest jumped into the Jordan and swam to the safety of the other side. Bacchides' army did not follow them into the river. ⁴⁹ About a thousand of Bacchides' soldiers died in this fight.

⁵⁰ After this, Bacchides returned to Jerusalem. He began to fortify the cities of Judea: Jericho, Emmaus, Beth-horon, Bethel, Timnath, Pharathon and Tephon. ⁵¹ In each he stationed garrisons of troops to harass the people. ⁵² He also built up the fortifications of Beth-zur and Gezer, as well as the citadel in Jerusalem. He reinforced the garrisons of each and provisioned them well. ⁵³ Then he took as hostages the youths of the leaders among the Jewish people, and held them in the citadel of Jerusalem.

⁵⁴ In the second month of the 153rd year, Alcimus gave orders to tear down the wall of the inner court of the sanctuary. This would mean the destruction of the work of the prophets.

⁵⁵ But just as the work began, Alcimus had a stroke, and the work came to a grinding halt. Paralyzed and unable to open his mouth, Alcimus could not even make his own wishes known to his family. ⁵⁶ He died in agony.

⁵⁷ When Bacchides learned that Alcimus was dead, he returned to Demetrius, and the land of Judea knew peace for a space of two years.

⁵⁸ But soon the apostates began to regroup. They said, "Look: Jonathan and his band are living in peace and security. If we bring Bacchides back now, he will capture them all in a single night." ⁵⁹ They traveled to discuss the matter with Bacchides, who then set out with a great army. ⁶⁰ He sent secret letters to allies in Judea asking them capture Jonathan and the rebels, but the plot became known, and failed. ⁶¹ Jonathan and the rebels captured fifty of the apostate leaders of this conspiracy, and put them to death.

⁶² Then Jonathan and Simon withdrew their forces to Bethbasi, in the wilderness. They rebuilt the walls and strengthened the town's defenses. ⁶³ When Bacchides learned they were there, he assembled his army, and, summoning his allies in Judea, moved against Bethbasi. ⁶⁴ They fought there for many days, and built large siege platforms.

⁶⁵ After the battle had gone on for some time, Jonathan slipped out into

the countryside with a small band of fighters, leaving Simon in charge of the town. ⁶⁶ He attacked Odomera and his people, and then the Phasirite camp, defeating them, and the came around to attack Bacchides from the rear. ⁶⁷ In the ensuing confusion, Simon and those remaining with him made a sally out of the gates and set fire to the siege platforms. ⁶⁸ They pressed Bacchides' forces hard, and crushed them. All of Bacchides planning, and his entire expedition, was brought to nothing. ⁶⁹ He turned in fury on the apostates who had urged him to return to Judea, and put many of them to death. He then resolved to return to his own country.

⁷⁰ When Jonathan heard of this, he sent emissaries to Bacchides to arrange for a peace treaty and the release of captives. ⁷¹ Bacchides agreed to this, and he kept his word; he furthermore vowed to Jonathan that he would seek no more harm against him for as long as he lived. ⁷² He freed all his prisoners, from earlier engagements as well as this one; and then Bacchides returned to his own land and never set foot in Israel again. So it was that the sword was lifted from Israel's neck.

⁷³ Jonathan settled in Michmash and began the governing of the people, and he sought to purge the land of the apostates who had betrayed their own people.

☙ ☙ ☙

10:1 In the 160th year, Alexander Epiphanes, begot of Antiochus IV, landed at Ptolmais and captured it. The people there welcomed him as their ruler. Alexander established his reign in that city.

² When Demetrius heard of this, he assembled a large army and came to face Alexander in battle. ³ Demetrius sent to Jonathan with offers of peace, ⁴ reasoning, "If we don't make an ally of Jonathan, Alexander will. ⁵ And then Jonathan will surely remember the wrongs committed against Israel."

⁶ So Demetrius signed a treaty with Jonathan, authorizing him to raise troops and arm them. He ordered, as well, that the hostages remaining in the citadel be released to Jonathan.

⁷ Jonathan traveled to Jerusalem and read the letter to the people there and to those in the citadel. ⁸ The guards in the citadel were alarmed to hear that Demetrius had given Jonathan the authority to raise an army, ⁹ but they turned the hostages over to him, and he returned them to their families.

¹⁰ Jonathan established himself in Jerusalem and began to rebuild and restore the city. ¹¹ He directed the builders to build walls of hewn stone around Mount Zion to protect it, and it was done. ¹² The foreigners slipped

away from the fortresses that Bacchides had built, ¹³ abandoning their posts and returning to their own lands. ¹⁴ A few of those who had abandoned the Law of Moses remained in Beth-zur, which served as a refuge for them.

¹⁵ Alexander learned of the promises that Demetrius had made to Jonathan. He had heard stories of Jonathan—of the battles he had fought, and the courage he had shown, and the troubles that he and his fighters had endured. ¹⁶ Alexander was certain that there was no other who could ever be compared to Jonathan, and he made up his mind that Jonathan must be his ally. ¹⁷ So he wrote the following letter to Jonathan:

¹⁸ "Alexander the ruler sends greetings to our brother Jonathan.

¹⁹ "Your deeds are well-known to us; you are a great warrior and have every right to be called our friend. ²⁰ And so, on this day, I appoint you high priest of your people; and you are to be called, 'Friend of the Ruler.' You are to be our ally, and will lend us your support."

He also sent Jonathan a purple robe and a golden crown. ²¹ Jonathan put on the robes of the high priest at the Feast of Booths in the seventh month of the year 160. And he raised an army, and stockpiled many weapons.

²² Demetrius was deeply disturbed when he heard about this. ²³ "How could we have let this happen?" he said. "We have let Alexander get to Jonathan ahead of us and form a friendship with the Jewish nation. Now his position is stronger. ²⁴ I will also write them a letter of friendship and offer them honors and gifts in exchange for their support." ²⁵ So Demetrius wrote the following message:

"Demetrius sends greetings to the Jewish people. ²⁶ We are encouraged to learn that you have kept the terms of your treaty with us, and have remained loyal to us and supported our enemies. ²⁷ As you continue to remain loyal to us, we shall reward you well. ²⁸ We grant you relief from taxes, and other privileges.

²⁹ "I now grant your nation release and exemption from regular taxes, from the salt tax, and other special taxes. ³⁰ From this day forward, forever, you are no longer obliged to hand over one-third of your grain harvest or fruit harvest to me. I will no longer require such payments from the people of Judea or from those territories which have been added to Judea, namely Samaria and Galilee. ³¹ Jerusalem and the surrounding vicinity is to be recognized as a holy city and will be exempt from all taxes. ³² I relinquish all authority over the citadel at Jerusalem, and place it under the authority of the high priest, who may select as guards any soldiers he wishes. ³³ I will grant a general amnesty to all Jewish people who are currently held pris-

oner anywhere in my realm. I will set them free without ransom, nor with any taxes, even on their livestock.

[34] "No taxes will be collected during the feasts of the New Moon and on Sabbaths, or any other holy day. Furthermore, no taxes will be collected three days prior to or three days following any holy day. [35] No one will be given authority to collect anything from you or bother you in any matter during these times.

[36] "Thirty thousand of the Jewish people are to be enrolled in the royal army, to be paid the same wages as any of our soldiers. [37] Some of them are to be placed in the great fortresses of the ruler, and some of them are to be given positions of great responsibility in the realm. Your officers and leaders are to be selected from your own people, and you will live by your laws and customs, just as I have commanded throughout the land of Judea.

[38] "The three districts added to Judea from the territory of Samaria are to be incorporated into Judea and placed under the authority of the high priest alone. [39] Taxes collected from the city of Ptolemais and the lands belonging to it will be given for the maintenance of the Temple.

[40] "Besides this, fifteen thousand silver shekels will be given each year from the royal treasury. [41] And the surplus funds, which government officials have neglected to pay in the past five years, will be given for the upkeep of the Temple from now on. [42] In addition to this, we will no longer require the annual payment of five thousand shekels from the Temple treasury. This money will go to the priests who serve in the Temple.

[43] "Any person, owing a debt to the government, or any other debt, who takes refuge in the Temple in Jerusalem or any place that belongs to it, may not be arrested, nor may any property they own be confiscated. [44] In the same manner, all the expenses for rebuilding the Temple will come out of the royal treasury. [45] So too, the expenses for rebuilding the walls of Jerusalem and the surrounding fortifications, as well as the walls of designated towns throughout Judea, will be paid out of the royal treasury."

[46] When Jonathan and people heard the lavish promises that Demetrius made to them, they grew deeply suspicious. They remembered the things that Demetrius had done to Israel and how he oppressed the people. [47] They favored Alexander because he was the first to approach them with a treaty of peace, and they remained Alexander's constant allies.

[48] Now Alexander raised a large army and set up headquarters opposite of Demetrius. [49] The two rulers met in battle, and Demetrius' army fled. Alexander pursued them, harrying them [50] and pressing the battle until night fell. It was on this day that Demetrius died.

⁵¹ Alexander then send ambassadors to Ptolemy, the ruler of Egypt with this message: ⁵² "I have returned to the land of my ancestors and taken my seat to rule over their realm. I established my government and have secured control over the whole country. ⁵³ I made war with Demetrius and defeated him, and have taken his place on the throne. ⁵⁴ Let us now make an alliance. Let me marry your daughter and become your son-in-law, and I will bestow upon you such gifts as befits your position."

⁵⁵ Ptolemy sent a reply: "It was a happy day when you returned to the land of your ancestors. ⁵⁶ I will accept your proposal; but first, meet with me at Ptolemais. We will get to know each other better there and then my daughter will marry you."

⁵⁷ Ptolemy left Egypt, with his daughter, Cleopatra;* and they arrived in Ptolemais in the year 162. ⁵⁸ They met there, and Alexander married Cleopatra with all the pomp and ceremony of which rulers are so fond.

⁵⁹ Alexander wrote to Jonathan, asking that he come to meet him. ⁶⁰ So, Jonathan went to Ptolemais and met the two rulers with great pomp. He gave them gifts of silver and gold, and gave many gifts to the Friends who accompanied them. The rulers were greatly pleased with him; ⁶¹ but at the same time, some of the Jewish apostates who wanted revenge on Jonathan, approached with accusations against him. But Alexander was not impressed. ⁶² He ordered that Jonathan be given robes of purple and gave him the place of honor at his side. ⁶³ Alexander instructed his officers to take Jonathan into the middle of the city and make a public announcement forbidding anyone from accusing Jonathan of anything or causing him any trouble.

⁶⁴ When his accusers saw the honors Jonathan was given, and heard the announcement and saw his purple robes, they fled. ⁶⁵ So Alexander placed Jonathan among his royal inner circle of Friends; and appointed him general and governor of Judea. ⁶⁶ Jonathan returned to Jerusalem in joy and satisfaction.

ೞ   ೞ   ೞ

⁶⁷ In the year one hundred sixty-five, Demetrius' heir, Demetrius II, left Crete and arrived in the land of his ancestors. ⁶⁸ When Alexander heard of this, he was gravely concerned and returned to Antioch. ⁶⁹ Demetrius appointed Apollonius governor of Coele-Syria. Apollonius gathered a large army and established a headquarters in Jamnia. He sent the following message to Jonathan the high priest:

---

* Cleopatra III, not to be confused with Cleopatra VII (69-30 BCE) of Caesar and Mark Anthony fame.

⁷⁰ "You alone have challenged our authority, and because of you we have become the laughingstock of the realm. Why do you continue this mountain rebellion when no one supports you? ⁷¹ If you truly believed in your forces, you would come down to the plain to meet us. There we can truly test each other's strength. ⁷² Inquire, and you will find that I have the support of the cities. You will learn who I am and who truly supports you, and will discover that your puny rebellion has no chance of success. Those who came before you have already been beaten twice on their own ground. ⁷³ What chance do you expect to have against my cavalry and the army I have assembled here on the plains? Down here, there is not so much as a pebble for you to hide behind, and no place for you to run away."

⁷⁴ As Jonathan read Apollonius' words, he was infuriated. He gathered 10,000 cavalry and a large infantry and set out from Jerusalem. ⁷⁵ Simon also brought troops, and the two armies camped outside of Joppa. The people of the city closed the gates—Apollonius kept a garrison there—⁷⁶ so they assaulted the city, and the people became afraid and opened the gates to them. Thus Jonathan captured Joppa.

⁷⁷ Apollonius, hearing of this, gathered 3,000 cavalry and a large infantry and went to Azotus, feigning that he would press on further. At the same time, his troops advanced on the plain, for he trusted the strength of his cavalry. ⁷⁸ Jonathan pursued them to Azotus, and there the two armies met in battle.

⁷⁹ Apollonius had secretly moved the cavalry around behind Israel's battle lines. ⁸⁰ When they attacked, Jonathan saw that he was ambushed; his army was surrounded and the enemy's arrows rained down from all sides from morning until evening. ⁸¹ But the troops stood their ground, following Jonathan's lead, and the attacking forces became weary. ⁸² As they grew exhausted, Simon and his forces arrived on the scene, and attacked the enemy troops, who broke and fled.

⁸³ The cavalry scattered across the plain and then retreated to Azotus and took refuge in the temple of Dagon. ⁸⁴ Jonathan set fire to the city and to the temple of Dagon, burning to death all who were hiding inside. ⁸⁵ That day, about 8,000 soldiers were killed in battle or burned alive in the fire. ⁸⁶ Jonathan left Azotus and set up headquarters in Ascalon, and the people of the city came out to welcome and honor him. ⁸⁷ Jonathan and the army returned to Jerusalem with much plunder.

⁸⁸ When Alexander heard of these deeds, he bestowed on Jonathan even greater honors. ⁸⁹ He sent a golden clasp, which is only given to those who bear the title "Member of the Royal Family." He also gave Jonathan control of the city of Ekron and all its territories.

11¹ Ptolemy IV of Egypt gathered a large number of soldiers—more numerous than the grains of sand on the seashore—and a great fleet of ships. He planned to take Alexander's realm by treachery and add it to his own.

² He set out for Syria with peaceful pretensions, and the people of the cities opened their gates to him when he arrived. Alexander had ordered that they do this—Ptolemy was his father-in-law. ³ But as Ptolemy continued north, he stationed troops in the cities he passed through.

⁴ When he reached Azotus, the citizens there showed him the damage that Jonathan had done: the burned temple of Dagon and the ruins of the city and surrounding villages. Corpses were piled high everywhere—the bodies of soldiers whom Jonathan had burned alive were piled up high along the road as Ptolemy passed. ⁵ The people told him all that Jonathan had done, hoping that he would take a vow of vengeance against Jonathan. But Ptolemy said nothing. ⁶ Jonathan went to Joppa to meet Ptolemy with all the pomp and circumstance of a high head of state. ⁷ Jonathan accompanied Ptolemy as far as the Eleutherus River before returning to Jerusalem.

⁸ So Ptolemy gained control of all the coastal cities as far as Seleucia, all the while developing his diabolical schemes against Alexander. ⁹ He sent messengers to Demetrius, saying, "Let's make a treaty with each other. I will give you my daughter in marriage—the same daughter I gave to Alexander—and you will rule over your ancestral lands. ¹⁰ I now regret that I made a treaty with him. Since then, he's tried to kill me."

¹¹ Ptolemy accused Alexander because he desired his realm. ¹² He called his daughter away from Alexander and gave her to Demetrius. It was at this point that he and Alexander became open enemies and their hostility began. ¹³ Ptolemy entered Antioch and put on the crown of Syria, thus wearing two crowns: those of Egypt and Syria.

¹⁴ Alexander happened to be in Cilicia at the time, curbing a local revolt. ¹⁵ When Alexander heard of Ptolemy's actions, he moved his forces to attack him. But Ptolemy met Alexander with a stronger force and forced him to retreat. ¹⁶ So Ptolemy was triumphant, and Alexander fled into Arabia to find protection. ¹⁷ Zabdiel the Arabian cut off Alexander's head and sent it to Ptolemy.

¹⁸ Just three days later, Ptolemy died and the troops left inside the fortress were killed off by the local people. ¹⁹ So, in the year 167, Demetrius II became ruler of Syria.

²⁰ At the same time, Jonathan was gathering forces in Judea to attack the citadel at Jerusalem. They built large siege platforms to use in the attack.

21 Some of the apostates, haters of their own people, went to Demetrius II and told him of Jonathan's preparations to attack the citadel. 22 Demetrius was angered at this, and immediately moved to the city of Ptolemais. From there he wrote Jonathan, ordering him to cease the attack and to meet him for a conference at Ptolemais as quickly as possible.

23 But when Jonathan read the message, he ordered the siege to continue. He then chose a number of the leaders of the Jewish community and some priests to go to Ptolemais with him.

24 Risking his life, Jonathan met with Demetrius in Ptolemais, bringing fine robes, silver and gold, and many other gifts. Demetrius was well pleased with him. 25 And although lawless apostates among his own people made accusations against Jonathan, 26 Demetrius treated him as the previous rulers had done, honoring him in the midst of all the high officials of the realm, 27 confirming him as high priest, and conferring all former benefits as a Friend of the Ruler.

28 Jonathan then asked Demetrius to exempt all the territory of Judea and the three districts of Samaria from taxes in exchange for three hundred talents.* 29 Demetrius assented, and wrote the following letter to Jonathan:

30 "Demetrius the ruler, to my Friend Jonathan and to the entire Jewish nation: Greetings.

31 "I have written to my cousin Lasthenes about your situation. Here is a copy of the letter I sent to him: 32 'I, Demetrius, send greetings to the honorable Lasthenes. 33 I have decided to grant to the Jewish people certain benefits because of the friendship they have shown to us in keeping their treaty obligations. 34 I confirm their claim to authority over the territories of Judea and to the three districts of Aphairema, Lydda and Rathamin, as well as their surrounding territories, which were added to Judea from Samaria. To all who offer sacrifices in Jerusalem, I grant exemption from all royal taxes that have been levied by past rulers on the produce of their fields and orchards. 35 Hereafter, all payment of taxes in these regions will no longer be made to the royal treasury, but to the Temple. I also grant an exemption on other tithes, tolls, salt taxes and other special taxes that were formerly due to the royal treasury. 36 These exemptions are to be observed in perpetuity. 37 See that a complete copy of this order be given promptly to Jonathan to be placed in full viewing on the Temple hill.' "

38 Demetrius saw that the realm was at peace under his rule and that all rebellions had ceased. He disbanded his army and sent everyone home,

---

* A little over eleven tons of silver, the traditional sum given to the ruler by the high priest.

except the troops he had recruited from foreign lands and the island territories. As the numbers of jobless soldiers swelled, they began to hate Demetrius.

³⁹ There was a certain Trypho, a former supporter of Alexander, was aware of this growing dissention among those soldiers whom Demetrius had dismissed. He went to Imalkue, the Arab who was fostering Alexander's heir, Antiochus. ⁴⁰ Trypho strongly urged Imaklue to place Antiochus in his custody so that he could be raised to take Alexander's place as ruler. He told Imaklue of how Demetrius had dismissed his entire army, and of the hatred which the soldiers held for him; and he stayed with Imaklue for many days.

⁴¹ Jonathan sent Demetrius a message requesting that the troops be removed from the citadel in Jerusalem and the surrounding fortresses, because they kept harassing the people of Israel. ⁴² Demetrius wrote back, saying, "I will do this favor for you, and will bestow even greater honors upon you and your people. ⁴³ I ask you this one favor: send soldiers here to fight for me because my own troops have revolted." ⁴⁴ So Jonathan sent 3,000 valiant warriors to Demetrius in Antioch. When they arrived there, Demetrius rejoiced.

⁴⁵ The people in the city rose up in a riot of 120,000, all calling for Demetrius' death. ⁴⁶ Demetrius hid in the palace, and the crowd seized the main streets of the city and began to fight. ⁴⁷ Demetrius called the Jewish soldiers to his aid and they rallied around him. They went through the entire city, killing about 100,000 people in their path. ⁴⁸ Demetrius' life was spared, but the city was despoiled and burned.

⁴⁹ When the people saw the might of the Jewish soldiers, and that they were in complete control over the city, they lost courage. ⁵⁰ They abandoned their arms and sent a message to Demetrius asking for peace. ⁵¹ Respect for the Jewish people grew among the ruler and the people, and they returned to Jerusalem with a large amount of spoil.

⁵² Finally Demetrius' rule was firmly reestablished, and the realm was at peace. ⁵³ But he began to break his promises to the Jewish people, and grew distant from Jonathan, not only refusing to fulfill the favors he had promised, but continuing to harass him.

⁵⁴ Some time later, Trypho returned with the young Antiochus and crowned him ruler. ⁵⁵ All the soldiers whom Demetrius had dismissed now rallied around the young ruler. They defeated Demetrius, who fled.

⁵⁶ Trypho took elephants and captured Antioch. ⁵⁷ The young Antiochus wrote to Jonathan saying, "I confirm you in the station of high priest, and

give you authority over the four districts, and make you one of the Rulers inner circle." ⁵⁸ He sent Jonathan gold plate and table service and authorized him to drink from the royal vessels and to dress in purple robes and wear the golden clasp. ⁵⁹ Antiochus appointed Jonathan's brother Simon as governor of the land between the Ladder of Tyre and the borders of Egypt.

⁶⁰ Now Jonathan traveled beyond the river and among the villages, joined by the Syrian army as allies. When he came to Askalon, the people of the city greeted him with great honors.

⁶¹ From there, he went to Gaza, but the people there would not let him enter the city. So he attacked the city and burned and plundered its surrounding villages. ⁶² Then the people of Gaza pleaded for Jonathan to stop, so he made peace with them. He took the children of their rulers as hostages of war and sent them to Jerusalem. Then he marched on until he reached Damascus.

⁶³ Jonathan heard that Demetrius' officers had come to Kedesh in Galilee with a large army, intending to remove him from office. ⁶⁴ He left his brother Simon in Judea and set out to meet them in battle. ⁶⁵ Simon attacked Beth Zur and fought against it for a long time. ⁶⁶ The people then asked for peace, and Simon granted it. He then took over the city, moved its inhabitants out, and stationed a garrison of troops there.

⁶⁷ Jonathan and his army set up headquarters by the shores of Gennesaret. Early in the morning, he marched his troops to the plain of Hazor, where the main force of the army was advancing to meet him. ⁶⁸ Unknown to Jonathan, they had staged an ambush for him in the mountains, ⁶⁹ and when this force descended on Jonathan's army, ⁷⁰ his people turned and ran. Only Mattathias begot of Absalom and Judas begot of Chalph, who commanded the forces, remained with Jonathan.

⁷¹ Jonathan tore his clothes and threw dirt over his head and cried out to heaven. ⁷² Then he turned back to the battle against the enemy, crushing them until they fled. ⁷³ When the soldiers who had run away saw this, they returned to Jonathan and joined in the pursuit of the enemy as far as Kedesh, where they set up camp. ⁷⁴ As many as 3,000 enemy soldiers died that day. Then Jonathan returned to Jerusalem.

∝ ∝ ∝

12:1 Now, when Jonathan saw that things were going well for him, he sent emissaries to Rome to confirm and renew the alliance which had been made with them. ² He also sent letters of similar intent to the Spartans and to other places.

³ When his emissaries arrived in Rome, they went to the Senate chambers and said, "The high priest Jonathan and the whole Jewish nation sent us to renew the former friendship and alliance with you."

⁴ The Romans gave them letters to the authorities of each of the countries through with they would pass guaranteeing them safe passage back to the land of Judea.

⁵ This is a copy of the letter Jonathan wrote to the Spartans:

⁶ "Jonathan, the high priest, the Grand Council of Elders, the priests and the rest of the people of Judea, to our friends in Sparta: Greetings.

⁷ "In times past, your ruler Arius sent a letter to our high priest Onias, stating that our two nations are related, as the attached copy shows. ⁸ Onias welcomed the emissary with great honor and received the letter which contained a clear declaration of alliance and friendship. ⁹ So, even though we have no need of these things, having in our possession the holy books, ¹⁰ we are writing to you to renew our family ties and friendship so that we might not be estranged from you, because so much time has passed since you sent your letter to us. ¹¹ Through the years, we have taken every occasion on our festival days to remember you as we offer our sacrifices and pray, as it is fitting and proper for member of the same family to do for one another.

¹³ "We have had one set of troubles after another, and have had to fight many wars because we are under constant attack from the surrounding nations. ¹⁴ We did not want to trouble you or our other allies and friends, ¹⁵ since we rely on the help of Our God—who has conquered our enemies and rescued us from them. ¹⁶ We have chosen Numenius, begot of Antiochus, and Antipater, begot of Jason, and sent them as emissaries to Rome to renew our ties of alliance and friendship with them. ¹⁷ We have also instructed them to bring our greetings to you, and to deliver to you this letter concerning our renewal of family ties. ¹⁸ We now request an answer to this letter."

¹⁹ The following is a copy of the earlier letter, sent to Onias:

²⁰ "Arius, ruler of Sparta, to Onias the high priest: Greetings. ²¹ We have found a document about the people of Sparta and the Jewish people which indicates that we are related and that both our peoples are descendants of Abraham. ²² Now that we have discovered this, please let us know about your situation. In reply, we will send a letter telling us of your situation. ²³ For our part, we want you to know that our property and livestock belong to you as much as yours belong to us. We have ordered our emissaries to give you a detailed report on these matters."

²⁴ Jonathan then learned that Demetrius' officers had returned to attack him with an even larger army than before. ²⁵ Jonathan did not want to give them the advantage of penetrating into the Judean territory, so he left Jerusalem and met them in the region of Hamath.

²⁶ Jonathan sent spies into the enemy encampment, who reported that the enemy forces were assembling with plans to attack them by night. ²⁷ At sunset, Jonathan ordered his troops to remain vigilant and keep their arms ready, and he stationed outposts around the camp so that they would be prepared for battle that night.

²⁸ When the enemy heard that Jonathan and the troops were prepared for battle, they grew deeply afraid. They kindled the fires in their camp, and then stealthily withdrew. ²⁹ Jonathan and his army saw the campfires burning, and so didn't realize they had left until the next morning. ³⁰ They set out in pursuit, but could not overtake them because they already crossed the Eleutherus River.

³¹ So Jonathan turned aside and attacked the Arabian tribe known as the Zabadeans. He conquered them and plundered their possessions. ³² Then he broke camp and marched to Damascus, inspecting the entire region along the way.

³³ Meanwhile Simon also set out and marched as far as Askalon and the neighboring villages. He then turned on Joppa and attacked it by surprise, ³⁴ having heard of their intention to hand over the fortress to Demetrius' allies. Simon left a garrison there to defend it.

³⁵ When Jonathan returned, he called a meeting of the Elders of the people. Together, they decided to build fortifications around Judea, ³⁶ to fortify the walls around Jerusalem, and to erect a high barricade between the citadel and the city to separate it from the city and to isolate and blockade it.

³⁷ They came together and rebuilt the city. Part of the wall over the eastern valley had fallen; they rebuilt this, and also restored the quarter called Chaphenatha. ³⁸ Meanwhile, Simon rebuilt Adida in the Shephelah, fortifying it and building bolted gates.

³⁹ At this time, Trypho plotted to become ruler of Syria, to take the crown, and overthrow Antiochus. ⁴⁰ He feared that Jonathan would stand in his way, and might make war on him if he did. So Trypho set out for Bethshan, hoping to find some pretext on which to arrest Jonathan and have him executed.

⁴¹ Jonathan met him at Bethshan, with 40,000 soldiers. ⁴² When Trypho saw Jonathan there with a large army, he hesitated to move against him. ⁴³ Instead, he received Jonathan with honor, commended him to all his

friends, presented gifts to him, and told his friends and his troops to obey him as they would himself. ⁴⁴ He said to Jonathan, "Why have you worn all these people to the bone, when there is no hostility between us? ⁴⁵ Send them home. You can choose yourself a few soldiers to be your bodyguard. Then come with me to Ptolemais. I will surrender it to you, with the other fortresses and the remaining troops and their officers. Then I will return home, for that was my only reason for coming here."

⁴⁶ Jonathan trusted Tryphos and did as he said. He dismissed his troops, who returned to Judea. ⁴⁷ Jonathan kept 3,000 soldiers, of whom he left 2,000 in Galilee, while 1,000 accompanied him. ⁴⁸ But as soon as Jonathan had entered Ptolemais, the people of Ptolemais closed the gates, arrested him, and killed all who had come with him.

⁴⁹ Trypho sent troops and cavalry into Galilee and the Great Plateau to destroy Jonathan's soldiers. ⁵⁰ Believing that Jonathan had been captured and had died with his companions, they rallied one another and closed their ranks as they prepared for battle.

⁵¹ When their pursuers saw that they were ready to fight for their lives, they turned back. ⁵² So Jonathan's fighters arrived home in Judea safe and sound. There, they wept for Jonathan and his companions, and with them, all Israel was plunged into shock and mourning.

⁵³ All the Gentiles in the surrounding regions now looked to destroy the Jewish people: "They have no leader," they said, "no allies! If we attack them now, we will wipe out their very memory from among the nations."

13:1–16:24

now Simon heard that Trypho was gathering forces to invade the land of Judea and destroy it. ² Seeing that the people were in anguish and in fear, he travelled to Jerusalem, and called the people together. He said, ³ "You have heard of the great battles I and my brothers—indeed, my whole house—have fought in defense of the Law and the Temple. You also know the trials we have experienced: ⁴ one by one, members of my family have lost their lives for Israel's sake. I alone am left. ⁵ But, far be it from me to spare my own life in times of trouble— I am no better than the others who have died. ⁶ I vow to avenge my nation and the Temple, and our families. Indeed, all the Gentiles are joining forces to destroy us out of mere malice."

⁷ As soon as they heard these words, the people took heart. ⁸ They answered with a loud voice, and said, "You are our leader—you stand in place

of place of Judas, and Jonathan. ⁹ Lead us in our battles, and we will obey your words."

¹⁰ So Simon called together all the warriors and rushed to finish the walls of Jerusalem, making it strong all around. ¹¹ He also sent Yohanan begot of Absalom to Joppa with a new army, where he threw out all the residents, and established himself there.

¹² Trypho now marched from Ptolemais with a great army to invade the land of Judea, and took Jonathan with them as a hostage. ¹³ Simon set up headquarters in Addus, facing the plateau. ¹⁴ When Trypho realized that Simon had taken his brother Jonathan's place as leader of the Jewish people, and that he intended to engage in battle with him, Trypho sent messengers to him and said, ¹⁵ "We have detained Jonathan for the money that he owed the royal treasury, because of the affairs which he had been given authority over. ¹⁶ Send us four tons of silver, and two of his children as hostages, so that when we set him free, he will not stage an uprising. Then we will release him."

¹⁷ Now Simon knew that Trypho was lying. Nonetheless he ordered the money and the children to be sent. He wished to avoid upsetting the people of Israel, who might have said, ¹⁸ "Because Simon has not sent the money or the children, Jonathan is doomed." ¹⁹ So Simon sent the children and the four tons of silver. But Trypho lied, and did not let Jonathan go.

²⁰ After this, Trypho entered Judea to destroy it, and the army marched along the road to Ador. Simon and the Judean army shadowed Trypho's army wherever they went.

²¹ The people of the citadel sent messengers to Trypho telling him to hurry through the wilderness and bring them provisions. ²² Trypho prepared the cavalry to march that night, but when night came, a great snow fell and they could not go, but instead marched into the region of Gilead.

²³ When Trypho approached to Bascama, he killed Jonathan and his sons there ²⁴ and then returned to his own country. ²⁵ Simon sent out soldiers to recover the bodies, and took the bones of Jonathan and buried them in Modein, in the city of their ancestors. ²⁶ All of Israel mourned Jonathan for many days.

²⁷ Simon built a monument, a sight magnificent to behold with brightly polished stones, over the family tomb, ²⁸ And then set up seven pyramids side by side, for their parents, his four brothers, and himself. ²⁹ Around these he set great pillars. On each pillar he placed suits of armor, and carved ships so large that they could be seen by all who sail the seas. And the monument stood as a perpetual memory. ³⁰ This same monument can be seen even today in Modein.

³¹ Trypho designed treachery against Antiochus. He assassinated him, ³² and then took his place, putting on the crown of Syria, and bringing nothing but violence to the land.

³³ Simon fortified the strongholds of Judea, building high towers and great walls and massive gates with bars, and stockpiling provisions in the fortresses. ³⁴ He selected emissaries and sent them to Demetrius, seeking relief for the people—for all that Trypho did was despoil.

³⁵ Demetrius responded with the following letter:

³⁶ "Demetrius the Great, to Simon the high priest and friend of rulers, and to the elders, and to the nation of Israel: Greetings.

³⁷ "I have received the golden crown and the palm branch which you sent. We are prepared to make a firm treaty with you, and to write to our chief officers granting you release from tributes. ³⁸ All that we have given you will remain in force. The strongholds which you have built shall remain in your own hands. ³⁹ As for any oversight or fault committed by you prior to this, as well as any royal tax which you owe, all is forgiven. What taxes are now being collected in Jerusalem will no longer be levied. ⁴⁰ Those of you who are fit to be enrolled among our soldiers shall be so enrolled; and let there be complete peace between us."

⁴¹ So, in the year 170, Israel was freed from the yoke of the Gentiles. ⁴² And at that time, the people of Israel began to date their documents and public records thus: "The first year under Simon the high priest, the great leader and ruler of Israel."

Then Simon began a campaign against Gazara, and camped his army around it. He built a large attack tower and moved it to the city walls, where they broke into and seized one of the city's towers. ⁴⁴ From here, the soldiers burst into the city and attacked from within, and a great uproar ensued. ⁴⁵ The citizens of Gaza rushed to the wall, ripping their garments and pleading loudly for Simon to make peace with them: ⁴⁶ "Do not deal with us according to our violent past," they cried, "but treat us with mercy. "

⁴⁷ Simon was moved and did not destroy them, but he did expel them from the city. He cleansed the shrines where they had kept idols, and then entered the city singing hymns and praising the Most High. ⁴⁸ When the place had been purified of uncleaness, Simon settled new people there who were devout observers of the Law. He fortified the city, and built a residence for himself there.

⁴⁹ The Gentiles who were in the citadel at Jerusalem had been locked in, and precluded from any commerce. There was famine, and many died of starvation, ⁵⁰ so they petitioned for peace. Simon granted their petition, but

made them leave the citadel. He then purified the place; ⁵¹ and on the twenty-third day of the second month, in the year 171, they entered the citadel with thanksgiving, waving palm branches, and sounding harps, and cymbals—singing songs and hymns of praise because a great enemy of Israel had finally been destroyed. ⁵² Simon ordered that this day be commemorated with celebration each year.

⁵³ He strengthened the walls around the Temple Mount near the citadel, and took up residence there with others. ⁵⁴ Seeing that John his son had become an adult, Simon made him commander of all the forces. John then took up residence in Gazara.

෮   ෮   ෮

14₁ In the year 172, Demetrius the ruler assembled an army and marched into Media in order to plunder it so that they would have the resources to sustain a fight against Trypho.

² Arsaces, ruler of Persia and Media, hearing that Demetrius had invaded his realm, sent one of generals to take him alive. ³ This general defeated the army of Demetrius, and Demetrius was captured and brought to Arsaces as a prisoner of war.

⁴ Judea was at peace throughout Simon's reign;
    he sought the good of the nation;
the people were pleased with his reign,
    and they honored him throughout his days.
⁵ As a crown upon his achievements,
    he took Joppa and made it into a harbor,
    opening the way to the islands in the sea.
⁶ He expanded the reaches of his realm,
    and established himself as the ruler unchallenged.
⁷ He gathered up a great flock of prisoners of war,
    and extended his rule over Gazara, Bethsura,
    and the citadel—
cleansing the citadel of its vileness—
    and there was none that could oppose him.

⁸ The land was cultivated in quiet;
    all Judea flowered with abundance,
    and the trees of the fields bore their fruit.
⁹ The elders of the people sat in the streets,
    talking among themselves about the bounty of the land;
    the youths adorned themselves in fine clothing and armor.

10 The towns were provided for in plenty,
  and were well fortified in their defenses;
  the fame of Simon spread out across the earth.
11 He brought peace to the land,
  and Israel was full of joy.
12 People rested in the shade of their vines and fig trees,
  and there was nothing for them to fear.
13 There was no one in the land to rise against them;
  the rulers of the nations had been crushed.
14 Simon gave help to those who were brought low,
  and protected them under the Law;
  the violent and the unjust were banished.
15 Simon restored the sanctuary's glory,
  and increased the vessels of the holy places.

16 News reached Rome, and as far as Sparta, that Jonathan was dead, and they were saddened. 17 But they heard that Simon was made high priest, and was in control of the nation and the cities, 18 and so they sent letters to him on bronze tablets, renewing the friendship and alliances which had been made with Judas and with Jonathan. 19 The tablets were read before the Assembly in Jerusalem. This is the letter that the Spartans sent:

20 "The leaders and citizen of Sparta, to Simon the high priest, and to the elders, the priests, and the rest of the people of the Israel: Greetings.

21 "The emissaries you sent here have told us of your glory and honor, and joy. We celebrate their arrival. 22 We have written what they have said to us in the records of the people in this manner: Numenius, begot of Antiochus, and Antipater, begot of Jason, of the Jewish people, came to us to renew our old bond of friendship. 23 We were pleased to welcome them with honor, and to place a copy of their words in the public records for the memory of the people of Sparta. We have sent a copy to Simon the high priest."

24 After this Simon sent Numenius to Rome, with a great shield of gold weighing over a thousand pounds, to confirm their alliance. When the people of Rome heard 25 of the things that had happened, they said, "How can we show our gratitude to Simon and those who have stood by him? 26 All of the house of his father have acted with honor; they have struggled, and have thrown out the enemies of Israel, and have set their people free."

They inscribed these words on bronze tablets, which were mounted on pillars in mount Zion: 27 "The eighteenth day of the month Elul, in the year 172, in the third year under Simon the high priest at Asaramel. 28 In the great counsel of the priests and the people, in the presence of the leaders of the nation and the elders of the land, these things were recorded.

"During the long history of wars in our land, ²⁹ Simon, begot of Mattathias of the children of Jarib, and his family, placed themselves in danger to resist the enemies of their people, and to preserve the Holy places, and the Law. In doing so, they have raised their nation to great glory.

³⁰ "Jonathan unified the nation, and became their high priest, and is now at rest among his people. ³¹ Then the enemies of Israel wanted to overrun the nation and destroy them, and violate their holy places; ³² but Simon rose to the cause and fought for the nation, paying out of his own funds for arms and wages for their soldiers. ³³ He strengthened the cities of Judea, and Bethsura that lie at the borders of Judea, where the armory of the enemies was before; and he placed a garrison there. ³⁴ Jonathan fortified the seaport of Joppa, as well as Gazara, on the border of Azotus, where enemies once guarded. He settled the Jewish people there, and provided for the restoration of those towns.

³⁵ "When the people saw the integrity of Simon, the glory which he brought to his people, the way he preserved them in justice and faith, and the ways he sought the betterment of the people, they made him their leader and high priest. ³⁶ During Simon's lifetime, the people prospered; and their enemies—those scattered around the country, and those who had made their home in the City of David in Jerusalem in the citadel, from where they would come out and profane the places around about the sanctuary—were thrown out of the nation, ³⁷ and settled the Jewish people in their place. And for the defense of the country and the city, he built up the walls of Jerusalem.

³⁸ "In light of these things, the ruler Demetrius confirmed him in the high priesthood, ³⁹ and called him his Friend, and gave him great honor. ⁴⁰ For he had heard that the Romans had called the Jews their friends, and confederates, and brethren, and that they had received Simon's ambassadors with honor.

⁴¹ "So the Jewish people and the priests agreed that Simon should be their leader and high priest forever—or until a faithful prophet should appear—⁴² that he should be their governor, and should take charge of the sanctuary, and should appoint ministers over their works, as well as over the country, and the armory, and the strong holds. ⁴³ They agreed that he should be in control of the holy places, that he should be obeyed by all, and that all the writings in the country should be made in his name—and that he should be clothed with purple and gold. ⁴⁴ They further agreed that it would be unlawful for any of the people or the priests,

to revoke any of these things, or to go against his words, or to call an assembly in the country without his permission, or for anyone else to be clothed with purple or to wear a buckle of gold— ⁴⁵ and that anyone who went against these things in any way would be punished."

⁴⁶ All the people agreed that these rights and privileges would be accorded to Simon, as it was written. ⁴⁷ Simon accepted, and was pleased to execute the office of the high priesthood, as well as that of commander and governor of the Jewish nation and its priests, and to be a guardian over them all. ⁴⁸ They decreed that this would be written on bronze tablets, which would be set up around the sanctuary in conspicuous places, ⁴⁹ with another copy to be put in the treasury, for Simon and his heirs to keep.

ଔ   ଔ   ଔ

15₁ Antiochus, the heir of Demetrius, sent this letter from the islands of the sea to Simon, priest and governor of the Jewish nation, and to all the people:

² "The ruler Antiochus, to Simon the high priest, and to the nation of the Jewish people: Greetings.

³ "You see that certain wretches have usurped the realm of my ancestors. It is now my intent to challenge their rule, and to restore the realm to its former state. I have recruited a large mercenary army, and have built warships. ⁴ I intend to sweep through the country, and have revenge on those that have destroyed it, and make its cities desolate.

⁵ "I now confirm all the rights and privileges that the rulers who preceded me had given to you, and any gifts that they may have given you. ⁶ I grant you permission to coin your own money in your nation; ⁷ and I promise that Jerusalem will be holy and free. All the weaponry that you have, and the fortresses which you have built and hold, remain yours. ⁸ Any debts which you owe to the realm, or that you might owe in the future, are cancelled now and permanently. ⁹ When I have recovered my realm, I will honor you and your nation and your Temple. The honor that I show to you will be such that it will shine throughout the earth."

¹⁰ In the year 174 Antiochus returned to the land of his ancestors. So great were the numbers that rallied to him that Trypho was left with nothing. ¹¹ Antiochus pursued him, and he fled along the sea coast to Dora. ¹² He knew that he was in deep trouble, with all his troops having forsaken him. ¹³ Antiochus set up camp above Dora with 120,000 warriors, and 8,000 cavalry. ¹⁴ His troops closed around the city, and his ships shut off all entry by sea. They besieged the city both by land and sea, and sealed it so that no one could get in or out.

¹⁵ Numenius and his party arrived at this time from Rome, with letters written to the various rulers and nations. The contents of these were as follows:

¹⁶ "Lucius the consul of the Romans, to Ptolemy the ruler: Greetings.

¹⁷ "The ambassadors of our friends the Jews visited us, sent by Simon their high priest, and by their people, to renew our old friendship and alliance. ¹⁸ They brought us a shield of gold weighing over a thousand pounds. ¹⁹ It seems a good thing to us to write to the various rulers and nations, asking that they do our friends no harm, and not attack them, either their cities or their nation; and further that they give no aid to any that might attack them.

²⁰ "We have been pleased to accept their golden shield. ²¹ If any outlaws from their country seek refuge with you, please deliver them to Simon the high priest, so that he may punish them according to their laws."

²² This same message was written to the ruler Demetrius, and to Attalus, and to Ariarathes, and to Arsaces, ²³ and to all the nations: to Lampsacus, and the Spartans, and Delus, and Myndus; to Sicyon, and Caria, and Samus, and Pamphylia; to Lycia, and Alicarnassus, and Cos, and Side; to Aradus, and Rhodes, and Phaselis, and Gortyna; and to Gnidus, and Cyprus, and Cyrene. ²⁴ And a copy was sent to Simon the high priest, and to the Jewish nation.

²⁵ Antiochus renewed his siege against Dora, assaulting it continually. They built siege engines, and Trypho was unable to move. ²⁶ Simon now sent Antiochus 2,000 of his best fighters for his aid, and silver and gold, and much equipment as well. ²⁷ But Antiochus would not receive them; he broke the promises which he had made before, and behaved as though they were strangers to him. ²⁸ He sent Athenobius, one of his friends, to Simon to negotiate with him, with this message: "You hold Joppa, Gazara, and the citadel that is in Jerusalem. These are cities of my realm. ²⁹ You have laid waste to their borderlands; you have created chaos in the land, and have taken control of many places in my realm. ³⁰ Surrender to me the cities which you have taken, and the tribute money as well that you have extracted from the lands you control outside the borders of Judea.

³¹ "If you will not do this, then give to me nineteen tons of silver for the destruction you have caused, and another nineteen tons for the tributes of those cities. If you will not do this, we will bring our war to you."

³² So Athenobius, the friend of Antiochus, arrived in Jerusalem. He saw Simon's magnificence, and the riches of gold and silver, and all the trappings, and he was astounded. He relayed the message of Antiochus to Simon, ³³ who replied, "We have taken no lands that were not ours, nor do

we hold anything that is not ours. What we hold is the inheritance of our ancestors, which for some time was usurped by our enemies; ³⁴ but we seized the opportunity reclaim our inheritance.

³⁵ "As for your complaining about Joppa and Gazara—they did nothing but harm to our people and our country. Nonetheless, for these we will give 7,500 pounds of silver."

Athenobius kept his silence, ³⁶ but he returned to Antiochus in a rage, and told him of Simon's words, and also of Simon's wealth, and of all that he had seen. Antiochus was infuriated.

³⁷ Trypho, in the meantime, escaped by a boat to Orthosias. ³⁸ Antiochus appointed Cendebeus to control the sea coast, and gave him an army of both soldiers and cavalry. ³⁹ He commanded him to march with his army towards Judea; and to rebuild Kedron, and to fortify its city gates, and to war against our people. Antiochus himself went in pursuit of Trypho.

⁴⁰ So Cendebeus arrived in Jamnia, and began to attack the people there; he also invaded Judea, taking prisoners and killing the people, all while building up Kedron. ⁴¹ He installed his cavalry there, and his army, so that they could easily make forays into Judea, as Antiochus had commanded.

16¹ Now John came up from Gazara, and told his father Simon what Cendebeus was doing to their people. ² Simon summoned his two eldest, Judas and John, and said to them: "I, and all those of my father's house, have fought against the enemies of Israel from the days of our youth until now; and we have done well at times; we have often saved Israel from great danger. ³ Now I am too old; now you, instead of me, must go out, and fight for our nation. May Heaven's help go with you."

⁴ John then chose 20,000 of the nation's warriors and cavalry, and they went out to face Cendebeus. They camped in Modein. ⁵ When they rose in the morning and went out on the plain, they saw a huge army of infantry and cavalry approaching them. There was a river running between them. ⁶ John prepared his battle lines, but he saw that his people were afraid to cross the river, so he went over first; the rest, seeing him, followed.

⁷ He divided his infantry in half, with the cavalry in between, because the enemy's cavalry outnumbered theirs. They sounded their holy trumpets, and Cendebeus' army fled; many fell, wounded, and the rest escaped into their stronghold. ⁹ Judas, John's brother, was wounded; but John pursued them to Kedron, which Cendebeus had fortified. ¹⁰ They fled also to the towers in the plains of Azotus; these, John burned. Two thousand men died in all before John returned to Judea in peace.

¹¹ Ptolemy, begot of Abobus, had been appointed the governor over Jeri-

cho. He was very wealthy, ¹² and was married one of the daughters of the high priest. ¹³ He grew arrogant, and plotted to make himself the ruler of the land; to this end, he devised treachery, making plans to destroy both Simon and his heirs.

¹⁴ Simon was touring through the cities of Judea, taking care to see that they were in good order, and in the course if this journey, went down to Jericho. He had with him Mattathias and Judas, two of his heirs. This was in the year 177, in the eleventh month, which is the month of Shebat.

¹⁵ This spawn of Abobus, pretending to welcome them, lured them into a little fortress called Dok, which he had built. There he served them a great feast, while his cutthroats hid. ¹⁶ And when Simon and his sons were drunk, Ptolemy's men drew their weapons, bursting in on them in the banquet hall, and murdered him and Mattathias and Judas, and some of his servants. ¹⁷ Thus Ptolemy committed great treachery against Israel, rendering evil for good.

¹⁸ Then Ptolemy wrote to the ruler about these matters, asking him to send an army to help him, and promising to deliver to him the country, the cities, and their tributes. ¹⁹ He sent others to Gazara to kill John; and to the military commanders he sent letters offering them gifts of silver and gold in exchange for their support to him. ²⁰ Still others he sent to take Jerusalem, and the Temple mount.

²¹ One who was loyal to John reached him first in Gazara, telling him that his father and brothers had been killed, and warning him that others had been sent to kill him also. ²² When he heard of these things he was in shock. He apprehended the men that had come to kill him and, knowing of their intent, put them to death.

²³ As for the rest of the acts of John—the wars that he fought, and his fine deeds, the walls that he built, and all the other things he accomplished— ²⁴ these stories are recorded in the accounts of his priesthood, from the time when he was appointed high priest after Simon.

2 maccabees

to our sisters and brothers, the jewish community in Egypt, from your sisters and brothers in Jerusalem and in Judea:

May prosperity and peace be yours! [2] May God be good to you, and may you always keep in mind the covenant made with Abraham and Sarah, Isaac and Rebecca, and Jacob, Leah and Rachel. [3] May God give each of you the heart of worship, with which you can do God's will with an open mind and willing spirit. [4] May God open your minds to the Law and the ordinances. May God bring you peace, [5] and an answer to all your prayers. May God be reconciled to you and never abandon you in time of temptation. [6] This is our prayer for you.

[7] In the year 169, during the reign of Demetrius, we wrote the following letter to you:

"In the hopeless crisis enveloping us after Jason and his band revolted

---

* This first section is comprised of two letters to the Jewish community of the Diaspora establishing the feast of the Rededication of the Temple, or Hanukkah. The first letter, dated forty years later than the second one, suggests that this new December festival should be accorded the stature and import of the Feast of Tabernacles—the harvest festival celebrated in October—by calling it the "December Tabernacles."

from the holy land and the realm, ⁸ they burned the porch of the House of Our God and spilled innocent blood. We then prayed to Our God, who heard our plea. We offered a sacrifice and a grain offering, lit the lamps and set out the loaves."

⁹ Accordingly, we recommend that you celebrate the Feast of Tabernacles in the month of Chislev, beginning in the year 188.*

CR CR CR

¹⁰ From the people of Jerusalem and Judea, together with the Sanhedrin, and Judas,**

To Aristobulus, tutor of Ptolemy the ruler, of the family of anointed priests, and to all Judeans in Egypt:

Greetings and good health. ¹¹ We give profound thanks to God, for we have been saved from great dangers. For God took up our cause against Antiochus the ruler, ¹² and has expelled the enemy from the Holy City.

¹³ When Antiochus reached Persia with a force that seemed invincible, they were cut to pieces. This came about in the temple of the Goddess Nanea, by means of a ruse employed by her priests. ¹⁴ Antiochus, accompanied by his courtiers, came to the temple on the pretext of entering into a ritual marriage with Nanea. His intent was to take most of the temple treasures as a dowry. ¹⁵ When the priests of Nanea had brought out these treasures, the ruler, with a small bodyguard, entered the temple. Then the priests closed the temple doors, ¹⁶ and, opening a secret door in the ceiling, hurled stones down on them, striking them all down. They dropped as if struck by lightning. The priests hacked off their heads and limbs and threw them to the people waiting outside. ¹⁷ Blessed in all things be our God, who returned the wicked to naught!

¹⁸ We feel it proper to inform you that we will celebrate the Purification of the Temple on the twenty-fifth of Chislev, so that you may celebrate the Feast of Tabernacles. It is in honor of the fire that appeared when Nemehiah offered sacrifices after rebuilding the Temple and the altar. ¹⁹ For when our ancestors were being exiled to Persia, the pious priests of that time took some of the fire from the altar and secretly concealed it inside a dry cistern. This proved a safe haven, for they concealed it in such a way that no one knew of it. ²⁰ After many years, when God's good time arrived, Nemehiah, at the request of Persia's ruler, sent the descendants

---

* The 188th year of the Selucid era translates to 124 BCE in our calendar.
** This is Judas—that is, Judah—Maccabeus, who here and in 1 Maccabees is a symbol for the entire nation of Israel.

of the priests who hid the fire to retrieve it. When they reported that there was no fire but only a thick liquid, Nehemiah told them to draw some out and bring it back. When the materials for the sacrifice were set out, the governor ordered the priests to sprinkle the wood and the sacrifice. 22 When this was done, and the clouds had cleared, to everyone's amazement, the sunlight ignited the liquid on the altar. 23 While the sacrifice was being consumed, the priests and all those present offered prayers, with Jonathan leading, and all those present responding with Nehemiah.

24 This was their prayer: "O Sovereign God, God Most High, Creator of all that is, the terrible and the mighty, the just and the merciful: you alone are the kind ruler, 25 you alone are bountiful, just, almighty and everlasting, the deliverer of Israel from all evil, who chose our ancestors and consecrated them! 26 Accept this sacrifice on behalf of all your people Israel, protect and consecrate your people—they are your own possession. 27 Bring together those of us who are scattered, set free those in slavery among the heathens, bless those who are rejected and despised, and let the Gentiles know that you are our God. 28 Punish the oppressor and the arrogant; 29 and, as promised by Moses, plant your people in your holy land."

30 Then the priests chanted the hymns. 31 Once the sacrifice was consumed, Nehemiah ordered the remaining liquid to be poured over large stones. 32 As this was done the flames shot up, but they soon burnt themselves out, and the altar fire outshone them.

33 When these events came to be known, and the ruler of Persia learned that in the place where the exiled priests had hidden the fire, a liquid had appeared which Nehemiah and his people had used to burn the sacrifice, 34 the ruler ordered that the site be enclosed and be declared sacred. 35 The guardians appointed to care for the site received a share of the huge revenues it generated for the ruler. 36 Nehemiah and his people called the liquid "nephthar," which means "purification." Most people call it naphtha.*

2:1 The old books tell us that the prophet Jeremiah ordered the exiles to hide the fire, as it has been described here. After giving them the Law, the prophet admonished them not to neglect the commandments of Our God, nor to let their minds be led astray with thoughts of the finery of gold and silver images. 3 The prophet also warned them never to let the Law be far from their hearts.

4 The same account also tells how the divinely enlightened prophet ordered that the Tent of Meeting and the Ark should accompany him. So

---

* Crude petroleum.

Jeremiah left for the mountain from which Moses saw God's promised land.

⁵ Once at the mountain, Jeremiah found a cave-dwelling, where he hid the Tent, the Ark, and the altar of incense. Then the prophet blocked up the entrance. ⁶ Some of his companions came back to mark the site, but were unable to find it. ⁷ Jeremiah, hearing of this, admonished them, "This place is to remain unknown until God finally brings us together again and favors us. ⁸ Our God will then bring these things to light. And Our God's glory will be seen, along with the cloud, as it was revealed in the time of Moses and in the time when Solomon prayed that this site would be appropriately consecrated."

⁹ It was noted also that Solomon, blessed with the gift of wisdom, offered a dedication sacrifice at the completion of the House of Our God; ¹⁰ and that just as Moses prayed to Our God and fire descended from heaven to consume the sacrificial offering, so in answer to Solomon's prayer, fire descended and consumed the whole offering. ¹¹ As Moses said, "The sin offering was consumed in the same way because it was not eaten." ¹² And Solomon also kept the feast in the same way for eight days.

¹³ In addition to the above, it is recorded in the archives and in the memoirs of Nemehiah that the prophet also founded a library, and there collected the books about the rulers, the writings of the prophets, and the works of David, as well as royal letters on the subject of sacred offerings.

¹⁴ In this same way Judas collected for us all the documents that were scattered as a result of the recent war. We now have them in our possession. ¹⁵ If ever you have the need, send messengers for them.

¹⁶ Since we are now about to celebrate the Purification of the House of Our God, we are writing you today to impress upon you the importance of keeping this festival. ¹⁷ It is God who saved us all, and returned our inheritance, the holy land, our rulers, the priesthood and the consecration, ¹⁸ promised by the Law. We are confident that God will soon have mercy on us and gather us to the holy land from our dispersion; for God has delivered us from great evils and purified the Temple.

2:19–7:42

Jason of Cyrene set out in five books the story of Judas Maccabeus and his brothers, of the purification of the great House of Our God, and of the dedication of the altar. ²⁰ Jason also gave us an account of the wars against Antiochus Epiphanes and his heir Eupator. ²¹ He described the apparitions that came from heaven to inspire those who fought bravely for Judaism, so that, though few in numbers, they overran the whole country, plundering and routing the barbarian hordes. [22] With the grace of God's kindness, they regained possession of our renowned Temple, liberated the city of Jerusalem, and reestablished the laws which were on the verge of being abolished.

[23] All of this, related in Jason's five books, I hope to condense into one volume. [24] I was concerned about the flood of statistics and the challenge that the sheer bulk of material presented to someone intent on learning this history. [25] I attempted to tell a story for those who read for pleasure, for those who want to memorize it, and for the benefit of all readers. [26] The task I took on in condensing the story was no light one; it cost me much sweat, and loss of sleep. [27] It is no easy thing, preparing a feast that will please the guests. Still, I gladly take on these difficult tasks for the sake of many. [28] I concentrated on presenting an overview, leaving the fine details to the original writer. [29] A builder putting up a new house must be concerned with every detail of the building, but one responsible for the paint work need only concentrate on the details of decoration. This describes my case. [30] The original author of a work of history must survey the field, and consider every detail, in order to do a thorough job. [31] But the person who abridges must be allowed to focus on cogency and brevity.

[32] Here, then, let us begin the narrative, and not add anymore to what has been said. It would be nonsense to expand the introduction while abbreviating the narrative!

જ જ જ

3[1] While Onias, the high priest, ruled the Holy City, it enjoyed unbroken peace, and the Law was observed as perfectly as possible. This was due to the piety of Onias, who hated wickedness. [2] The rulers themselves came to esteem the Sanctuary and added to its glory with their magnificent gifts, to such extent that [3] Seleucus of Asia underwrote the entire cost of the sacrificial services.

[4] But a person named Simon, of the Bilgah clan, the administrator of the Temple, had a falling out with the high priest over the supervision of the city market. [5] Unable to get satisfaction from the high priest, the administrator went to Apollonius of Tarsus, governor of Coele-Syria and Phoenicia, [6] and reported to the governor that the treasury in Jerusalem was so full of untold riches that the sum was incalculable, that it was

utterly disproportionate with the cost of the sacrifices, and that it was possible for these funds to fall under the control of the ruler.

7 Apollonius met with the ruler and related what had been reported to him about the riches. The ruler sent the chief minister, Heliodorus, to see to it that the treasures be removed immediately. 8 Heliodorus left at once, ostensibly on a tour of the cities of Coele-Syria and Phoenicia, but in reality to carry out Apollonius' order.

9 When the chief minister arrived in Jerusalem, after a gracious welcome, he disclosed the reason for the visit, told of the allegations, and asked if they were true. 10 The high priest explained that some of the funds were set aside for widows and orphans, and some of the funds belonged to Hyrcanus, begot of Tobias, a prominent member of the community. The total of the entire fund, contrary to what the godless Simon reported, was nearly fourteen tons of silver and seven tons of gold. 12 The high priest added that it was utterly impossible to deal unjustly with those who had put their trust in the sanctity of the place, the holy inviolability of the Temple which was venerated worldwide.

13 But Heliodorus, under the orders of the ruler, insisted that the funds be confiscated for Apollonius' treasury. 14 So on the day appointed, when the chief minister entered the Temple to inventory funds, turmoil reigned throughout the city. 15 Fully vested priests prostrated themselves before the altar and prayed to Heaven, whose Law made deposits sacred, to protect them for the original owners.

16 The appearance of the high priest pierced the hearts of the beholders. The gray of his face disclosed his anguished soul. 17 Onias, overwhelmed with fear and trembling, plainly showed the pain in his heart. 18 Crowds of people rushed from their houses to join in a general supplication over the dishonor threatening the holy place. 19 Bare-breasted women wearing skirts of sackcloth thronged the streets. Young women who were normally secluded ran to the gates, and others to the walls, while some leaned out the windows. 20 They all, as if one, stretched out their hands to heaven. 21 It was a tragic scene—the crowd prostrated in utter disarray and the high priest dreadfully anguished.

22 While the people implored Almighty God to keep that which had been entrusted to the Temple intact and safe for its depositors, 23 Heliodorus proceeded with his task. 24 But when the chief minister approached the treasury, the Sovereign of Spirits caused so great an apparition that Heliodorus' retinue collapsed in terror, struck with panic before God's might. 25 A horse in rich trappings appeared, with a rider in golden armor—an appearance both awesome and fearsome. Ferociously, it rushed Heliodorus and struck with its front hoofs. 26 Two strong and handsome

youths, magnificently attired, appeared on either side of Heliodorus, and flogged him continuously. ²⁷ He collapsed to the ground, unconscious. Members of his retinue put him on a stretcher and carried him away— ²⁸ the one who so recently had forged his way into the treasury with body-guards and an attendant crowd, was now a motionless heap. The sover-eign power of God was overwhelmingly clear.

²⁹ While Heliodorus lay rendered unconscious by this divine interven-tion, with no hope of recovery, ³⁰ the people praised God for working this miracle in the holy place. The Temple, which moments before had been filled with chaos and fear, was now filled with joy and gladness for the deliverance of Almighty God.

³¹ Some of those who had accompanied Heliodorus begged Onias to pray that the Most High would spare his life, since he lay at death's door. ³² Fearing that the ruler might believe Heliodorus had met with foul play at the hands of the Jewish community, the high priest offered a sacrifice for the chief minister. ³³ While the high priest offered the sacrifice of atone-ment, the same two handsome youths, dressed as before, appeared once more and stood over Heliodorus, saying, "Be very grateful to Onias, for God has spared your life through his intercession. ³⁴ You have been flogged by God. Now proclaim God's mighty power to all." With these words they vanished.

³⁵ Heliodorus then offered sacrifice and made many free-will offerings to the God who had spared his life. Then, bidding Onias farewell, he re-turned with his retinue to the ruler. ³⁶ Openly speaking about the miracle of the Most High God who saved his life, Heliodorus gave witness to one and all. ³⁷ When the ruler asked the chief minister what sort of person he should send to Jerusalem the next time, Heliodorus replied, ³⁸ "If you have enemies or someone plotting against you, send them to that place, for they will return thoroughly flogged, if they survive at all. There is most cer-tainly some power of God there. ³⁹ The One who resides in heaven watches over the place and protects it. Those who come to it intending harm are struck down and destroyed."

⁴⁰ And that is the story of Heliodorus and the preservation of the Trea-sury.

ଔ   ଔ   ଔ

4:1 Simon, mentioned earlier—who had testified against his own country concerning the money in the Temple—now began slander against Onias, saying that it was the chief priest who had brought about these events and mistreated Heliodorus. ² Simon had the audacity to accuse this benefactor of the city, a protector of citizens and a fervent upholder of the Law, of collusion against the government. ³ The growing enmity reached such a pitch that in one case, a follower of Simon committed murder.

⁴ Onias came to realize the depth of the rivalry, and was aware that Apollonius, begot of Menestheus, governor of Coele-Syria and Phoenicia, was fomenting Simon's animosity. ⁵ So Onias went to the ruler, not to accuse the rivals, but as a fellow citizen concerned about the public and private welfare of all the Jewish people, both individually and as a nation. ⁶ He believed that without the ruler's intervention, public affairs could not be peacefully settled, and Simon would not stop disrupting the peace.

⁷ When Seleucus had died, Antiochus, known as Epiphanes, succeeded him; and Jason, Onias' peer, became high priest by bribery. ⁸ Jason offered Antiochus twelve tons of silver immediately, and two-and-a-half tons from future revenue, ⁹ and proposed to pay an additional five tons of silver in return for the authority to establish a gymnasium for the training of the young, and to enroll the people of Jerusalem as citizens of Antioch. ¹⁰ The ruler agreed. And Jason, with the title of high priest, immediately began pushing the Jewish citizens to conform to the Greek culture.

¹¹ Jason set aside the royal privileges which had been gained for the Jewish citizens by John, the father of Eupolemus, who had gone on a mission to nurture friendship and alliance with the Romans. The high priest suppressed the institutions founded on the Law and replaced them with activities contrary to their customs. ¹² Jason immediately set up a gymnasium at the very foot of the citadel, and began training their brightest and best young people in serious gymnastics—even to dressing them like the Greek athletes. ¹³ Hellenization and the adoption of these foreign customs became so advanced through the corruption of Jason, an apostate and not a high priest, ¹⁴ that the priests became disinterested in their altar duties. They lost their respect for the Temple and neglected the sacrifices, but were quick to respond to the signal to join in the activities on the training grounds—all in defiance of the Law. ¹⁵ They disdained all that their ancestors had held in honor, and set a higher value on these Greek customs.

¹⁶ All this brought down its own reprisal on them. The very people whose life they chose to emulate, whose customs and values they so envied, came to be their enemies and oppressors. ¹⁷ It is no small matter to profane the divine laws, as is shown by the account that follows.

¹⁸ When the quadrennial games* were held in Tyre in the presence of the ruler, ¹⁹ the vile Jason sent Antiochians representing Jerusalem with

---

* I.e., the Olympics.

three hundred silver drachmas to offer a sacrifice to Hercules. But those in the entourage felt that it was unfitting that the money be spent on sacrifice; that it should be used to some other purpose. ²⁰ So the funds that had been sent for the purpose of sacrifice to Hercules were actually applied, by those who delivered them, to the construction of galley ships.

²¹ When Apollonius, begot of Menestheus, was sent to Egypt to attend the enthronement of Philometor there as ruler, Antiochus learned that Philometor had grown hostile to him. Antiochus, taking measures for his safety, fled to Joppa and then to Jerusalem. ²² Jason and the city welcomed the ruler extravagantly with torchlight parades and acclamations. Then Antiochus marched his army on to Phoenicia.

²³ After three years Jason sent Menelaus, the brother of the Simon mentioned above, to deliver funds to Antiochus and receive decisions on various pending matters. ²⁴ But Menelaus, upon being presented, flattered Antiochus with such skill and such authority that he secured the high priesthood for himself, outbidding Jason by ten tons of silver. ²⁵ Menelaus returned bearing the royal mandate but lacking anything worthy of the title; he had nothing except the temper of a cruel tyrant and the rage of a savage animal. ²⁶ Jason, who had replaced his own brother through scheming, was replaced now by yet another schemer, and fled as a fugitive into Ammon.

²⁷ While holding the office of high priest, Menelaus failed to deliver the promised payments to the ruler, despite the frequent requests of Sostratus, who was commander of the citadel, ²⁸ and who was charged with the collection of revenues. Subsequently, the two were summoned before the ruler for an accounting. ²⁹ Menelaus left his brother Lysimachus as deputy in charge of the high priesthood; while Sostratus, for his part, left Crates as commander of the Cypriot guard.

³⁰ In the meantime, it happened that the people of Tarsus and of Mallus had risen up in revolt because their cities had been given as a gift to Antiochis, the ruler's concubine. ³¹ The ruler immediately set out to put down the revolt, leaving Andronicus, a minister, as deputy.

³² Menelaus, thinking to take advantage of the empty judgment seat, stole several golden vessels from the Temple, and gave them to Andronicus. Several other vessels were sold in Tyre and other nearby cities. ³³ Onias, learning of all this on good authority, withdrew to a place of sanctuary and publicly denounced Menelaus. ³⁴ Menelaus then conspired with Andronicus to murder Onias. Andronicus approached Onias, and

by means of sworn oaths persuaded him to come out of the sanctuary. Onias, though still suspicious, acceded; whereupon, with no regard for justice, Andronicus killed him.

³⁵ This murder by treachery and sacrilege left both the Jewish community and the surrounding nations appalled and indignant. ³⁶ Antiochus, recently returned from Cilicia, received a petition from the Jewish community of Antioch concerning this vile murder. ³⁷ Antiochus grieved deeply to think of one of such high character and wisdom being so treated. ³⁸ In a rage, he stripped Andronicus of his purple robes and paraded him naked through the streets and then to the site of this travesty, where the murderer was killed. Thus Our God gave Andronicus his just punishment.

³⁹ Menelaus in the meantime was in league with a certain Lysimachus, who committed sacrilegious thefts throughout the city. When Lysimachus had stolen many of the gold sacred vessels, word of this began to get around, and the people rose in anger. ⁴⁰ When an enraged crowd began gathering, Lysimachus armed about three thousand of his own and launched an attack against the crowd, led by a certain Auranus—a man well-advanced in years, but not in wisdom. ⁴¹ Those in the crowd grabbed stones, sticks for clubs, even handfuls of ash from nearby ash heaps, and hurled them at Lysimachus' mob. ⁴² Many were wounded in this melee, some were killed, and the rest were routed. The Temple robber himself they put to death outside the treasury.

⁴³ As a result of this incident, charges were brought against Menelaus. ⁴⁴ When Antiochus came to Tyre, three defendants were sent by the Sanhedrin to present their case before him. ⁴⁵ Menelaus, looking defeat in the eye, promised a substantial bribe to Ptolemy, begot of Dorymenes, if he should win the ruler to his cause. ⁴⁶ Then Ptolemy, taking Antiochus aside into a colonnade as if for a breath of air, presented Menelaus's case for him. ⁴⁷ The charges against Menelaus, the cause of so much chaos, were dropped; and the unfortunate three who presented the case—who would have been released as innocent even by the Scythians—were instead condemned to death. ⁴⁸ Thus, these who had spoken on behalf of the city and the villages about the holy vessels suffered a quick and unjust penalty. Even the Tyrians, having no interest in the case, were outraged by the unjust penalty, and provided richly for the funeral of the victims.

⁵⁰ And all the while, due to greed high places, Menelaus remained in high office, growing in wickedness and plotting against his fellow citizens.

5:1 About this time, Antiochus began a second invasion of Egypt. ² For forty days, apparitions were seen throughout the entire city: golden armored cavalry galloping in the sky, ³ companies of armed troops ready for battle, more troops armed with swords in battle formation, attacks and counterattacks back and forth, emblazoned shields, a stand of pikes, brandished spears, flying javelins, singing arrows, golden ornaments glittering among all sorts of armor. ⁴ Everyone prayed that these apparitions were a good omen.

⁵ When a false rumor made the rounds that Antiochus was dead, Jason gathered no fewer than a thousand troops and launched a sudden attack on Jerusalem. The defenders on the wall fell back, the city was captured, and Menelaus took refuge in the citadel. ⁶ But Jason continued with the slaughter, giving no thought that to win the day against one's own fellow citizens is a grievous victory indeed, but imagining instead the trophies of victory over an enemy, and not his own flesh and blood.

⁷ Yet in the end he gained no victory at all—only disgrace for his conspiracy—and fled once again into the Ammonite territory. ⁸ He came to an unhappy end: accused before Aretas, the ruler of Arabia, he fled from city to city, pursued as a fugitive, hated as a lawbreaker, abhorred as a butcher of his own people and land. He fled into Egypt; ⁹ then sailed to Sparta, hoping to find some refuge among kindred there. ¹⁰ Jason, who had left so many to lie unburied, died unmourned, with no funeral, and no place in the tomb of his ancestors.

¹¹ Antiochus, having learned of these events, believed Judea to be in revolt. He marched out of Egypt, raging like a wild bull, and stormed Jerusalem. ¹² He ordered the troops to cut down everyone they encountered without mercy, even to pursuing them into their homes. ¹³ A massacre ensued of young and old, of women and children and infants. ¹⁴ There were eighty thousand casualties in three days: forty thousand died a violent death, and a like number were sold into slavery.

¹⁵ Still dissatisfied, the ruler boldly entered the Temple, that holiest of places in all the world, guided by Menelaus, a traitor to both the holy Law and his people. ¹⁶ With unclean and unholy hands, Antiochus seized the sacred vessels and the gifts that had been offered by other rulers to the glory and splendor of this place.

¹⁷ In his frenzied and spirited state, Antiochus gave no thought to the fact that Adonai was for the moment enraged by the sins of the people of Jerusalem—that the Temple would not otherwise have been left to such a

fate. [18] Had it not happened that the people were enmeshed in their own wickedness at this time, Antiochus would have fared no better than had Heliodorus, who had been sent by Seleucus to inspect the treasury. [19] But God did not choose this people for the sake of the Holy Place, but the Holy Place for the sake of the people. [20] Thus the Holy Place shared in the misfortune that befell the people—and in the end, in their good fortune. What was forsaken in this moment of God's wrath was restored again in full glory when the people were reconciled with the Holy One.

[21] Antiochus returned quickly to Antioch, looting twelve hundred pounds of silver from the Temple. So carried away was he with arrogance that he believed that he could sail on land and walk on the sea.

[22] He left behind governors to torment the people. Philip, a Phrygian by birth, was left as governor of Jerusalem; he was a brute by disposition, more ruthless than the one who had appointed him. [23] At Mount Gerizim he left Andronicus. And over them both he left Menelaus, the worst one of all, who held a harsh and arrogant hand over his compatriots.

Antiochus, in his antipathy to the Judeans, [24] sent Apollonius in command of twenty-two thousand Mysian mercenaries with orders to kill all the grown men and sell the women and children into slavery. [25] Apollonius arrived in Jerusalem under the pretence of being a peacemaker. He waited until the holy Sabbath day and then, while the Judeans were enjoying their day of rest, put his troops on parade, fully armed. [26] Those who came out to watch were put to the sword; then Apollonius charged his troops into the city, cutting down the people in great numbers.

[27] But Judas, nicknamed Maccabeus, escaped with about nine others into the wilderness, where they lived in the hills, eating plants the way animals do. In this way they avoided the abominable desecration wrought by Antiochus.

છ છ છ

[6:1] Shortly after this, Antiochus sent Gerontes the Athenian to compel the Jews to abandon the ways of their ancestors and to abandon God's Law. [2] He was also ordered to desecrate the Temple and rededicate it to the Olympian Zeus. It was to be the same on Mount Gerizim, except that here it would to be dedicated to Zeus the Hospitable, by the request of some of the inhabitants.

---

* "Maccabeus" has multiple meanings: "Designated by God," "Hammerer," or "Hammerhead."

³ The evil of this was oppressive and intolerable. ⁴ The Gentiles filled the Temple with debauchery, revelry, prostitution, and sexual intercourse in the sacred precincts. ⁵ The altar was covered with sacrifices forbidden by the law. ⁶ Observing the Sabbath and keeping the traditional feasts was forbidden; so was even admitting to being Jewish. ⁷ Every month, at the celebration of Antiochus' birthday, people were forced to eat of the sacrifices. At the festivals of Dionysus they were compelled to wear wreaths of ivy in processions honoring that god. ⁸ On the recommendation of the citizens of Ptolemais, a decree was sent to the neighboring Greek cities that they should adopt this same policy toward the Jews who lived there—that they should be required to eat of the sacrifices, ⁹ and that any that refused to participate in these Greek customs should be executed.

The weight of their oppression was self-evident. ¹⁰ Two women, for example, were charged with having their babies circumcised. They were paraded throughout the city with their babies hanging at their breasts, and then thrown from the top of the city wall. ¹¹ Others, secretly gathering in caves to keep the Sabbath, were betrayed to Philip, who had them all burned alive. None offered resistance, for they would not defend themselves out of respect for the holiness of the day.

¹² I urge the reader not to be depressed by these tragedies, but to meditate on the fact that such misfortunes are intended not to destroy our people but to discipline us. ¹³ In fact, it is a sign of great tolerance to punish sinners quickly rather than have them go on for some time. ¹⁴ In the matter of other peoples, Our God waits patiently for them to reach the fullness of their wickedness before punishing them. ¹⁵ But God treats us differently, not waiting for our sins to reach their fullness. ¹⁶ In this way, Adonai never withdraws mercy. We may be decimated with calamities, but God does not abandon us, ever. ¹⁷ Let this little message be but a reminder, and I will continue with the story.

¹⁸ Eleazar, who was one of the foremost scribes—of noble demeanor, and well advanced in years—was being forced to open his mouth to eat pork. ¹⁹ But preferring an honorable death to a life defiled, Eleazar spat out the meat, quite preferring to face torture ²⁰ rather than to eat that which is unlawful. So should anyone do in such a case, if they have the courage, even though they may love life.

²¹ Those in charge of this unlawful banquet took the scribe to one side privately. Having been long acquainted with him, they urged him to bring meat of his own, something ritually correct, so that he might make a pretense of eating the meat of the sacrifice prescribed by the authorities; ²² in

this way he would escape death, and be treated kindly because of their old friendship.

²³ But Eleazar had a noble mind, worthy of his years, worthy of the distinction presented by his gray hair and his dignity, and worthy of the admirable life that he had lived since childhood. He declared that he would be loyal above all to the holy laws given by God. Telling them that he was ready to go to the abode of the dead, the scribe explained, ²⁴ "At my age it would be unbecoming to make such a pretense; many young people would think the ninety-year-old Eleazar had embraced an alien religion. ²⁵ If I dissimulated for the sake of a brief moment of life, they would be scandalized by me, and I would bring shame and dishonor on my old age. ²⁶ Even if, for the moment, I avoided the punishment of mortals, I would never, alive or dead, escape the hands of the Almighty. ²⁷ If I therefore have the courage to give up my life now, I will show myself worthy of my years, ²⁸ and I will leave to the young a noble example of how to die willingly and gracefully for the sake of the holy Law that we revere."

Having said this, he went straight to their instruments of torture. ²⁹ Those who had shortly before been kindly disposed to him now became hostile, for his words seemed to them utter madness. ³⁰ On the edge of death beneath the blows, Eleazar groaned out, "God, whose knowledge is holy, knows that I might have escaped death, and that I suffer terrible pain from this scourging, and suffer it with joy in my soul for the sake of the Holy One." ³¹ Thus Eleazar died, leaving in his death a model of courage and unforgettable virtue, not only for the young but for the whole nation.

7:1 In another case, a mother and her seven children* were arrested and tortured with whips and scourges by the authorities, to force them to eat pork in violation of God's law.

² But one, speaking for them all, said, "What do you hope to learn by questioning us? We are ready to die rather than break the laws of our ancestors."

³ The furious ruler ordered huge pans and caldrons to be heated over a fire. ⁴ Meanwhile he ordered that the youth's tongue be cut out first, and that he then be scalped, and his hands and feet cut off, before the eyes of his mother and family. ⁵ Thus mutilated and helpless, but still alive, the ruler ordered that he be fried alive in one of the pans. As the smoke from

---

* Traditionally, these seven famous Maccabean martyrs are all male; but because the word for "children" can indicate both sons and daughters, we alternate the genders for the sake of inclusivity.

the cooking drifted throughout the area, the mother and her children encouraged each other to die nobly, saying, ⁶ "Our God is watching us, and will surely have mercy on us. Didn't Moses say to Israel in his song condemning their apostasy, 'God will have compassion on the faithful'?"

⁷ After the first child had died in this way, they dragged forward a second for their games. Tearing the skin off her head by the hair, they asked her, "Shall we tear you apart limb by limb, or will you eat?"

⁸ "Never!" the second replied, in the language of her ancestors. She then underwent the same tortures as had her brother. ⁹ Near death, she gasped, "Wretch! Fiend! You only free us from this life; but the Ruler of the universe will raise us to everlasting life, for we die for God's laws."

¹⁰ As with the second, so with the third. When asked the same question, he offered his tongue and his hands, ¹¹ saying, "The heavenly God gave these to me; and for the sake God's law I surrender them; and from God, I hope to receive them back again." ¹² Both ruler and torturers were amazed at the courage of this youth, and his utter disregard for the pain.

¹³ After the death of the third youth, they tortured the fourth in the same way. ¹⁴ At the point of death, she said, "It is better to meet death at the hands of mortals in the hope of God's promise of resurrection! But for you, there will be no resurrection!"

¹⁵ Next the fifth was dragged forward for torture; ¹⁶ looking at the ruler he said, "You are only mortals. As you have authority over people, you do as you like. But don't think that Our God has abandoned us. ¹⁷ Wait a little while, and you will face God's might, and there will be torment, both for you and your descendants."

¹⁸ After the fifth, they brought forward the sixth. About to die, she said, "You deceive yourself if you believe that we suffer for anything but our own faults. We sinned against Our God; therefore terrible things have happened. ¹⁹ But don't think that you will go unpunished for vying with the Most High God."

²⁰ Even more admirable and unforgettable was the mother who, watching her seven children die on this one day, suffered it courageously because of her hope in Our God. Filled with a noble spirit that stirred her heart with extraordinary courage, ²¹ she exhorted each of them in the language of her ancestors: ²² "I do not know how you came into being in my womb. It was not I who gave you the breath of life, nor who set in order the elements of which you are composed. ²³ Since it is the Creator of the universe who shapes our beginnings, and the Creator who brings about the origin of everything, the Creator will mercifully give back to you both your breath and your life, because you now disregard yourselves for the sake of the Law."

²⁴ Antiochus suspected insult in the tone of her voice ,and thought himself ridiculed. The youngest being still alive, the ruler appealed to him, not only with words but with oaths, to make him both rich and happy if he would abandon the ways of his ancestors: Antiochus would call him "Friend" and entrust him with high office.

²⁵ When the youth paid no attention at all, the ruler appealed to the mother, urging her to advise the child to save his life. ²⁶ After Antiochus had urged her for a long time, the mother made motions of persuading the child.

²⁷ Deriding the cruel tyrant, she leaned close to her son and whispered in their native language, "Child, have pity on me, who carried you in my womb for nine months, nursed you for three years, brought you up, educated and supported you to your present age. ²⁸ I beg you, child, to look at the heavens and the earth and see all that is in them; see that God made them out of nothingness; and in the same way made the human race. ²⁹ Do not be afraid of this butcher, but be worthy of your family and accept death, so that in the time of mercy I may receive you again with them."

³⁰ Not even waiting for her to finish, the youth said, "What are you waiting for? I will not obey the ruler's command. I obey the command of the Law given to our ancestors through Moses.

³¹ "But you, Antiochus, who have contrived every kind of torment for the Hebrews, will not escape the hands of God. ³² We suffer for our own sins. ³³ Perhaps our living God is angry now, and reprimands and disciplines us, but we will be reconciled with the God we serve. ³⁴ But you, who are an unclean thing, the most foul among humankind—don't let yourself be carried away with vain hopes, as you raise your hand against the children of heaven. ³⁵ You are not yet free of judgment of the all-seeing, omnipotent God. ³⁶ Each of my family, after brief suffering, now drink the water of everlasting life through God's covenant. But you, by God's judgment, will pay the just penalty for your arrogance.

³⁷ "I, like my kin, abandon my body and my life for the laws of our ancestors. I call on God to show mercy to our people soon, and by trials and suffering, force you to admit that Our God is the only God. ³⁸ May the just anger of the Almighty, which now purifies us, cease here with me and my family!"

³⁹ The ruler, enraged by this condemnation, treated this son to even worse torments than the others. ⁴⁰ The youth, totally trusting in God, died undefiled.

⁴¹ The mother died last, after her children.

⁴² Enough said, then, about the eating of sacrifices and the grotesque tortures.

8:1–10:9

Ín the meantime, Judas Maccabeus and his companions secretly made their way into the villages to summon their kin and recruit those who remained faithful to Judaism. They gathered together about six thousand.

² Together they appealed to God to hear their pleas for release from oppression; to take pity on the Temple which had been so defiled; ³ and to have mercy on Jerusalem, so nearly destroyed, all but leveled to the ground. They prayed to God to hear the blood crying out for vengeance; ⁴ to never forget the slaughter of innocent babies and all the blasphemies against God's Name, and to show his hatred for these evils.

⁵ Once Maccabeus had got his guerrilla band mobilized, the Gentiles could not stand against it, for God's wrath now turned to mercy. ⁶ Descending on towns and villages in surprise attacks and torching them, Maccabeus soon captured many strategic sites, routing the enemy time and again. ⁷ His night raids proved most successful, and soon talk of Maccabeus' valor was spreading through the countryside.

⁸ When Philip saw that the small gains of the Maccabeans were growing with each action, and their frequency as well, he wrote to Ptolemy, the governor of Coele-Syria and Phoenicia, asking for aid. ⁹ Ptolemy immediately appointed Nicanor, begot of Patroclus, a member of the order of the ruler's First Friends, in command of an army of twenty thousand troops of various nationalities. He sent them with orders to exterminate the entire Jewish people. With Nicanor, Ptolemy sent Gorgias, a general well-experienced in military action, as co-commander.

¹⁰ It was Nicanor's intent, by the sale of captive Judeans into slavery, to gather the two thousand talents—sixty-seven tons of silver—owed by Ptolemy as tribute to Rome. ¹¹ So he immediately offered Judean prisoners to the seacoast towns: ninety prisoners per talent, delivered. Little did he know that the judgment of the Almighty was soon to overtake him.

¹² When the news of Nicanor's invasion reached their encampment, Judas briefed his band. ¹³ Some fled—those who were fainthearted, and failing in their faith in God's justice. ¹⁴ Others sold what possessions they had left to help finance their campaign, all the while praying to the Holy One for the deliverance of those whom the godless Nicanor had already sold,

before they ever had a chance to give battle. ¹⁵ They prayed to God, saying, "If you won't hear us on our own sake, then remember the covenants you made with our ancestors, those who upheld your holy and glorious Name."

¹⁶ Maccabeus called together his six thousand followers and encouraged them. He exhorted them not to fear this great horde of Gentile invaders, but to fight nobly ¹⁷ and keep in their mind's eye the outrages that the Gentiles had inflicted on the Temple and their tortured city; and no less, the attempts to destroy their own traditional way of life. ¹⁸ "These people put their trust in their arms and their exploits," he added; "we put our trust in Almighty God, who could with a single nod destroy these present invaders; or even the whole world."

¹⁹ He reminded them of how often God had come to the rescue of their ancestors; of how in Sennacherib's time, one hundred and eighty-five thousand invaders had been destroyed. ²⁰ He recounted to them of the battle against the Galatians in Babylon, where a force of eight thousand Judeans fought side by side with four thousand Macedonians, and of how, when the Macedonians were hard pressed, those eight thousand Judeans, by divine intervention, had destroyed and plundered one hundred twenty thousand Galatians.

²¹ Judas' words gave them the courage they needed to die for their laws and for their country. ²² He divided the army in four squadrons of about fifteen hundred warriors each; he led one, and his brothers Simon, Josephus, and Jonathan, each took another. ²³ Then he asked Eleazar to read from the holy Book, after which he gave them their battle cry: "God is our help!" And then, taking lead of the first division, he joined in battle with Nicanor.

²⁴ With Almighty God on their side, they destroyed more than nine thousand of the enemy, wounding or disabling most of Nicanor's army and turning the day into a complete rout. ²⁵ They captured as well the funds of those who had come planning to buy them as slaves. Their hot pursuit of the enemy was ended only by the late hour, ²⁶ for it was the eve of the Sabbath.

²⁷ After gathering up the enemy's weapons and stripping them of their spoils, they then kept the Sabbath with deep gratitude, giving thanks and praise to the Holy One who had preserved them for that day and had granted them these first few drops of divine mercy. ²⁸ After the Sabbath, they distributed some of the spoils among those who had been tortured, and the widows and orphans. The rest they divided among themselves and their children. ²⁹ This being finished, they joined together in prayer to their merciful God, that their reconciliation with him might be complete.

³⁰ In ensuing encounters with the armies of Timotheus and Baccides, they inflicted over twenty thousand casualties, as well as gaining control of several important fortresses. Again they divided equal shares of the great spoils, allocating shares to those persecuted, and to the widows and orphans, as well as the elderly. ³¹ Captured arms of the enemy were collected and stored in strategic places; the rest of the spoils were taken to Jerusalem. ³² They executed the officer commanding Timotheus' forces—an utterly godless man who had caused much suffering among the Judeans. ³³ During the victory celebration in Jerusalem, they burned alive certain enemy troops who set fire to the sacred gates—Callisthenes and several others, who had taken refuge in a small house. It was a reward suitable to their impiety.

³⁴ Nicanor—that much accursed one—who had brought with him a thousand merchants to buy Judean prisoners, ³⁵ had been humiliated, with the help of God, by the very people he had reckoned to be of no account. He escaped by abandoning his magnificent apparel and sneaking through the country alone like a runaway. Eventually he succeeded in reaching Antioch, his chief success having been the destruction of his own army. ³⁶ So Nicanor—who had set out vaunting that he would gather the Roman's tribute money by the sale of Judeans into slavery—now announced to the world that the Judeans had a Champion, and that they were indestructible because they abided by the laws of this Champion.

ର ର ର

9.1 It was at about this same time that Antiochus had been driven out of Persia in complete disarray. ² He had entered Persepolis intending to pillage the temples and take control of the city. But its people had risen up in arms and defeated him and his army soundly, and he had been forced into a humiliating retreat.

³ As he reached Ecbatana, he learned of the failure of Nicanor and the troops of Timotheus. ⁴ This so enraged him that he became possessed by the notion that he would humiliate the Jews as he had been humiliated. Antiochus instructed his charioteer not to stop until they reached their destination.

⁵ But divine judgment was a third passenger on the journey, for he had boasted, "When I reach Jerusalem, I will make it one burying ground of Jews." And the all-seeing God, the God of Israel, struck him a deadly and invisible blow; no sooner had he made this remark than he was seized with intense pain in his bowels, sharp pain without relief. ⁶ It was a pun-

ishment fitting for one who punished the bowels of others with many strange and inhuman torments.

⁷ Yet even this did not end his insolence; full of arrogance, and spitting flames of rage against the Judeans, he ordered yet more speed. Now—the chariot moving at a dangerous pace—the ruler was hurled into the air, and in a violent fall wracked every limb in his body. ⁸ He who in his arrogance only moments before had so believed in himself that he fancied he could tame the waves of the sea and weigh mountains on a scale, was now struck down, and finished his journey on a stretcher. Thus was God's power shown to all.

⁹ In no time, the ungodly one's body was infested with maggots, rotting while he was still alive and in agony. The sight and the stench sickened the whole army, ¹⁰ and became so intolerable that no one could bear to carry his stretcher—he who so short a time before had believed that he could reach out and touch the heavenly stars.

¹¹ Toward the end, broken in spirit, Antiochus' overweening arrogance began to abate. In unbearable pain and scourged by God, he began to see things more clearly. ¹² Unable to bear his own stench, the ruler declared, "It is right to submit to God. Mortals must not think themselves equal to the Almighty One." ¹³ Then this despised creature, bereft of divine mercy, made a vow to God ¹⁴ that he would free the Holy City, the city which he had been racing to raze and turn into a graveyard. ¹⁵ All the Jewish people and their children—people whom he had considered unfit for burial, worthy only to be thrown out like carrion for the wild animals and birds to eat—he would make citizens, equal to the Athenians. ¹⁶ The House of Our God, so recently plundered by his troops, he would furnish with the finest gifts. The holy vessels would be more than returned, and their value many times over; and the cost of the burnt offerings he would give from his own funds. ¹⁷ Beyond that, he would convert to Judaism and visit every inhabited place in order to proclaim God's power.

¹⁸ But when his agony continued unchecked—for God's just judgment was on him—Antiochus, despairing for himself, wrote this conciliatory letter to the Judeans:

¹⁹ "From Antiochus, the ruler and commander-in-chief, to my worthy Judeans: Greetings and good wishes for your health and happiness. ²⁰ If you and your children are well and if your affairs are to your liking, then I give great thanks to God, as my hope is in heaven.

²¹ "As for me, I have been weak; otherwise I would have remembered with kindness the loving memories of your esteem and good will. While

returning from Persia I have been stricken grievously ill, so I consider it best that I plan for the common welfare of all. ²² I do not despair of my health, for I hold great hopes of a full recovery. ²³ Yet I recall that my father, when undertaking expeditions into unfamiliar territory, always named a successor, ²⁴ so if anything unexpected happened or if any bad news came back, the people of the realm would have no cause for alarm, for they would know to whom the state was entrusted.

²⁵ "Again, I am aware of the watchful neighbors of the realm along our borders, who look always for something to happen and await their opportunities . Therefore, I have appointed my heir Antiochus to become ruler; I often entrusted and commended him to most of you, when traveling to the outlying provinces.

"I have written to Antiochus as I have written here.

²⁶ "I beg you, therefore, to bear in mind the official and the private benefits I provided you, and to continue in your good will to us both. ²⁷ For I am confident that he, understanding my good will toward you, will yield favorably and graciously toward you in all your desires."

²⁸ And so, this murderer and blasphemer, writhing in agony comparable to that which he had inflicted on others, met a miserable end in foreign mountains. ³⁰ Philip, the ruler's close friend, returned with the body; but later, fearing Antiochus the heir, he fled into Egypt to the protection of Ptolemy Philometor.

ભ ભ ભ

10:¹ By now Maccabbeus and his followers, under the guiding hand of the Holy One, had recaptured the city of Jerusalem and the Temple. ² They tore down the altars that the foreigners had set up in the public squares, and likewise their shrines.

³ They purified the sanctuary and constructed a new altar; then struck fire from flint and offered sacrifice—the first in two years. They burned incense, lighted the lamps, and set out the bread of Presence.

⁴ Then they prostrated themselves and begged God that they might never again fall into such degradation; but if in the event they fell again into sin, that they might be disciplined more gently, and not be given over to the blasphemous and barbarous Gentiles.

⁵ This purification of the Temple took place on the twenty-fifth day of Chislev, which is the anniversary of the day when the Gentiles desecrated it.

⁶ The Judeans celebrated with joy for eight days, just as in the Feast of the Tabernacles, bearing in mind how so recently they had kept that feast while wandering like animals in the caves and mountains. ⁷ Therefore, carrying poles wreathed with ivy, green branches and palm fronds, they chanted hymns of thanksgiving to the One who brought about the purification of this place. It was decreed by a public vote that the whole nation of Judea should celebrate these days annually.

⁹ This, then, was the end of Antiochus, also called Epiphanes.

10:10–14:26

Now we will tell you about Antiochus Eupator, begot of that godless one, and will relate briefly the disastrous effects of his wars.

¹¹ When he had succeeded as ruler, Eupator appointed as minister over the affairs of the realm a certain Lysias, who had been the officer in charge of Coele-Syria and Phoenicia.

¹² Lysias took the position that had been held by Ptolemy, also known as Macron, who had been foremost in showing fairness to the Judeans in light of the wrongs that had been done to them. ¹³ For this, he was denounced to Eupator by the ruler's Friends—for supposedly having abandoned Cyprus, which Philometor had appointed him to govern, and for the treachery of having supported Antiochus Epiphanes. Treated without the respect due his office, he committed suicide by taking poison.

¹⁴ Gorgias became governor of the region after Lysias was promoted. He maintained a force of mercenaries and took advantage of every opportunity to attack the Judeans.

¹⁵ During this time, the Idumeans, entrenched in certain strategic strongholds, were also harassing the Judeans. They welcomed Judean outcasts and maintained constant hostilities.

¹⁶ But Maccabeus and his forces, after making solemn supplications, and praying to God to take their side, rushed the Idumean strongholds. ¹⁷ In vigorous attacks, they captured the fortresses, swarming over those guarding the walls and cutting down all they encountered. They killed no less than twenty thousand. ¹⁸ But nine thousand more took refuge in two extremely strong towers well provided to withstand a long siege.

¹⁹ Maccabeus left Simon and Josephus with Zacchaeus and his troops,

a force adequate to carry on such a siege, while he himself left for places where he was more needed. ²⁰ But there were those with Simon's troops who were greedy for money, and they accepted a bribe of seventy thousand drachmas to let a number of the enemy slip away.

²¹ When Maccabeus heard of this, he called together the leaders of the army and denounced those guilty for selling their kin for money by allowing the enemy to slip away to fight again. ²² These traitors he executed, and then turned suddenly on the two towers and captured them. ²³ He was successful in every military endeavor he attempted; and here more than twenty thousand enemy troops were slain.

²⁴ Then Timothy, who had suffered defeat before at the hands of the Judeans, put together a vast army of mercenaries, as well as a large number of Asian cavalry. They marched on Judea, intending to storm it.

²⁵ As the intruder approached, Maccabeus and his followers prayed to God, sprinkled dust on their heads, and wrapped themselves in sackcloth. ²⁶ Lying prostrate before the altar, they implored God to bless them with victory and "to be a foe of their foe and an adversary to their adversaries," as it says in the Law.

²⁷ Rising from their prayer, they took up arms and marched a considerable distance from Jerusalem, drawing up within sight of the enemy. ²⁸ At first light, the two armies joined battle. The Judeans were sure of victory, for they were both courageous and secure in Adonai's protection, while the enemy made their fury their leader in battle.

²⁹ In the height of the battle, the enemy saw coming from heaven five radiant riders on horses with golden bridles, leading the Judeans. ³⁰ Two of these took Maccabeus between them, screening him with their armor to keep him safe. They hurled arrows and thunderbolts at the enemy, who, blinded and disoriented by the assault, broke in utter disarray. ³¹ Twenty thousand five hundred of the infantry were slain, along with six hundred cavalry.

³² Timothy fled to the fortified stronghold called Gazara, commanded by Chaereas. ³³ This fit well into the strategy of Maccabeus and the army, and they readily besieged it for four days. ³⁴ Those within, confident in their stronghold, shouted wicked blasphemies and obscenities at them.

³⁵ At first light of the fifth day, twenty young Maccabean soldiers, angered over the abuses hurled at them, stormed the wall and savagely cut down all who stood against them. ³⁶ Meanwhile, in the confusion of the attack, more soldiers climbed the wall in the same place and set the towers ablaze, burning the blasphemers alive. Still others opened the gates to let the rest of the army in, and so the city fell.

[37] They killed Timothy, finding him hiding in a cistern, and likewise his brother Cheares, and Apollophanes.

And when the fighting was done, the Judeans celebrated their victory with hymns and thanksgiving to God who shows great kindness to Israel and gives them victory.

☙ ☙ ☙

11[1] Soon after this, Lysias—the ruler's guardian and cousin, who was in charge of the government—enraged at these events, [2] mobilized about eighty-thousand infantry, along with all his cavalry, and marched against the Judeans. He intended to make Jerusalem a domicile for Gentiles, [3] and levy taxes on the Temple as he did on the places of worship of other nations. The office of high priest he would sell to the highest bidder. [4] He gave no thought whatever to the power of God, but only delighted in his tens of thousands of infantry, and thousands of cavalry, and eighty elephants. [5] Invading Israel, he came up on Bethsura, pushing hard.

[6] When Maccabeus and his company heard of Lysias attacking their strongholds, they and all the people cried out to God to send a good angel to save Israel. [7] Maccabeus was first to take up arms, and urged the others to follow, risking everything to aid their sisters and brothers. As one person, they rushed off eagerly.

[8] While they were still near Jerusalem, there appeared before them a mounted rider, dressed all in white, with weapons of gold. [9] This moved all to praise of their merciful God; their spirits surged, and they felt ready to attack not only soldiers but the most savage beast, or walls of iron. [10] They advanced in battle formation behind their heavenly guide—God's mercy was with them. [11] They charged on their enemy like lions. Eleven thousand infantry and sixteen hundred cavalry were destroyed, and the rest were routed; many were wounded, and most abandoned weapons and armor in their haste to flee. Lysias, like the rest, saved himself by ignominious flight.

[13] Lysias was no fool; reflecting on his defeat, he concluded that the Hebrews were invincible because Almighty God fought with them in battle. He sent emissaries [14] suing for a just peace, promising to persuade Antiochus to accept them as friends. [15] Maccabeus, whose concern was for the common good, accepted Lysias' supplication; and Antiochus, for his part, agreed to all that Maccabeus requested on the behalf of the Hebrews .

[16] Lysias' letter to the Hebrews was as follows:

"Lysias, to the Jewish community: Greetings.

¹⁷ "Your envoys, John and Absalom, delivered your signed document and asked for its approval. ¹⁸ I have put the matters before Antiochus, and he has granted as much as was possible. ¹⁹ If you maintain good will toward the government, I will endeavor to promote your interests in the future. ²⁰ I charged your envoys and mine to confer with you concerning the details. Farewell.

"The twenty-fourth day of Dioscorinthius in the year 148."*

²² The ruler's letter is as follows:

"From Antiochus, the ruler, to his cousin Lysias: Greetings.

²³ "Now that my father is among the gods, it is our desire that the subjects of the realm be left undisturbed to attend to their own affairs. ²⁴ It is my understanding that the Judeans are not prepared to accede my father's policies by adopting the Greek ways. They prefer their own ways, and request that their own customs be allowed to them. ²⁵ It is our desire that this people be free also from outside disturbances.

"Therefore it is our decision is that their Temple be restored to them and that they conduct their affairs according to the customs of their ancestors. ²⁶ You will be well advised, therefore, to inform them of this and give them pledges of friendship, so that they will know our policy and be of good cheer, and will manage their own affairs peacefully."

²⁷ The ruler's letter to the Jewish nation is as follows:

"From Antiochus, the ruler, to the Jewish Sanhedrin and to the Jewish people: Greetings.

²⁸ "We pray that all is well with you. We, too, enjoy good health. ²⁹ Menelaus has made it clear that you desire to return to your home and look after your own affairs. ³⁰ Therefore, to all who return by the thirtieth day of Xanthicus, we grant our pledge of friendship, as well as full permission that ³¹ the Jews be allowed to follow their own food laws as in former times. None of them will be harassed for any previous unwitting offenses.

³² "I send Menelaus to set your minds at rest. ³³ Farewell.

"The fifteenth day of Xanthicus in the year 148."

---

* Spring, 164 BCE. Dioscorinthius is another name for the Cretan month of Xanthicus mentioned in verses 30 and 32.

³⁴ The Romans also sent them the following letter:

"From Quintus Memmius, Titus Manilius, and Manius Sergius, Roman envoys, to the Judean people.

³⁵ "Regarding everything Lysias, the cousin of Antiochus, has granted to you, we equally grant our consent. ³⁶ Regarding the questions which Lysias referred to the ruler, consider them promptly and then send an envoy to us so we may make appropriate proposals on your behalf, for we are on our way to Antioch. ³⁷ Send envoys immediately, therefore, to inform us of your intentions. ³⁸ Farewell.

"The fifteenth day of Xanthicus in the year 148."

℘ ℘ ℘

12·1 Once the agreements were finalized, Lysias returned to the ruler while the Judeans went back to their farming.

² But certain of the governors—Timothy, and Apollonius begot of Gennaeus, together with Hieronymus and Demophon, as well as Nicanor, governor of Cyprus—would not allow the Judeans to live in peace and serenity.

³ Nor did the people of Joppa, who executed a scheme of supreme wickedness: they invited the Judeans living among them, including all the women and children, to go on a boat ride. It was a public invitation offered by the whole town. The invitation, giving no hint of animosity, was proffered kindly; the Judeans, having no reason to suspect perfidy, and wishing to maintain good will, accepted. ⁴ But once out in the open sea, the people of Joppa drowned them—two hundred, at the least.

⁵ As soon as Judas got news of this atrocity, he issued orders to his followers, ⁶ and, calling upon God the just Judge, he attacked these murderers. Under the cover of dark, they set the Joppa harbor on fire, burned the boats, and killed everyone who took refuge there. ⁷ Finding the city gates closed, he withdrew with the intention of returning to wipe out the whole community.

⁸ He then learned that the people of Jamnia had made plans to do the same thing to their Judean neighbors, ⁹ and so in the same way he struck them at night, setting both town and harbor afire. The glow of the flames was seen in Jerusalem, thirty miles away.

¹⁰ Then they marched against Timothy. But having gone only a short way from Jamnia, they were ambushed by about five thousand Arabs with five hundred horses. ¹¹ After a fierce battle, and with God's help, they prevailed.

The defeated nomads begged Judas's friendship, with promises to supply them with livestock and help them in every way they could. ¹² Seeing how useful this might be, Judas agreed to make peace with them. Assurances were exchanged and they returned to their tents.

¹³ Judas also attacked Caspin, a heavily fortified town, inhabited by Gentiles of all nationalities. ¹⁴ Confident that their walls were impregnable and their stores sufficient, the defenders treated Judas and his followers insolently with abusive and blasphemous talk. ¹⁵ But Judas and the troops, calling upon the great Sovereign of the universe—who had overrun Jericho in the time of Joshua without battering rams or siege engines—initiated a furious assault on the walls. ¹⁶ Taking the town by God's will, they inflicted such slaughter that the adjacent lake, a quarter mile wide, appeared to overflow with blood.

¹⁷ About ninety-five miles from there, they reached Charax, where Jewish inhabitants known as Tubians resided. ¹⁸ They did not find Timothy, who had left the region, having accomplished nothing. He had, however, left one very strong garrison; ¹⁹ against this were sent Dositheus and Sosipater, two captains under Judas. They destroyed a force of more than ten thousand troops that had been left behind to defend the stronghold.

²⁰ Maccabeus, breaking the army into divisions and appointing commanders for each, raced after Timothy, with his infantry of one hundred and twenty thousand, and twenty-five hundred cavalry. ²¹ When Timothy learned that Judas was approaching, he dispatched the children and women, along with the baggage train, to a place known as Carnaim. It was a place difficult to reach, let alone besiege, because of its narrow approaches.

²² When Judas' first division came into view, panic broke through the enemy, for they saw a manifestation of the all-seeing One. Fleeing headlong in all directions, the fell into such mass confusion that many died on the swordpoints of their own comrades. ²³ By this chaos and by the swords of Judas's army, in hot pursuit, fully thirty thousand died.

²⁴ Timothy was captured by the soldiers of Dositheus and Sosipater. With cunning words he talked himself free, for he held captive the parents of many of them and the children of some, and they could expect no mercy if he died. ²⁵ After assuring them with endless words that their kin would be freed unharmed, he was released for their sake.

²⁶ Judas then marched on Carnaim and the temple of Atargatis, where he slaughtered twenty five thousand. ²⁷ After this destruction, he marched on Ephron, the dwelling place of Lysias. It was a fortified town with a

large population consisting of peoples of many nationalities. Rugged young soldiers stood before the walls, putting up a strong defense, while inside was a great supply of catapults and missiles. ²⁸ But the Jewish attackers, calling on the Sovereign One whose power shatters mighty enemies, overran the town, killing twenty-five thousand.

²⁹ Pressing on hard, they reached Scythopolis, about seventy-five miles from Jerusalem. ³⁰ Here the Jewish inhabitants assured Judas that the people of that place had always treated them justly, and showing great kindness when the Jews came on hard times. ³¹ Judas thanked them, reminding them to be no less kind to the Jewish residents in the future.

By this time the Feast of Weeks was at hand, so they returned to Jerusalem.

³² Immediately after Pentecost, as the Feast of Weeks is called, they marched against Gorgias, the governor of Idumea, ³³ who faced them with three thousand infantry and four hundred cavalry. ³⁴ When the fighting began, a few of the Judeans fell. ³⁵ Dositheus, one of Bacenor's men—who was on horseback, and known for his strength—caught hold of Gorgias' cloak and was carrying him off bodily, thinking to take him alive, when one of the Tracian cavalry bore down on them and cut off his arm. Gorgias escaped to Marisa.

³⁶ The fighters under Esdrias being exhausted and battle-weary, Judas appealed to God to show them divine support and leadership. ³⁷ He raised the battle cry of their ancestors, and chanted hymns; then suddenly he charged Gorgias' troops, catching them off guard, and put them to flight.

³⁸ The fighters then reassembled and withdrew to Adullam. The seventh day approached, and so, according to custom, they purified themselves and kept the Sabbath there. ³⁹ On the next day it was necessary that they collect the bodies of their fallen, to bury them in their ancestral graves. ⁴⁰ Beneath the tunics of those who had died they found sacred tokens of the idols of Jamnia, which were forbidden to them by Jewish law. So they knew that this was why these fighters died, ⁴¹ and they praised God's ways, the just Judge, the revealer of hidden things. ⁴² Then they asked God in their prayers that every trace of this sin be blotted out. Brave Judas urged those gathered to free themselves of sin, for they had seen with their own eyes what happened as a result of the others' sin.

⁴³ He took up a collection from every fighter, and sent to Jerusalem two thousand silver drachmas for an atonement sacrifice—an act fitting and appropriate for those cognizant of the resurrection. ⁴⁴ Had they not expected that the dead would rise again, it would have been superfluous and foolish to pray for them. ⁴⁵ But Judas, anticipating the joyous reward

reserved for those who die after a godly life, was holy and devout in his purpose, and so made the atonement sacrifice for them, that they might be freed of their sin.

ൠ ൠ ൠ

13¹ In the year 149, Judas and his followers learned that Antiochus Eupator, accompanied by his guardian Lysias who held charge of his government, was advancing on Judea with a large army. ² Each of them commanded a Greek force of one hundred and ten thousand infantry, fifty three hundred cavalry, twenty-two elephants, and three hundred chariots equipped with scythe blades.

³ Menelaus also was with them, hypocritically urging Antiochus on— not out of any patriotic fervor, but in the hope of gaining some position for himself. ⁴ But the Sovereign of all rulers aroused Antiochus's wrath against him, and when he heard from Lysias that Menelaus was the person responsible for all this trouble, Antiochus ordered that he be taken to Beroea and executed in the manner that was used there. ⁵ In Beroea there is a seventy-five foot tower filled with ash. At the top, it slopes precipitously into the ash. ⁶ Into this, the locals push anyone who is guilty of sacrilege or of other heinous crimes. ⁷ By such a death it was fitting for the recreant Menelaus to die, without even a normal burial; ⁸ for often he had desecrated the altar, whose very ashes were holy, and so by ashes he died.

⁹ Antiochus, with savage arrogance, intended to give the Judeans a lesson far worse than any they had had in his father's time. ¹⁰ But when Judas learned of this, he ordered the people to pray to the Creator day and night. They must pray that now more than ever there would be help for those who might otherwise soon be deprived of the Law, of their homeland, and their Holy Temple; ¹¹ that God not allow them, now on the verge of revival, to fall into the hands of these blaspheming Gentiles.

¹² All joined together in continuous petition, crying out to the merciful God with weeping, fasting, and prostration for three days. Then Judas called upon them to stand ready. ¹³ After a council of war with the elders, Judas decided to march out to resolve the issue with God's help before these armies could enter Judea and take the city. ¹⁴ So, committing the decision to the Creator of the world, Judas called upon his soldiers to fight bravely to the death for Law and the Temple, for city and country, and the common good of all. They set up camp near Modein.

¹⁵ He gave his troops the watchword, "God's victory!"; and, with a hand-picked force of the bravest, he attacked at night near Antiochus' tent, killing two thousand of the enemy, as well as stabbing to death the

lead elephant and its driver. ¹⁶ When they left, the camp was in a state of terror and chaos, and they returned to their own in triumph. ¹⁷ By dawn, everything had been accomplished, by the protection of Our God.

¹⁸ Having tasted the Jews' daring, Antiochus attempted a strategy in attacking their positions. ¹⁹ Advancing against Beth-zur, a strong Jewish fortress, he was repelled; again he attacked, and again met defeat. ²⁰ Judas, meantime, kept the fortress supplied. ²¹ A certain Rhodocus, of the Judean army, was caught and imprisoned after giving out secret information to the enemy. ²² Antiochus negotiated a second time with the people of Beth-zur, making pledges and receiving them in return; withdrawing then, he attacked the Maccabean army, and was defeated.

²³ He now received a report that Philip, who had been left in charge of affairs of state in Antioch, had revolted. Highly distraught, he summoned the Judeans, yielding to them and swearing to honor all their rights.

Having settled with them, he offered a sacrifice and paid honor to the sanctuary with generous gifts. ²⁴ He received Maccabeus in the spirit of friendship, and then, appointing Hegemonides governor of the region from Ptolemais to Gerrafor, he left ²⁵ for Ptolemais. The people there were angry over the treaty, and wanted to abrogate it. ²⁶ Lysias addressed them in a public forum, and so convincing were his arguments in favor of the terms that they were calmed and persuaded. Having gained their support, Antiochus now left for Antioch.

Such is the full account of Antiochus Eupator's attack on Judea, and his subsequent withdrawal.

*t*hree years later, Judas and his followers learned that Demetrius, begot of Seleucus, had sailed into Tripoli's harbor with a strong army and fleet, ² and had occupied the surrounding country, having killed Antiochus and his guardian Lysias.

³ There was certain Alcimus, who had been a high priest but who had willfully defiled himself during the time of the Gentiles' occupation. Alcimus knew that his safety was uncertain and that there was no chance that he would again have access to the holy altar. ⁴ He approached Demetrius the ruler, in about the year 151, and presented him with a gold crown and a palm, as well as with some of the customary olive branches

from the Temple. For the time being, he kept his silence; ⁵ but an opportunity came to advance his foolish scheme when Demetrius summoned him to a meeting of the council.

When he was asked about the attitude and intentions of the Judeans, he replied, ⁶ "The Hasidean Jews, led by Judas Maccabeus, are warmongers who continually stir up sedition, and will not let the realm be at peace. ⁷ Having been deprived of the dignity of my ancestral right—that is, the high priesthood—I have come here; ⁸ first, because I am truly concerned for the ruler's interests; and also because I am concerned for my fellow Judeans. It is through the foolish behavior of those whom I have mentioned that our nation has suffered much ill fortune. ⁹ As you are well acquainted, my Sovereign, with these matters, and as you show graciousness to all, you might perhaps give your attention to the welfare of our country and our oppressed nation. ¹⁰ For so long as Judas continues to live, there will be no peace for the state."

¹¹ Others present, the ruler's Friends, who were hostile to Judas, quickly followed up on this rhetoric and further agitated Demetrius with their comments.

¹² He promptly appointed Nicanor, who held command of the elephants, as governor of Judea. He charged him ¹³ that Judas must be killed and his followers dispersed, and Alcimus be installed as high priest in the great Temple. ¹⁴ The Judean Gentiles, who had fled from Judas, flocked to join Nicanor, with thoughts of the misfortune and defeat of the Jews, and of the opportunities this would provide for them.

¹⁵ When the Jews learned of the coming of Nicanor, with his following of Gentiles, they sprinkled dust on their heads and prayed to the One who established the people of God forever, who upholds them by revealing the divine power in times of need.

¹⁶ At their leader's command, they moved out immediately, and encountered the enemy at the village of Adasa. ¹⁷ Simon, Judas' brother, met Nicanor's forces; but he temporarily checked his attack, uncertain of the enemy's intent, because they remained passive. ¹⁸ Nicanor had heard of the bravery of Judas's army, and of how ferociously they would fight for their country; and he hesitated to settle the issue with bloodshed.

¹⁹ Instead, he sent Posidonius, Theodotus, and Mattathias to make peace.

²⁰ After reviewing the proposed terms of treaty, Judas put them to the troops; they were amenable, and so an agreement was reached. ²¹ On an appointed day, the leaders met alone; a chariot moved forward from each encampment, and seats of honor were set up. ²² Judas posted his fighters

in strategic places, as a precaution against any treachery that might be planned, but the discussion proceeded as arranged.

²³ Nicanor remained in Jerusalem, doing nothing that might arouse concern, and sending away the masses of people who had followed him. ²⁴ And always he kept close to Judas, for he developed a great affection for the leader. He counseled Judas to marry and raise a family, and this Judas did, settling down to lead a quiet and everyday life.

²⁶ But Alcimus saw the harmony between the two; and taking a copy of the treaty they had made, went to Demetrius.

The high priest told Demetrius that Nicanor was plotting against the state, that he had appointed Judas, a rebel and conspirator against the state, to succeed him.

²⁷ The ruler, angered and provoked by the slanders of that madman, wrote to Nicanor, expressing displeasure with the treaty, and ordering him to arrest Maccabeus immediately and send him to Antioch. ²⁸ Nicanor read the letter with a heavy heart, for he was required to abrogate his own agreement with a person who had kept good faith. ²⁹ But he could not defy the ruler's orders, so he watched for an opportunity to carry them out by craft.

³⁰ But Maccabeus, seeing that Niconar was less friendly than before, sensed that their relationship had changed, and that this change was not to the good. Calling together a sizable number of his followers, he went into hiding.

³¹ When Nicanor realized that he had been outwitted, he went to the great and holy Temple at the time of the customary burnt offerings, and ordered the priests to surrender Judas. ³² When they protested on oath that they did not know where Maccabeus was, ³³ Nicanor pointed toward the Temple and swore, "Unless you surrender Judas to me as a prisoner, I will level this shrine of God to the ground. The altar I will destroy, and in its place I will build a splendid shrine to Dionysus." ³⁴ With these words, he left.

Then the priests, with arms outstretched to heaven, pleaded with the eternal Defender of the nation, "O God, you need nothing of this world, yet it pleased you that there should be among us a shrine as your dwelling place. ³⁶ Now, Holy God, the One from whom all holiness flows, save forever from defilement this House, so newly purified."

³⁷ A certain Razis, an elder of Jerusalem, was denounced to Nicanor. Razis was one who loved his fellow Jews, and because of his loyalty was

regarded as the Elder of the Jewish people. ³⁸ In the early days of the Jewish rebellion, he had been convicted of practicing Judaism, and had zealously risked body and soul rather than denounce his faith.

³⁹ Nicanor, resolving to show his enmity for the Jewish people, sent five hundred soldiers to arrest Razis, ⁴⁰ thinking that by this he would do them some harm. ⁴¹ The soldiers were at the point of overrunning the tower of the house, and at the outside gate they called for fire to burn the inner doors.

Completely surrounded, Razis resolved to fall on his own sword, ⁴² for he preferred a noble death rather than to fall into the hands of the wicked and suffer outrages unworthy of his noble birth. ⁴³ In the midst of the confusion, the blade did not kill him cleanly; and, with soldiers rushing through the door, he climbed up on the wall and bravely threw himself off and into the crowd. ⁴⁴ They quickly pulled back, and he fell to the ground; ⁴⁵ but, though wounded and severely bleeding, he was still alive and burning with anger. Rising again, he ran through the crowd and up onto a steep rock, ⁴⁶ and now completely drained of blood, he tore out his own entrails, and threw them into the crowd, calling on the God of his life and spirit to give them back some day.

And that is how he died.

15·¹ Nicanor, learning that Judas and his followers were in the region of Samaria, planned an attack on their day of rest, at no risk to themselves. ² The Jews who were forced to accompany him begged him not to do such a barbarous and wicked thing. "Have respect for this day made holy above all others by the All-Seeing One," they urged him.

³ This much accursed blasphemer then asked, "Is there a ruler in heaven who orders the keeping of the Sabbath?"

⁴ The Judeans declared, "It is the living God, the ruler of the heavens, who commands that the seventh day be held sacred."

⁵ "Yet I too am a ruler, here on earth," he countered, "and I order you to take up arms and carry out the ruler's business."

As it happened, he did not succeed in carrying out his atrocious scheme. ⁶ This Nicanor, in his extreme arrogance, had already planned a monument for his victory over Judas' army. ⁷ But Maccabeus never wavered in his trust in God's help. ⁸ He urged the troops not to fear the Gentiles' attack, but to recall times past when help had come to them from heaven, and to look for the victory God would send.

⁹ Building up their confidence, citing the Law and the prophets, and recalling for them the struggles they'd already won, he honed them to a

point of readiness. ¹⁰ As their courage peaked, he issued their orders and reminded them of the Gentiles' treachery and their violation of oaths. ¹¹ His armor for them was less the protection of shield and spear, and more the power of brave and reassuring words; and he cheered them up by telling them of a recent dream, a sort of vision which was well worth belief.

¹² This is what Judas saw: Onias, who had been good and noble, a former high priest, gentle and modest, eloquent, and trained from youth in the way of justice, was praying with upraised hands for the whole Jewish community. ¹³ Then another appeared, marked by his gray hair and his great dignity, and an air of majestic authority. ¹⁴ Onias then said, "Here is one who loves Israel and who prays for its people and for the Holy City—Jeremiah, the prophet of God." ¹⁵ Jeremiah stretched out his right hand to Judas, giving him a golden sword; and as he did so, he said, ¹⁶ "Take this gift of God, a holy sword; with it, you will cut down your enemies."

¹⁷ Judas' brave words gave heart to everyone, rousing the courage of even the youngest and most inexperienced among them. They resolved that they would carry on no long campaign, but attack full force and settle the issue with quick courage in hand-to-hand combat. The city of Jerusalem, their holy religion, and their Temple were endangered. ¹⁸ Even their fear for their families and children, sisters and brothers and relatives, weighed on them less than this first and foremost fear for the consecrated sanctuary. ¹⁹ Those left behind in the city were no less anxious over this battle in the open country.

²⁰ Everyone anticipated the decisive conflict; the enemy was already at hand: the army was drawn up in battle formation; the elephants held a strategic position, with the cavalry ready on the flanks.

²¹ Maccabeus, viewing the battle arrangement of the enemy with their many weapons and the ferocity of their elephants, raised his hands to heaven and called on God who works miracles. He knew that victory is decided not by arms but by the will of God; that God grants victory to those who deserve it. ²² He prayed these words: "O God, in the days of Hezekiah, the ruler of Judea, you sent your angel, and it destroyed one hundred eighty-five thousand troops in Sennachrib's camp. ²³ Now, O heavenly Sovereign, send a good angel again to lead us, spreading fear and trembling. ²⁴ May these blasphemers coming to attack your holy people be struck down by your strong arm." This was his prayer.

²⁵ Nicanor and his troops advanced to the blaring of trumpets and war songs, ²⁶ but Judas and his troops met them in battle with invocations and

prayers. ²⁷ So, fighting with their hands and praying to God with their hearts, they put to death at least thirty-five thousand in hand-to-hand combat, and were elated by God's manifestation.

²⁸ With the action over, they were returning in triumph when they spotted Nicanor's fully-armored body. ²⁹ Shouting and commotion broke out as they blessed the Sovereign God in the language of their ancestors.

³⁰ Then Judas, who as protagonist had devoted himself body and soul to the service of the people, who always maintained the love he had carried for his people ever since he was a child, ordered them to cut off Nicanor's head and right arm and bring them to Jerusalem.

³¹ When they arrived in Jerusalem and had called the people together, he stationed the priests before the altar and sent for the keepers of the citadel. ³² He showed them the head of the notorious Nicanor and the arm which the blasphemer had stretched out so arrogantly against the holy House of the Almighty. ³³ He cut out the tongue of the ungodly Nicanor and announced that he would feed it bit by bit to the birds; that he would hang up these rewards of Nicanor's folly opposite the shrine.

³⁴ And everyone, looking up to heaven, blessed the God who showed divine power: "Praise to the God who preserved this holy sanctuary undefiled!"

³⁵ Judas hung Nicanor's head from the citadel, a clear and conspicuous sign to all of God's help.

³⁶ By public vote they decreed that this day should not go unnoticed, but that the thirteenth day of the twelfth month—called Adar in Aramaic—the eve of Mordecai's Day—should be appropriately celebrated.

³⁷ This, then, is how things ended with Nicanor; and from that time on, the city has been in the Hebrews' hands.

CR   CR   CR

Here I end the story. ³⁸ If it is well told and well heard, then it is as I wished; if poorly told and mediocre—it was the best I could do. ³⁹ Just as it is not wise to drink wine or water by themselves, yet wine mixed with water is sweet and delicious and pleasurable, so too the skillfully composed story delights the ears of those who read the work. And here it ends.

the wisdom of solomon

1:1–5:23

Desire justice,
    you who hold seats of power;
make sure your prayers to the Holy One
    are done with the right intentions;
2   for God is sought with singleness of heart,
        and is found by those who do not test God's power;
        God is revealed to those whose trust is real.

3   But selfish desires separate us from God;
        and any fool who tests the power of God will be flustered.
4   No, Wisdom will never come into a devious soul
        nor stay in a body entrapped in sin;

⁵ the holy Spirit of instruction avoids liars,
  withdraws from those of reckless purpose
  and takes offense at the sight of iniquity.
⁶ Wisdom is a spirit, a friend to us mortals,
  though She will not tolerate the words of blasphemers;
for God can see our innermost being,
  observes our heart, and listens to our speech.
⁷ For the Spirit of God that fills the world
  is all-embracing and knows what we say.
⁸ No one can speak unjustly and not be discovered,
  and justice, God's avenger, will take care of those who do.
⁹ The schemes of the rebellious will be laid bare,
  and their plans will be reported to Our God
  to make sure they receive their judgment;
¹⁰ No sound will escape that jealous ear,
  and your mutterings are no longer secret.
¹¹ So be on guard against all your grumbling,
  and avoid all your murmuring complaints;
for even the most silent whisper will be heard,
  and a liar's tongue is a soul-killer.

¹² So don't tempt death by living a corrupt life;
  don't call destruction down upon you by your deeds.
¹³ For God is not the author of death
  and does not delight in desolation;
¹⁴ God created all things to be alive.
All things of the world are made to be wholesome,
  and there is no poison in them.
The netherworld has no power over the earth,
¹⁵ for justice lasts forever.

¹⁶ But rebels court death with their actions and words—
  they call death "friend," and long for its company.
They make deals with death,
  and are death's worthy partners.
^{2·1} Hear what these poor deluded people
  say to themselves:

"Our lives are too brief and filled with worries,
  and there is no cure for death:
  no one has ever returned from the grave.

2 Our birth was a random accident,
　　and after we're gone, it won't matter if we ever existed.
The breath that fills our nostrils is like a mist,
　　our mind just a spark kept alive by the beating of our hearts,
3 and when that leaves us, we will turn to dust
　　and our spirit will disperse like the wind.
4 With the passing of time, nobody will remember our names
　　or remember what we have done.
Our life will fade away like a cloud,
　　and we'll evaporate like a mist
that is chased by the sun's rays
　　and overpowered by its heat.
5 An all-too-brief shadow—that's all life is,
　　and there is no deferral of our end.
Our fate is sealed:
　　no one returns.

6 "So let's just enjoy the good things of life while we can,
　　and take full advantage of this world
　　with all the gusto of our youth!
7 let's enjoy expensive wines and perfumes to our heart's content
　　and not miss even a single flower of spring;
8 let's adorn ourselves with roses before they wither
9 　　and revel in everything that comes our way,
leaving behind signs of our debauchery wherever we go.
　　This is our life: we deserve no less than this!

10 "Let's take advantage of the poor and the honest!
　　Let's show no sympathy to the bereaved
　　or respect to those whose hair has turned gray.
11 Strength is our justice!
　　Those who are weak don't deserve to live!
12 Let's set a trap for the just,
　　who greatly annoy us by opposing what we do
and reproaching us for breaking the Law.
　　They call us traitors to our heritage.
13 They claim to know God personally,
　　and to be children of God.
14 Their life is an affront to our ways.
　　The very sight of them makes us sick,
15 because they don't live like other people,
　　but follow their own path.

16 They consider us contemptible
    and avoid us like a pile of filth,
claiming that those who are just will die a happy death
    and boasting that God is their parent.
17 So let's test these spurious claims
    and see what happens to the just when they meet their end.
18 For if the just are God's children, God will reach down
    to rescue them from the hands of their enemies.
19 Let's test them with insults and torture
    to see how long they will hold out
    and learn how long their patience will last.
20 Let's condemn them to die in shame:
    Why should they worry?
    If what they say is true, they will be protected!"

21 Such are the thoughts of the corrupt—
    but they are seriously deluded!
22 They cannot see beyond their own ill will,
    and they fail to comprehend the hidden ways of God.
They don't consider that
    a life of righteousness will be rewarded.
23 For God created us to be imperishable,
    and modeled us on the divine nature;
24 it was the devil's envy that brought death to the world,
    as those who call themselves partners of the devil
    will soon find out.

3:1 But the souls of the just are in the hand of God,
    and no affliction will ever touch them.
2 To the eyes of fools, they seem to be dead;
    their departure will be interpreted as a defeat
3 and their going away will be considered a disaster—
    but they have found peace!
4 For though, to mortals, they may have suffered punishment,
    their hope is in life everlasting,
5 and after a time of trial they will receive great blessings,
    because God has tested them and found them worthy.
6 God purified them like gold in a crucible
    and found them as acceptable
    as a whole burnt offering on the altar.
7 When their time of judgment comes, they will shine,
    and will sweep over the world like sparks through the chaff.

⁸ They will be appointed as judges and leaders
   over all nations and peoples,
   and the Holy One will be their Sovereign forever.
⁹ Those who have put their trust in God
   will find out that this is all true,
and those who are faithful
   will dwell in God's love.
These are God's chosen ones,
   and grace and mercy belong to them.

¹⁰ But the rebellious will get the punishment
   their thoughts deserve,
since they ignored justice
   and turned away from Our God.
¹¹ Those who scorn wisdom and instruction are to be pitied:
   their hopes are all empty,
   their labors bear no fruit,
¹² their spouses are unfaithful,
   their children are criminals,
   and their descendants are cursed.

¹³ The childless couple, if they have been blameless and faithful,
   will now feel themselves blessed, not cursed—
   for they will bear fruit on the Day of Judgment.
¹⁴ Eunuchs,* if they have committed no crime
   and held no thoughts of angry resentment against God,
will be rewarded for their loyalty
   with "most favored" status in the Temple of Our God.
¹⁵ The fruit of honest work has a glory all its own,
   and wisdom grows from roots that are imperishable.

¹⁶ But the children of unfaithfulness
   are like fruit that never ripens;
they have sprung from an illegitimate union
   and will come to nothing.
¹⁷ Even if they live a long life, they will be shunned,
   and in the end, their old age will be dishonored.

---

* The Torah excluded eunuchs from the religious life of Israel; however, Isaiah prophesied that in the messianic reign eunuchs would enjoy an inheritance greater than that of daughters and sons. Because individuals who held the office of eunuch for a ruler's harem were frequently homosexual, many in the lesbian and gay community have embraced passages like this one as an affirmation that there are indeed no outcasts in the kindom of God.

¹⁸ And if they die when they are young,
they will have neither hope nor comfort at the Judgment.
¹⁹ A savage fate awaits the progeny of evildoers.

4:1 So it is better to be childless and upright—
your immortality is now the memory of your just deeds,
bringing recognition from God and humankind alike.
² When justice is alive, people imitate it;
when it is missing, people long for it.
Throughout history, justice will make triumphal progress;
because it strives for incorruptibility, it is always victorious.

³ But the teeming offspring of the corrupt will come to naught;
these ill-begotten offspring will never take deep root
or establish firm foundations.
⁴ Their branches may bloom for a brief time,
but since they have no firm hold in the earth,
the wind will shake them to the foundations
and they will be uprooted in the next storm.
⁵ Their branches will be torn off before they are half-grown,
and their fruit will be worthless—
unripe, inedible, and not fit for anyone.
⁶ Children born of evil will bear witness
against their parents' sin on the Day of Judgment.

⁷ But those who are just, even when they die prematurely,
will be at peace.
⁸ It is neither the length of life nor the number of years
which brings honor to old age:
⁹ understanding—this is gray hair;
a life of justice—this is a ripe old age.
¹⁰ There were those who pleased God,
and out of great love, God took them away
from this sinful world,
¹¹ and carried them off,
so that corruption would never pervert their understanding
and or deception tempt their soul.
¹² For evil's seductivenss can overshadow what is good,
and the carnival of desire can defile the innocent heart.
¹³ So, in a very short time, they achieved the same perfection
as those who have lived a long life.

¹⁴ The souls of the just were pure,
   so God hurried them away from this depraved world.

¹⁵ Many people see this, but don't understand it;
   they don't consider the true meaning of what has happened:
   that those whom God has called away are blessed,
   and that God comes to the aid of those who are holy.
¹⁶ In death, the just are a condemnation of the godless who live,
   and the young, perfected so early,
   condemn the advanced old age of evildoers.
¹⁷ Fools see the death of the wise
   and never understand Our God's plans
   or why God snatched them safely away.
¹⁸ They see what is happening and mock it,
   but it is God who will laugh at them:
   when they die, their bodies will be treated without respect,
   and they will be vilified by the inhabitants of Sheol.
¹⁹ God will fling them broken and speechless to the ground
   and shake them to their foundations,
   leaving them utterly ruined and in anguish,
   forgotten for all time.

²⁰ On the Day of Judgment, they will come crawling—
   their own crimes testifying against them
5:1 Then the just will rise up, filled with confidence,
   to face those who had oppressed them
   and mocked their suffering;
² the sight of the just will make them cower in fear,
   amazed at the unexpected way God had saved the upright.
³ Filled with regret, they will say to each other,
   groaning and gasping for breath:
   "Weren't these the people we made the butt of our jokes
   and the target of our ridicule?
   What fools we were
⁴   to have thought them crazy for the way they lived,
   and dishonored for the way they died!
⁵ Who would have thought
   that they would be counted among the children of God
   and assigned a special place among the holy ones?
⁶ Just look how far we have strayed from the truth!
   The lamp of justice never lit our way
   and the sun never rose on us!

7   We left no path of corruption or destruction unexplored,
        wandering through unmarked wastelands
        and ignoring the clearly marked path of God.
8   What good was all our boasting?
        What do we have to show for all the wealth we flaunted?
9   All these things have disappeared like a shadow,
        as fleeting as a rumor;
10 or like a ship that passes over the waves
        leaving no trace to show where it has been;
11 or like a bird that flies through the sky
        and leaves no sign of its passage,
    but with a stroke of the wing,
        it whips through the insubstantial breeze and parts it,
        leaving no evidence behind that it had been there;
12 or like an arrow that is shot at a target,
        the pierced air closing up instantly,
        with no one able to tell where the arrow passed.
13 So it is with us:
        no sooner were we born than our lives were over,
    and we left no trace of justice to show for our lives!
        We wasted our lives, consumed by our own depravity!"

14 The desires of the godless
        are like dust in the wind,
    like a fine mist carried away by the squall,
        like a puff of smoke which the wind blows away,
    passing like the memory of a nomad
        who made camp only for a night, then travelled on.
15 But the just will live forever,
        and their reward is with Our God,
        for the Holy One will take care of them.
16 From God's own hand they'll receive
        the crown of glory and the diadem of beauty—
    they'll be protected by God's right hand
        and shielded with God's arm.

17 A fierce love is all God will need for armor
        when creation itself is turned against the earth's enemies:
18 God will use justice for a breastplate,
        strong judgment for a helmet,
19   and unassailable holiness for a shield;

20 with a sword forged from God's absolute rage,
      the whole universe will join the struggle
      to conquer the madness of these foes.
21 Bolts of lightning will fly
      as if the bow of the clouds were drawn to full arc,
      hitting their mark with precision,
22 and hailstones of wrath
      will be hurled from God's catapult.
The seas will rage and overtake the unjust;
      the rivers will overwhelm them without mercy.
23 A great storm will rise against them
      and scatter them like chaff in a whirlwind.
Their crimes will bring destruction to the whole earth,
      and their evil ways will destroy entire governments.

6:1–8:21

*n*ow listen well, you leaders, and take this to heart!
      You who hold power at the ends of the earth, take heed!
2 Pay close attention, you who govern the masses,
      who take pride in the multitudes under your control:
3 any authority you have
      was given to you by the Most High.
God will examine all your actions
      and scrutinize all your intentions.
4 Even though you are but attendants appointed by the ruler,
      you have not been just in your dealings;
you have not obeyed the Law
      or guided your steps by the will of God.
5 God will come down on you swiftly and terribly,
      for judgment shows no mercy to those of high estate.
6 Those of low estate may find mercy and forgiveness,
      but those who hold power will be held to account,
7 for the One who is Sovereign over all is servile to none
      and shows no favor to anyone of high estate.
God made the powerful and the weak alike,
      and all are held equal under God's authority.
8 But God will severely cross-examine
      those who hold authority over people.

9 I speak, then, to you who hold power over the people,
       that you may learn wisdom and not be led astray;
10 those who remain holy and walk the way of holiness
       will be regarded as holy,
    and those who have learned the lessons of justice
       will be able to defend themselves upon examination.
11 So give this your full attention:
       desire this lesson and you will learn it.
12 Wisdom shines brightly and never fades.
       She is seen by those who love Her
       and is found by those who seek Her.
13 She reveals herself
       to all who desire to know Her,
14 and those who rise early to search for Her
       will not grow weary of the journey,
    for they will find Her seated at the door of their own homes.
15 To ponder Her is the fullness of Wisdom
       and to be loyal in Her pursuit
       is the shortcut to freedom from care.
16 She searches the far ends of the earth
       for those who are worthy of Her,
    and She appears to them on their daily path with kindness,
       meeting them half-way in all their journeys.
17 The true meaning of Wisdom is the desire to learn,
       and to be passionate about learning is to love Her.
18 The love of Wisdom
       means keeping Her laws at all times—
    keeping Her standards assures you of immortality,
19   and staying pure brings you close to God.
20 In this way, the desire for Wisdom
       leads you to true sovereignty.
21 If you who rule over people
       wish to keep your thrones and symbols of power,
    then honor Wisdom
       so that you may lead forever!

            ೞ   ೞ   ೞ

22 I will now tell you about Wisdom and how She came to be,
       and I will not conceal Her mysteries from you.

I will trace Her path right from the beginning
  and make the knowledge of Her as bright as the day.
  I will not leave the truth untold.
23 Nor will I make the hunger for power my companion,
  for it and Wisdom have nothing in common.
24 The wise, in great numbers, are the world's safety,
  and a sage leader is the people's security.
25 So learn what I have to teach
  and you will prosper.

7:1 I am mortal, like everybody else,
  a descendant of our first parents, molded out of clay.
2 In my mother's womb,
  my flesh was knit together for ten lunar months,
  taking shape in her blood.
  I was born of my father's seed
  and the pleasure that two people take in each other.
3 After I was born, I breathed the same air
  and was laid on the same ground that all other mortals tread;
  the first sound I made was a cry, like everyone else.
4 They swaddled me and nursed me and cared for me—
5 no leader begins life in any other way,
6 for they all came into the world in the same way
  and they all go out of the world in the same way.

7 So I prayed, and understanding was given to me;
  I called for help and the spirit of Wisdom came to my aid.
8 I valued Her above even my throne and scepter
  and all my great wealth was nothing next to Her.
  I held no precious jewel to be Her equal,
9 because all the gold in the world
  was just a handful of sand compared to Her,
  and all the silver in the world
  was worth no more than mud.
10 I loved Her more than health and beauty;
  I preferred Her to the light of day,
  for Her countenance shone unceasingly.
11 Through Her, I received all good things,
  and because of Her, I had wealth beyond counting.
12 Everything was given to me to enjoy,
  for all follow where Wisdom leads,
  but I did not yet know that She was the source of it all.

13 What I learned over time, I now share freely with you,
    for I do not want to hide Her abundance.
14 She is an inexhaustible treasure to humankind,
    and those who acquire this treasure become God's friends:
the gifts they receive through Her teaching
    makes them worthy to stand in God's presence.
15 So may God grant me the gift of speaking the divine will,
    and make my own thoughts worthy of the Holy One's gifts;
for even Wisdom is under God's jurisdiction,
    and God gives direction to those who are wise.
16 All that we are, and all that we say, are in God's hands—
    all of our knowledge, and all of our skill.

17 It was God who gave me certainty
    in understanding the way things are:
the organization of the universe
    and the working of the elements;
18 the beginning and end of an era,
    and all that occurs in between;
the cycles of the solstices
    and the changing of the seasons;
19 the circle of the year
    and the positions of the stars;
20 the nature of animals
    and the instincts of wild beasts;
the power of spirits
    and the thoughts of human beings;
the uses of plants
    and the properties of roots.
21 Whether it was hidden or apparent,
    I learned it all,
22 for Wisdom was my teacher,
    and it was She who designed all these things.

Inside Wisdom, there is a spirit of intelligence and holiness
    that is unique and unmistakable:
subtle, dynamic, perceptive, pristine, unclouded,
    unconquerable, compassionate, shrewd, compelling, generous
23 and loving toward mortals, faithful,
    faultless, serene, directing all, knowing all,
    and pervading every intelligent, pure and most subtle spirit.

²⁴ For Wisdom moves more swiftly than motion itself;
    She is so pure that She pervades and permeates
    all living things.
²⁵ She is a breath of the power of God,
    a pure light of the glory of the Most High,
and nothing that is base
    can come into Her presence in secret.
²⁶ She is the light that shines forth from everlasting light,
    the flawless mirror of the dynamism of God
    and the perfect image of the Holy One's goodness.
²⁷ Though alone of Her kind, She can do all things;
    though unchanging, She renews all things;
generation after generation She enters into holy souls
    and makes them friends of God and prophets,
²⁸ for God loves the one
    who finds a home in Wisdom.
²⁹ She is more beautiful than the sun
    and more magnificent than all the stars in the sky.
When compared with daylight,
    She excels in every way,
³⁰ for the day always gives way to night,
    but Wisdom never gives way to evil.
8:1 She stretches forth Her power
    from one end of the earth to the other
    and gently puts all things in their proper place.

² I loved Wisdom and sought Her when I was young;
    I longed to marry Her, so in love was I with Her beauty.
³ Her closeness to God adds splendor to Her regal beginning,
    for the Guide of the universe has loved her always.
⁴ She shares intimately in the thoughts of God,
    and it is She who chooses the works that God is to do.
⁵ If great wealth is desirable in this life,
    how much more desirable are the riches of Wisdom,
    who is the initiator of all things?
⁶ If prudence is demonstrated through actions,
    who more than Wisdom is the initiator of action?
⁷ For those who love justice, the fruits of Wisdom are virtues:
    she teaches moderation, prudence, justice and courage—
    and nothing in life is more useful than these!
⁸ For those who desire breadth of experience,
    She knows all that is past and what will occur in the future;

She understands the subtleties of arguments
and the resolution of perplexities;
She can tell when omens will be given and miracles will occur,
and knows how the times and the ages will unfold.

9 So I was determined to bring Her home to share my life,
knowing that She would be
my counselor through the good times
and my consoler in times of grief and anxiety.
10 Through Her, I would win fame in the eyes of the people
and respect from the Elders, despite my youth.
11 I would prove myself to be astute in all my judgments
and win the admiration of rulers;
12 when I was silent, people would wait for me to speak,
and when I spoke at length, everyone would remain silent
and hang on my every word.
13 Through Wisdom, I would gain immortality
and leave behind a perpetual memory for all generations.
14 I would lead entire peoples,
and all nations would follow me.
15 Even the most dreaded tyrants
would tremble when they heard of me
and my own people would regard me as a just guide
and the bravest one in any battle.
16 When I was home, I would find tranquility in Her,
for resentment cannot remain in Her company
nor can pain persist in Her presence:
only gladness and joy.

17 I pondered this deeply and came to the conclusion
that immortality is found in relationship with Wisdom,
18 that Her friendship gives pure delight;
that doing Her work brings boundless wealth;
that being Her disciple brings understanding;
and that talking with Her creates an honorable reputation.
So I sought some way
to become close to Her.
19 When I was a child, I had a naturally happy disposition
and I had a good soul from the beginning—
20 or rather, because I was good,
I was given a body that was unblemished.

21 Yet I understood that there was no way to gain Wisdom
    unless God were to give Her to me,
and indeed it was proof of my understanding
    to know from whom this gift comes.
So I entreated the Holy One,
    and from the depths of my being, I prayed these words:

God of our ancestors, God of mercy,
    you who made all things by your word,
2 and in your wisdom
    gave mere mortals stewardship over all creation
3 to care for the world in holiness and uprightness,
    and to administer justice with a pure heart:

4 Give me Wisdom, who sits beside your Judgment Seat,
    and do not reject me from those you call your own.
5 For I am your subject, the child of those who attend to you.
    I am weak and have only a short time to live
    and lack comprehension in matters of justice and law.
6 Even if anyone among the human race were perfect,
    if they lacked your Wisdom, they would count for nothing.
7 You chose me to lead your own people
    and to act as judge over your children.
8 You instructed me to build a Temple on your sacred mountain,
    and an altar in the city where you have chosen to dwell—
a copy of the sacred tabernacle
    prepared by you from the beginning
9 Wisdom is beside you and knows all your ways
    and was present when you created the universe.
She is aware of what is acceptable to you
    and what is in keeping with your Law.
10 Send Her forth from your holy heavens,
    and dispatch Her from your glorious Judgment Seat
to work at my side
    and teach me to do what is pleasing to you.
11 She knows and understands all things
    and will lead me with discernment in everything that I do,
    guarding me with Her radiance.

¹² Then my life's work will be acceptable to you,
and I will be able to judge your people rightly
and be worthy of the judgment seat of my ancestor.

¹³ For how can any mortal know the mind of God?
Who can discern the will of the Holy One?
¹⁴ Mortal reasoning is faulty
and our plans are shaky,
¹⁵ because a corruptible body weighs down our soul
and our frame of clay weighs heavy
on a mind already so filled with cares.
¹⁶ Our best guesses about the things of this earth
are only approximate,
and we toil to discover
even those things which are within our grasp.
¹⁷ But who has ever mapped out the ways of heaven?
Who has ever discerned your intentions
unless you have given them Wisdom
and sent your Holy Spirit from heaven on high?
¹⁸ It was because of Her
that we on earth were set on the right path,
that we mortals were taught what pleases you
and were kept safe under Her protection.

଼ଆ   ଼ଆ   ଼ଆ

10^{·1} It was Wisdom who kept guard over our first parents,
the founders of the human race, then they alone were created.
And after they sinned, it was She who rescued them
²   and gave them the power to direct all things.

³ It was because of one unjust person who renounced Her
that, in a fit of rage, he murdered his own brother
and so became accursed.

⁴ Because of the consequences of this fault,
the world was engulfed in a flood,
but again Wisdom came to the rescue
and taught one just person
to steer a wooden craft through the raging waters.

⁵ While the godless nations conspired in their sinful ways
and were thrown into a babble of confusion,

it was She who recognized one just person
   and kept him blameless in the sight of God,
   giving even the strength to resist pity for his own offspring.

6   She saved those who were just
      when the godless were being destroyed,
   and they escaped the fire
      that rained down on the Five Cities.
7   In witness to their sinfulness, that desolate land still smolders,
      its trees bear fruit that never ripens,
   and a pillar of salt still stands in memory
      of a doubting soul.
8   They all renounced Wisdom and suffered for it.
      They lost the power to recognize what is good
   and left behind them a monument to their foolishness,
      so that their crimes could not be ignored—
9   but Wisdom guided Her disciples safely
      though all the tribulations.

10   And when one just person fled from his twin brother's anger
      She guided him on the right paths
   and gave a vision of the loving concern of God
      and a knowledge of holy things.
   She brought success to all the works of that one just person
      and made them fruitful and abundant.
11   When others became greedy and tried to exploit him,
      She stood by and only increased his wealth.
12   She protected him from all his enemies
      and gave shelter from all treacheries;
   after the battles, She awarded him the victory
      and taught him that reverence for God
      is the most powerful force on earth.

13   It was She who refused to abandon one just person
      who was sold into slavery,
   preserving him from sin
14   and accompanying him into prison.
   She did not abandon him in his chains
      and won for this one the authority over a whole nation
      and command over all his oppressors.
   She turned the tables on those who had accused him falsely
      and gave him undying glory.

¹⁵ And it was She who delivered a holy people, a blameless stock,
   from a nation of oppressors;
¹⁶ She entered the soul of one of Our God's faithful,
   who, with signs and wonders,
   was able to stand against an imposing ruler.
¹⁷ She rewarded the labors of a holy people
   and guided them on a wondrous quest,
becoming their shade by day
   and their starlight at night.
¹⁸ She led them across the Sea of Reeds,
   brought them safely through the deep waters,
¹⁹ but She engulfed their enemies
   and spewed them up from the fathomless depths.
²⁰ And when these just people stood in victory over the godless,
   they sang of your glory, God our Deliverer,
and in one voice praised your power
   and called you their champion.—
²¹ because Wisdom gave speech to those who could not speak
   and brought eloquence to the lips of infants.

11:1 Wisdom spoke through a holy prophet
   and brought them victory in all things.
² They roamed across a barren desert
   and made their camp in a wasteland.
³ They were able to withstand their enemies
   and were paid back for their foes' actions.
⁴ When they were thirsty, they called out to you
   and you gave them water from sheer rock,
   quenching their thirst from hard stone.

     ભ   ભ   ભ

⁵ The very means used to punish their enemies
   became a blessing to them in their time of need:
⁶ the godless were not given an everlasting spring,
   but a foul and bloody river
⁷   as punishment for their order to kill all infants;
to the faithful, though, you gave abundant streams
   in a way they could never have hoped for—
⁸ after they had understood, through their own thirst,
   how greatly you had punished their enemies.
⁹ So from their tribulations,

which were no more than expressions of your mercy,
they recognized the agonies
your wrathful judgment inflicts upon the corrupt.
10 Those far away and those near by
were each brought low—
11 you tested your own, correcting them like a parent,
but the godless you scrutinized and condemned like a tyrant:
12 they experienced grief twice—their own torment,
and their anguish at remembering those who had escaped.
13 When they heard that the means you had used to punish them
had been used to bless your people,
they recognized your hand in it, O God.
14 The one who had been abandoned
and exposed to the elements many years earlier,
whom they had mocked and snubbed,
in the end became the object of their awe and respect—
when their thirst, compared with that of the just,
came by such extraordinary means!
15 And when their foolish and sinful ideas led them astray,
and they worshiped senseless reptiles and loathsome beetles,
you sent swarms of mindless creatures to punish them
16 and to teach them that the instruments of our sins
will become the means by which we are punished.

17 Indeed, your strong hand,
which created all things out of nothingness,
did not lack the means to set
hordes of bears or ravenous lions upon them,
18 or even beasts not yet known—
newly created and filled with fury, breathing out blasts of fire,
or roaring and belching smoke,
or flashing terrible sparks like lightning from their eyes.
19 Such beasts would not only have the power to annihilate them,
but their very appearance could slay them.
20 But even without creatures like these,
they could have been killed with a single breath from you,
pursued by your justice
and winnowed like chaff by your mighty breath.
For you have set all things in order
by measure, number and weight;
21 you can exert your great strength at any moment—
who can resist the power of your arm?

²² With you, the entire universe is nothing more
than a grain of sand that barely tips the scales,
or a drop of dew settling on the grass in the morning.
²³ But because you can do all things,
you are merciful to all and overlook the sins of the people
so that they may be brought to repentance.
²⁴ You love everything that exists
and you don't hate anything you have created:
for what other reason would you have made everything?
²⁵ How could anything remain in existence
had it not been your will?
How could anything have lasted
unless you called it into being?
²⁶ You save all things because they are yours, O God,
and you love all that lives,

12¹ for your imperishable breath
fills every one of them.
² For this reason,
you gradually correct those who break your Law,
disciplining them and reminding them of their sins
so that they may abandon their evil ways
and put their trust in you, O God.

³ Do you remember the ancient inhabitants
of your holy land?
⁴ You scorned them for their unholy ways,
for their sorcery and profane rituals,
⁵ their callous killing of children,
their cannibal feasts on human flesh and blood,
They practiced secret rituals
⁶ in which parents slaughtered their own defenseless children.
So you resolved to destroy them
by the hand of our forebears,
⁷ so that this land, which is most beloved to you,
may have in God's children settlers worthy of it.
⁸ Yet you showed mercy to them too,
since you knew that they were only human.
You sent hornets as the advance guard of your army
to wear them down bit by bit.
⁹ It was well within your power
to have the just overpower evildoers in a heated battle,

or to annihilate them instantly with fierce beasts
    or with a single decisive word.
10 But by punishing them in stages,
    you gave them opportunities to repent,
though you knew that their depravity was deeply ingrained,
    that they were corrupt to the bone
and that they had closed their minds to you
11   because they were an accursed people from the beginning.
Nor was it out of deference to anyone else
    that you gave them immunity for their crimes.

12 After all, no one can say to you, "Why have you done this?"
    Who can question your decisions?
Who can blame you for destroying nations
    which you yourself created?
Who can take the stand against you
    to plead the cause of the guilty?
13 For there is no other god but you;
    you care for the whole world
    and you need not justify your decisions to anyone.
As for those you have punished,
14   there is no ruler or potentate
    who can rebuke you to your face.
15 For you are just and you direct all things justly,
    holding it unworthy of your power
    to condemn those who don't deserve reproof.
16 For your power is the source of your justice,
    and it is because you are the Maker of all
    that you are merciful to all.
17 You demonstrate your strength
    when people question whether your power is absolute—
it is only when they know your power and still rebel
    that you punish them.

18 But even with all your great power,
    you judge us with mercy and guide us with great kindness,
    for you exercise your strength as you choose.
19 By acting in this way, you taught your people
    that those who are just must also be kind,
and you have given your children hope
    by offering them repentance for their sins.

²⁰ So if you exercised such care and tolerance
in punishing your children's enemies, who deserved to die,
by giving them time to repent of their evil ways,
²¹ then how much more will you show mercy to your people,
to whose ancestors you gave sworn covenants
and promised them all good things?
²² Even though you punish us,
you trounce our enemies ten thousand times more,
so that we may remember your goodness when we judge others
and may hope for mercy when we ourselves are judged.

²³ This is why you tormented evildoers,
who lived their lives brashly and foolishly,
with the consequences of their own atrocities.
²⁴ They wandered far down the path of error,
making despicable and repulsive creatures their gods;
they behaved like foolish children.
²⁵ So you treated them like children
who had not learned to reason,
and ridiculed them with your judgments.
²⁶ Yet those who did not learn from your derisive scolding
would experience a condemnation worthy of God.
²⁷ They became incensed at their own suffering,
finding that they were punished by the very creatures
they had set up as gods,
and recognized that the one they had refused to seek
was the one true God.
This is why they received
the most severe punishment.

13:1 How inherently obtuse are those who do not know God!
They see all the good things before them,
but don't recognize, through careful study of these things,
the Maker of all!
² Fire, wind, squall,
the vault which holds the stars, surging waters,
or the great lights in heaven that rule the earth—
they consider these things to be gods.
³ Since they were enchanted by the beauty of these things
and presumed these things to be gods,

let them now know that the Holy One
  is the noblest of all,
    since God is the Author of all beauty.
4 Since they stood in awe
    of the power and influence of creation,
  they should now know how much greater
    is the One who made them.
5 For the greatness and beauty possessed by created things
    is but a pale reflection of the One who created them.
6 Yet we cannot blame these people too much,
    for even when they go astray, they may be seeking God,
    really desiring in their hearts to know the Holy One.
7 Because they live their lives among the works of Our God,
    making a close study of them,
  they are convinced by the beautiful facade
    of the things they see.
8 But, this should not let them completely off the hook,
9   for if they possess enough understanding
  to speculate about the universe,
    why are they slow to recognize its Maker and Guide?

ᘉ   ᘉ   ᘉ

10 The really deluded ones are those who worship lifeless things,
    calling artifacts as their gods—
  skillfully formed images of animals, made of gold and silver
    or of useless stone carved by a stonemason long ago.
11 Consider a woodcutter who cuts down a suitable tree,
    neatly strips off all its bark
    and then skillfully carves it into some useful household object,
12 using all the leftover pieces of wood for fuel to cook food
    enough to sate an appetite.
13 But among the wood that is left over,
    there is one useless piece, gnarly and full of knots,
  and the woodcutter takes this piece and whittles away at it
    just to fill up some idle time.
  The woodcutter forms the piece into
    a caricature of a human being,
14   or perhaps forms it into some weird animal,
  then smears it with red stain
    so that every natural flaw is covered over.

15 Then the woodcutter makes a shrine for the carving,
     nailing it securely to the wall.
16 It is the woodcutter who has taken all the precautions
     to prevent the image from falling,
   for it cannot fend for itself—
     it needs help because it is only an image.
17 Yet the woodcutter prays to the image
     about possessions and spouse and children,
     feeling no shame in talking to a lifeless object.
18 The woodcutter prays for health from a thing that is weak,
     for life from a thing that is dead,
   for help from something that is completely inert,
     for a prosperous journey from something that cannot walk,
19 for success in business—for skillful hands—
     from a thing whose hands are completely useless.

14:1 Likewise, consider someone who prepares for a voyage
     and plans to set forth through surging seas
     by praying to a piece of wood more fragile than the ship itself!
2 Ambition invented the ship,
     and it was skillfully built by the shipbuilder,
3 but your providence, Abba, is the pilot
     and you have cleared a path for it through the seas
     and a given it safe passage over the waves,
4 demonstrating that you can rescue the ship from every danger,
     so that even the most inexperienced sailor can put out to sea.
5 Because you want all that Wisdom has created to prove useful,
     people entrust their lives to a small piece of wood,
   using it as a raft to cross the high seas
     and come into safe harbor.
6 Even in ancient times,
     when that arrogant race of giants was being destroyed,
   the hope of humanity escaped on a raft
     and, guided by your hand,
   ensured that the world would have a progeny
     for many ages to come.
7 So even though the wood by which the right prevails
     is a blessed thing,
8 the wooden image, carved by human hands,
     is cursed along with its maker, the artist—
   the artist, for having made it;
     and the carving, because it is deemed a god

even though it will rot
  like any other piece of wood.
9 God hates both equally:
    the godless person, and the fruit of that godlessness—
10 both the doer and the deed will be punished.
11 So even the nation's idols will have their day of visitation,
    since, even though they are a part of creation,
  they have been twisted into an abomination
    to make people stumble
    and trap the feet of the foolish.
12 The making of idols is the beginning of impurity:
    they are inventions that have corrupted human lives.
13 They did not exist from the beginning,
    nor will they remain with us forever.
14 They are the products of human arrogance,
    so an abrupt end has been planned for them.

15 Consider a parent who,
    overwhelmed with grief by the untimely death of a child,
  then constructs an image of the child,
    thereafter honoring as a god
    what had previously been nothing more than a corpse,
  then hands down to future generations
    the duty to perform these customs and rituals.
16 Then, over the passage of time, this blasphemous practice
    becomes standard and is observed as law,
    and carved statues are worshipped by royal command.
17 When people live so far away
    that they aren't able to pay homage to the ruler in person,
  they make a portrait of that faraway face
    and create a public image of the one they seek to honor,
  in their zeal to flatter the absent ruler
    as if their sovereign were present.
18 As the intensity of their devotion grows,
    those who mindlessly pay homage to a distant ruler
    are incited to continue the practice by opportunistic artisans.
19 Out of ambition, perhaps, to win favor with the tyrant,
    the artist skillfully crafts the image into an ideal form,
20 and the masses of people, enthralled by the beauty of the statue,
    begin to worship as a god
    one whom they had previously honored as human.

²¹ So this is the great trap for many people:
    held in bondage by grief or misgovernment,
they ascribe the Name that cannot be spoken
    to mere sticks and stones.
²² And worse than erring in their knowledge of God,
    they soon engage in wars of ignorance—
    yet call their atrocities "peace."
²³ They begin to perform child sacrifices in secret ceremonies
    or participate in the frenzied orgies of bizarre cults;
²⁴ they don't maintain virtue in their own lives
    or in their marriages;
they murder one another through treachery
    and harm each other with their infidelities.
²⁵ Chaos is all around them:
    blood and murder, theft and fraud,
    corruption, betrayal, riots, perjury,
²⁶ molestations, bail-jumping, depravity, perversity,
    domestic violence, adultery, drunkenness.
²⁷ The worship of idols, whose names are too heinous to mention,
    is the cause and end of every evil.
²⁸ In the names of these idols,
    people indulge themselves to the point of insanity,
pass off lies as prophecies, live dishonest lives,
    and break promises without remorse.
²⁹ And since the gods they take oaths upon are lifeless,
    they expect no retribution when they perjure themselves.
³⁰ But they will be charged on two counts:
    because they think little of God in worshipping idols,
and because they think even less of what is sacred
    in deliberately perjuring themselves.
³¹ In the end, what always overtakes those who are guilty
    is not the power of the things by which they swear,
    but rather the retribution that sinners receive.

15¹ But you, my God, are kind and true and patient—
    a merciful ruler of all creation.
² Even if we sin, we are yours
    because we acknowledge your authority.
And because we know that we belong to you,
    we keep ourselves from sin.

3   To know you is the foundation of justice,
        and to know your power is the source of immortality.
4   We have not been led astray by the misuse of human skills
        or the empty work of painters,
    a shape carefully painted with lifelike colors,
5   the sight of which stirs in fools
        an intense yearning for an image without life or breath.
6   Those who make these images,
        and those who lust after them and worship them,
        love evil and deserve nothing better to trust in.

7   Consider a potter, thoroughly kneading the soft clay
        and using it to shape all sorts of things for our use.
    Some of the clay makes vessels intended for clean purposes,
        and some for unclean—it doesn't matter which,
    because the purpose that each will have
        is determined by the potter alone.
8   If the potter chooses to use some of the clay for evil purposes,
        using it to construct a meaningless idol,
    even though that potter was molded
        out of the same earth not long before
    and must return to that earth
        when the life that was loaned is demanded back.
9   Even so, this person does not waste time
        thinking about the suddenness of death
        or the shortness of life.
    Rather, the potter tries to outshine
        all the goldsmiths and silversmiths,
    imitating even those who work in bronze,
        taking pride in the uselessness of all these handmade images,
10   but ends up with heart filled with ashes,
        with a hope worth less than the dust of the earth,
        and a life that is cheaper than clay—
11   never acknowledging the potter's own creator,
        from whom the artisan received an active imagination
        and was infused with the breath of life.
12   No, this person considers life to be nothing but a game
        and our existence a market where money can be made:
    "By hook or by crook," this one says,
        "one must make a living!"
13   But those who make fragile pots and idols from earthy stuff
        should know the truth better than most.

14 But most foolish of all, far worse than the childish,
    are the enemies and oppressors of your people, the Egyptians.
15 They looked upon all their statues as gods,
    even though the eyes of their idols couldn't see,
they couldn't draw breath through their noses,
    their ears couldn't hear, their hands couldn't feel—
    and their feet were useless for walking.
16 For they were made by human hands;
    one with borrowed breath gave them their shape.
But no human being has the power to craft a god:
17   for each of us is mortal,
    and the things made by human hands are dead.
So the makers of idols are better
    than the objects that they make to worship,
for they at least are alive,
    whereas the images that they make are completely lifeless.
18 They even worship reptiles, those most hideous beasts,
    stupider than all other creatures,
19   and ugly even for animals!
When God called all creation good,
    they were left out.

ର   ର   ର

16:1 How fitting, then, that they were punished by means of them:
    they were tormented by hordes of vermin.
2 But even as our oppressors were punished,
    you treated your own people with mercy,
sending quail for them to eat—
    an exotic food to satisfy their hunger.
3 Our oppressors, hungry as they were,
    were so sickened by the loathsome creatures sent to them
    that they lost all appetite for food;
whereas your people, after a short period of wanting,
    delighted in wondrous foods.
4 It was right that unyielding hunger
    should overtake our oppressors;
it was also right that we should learn through a taste of the same
    how our enemies were tortured.

5 So when fierce poisonous snakes stormed against us,
and we were dying from the bites of these writhing creatures,
your anger did not last to the bitter end.

6 Our short-lived trouble was sent to us to teach us,
and afterward we were given a symbol of salvation
to remind us of the requirements of the Law.

7 Anyone who looked upon it was saved by you,
the Savior of all.

8 And through reports of your deeds,
you also convinced our enemies
that you are the One who delivers from every evil.

9 They died from the sting of locusts and flies,
finding no cure to save their own lives
because they deserved to be punished by such creatures.

10 But your people did not perish from the bites of snakes,
even the most poisonous of snakes,
because in your mercy
you came to their aid and cured them.

11 They were bitten
so that they would remember your decrees;
they were quickly healed
so that they would not forget you
or become callous toward your mercy.

12 It was no herb or poultice that cured them;
rather, it was your all-healing word, my God.

13 You have the power over life and death;
you cast us down to the gates of death
and you bring us back up again.

14 One human being may maliciously kill another,
but no one can bring back the breath of life once it has left
or release a soul held prisoner by death.

15 But there is no escape from your hand, O God;

16 you struck down with your arm the impious
who refused to acknowledge your authority.
They were beset by endless torrents of rain and hail,
and fire completely consumed them—

17 how strange that in water, which quenches everything,
the fire should burn so much more intensely!
All of creation comes to the defense of the just!

18 At one point the flame died down
so that it would not destroy all the animals

sent to attack the godless
and to teach them that this was the judgment of God;

¹⁹ at another time, the flame burned even brighter in the water,
with a greater intensity than any natural fire,
and destroyed all the harvest of the land.

²⁰ By contrast, your own people were given
the food of the angels.
You sent your people bread from heaven
that they might eat without toiling for their food:
a bread ready to eat and rich in flavor
and suitable to everyone's taste.

²¹ You demonstrated your sweet kindness toward your children
by sustaining them with a food that satisfied every taste,
transforming itself into whatever
each person desired it to be.

²² Though it looked like snow and ice,
it resisted fire and did not melt,
so that your children might understand that,
even though you destroyed their enemies' harvest
with fire in the hailstones
and lightning in the torrential rains,

²³ that same fire had been made powerless
so that the just might be fed.

²⁴ For creation, in imitation of you, its Maker,
seeks to punish the unjust,
but is benevolent toward those who trust in you.

²⁵ It was true at that time too:
nature adapted itself unceasingly
to the service of your great bounty
according to the desires of those who called upon your Name.

²⁶ So these people whom you loved, Adonai,
were to learn that we are not nourished by food—
but that those who trust you are sustained by your word!

²⁷ That food, which even fire could not destroy,
simply melted away when warmed by the sun's first rays

²⁸ so that they might learn to rise before the sun
and give thanks and praise to you as the new day dawns.

²⁹ The hope of the ungrateful will melt like the snow
and drain away like water that runs to the cistern.

17 1 Your judgments are magnificent and beyond description,
  and this is why those unruly souls went astray.

2 The lawless thought they could oppress your holy people,
  but as prisoners of shadow and captives of unending night,
they themselves were caged in by their own roofs,
  fugitives from divine providence.

3 Thinking that their secret sins would remain hidden
  beneath the dim shadow of the void,
they lived chaotic lives,
  always terrified by specters.

4 Not even the dim recesses in which they hid
  offered any relief from their fear,
but loud, intimidating noises reverberated around them
  and grim-faced phantoms haunted them.

5 No fire, however bright,
  was strong enough to give them light,
nor were even the brightest stars
  enough to pierce their fear-filled night.

6 The only light they had
  was a terrifying blaze that no human being had made,
and in their panic they thought their lives more unbearable
  than even the sight conjured up by their own imaginations.

7 The tricks of their sorcerers failed,
  a mockery of the false wisdom they so vaunted,

8 for those who tried to banish dread and trouble from sick souls
  were themselves so sick and filled with dread
  that they proved themselves ludicrous.

9 Even if there were nothing real that could terrify them,
  they had already been frightened
  by the plague of vermin and hissing of snakes,

10 and so they died convulsed with fear,
  refusing even to look at the air,
  which no one can escape anyhow!

11 Wickedness proves itself cowardly and is its own condemnation;
  when confronted by conscience, it always assumes the worst.

12 Fear is nothing other
  than the abandonment of the aid that reason gives,

13 and the less they relied on reason,
  the more shocking it was that they didn't understand
  the cause of their suffering.

¹⁴ So all through the night, which really had no hold on them
   because it came upon them from a powerless netherworld,
   they had the same haunted dreams over and over:
¹⁵ here chased by ominous wraiths,
   there held captive by the treachery of their own souls,
   then suddenly an unexpected fear would overwhelm them.
¹⁶ They would fall down wherever they were
   and would be bound by that prison that has no bars.
¹⁷ A farmer, a shepherd, a laborer toiling in the fields—
   they were all overcome and awaited impending destruction;
   the same chain of shadows bound all alike.
¹⁸ The whispering breeze,
   the sweet song of birds in the spreading branches,
   the constant babble of running water,
¹⁹ the headlong crash of falling rocks,
   the noise of animals running away unseen,
the roar of untamed beasts
   or the echo reverberating from the valleys between the hills:
   all these things caused them to fall down in fear.
²⁰ While the world was bathed in light of day
   and went on about its tasks unconcerned,
²¹ these people alone were covered with a pall of heavy night—
   a fitting prelude to the eternal night that awaited them.
For even heavier than the night
   was the burden of themselves that each of them bore.

18:1 But for your holy people, there was a radiant light.
   Their enemies heard their voices, but could not see them,
   and called them fortunate because they had not suffered also.
² They thanked your holy people
   for not avenging the injustices inflicted upon them,
   and begged them to forgive all their past crimes against them.
³ In place of the night, you gave them a pillar of fire
   to guide them in their trek through uncharted land—
   a sun that would not scorch them on their ambitious journey.
⁴ But their enemies deserved to be deprived of the day
   and imprisoned in perpetual night,
because they had subjugated your children,
   through whom the imperishable light of the Law
   was to be given to the world.

5 They planned to kill all the newborns among your holy people,
      but though many were endangered, one child was saved.
   In retaliation, you seized up thousands of their children
      and drowned them all in the swelling waves.
6 Our ancestors were warned in advance
      about the things that would happen that night,
   and so warned, they were given the courage
      to trust your promises.
7 Your people awaited the salvation of the just
      and the destruction of their enemies,
8 for you used the same means to pull down our oppressors
      as you used to lift us up when we heard your call.
9 The holy children of an upright people
      offered you sacrifices behind closed doors,
   conspiring among each other to keep the Law of God,
      sharing together in both the benefits and the dangers—
      then singing ancestral songs of praise in the night.

10 But from their enemies there came only a discordant cry,
      the wail of those lamenting the death of their children.
11 The lowborn received the same punishment as the nobles;
      rulers and subjects suffered the same fate.
12 There were countless dead—
      all struck down by one common agent of death.
   There were too few left to bury the dead;
      in one stroke, their most cherished heirs were slain.
13 Because they put their trust in their sorcery,
      they ignored all warnings;
   but when they saw the destruction of their firstborn,
      they admitted that this people are the children of God.
14 When all was calm and silent,
      and the night was half-spent,
15 your all-powerful word bounded from your throne in heaven
      and descended on that cursed land like a fierce warrior,
16 brandishing the sharp sword of your inflexible ruling;
      its head was in the heavens, its feet firmly on the ground,
      as it spread death everywhere.
17 Suddenly, terrifying nightmares tormented the godless
      and unforeseen horrors overwhelmed them.
18 They flung themselves to the ground—
      a half-dead one here, another one there—
      and made it very clear why they were dying;

¹⁹ for the dreams that tortured them
   had instructed them before they died,
so that they would not die ignorant
   of the reason for their suffering.

²⁰ The just also had a brush with death
   when large numbers were struck down in the wilderness.
But God's anger did not last for long,
²¹   for one just person was willing to champion them,
wielding the weapons of sacred office
   prayer, and propitiatory incense—
to temper God's anger
   and set a limit on the disaster.
By this, the high priest proved to be true,
²²   for God's anger was subdued neither by bodily strength
   nor by force of arms,
but assuaging you by words,
   and appeals to sworn covenants made with our ancestors.
²³ The dead were already piling high on the earth
   when the high priest stepped in
and drove back your anger,
   barring your line of attack on those still alive.
²⁴ The whole world was depicted
   on the high priest's vestments,
the glories of our ancestors were engraved
   on four rows of precious stones
and your glory was the crowning jewel
   on the high priest's head.
²⁵ The angel of death flinched at the sight of these things,
   and became terrified.
It was only a brush with death,
   but it was enough.

19¹ But evildoers were attacked by merciless anger to the very end,
   for God knew what they would do:
²   God knew that, even after allowing the people to go,
   insisting on their exodus,
they would change their minds
   and set out in hot pursuit.
³   While they were still mourning
   and wailing over the graves of their dead,

they rushed into yet another foolish decision
    and pursued those whom they had begged to leave
    as if they were fugitives.
4   Their obsession pushed them on to a fitting end,
    forgetting everything that had just happened,
    so that all their torments might add up
    to one outstanding punishment,
5   and your people might embark on an incredible journey
    while their enemies met an extraordinary end.
6   All creation, with all the elements,
    was made obedient to your commands
    so that your children could pass through unscathed.
7   Hovering over their encampment
    was a cloud into which the waters rose,
    creating dry land where water once was;
    the Sea of Reeds became a clear path
    and raging waves became a green plain.
8   Under your protection, the whole nation safely passed through,
    witnessing this amazing occurrence.
9   They were like horses grazing in the pasture,
    like lambs skipping in the fields,
    singing your praises, Adonai, our deliverer.
10 They still recalled the time of their exile,
    and how the land, instead of nourishing livestock,
    nourished mosquitoes instead;
    and how the river became the breeding ground
    for frogs instead of fish.
11 Later, when they were hungry and asked to be fed,
    they saw birds born in a new manner.
12 You sent quail out of the sea
    for them to feast on.

13 You continued to punish their corruption—
    this time with violent thunder to warn them.
    And they justly suffered for their crimes
    because they showed an even greater hatred toward foreigners.
14 The inhabitants of Sodom had refused hospitality
    to their unfamiliar visitors,
    but the Egyptians had enslaved
    their own beneficent guests.
15 And what a punishment Sodom received
    after giving strangers such a hostile welcome!

¹⁶ But the Egyptians welcomed your people with great feasts
    and gave them equal rights among their people—
    then changed their minds and enslaved them!
¹⁷ So you struck them with blindness,
    just as you did to the citizens of Sodom.
  Night encircled them completely,
    and they had to grope through the darkness
    just to find their own doorways.

¹⁸ Just as the strings of a harp make music when played together,
    though each string is separate and retains its own pitch,
  so the elements worked together in harmony,
    as can be observed from these great occurrences.
¹⁹ Land creatures became aquatic
    and sea creatures took to dry land;
²⁰ fire retained its normal power even in water,
    and water forgot that it could quench fire;
²¹ fire failed to consume the flesh
    of delicate creatures that wandered in the flames,
  nor did it melt the food from heaven,
    that looked so like ice and dissolved quickly on its own.

ଓ   ଓ   ଓ

²² In all things, Adonai,
    you have made your people great and glorious,
  and throughout every time and place,
    you have been our constant help.

sírach

prologue*

an invaluable legacy has been passed on to us through the Law, the prophets, and later authors. It is a schooling in wisdom which redounds to the glory of Israel. These blessings of learning are for our scripture scholars and their work, and for the edification and learning of others through their words and writings.

It was for the learning and edification of others that my grandfather Yeshua, after a time of intense study of the Law, the prophets, and other ancient scriptures, was inspired to write. He compiled a book on the themes of knowledge and wisdom for conscientious students and responsible ministers of the Law. The goal of the book was to assist them in making even greater progress in fulfilling the Law.

We ask you to read the book with thoughtful good will. Please be lenient wherever, in spite of our efforts to do justice to the translation, our rendi-

---

* The book is named for the author, Yeshua begot of Eleazar, begot of Sirach. Some may be more familiar with its Latin name, *Liber Ecclesiasticus*—usually shortened to Ecclesiasticus—which means "Church Book," probably because the Church used it so extensively in its liturgy. This prologue, which was never given verse numbers, is a later addition, written by the author's grandson. He translated his grandfather's Hebrew original book, now lost, into this Greek version, and prepared the manuscript for publication around 130 BCE.

tion seems inadequate. For words originally spoken in Hebrew don't have the same impact when translated into another language. This holds true not only for this book, but also for translations of the Law, the prophets, and the rest of the books: the differences between them and their original versions are often significant.

When I settled in Egypt in the thirty-eighth year of the reign of Euergetes, I came across a copy of this invaluable instruction. This inspired me to devote my time to diligently laboring to translate them. I spent countless sleepless hours working to get the book ready for publication. It is being published especially for those living abroad who wish to study and discipline themselves according to the teachings of the Law.

1:1*–42:14

*W*isdom comes from Our God;
  She dwells with God forever.
2 Who can count the sand in the sea,
  the drops of rain, the days of eternity,
3 the height of the sky, the width of the earth,
  the depth of the abyss?
4 Only Wisdom can—the first of all creation;
  judicious understanding from the beginning.
5 To whom has the root of wisdom been disclosed?
  Who understands Her resilience?
6 There is only One, wise and awe-inspiring;
  One who sits upon the judgment seat.
7 It is Our God who created Her;
  espied Her; appraised Her;
8 who has poured Her forth upon all God's works,
  upon every living creature, as a gift,
  and lavished Her upon those who love the Most High.

9 Reverence for Our God is honor and glory,
  a blessing and a wreath of joy.
10 Reverence for Our God makes the heart glad,
  happy and joyful and long-lived.

---

* The verse numbering of several chapters in Sirach varies from translation to translation. We have followed the verse numbering of the New Revised Standard Version throughout.

11 Those who revere Our God will die happy;
  they will be blessed on the day of their death.
12 Reverence for Our God is where Wisdom begins;
  She bonds with the faithful in the mother's womb;
13 She has set up an eternal residence among humankind,
  and she continues to dwell with its ancestors.
14 Reverence for Our God is Wisdom in Her fullness;
  Her wine is intoxicating.
15 Her home overflows with rich fare;
  She stores the harvest.
16 Reverence for Our God is Wisdom's wreath:
  blossoms of peace and good health.
17 She showers the earth with insight and intelligence,
  and rewards those who espouse Her gifts.
18 Wisdom is planted in reverence for Our God,
  and Her branches are long-lived.

19 Unjust anger can never be justified,
  it is the ruin of the corrupt.

20 Those who are patient hold out till the right moment,
  and joy returns to them;
21 they know how to marshall their hidden thoughts,
  and many lips celebrate their wisdom.

22 Wise proverbs reside in Wisdom's treasury;
  but reverence for Our God is loathsome to the arrogant.
23 If you desire Wisdom, keep the commandments,
  and Our God will bless you with Her.
24 Reverence for Our God is wisdom and enlightenment;
  the Most High delights in faithfulness and gentleness.

25 Do not reject reverence for Our God
  or approach the Almighty with duplicity.
26 Don't be a hypocrite;
  keep watch over your lips.
27 When you exalt yourself,
  you risk disgracing yourself;
28 for the Almighty will expose your secrets
  and publicly humiliate you,
29 because you were motivated not by reverence for Our God,
  but by a deceitful heart.

2·1 Daughters and sons, if you hope to follow Our God
    prepare yourself to be tested.
2   Be clear-minded about your goals, and persevere;
    and be brave when faced with challenges.
3   If you want a long and successful life,
    put yourself in the presence of God and stay there.
4   Endure every adversity
    in patient humility,
5   for even gold must be tested by fire—
    and so are the chosen, in fires that dethrone the ego.
6   Trust in God, and God will help you;
    keep to the narrow path of goodness, and have hope.

7   You who revere Our God must wait for God's mercy;
    if you fear falling, you will fall.
8   You who revere Our God must also trust God,
    and you will not forfeit your reward
9   You who revere Our God should hope to prosper,
    to find joy and God's favor.

10 Study the generations who went before us:
    were any who hoped in Our God denied?
    Were those who persevered in reverence for Our God abandoned?
    Were those who prayed to God ever ignored?
11 Our God is compassionate and merciful,
    the forgiver of sins and our savior in troubled times.

12 Woe to cowardly hearts and fearful hands!
    Woe to hypocritical sinners!
13 Woe to the feeble-hearted who have no faith,
    for they have no one to rely on!
14 Woe to you who have despaired!
    What will you say when Our God comes to you?

15 Those who revere Our God don't disobey God's word;
    those who love Our God follow God's path.
16 Those who revere Our God strive to please the Almighty,
    and immerse themselves in the Law.
17 Those who revere Our God are always alert,
    and humble themselves in the presence of the sacred.

18 Let us fall into the hands of Our God,
    and not into the hands of mortals;
  for as great as God's majesty is,
    God's mercy is just as great.

3.1 My children, listen to your parents:
    do what we say and you will live—
2 for Our God gives a father honor over his daughters and sons,
    and upholds a mother's authority over her children.

3 Respect your father, and you atone for sin;
4   revere your mother, and you accrue great wealth.

5 Children are the reward for those who respect their parents,
    and their prayers will always be heard.

6 Those who esteem their father will be long-lived;
    those who comfort their mother are obeying Our God.
7 Those who revere Our God honor their parents,
    and gives them the respect that is due a sovereign.

8 Honor your parents in word and deed,
    and their blessing will come upon you.
9 For a parent's blessing gives a family deep roots,
    but their curse rips up its foundation.

10 Don't seek glory at the expense of your parents.
    How can their loss of face glorify you?

11 If your parents are honored, you receive the glory;
    if your parents are shamed, you receive the denigration.

12 My children, care for your parents in their later years;
    don't do anything to give them grief while they are alive.
13 Make allowances for their feebleness in age;
    don't despise them because you're in the prime of life.
14 For kindness to your parents will never be forgotten,
    and it will make reparation for your sins;
15 in time of trouble, it will be remembered to your advantage,
    and your sins will melt away like frost in sunshine.

16 Renouncing one's parents is tantamount to blasphemy:
    those who curse them tempt the Creator's wrath.

17 My children, be gentle in all that you do,
   and you will be loved by the blessed.
18 The bigger you become, the more you should humble yourself,
   and will find favor with God;
19 for as great as God's power is,
   it is to the humble that God's secrets are revealed.

20 Don't pry into things beyond your circumstances,
   or delve into what is beyond your limits.
21 Know what you can—and can't—take on;
   don't fret about what is hidden.
22 Don't trouble yourself with things beyond you,
   or when shown things beyond human comprehension.

23 People's own opinions lead many of them astray,
   and stubborn illogic impairs good judgment.
24 If your eye is bad, light can't get in;
   if your reasoning is bad, wisdom can't get in.

25 Obstinacy comes to grief;
   to tempt danger is to tempt death.
26 Obstinacy leads to stupidity;
   sinners stack sin on sin.
27 There is no cure when disaster afflicts the arrogant;
   corruption has already established itself here.

28 The wise take proverbs to heart;
   every sage is a good listener.

29 As water douses flames,
   so charitable giving atones for sins.
30 Those who do kind things are long remembered;
   when they fall, they are supported.

4·1 My children, don't cheat the poor of their livelihood;
   don't antagonize the needy.
2 Don't inflict pain on the hungry;
   don't taunt the needy.
3 Don't add trouble to the troubles of the desperate
   or keep them waiting for relief.
4 Don't reject the plea of the distressed,
   or turn your face from the beggar;

5 don't turn away when they ask you for something,
   and give no one a reason to curse you—
6 for if they curse you in their embittered state,
   the Creator will hear their prayer.
7 So gain the respect of the community,
   and bow your head to those who are rightly in authority.
8 Attend to the poor when they approach you
   and answer their plea with a kind word.
9 Rescue the oppressed from the hand of the oppressor;
   be just in your judgments.
10 Be like a parent to orphans,
   like a spouse to the widowed;
   then you will be like a child to the Most High,
   and God will be more tender than a mother to you.

11 Wisdom rears Her children to greatness
   and aids them when they search Her out.
12 To love Her is to love life;
   those who seek Her win Her favor.
13 Those who hug Her tightly inherit glory;
   wherever they go, Our God will bless them.
14 Those who follow Her follow the Holy One;
   the Most High loves those who love Her.
15 Obey Her, and you'll be in a position of supreme authority;
   listen to Her, and you'll live in Her heart of hearts.
16 If we trust Her, She is ours forever,
   and we pass Her on to our descendants.
17 Wisdom walks with us as a stranger, at first,
   and puts us to the test:
   She brings fear and trembling upon us
   and winnows us with her discipline.
   Her decrees test us again and again
   until we trust Her with all our heart.
18 Then She leads us back to happiness
   and reveals Her secrets to us.
19 But if we stray, She cuts us loose,
   and abandons us to our fate.

20 Use your time well, and avoid evil;
   but don't be unduly ashamed of your past.
21 Shame can choke you;
   but humility can bring you honor and respect.

22 Don't give undue deference to others,
    or be timid to a fault.

23 Don't sit on your hands when a single word can set things right;
    and don't hide your wisdom.
24 For your wisdom will be obvious in your speech,
    and your understanding will be evident in what you say.

25 Never deny the truth,
    and never swim against its current.

26 Admitting your mistakes is not shameful;
    being willfully ignorant is.

27 Never grovel to a fool,
    or be partial to the influential.

28 Fight to the death for truth
    and Almighty God will be on your side.

29 Don't have a bold tongue
    and a lazy body at the same time;
30 don't be a beast at home
    and a coward in public;
31 and don't hold your hand open to receive
    and closed to give.

5:1 Don't rely on your wealth, and say,
    "I am powerful."
2 Don't be driven by your appetites and ambition
    and succumb to the passions of the heart.
3 Don't say, "I am my own authority,"
    for the Almighty will certainly call you to judgment.
4 Don't say, "So I sinned; nothing has happened to me!"—
    Our God can wait as long as necessary.
5 Don't presume God's forgiveness—
    that's adding sin to sin.
6 Don't say, "God is so merciful
    that even all my sins will be forgotten,"
7 for God is both merciful and jealous;
    the corrupt feel the heavy hand of God's wrath.
8 Don't procrastinate about returning to Our God;
    don't put it off another day,

9 for God's vengeance can be sudden and swift,
       and you'll be completely destroyed in a flash.
10 Don't trust in your money or your ill-gotten gains;
       it will have no value on the day of your judgment.

11 Don't be blown about by every breeze
       or try to walk in every direction at once.
12 Stand your ground about what you know;
       sincere about what you say.
13 Be quick to listen,
       slow to answer.
14 Say your piece when you know the answer;
       keep quiet when you don't.
15 For our words can honor or dishonor us;
       our tongue can be our downfall.
16 Don't get a reputation as a gossip,
       or use your tongue to tear someone down.
17 If you do, you're no better than a thief,
       and being duplicitous will earn your neighbor's reproach.
6:1 Say nothing hurtful, whether in large matters or small ones;
       don't alienate when you can be a friend instead.
       You'll earn a bad reputation,
       and a curse for being "that person with the forked tongue!"

2 Don't let desires sap all your energy.
       For they can tear you apart like a boar;
3 they strip off your leaves, devour your fruit,
       and leave you with a naked stump.
4 Wicked desires destroy their clients,
       and give foes cause for ridicule.
5 Kind words multiplies the number of friends you have,
       and pleasant talk bonds neighbors together.

6 Be friendly with many,
       but take few into your confidence.
7 Begin friendships cautiously:
       trust takes longer to create.
8 One kind of friend is reliable only when it's convenient,
       and won't give you support when it really counts.
9 Another kind of friend friend becomes a rival
       and tells everyone of your quarrels, to your shame.

10 Yet another friend breaks bread with you,
  but disappears in your time of grief;
11 when you prosper, this friend is like family—
  acts like a member of your household—
12 but at you lowest point, this "friend" turns against you,
  and avoids you on the street.
13 So keep your rivals at a distance,
  and be cautiously optimistic about your friends.
14 Faithful friends are a well-built shelter;
  find one, and you have found a treasure.
15 Faithful friends are priceless;
  their value is beyond counting.
16 Faithful friends are the essence of life,
  a blessing for those who revere Our God.
17 Those who revere Our God treat others with respect;
  and their friends will behave the same way.

℘   ℘   ℘

18 My daughters and sons, if you seek discipline early in life,
  you will find Wisdom when your hair is gray.
19 Cultivate Her like the farmer who plows and plants,
  and enjoys the crop in anticipation of the harvest.
20 Cultivating Her is a small matter
  compared with the bounty to come.
21 She is severe with the undisciplined;
  fools cannot submit to Her.
22 She is a boulder testing their endurance;
  they lose no time in shaking Her off.
23 She is Discipline;
  you must earn access to Her.
24 Pay attention, daughters and sons, and heed what I say;
  don't reject my advice:
25 slip on Her shackles,
  put Her collar around your neck;
26 lift Her yoke onto your shoulders,
  and willingly accept Her reins.
27 Draw close to Her with all your heart,
  and keep to Her discipline at all cost;
28 pursue Her, look for Her, seek Her,
  and you will find Her—

and once you hold Her,
>   never let go.
29 In time you will be two in one,
>   and She will be your joy.
30 Her shackles will become your strong defense,
>   Her collar a robe of honor;
31 Her yoke will be a gold pendant,
>   and Her reins lavender ribbons;
32 you will carry Her like a splendid gown
>   topped with a wreath of joy.

33 If you have the desire, children, you will receive instruction;
>   if you do well, you will grow in competence;
34 if you love to listen, you will learn;
>   if you give your mind to it, you will grow wise.
35 When you attend the gathering of the elders,
>   pick out the wisest and stay close to them.
36 Be especially attentive when the discourse is of God;
>   remember every wise proverb.
37 Rise early and visit those you discover to be wise,
>   wear a path to their door.
38 Meditate on the admonitions of Our God,
>   and busy youself with the Commandments always;
> then God will enlighten your mind,
>   and the wisdom you yearn for will be yours.

7:1 Avoid evil, and evil will avoid you;
2   eschew wrongdoing, and it will avoid you.
3 Don't sow in the furrows of corruption,
>   lest you reap it sevenfold.

4 Don't seek the highest glory from Our God,
>   or the highest honors from the ruler.
5 Don't justify yourself before the Almighty
>   or display your wisdom before the magistrate.
6 Don't strive for a judgeship
>   unless you are capable of driving out injustice;
> for you may risk losing your integrity
>   by favoring a prominent citizen.

7 Don't wrong the members of the community
>   and suffer public disgrace.

8 Don't add sin upon sin to your conscience;
     one makes you guilty enough.

9 Don't brag, "God will be pleased to accept my many gifts
     when I make my offering."
10 Don't be impatient when you pray,
     and don't neglect the giving of alms.

11 Don't mock those whose lives seem pathetic;
     keep in mind the One who humbles and exalts.

12 Don't plot wrongdoing against your own family,
     or against a friend.
13 Don't get caught up in a habit of lying;
     it never brings anything good.

14 Don't be long-winded in the presence of the elders;
     don't repeat yourself when you pray.

15 Don't shun labor-intensive work,
     or farming, for it was instituted by the Most High.

16 Don't think yourself better than others;
     nothing makes God angrier.
17 Do everything you can to dethrone your ego;
     remember—death awaits us all.

18 Don't give away a friend for money;
     don't sell a soulmate for all the gold of Ophir.

19 When you find a good and wise spouse, hold on tight;
     a kind-hearted spouse is worth more than gold.

20 Don't mistreat a bonded laborer who is a faithful worker,
     or a wage earner who is gives an honest day's work.
21 Love a wise employee as you love yourself;
     treat all your workers with the greatest justice and respect.
22 See that your livestock receive good care;
     if they are making you a profit, keep them.

23 See that your children receive an education;
     teach them the rules of conduct early in life.
24 Raise your children to be good and honorable;
     don't spoil them.

25 Getting your children grown and settled is a worthy goal,
    but make sure their relationships are healthy and loving.

26 A couple must work at mutuality;
    lack of trust can destroy a relationship.

27 Honor your father with your whole heart,
    and never forget your mother's birth pangs.
28 You owe your birth to them;
    can you ever repay them for what they did?

29 Revere God with your whole heart,
    and treat priests with respect;
30 love your Creator above all else,
    and don't forsake God's ministers.
31 Revere Our God and honor the priests
    and give them their due as it was commanded:
the firstfruits, contributions,
    sacrifices, and sacred offerings.

32 Reach out your hand to the homeless, the needy,
    and your blessing will be full.
33 Be generous to all living things;
    even the dead deserve our kindness.
34 Don't turn your back on those who grieve;
    mourn with those who mourn.
35 Be diligent in visiting the sick;
    your deeds will gain you affection.
36 In all you do, keep in mind the fate that awaits you,
    and you will never sin.

8:1 Don't contend with the influential,
    lest you fall into their power.
2 Don't quarrel with the wealthy
    for they may turn their wealth against you;
for gold has destroyed too many—
    has twisted the soul of rulers.
3 Don't argue with the talkative;
    it just encourages them.
4 Don't joke with an ill-mannered person;
    you may hear your ancestors abused.

5 Don't mock a repentant sinner;
    bear in mind that we all are guilty.
6 Don't look down on the elderly,
    for you too will grow old.
7 Don't gloat over anyone's death;
    remember that all of us will die.

8 Don't neglect the colloquies of the wise;
    reflect on their proverbs;
  for they will make you fit
    to minister to powerful people.
9 Learn from the tradition of the elders;
    for they got their understanding from their own elders.
  They can teach you how to think,
    and how to answer in the time of need.

10 Don't fuel the coals of a sinner,
    or you may be burned in the flames.
11 Don't be intimidated by the arrogant;
    it only spurs them on to trap you in your words.

12 Don't lend to those more powerful than you;
    if you do, write it off as a loss.
13 Don't guarantee loans beyond your means;
    if you do, be prepared to pay.

14 Don't take a judge to court
    if you hope for a favorable decision.

15 Don't travel with irresponsible people,
    or you'll find yourself in deep trouble:
  for they will start directing your every step,
    and you'll follow them into danger.
16 Don't argue with the hot-tempered
    or travel with them across the desert;
  they court bloodshed, and will turn against
    you when things grow dangerous.

17 Don't seek advice from fools;
    they cannot keep a confidence.
18 Don't do anything of a private nature in front of strangers;
    you don't know what use they might make of it.

¹⁹ Don't open your heart to just anyone,
   or you'll say goodbye to your happiness.

9¹ Don't be jealous of your beloved spouse,
   lest you teach your partner how to hurt you.
² Don't surrender yourself to anyone
   who will tear down your self-esteem.
³ Don't even approach the promiscuous,
   for they will draw you into their net.
⁴ Don't dally with hustlers;
   they only want to entrap you.
⁵ Don't let your mind wander at the sight of innocent purity;
   you might find yourself tumbling toward disaster.
⁶ Don't give your soul to gigolos or prostitutes;
   they will steal your inheritance.
⁷ Don't lurk around the city streets
   or frequent its seamier quarters.
⁸ Avert your eyes when you find someone attractive;
   don't lust after those who are already partnered,
for physical beauty has brought many to their death:
   the hunger for it can consume you like a fire.
⁹ Don't let yourself be alone with someone who is married,
   and don't go out for drinks,
lest you find yourself uncontrollably attracted,
   with deadly consequences.

¹⁰ Don't desert old friends;
   new ones have no past to honor;
friends, like wine,
   are best enjoyed with age.

¹¹ Don't envy the corrupt their successes;
   you don't know the disaster waiting for them.
¹² Don't enjoy the pleasures of the arrogant;
   they won't reach death unpunished.

¹³ Avoid those who have the power over life and death,
   and the fear of death won't haunt you.
If you do approach them,
   be careful, for your life is at risk.
Recognize that you are walking among trip lines,
   wandering through fields planted with traps.

¹⁴ Size up your neighbors to the best of your ability,
and associate only with the wisest of them.
¹⁵ Seek out the intelligent for conversations,
and let all your talk concern the Law of Our God.
¹⁶ Break bread with those who love justice;
let your reverence for God be your glory.

¹⁷ As a craftsperson is recognized by skilled hands,
and a counselor by wise words,
¹⁸ so loudmouths are the bane of the community;
the rash talker is detested.

10¹ The wise magistrate brings stability to the people,
and the wise government keeps its own house in order;
² as goes the head of government, so go the cabinet members;
as goes the mayor of a city, so go its citizens.
³ A ruler without a moral compass destroys the country,
but a community grows with the wisdom of its leaders.
⁴ But ruling over it all is the hand of God,
who provides the right caretakers at the right time.
⁵ All human sovereignty is in the hands of God,
who honors individuals to legislate and judge.

⁶ No matter how a neighbor wrongs you,
never raise your hand in violence;
don't let your arrogance dictate your actions.
⁷ Conceit is odious to God and humankind,
and injustice offends both.

⁸ Sovereignty passes from nation to nation
because of injustice, oppression, and greed.

⁹ What reason do dust and ashes have to be proud?
Even while we're alive, we're decaying.
¹⁰ A long illness derides the doctor's skill;
a ruler today, a corpse tomorrow.
¹¹ At death, we inherit corruption,
worms, maggots, and vultures.

¹² Pride begins with our stubbornness,
in a turning of our heart from our Creator;
¹³ it begins through the sin of the proud,
and runs its course to their utter depravity.

To them God sends new and crushing afflictions,
    to bring on their complete ruination.
14 Our God brings down arrogant leaders
    and establishes humble people in their place.
15 God plucks up the arrogant by the roots
    and puts the lowly in their stead:
16 God cuts down their tree, leaving only a stump,
    then digs out the stump, roots and all.
17 God sweeps away every trace that they lived,
    and erases their memory from the earth.

18 Pride was not part of the Maker's plan for humankind,
    nor boiling rage for those born of woman.
19 What breed is able to receive honor?
    Humankind.
What breed actually receives honor?
    Those who revere God.
What breed is able to receive contempt?
    Humankind.
What breed actually receive contempt?
    Those who break the commandments.

20 A family honors the head of its household;
    a people honors those who revere God.
21 Whether tenant, or traveler, or foreigner, or homeless—
    their glory is in their reverence for Our God.
22 It is unjust to revile the wise because of their poverty,
    and wrong to honor the sinner because of their wealth.
23 Magistrates, rulers, and judges are all worthy of honor;
    but none is as great as the one who reveres God.
24 When the high-and-mighty serve the sagacious pauper,
    wise people will approve.

25 In managing your affairs, don't boast of your wisdom;
    when you're in trouble, don't be full of bluff and bluster.
26 It is better to be a simple worker and have all your needs met
    than to be an arrogant pretender who doesn't have bread.

27 Children, be unpretentious; maintain your self-respect;
    value yourself at your proper worth.
28 Who speaks for those prone to self-destruction,
    or respects those who scorn themselves?

29 The poor are honored for their wisdom;
    the rich for their wealth.
30 To be honored in poverty is to be more than wealthy;
    to be dishonored in wealth is to be the poorer for it.
11:1 The wisdom of the poor lets them hold their head high
    and take their place among the mighty.

2 Don't praise people for their beauty,
    or despise them for their plainness.
3 The bee is one of the smallest winged creatures,
    yet its honey is the sweetest of sweets.
4 Don't mock another's shabby clothes
    or laugh when they're having bad times,
  for Our God works strange wonders,
    and does things hidden from our view.
5 Many of oppressed rise to a position of great authority,
    and the unlikliest of all is given a crown;
6 and many a ruler has been made to sit on the ground,
    and the prominent are delivered into the hands of their enemy.

7 Don't find fault without examining the evidence;
    think about it at length, then judge.
8 Listen, then answer;
    don't interrupt while another is speaking.
9 Don't be drawn into an argument not of your concern,
    or interfere in the conflicts of the corrupt.

10 My daughters and sons, don't take on too much work:
    it is the fast lane to grief;
  you will find yourself in the rat race,
    from which there is no relief—
11 we struggle and labor and press on,
    only to realize that we fall further behind.
12 Or take those sad people who fail at each new endeavor,
    weak and full of misery—
  suddenly Our God looks with favor on them
    and frees them from their wretchedness,
13 lifts their head and raises them up,
    to the amazement of all.

14 The good and the bad, life and death,
    poverty and wealth—all from Our God.

15 Wisdom, understanding, knowing how things work,
    love, and the path of justice—all from Our God.

16 Error and darkness are ingrained in the corrupt from birth,
    and as evildoers grow, do does their evil.
17 But the grace of Our God remains upon those who are just,
    and God's favor brings them unbroken success.

18 People can get ahead by holding onto money like misers,
    but this is how they're rewarded:
19 they say, "Now I can sit back and enjoy my wealth,"
    without knowing how little time they have left,
    and dying, leave everything to others.

20 Stand fast in your duties, enoy your work,
    and grow old doing your craft.
21 Don't envy the corrupt and what they accomplish;
    put your trust in Our God and stay the course;
    for Our God, in the blink of an eye,
    can make the rich poor and the poor rich.
22 The devout are rewarded with God's blessing;
    it happens in a moment.
23 Don't say, "What more do I need?
    What new bauble can I buy myself?"
24 And don't say,"I'm completely independent!
    Nothing can go wrong now!"
25 For in a time of good fortune, adversity is forgotten,
    and in a time of adversity, good fortune is lost to memory;
26 and it's a simple thing for Our God
    to pay us what we deserve on the day of our death.
27 A minute's misery erases a lifetime of pleasure;
    in our last hour, our deeds tell how we lived.
28 No one is called fortunate before death;
    we are best known by how we die.

29 Don't invite just anyone into your household;
    the crafty have many ways to deceive.
30 They may seem as safe as a caged bird,
    but they're like spies searching for weaknesses.
31 With a word they can turn good into evil;
    a roaring fire can start from a single spark.

32 These corrupt wait for a chance to spill your blood;
    they plot to steal your most precious belongings.
33 Beware of such reprobates and their evil schemes;
    they can ruin you for forever.
34 Take in a stranger, and you set yourself up for trouble;
    you'll become a stranger to your own family.

12:1 When you do a kindness, actually get to know the person—
    then your kindness will have its full effect.
2 Help someone who is just, and you'll be rewarded—
    if not by the recipient, certainly by Our God.
3 Help someone who is corrupt, and no good will come of it—
    to do so isn't even an act of mercy.
4 Give to good people, but not to reprobates;
    comfort the oppressed, but shun the arrogant.
5 Don't give them weapons for protection,
    lest they use them against you,
6 and for every good deed you do for them,
    they repay you with twice as many evils.
7 The Most High especially abhors the corrupt,
    and repays them with a vengence.

8 When you're prosperous, you don't know who your friends are,
    but adversity reveals all our enemies.
9 Even our enemies are friendly when we're successful,
    but in our adversity, even our friends avoid us.
10 Don't trust your enemies, for their perversity is as certain
    as oxidation is to bronze.
11 Even when they bow and scrape as if humbled,
    be on your guard and keep a safe distance.
Rub them as if you were polishing bronze,
    to test the persistence of their corrosion.
12 Don't go near them lest they betray you and topple you;
    don't seat them at your table lest they demand your chair.
In the end you'll realize the truth in what I say,
    and regret that you didn't heed my warning.
13 Does anyone sympathize with snake charmers who get bitten
    or lion tamers who get mauled?
14 It is the same with those who run in the wrong crowd
    and are accomplices in their crimes;
15 they may support you awhile,
    but their friendship lasts only as long as your good fortune.

16 Foes may speak with honeyed words,
    but they are scheming to topple you into a ditch.
  They may have eyes full of tears,
    but given the chance, they'll tear you limb from limb.
17 Should you meet with misfortune, you'll find them at your side,
    feigning aid, but intending to trip you up.
18 They will nod their heads and throw out their arms to you;
    but their whispered words will show their true selves.

13:1 Just as putting your hand in tar covers it with pitch,
    those who accompany the arrogant grow arrogant.

2 Don't carry too heavy a burden;
    don't associate with those greater and wealthier than you.
  Clay pottery and iron pots don't mix;
    when they collide, the pottery suffers.
3 The wealthy deceive and brag about it;
    the homeless are deceived and apologize for it.
4 As long as the wealthy can exploit you,
    they will keep you under their control;
  once you are useless to them,
    they abandon you.
5 If you have money, they're always at your side,
    winning your confidence, smiling all the time;
6 if they need anything from you, they'll flatter you wildly,
    but they'll drain you dry without a qualm of conscience.
7 They'll seduce you with friendship,
    until they milk you two or three times over, humiliating you.
  Later, when they run into you, they'll ignore you,
    or shake their heads as if ashamed of you.
8 So don't presume that they really like you,
    and keep your head on your shoulders.

9 Accept the overtures of influential people with caution;
    test the degree of their desire to meet you.
10 Don't press your luck and suffer rejection,
    but don't be aloof and get ignored.
11 Don't be presumptuous and act as an equal;
    don't trust their ebullient words.
  For all this flow of words is a test,
    checking you out between the smiles.

¹² These people of influence are pitiless creatures;
   they'll hurt you, or they'll enslave you.
¹³ Be on your guard and very, very careful;
   associate with them, and you risk great violence.

¹⁴ Every creature loves its own kind,
   and we all love someone like ourselves.
¹⁵ Every animal is drawn to its own species,
   and all people associate with their own kind.
¹⁶ Can a wolf and a lamb agree?
   Neither can the just and the depraved.
¹⁷ Can the dog and the hyena be at peace?
   Can there be peace between the wealthy and the homeless?
¹⁸ As wild donkeys are victims of lions in the wilderness,
   so the poor are the game of the rich.
¹⁹ The proud abhor humility
   as much as the wealthy abhor the poor.
²⁰ If the wealthy falter, support is always there;
   if the poor falter, they risk abandonment.
²¹ When the wealthy slip, many hands support them;
   if they talk nonsense, they are excused.
   When the poor slip, they are condemned;
   even if their words make sense, they are ignored.
²² When the wealthy speak, all stop and listen—
   then they praise the speakers for their wisdom.
²³ When a poor person speaks, they say, "Who's this?"—
   and dismiss the speaker if even a minor stumble is made.
²⁴ Wealth is a virtue—but only in a sinless society.
   Yet the arrogant always claim that poverty is evil.

²⁵ Our heart determines the expression of our face,
   whether it's good or bad.
²⁶ A cheerful countenance is the token of a good heart;
   but one who schemes laboriously looks withdrawn and sour.

14:1 Blessed are those whose mouth brings them no grief,
   who have never felt the pain of guilt.
² Blessed are those who have a clear conscience,
   who are always hopeful.

³ Wealth is unbecoming to a tightwad;
   what use can a miser make of gold?

4 Those who are stingy are hoarding for strangers
   who will live luxuriously on the what the miser collected.
5 How can those who are overcautious with money be generous?
   They can't even enjoy what is theirs!
6 No one is stingier than those who are stingy to themselves;
   they punish their own stinginess.
7 They are generous only by accident;
   in the end they expose their own greed.
8 The eye that is grudging bespeaks the wickedness of the greedy;
   by refusing to share, they condemn themselves.
9 The eye of the greedy looks beyond its share;
   greed dries up the soul.
10 The tight-fisted deny themselves even bread,
   and their own table is bare.

11 Daughters and sons, be as good to yourself as you can;
   let your offerings be worthy of you.
12 Be mindful that death is not slow in coming,
   and its hour cannot be foretold.
13 Be good to your friend before you die—
   be as generous as your means allow.
14 Don't deny yourself good things,
   or let innocent pleasure escape you—
15 for won't you leave all your possessions to others?
   Won't they draw straws for what you amassed?
16 Give and receive, be good to yourself;
   there is no pleasure in the grave.
17 Every thing alive grows old like a garment;
   it is the law of the ages that all will die.
18 We are like leaves on a healthy tree;
   some fall off, others flourish.
   So it is with the generations of flesh and blood;
   one dies off, another comes alive.
19 The fruit of all our labor decays and perishes,
   and so do we in our time.
20 Blessed are those who meditate on Wisdom,
   and seek understanding,
21 who study Her ways
   and dwell on Her secrets;
22 who shadow Her like the hunter
   and lie in ambush by Her gate;

23 who sneak a glance through the window,
    and listen at the door;
24 who set up camp near Her dwelling,
    and drive tent-pegs at Her walls;
25 who let their children play in Her shade
    and camp under Her branches—
26 She gives them shelter from the heat,
    they abide in Her home.

15:1 Those who fear Our God will live this way,
    and once adept in the Law, they'll possess Wisdom.
2 She will come to them like a mother,
    will greet them like a young bride.
3 Her food is the bread of understanding;
    Her drink the water of knowledge.
4 They will lean on Her for support,
    and rely on Her without shame.
5 She will place them high above their neighbors,
    and give them words to speakl in the Assembly.
6 They will be blessed with a wreath of joy,
    and She'll establish an everlasting name for them.
7 The foolish will never possess Her;
    the corrupt will never glimpse Her.
8 She is aloof to pride,
    and liars don't remember Her.
9 Praise is out of place on the lips of the vile,
    for Our God has not placed it there;
10 for praise expresses Wisdom,
    and only with God's assent.

11 Don't ever say, "God made me fall,"
    for you must shun what God hates.
12 Don't say, "God led me into error,"
    for God has no use for sinners.
13 Our God hates all that is evil,
    and we will too, if we fear God.
14 God alone created us at the beginning,
    and abandoned us to our free will.
15 You are free to keep the Commandments;
    it is in your power to be faithful.
16 Our God has placed fire and water before us all;
    each must choose one.

17 We have before us life and death;
    we are to choose between them.
18 For God's wisdom is immense,
    it is all-powerful, all-seeing;
19 God sees everthing in all creation;
    nothing escapes God's eyes.
20 No one has God's permission to sin;
    none is given license to lie.

16:1 Don't plan a family of worthless children,
    don't take pride in godless offsprings.
2 Whatever the size of your family,
    delight in them only if they revere Our God.
3 Don't depend on them to be long-lived,
    and don't put too much trust in their future.
    It's better to have one good child than a thousand reprobates;
    dying childless is better than having a blasphemous child.

4 A single sage can establish a city;
    but it takes a whole generation of rebels to destroy it.
5 My eyes have seen as much,
    and my ears have heard things even more significant.
6 Fire kindles wherever the debauched gather;
    flames of wrath envelop a disobedient nation.
7 The giants of old got no pardon from God
    who rebelled, emboldened by their strength.
8 God didn't spare Lot's neighbors,
    who invited doom by their pride;
9 God had no pity on that condemned nation,
    which ceased to exist in their sinfulness.
10 God had no mercy on the six hundred thousand who wandered
    and perished in the desert for their hardness of heart.
11 But had only one of them been rebellious,
    it would still have been miraculous had that one survived—
    for mercy and anger are one and the same with God;
    now God's power saves, now God's power condemns.
12 God's mercy is immense, as is God's punishment;
    God judges everyone according to each one's merits:
    sinners don't escape with their booty,
    nor is the patience of the devout ignored.
14 God's mercy is broadly dispersed;
    all are judged by their deeds.

¹⁵ Don't say, "I will hide from sight,
    so that all those up there will forget about me;
  in a place of such size, surely I can be missed;
    what am I in the vastness of creation?"
¹⁶ Just look—see the heavens, the firmament,
    the deep, and the earth—all of them wilt at God's visitation;
¹⁷ the footings of the earth and the mountains
    tremble and quake at a mere glance from the Almighty.
¹⁸ So who would even think about me?
    Who would be concerned with my little ways?
¹⁹ If I sin, who will see me?
    If all my treachery is done in secret, who will know?
²⁰ Who tells God about the good things I do?
    What do I get for doing what I should?"
²¹ These are the thoughts of the misguided,
    the arguments only fools make.

ʘ   ʘ   ʘ

²² Listen to me, daughters and sons,
    listen closely to what I say,
²³ as I provide you with sound instructions
    and teach you accurate information.
²⁴ In the beginning, when God created everything
    and assigned each its place in the order of creation,
²⁵ the Almighty placed each of them within an eternal rhythm,
    and fixed their limits for all time.
²⁶ They would not know hunger,
    or grow tired, or desert their posts.
²⁷ None of them would ever disturb its neighbor
    or disobey God's word.
²⁸ Then Our God looked down on the earth,
    and filled it with innumerable blessings,
²⁹ populating its surface with every form of life,
    life that must go back into it when its work is done.

17:1 Our God formed humankind from the earth,
    and made us in the divine image;
² God gives us a limited number of days on earth,
    and makes us go back into it when our work is done.
³ God endows humankind with strength,
    and makes us responsible for everything on the earth.

4 God puts into all living things a fear of us,
   and grants us preeminence over animals and birds.
5 God shapes for us mouths and tongues, eyes and ears,
   and gives us an understanding heart.
6 God fills us with wisdom and knowledge,
   and shows us both good and evil.
7 God tends our hearts,
   and lets us appreciate the splendor of God's work.
8 We in our turn are to praise God's holy Name,
   and tell the splendor of everything God does.

9 God gave us knowledge
   and endowed us with life's laws.
10 God joined in an eternal covenant with humankind,
   and disclosed to us the commandments.   \
11 We saw God's glorious splendor with our own eyes;
   we heard the glory of God's voice with our own ears.
12 God said to us, "Do no evil!"
   and gave each of us rules of conduct toward our neighbor.
13 Our conduct is always visible to the Almighty,
   we cannot hide from God's view.
14 God sets us rulers for each nation—
   except Israel: here God alone reigns.
15 Everything we do is as clear as the sun to the Most High,
   God's eyes see everything we do.
16 Our injustices cannot be hidden from the Most High,
   and all our sins are before Our God.
17 God treasures our acts of charity ike a signet ring;
   our good works makes us "the apple of God's eye."
18 And later God will rise up and repay us,
   give each of us what what we deserve.
19 But God also opens a way to the penitent,
   and encourages those who are losing hope:
20 return to Our God and abandon your sin,
   face God and cease your offenses;
21 return to the Most High and renounce evil;
   hate what God hates.
22 Who can worship the Most High from the grave,
   when it's the living who offer their praise?
23 The dead can't praise God any better than those who never lived;
   people express their gratitude only when alive and well.

²⁴ How great is Our God's mercy!
　God's forgiveness is open to all who come back!
²⁵ Humans don't have that capacity for forgiveness,
　for we are not immortal.
²⁶ Is anything brighter than the sun? Even it undergoes eclipse.
　How much more in shadow, then, are the thoughts of mortals?
²⁷ God judges hosts of heavenly beings—
　but all we are is dust and ashes.

18:1 The One who lives forever is supreme judge, without exception;
　Only Our God knows true justice.
² Who has the capacity to proclaim all God's creation,
　who is there who can tell all God's mighty acts?
³ Who can measure God's majestic power,
　let alone tell the story of all God's mercies?
⁴ No one can add to the marvels of Our God,
　or take away from them, or even comprehend—
⁵ when we think we've finally understood, we're only beginning,
　and when we stop, we're as confused as ever.
⁶ What is a human being, and what is its purpose?
　what does its good signify, and its evilness?
⁷ A person's life span is considered great
　if it runs one hungred years;
⁸ compared to eternity,
　our few years here are a drop of water, a grain of sand.
⁹ Now you can understand Our God's patience with us;
　now you see why God showers us with mercy.
¹⁰ The Almighty sees and understands how grievous death is to us,
　and so forgives us all the more.
¹¹ Our compassion is for our neighbor;
　Our God's compassion is for us all.
¹² The Most High disciplines, corrects, and teaches us,
　and reclaims us as the shepherd does the flock.
¹³ The Almighty is compassionate to those who agree to discipline,
　who eagerly obey God's laws.

ભ　　　ભ　　　ભ

¹⁴ When you give charity, my children, don't scold the recipients—
　don't spoil your kindness with words that hurt.
¹⁵ As the dew gives relief from the heat,
　so a kind word improves a gift.

16 Sometimes kind words do more than gifts,
so truly kind people offer both.
17 Chastizing the recipient when giving charity is foolish—
eyes of hope dim when the gift is given grudgingly.

18 Before you talk, learn;
before you attend the sick, study the cure.
19 Before the judgment falls, examine yourself,
so that on your day of visitation, you'll be vindicated.
20 Before you fall, humble yourself;
once you have sinned, repent.

21 Don't delay in forsaking your sin;
don't wait until you need God's help.
22 Be prompt about fulfilling your vows;
fulfill them before you're at death's door.
23 Give careful thought before you make a vow;
don't be like those who test God's patience.
24 Contemplate the wrath you must face on your day of death;
the time of judgment when God's face is turned aside.
25 Be mindful of famine times in times of plenty;
poverty and longing in times of wealth.
26 Weather can change dramatically in a single day,
but before Our God, everything is fleeting.

27 The wise are prudent all the time;
the greater the danger of sin, the more they watch themselves.
28 The astute recognize wisdom when they see it,
and honor those who possess it.
29 The learned prove the character of their wisdom
when they pour forth the right proverbs.

30 Don't pursue your lusts;
rein in your desires.
31 When you give in to the satisfaction of your desires,
you become a fool to your foes.
32 When you enjoy too much luxury,
you bring on poverty twice as fast.
33 Luxurious living and excessive drinking
have ruined many a fortune—
19:1 those who do never get ahead;
while those who waste what little they have will be ruined.

² Liquor and sex waste the mind,
    and promiscuity breeds recklessness—
³ corruption and ruin follow,
    and consuming lust destroys its owner.
⁴ Those who trust in such things are senseless,
    and those who run after them are sinning against themselves.

⁵ Those who gossip about others' misfortunes
    will have misfortune come upon them;
    those who repeat an evil report are fools.
⁶ Never repeat gossip
    and you won't be gossiped about.
⁷ Keep your secrets to yourself,
    don't reveal them to anyone, not even friends—
⁸ those who hear your secrets may have power over you,
    and that can turn friends into foes.
⁹ So you heard something juicy? Give it a funeral.
    Restrain yourself. It won't make you burst!
¹⁰ Fools hear a piece of gossip, and go straight into labor,
    desperate to let this news come to birth;
¹¹ until they spread the gossip, they're in pain
    as sharp as an arrow in the thigh.

¹² Challenge your friend—"Did you really do this?"—
    and if it's true, perhaps your friend won't do it again.
¹³ Challenge your neighbor—"Did you really say this?"—
    and if it's true, perhaps your neighbor won't say it again.
¹⁴ Challenge your friends—but maybe it's not true,
    so don't believe everything you hear.
¹⁵ A person may let something slip untentionally;
    who among us hasn't said something wrong?
¹⁶ So challenge your neighbor before breaking the friendship;
    doing so fulfills the Law of the Most High.

¹⁷ The Law is perfectly fulfilled by following wisdom,
    and all wisdom comes from reverence for Our God.
¹⁸ But knowing all wickedness doesn't consitute wisdom;
    there is no good judgment in the advice of sinners.
¹⁹ Sometimes being shrewd is detestable;
    sometimes it's better to be simple-minded.
²⁰ It is better to be less intelligent and godfearing
    than to be brilliant and violate God's Law.

21 There are those who skillfilly promote injustice,
    who bend the law to justify their claim.
22 Some people display grief and sorrow
    with a deceitful heart;
23 they cover their face and pretend they hear nothing,
    then gain an advantage when no one is looking.
24 Their saving grace is the lack of ambition,
    but they'll still harm you given the chance.
25 You can read a lot in a person's appearance;
    you can ascertain wisdom by the look of the face.
26 The clothes we wear, the way we laugh, the way we walk,
    all reveal us for who we are.

 C3   C3   C3

20·1 A rebuke that is out of order
    is best received in silence.

2 An honest confrontation is better than losing one's temper;
    if they can admit their fault, you've kept them from disgrace.

3 Violence in the struggle for justice
    is like the lust of someone sworn to celibacy.

4 Better to be silent and appear wise,
    than to be talkative and be disliked.*

5 When some are silent, they're at a loss for words;
    when others are silent, they're just biding their time.

6 The wise are silent until the right time arrives;
    blustering fools have no sense of timing.

7 The loquacious bring disdain,
    as do those who assume an authority that is not theirs.

8 Some people turn misfortune into gain,
    some people gain only to lose.

9 There are times when generosity is actually a loss,
    and times when it doubles its value.

10 One can be brought low by fame;
    another can come to fame from obscurity.

---

* Contrast this proverb with Mark Twain's famous saying: "It is better to keep your mouth shut and appear stupid than to open it and remove all doubt."

11 When you pay too little for too much,
   you often pay for it seven-fold.

12 The wise can endear themselves to others through words;
   fools lavish their compliments on people in vain.

13 Gifts from the corrupt are worthless:
   they think their one gift is worth seven from anyone else.

14 They donate little and bad-mouth a lot;
   they are outspoken in public;

15 they lend today and expect payment tomorrow.
   They are hateful people.

16 Fools say, "I have no friends,
   no gratitude for my generosity,

17 and those who break bread with me ridicule me."
   How often they are despised, and by so many!

18 A slip of the tongue happens faster than a slip on the ground;
   that's why the corrupt have such quick downfalls.

19 The boring story is like unsalted food,
   especially when people tell them again and again.

20 Proverbs spoken by fools are just as unwelcome,
   because their timing is always atrocious.

21 Poverty often prevents opportunity for sin,
   but that doesn't let poor people sleep any easier.

22 Some people are eaten up with false shame,
   shame brought on by the intimidation of a fool.

23 When people are shamed into making promises to a friend,
   they waste a friendship.

24 Lies are grotesque stains on our character,
   and always on the lips of the corrupt.

25 A thief is more honorable than an habitual liar;
   but both are doomed to disgrace.

26 Liars will always suffer disgrace;
   a shame never to be rid of.

27 The wise promote themselves through discourse;
   the cunning always please the people in charge.

28 Farmers work the soil for a bountiful harvest;
   the cleaver work the ruler for favorable judgments.

29 Gifts and favors dull the eyes of the wise,
   and stifle their reprimands like a muzzle.

30 Hidden wisdom is like buried treasure—
   what's the use of either of them?

31 It's better for people to hide their folly
   than to repress their wisdom!

ʒ ʒ ʒ

21:1 If you have you sinned, my children, stop now—
   seek forgiveness for all your sins.
2 Flee from sin as you would flee from snakes:
   both bite when you go near;
3 their teeth are like lion's teeth,
   they can kill you.
4 All lawbreaking is sharp as a two-edged sword—
   once it cuts, there's no cure.

5 Arrogance and violence despoil the wealthy
   and desolate the household of the proud.
6 But God hears the appeal of the lowly,
   and God's reply is prompt.

7 To hate admonition is to tread the path of the sinner;
   to revere God is to repent with all one's heart.

8 The loquacious are known far and wide;
   the wise know their own failings.

9 To build a house on funds of another
   is like gathering stones for your tomb.

10 A gathering of the corrupt is like a bundle of hemp waste:
   they both end up in a blazing fire.

11 The path of the corrupt is smoothly paved;
   it leads straight to Sheol's pit.

12 Those who keep the Law control their instincts;
   reverence for Our God gives birth to wisdom.

13 Some people have little capacity for learning;
   others, a cynicism which masquerades as intelligence.

14 The knowledge of the wise expands like a flooded stream,
   and their advice is like a living spring;

15 but a fool's mind is a bottle with a crack;
   anything it acquires leaks out.

16 When the learned hear a wise saying,
   they acclaim it and improve on it;
17 when the fools hear it, they mock it,
   and toss it away.

18 Listening to a fool is like carrying a heavy load on a journey;
   listening to a wise person is uplifting.

19 The assembly listens closely to the words of the wise,
   and spends time reflecting on them.

20 Fools treat wisdom as one would an abandoned house;
   they see it as useless and of no value to them.

21 To the fool, learning is like chained ankles
   and handcuffed arms.

22 Fools laugh out loud;
   the wise smile quietly.

23 To the wise, learning is like a gold pendant,
   like a bracelet on the arm.

24 Fools rush into a house,
   while the wise approach slowly;
25 fools rudely peer through the door
   while the wise wait to be greeted.

26 Listening at the doorway is rude and ill-mannered;
   the well-trained person would be embarrassed by it.

27 The lips of gossips repeat what others say;
   the words of the wise are deliberately stated.

28 The thoughts of fools come out of their mouths,
   while wise words tell what is in the heart.

29 When the profane curse the enemy,
   they're actually cursing themselves.

30 When the backbiters defile themselves,
   they win the loathing of their neighbors.

22:1 The sluggard is like a muddy rock:
   everyone sneers at such a disgrace.

2 A shirker is like a lump of dung;
   all who touch it wipe off their hands.

3 An ill-mannered child embarrasses the parents;
       unruly children can bring their parents to poverty.
4 Sensible children enter into good marriages;
       shameless ones bring grief to their parents.
5 Insolent children shame their parents
       and ruin every relationship they enter.
6 Inappropriate talk is like whistling during a funeral;
       a good spanking and bridling are always wise moves.

7 Teaching a fool is like gluing a broken pot,
       like rousing a sleeper from a deep sleep.

8 Talking to a fool is like talking to someone dozing:
       sooner or later both will ask, "What did you say?"

9 Weep for the deceased, for they leave the light behind;
       weep for the fool, for they leave their wits behind.

10 Weep just a few tears for the dead, for they are at rest;
       but life for the fool is worse than dying.

11 Mourning for the dead is a seven-day ritual;
       for the ungodly fool, it lasts a lifetime.

12 Don't indulge in extended words with fools,
       or even approach the senseless.
13 Avoid them, for they are trouble;
       contact with them will leave you soiled.
    Turn away from them and you'll have rest,
       and won't be burdened with their stupidity.

14 What is heavier than lead?
       What is the name of a fool?

15 Bags of sand and salt and a lump of iron
       are easier to carry than a fool.

16 A crossbeam welded into the superstructure
       cannot be brought down by an earthquake,
17 just as a conscience that is clear even after ample consideration
       cannot be overridden in a crisis.
18 A mind affirmed by careful reflection
       will not quake in confrontation.
19 Gravel lying on a high ridge
       will be blown away in a gale;
    and a resolve fortified by hasty judgments

will evaporate when challenged.

20 A jab in the eye brings tears;
   a jab in the heart brings feelings into the light.

21 Toss rocks at birds, and you scatter them;
   you scatter your friends when you slander them.

22 When you have a fight with a friend, don't despair—
   there's still time to renew the friendship.
23 If you have bad-mouthed a friend, don't be afraid—
   reconciliation is still possible.

24 Gain your neighbors' confidence while they are still poor,
   and you will merit their largess when they are wealthy;
   when troubles come, stand by them,
   and you will be blessed by their gratitude.

26 Fumes and smoke precede the flame,
   insults before bloodshed.

27 I will never be ashamed to support my friends,
   and I will never hide from them;
28 if I am ever harmed by them,
   all who hear of it will see their true colors.

℆   ℆   ℆

29 Who will place a sentry before my mouth,
   a judicious seal on my lips,
   to assure that they never cause my downfall,
   that my tongue never ruin me!
23:1 O God, my Creator, the Ruler of my life,
   don't abandon me to my tongue's excesses,
   or let me fall because of them.
2 Who will rein in my thoughts—by force, if necessary!—
   or bring wisdom's discipline to my mind?
   Be strict with my failures,
   and punish me for my sins!
3 Then my faults will cease,
   and my sins will diminish;
   then I won't fall to my enemies,
   nor will they rejoice at my plight.
4 O God, Creator, Ruler of my life,

take away my aloofness;

5 don't allow me a single licentious glance,
   shield me from lustful drives,
6 snatch me from the grip of lust and debauchery,
   and don't abandon me to a life of shame.

7 My children, pay attention to this lesson:
   if you keep it you will not be ensnared by vice.
8 Sinners are entrapped by their own lips;
   pride and arrogance are their prisons.
9 Don't let swearing become a habit,
   nor the taking of the holy Name.
10 Notice how the laborer who requires constant supervision
   wears a multitude of scars,
   and you will learn the consequences of constantly
   taking oaths and swearing by the holy Name.
11 Those who habitually swear are vile to the core;
   the whipping cane will always be near their household.
   When they offend, their sins multiply;
   frivolous swearing bears a double dose of guilt.
   Casual swearers cannot justify themselves,
   and their guilt extends to their whole household.
12 There is a style of talking that is deadly;
   may it never take root in the heritage of Jacob.
   The god-fearing who stay at arm's length from it
   won't wallow in sin.
13 Don't develop the habit of foul language,
   for the words themselves will be sinful.
14 Think of your mother and father
   when you are seated among the mighty,
   lest you forget yourself while among them
   and make a fool of yourself;
   and then you would wish you had never been born
   and curse the day of your birth.
15 Those who habitually swear and take oaths
   will never break the habit all their days.
16 Two types of people compound sins;
   a third draws down God's wrath,
17 for torrid lust has flames like fire,
   which cannot be cooled until it has been sated:
   those who lust for their own body

and only give up when consumed by fire;
  the lecher to whom every morsel is sweet,
    until death ultimately stills the appetite;
18 and those who wander from their own marriage bed,
    thinking to themselves, "Who can see me?
  It's dark outside, and the walls hide me;
    I'm so well hidden nobody can see,
    And the Almighty won't notice it."
19 They fear human eyes;
    they fail to know that God's eyes
  are ten thousand times brighter than the sun;
    they see our every move and penetrate every hidden place.
20 All things are known to God even before they were created,
    and remain known to God.
21 These people will find punishment in view of everyone;
    it will happen when least expected.
22 It is the same with spouses in adultery,
    whose sin brings forth children—
23 first, the adulterer disobeyed the Law of the Most High;
    second, a spouse has been wronged;
  and third, in their careless adultery,
    they have created an unwanted child.
24 Such adulterers will be dragged before the assembly,
    and their punishment will extend to their children.
25 The children will not set down roots,
    nor will they multiply.
26 The adulterers will leave an accursed memory
    with a long-remembered shame.
27 What will be learned and remembered
    long after they are gone
  is that reverence for Our God is the best food;
    keeping the commandments is the sweetest fruit.

ଓ   ଓ   ଓ

24:1 Hear Wisdom sing Her own praises;
    She proclaims Her glory among Her own people.
2 She speaks out in the assembly of the Most High,
    in the presence of the God's host:

³ "I am the word come forth from the mouth of the Most High,
    I enveloped the earth like a mist.
⁴ I dwelt in the high heavens,
    my judgment seat a cumulus cloud.
⁵ Alone I encompassed the vault of the sky,
    I wandered across the abyss.
⁶ Over the waves of the sea, over the whole earth,
    over all peoples and nations I reigned.
⁷ I searched for a place to rest among all these places,
    where would I dwell within all of creation.
⁸ Then the Creator of all these things
    chose a place for my dwelling and commanded me,
  'Dwell in the land of Jacob;
    make Israel your inheritance.'
⁹ Before motion began to be measured, God created me,
    and my heritage will last forever.
¹⁰ In the holy tabernacle I ministered in God's presence;
    in Zion I established my domicile.
¹¹ God settled me in the beloved city of Jerusalem,
    it is here my authority is acknowledged.
¹² I have put down roots among an honored people,
    selected to be God's portion.
¹³ There I flourished like a cedar of Lebanon,
    as a cypress on Mount Hermon;
¹⁴ there I grew like the date palm of Engedi
    and the roses of Jericho,
  like an olive tree in the orchards,
    a plane tree growing tall.
¹⁵ I exuded aromas like cinnamon and acacia,
    like sweet balm, precious myrrh,
  galbanum, and gum resin,
    like burning incense in the tabernacle.
¹⁶ I spread my branches like a terebinth,
    branches heavy with grace and beauty.
¹⁷ I put out graceful shoots like a vine;
    my blossoms bear fruit of honor and wealth.

¹⁸ "Come near, all you who yearn
    to eat heartily of my fruit,
¹⁹ you will be reminded that I am sweeter than honey,
    more precious than the honeycomb.
²⁰ Once you feed on me, you'll yearn for more;

once you drink of me, you'll thirst for more.
21 Once you hear me out, you are beyond disgrace;
    once you follow my rule, you'll fail no more.
22 All this is the book of the Covenant of the Most High,
    the Law that Moses ordained for us,
    as the heritage for the assemblage of Jacob.
23 It floods with wisdom like the Pishon,
    like the Tigris in the growing season;
24 it overflows with understanding, like the Euphrates,
    like the Jordon at harvest;
25 it flows with discipline, like the Nile,
    like the Gihon when the grapes are ripe.
26 Our ancestors never fully understood its message,
    and even now our grasp of it is weak.
27 Its thoughts are wider than the oceans,
    its ambition deeper than the abyss.

28 "And I, I was like a stream branching off a river,
    like a waterway running through a field
29 I said, 'I will water my garden,
    soak my flower beds.'
30 And look! My waterway became a stream
    and my stream, a river.
31 Once again I will send forth my teachings, shining like the dawn,
    that its light may be viewed far and wide.
32 I will send forth my teaching like prohecy,
    and will it to future generations.
33 Let it be known that I have toiled not only for myself,
    but for all who thirst for wisdom.

25:1 There are three relationships that I value;
    they are delightful to God and humankind as well:
2 harmony between sisters and brothers,
    friendship among neighbors
    and mutual love of husband and wife.

3 There are three types of people I hate with all my heart,
    whose very existence I abhor:
4 the poor when puffed up with pride,
    the rich when they lie,
    and elders when they are adulterous and senseless.

5   If you have not grown in wisdom in your early years,
        will you gather it in later in life?
6   A fine thing to behold is sound judgment from gray hairs;
        good counsel coming from the elderly.
7   A fine thing to behold is wisdom in seniors,
        sound advice from the esteemed!
8   The diadem of our first citizens is vast experience,
        who glory in their reverence for Our God.

9   There are nine things I can reflect on that make me happy,
        and a tenth thing I have on my mind:
10 parents who delight in their children;
        living long enough to see their enemy's downfall;
11 a happy household with sensible parents;
        a farmer who doesn't plow with an ox yoked to an ass;
12 those who never sin with their tongue;
        not having to work for a poor supervisor;
13 good friendships;
        people who want to hear what you say;
14 and those who attain wisdom—they are great indeed,
        but no greater than those who revere Our God.
15 Reverence for Our God transcends everything;
        those who have it have no superior.

16 There are wounds,
        and there are wounds of the heart;
    there is evil,
        and there is the evil of a deceiver.
17 There is suffering,
        and there is suffering at the hands of a foe;
    there is vengeance,
        and there is the vengeance of an enemy.
18 There is snake venom,
        and there is the venom between intimates.
19 I would rather live in a household with a lion or a dragon
        than with a spouse who has a nasty temperament.
20 Spite changes the appearance of people—
        they look as grim as a bear.
21 When couples in disharmony go out in public,
        they're not even aware that their tone of voice betrays them.
22 No bitterness exceeds rejection after intimacy;
        may it always be the lot of the adulterer!

23 As difficult as it is for the elderly to climb sand dunes,
     even more difficult are spouses who rail at their mates.
24 So don't be enamored of someone's physical attractivness,
     or be attracted to someone for their wealth:
25 one person totally dependant upon another
     is oppression and a cause for shame.
26 A broken heart, deep sadness, abject depression—
     all come from a worthless spouse.
27 Nervous hands and quaking knees—
     all from marital unhappiness.
28 Through that first couple, sin entered the world,
     and because of them, we all die.
29 Stop a trickle before it becomes a flood;
     that goes for a erring spouse, too;
30 if that doesn't work,
     end the relationship.

26:1 When a couple nutures a happy marriage
     the partners double their days together.
2 A good spouse brings joy to the relationship,
     and together their life is peaceful and full.
3 A good spouse is a great blessing
     accorded to those who revere Our God;
4 rich or poor, they carry a glad heart,
     and they always wear a smile.

5 Three things bring dread to my heart;
     the fourth terrifies me:
6 a town of slanderers; a trial by public judgment;
     a false accusation—they're worse than death;
7 but a jealous spouse brings heartbreak and anguish,
     and a has a tongue that is the worst kind of scourge.

8 A bad spouse is a dreadful yoke;
     scorpions are easier to control.
9 A drunken spouse always goads anger;
     it is a degrading vice as well.
10 Licenteousness shows itself in the face,
     in seductive eyes and a wanton expression.
11 Relationships need strong commitments;
     otherwise the temptation to leave is always there.

12 Learn to assess when your partner is restless,
and prepare yourself for the worst—
13 for as thirsty travelers with parched lips
will drink from the first water they spot,
so will unfulfilled partners open their embrace to one and all
and offer themselves to any vice.

14 A loving partner is a continual delight;
mutual thoughtfulness enriches the union.
15 A judicious mouth is a holy gift in a spouse,
and strong character is beyond price.
16 Modesty is a special blessing,
and a welcoming home brings grace to the whole family.
17 View the sun coming up over God's mountains
and you witness good mates in a happy household.

18 Radiant as the light from the sacred lampstand
is the beauty and grace of a couple bonded by love.
19 Handsome as the pillars in the Temple
are the bodies of two lovers.

20 Two things make my heart ache
and a third makes me angry:
21 a person of means and skills going idle;
the wise humiliated;
22 and a person who turns from justice to injustice—
whom Our God has destined for the sword.

23 Merchants are constantly tempted to be dishonest,
and shopkeepers are always being tested.
27:1 Many cheat for profit,
and the struggle for wealth blinds one to what is right.
2 Like a peg between fitted stones
is the fine line of sin between buying and selling.
3 Unless you are resolute in our reverence for Our God,
your house will fall without warning.

4 Sift the grain and the husks come up;
so do the faults of people when they speak up.
5 Just as the potter's work is tested in the kiln,
so to are we tested when we open our mouths.

6 Trees in the orchard are judged by the quality of their fruit;
  our character is tested by the quality of our words.
7 Don't praise anyone before you hear them in a discussion,
  for this is the test of character.

8 If you strive for justice, you will receive it,
  and wear it like a splendid coat.
9 "Birds of a feather flock together"—
  and faithfulness roosts where it is practiced.

10 As the lion lies in wait for its prey,
  so does sin for the corrupt.

11 The conversation of the good is bathed in wisdom,
  the fool changes like the moon.
12 Take your leave quickly when among fools,
  and linger with the wise.
13 The jabbering of fools is offensive;
  their rowdy snickering betrays a life of license.
14 The gabble of the wicked is chilling,
  their brawls force one to cover the ears.
15 When the proud quarrel, blood is shed;
  their cursing is painful to hear.

16 Betrayers of secrets forfeit trust;
  they will never have a close companion.
17 Value your friends and be faithful to them;
  but if you betray a confidence, you'll lose them;
  for as a bird can slip away in a moment of carelessness,
  you have let a friend slip away—forever.
18 No need to search—your friend has gone,
  and fled like a gazelle freed from a trap.
19 Wounds can be bandaged, rebuffs can be forgiven,
  but there is no hope for betrayers of secrets.

20 People with a sly wink are mischief-makers,
  and no one can dissuade them from their designs.
21 To your face, their speech drips with honey,
  they admire everything you say;
  behind your back they sing another song,
  and use your own words against you.
22 There's nothing I hate more then them—
  and Our God hates them, too.

23 Throw a rock in the air, and you hurt yourself when it falls;
   that's how treachery affects the betrayer.
24 Those who dig pits fall into them;
   those who set traps get caught in them.
25 Evil recoils on evildoers,
   though they'll never know where it came from.
26 The arrogant are skilled at mockery and sarcasm;
   but vengeance awaits them like a hungry lion.
27 The trap is set for those who take pleasure in pitfalls;
   pain will consume them up to their time of death.
28 Hostility and anger are just as hateful;
   yet sinners hug them close.

28.1 To take vengeance is to expect Our God's vengeance,
   who keeps a strict account of our sins.
2 Forgive your neighbors when they offend you,
   then you will be forgiven when you pray.
3 When we tend our anger against another,
   how can we expect compassion from Our God?
4 If we refuse mercy to our neighbor,
   can we ever seek God's forgiveness of our sins?
5 If mere mortals cherish rage,
   to whom will they turn for forgiveness?
6 Meditate on the last things, and end your quarrelling;
   meditate on your end, and stop sinning.
7 Meditate on the commandments, and don't hate your neighbor;
   meditate on God's covenant, and forgive all who offend you.
8 You will sin less if you avoid quarrels,
   for the hotheaded provoke them;
9 sinners provoke dissention among friends,
   and introduce friction between peacekeepers.
10 An excess of fuel makes an excess of fire;
   an excess of hostility makes an excess of bloodshed.
11 Our rancor is equal to our power;
   our ferocity is equal to our wealth.
12 Sudden outbursts kindle fires;
   rash disputes lead to bloodshed.

13 Blow on a spark to make it flame, or spit on it to put it out;
   but you do both with your mouth.
14 Curse the gossips and the talebarers!
   They've disturbed many who once lived peacefully.

¹⁵ Meddlesome words have ruined many lives,
   driven them from land to land;
  they have destroyed mighty cities,
   have brought down great households.
¹⁶ Meddlesome words have driven away virtuous spouses,
   and destroyed once happy homes;
¹⁷ whoever listens to them will not know peace of mind,
   or ever live in peace again.
¹⁸ The snap of a whip raises a welt,
   but the slash of a tongue breaks bones.
¹⁹ Many are dead from the edge of a sword,
   but many more have fallen by the tongue.
²⁰ Happy are those who have found shelter from it,
   have not endured its onslaught;
  happy are those who have not endured its yoke
   or been shackled in its chains;
²¹ for its yoke is an iron yoke
   and its chains are of bronze;
²² the death it exacts is hideous—
   Sheol is a better choice.
²³ It has no effect on the just,
   and it will not singe them in its fires.
²⁴ But those who abandon Our God end up in its flames;
   its burning will be unending.
  It will hurl itself at them like a lion,
   rip them like a leopard.
²⁵ As you put a thorn hedge around your place,
   as you lock your silver and gold into the safe,
²⁶ so you must weigh and measure your words
   and make a door with locks across your mouth.
²⁷ Take care not to foiled by your tongue
   and be vicitmized by those lying in wait.

⋄   ⋄   ⋄

29¹ Those who have compassion lend freely to their neighbor;
   those who serve others fulfill the commandments.
² So lend to your neighbors when they are in need
   and repay what you owe them on time.
³ Be true to your word; keep your promises,
   and your needs will always be met.

4 There are many who are not responsible with a loan—
       they cause trouble to those who have helped them.
5 People like this will kiss their neighbors' hand
       before the loan is given,
   but when the money is in hand,
       they are distant, and slow with repayment,
   making only small payments
       and complaining of difficult times.
6 If those whom they owe demand quick payment,
       they will receive only half what is due.
       and be fortunate to receive even that.
   If they don't demand quick payment,
       they will lose all the money they loaned
       and gain an enemy in the bargain.
7 Because of such dishonesty, many refuse to lend,
       fearing that they will be parted from their money
       while gaining no profit.

8 Nonetheless, be patient with those who have nothing,
       and don't make them wait for your help;
9 give to the poor for the sake of the commandments,
       and don't send them away empty handed.
10 Lose money on your family and friends
       rather than hide it under a stone to rust away.
11 Give of your wealth, as commanded by the Most High;
       that in itself is of more benefit than your gold.
12 Let generosity be the treasure you store,
       and it will deliver you from every harm.
13 It will protect you against an enemy
       better than a sturdy shield or strong spear.
14 For those who are virtuous
       will stand firmly for their neighbors;
   only those who have no shame
       will disappoint them.

15 If someone takes a stand for you, don't forget the favor—
       for they have staked their honor on your behalf.
16 A dishonest person is careless with the property of another;
       the ungrateful will desert their benefactors in a crisis.
17 Many honest people have been ruined
       by cosigning for another's debts—
       they have been rocked like the ocean's waves.

18 Many have lost their homes,
   left to wander through foreign lands.
19 Sinners who make loose promises of backing just to close the deal,
   will freely involve themselves in lawsuits.
20 So help your neighbor when you are able,
   but beware of becoming too deeply involved.

21 The basic things of life are water, bread and clothing,
   and a house for privacy.
22 It is better to be poor and live in your own shanty,
   than to live extravagantly in another's house!
23 Be content with what you have,
   whether it is much or little—
   don't come to be known as a freeloader.
24 It's a wretched way to live, going from house to house,
   always bowing to the will of others because you're their guest.
25 You would be forever a stranger,
   tasting humiliation and stinging from bitter words:
26 "Come now, Stranger, earn your keep, set the table for us,"
   and, "Whatever you have, give it to me," or,
27 "You have to leave, now, Stranger,
   we have important guests coming—
   my family is coming,
   and we need the guest room."

28 There are two things that any sensitive person finds hard to bear:
   criticism at home, and abuse from a creditor.

☙   ☙   ☙

30:1 Parents who love their children
   will not fear being strong with them.
   When they are old, their children will bring them much joy.
2 Parents who raise their children well will reap a great reward:
   they will take pride in them in front of their friends.
3 Parents who teach their children well are envied by their enemies;
   they can boast about them among their friends.
4 When parents die, it's as if they were still alive,
   for they leave behind an image of themselves.
5 During their life, they see and they rejoice;
   they will have no regrets on their deathbed.

6 They'll leave heirs to take vengeance against their enemies
   and repay their friends with kindness.
7 Those who spoil their children
   will bandage every scratch,
   and come running at every cry.

8 Untrained horses become stubborn;
   unsupervised children become obstinate.
9 If you pamper your children, they will shame you;
   if you indulge them, they will bring you grief.
10 If you join in their play, you'll join in their sorrow
   and end up grinding your teeth.
11 Don't give them too much freedom when they are young,
   and don't make light of their mistakes.
12 While they are young, break them in;
   be strong with them when they are young,
   or they will grow up stubborn and disobedient
   and cause you great pain.
13 Teach your children discipline;
   take care with them when they are young,
   or they may bring you shame
   through some disgraceful act.

ଊ   ଊ   ଊ

14 It is better to be poor, and be healthy and fit,
   than to be rich and always sick.
15 Health and fitness are better than any wealth;
   a healthy body is better than endless prosperity.
16 No amount of money can compare to good health,
   and there is no pleasure better than joy in the heart.
17 It is better to die than to live in misery;
   to rest forever, than to linger in illness.
18 Fine foods offered to someone with no appetite
   might as well be placed before a tomb.
19 What use is sacrifice to idols
   that can neither taste nor smell?
20 It's the same with those afflicted by Our God:
   they gaze at their food and groan, unable to partake,
   as a eunuch goans when embracing a lover.

²¹ Do not surrender yourself to your sorrow
    or be quick to cause yourself distress.
²² A cheerful heart will keep you alive,
    and joy will add years to your life.
²³ Rejoice and be content with yourself,
    and banish your grief;
for grief has caused the death of many
    and has brought profit to no one.
²⁴ Envy and anger will shorten your life;
    anxiety will turn your hair turn gray.
²⁵ Those who have a light heart have a good appetite
    and enjoy the food they eat.

31 ¹ Restless nights make the rich person lose weight,
    when the cares of their wealth weigh down their sleep.
² Sleepless worries keep them wide awake,
    like an illness that makes them toss and turn.
³ The rich struggle to pile up great wealth,
    so that when they relax that they can enjoy every luxury.
⁴ The poor struggle to earn a meager living;
    when they rest, they know only hunger.

⁵ Lust for gold can never be justified;
    chasing after profits leads many astray.
⁶ Many have met their downfall
    running recklessly after gold, only to find
    themselves face to face with ruin.
⁷ Gold is a trap for those who make it their god,
    a trap that every fool is sure to fall for.
⁸ The rich who remain blameless—who don't let gold
    be the ruler of their lives—these are the happy ones!
⁹ Show them to me, and I will congratulate them;
    for what they have accomplished is a great deed.
¹⁰ Have any passed this test with honor intact?
    If so, they have good reason to be proud.
Have any had the chance to commit injustice, yet not done so—
    to do what is wrong, yet chosen not to?
¹¹ Then they will prosper, and people
    will cheer them as great benefactors.

12 When seated at a great banquet,
 don't slaver at the table and say, "What a feast!"
13 Remember, it is a bad thing to have greedy eyes.
 Is anything in creation more full of greed than the eye?
 This is why it must always be shedding tears.
14 Don't try to grab everything in sight,
 or fight with other guests over food.
15 Care for the feelings of others as you would your own,
 and always behave with consideration.
16 Eat what is set before you, but not like an animal—
 don't wolf down your food and act rude.
17 For the sake of good manners, be the first to stop eating;
 don't act like a glutton, or you will offend your host.
18 If you are dining in a large group,
 don't reach across the table in front of others.
19 Those who are well-mannered are content with little,
 and they are not short of breath when they go to bed.
 Those who eat moderately enjoy healthy sleep:
  they rise early and rested—
20 but sleeplessness, nausea and colic
 are what the glutton lives with.
21 If you cannot avoid overeating at a banquet,
 leave the table and find relief.

22 Listen closely, my child;
 don't ignore my words:
 in the end, my advice will benefit you.
 Avoid extremes in everything you do,
  and you will never become sick.
23 Everyone speaks well of a generous hosts;
 their generosity speaks of who they are.
24 The whole town talks of ungenerous hosts;
 their stinginess tells who they are.

25 Don't try to use wine to prove your maturity,
 for wine has been the downfall of many.
26 As the furnace tests the tempering of metal,
 so will wine test one's mettle at the bacchanalia of braggarts.

²⁷ Yet wine gives life to those who drink modestly.
　　What would life be without wine?
　　Wasn't it made to gladden the heart?
²⁸ Wine brings laughter and a cheerful disposition
　　to those who know when to drink and when to stop.
²⁹ But too much wine has been the cause of ill will,
　　leading to attacks and revenge.
³⁰ Drunkenness ignites the bitterness of fools
　　in their foolishness; it drains their strength
　　and becomes the cause of injuries.

³¹ Don't scold your neighbors at a banquet
　　or belittle them when they are enjoying themselves.
　This is no time to deride them
　　or badger them to pay their debts.

32:1 If you are the host of a banquet, don't be conceited;
　　mingle with everyone, as one of the party.
　Care for the needs of your guests first,
　　and only then take your seat;
² do your duties to them
　　before you sit down.
　Let their enjoyment be your pleasure
　　and your good manners will be their own reward.

³ When you are the elder, it is your place to speak;
　　but make your point quickly, and don't interrupt the music.
⁴ During the entertainment, stop your stream of talk;
　　this is not the time to show how clever you are.
⁵ Like a garnet in a ring of gold,
　　so is a concert at a feast.
⁶ Like an emerald set in pure gold,
　　so are stringed melodies and good wine.

⁷ If you are young, speak only if it is necessary,
　　but twice at most, and then only when asked.
⁸ Be succinct: say your piece in few words,
　　like the sages who can hold their tongues.
⁹ When you are in the company of important people,
　　don't pose as their equal,
　　and don't chatter incessantly when someone else is speaking.

10 As lightning always precedes thunder,
    so dignitaries precede the common folk.
11 Leave at a reasonable hour and go straight home;
    don't wait around for everyone else to leave.
12 You may amuse yourself there, and do as you please,
    but do not offend people with bragging.
13 And one more thing to remember—
    always give thanks to your Maker
    who has given you all these good things.

ભ   ભ   ભ

14 Those who honor the Most High
    will accept correction;
those who never cease their search for God
    will win God's approval.
15 Those who study the Law will find peace through the Law;
    but always, the Law will trip up hypocrites.
16 Those who respect the Most High will reveal God's intentions;
    they will make the decrees of God shine like a lighthouse.
17 Those who are unscrupulous never accept criticism;
    they always have reasons to justify their deeds.
18 Those who are conscientious will always take a hint,
    but pretentious social climbers are shameless.

19 Never do anything without considering the consequences;
    but once you have begun, don't waver in your course.
20 Don't walk down a path full of obstacles,
    stumbling on all the rocks.
21 Don't daydream when the road is clear—
22   always pay attention to where you are going.
23 In whatever you do, be conscientious,
    for this is the essence of the commandments.
Those who trust in the Law will obey the commandments;
Those who trust in the Most High will not be let down.

33:1 Those who trust in the Most High will never meet disaster:
    they will be rescued from trouble again and again
2   Those who are wise
    will not hate the Law;

but those who live hypocritically toward the Law
    will be like a ship in a storm.
3 Those who are reasonable, trust in the Law,
    and find it a trustworthy oracle of God.

4 If you want your opinion to be heard,
    prepare what you have to say;
organize all your knowledge
    before you speak.

5 The feelings of fools turn like a wagon wheel,
    and their thoughts go in circles.

6 A cynical friend is like a wild horse
    that tosses its head, caring nothing for the rider.

ℭ   ℭ   ℭ

7 Why should one day be better than another?
    The light of each day of the year is of the same source.
8 Each day is important in the mind of the Most High,
    who has set the seasons with their festivals:
9 some days were made High Holy Days,
    while others were made for ordinary living.

10 Humankind comes from the earth—
    ha'adam was created from clay—
11 yet in the mind of Our God, each of us is unique,
    and we each walk our own paths:
12 some will be blessed and exalted,
    some will be brought close to God, and made holy,
while others will be cursed and laid low
    and removed from their places of honor.
13 As clay in the hands of a potter
    is molded by the will of the potter,
so shall we, in the hands of our Maker,
    be clay to the divine will.

14 As good is the opposite of evil, and life is the opposite of death,
    so are the corrupt the opposite of the virtuous.
15 Look at the doings of the Most High—each has its opposite;
    each is the perfect compliment to the other.

16 I myself was the last to attend to these things,
    like a gatherer following the grape pickers,
17 and it was by the grace of Our God that I arrived
    in time to fill my own wine press
    with as much of the harvest as anyone.
18 Notice that I didn't work for my benefit alone,
    but for the benefit of all who seek knowledge.

19 So listen, you who are regarded highly by many;
    you who lead the Assembly, pay attention to me:
20 As long as you live, give power over yourself to no one—
    whether it be your spouse or your children,
    your siblings or your friends.
21 Do not give your possessions to another,
    for you might change your mind and ask for them back.
    As long as you live and are breathing,
    give power over yourself to no one—
22 it is far better that your children should depend upon you
    than for you to depend upon them.

23 Maintain an advantage in all that you do,
    and let nothing spoil your reputation.
24 Let your life run its full course,
    and then, when it is your time to die,
    give away your possessions.

CR   CR   CR

25 The lot of the donkey is fodder, the stick, and the burden;
    the lot of the worker is bread, discipline, and hard labor!
26 Let your workers keep busy if you want peace for yourself;
    let them get lazy, and they will lose all respect.
27 The ox is tamed by the yoke and the harness,
    and lazy workers by virtue and strong will.
28 So put them to work and don't let them be idle,
    for idleness is a great teacher of discontent.
29 Give them work to do: that is their role;
    and if they won't do their share,
    you must deal with them firmly.
30 Do not give your workers more than they can do
    or treat them in ways that are unjust.

³¹ Treat your workers as you would treat yourself,
and they will be worth the high cost of their labor.
³² Treat your workers as if they were family—
you need them as much as you need yourself.
³³ If you treat workers poorly, and they leave you,
where will you find others to replace them?

જી   જી   જી

34^{:1} Vain and empty hopes cloud the minds of fools
and dreams give flight to their fancy.
² Worrying about dreams is like grasping at shadows
or chasing the wind.
³ What you see in a dream is only illusion—
the reflection of your face in the mirror.
⁴ For truth cannot come out of fantasy
nor can purity come out of corruption.

⁵ Fortune-telling, omens and dreams: all are empty—
mere fabrications, like a feverish vision.
⁶ Unless they are sent by the hand of the Most High,
don't even pay attention to them.
⁷ Dreams have led many people astray,
causing the downfall of those who follow them.
⁸ The Law is complete, with no need of such fantasies;
you need only Wisdom,
spoken to those who are faithful to the Law.

જી   જી   જી

⁹ Those who have traveled much know much,
and those who have experienced much
know what they are talking about.
¹⁰ Those with little experience know little,
but travel increases the storehouse of knowledge.
¹¹ In my own travels, I have seen many things
and have encountered more than I can put into words.
¹² I have gone through times of great danger and escaped,
grateful for the experience that I gained.

¹³ Those who revere Our God will continue to live;
because of their trust, God will keep them safe.

14 Those who revere Our God will have nothing to fear;
  those who trust in Our God will never be thwarted.
15 Happy are those who revere Our God!
  They know where to look for help.
16 The Most High watches over those who show their love,
  and is their strong shield and firm support,
  a respite from the scorching wind and heat of midday,
  a defense against stumbling and a help against falling.
17 God gives zest to life and makes your eyes sparkle;
  with God, there is wholeness and happiness and life.

℘   ℘   ℘

18 A sacrifice of ill-gotten gains is dirty,
  and the gifts of the corrupt will go unnoticed.
19 The Most High disdains the offerings of the corrupt,
  their countless sacrifices will never win God's forgiveness.
20 To offer sacrifice from what has been extorted from the poor
  is like killing a child before its parent's eyes.
21 Bread is life for those in need,
  and to take that away from them is murder.

22 To steal your neighbors' livelihood is to kill them,
  and one who cheats a worker out of wages sheds blood.
23 When one person builds up and another tears down,
  what has either gained except needless toil?
24 When one person offers blessing and another offers curses,
  to which will the Most High listen?

25 If you wash yourself after touching a corpse, then touch it again,
  what good is it to have washed?
26 It's the same for those who fast for their sins,
  and then turn around and do the same thing again—
  who will listen to their prayer?
  What has been gained through their penance?

35:1 Those who keep the Law lend strength to their sacrifices,
  for to obey the commandments is a communal offering.
2 A kindness repaid is a grain offering,
  and the giving of alms, a thank-offering.
3 The way to please the Most High is to avoid doing evil,
  and keeping from future wrongs is an atonement for the past.

⁴ But do not come before God empty-handed—
  perform all sacrifices, for that is the Law.
⁵ The sacrifices of the just enrich the altar,
  and their fragrance rises to the presence of the Most High.
⁶ God accepts the sacrifices of the just,
  and their offering will never be forgotten.
⁷ So be generous when you worship the Most High,
  and don't hold back the first fruits of your labor.
⁸ Give your gifts cheerfully at all times,
  and dedicate your tithing with eagerness.
⁹ Give back to God as God has given to you,
  as generously as your means will allow.
¹⁰ For the Most High always repays
  and you will be repaid seven times over.

¹¹ Don't try to bribe God, for that will never be accepted;
  don't expect good from an ill-gotten sacrifice.
¹² For the Most High is a judge
  who does not respect individuals or grant favors
¹³ at the expense of the poor; God listens
  to the prayers of those who are exploited.
¹⁴ God will never ignore the pleas of the orphan
  or the widowed, as they pour out their heart.
¹⁵ See how the tears run down the cheeks of the bereaved
  and their cries indict their persecutors!

¹⁶ To be accepted, you must give of yourself
  as the Most High requires—
  then your prayer will reach the clouds.
¹⁷ The prayer of the humble pierces the clouds.
  Until it is heard, there is no comfort for them;
¹⁸ yet they do not give up until the Most High answers them,
  giving the just what is theirs, and granting them justice.

¹⁹ The Most High will not be neither slow nor patient
  when dealing with the corrupt,
²⁰ until the bones of the ruthless are broken
  and vengeance is dealt out to the corrupt;
²¹ until God wipes away their arrogance,
  and breaks the will of the unjust;
²² until God gives all people their due,
  measuring their actions against their intentions;

23 until God gives the people their rights,
    and gladdens them with every mercy.
24 During troubled times, mercy is as welcome
    as rain clouds during a drought.

36:1 Be merciful to us, Most High God of all,
    and strike fear into every nation.
2 Raise your sword against the corrupt
    and let them see your power.
3 As they have seen your holiness displayed among us
    so let them see your might displayed among them.
4 Let them learn, as we had to learn,
    that there is no god but you, Most High.
5 Show us your wonders again, all your miracles,
    and demonstrate the glory of your mighty hand and right arm.
6 Rise up in anger and pour out your vengeance
    to destroy those who attack us; to annihilate our enemies.
7 Remember the day you have chosen and let it come quickly,
    so that all people will remember your deeds.
8 May the fire of your rage devour all survivors,
    may those who oppress your people meet their doom.
9 Smash the heads of hostile leaders
    who say, "There is no one higher than we."

10 Gather up the tribes of Leah, Rachel and Jacob,
    and return their inheritance of so long ago.
11 Oh God, have mercy on the people who called upon you,
    on Israel, whom you have called "firstborn."
12 Be merciful on the city of your dwelling,
    the city of Jerusalem where you have made your home.
13 Fill Zion with the praise of your triumph;
    fill the Temple with your Glory.
14 Accept those whom you created first of all,
    and fulfill all that has been prophesied in your name.
15 Reward those who look to you in trust
    and show your prophets to be worthy of belief.

16 Oh God, hear the prayer of your faithful
    who tell of the blessings of Miriam and Aaron
    on your people.
17 Let all who live on earth proclaim that you are God,
    the Eternal God.

18 The stomach will accept all food,
      but some foods are better than others.
19 As the tongue knows the taste of game,
      so the prudent mind tastes lies.
20 A depraved mind creates problems,
      but the experienced know how to repay a troublemaker.
21 Some choose their companions indiscriminately,
      but others know how to choose well.

22 Beauty brings happiness to the heart,
      so that nothing more will be desired.
23 Those who are kind and gentle
      will not find their spouses seeking the company of others.
24 Those who find true love are at the beginning of their fortune,
      for they have a friend to match their needs
      and a pillar to support them.
25 Without a wall, a vineyard will be plundered;
      without a companion, a person will wander in misery.
26 Who will trust the well armed outlaw
      who plunders village after village?
27 Will anyone trust loveless vagabonds
      who will sleep wherever night overtakes them?

37:1 Many people claim, "I'm your friend!"
      But some will be friends in name only.
2   It is the cause of great pain
      when a cherished friend becomes your enemy!
3   Oh evil desires, when did you sneak in
      to cover the earth with so much misery?
4   A false friend will be all smiles in your time of contentment,
      but turn against you in your hour of need.
5   A true friend will stand with you against your enemies,
      and be your shield-bearer in times of strife.
6   Don't forget those who stand by your side,
      and don't neglect them when good times return.

7   Those who give advice think theirs is the best,
      but usually have their own interests at heart.
8   So be careful of those who give their advice freely,
      find out first where their interests lie—
      for their advice will be given to their own best advantage.

9 They may tip the scales against you, like the one who says,
       "Your road is clear," and then stand aside to watch you fall.
10 Don't seek the advice of those who don't trust you,
       or reveal your interests to those who envy you.
11 Never consult a suitor about their rivals,
       or the coward about war,
   a merchant about a bargain,
       or a buyer about a sale.
   Don't ask an ingrate how to show appreciation,
       or the cynic about kindness,
   or the indolent about work,
       or the seasonal worker about the season's end,
   or the careless person about an careful task—
       don't seek advice of any of these people.
12 Seek, rather, the advice of those who have honor,
       and those whom you know keep the commandments—
   those who are like you, heart and soul,
       and who will be compassionate if your fortunes fail.
13 But trust your own judgment also,
       for you have no better counselor than this.
14 Your own reason gives you better advice
       than seven sentries on a watchtower.
15 But above all, pray to the Most High
       to guide you on the path of truth.

ରେ   ରେ   ରେ

16 Discretion must precede every action
       and planning must precede every task.
17 Thoughts have their roots in the heart
       and from there they send out four branches:
18 of good and evil; of life and death.
       And it is always your judgment that decides the issues.
19 Some may be wise enough to teach many people
       and yet their own advice is of little use to themselves.
20 The most eloquent speakers may make enemies
       and in the end, die hungry,
   if the Most High withholds grace and fortune
       by depriving them of Wisdom.
21 Those who are wise in living their own life
       should be trusted when they advise others.

22 If someone is wise and instructs the people in Wisdom,
      then their good sense is to be trusted.
    The wise will be praised by many people,
      and all who seek them will consider them blessed.

23 Human life spans only so many days,
      but the life span of Israel is endless.
24 Those who rely on their own wisdom find joy,
      and win the praise of the people.
25 Those who are wise will be trusted by the people,
      and their name will be remembered forever.

CR   CR   CR

26 My child, question yourself throughout your life;
      take note of what is bad for you and leave it alone;
27 for not everything is good for every person;
      nor does everyone enjoy the same things.
28 Don't grasp at every delight,
      or indulge yourself unrestrained,
29 for overeating is the cause of many illnesses,
      and gluttony leads to nausea.
30 Gluttony has caused the death of many,
      but restraint will lengthen life.

38:1 Give physicians the respect due their services,
      for their place has been given by the Most High.
2   Their skill was given them by God,
      and they are rewarded by great rulers.
3   The knowledge of doctors brings them a place of honor,
      and earns them the respect of the great.
4   The Most High has created medicines from the earth,
      and those who are sensible will not reject them.
5   Didn't a branch once sweeten the water,
      thus revealing the power of Our God?
6   The Most High has given knowledge to mortals,
      so that by the use of the marvels of the earth,
      God may be praised.
7   Through the properties of the earth, physicians relieve pain,
      and from them the apothecary mixes potions.

8 There is no limit to the works of the Most High,
    who increases the health of all the earth.
9 My child, when you are ill, don't be neglectful,
    but pray to Our God that you be healed.
10 Stay away from vices and change your ways;
    keep your heart clean from all sin.
11 Let your life be a fragrant offering and
    and a memorial sacrifice of wheat—
  pour oil on the sacrifice
    and be as generous as you are able!
12 Then call your physician—
    but show due respect, for you are the one in need.
13 It may be that your very health
    will depend on your doctor's skill—
14 and a physician will pray to Our God
    for success in relieving your pain
    and finding the cure that will save your life.
15 Those who sin before their Maker
    also show disrepect for their physician.

          ભ   ભ   ભ

16 My child, shed a tear for those who have died;
    cry loudly for your great loss.
  Clothe yourself as is apprpriate for grieving,
    and then bury the dead.
17 Through your weeping and heartfelt cries,
    let your mourning be worthy of the one who has died.
18 Mourn for a few days and avoid bitter memories,
    then take some comfort from your grief,
    for prolonged grieving may lead you to death—
    grieving itself will drain your strength.
19 After the burial, let your grief pass;
    a life of mourning is an obstacle to the mind.
20 Don't surrender yourself to your grief;
    keep it at arm's length by remembering
    that you too will die one day.
21 Don't forget that fact: there is no return;
    you cannot help the dead and you can only harm yourself.
22 Keep in mind that you too will one day meet the same end:
    "Mine today, yours tomorrow."

²³ When you have put the dead to rest,
    put their memory to rest also,
  as their spirit passes,
    rejoice in their release.

ଔ   ଔ   ଔ

²⁴ Freedom gives opportunity for the scholars' wisdom;
    to gain knowledge, they must be freed of menial tasks.
²⁵ How can anyone gain knowledge behind a plow?
    Who takes pride in the use of the shepherd's crook
    or the study of the driving of cattle?
²⁶ These people concentrate on plowing their fields,
    and work late feeding their cattle.
²⁷ So it is with the artisan and skilled worker,
    who works both day and night.
People like these, who carve designs on household seals,
    work carefully on every emblem,
and apply themselves to make a perfect image,
    working late into the night until they are done.
²⁸ So, too, with ironsmiths at the anvil,
    intent on the hammering of iron,
as hot fumes sear their flesh
    and they battle with the heat of the forge.
The sound of the hammer rings again and again in their ears
    as they concentrate on the design that they make,
as they stuggle to perfect their work,
    late into the night, until their task is done.
²⁹ So, too, with potters sitting at the wheel,
    turning the wheel with the their feet
    forever absorbed in their work.
³⁰ Each movement of their finger carefully measured—
    the kneading of clay with strong arms,
    throwing all their weight into the task—
their hearts are set on perfecting the glaze
    as they work late into the night at their kiln.
³¹ All of these trust in their hands
    and each is skilled in an art.
³² Without them, the village would never have been built,
    and no settlers or travelers would come to it.

33 Yet you will find them at no public debates,
    in no high office in the Assembly.
None of them sits on a judge's bench
    or understands the intricacies of the law.
They don't make great speeches on moral or legal issues,
    nor are they quick with the right proverb.
34 But they keep this world going,
    and the practice of their craft is their prayer.

39:1 Compare them with scholars who devote their lives
    to studying the Law of the Most High,
exploring the great wisdom of ages past,
    and busy themselves in the study of the prophets!
2 They preserve the teachings of the venerable
    and plumb the subtleties of the parables.
3 They explore the hidden meanings in the sayings
    and find a way through the most puzzling parables.
4 Those who are in power will seek their service,
    and they make their company with the leaders of nations.
5 They travel to distant lands to learn firsthand
    of the good and the evil people do.
6 They are sure to rise before the sun,
    to search for the Most High their Maker,
and to pray to the Most High
    asking God to forgive their sins.
If our mighty God is willing
    they will be filled with the spirit of wisdom,
speaking proverbs of their own
    and giving thanks to the Most High in prayer.
7 They are led by the Most High
    in all their wisdom and knowledge,
    and the mysteries of Our God are their constant study.
8 Their teaching will manifest their learning,
    and their pride is in the Law of the Covenant of Our God.
9 Many will praise their intellect
    and their reputation will spread far and wide.
10 The nations will speak of their wisdom,
    and the Assembly will honor them in song.
11 If they live a long life, they will be more respected
    than a thousand of others; when they go to their rest,
    their reputation will hold firm.

¹² There is still so much that I want to say;
　　I am as full as the moon at mid-month.
¹³ Listen to me, my faithful children,
　　and grow like a rose planted beside a river.
¹⁴ Let your fragrance spread like frankincense
　　and blossom like a lily.
¹⁴ Spread your fragrance, lifting your voices in song,
　　and praising all that the Most High has done.
¹⁵ Proclaim the glory of God's Name
　　and give God thanks and praise,
　playing the harp and singing your songs—
　　pray this prayer to the Most High:
¹⁶ "Everything that comes from you, my God, is wonderful,
　　and everything that you command
　　will take place in its own time.
¹⁷ The waters become as still as in a pot
　　at the sound of your voice;
　　when your spoke, the great reservoirs were made.
¹⁸ At your command, your will was done;
　　nothing can stand in the way of your will.
¹⁹ The works of all peoples are present to you
　　and there is nothing that you do not see.
²⁰ Your vision spans all ages,
　　and nothing is unforeseen to you"

²¹ So don't ask, "What is this?" or "Why is that?"—
　　everything that is has its purpose and design .
²² The blessings of Our God are a river flowing out of its banks,
　　which soaks the scorched plains.
²³ As God turns fresh water into sea water,
　　so will the evil awaken God's anger.
²⁴ For the faithful, God's ways are clear,
　　but for the corrupt, there are many hidden traps.
²⁵ In the beginning, good was created for those who were good,
　　and evil for those who do evil.

²⁶ The basic elements for living a good life are:
　　water, fire, and iron;
　salt, flour, honey, and milk;
　　wine, oil, and clothing—

27 all these thing are made for the devout
   but become evil for those who do evil.

28 The purpose of some winds is to punish,
   whipping about to demonstrate their fury;
   unleashing their full force on a day of destruction—
   all this is to express the anger of the One who created it.

29 Fire and hail, famine and disease—
   all these things were created to punish.

30 Wild animals at prey, scorpions, cobras—
   and the sword of vengeance that vanquishes the ungodly.

31 All of these rejoice
   in fulfilling the commands of the Most High,
   and are always ready to carry out
   God's will on the earth.
   When their time comes,
   they never act against the word of Our God.

32 I came to this conclusion a long time ago,
   carefully considering it before I left it to you in writing:

33 everything that Our God made is good,
   and God gives us everything we need at the right time.

34 So don't complain, "This is not as good as that,"
   for all things are good in their own time.

35 So sing with all your heart and with full voice,
   and give praise to the Name of the Most High.

40:1 Hardship is the lot of all mortals: a great burden
   to be carried by the children of our first parents;
   it begins on the day we are born,
   and ends on the day we return to the earth—
   the mother of us all.

2 Our lives are full of fears and troubles
   and anxious broodings over our coming death.

3 It doesn't matter whether you sit on a high throne
   or low in a pile of dirt and ashes;

4 whether you wear a purple robe and golden crown
   or a garment of sackcloth—

5 your life will be filled with anger and envy
   and your mind will be troubled with anxiety,
   fear of death, guilt and struggle.
   Every night when you go to bed,
   your dreams will bring new worries to trouble your mind.

6   There will be little rest, if any —
        for sleep is as troubling as the time when you are awake.
    If you have a nightmare, you may imagine yourself
        fleeing from the front lines of a battle,
7   and at the moment you reach safety, you wake up,
        only to find all your fears unfounded.

8   All living creatures, both human and animal—
        and even more so, the sinner!—
9   will find their death in bloodshed,
        in fighting and the sword;
        or in disaster and famine, upheaval and plague.
10 All these things were created for the corrupt,
        on account of whose deeds the great flood was unleashed.
11 All things of the earth will return to the earth,
        and all things from the sea will return to the sea.
12 Bribery and injustice will vanish forever,
        but trust will remain for all times.
13 Ill gotten profits will dry up like a stream,
        and fade like thunder in a storm;
14 when the waters rise, the rocks are washed away,
        but just as suddenly, the waters will dry up forever.
15 Few shoots will sprout from the branches of a corrupt stock
        whose poisonous roots cling desperately to rocky cliffs.
16 The rushes that grow on the river banks
        dry up before any other grass.
17 But kindness is a garden of happiness
        and almsgiving will last for all times.
    Worker or employer—both are good,
        but it is better still to find a treasure.

18 Having children or founding a city will perpetuate a name—
        but it is better to seek after Wisdom.
19 Flocks of sheep and orchards are a source of well-being,
        but it is better to have a devoted spouse.
20 Wine and song give joy to the heart—
        but the greater joy comes of making love.
21 The flute and harp make beautiful music—
        but even more beautiful is the speaking of truth.
22 The eye delights in beautiful and elegant possessions—
        but the flowers of the field are even more beautiful.

23 A friend or colleague is a welcome partner—
       but better still is the partnership of marriage.
24 Family and friends are a shelter in troubled times—
       but even more so is almsgiving.
25 Gold and silver provide stability—
       but even better is good advice.
26 Wealth and power fortify the heart—
       but even better is to stand in awe of Our God.
27 Revering Our God, we lack nothing,
       and need no other support.
    To revere Our God is to stand in a garden
       of happiness which provides more protection
       than holding any high office.

28 My child, don't live your life begging from others—
       better to die than to beg!
29 When you have to start looking to the table of another,
       your existence will be unworthy to be called life.
    It's degrading to live on the food of another,
       and those who are wise and self-disciplined
       will be on guard against this.
30 Those who have lost all shame speak as if begging were good,
       but their hearts burn with resentment.

41:1 Death—how obnoxious you are
       to those who find security in their possessions,
    who are carefree and successful in their affairs,
       and have vigor for fine dining!
2   And yet, Death, how welcome you are to the poor,
       whose strength has been drained,
    who are tired from many years of endless anxiety,
       who are tired and at the end of their endurance!

3   Don't fear Death's judgment:
       always remember those who came before you
       and those who will come after you.
4   This is what the Most High desires of all mortals—
       what use is it to argue with God's will?
    Whether our life lasts ten years, a hundred or even a thousand—
       the number of your days will not matter in Sheol.

5   The children of the corrupt are wicked,
        sustained in the haunts of the godless!
6   They will squander their inheritance
        and their children will live in disgrace forever.
7   Godless parents become a curse to their children,
        and that disgrace continues even to their descendants.

8   Life will not go well for you blasphemers
        who have forsaken the Law of Our God!
9   The moment you are born, your life becomes a curse;
        when you die, your memory will be a curse.
10 As everything that comes from the earth will return to the earth,
        the godless will be born in their curse and die in their curse.
11 There may be grief over the death of the body,
        but the corrupt will have no good reputation to survive them.
12 So consider your reputation—it will outlive you far longer
        than a thousand vast treasure rooms full of gold.
13 A good life has only so many days,
        but a good reputation lasts forever.

14 My children, listen to my teaching about shame,
        and learn when you should feel disgrace—
    for it's not good to always be ashamed,
        and disgrace isn't always warranted.
15 Be ashamed before your parents if you've been promiscuous,
        or before an employer, if you've lied;
16 be ashamed before judges or magistrates, for flattering them,
        or before the jury, if you've committed a crime,
17 or before partners or friends, if you've been disloyal
        and broken your promises to them.
18 Be ashamed if you steal from a neighbor,
        or if your table manners are crude,
19 or you refuse to give charity when asked,
        or defraud others of their proper share,
20 or you fail to return a greeting,
        or rebuff a friend,
21 or you lust after someone who's married,
        or covet the spouse of another,
    or you attempt to seduce one who works under you,
        or violate their privacy,
22 or you ridicule your friends,
        or follow your generous act with an insult,

²³ or you gossip
>> or break a confidence.
²⁴ These are things that you should rightly feel shame for,
>> and if you avoid them you'll be respected by everyone.

42:1 But there are times when it's inappropriate to feel shame,
>> for then you might act unjustly, bending to others' opinions.
² Don't be ashamed of following the Law and the Covenant,
>> or of acting justly even if the impious are acquitted,
³ or of settling a debt with a partner or traveling companion,
>> or of sharing your inheritance with your siblings.
⁴ Don't be ashamed of using accurate weights and measures,
>> or being fair in your business dealings,
⁵ or acquiring new possessions—whether few or many,
>> or making a profit in business,
> or instilling discipline in your children,
>> or treating a dishonest worker with severity.
⁶ Don't be ashamed of paying attention to your spouse,
>> or locking things up if there are many hands around,
⁷ or watching your money as it's counted and weighed,
>> or asking for a receipt whenever you pay for something.
⁸ Don't be ashamed of admonishing the ignorant or foolish
>> or even the elderly for loose conduct.
> By this, you will show the character of your upbringing,
>> and you will be respected by everyone.

⁹ Children are a treasure,
>> but they keep their parents awake at night,
>> and worry about them keeps rest at bay—
¹⁰ whether they'll get married,
>> whether they'll stay married,
> whether they'll have children out of wedlock,
>> whether they'll have children at all.
¹¹ So keep a close watch on your offspring,
>> lest give your enemies reason to be happy,
> and you be the subject of gossip in the village,
>> shaming you in the eyes of your neighbors.
¹² Make sure their bedrooms don't have easy access;
>> watch that they don't sneak out at night.
> See that their clothing is appropriate,
>> and see that their friends are appropriate as well—

¹³ for just as moths are bred in clothes,
    so harm to young people comes from other young people.
¹⁴ Better to be too strict as a parent than too lenient;
    a child who's out of control is a shame and a disgrace.

42:15–51:30

I will now recount the works of Our God
    and tell you all that I have seen,
    the many works that were made by God's word.
¹⁶ Just as all things reflect the light of the sun,
    so all the works of creation reflect the light of God's glory.
¹⁷ God has not given even to the angels sufficient knowledge
    to tell the full tale of the wonders the Most High has done;
God has only given them, the heavenly host,
    the strength to stand in the divine presence and live.
¹⁸ God explores both the Abyss and the human heart,
    and is intimate with them to their depths;
Our God knows all things,
    and watches over the signs of the times.
¹⁹ God declares the past and future
    and discloses the traces of things held in secret.
²⁰ Not a single thought is unnoticed by God,
    and not a word is hidden from the Most High.
²¹ God has given an order to all the great works of Wisdom,
    and is their Source for ages and untold ages;
nothing can be added to God and nothing can be taken away,
    and God needs the counsel of no one.
²² All of God's works are excellent,
    even the smallest spark visible to the eye!
²³ God's works endure, each of them active
    and each of them fulfilling many purposes.
²⁴ Each thing has its twin, one a perfect mate to the other,
    for God has made nothing incomplete.
²⁵ Each thing complements the qualities of another.
    Who can ever have too much of God's glory?

43¹ How wonderful is the vault of the clear night sky,
    and how magnificent are the stars in all their glory!

2   As the sun rises, it proclaims its greatness,
         a reflection of the glory of its Maker.
3   At noonday, it scorches the land,
         and none can survive its blazing heat.
4   The stoker might withstand the heat of the furnace,
         but the hill-scorching sun is three times as hot.
     Its breath is fire
         and the glare of its rays blinds the eyes.
5   How great is the Most High, its Creator,
         whose word keeps it in its path.

6   God also made the moon to serve its turn,
         as a eternal sign to mark the divisions of the year.
7   By the turning of the moon, the feast days are determined;
         and as it completes it journey, its light fades.
8   The moon gives a name to each month,
         it wonderfully goes through its changing phases,
     a light to the armies of heaven.

9   The stars, in their brilliance, are the ornaments of the skies,
         a glittering display of the glory of Our God.
10   At the word of the Holy One
         each one takes its place in the sky
         and never abandons its sentry post.
11   Look at the rainbow and praise its Maker;
         is shines with a matchless beauty;
12   its shining arch bridges the heavens—
         a bow bent by the hands of the Most High.

13   At the command of Our God, the snowstorm advances,
         and lightning bolts execute the judgment of God.
14   In the same way, the treasures of heaven are opened,
         and the clouds fly out like birds.
15   By God's powerful hand, the clouds are gathered
         and God breaks them into pieces of hail.
16   The thunder of God's voice makes the earth tremble,
         and at the sight of the Most High, the hills quake.
17   By the will of Our God, the south wind blows,
         as do the cold winds and ice from the north.
     God scatters the snowflakes like birds lighting;
         and they fill the sky like swarms of locust.
18   Their purity dazzles the eye, and their falling

hypnotizes the mind of the watcher.

19 God sprinkles frost like salt across the land,
    and it shimmers like flowers on a thornbush.
20 God sends a blast of cold from the north
    to turn the water in the wells hard with ice,
    as if the water itself put on armor.
21 Our God scorches the mountains and desert,
    the desert flowers wilt in the heat.
22 Then God sends the clouds to rejuvenate them,
    and the morning dew brings relief from the blaze.

23 It was God's plan to imprison the Deep
    and to create islands.
24 Those who sail the sea tell many stories of its danger—
    stories which amaze all who hear them.
25 There are stories of strange and wonderful animals,
    and all kinds of things—great sea monsters.

26 It is by God's plan that each of these fulfills its own purpose;
    by the word of the Most High, they are held together.
27 No matter how much we say, our words are inadequate;
    in the end, God is everything.
28 Where can we find the skill to sing God's praises?
    God is greater than all creation.
29 The Most High is great and all powerful
    and inspiring of awe.
30 Worship Our God as well as you are able,
    knowing that the Most High is above all praise.
Gather all your strength to glorify Our God;
    let your praise be unceasing,
    though God is beyond all your power to praise.
31 Who has seen, and how can we describe, Our God?
    Who can give God truly fitting praise?
32 We have seen only a fraction of God's work,
    and there are still many mysteries that are far greater.
33 For Our God has created all things,
    and to the pious, God has given Wisdom.

CR   CR   CR

44:1 Now we will praise our great heroes,
    the ancestors of our people from times long past.

2 Our God gave them greatness and honor,
   they too reflected to greatness of God in ancient times.
3 Some of them had power over great domains
   and gained their fame through their strength.
   Others were advisors who possessed great foresight
   and spoke with the power of prophets.
4 Some led the people through their wisdom,
   and by their knowledge of the Law of Israel,
   teaching the people from their wealth of understanding.
5 Some composed great music,
   and others wrote great poetry.
6 Still others possessed great wealth and power,
   living a life of ease in their estates.
7 All of these were known for great honor
   and those among them took great pride in them.

8 Some left behind them renown,
   and their stories are told to this day.
9 Others are forgotten; passed away, as though
   they had never existed,
   as if they had never been born—
   and their children after them did the same.
10 But it was different with our ancestors
   who were true to their faith;
   their virtuous deeds will be remembered forever.
11 They passed down their treasures to their descendants,
   their inheritance to future generations.

12 Because of them, their children are included in the Covenant—
   every one of their descendants included.
13 Their progeny will last for all time
   and respect for their names will never die.
14 Their bodies are at peace
   but their names will continue forever.
15 Nations will tell of their wisdom,
   and their praises will be sung in the Assembly.

16 Enoch pleased the Most High, and was taken into heaven,
   to be an example of repentance for all times.

17 Noah was found perfect and virtuous,
   and made a sacrifice of atonement when God was angry.

This is why, the when the floods came,
    a small group survived on the earth.

¹⁸ God made an everlasting pact with them, that never again
    would life on earth be washed away in a flood.

¹⁹ Sarah and Hagar and Abraham were great,
    and founded many nations,
    no one has ever matched their fame.

²⁰ They kept the Law of the Most High
    and entered into an agreement with Our God,
    a pact ratified by circumcision.
When Abraham was tested, he was shown to be faithful,

²¹   and so the Most High made a covenant that the nations
    descended from them would always be blessed;
that their family would number more than the sands of the
    earth, and their land would extend from one sea to the other,
    from the river to the ends of the earth.

²² Rebecca and Isaac, for the sake of Sarah and Abraham,
    were given the same promise
    of a blessing and a covenant before all other peoples.

²³ That blessing was given to the second-born, Jacob,
    whom God acknowledged as the firstborn
    by ratifying Isaac's blessing and giving him the inheritance.
Jacob fixed the boundaries for his tribes,
    and divided it into sections, one for each of the twelve.

45:1 From the house of Leah, Rachel and Jacob,
    the Most High brought forth a faithful one,
    who was esteemed in the eyes of all:
Moses, of cherished memory,
    whom both God and the people loved.

² The Most High gave him the power of the angels,
    and made him the terror of his enemies.

³ God sent sign after sign as Moses asked,
    and so his reputation grew in Pharaoh's house.
God gave Moses a mission to the People of Israel
    and showed Moses a part of the Glory.

⁴ Moses was set above all others
    for his loyalty and his humility.

⁵ Moses heard the voice of the Most High
    and met with God face to face in a dark cloud,

where God revealed to him the commandments—
    the Law that is the source of all life and knowledge—
that God's covenant might be taught
    to the offspring of Leah and Rachel and Jacob,
    and the decrees to the House of Israel.

6 Aaron and Miriam were raised up
    from the tribe of Levi, holy like their brother.
7 God made an eternal covenant with them,
    granting them priestly authority over the nation.
  Aaron was honored and adorned,
    clothed in splendid vestments
8   and wrapped in full array.
  He was given emblems of the priestly office:
    the linen trousers, the tunic and robe.
9 And around the robe were placed pomegranates
    and circled with golden bells
  so that music was heard wherever he walked, ringing loudly
    through the sanctuary to remind the people.
10 Aaron was given the sacred vestment,
    adorned with symbols, gold, violet and purple
    and an oracle of judgment with its truth telling objects.
11 A scarlet thread spun with the skill of an artisan;
    the precious stones carved into seals
  and mounted onto a plate of gold by a jeweler,
    each inscribed with an emblem for a tribe of Israel;
12 the golden diadem upon the turban,
    carved into a seal saying, "Holy to the Most High."
  A great ornament! A work of true art!
13 How wonderful it is
    to see things of such beauty!
  Only Aaron's successors have worn them throughout the ages,
    only the heirs of Aaron and his descendants.
14 They present their sacrifice without fail every day—
    a whole offering.
15 Moses installed Aaron
    and anointed him with sacred oil,
  as a sign of the pact made with him for all times
    and with his descendants as long as the heavens last,
  and he commanded that they attend to Our God
    fulfilling the duties of their priestly office
    and blessing the people in God's Name.

¹⁶ The Most High chose Aaron from among all others
     to offer the sacrifice—incense and the sacrificial offering—
     as an atonement for the people.
¹⁷ God entrusted the commandments to Aaron,
     and gave authority make legal judgments
   and to teach the decrees of Israel
     and enlighten the people about the Law.
¹⁸ Yet the rebellious became envious,
     and conspired against Aaron in the desert:
   Dathan and Abiram and their lot,
     and the followers of Qorach grew bitter.
¹⁹ Our God saw all this, and in the heat of rage,
     destroyed them all—consuming them all in a blaze of fire.
²⁰ But to Aaron was given greater honor, and a rich heritage,
     by assigning to the priests the choicest offerings,
   thus assuring that they, more than any others,
     should have bread in plenty;
²¹ for the priests consume the sacrifice to Our God
     since the privilege was given to Aaron and his descendants.
²² Yet Aaron was to inherit nothing;
     of the lands of the people, no parcel was given to him—
   for God was Aaron's portion and inheritance.

²³ Phinehas, begot of Eleazar, held third place in honor
     for his fervor in worshiping the Most High
   and for taking a courageous stand
     when the rest of the people ran away;
     by doing this, he atoned for Israel.
²⁴ So God made a pact with him,
     giving him charge of the sanctuary of the people,
   and passing on to his descendants,
     the high priesthood for all times.
²⁵ Just as with the pact made with David,
     begot of Jesse, of the tribe of Judah,
     that the royal succession would pass on in his line,
   so it was that the priestly succession would pass on
     in the line of Aaron.

²⁶ Praise Our God who is good,
     and who crowns you with glory!
   May God grant you Wisdom
     so that you will judge the people justly,

that their prosperity will last forever
and their tales of glory be passed on to future generations!

46:1 Joshua begot of Nun was a mighty warrior
and succeeded Moses in the office of prophet.
His name was well deserved,
because he was the great deliverer of God's chosen people.
Joshua wrought vengeance on the attacking hoards
and returned Israel's inheritance to the people.

2 Joshua shone with light when,
with his sword raised high above his head,
he charged to attack the city.

3 Joshua led the battles of the Most High,
and no one could defeat him.

4 The sun stood still at his command
and one day stretched into two.

5 When their enemies had surrounded them,
Joshua called upon the Most High—the Mighty One—
and his prayer was answered by Our Great God

6 who demonstrated power in form of a hailstorm.
Joshua conquered the aggressors;
defeating the attackers as they passed through the valley,
so that the nations would grow to fear his great valor,
knowing that the Most High was on his side,
and that he followed wherever the God of Might led.

7 During the days of Moses, Joshua proved his faithfulness,
when he and Caleb, begot of Jephunneh,
stood their ground against the assembled people,
keeping them from grievous sin,
and silencing their ceaseless complaint.

8 Only these two, from the six hundred thousand warriors,
survived to lead the people into their inheritance—
into the land flowing with milk and honey.

9 The Most High gave Caleb great strength
that lasted even into his later years,
and he was able to lead invasions into the hills,
and gather spoils for the descendants of Israel.

10 So all of Israel witnessed the benefits
of following Our God.

¹¹ Then there were the judges, each of them,
  whose hearts weren't deceived by idols
 and never turned away from serving the Most High—
  may their memory last forever!
¹² May their bones nurture new life even from the grave!
  May the legacy of the dead live on in their children!

¹³ Samuel was loved by the Most High.
  He was the prophet who set up the monarchy
  and established the rulers over the people.
¹⁴ He proclaimed justice according to God's Law,
  and the Most High kept watch over the descendants of Jacob.
¹⁵ Through his faith, Samuel showed himself a true prophet;
  by the truth of his words was his faith made manifest.
¹⁶ When enemies surrounded him, he called on the Most High,
  offering a newborn lamb for a sacrifice.
¹⁷ Then the Most High sent down thunder from heaven,
  and God's voice was heard in the tumult,
¹⁸ and all the chiefs of the enemy grew afraid—
  all the leaders of the Philistines.

¹⁹ Before Samuel's time came to pass on, he spoke
  before the Most High and before witnesses, saying,
 "I have never taken another's things,
  not even a pair of sandals."
 and there was no one who would take issue with him.
²⁰ Even as he lay dying, he prophesied,
  telling the ruler of the fate in store for him,
 raising his voice in prophesy from his bed
  to blot out the corruption of the people.

47¹Samuel was succeeded by Nathan
  who prophesied during the reign of David.
² As the choice fat is set aside for the daily sacrifice,
  so David was set aside for all of Israel.
³ He played with lions like young goats
  and with bears as though they were lambs.
⁴ While still a youth, he killed a giant,
  taking away the shame of the people,
 by hurling a stone with his sling,
  bringing down the arrogant Goliath.

5   David called on the Most High, to give strength to his arm
        to strike down the mighty warrior,
6   leading the people to victory.
    So David was hailed as conqueror of ten thousand,
        and his praises were sung for the favors given by Our God.
    And when David was crowned,
7   he fought and conquered the surrounding enemy
        and crushed the Philistine resistance,
        whose power remains scattered to this day.

8   In all he did, David gave thanks,
        giving credit to the Holy One, the Most High,
    and sang songs of praise to Our God,
        showing his love for the Creator.
9   He assigned musicians for the sanctuary
        to sing and play soothing tunes on the harp.
10 He established celebrations of great grandeur,
        and set the festivals of the seasons for ages to come—
    those times when the sanctuary echoes with music
        from sunrise to sunset.
11 The Most High forgave David,
        and established his judgment seat forever.
    By sacred pact, God gave David the rulership
        and a glorious throne in Israel.

12 David was succeeded by Solomon the Wise,
        who, thanks to David, ruled during prosperous days
13 and reigned over a time of peace—
        for God had granted Solomon lasting tranquility
    so that he could build up the House of God,
        a sanctuary built to last for all time.

14 How wise you were, Solomon, even in your youth,
        flowing with wisdom, like a river!
15 Your mind could fathom the whole universe,
        and you passed on your learning
        through proverbs and riddles.
16 Your renown reached distant shores
        and you were loved because you kept the peace.
17 Your songs and your sayings, your proverbs
        and your judgments were the wonders of the world.

¹⁸ In the Name of the Most High God,
  whom Israel calls their own,
you filled your treasuries with gold and silver
  as if they were tin or lead.
¹⁹ But you took foreigners to your side
  and allowed them to undermine your authority.
²⁰ You sullied your reputation
  and sullied your descendants.
You brought God's anger down upon your children;
  the Most High raged against your foolish ways
²¹ because you divided your authority.
And so a breakaway dynasty was established in Ephraim.

²² But Our God is always merciful
  and what God has established will not be destroyed.
God will never abandon the children of the faithful one
  or sever the lineage of the one who loved Our God.
Our God granted a faithful remnant to Jacob
  and allowed a descendant of David to survive.
²³ When Solomon was laid to rest with his ancestors,
  one of his own children ascended the throne:
Rehoboam—a dimwit, a laughingstock of the nations—
  whose policies drove the people to rebellion.
Jeoboam, begot of Nebat, broke away,
  leading Israel into iniquity and Ephraim into idolatry.
²⁴ They became increasingly corrupt, until they were conquered,
  to be scattered among the nations far from their homeland.
²⁵ They experimented with every kind of base behavior
  until they were conquered and punished.

48:1 Then the prophet Elijah came blazing like a fire,
  whose words glowed like a torch.
² Elijah called down a drought upon the people
  and their numbers shrank at the rage of his words.
³ Through the word of Our God,
  Elijah shut up the floodgates of heaven
  and three times called down fire from the sky.

⁴ How magnificent you were, Elijah,
  in the full array of your wonders!
  What other person can vaunt such awesome deeds?

5 Through the power of Our God,
    you brought a dead body back to life;
6 you brought sickness upon rulers and leaders
    and brought them to their end.
7 You heard God's words of reprimand at Sinai,
    God's promise of punishment at Horeb.
8 You anointed rulers to carry out your punishment
    and a prophet to be your successor.
9 You were carried off to heaven in a whirlwind of flames,
    in a chariot drawn by horses of fire.
10 It was foretold that you will return at an appointed time
    to reunite estranged parents and children
and restore the tribes of Leah, Rachel and Jacob—
    to alleviate God's anger before that great Day of Judgment.
11 Those who see you will be counted fortunate,
    as will all who fall asleep in love—as we surely will.

12 After Elijah disappeared into the whirlwind,
    the spirit of prophecy came upon Elisha.
Elisha stood before great rulers without fear,
    and no one was his ruler.
13 There was no task that was too difficult,
    and his body kept its prophetic power even in the grave.
14 During his life, Elisha worked great wonders,
    and his wonders continued even after his death.

15 Yet still the people did not repent
    and renounce their evil ways;
and so were conquered and exiled far from their land,
    and scattered throughout the earth.
Only a small remnant was left
    with a ruler from the house of David—
16 some of them did what pleased Our God,
    while others continued their evil ways.

17 Hezekiah turned the city into a fortress
    and stored water inside its walls;
with great iron tools, the people cut through the rock,
    building reservoirs for the water.
18 During Hezekiah's rule, Sennacherib invaded the land
    and sent Rabshakeh from Laschish,

with arrogant boasts,
    to deliver an ultimatum to Zion.
19 Panic spread through the city,
    and the people screamed in fear,
20 calling upon God's mercy
    and raising their hand to heaven in prayer.
And God in heaven quickly answered their prayers,
    sending Isaiah to their rescue;
21 sending an avenging angel
    to attack the Assyrian camp.
22 For Hezekiah was faithful to Our God,
    and followed in the ways of David his ancestor,
just as Isaiah told him to do,
    for Isaiah was a great prophet
    whose vision was true.

23 During the time of Isaiah,
    the sun reversed its course
    and many years were added to the ruler's life.
24 Isaiah saw into the future with awesome power,
    and comforted those who were grieving in Zion.
25 He told them what to expect at the end of time,
    and the secrets of things yet to come.

49:1 The memory of Josiah lingers like the fragrance of incense
    prepared by the finest perfumer,
sweet as honey to every tongue,
    like soothing melodies at a great feast.
2 Josiah followed the way of virtue and reformed the nation,
    uprooting despicable and uncivil habits.
3 Josiah was loyal to Our God in every way
    and during an age of incivility, made virtue prevail.

4 Save for David, Hezekiah and Josiah,
    all others were guilty of grave offenses,
    for they had rejected the Law of the Most High.
So the royal line of Judah was brought to an end—
5   they surrendered their authority to another
    and their majesty to foreign conquerors.
6 The chosen city, the city of the sanctuary, was set on fire,
    and its streets laid in ruins, as Jeremiah had predicted.

7 Jeremiah was ridiculed, though he was a prophet
   consecrated before his birth
to uproot and tear down and raze,
   but also to plant and to build.

8 A vision of Glory was revealed to Ezekial,
   seated on a chariot of cherubim.
9 Our God remembered the enemies and sent a storm,
   but to those in the path of virtue, God sent blessings.

10 As for the twelve prophets,
    may their bones bloom once again in their graves!
They put a new heart into Israel,
    and through their faith and hope, rescued the people.
11 Just how will we tell the greatness of Zerubbabel,
    who was like a royal seal worn on God's right hand,
12 as was Joshua, begot of Jozadak,
    who in their own time rebuilt the House,
setting up the holy Temple of the Most High God,
    destined for eternal glory?
13 Also of renown is the memory of Nehemiah,
    who rebuilt the walls that had been torn down
assembling the secured gates
    and restoring our ruined homes.

14 There has never been an equal to Enoch on the earth,
    for he was taken up from earth into heaven.
15 No one has ever equaled Joseph,
    the leader of his family and help of the people—
    his bones were guarded at all times.
16 Shem and Seth were held in high esteem
    but our first parents hold the first place over all of creation.

50:1 The priest Simon, begot of Onias,
    was the greatest of his family
    and was held in esteem by all people.
It was during his life that the house was rebuilt;
    in whose days the Temple was set up.
2 Simon laid the foundation for the high double wall;
    the retaining wall surrounding the Temple.

3 During this time, a great reservoir was dug,
    a well as wide as the sea.

⁴ Simon thought to fortify the people against disaster,
   and built many fortifications to protect the city from siege.

⁵ He was dazzling as he walked through the Temple
   and emerged from behind the veil of the sanctuary!
⁶ He was like the star of the morning
   that reveals itself through the clouds
   or the full moon that shines over the holy days;
⁷ like the sun shining over the Temple of the Most High,
   or the light of the rainbow reflecting on the clouds;
⁸ like a rose in the spring,
   or lilies by a fountain of water;
   like a green tree growing in Lebanon on a summer's day,
⁹ or frankincense burning in the censer;
   like a golden chalice covered with precious stones,
¹⁰ or an olive tree heavy with fruit,
   or a cypress with its branches in the clouds.

¹¹ When Simon put on his sacred robes,
   and was covered in splendor,
   he ascended to the altar
   and became a brilliant light in the sanctuary.
¹² When Simon accepted the sacrifices from the priests,
   standing at the altar, with the other priests
   around him like a necklace,
   he was like a young cedar of Lebanon
   surrounded by tall palm trees.
¹³ All the priests of Aaron's stock in their robes,
   stood before the Assembly of Israel
   holding the offering to the Most High in their hands.
¹⁴ At the end of the sacred rites at the altar,
   Simon raised the offering to the Most High, the Almighty;
¹⁵ he reached out and took the cup
   and made the drink offering from the blood of the grape,
   pouring out the sweet nectar at the base of the altar,
   to the Most High God, Ruler of all.
¹⁶ Then the priests of Aaron's stock shouted
   and sounded their silver trumpets;
   they played a rousing chorus
   in honor of the Most High.
¹⁷ And then all the people fell prostrate
   to pay homage to the Most High.

¹⁸ The choir sang praises,
  accompanied by sweet melodies and resounding tunes,
¹⁹ while the people prayed to the Most High, the Merciful One,
  until the rite of Our God was done.
²⁰ Then Simon descended the altar,
  raised his hands over the whole over the Assembly of Israel
and pronounced the blessings of Our God
  to the glory of God's Name.
²¹ And so the people bowed in homage
  and received the blessing of the Most High.

ଓ   ଓ   ଓ

²² Let us praise the God of the Universe
  who alone works great wonders,
who from the day we were born sustains us
  and treats us with mercy!
²³ May God give us a heart filled with joy
  and may we live all our days in lasting peace in Israel.
²⁴ May God show mercy towards us
  and with compassion rescue us.

²⁵ There are two nations I hate,
  and a third which is no nation at all:
²⁶ Those who live on Mount Seir, and the Philistines,
  and those ridiculous people who live at Shechem!

ଓ   ଓ   ଓ

²⁷ I, Yeshua begot of Sirach Eleazar of Jerusalem,
  whose mind is a fountain of wisdom,
  have given instruction in good sense
  and understanding through this text.
²⁸ Happy are those who occupy themselves
  thinking on these things—
  all who memorize these things will be wise!
²⁹ If you follow this advice, you will be ready for anything,
  for the light of the Most High will shine on your path.

51:1 I will give you thanks, my God, my Ruler,
  I will give you praise,

² for you have protected me and come to my aid,
   delivering me from destruction
and from the traps laid by those who slander me;
   from the lips of those who tell lies about me.
You came face to face with my attackers to help me,
³ and in your resplendent mercy and honor, rescued me
from the gnawing teeth that waited to devour me,
   from the hands of those who threatened my life,
   and from my many problems,
⁴ from the consuming fire that surrounded me,
   from the flames I had not even ignited,
⁵ from the depths of Sheol,
   from the bitter tongue and the lying words—
⁶ an evil lie spoken in the presence of the ruler.
I nearly died—I was on the brink of death.
⁷ I was surrounded and there was no one left to help me.
I looked to other people for aid, but found none.
⁸ Then I remembered your kindness, my God,
   and what you did long ago—
how you delivered those who put their trust in you
   and freed them from their powerful enemies.
⁹ I prayed to you from my lowly state
   and prayed that you would save me from death.
¹⁰ I cried, "My God, you are my Abba,
   don't abandon me now when I am in danger,
   when I am helpless in the face of arrogant foes.
¹¹ I will praise you at all times,
   I will sing hymns of thanksgiving."
Then you accepted my prayer
¹² and saved me from destruction,
   bringing me out of my desperation.

So now I will thank you and praise your Name;
   I bless your Name, O God!
¹³ In my youth, before I began my travels,
   I prayed for Wisdom.
¹⁴ I prayed in the Outer Court of the Temple for Her,
   and I will seek Her all my days.
¹⁵ From the first blossom to the harvested grape,
   She alone has been the delight of my heart.

From the days of my youth,
   I have followed Her unfailingly.
16 And I had barely begun to listen
   when I received my reward
   and was instructed in Her ways.
17 I progressed in my studies—
   for it is the glory of Our God that gives Wisdom!
18 I made up my mind to put into practice all that I had learned
   I followed the path of virtue with no regrets.
19 I sought Wisdom with all my strength
   and was careful in whatever I did.
   I held out my hands to the heavens,
   and asked forgiveness for all my faults;
20 I set out to attain Wisdom,
   keeping myself pure until I found Her.
   I gained understanding from the first moment I found Her,
   so that I will never be at a loss.
21 And because I sought her out with passion,
   I gained a noble possession:
22 for my reward, Our God made me eloquent
   so now I may praise the Most High.

23 Those of you who hear this,
   come to me and stay at my house.
24 Why do you continue to lack these things
   and leave your thirst unquenched?
25 I proclaim:
   "Purchase Wisdom for yourself without money.
26 Place your neck in the yoke
   and be ready to accept instruction—
   you don't need to go far to find it.
27 See for yourself how few were my labors
   when compared with my reward.
28 Your instruction may cost much silver,
   but you will receive a larger return in gold.
29 May you delight in Our God's mercy
   and not be ashamed to praise the Most High.
30 Do your duty in good time,
   and in God's own time, you will have your reward."